Anthropology 13/14

Thirty-Sixth Edition

EDITOR

Elvio Angeloni
Pasadena City College

Elvio Angeloni received his BA from UCLA in 1963, his MA in anthropology from UCLA in 1965, and his MA in communication arts from Loyola Marymount University in 1976. He has produced several films, including *Little Warrior,* winner of the Cinemedia VI Best Bicentennial Theme, and *Broken Bottles,* shown on PBS. He served as an academic adviser on the instructional television series *Faces of Culture.* He received the Pasadena City College Outstanding Teacher Award in 2006. He is also the academic editor of *Annual Editions: Physical Anthropology, Classic Edition Sources: Anthropology,* co-editor of *Rountable Viewpoints Physical Anthropology* and co-editor of *Annual Editions: Archaeology.* His primary area of interest has been indigenous peoples of the American Southwest.

McGraw Hill

Connect Learn Succeed™

ANNUAL EDITIONS: ANTHROPOLOGY, THIRTY-SIXTH EDITION

1 2 3 4 5 6 7 8 9 0 QDB/QDB 1 0 9 8 7 6 5 4 3 2

MHID: 0-07-805131-2
ISBN: 978-0-07-805131-9
ISSN: 1091-613X (print)
ISSN: 2162-3546 (online)

Managing Editor: *Larry Loeppke*
Marketing Director: *Adam Kloza*
Marketing Manager: *Nathan Edwards*
Senior Developmental Editor: *Debra A. Henricks*
Senior Project Manager: *Joyce Watters*
Buyer: *Nichole Birkenholz*
Cover Designer: *Studio Montage, St. Louis, MO*
Content Licensing Specialist: *DeAnna Dausener*
Media Project Manager: *Sridevi Palani*

Compositor: Laserwords Private Limited
Cover Image credits: © The McGraw-Hill Companies/Lissa Harrison (inset), © The McGraw-Hill Companies/Lissa Harrison (background)

Editors/Academic Advisory Board

Members of the Academic Advisory Board are instrumental in the final selection of articles for each edition of ANNUAL EDITIONS. Their review of articles for content, level, and appropriateness provides critical direction to the editors and staff. We think that you will find their careful consideration well reflected in this volume.

ANNUAL EDITIONS: Anthropology 13/14
36th Edition

EDITOR

Elvio Angeloni
Pasadena City College

ACADEMIC ADVISORY BOARD MEMBERS

Preface

In publishing ANNUAL EDITIONS we recognize the enormous role played by the magazines, newspapers, and journals of the public press in providing current, first-rate educational information in a broad spectrum of interest areas. Many of these articles are appropriate for students, researchers, and professionals seeking accurate, current material to help bridge the gap between principles and theories and the real world. These articles, however, become more useful for study when those of lasting value are carefully collected, organized, indexed, and reproduced in a low-cost format, which provides easy and permanent access when the material is needed. That is the role played by ANNUAL EDITIONS.

This thirty-sixth edition of *Annual Editions: Anthropology* contains a variety of articles on contemporary issues in social and cultural anthropology. In contrast to the broad range of topics with minimum depth that is typical of standard textbooks, this anthology provides an opportunity to read firsthand accounts by anthropologists of their own research. In allowing scholars to speak for themselves about the issues in which they are experts, we are better able to understand the kinds of questions anthropologists ask, the ways in which they ask them, and how they go about searching for answers. Indeed, where there is disagreement among anthropologists, this format allows the readers to draw their own conclusions. Given the very broad scope of anthropology—in time, space, and subject matter—the present collection of highly readable articles has been selected according to a certain criteria. The articles have been chosen from both professional and non-professional publications for the purpose of supplementing standard textbooks that are used in introductory courses. Some of the articles are considered classics in the field, while others have been selected for their timely relevance.

Included in this volume are a number of features that are designed to make it useful for students, researchers, and professionals in the field of anthropology. While the articles are arranged along the lines of broadly unifying themes, the *Topic Guide* can be used to establish specific reading assignments tailored to the needs of a particular course of study. Other useful features include the *Table of Contents* abstracts, which summarize each article and present key concepts in bold italics. In addition, each unit is preceded by an overview, which provides a background for informed reading of the articles, emphasizes critical issues, and presents *Learning Outcomes* that are tied to *Critical Thinking* questions at the end of each article. The *Internet References* section can be used to further explore the topics online.

Finally, it should be pointed out that an *Author's Note* has been added to several classic articles that have been in this book since they were originally published. These updates consist of fresh perspectives on important issues, written by the authors themselves exclusively for this book.

Instructors will appreciate a password-protected online *Instructor's Resource Guide* and students will find online quizzing to further test their understanding of the material. These tools are available at www.mhhe.com/cls via the *Online Learning Center* for this book.

Annual Editions: Anthropology 13/14 will continue to be updated annually. Those involved in producing the volume wish to make the next one as useful and effective as possible. Your criticism and advice are always welcome. Any anthology can be improved. This continues to be—annually.

Elvio Angeloni
Editor
evangeloni@gmail.com

The Annual Editions Series

VOLUMES AVAILABLE

Adolescent Psychology

Aging

American Foreign Policy

American Government

Anthropology

Archaeology

Assessment and Evaluation

Business Ethics

Child Growth and Development

Comparative Politics

Criminal Justice

Developing World

Drugs, Society, and Behavior

Dying, Death, and Bereavement

Early Childhood Education

Economics

Educating Children with Exceptionalities

Education

Educational Psychology

Entrepreneurship

Environment

The Family

Gender

Geography

Global Issues

Health

Homeland Security

Human Development

Human Resources

Human Sexualities

International Business

Management

Marketing

Mass Media

Microbiology

Multicultural Education

Nursing

Nutrition

Physical Anthropology

Psychology

Race and Ethnic Relations

Social Problems

Sociology

State and Local Government

Sustainability

Technologies, Social Media, and Society

United States History, Volume 1

United States History, Volume 2

Urban Society

Violence and Terrorism

Western Civilization, Volume 1

Western Civilization, Volume 2

World History, Volume 1

World History, Volume 2

World Politics

Contents

UNIT 1
Anthropological Perspectives

1. **Queer Customs,** Clyde Kluckhohn, from *Mirror for Man,* University of
   California 1994

   Intrinsic to anthropologists' efforts to **understand humans** is the **concept of culture,**
   which involves not simply explanations for people's particular ways of life, but an appreciation of the general fact that human beings do not simply act out of biological necessity, but behave according to the **precepts and customs that they have been taught.**
   In this classic article, Clyde Kluckhohn sets forth such notions as **"cultures produce
   needs as well as provides a means of fulfilling them"** and **"not all culture promotes
   physical survival . . . at times, indeed, it does exactly the opposite."** In other words, for
   Kluckhohn, and for anthropologists in general, **biology is not destiny.**   2

2. **Ethnographic Empathy and the Social Context of Rights: "Rescuing"
   Maasai Girls from Early Marriage,** Caroline S. Archambault, *American
   Anthropologist,* December 2011

   Child marriage among the conservative, pastoral Maasai has been **portrayed as a
   relic of tradition and malicious patriarchy.** The importance of the **ethnographic perspective** is emphasized, however, in the way the author shows the recent downward
   shift in the age of marriage is actually **a response to cultural change, increasing poverty and marginalization.**   7

3. **Eating Christmas in the Kalahari,** Richard Borshay Lee, *Natural History,*
   December 1969

   Anthropologist Richard Borshay Lee gives an account of the misunderstanding and
   confusion that often accompany **cross-cultural experience.** In this case, he violated a
   basic principle of the !Kung Bushmen's social relations—**food sharing.**   10

4. **Tricking and Tripping: Fieldwork on Prostitution in the Era of AIDS,**
   Claire E. Sterk, *Tricking and Tripping: Prostitution in the Era of AIDS,*
   Social Change Press, 2000

   As unique as Claire E. Sterk's report on **prostitution** may be, she discusses issues
   common to anthropologists wherever they conduct **fieldwork:** How does one build trusting relationships with informants and what are the **ethical obligations** of an anthropologist toward them?   14

5. **The September 11 Effect on Anthropology,** Lara Deeb and Jessica Winegar,
   Middle East Report, Winter 2011

   The September 11, 2001 attacks have had a considerable effect on **anthropological
   research in the Middle East** and beyond. Along with the fact that **job opportunities**
   have increased in some areas and diminished in others, anthropologists have become
   increasingly concerned about the **politics of funding** and the **ethics of particular
   kinds of projects** offered. In general, pressures are mounting with respect to scholars'
   ability to maintain **academic freedom** and, perhaps, even **tenure** itself.   20

The concepts in bold italics are developed in the article. For further expansion, please refer to the Topic Guide.

UNIT 2
Culture and Communication

UNIT 3
The Organization of Society and Culture

The concepts in bold italics are developed in the article. For further expansion, please refer to the Topic Guide.

UNIT 4
Other Families, Other Ways

The concepts in bold italics are developed in the article. For further expansion, please refer to the Topic Guide.

UNIT 5
Gender and Status

The concepts in bold italics are developed in the article. For further expansion, please refer to the Topic Guide.

UNIT 6
Religion, Belief, and Ritual

UNIT 7
Sociocultural Change

The concepts in bold italics are developed in the article. For further expansion, please refer to the Topic Guide.

The concepts in bold italics are developed in the article. For further expansion, please refer to the Topic Guide.

Correlation Guide

The *Annual Editions* series provides students with convenient, inexpensive access to current, carefully selected articles from the public press. **Annual Editions: Anthropology 13/14** is an easy-to-use reader that presents articles on important topics such as *cultural diversity, language, social relationships,* and many more. For more information on *Annual Editions* and other *McGraw-Hill Contemporary Learning Series* titles, visit www.mhhe.com/cls.

This convenient guide matches the units in **Annual Editions: Anthropology 13/14** with the corresponding chapters in three of our best-selling McGraw-Hill Anthropology textbooks by Kottak and Lenkeit.

Annual Editions: Anthropology 13/14	Mirror for Humanity: A Concise Introduction to Cultural Anthropology, 8/e by Kottak	Window On Humanity: A Concise Introduction to General Anthropology, 5/e by Kottak	Introducing Cultural Anthropology, 5/e by Lenkeit
Unit 1: Anthropological Perspectives	**Chapter 1:** What Is Anthropology? **Chapter 3:** Doing Anthropology **Chapter 12:** Applying Anthropology	**Chapter 1:** What Is Anthropology? **Chapter 3:** Doing Anthropology **Chapter 18:** Applying Anthropology	**Chapter 1:** Anthropology: What Are Its Subfields and Perspectives? **Chapter 3:** Fieldwork How Are Data Gathered? **Chapter 14:** Applying Anthropology: How Does It Make a Difference?
Unit 2: Culture and Communication	**Chapter 2:** Culture **Chapter 4:** Language and Communication **Chapter 11:** Ethnicity and Race	**Chapter 2:** Culture **Chapter 10:** Language and Communication **Chapter 17:** Ethnicity and Race	**Chapter 2:** Culture: What Makes Us Strangers When We Are Away from Home? **Chapter 4:** Language: Is This What Makes Us Human?
Unit 3: The Organization of Society and Culture	**Chapter 7:** Families, Kinship, and Marriage **Chapter 13:** Anthropology's Role in a Globalizing World	**Chapter 13:** Families, Kinship, and Marriage	**Chapter 5:** Subsistence Strategies and Resource Allocation I: What Challenges Face Foragers? **Chapter 6:** Subsistence Strategies and Resource Allocation II: How Did Food Production Transform Culture? **Chapter 10:** Political Order, Disorder, and Social Control: Who Decides?
Unit 4: Other Families, Other Ways	**Chapter 7:** Families, Kinship, and Marriage	**Chapter 13:** Families, Kinship, and Marriage	**Chapter 7:** Marriage, Family, and Residence: What Are the Possibilities? **Chapter 8:** Kinship and Descent: Are These the Ties That Bind?
Unit 5: Gender and Status	**Chapter 8:** Gender	**Chapter 14:** Gender	**Chapter 9:** Gender and Sexuality: Nature or Nurture?
Unit 6: Religion, Belief and Ritual	**Chapter 6:** Political Systems **Chapter 9:** Religion **Chapter 13:** Anthropology's Role in a Globalizing World	**Chapter 12:** Political Systems **Chapter 15:** Religion **Chapter 19:** Anthropology's Role in a Globalizing World	**Chapter 11:** Belief Systems: How Do We Explain the Unexplainable?
Unit 7: Sociocultural Change	**Chapter 5:** Making a Living **Chapter 10:** The World System and Colonialism **Chapter 12:** Applying Anthropology **Chapter 13:** Anthropology's Role in a Globalizing World	**Chapter 11:** Making a Living **Chapter 16:** The World System and Colonialism **Chapter 18:** Applying Anthropology **Chapter 19:** Anthropology's Role in a Globalizing World	**Chapter 13:** Culture Change and Globalization: What Have We Learned? **Chapter 14:** Applying Anthropology: How Does It Make a Difference?

Topic Guide

This topic guide suggests how the selections in this book relate to the subjects covered in your course. You may want to use the topics listed on these pages to search the Web more easily.

On the following pages a number of websites have been gathered specifically for this book. They are arranged to reflect the units of this Annual Editions reader. You can link to these sites by going to www.mhhe.com/cls

All the articles that relate to each topic are listed below the bold-faced term.

Acculturation
1. Queer Customs
2. Ethnographic Empathy and the Social Context of Rights: "Rescuing" Maasai Girls from Early Marriage
10. Breastfeeding and Culture
14. Cell Phones, Sharing, and Social Status in an African Society
19. Who Needs Love!: In Japan, Many Couples Don't
20. The New Monogamy: Forward to the Past
25. The Bride
28. The Untold Story of the Amputees
29. Shamanisms: Past and Present
31. Understanding Islam
35. The Arrow of Disease
36. The Americanization of Mental Illness
37. The Price of Progress
38. Last of Their Kind
41. Being Indigenous in the 21st Century

Aggression
24. Missing Girls
26. Rising Number of Dowry Deaths in India
27. Murder in Amman
31. Understanding Islam
35. The Arrow of Disease

Altruism
3. Eating Christmas in the Kalahari
13. Ties That Bind

Child care
10. Breastfeeding and Culture
17. Death without Weeping
23. Where Fat Is a Mark of Beauty
24. Missing Girls

Children
2. Ethnographic Empathy and the Social Context of Rights: "Rescuing" Maasai Girls from Early Marriage
10. Breastfeeding and Culture
17. Death without Weeping
23. Where Fat Is a Mark of Beauty
24. Missing Girls

Communication
6. How Language Shapes Thought
7. Famous Names: The World of Business
8. Fighting for Our Lives
9. Shakespeare in the Bush
13. Ties That Bind
14. Cell Phones, Sharing, and Social Status in an African Society
31. Understanding Islam

Cross-cultural experience
1. Queer Customs
3. Eating Christmas in the Kalahari
6. How Language Shapes Thought
9. Shakespeare in the Bush
12. The Inuit Paradox

17. Death without Weeping
18. Arranging a Marriage in India
25. The Bride
29. Shamanisms: Past and Present
31. Understanding Islam
36. The Americanization of Mental Illness
41. Being Indigenous in the 21st Century

Cultural change
2. Ethnographic Empathy and the Social Context of Rights: "Rescuing" Maasai Girls from Early Marriage
10. Breastfeeding and Culture
12. The Inuit Paradox
14. Cell Phones, Sharing, and Social Status in an African Society
15. The Invention of Marriage
19. Who Needs Love!: In Japan, Many Couples Don't
20. The New Monogamy: Forward to the Past
24. Missing Girls
25. The Bride
26. Rising Number of Dowry Deaths in India
28. The Untold Story of the Amputees
29. Shamanisms: Past and Present
34. Why Can't People Feed Themselves?
35. The Arrow of Disease
36. The Americanization of Mental Illness
37. The Price of Progress
38. Last of Their Kind
39. The Tractor Invasion
40. We Are Going Underwater
41. Being Indigenous in the 21st Century
42. Population Seven Billion

Cultural diversity
1. Queer Customs
6. How Language Shapes Thought
18. Arranging a Marriage in India
20. The New Monogamy: Forward to the Past
21. The Berdache Tradition
29. Shamanisms: Past and Present
31. Understanding Islam
36. The Americanization of Mental Illness
38. Last of Their Kind

Cultural identity
1. Queer Customs
12. The Inuit Paradox
23. Where Fat Is a Mark of Beauty
30. The Adaptive Value of Religious Ritual
31. Understanding Islam
41. Being Indigenous in the 21st Century

Cultural relativity
1. Queer Customs
3. Eating Christmas in the Kalahari
6. How Language Shapes Thought
12. The Inuit Paradox
18. Arranging a Marriage in India
31. Understanding Islam
36. The Americanization of Mental Illness

Internet References

The following Internet sites have been selected to support the articles found in this reader. These sites were available at the time of publication. However, because websites often change their structure and content, the information listed may no longer be available. We invite you to visit www.mhhe.com/cls for easy access to these sites.

Annual Editions: Anthropology 13/14

General Sources

American Anthropologist Association
www.aaanet.org

Check out this site—the home page of the American Anthropology Association—for general information about the field of anthropology as well as access to a wide variety of articles.

Anthropology Links
http://anthropology.gmu.edu

George Mason University's Department of Anthropology website provides a number of interesting links.

InfoTrac College Edition
http://infotrac.thomsonlearning.com

This site provides access to nearly 6,000 scholarly and popular periodicals, including more than 20 million articles, many of which are anthropologically related.

Latin American Studies
www.library.arizona.edu/search/subjects

Click on Latin American Studies to access an extensive list of resources—links to encyclopedias, journals, indexes, almanacs, and handbooks, and to the Latin American Network Information Center and Internet Resources for Latin American Studies.

The Royal Anthropological Institute of Great Britain and Ireland (RAI)
www.therai.org.uk

The world's longest established scholarly association dedicated to the furtherance of anthropology in its broadest and most inclusive sense.

A Sociological Tour through Cyberspace
www.trinity.edu/mkearl

This is an excellent starting point for anthropological resources, using links.

UNIT 1: Anthropological Perspectives

Archaeology and Anthropology Computing and Study Skills
www.isca.ox.ac.uk/index.html

Consult this site of the Institute of Social and Cultural Anthropology to learn about ways to use the computer as an aid in conducting fieldwork, methodology, and analysis.

The Institute for Intercultural Studies
www.interculturalstudies.org/main.html

Established by Margaret Mead, the institute is directed by her daughter, Mary Catherine Bates. With links, it promotes accessibility to Mead's work as well as that of several of her associates, including Franz Boas, Ruth Benedict, and Gregory Bateson.

Introduction to Anthropological Fieldwork and Ethnography
http://web.mit.edu/dumit/www/syl-anth.html

This class outline can serve as an invaluable resource for conducting anthropological fieldwork. Addressing such topics

as *The Interview and Power Relations in the Field,* the site identifies many important books and articles for further reading.

Theory in Anthropology
www.indiana.edu/~wanthro/theory.htm

These web pages cover sub-disciplines within anthropology, changes in perspectives over time, and prominent theorists, reflecting 30 years of dramatic changes in the field.

UNIT 2: Culture and Communication

Center for Nonverbal Studies
www.library.kent.edu/resource.php?id=2800

This site is from a private, nonprofit research center with links to relevant news stories.

Exploratorium Magazine: "The Evolution of Languages"
www.exploratorium.edu/exploring/language

Where did languages come from and how did they evolve? This educational site explains the history and origin of language. You can also investigate words, word stems, and the similarities of different languages.

Hypertext and Ethnography
www.umanitoba.ca/anthropology

Under the sponsorhip of the University of Manitoba, this site will be of great value to people who are interested in culture and communication. Schwimmer addresses such topics as multi-vocality and complex symbolization.

International Communication Association
http://www.icahdq.org

The I.C.A. sponsors conferences and publishes books and journals having to do with cross-cultural communication.

Intute: Anthropology
www.intute.ac.uk/anthropology

www.intute.ac.uk/socialsciences/cgi-bin/browse.pl?id=120052

This site provides links to linguistic associations, journals, and links to websites and data bases dedicated to the preservation and study of languages.

Language and Culture
http://anthro.palomar.edu/language/default.htm

This is a good introduction to the subject of linguistics and includes related websites.

Language Extinction
www.colorado.edu/iec

"An often overlooked fact in the ecological race against environmental extinction is that many of the world's languages are disappearing at an alarming rate." This article investigates language extinction and its possible consequences.

Nonverbal Behavior
www.usal.es/~nonverbal/researchcenters.htm

This site is the gateway to links to many other sites having to do with nonverbal behavior and communication. The site includes links to publications, research centers, experiments, and conferences.

Internet References

Showcase Anthropology
www.anthropology.wisc.edu

Examples of documents that make innovative use of the web as a tool for "an anthropology of the future"—one consisting of multimedia representations in a nonlinear and interactive form—are provided on this website.

UNIT 3: The Organization of Society and Culture

Smithsonian Institution Website
www.si.edu

Looking through this site, which provides access to many of the enormous resources of the Smithsonian, will give a sense of the scope of anthropological inquiry today.

Sociology Guy's Anthropology Links
www.trinity.edu/~mkearl/anthro.html

This list of anthropology resources on the web is suggested by a sociology professor at Trinity University and includes cultures of Asia, Africa, the Middle East; Aztecan, Mayan, and aboriginal cultures; sections on Mythology, Folklore, Legends, and Archaeology; plus much more.

UNIT 4: Other Families, Other Ways

Kinship and Social Organization
www.umanitoba.ca/anthropology

Kinship, marriage systems, residence rules, incest taboos, and cousin marriages are explored in this kinship tutorial.

Sex and Marriage
http://anthro.palomar.edu/marriage/default.htm

This is a good cross-cultural survey of marriage customs, residence rules, and the treatment of homosexuality. Related websites are included.

Wedding Traditions and Customs
http://worldweddingtraditions.com

Marriage customs are summarized for every region of the world.

UNIT 5: Gender and Status

Heal Africa
www.healafrica.org

The mission of Heal Africa is to provide holistic health care for the People of the Democratic Republic of Congo, train health professionals, strengthen communities, encourage women in community leadership roles and support education and vocational training.

Ideal Bride
www.idealbride.sg

Go to this site for a sense of what is involved in Asian matchmaking.

It's Time: African Women Join Hands against Domestic Violence
www.itstimeafrica.org/index.html

The is a unique project working to reform the justice systems and combat domestic violence in South Africa and Ethiopia, in partnership with the Justice Education Society of BC, the South African National Prosecuting Authority and the Ethiopian Women Lawyers Association.

Reflections on Sinai Bedouin Women
www.sherryart.com/women/bedouin.html

Social anthropologist Ann Gardner tells something of her culture shock while first living with a Sinai Bedouin family as a teenager. She provides links to sites about organization of society and culture, particularly with regard to women.

Women Watch
www.un.org/womenwatch/about

As part of the United Nations, Women Watch serves as a conduit for information and resources on the promotion of gender equality and empowerment throughout the world.

UNIT 6: Religion, Belief, and Ritual

Anthropology Resources Page
www.usd.edu/anth

Many topics can be accessed from this University of South Dakota website. Repatriation and reburial are just two.

Apologetics Index
www.apologeticsindex.org/site/index-c

This site offers resources on religious cults, sects, religions, and doctrines.

Magic and Religion
http://anthro.palomar.edu/religion/default.htm

This site deals with the various aspects of folk religion and magic along with related Internet links.

Yahoo: Society and Culture: Death
http://dir.yahoo.com/Society_and_Culture/Death_and_Dying

This Yahoo site has an extensive index to diverse issues related to how different people approach death, such as beliefs about euthanasia, reincarnation, and burial.

UNIT 7: Sociocultural Change

Association for Political and Legal Anthropology
www.aaanet.org/apla/index.htm

As a branch of the American Anthropological Association, this organization supports workshops, lectures, and publications having to do with issues of contemporary importance in the fields of political and legal anthropology, such as nationalism, colonialism, and post-colonial public spheres, multiculturalism, and globalism.

Human Rights and Humanitarian Assistance
www.etown.edu/vl/humrts.html

Through this site you can conduct research into a number of human rights topics and issues affecting indigenous peoples in the modern era.

The Indigenous Rights Movement in the Pacific
www.inmotionmagazine.com/pacific.html

This article addresses issues that pertain to the problems of the Pacific Island peoples as a result of U.S. colonial expansion in the Pacific and Caribbean 100 years ago.

Murray Research Center
www.radcliffe.edu/murray_redirect/index.php

This site promotes the use of existing social science data to explore human development in the context of social change.

Internet References

RomNews Network—Online
www.romnews.com/community/index.php

This is a website dedicated to news and information for and about the Roma (European Gypsies). Visit here to learn more about their culture and the discrimination they constantly face.

Small Planet Institute
www.smallplanet.org/food

This organization promotes the right of everyone to one of the essentials of life—wholesome, nutritious, and safe food. It is activist as well as educational in its search for solutions to the environmental crises facing us today.

WWW Virtual Library: Indigenous Studies
http://cwis.org

This site presents resources collected by the Center for World Indigenous Studies (CWIS) in Africa, Asia, and the Middle East, Central and South America, Europe, and the Pacific.

World Map

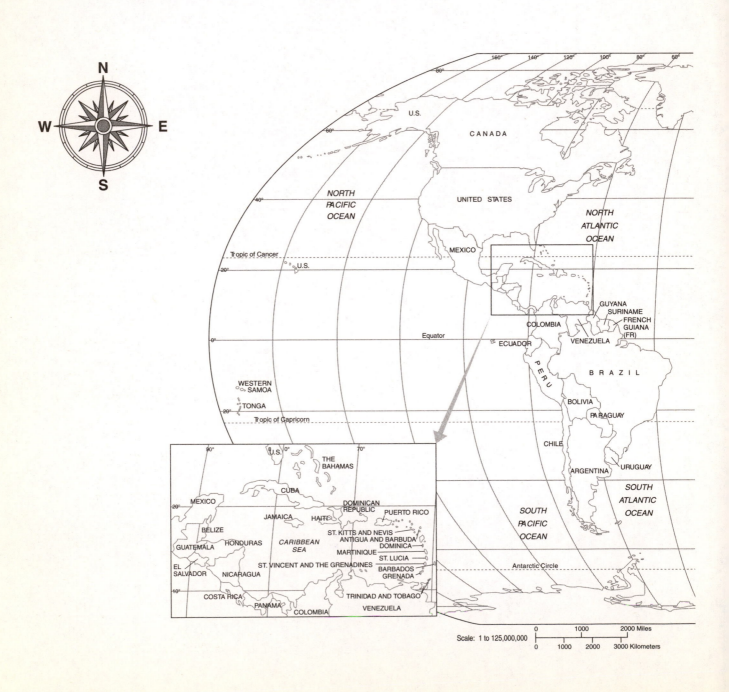

N
W   E
S

160° 140° 120° 100° 80° 60°

80°

U.S.

CANADA

60°

NORTH
PACIFIC
OCEAN

40°

UNITED STATES

MEXICO

NORTH
ATLANTIC
OCEAN

Tropic of Cancer

20°

U.S.

GUYANA
SURINAME
FRENCH
GUIANA
(FR)

COLOMBIA

VENEZUELA

Equator

0°

ECUADOR

P E R U

B R A Z I L

WESTERN
SAMOA

BOLIVIA

TONGA

20°

PARAGUAY

Tropic of Capricorn

CHILE

ARGENTINA

URUGUAY

SOUTH
ATLANTIC
OCEAN

SOUTH
PACIFIC
OCEAN

Antarctic Circle

90° 0° 70°

U.S.

THE
BAHAMAS

CUBA

20°

MEXICO

DOMINICAN
REPUBLIC

PUERTO RICO

JAMAICA

HAITI

BELIZE

ST. KITTS AND NEVIS
ANTIGUA AND BARBUDA
DOMINICA

GUATEMALA

HONDURAS

CARIBBEAN
SEA

MARTINIQUE

ST. LUCIA

EL
SALVADOR

NICARAGUA

ST. VINCENT AND THE GRENADINES

BARBADOS
GRENADA

10°

COSTA RICA

TRINIDAD AND TOBAGO

PANAMA

COLOMBIA

VENEZUELA

Scale: 1 to 125,000,000

0   1000   2000 Miles

0   1000   2000   3000 Kilometers

UNIT 1

Anthropological Perspectives

Unit Selections

1. **Queer Customs,** Clyde Kluckhohn
2. **Ethnographic Empathy and the Social Context of Rights: "Rescuing" Maasai Girls from Early Marriage,** Caroline S. Archambault
3. **Eating Christmas in the Kalahari,** Richard Borshay Lee
4. **Tricking and Tripping: Fieldwork on Prostitution in the Era of AIDS,** Claire E. Sterk
5. **The September 11 Effect on Anthropology,** Lara Deeb and Jessica Winegar

Learning Outcomes

After reading this Unit, you will be able to:

- Discuss the concept of "culture" and how it applies to the question of whether "biology is destiny."

- Describe some of the unique research strategies of anthropological fieldwork.

- Explain how anthropologists who become personally involved with a community through participant observation maintain their objectivity as scientists.

- Give examples of the kind of ethical obligations fieldworkers have toward their informants.

- Explain the ways in which the results of fieldwork depend on the kinds of questions asked.

- Identify some of the lessons that can be learned about one's own culture by doing anthropological fieldwork.

- What have been the effects of September 11 on the field of anthropology?

Student Website

www.mhhe.com/cls

Internet References

Archaeology and Anthropology Computing and Study Skills
www.isca.ox.ac.uk/index.html
Introduction to Anthropological Fieldwork and Ethnography
http://web.mit.edu/dumit/www/syl-anth.html
The Institute for Intercultural Studies
www.interculturalstudies.org/main.html
Theory in Anthropology
www.indiana.edu/~wanthro/theory.htm

For at least a century, the goals of anthropology have been to describe societies and cultures throughout the world and to compare and contrast the differences and similarities among them. Anthropologists study in a variety of settings and situations, ranging from small hamlets and villages to neighborhoods and corporate offices of major urban centers throughout the world. They study hunters and gatherers, peasants, farmers, labor leaders, politicians, and bureaucrats. They examine religious life in Latin America as well as revolutionary movements.

Wherever practicable, anthropologists take on the role of "participant observer." Through active involvement in the life ways of people, they hope to gain an insider's perspective without sacrificing the objectivity of the trained scientist. Sometimes the conditions for achieving such a goal seem to form an almost insurmountable barrier, but anthropologists call on persistence, adaptability, and imagination to overcome the odds against them. Read "Tricking and Tripping: Fieldwork on Prostitution in the Era of AIDS" to see how one anthropologist, Claire E. Sterk, solves the problems, both professional and personal, involved in trying to understand the precarious lives of prostitutes on the urban streets of America.

The diversity of focus in anthropology means that it is earmarked less by its particular subject matter than by its perspective. Although the discipline relates to both the biological and social sciences, anthropologists know that the boundaries drawn between disciplines are highly artificial. For example, while in theory it is possible to examine only the social organization of a family unit or the organization of political power in a nation-state, in reality it is impossible to separate the biological from the social, from the economic, from the political. The importance of the cultural aspects of our being is emphasized in the classic piece written by Clyde Kluckhohn, "Queer Customs," in which he makes the very important point that "biology is not destiny."

Richard Borshay Lee, in "Eating Christmas in the Kalahari," came to realize that what might be considered generous behavior

© Royalty-Free/CORBIS

in his culture conveyed a certain attitude incompatible with the values of his hosts. In the process, he learned an important lesson about how these hunter-gatherers have been able to survive for so long under conditions that we would consider marginal at best.

One might get the impression from some of the field experiences described in this unit that anthropology has to do with the exotic and the unusual and, therefore, is not particularly relevant to the larger world in which most of us live. On the contrary, much is at stake in our attempts to achieve a more objective understanding of the diversity of peoples' ways. Read the final article in this unit, "The September 11 Effect on Anthropology," to appreciate the importance of International understanding. After all, the purpose of anthropology is not only to describe and explain, but also to develop a special vision of the world in which cultural alternatives (past, present, and future) can be measured against one another and used as guides for human action.

Queer Customs

CLYDE KLUCKHOHN

Why do the Chinese dislike milk and milk products? Why would the Japanese die willingly in a Banzai charge that seemed senseless to Americans? Why do some nations trace descent through the father, others through the mother, still others through both parents? Not because different peoples have different instincts, not because they were destined by God or Fate to different habits, not because the weather is different in China and Japan and the United States. Sometimes shrewd common sense has an answer that is close to that of the anthropologist: "because they were brought up that way." By "culture" anthropology means the total life way of a people, the social legacy the individual acquires from his group. Or culture can be regarded as that part of the environment that is the creation of man.

This technical term has a wider meaning than the "culture" of history and literature. A humble cooking pot is as much a cultural product as is a Beethoven sonata. In ordinary speech a man of culture is a man who can speak languages other than his own, who is familiar with history, literature, philosophy, or the fine arts. In some cliques that definition is still narrower. The cultured person is one who can talk about James Joyce, Scarlatti, and Picasso. To the anthropologist, however, to be human is to be cultured. There is culture in general, and then there are the specific cultures such as Russian, American, British, Hottentot, Inca. The general abstract notion services to remind us that we cannot explain acts solely in terms of the biological properties of the people concerned, their individual past experience, and the immediate situation. The past experience of other men in the form of culture enters into almost every event. Each specific culture constitutes a kind of blueprint for all of life's activities.

One of the interesting things about human beings is that they try to understand themselves and their own behavior. While this has been particularly true of Europeans in recent times, there is no group which has not developed a scheme or schemes to explain man's actions. To the insistent human query "why?" the most exciting illumination anthropology has to offer is that of the concept of culture. Its explanatory importance is comparable to categories such as evolution in biology, gravity in physics, disease in medicine. A good deal of human behavior can be understood, and indeed predicted, if we know a people's design for living. Many acts are neither accidental nor due to personal pecularities nor caused by supernatural forces nor simply mysterious. Even those of us who pride ourselves on our individualism follow most of the time a pattern not of our own making. We brush our teeth on arising. We put on pants—not a loincloth or a grass skirt. We eat three meals a day—not four or five or two. We sleep in a bed—not in a hammock or on a sheep pelt. I do not have to know the individual and his life history to be able to predict these and countless other regularities, including many in the thinking process, of all Americans who are not incarcerated in jails or hospitals for the insane.

To the American woman a system of plural wives seems "instinctively" abhorrent. She cannot understand how any woman can fail to be jealous and uncomfortable if she must share her husband with other women. She feels it "unnatural" to accept such a situation. On the other hand, a Koryak woman of Siberia, for example, would find it hard to understand how a woman could be so selfish and so undesirous of femine companionship in the home as to wish to restrict her husband to one mate.

Some years ago I met in New York City a young man who did not speak a word of English and was obviously bewildered by American ways. By "blood" he was as American as you or I, for his parents had gone from Indiana to China as missionaries. Orphaned in infancy, he was reared by a Chinese family in a remote village. All who met him found him more Chinese than American. The facts of his blue eyes and light hair were less impressive than a Chinese style of gait, Chinese arm and hand movements, Chinese facial expression, and Chinese modes of thought. The biological heritage was American, but the cultural training had been Chinese. He returned to China.

Another example of another kind: I once knew a trader's wife in Arizona who took a somewhat devilish interest in producing a cultural reaction. Guests who came her way were often served delicious sandwiches filled with a meat that seemed to be neither chicken nor tuna fish yet was reminiscent of both. To queries she gave no reply until each had eaten his fill. She then explained that what they had eaten was not chicken, not tuna fish, but the rich, white flesh of freshly killed rattlesnakes. The response was instantaneous—vomiting, often violent vomiting. A biological process is caught in a cultural web.

A highly intelligent teacher with long and successful experience in the public schools of Chicago was finishing her first year in an Indian school. When asked how her Navaho pupils compared in intelligence with Chicago youngsters, she replied, "Well, I just don't know. Sometimes the Indians seem just as bright. At other times they just act like dumb animals. The other night we had a dance in the high school. I saw a boy who is one of the best students in my English class standing off by himself. So I took him over to a pretty girl and told them to dance. But they just stood there with their heads down. They wouldn't even say anything." I inquired if she knew whether or not they were members of the same clan. "What difference would that make?"

"How would you feel about getting into bed with your brother?" The teacher walked off in a huff, but, actually, the two cases were quite comparable in principle. To the Indian the type of bodily contact involved in our social dancing has a directly sexual connotation. The incest taboos between members of the same clan are as severe as between true brothers and sisters. The shame of the Indians at the suggestion that a clan brother and sister should dance and the indignation of the white teacher at the idea that she should share a bed with an adult brother represent equally nonrational responses, culturally standardized unreason.

All this does not mean that there is no such thing as raw human nature. The very fact that certain of the same institutions are found in all known societies indicates that at bottom all human beings are very much alike. The files of the Cross-Cultural Survey at Yale University are organized according to categories such as "marriage ceremonies" "life crisis rites," "incest taboos." At least seventy-five of these categories are represented in every single one of the hundreds of cultures analyzed. This is hardly surprising. The members of all human groups have about the same biological equipment. All men undergo the same poignant life experiences such as birth, helplessness, illness, old age, and death. The biological potentialities of the species are the blocks with which cultures are built. Some patterns of every culture crystallize around focuses provided by the inevitables of biology: the difference between the sexes, the presence of persons of different ages, the varying physical strength and skill of individuals. The facts of nature also limit culture forms. No culture provides patterns for jumping over trees or for eating iron ore.

There is thus no "either-or" between nature and that special form of nurture called culture. Culture determinism is as one-sided as biological determinism. The two factors are interdependent. Culture arises out of human nature, and its forms are restricted both by man's biology and by natural laws. It is equally true that culture channels biological processes—vomiting, weeping, fainting, sneezing, the daily habits of food intake and waste elimination. When a man eats, he is reacting to an internal "drive," namely, hunger contractions consequent upon the lowering of blood sugar, but his precise reaction to these internal stimuli cannot be predicted by physiological knowledge alone. Whether a healthy adult feels hungry twice, three times, or four times a day and the hours at which this feeling recurs is a question of culture. *What* he eats is of course limited by availability, but is also partly regulated by culture. It is a biological fact that some types of berries are poisonous; it is a cultural fact that, a few generations ago, most Americans considered tomatoes to be poisonous and refused to eat them. Such selective, discriminative use of the environment is characteristically cultural. In a still more general sense, too, the process of eating is channeled by culture. Whether a man eats to live, lives to eat, or merely eats and lives is only in part an individual matter, for there are also cultural trends. Emotions are physiological events. Certain

situations will evoke fear in people from any culture. But sensations of pleasure, anger, and lust may be stimulated by cultural cues that would leave unmoved someone who has been reared in a different social tradition.

Except in the case of newborn babies and of individuals born with clear-cut structural or functional abnormalities we can observe innate endowments only as modified by cultural training. In a hospital in New Mexico where Zuñi Indian, Navaho Indian, and white American babies are born, it is possible to classify the newly arrived infants as unusually active, average, and quiet. Some babies from each "racial" group will fall into each category, though a higher proportion of the white babies will fall into the unusually active class. But if a Navaho baby, a Zuñi baby, and a white baby—all classified as unusually active at birth—are again observed at the age of two years, the Zuñi baby will no longer seem given to quick and restless activity— *as compared with the white child*—though he may seem so as compared with the other Zuñis of the same age. The Navaho child is likely to fall in between as contrasted with the Zuñi and the white, though he will probably still seem more active than the average Navaho youngster.

It was remarked by many observers in the Japanese relocation centers that Japanese who were born and brought up in this country, especially those who were reared apart from any large colony of Japanese, resemble in behavior their white neighbors much more closely than they do their own parents who were educated in Japan.

I have said "culture channels biological processes." It is more accurate to say "the biological functioning of individuals is modified if they have been trained in certain ways and not in others." Culture is not a disembodied force. It is created and transmitted by people. However, culture, like well-known concepts of the physical sciences, is a convenient abstraction. One never sees gravity. One sees bodies falling in regular ways. One never sees an electromagnetic field. Yet certain happenings that can be seen may be given a neat abstract formulation by assuming that the electromagnetic field, exists. Similarly, one never sees culture as such. What is seen are regularities in the behavior or artifacts of a group that has adhered to a common tradition. The regularities in style and technique of ancient Inca tapestries or stone axes from Melanesian islands are due to the existence of mental blue-prints for the group.

Culture is a *way* of thinking, feeling, believing. It is the group's knowledge stored up (in memories of men; in books and objects) for future use. We study the products of this "mental" activity: the overt behavior, the speech and gestures and activities of people, and the tangible results of these things such as tools, houses, cornfields, and what not. It has been customary in lists of "culture traits" to include such things as watches or lawbooks. This is a convenient way of thinking about them, but in the solution of any important problem we must remember that they, in themselves, are nothing but metals, paper, and ink, What is important is that some men know how to make them, others set a value on them, are unhappy without them, direct their activities in relation to them, or disregard them.

It is only a helpful shorthand when we say "The cultural patterns of the Zulu were resistant to Christianization." In the directly observable world of course, it was individual Zulus who resisted. Nevertheless, if we do not forget that we are speaking at a high level of abstraction, it is justifiable to speak of culture as a cause. One may compare the practice of saying "syphilis caused the extinction of the native population of the island." Was it "syphilis" or "syphilis germs" or "human beings who were carriers of syphilis?"

"Culture" then, is "a theory." But if a theory is not contradicted by any relevant fact and if it helps us to understand a mass of otherwise chaotic facts, it is useful. Darwin's contribution was much less the accumulation of new knowledge than the creation of a theory which put in order data already known. An accumulation of facts, however large, is no more a science than a pile of bricks is a house. Anthropology's demonstration that the most weird set of customs has a consistency and an order is comparable to modern psychiatry's showing that there is meaning and purpose in the apparently incoherent talk of the insane. In fact, the inability of the older psychologies and philosophies to account for the strange behavior of madmen and heathens was the principal factor that forced psychiatry and anthropology to develop theories of the unconscious and of culture.

Since culture is an abstraction, it is important not to confuse culture with society. A "society" refers to a group of people who interact more with each other than they do with other individuals—who cooperate with each other for the attainment of certain ends. You can see and indeed count the individuals who make up a society. A "culture" refers to the distinctive ways of life of such a group of people. Not all social events are culturally patterned. New types of circumstances arise for which no cultural solutions have as yet been devised.

A culture constitutes a storehouse of the pooled learning of the group. A rabbit starts life with some innate responses. He can learn from his own experience and perhaps from observing other rabbits. A human infant is born with fewer instincts and greater plasticity. His main task is to learn the answers that persons he will never see, persons long dead, have worked out. Once he has learned the formulas supplied by the culture of his group, most of his behavior becomes almost as automatic and unthinking as if it were instinctive. There is a tremendous amount of intelligence behind the making of a radio, but not much is required to learn to turn it on.

The members of all human societies face some of the same unavoidable dilemmas, posed by biology and other facts of the human situation. This is why the basic categories of all cultures are so similar. Human culture without language is unthinkable. No culture fails to provide for aesthetic expression and aesthetic delight. Every culture supplies standardized orientations toward the deeper problems, such as death. Every culture is designed to perpetuate the group and its solidarity, to meet the demands of individuals for an orderly way of life and for satisfaction of biological needs.

However, the variations on these basic themes are numberless. Some languages are built up out of twenty basic sounds, others out of forty. Nose plugs were considered beautiful by the predynastic Egyptians but are not by the modern French. Puberty is a biological fact. But one culture ignores it, another

prescribes informal instructions about sex but no ceremony, a third has impressive rites for girls only, a fourth for boys and girls. In this culture, the first menstruation is welcomed as a happy, natural event; in that culture the atmosphere is full of dread and supernatural threat. Each culture dissects nature according to its own system of categories. The Navaho Indians apply the same word to the color of a robin's egg and to that of grass. A psychologist once assumed that this meant a difference in the sense organs, that Navahos didn't have the physiological equipment to distinguish "green" from "blue." However, when he showed them objects of the two colors and asked them if they were exactly the same colors, they looked at him with astonishment. His dream of discovering a new type of color blindness was shattered.

Every culture must deal with the sexual instinct. Some, however, seek to deny all sexual expression before marriage, whereas a Polynesian adolescent who was not promiscuous would be distinctly abnormal. Some cultures enforce lifelong monogamy, others, like our own, tolerate serial monogamy; in still other cultures, two or more women may be joined to one man or several men to a single woman. Homosexuality has been a permitted pattern in the Greco-Roman world, in parts of Islam, and in various, primitive tribes. Large portions of the population of Tibet, and of Christendom at some places and periods, have practiced completely celibacy. To us marriage is first and foremost an arrangement between two individuals. In many more societies marriage is merely one facet of a complicated set of reciprocities, economic and otherwise, between two families or two clans.

The essence of the cultural process is selectivity. The selection is only exceptionally conscious and rational. Cultures are like Topsy. They just grew. Once, however, a way of handling a situation becomes institutionalized, there is ordinarily great resistance to change or deviation. When we speak of "our sacred beliefs," we mean of course that they are beyond criticism and that the person who suggests modification or abandonment must be punished. No person is emotionally indifferent to his culture. Certain cultural premises may become totally out of accord with a new factual situation. Leaders may recognize this and reject the old ways in theory. Yet their emotional loyalty continues in the face of reason because of the intimate conditionings of early childhood.

A culture is learned by individuals as the result of belonging to some particular group, and it constitutes that part of learned behavior which is shared with others. It is our social legacy, as contrasted with our organic heredity. It is one of the important factors which permits us to live together in an organized society, giving us ready-made solutions to our problems, helping us to predict the behavior of others, and permitting others to know what to expect of us.

Culture regulates our lives at every turn. From the moment we are born until we die there is, whether we are conscious of it or not, constant pressure upon us to follow certain types of behavior that other men have created for us. Some paths we follow willingly, others we follow because we know no other way, still others we deviate from or go back to most unwillingly.

Mothers of small children know how unnaturally most of this comes to us—how little regard we have, until we are "culturalized," for the "proper" place, time, and manner for certain acts such as eating, excreting, sleeping, getting dirty, and making loud noises. But by more or less adhering to a system of related designs for carrying out all the acts of living, a group of men and women feel themselves linked together by a powerful chain of sentiments. Ruth Benedict gave an almost complete definition of the concept when she said, "Culture is that which binds men together."

It is true any culture is a set of techniques for adjusting both to the external environment and to other men. However, cultures create problems as well as solve them. If the lore of a people states that frogs are dangerous creatures, or that it is not safe to go about at night because of witches or ghosts, threats are posed which do not arise out of the inexorable facts of the external world. Cultures produce needs as well as provide a means of fulfilling them. There exists for every group culturally defined, acquired drives that may be more powerful in ordinary daily life than the biologically inborn drives. Many Americans, for example, will work harder for "success" than they will for sexual satisfaction.

Most groups elaborate certain aspects of their culture far beyond maximum utility or survival value. In other words, not all culture promotes physical survival. At times, indeed, it does exactly the opposite. Aspects of culture which once were adaptive may persist long after they have ceased to be useful. An analysis of any culture will disclose many features which cannot possibly be construed as adaptations to the total environment in which the group now finds itself. However, it is altogether likely that these apparently useless features represent survivals, with modifications through time, of cultural forms which were adaptive in one or another previous situation.

Any cultural practice must be functional or it will disappear before long. That is, it must somehow contribute to the survival of the society or to the adjustment of the individual. However, many cultural functions are not manifest but latent. A cowboy will walk three miles to catch a horse which he then rides one mile to the store. From the point of view of manifest function this is positively irrational. But the act has the latent function of maintaining the cowboy's prestige in the terms of his own subculture. One can instance the buttons on the sleeve of a man's coat, our absurd English spelling, the use of capital letters, and a host of other apparently nonfunctional customs. They serve mainly the latent function of assisting individuals to maintain their security by preserving continuity with the past and by making certain sectors of life familiar and predictable.

Every culture is a precipitate of history. In more than one sense history is a sieve. Each culture embraces those aspects of the past which, usually in altered form and with altered meanings, live on in the present. Discoveries and inventions, both material and ideological, are constantly being made available to a group through its historical contacts with other peoples or being created by its own members. However, only those that fit the total immediate situation in meeting the group's needs for survival or in promoting the psychological adjustment of

individuals will become part of the culture. The process of culture building may be regarded as an addition to man's innate biological capacities, an addition providing instruments which enlarge, or may even substitute for, biological functions, and to a degree compensating for biological limitations—as in ensuring that death does not always result in the loss to humanity of what the deceased has learned.

Culture is like a map. Just as a map isn't the territory but an abstract representation of a particular area, so also a culture is an abstract description of trends toward uniformity in the words, deeds, and artifacts of a human group. If a map is accurate and you can read it, you won't get lost; if you know a culture, you will know your way around in the life of a society. Many educated people have the notion that culture applies only to exotic ways of life or to societies where relative simplicity and relative homogeneity prevail. Some sophisticated missionaries, for example, will use the anthropological conception in discussing the special modes of living of South Sea Islanders, but seem amazed at the idea that it could be applied equally to inhabitants of New York City. And social workers in Boston will talk about the culture of a colorful and well-knit immigrant group but boggle at applying it to the behavior of staff members in the social-service agency itself.

In the primitive society the correspondence between the habits of individuals and the customs of the community is ordinarily greater. There is probably some truth in what an old Indian once said, "In the old days there was no law; everybody did what was right." The primitive tends to find happiness in the fulfillment of intricately involuted cultural patterns; the modern more often tends to feel the pattern as repressive to his individuality. It is also true that in a complex stratified society there are numerous exceptions to generalizations made about the culture as a whole. It is necessary to study regional, class, and occupational subcultures. Primitive cultures have greater stability than modern cultures; they change—but less rapidly.

However, modern men also are creators and carriers of culture. Only in some respects are they influenced differently from primitives by culture. Moreover, there are such wide variations in primitive cultures that any black-and-white contrast between the primitive and the civilized is altogether fictitious. The distinction which is most generally true lies in the field of conscious philosophy.

The publication of Paul Radin's *Primitive Man as a Philosopher* did much toward destroying the myth that an abstract analysis of experience was a peculiarity of literate societies.

Critical Thinking

1. Why do customs differ, according to Clyde Kluckhohn?

2. What is "culture"? In what sense does the term have a wider meaning than that of the "culture" of history and literature? Of what does this general, more abstract notion remind us?

3. Discuss, with examples, the explanatory importance of the concept of culture.

4. In what respects does nature play a role in shaping cultures?

5. What is Kluckhohn's view of cultural determinism vs. biological determinism?

6. Is culture a "disembodied force" or a "convenient abstraction"? Explain.

7. In what sense is "culture" a "theory"? How is it "useful"?

8. What is the difference between "culture" and "society"?

9. How can culture be thought of as a storehouse of pooled learning?

10. Why are the basic categories of all cultures so similar? To what extent are there variations on the basic themes?

11. Why does the author say "selectivity" is the essence of culture?

12. How might cultures create problems as well as solve them? Produce needs as well as provide a means of fulfilling them?

13. What are "survivals"?

14. What is the difference between a "manifest function" and a "latent function"?

15. How is culture like a map? Does it apply only to an exotic way of life? Explain.

Kluckhohn, Clyde. From *Mirror for Man: Anthropology and Modern Life,* 1994, pp. 6–12. Copyright © 1994 by Clyde Kluckhohn. Reprinted by permission of Clyde Kluckhohn's estate.

Ethnographic Empathy and the Social Context of Rights: "Rescuing" Maasai Girls from Early Marriage

Caroline S. Archambault

Esther was the first of five young women in line to talk to me. We sat on the steps of the boarding house of a Maasai school on the edge of town in southern Kenya. Esther is tall, thin, and, even at the young age of 17, has an air of confidence about her. Without much prompting on my part, she dove into her story—one she has clearly told many times before.

My father wanted to give me away. I went to my sister in Kiserian and she sent me to school. My mzee [father] came to remove me from school. I got help from my brother and a teacher. They brought me to the District Officer. He wrote me a letter to bring to the head teacher. I came here and started in class 2. Now I am in class 5. [interview, June 24, 2007]

Esther is one of several young Maasai girls in Kenya who have been "rescued" from early marriage, taking up residence in centers specifically created to shelter, feed, and educate them. The centers, first pioneered almost two decades ago, are largely funded by international donors. They have gained considerable momentum following Kenya's Free Primary Education initiative in 2002 and the growing popularity of a rights-based approach to development. The centers are part of a wider network of initiatives and organizations that support the second and third Millennium Development Goals: namely, gender equality, female empowerment, and the rights of all children to an education. Maasai practices of early marriage and the associated practice of female circumcision, in particular, have come under fire internationally, as they constitute some of the most obvious examples of gender-based violence and infringements on the rights of the child.

Several years prior to this meeting with Esther, as part of my doctoral fieldwork on Maasai education, I volunteered

at a Maasai boarding school known for pioneering the rescue-center service. I was encouraged by the administration to interview several of the 22 "rescued girls" that took refuge in this center. As they explained, getting their stories out to the public was an important strategy in finding sponsors to support the girls' continued studies. In 2007, I returned to follow up on these interviews and met Esther for the first time. Esther's story shared a distinct narrative structure with the stories told to me by the other girls. A typical narrative begins with a father or uncle's marriage plans for her, is followed by a brief explanation of her narrow escape, and concludes with the girl happily ever after in pursuit of an education. This story line is usually framed by a set of prevailing binaries that distinguish violators from victims, patriarchy from female empowerment, tradition from modernity, and collective culture from individual rights. I came to recognize this as the narrative form commonly used to depict early marriage in the international media, in development circles within Kenya, and even locally in Enkop, Esther's home. Although such a framework may be effective in mobilizing public support, it essentializes and renders static notions of "victimhood," "tradition," "culture," and "rights"; it obscures the real structural underlying factors that give rise to the practice of early marriage, among the Maasai; and it deflects attention from important policy interventions that could more effectively address the issue. Because Esther had run away from Enkop, the community where I have been working for more than seven years, the profound limitations of these conventional narratives were apparent to me. Interviews with her friends, family members, and other members of the community, as well as regular periods of fieldwork on a variety of topics, brought out the complexity of the issue of early marriage and the importance of ethnographic con-textualization for effectively addressing this problem.[3]

As my interview with Esther's father illustrated, the fathers, who are commonly viewed as responsible for these incidences of early marriage, are often not the cari-cature of the traditional, conservative, pastoral patriarch. Esther's father proclaims himself to be "a very good man of education" (interview, November 3, 2007). Formal education, he hopes, will offer his children alternatives to the exclusive practice of pastoralism in a region where rapid land fragmentation and dispossession, continued neglect by the state, increased climactic instability, and heightened population pressure have all compromised the viability of a pastoral livelihood for Maasai youth. With three wives and 26 children, his educational record is rather exceptional compared to the average family in Enkop. Despite never attending school himself and rais-ing his children in a time when it was uncommon to send many children to school, Esther's father has served for years as the chairman of the primary school management committee. He has managed to send all but eight of his 26 children to school. Esther's mother, who never attended school herself, has had three of her seven children (two boys and one girl) pursue secondary studies—a remark-able feat by Enkop standards. Esther, the fifth-born child and fourth-born daughter, together with her eldest sister, were the two children in her family who were not sent to school. "[Esther] was not a school girl," her father explained. "She was a girl of the home. . . . We tried to educate all our children but it depended on our cows and goats and poverty. . . . I have had children in six differ-ent schools, so I am a very good man for education. The problem is [too few] animals" (interview, November 3, 2007). Esther's father decided it best to secure her future as a pastoralist by marrying her to a good family and husband at the age of 14.

Esther resisted her status as a "girl of the home." Shortly before her marriage, she secretly enrolled herself in school under the pretense of visiting her sister. When news reached her parents, her mother was sent to retrieve her, and the wedding plans were expedited. The night of her wedding, when friends and family of the bride and groom were in attendance and the festivities had started, Esther ran away to the center with the help of her brother and a local teacher. The wedding had to be cancelled, and initial bridewealth payments returned to the groom and his family. Following her escape, domestic conflict ensued: Esther's father suspected his wife and son of colluding with his daughter and forced them to temporarily leave their home. On visiting the center to retrieve Esther, Esther's

father was told by the headmistress that she was now "a school child." "Esther will be your child," he replied. "You will give her a husband and she will never set foot in my house again. I don't count her as a child in my family" (interview, June 1, 2007). Esther was disowned.

Years have passed and because Esther has been suc-cessful in her studies, her father has now accepted her back as his daughter. He recognizes and appreciates her as a "girl of school" and hopes that education will provide her with a secure livelihood and a good husband.

There are significant limitations to the conventional view of Esther's story as a simple tension between culture–patriarchy–tradition and a girl's right to an education. In this article, I offer novel research findings by ethnographi-cally contextualizing the underlying factors giving rise to practices of early marriage among the Maasai in Enkop. The investigation provides a unique perspective on con-temporary predicaments that the practice of pastoralism encounters in the face of land-tenure reform, political mar-ginality and state neglect, climactic instability, and popula-tion growth. It demonstrates the insecurities and challenges associated with formal education. Through the intimate portrayal of Esther's case against this backdrop of societal change, early marriage is situated not as a relic of tradi-tion and malicious patriarchy but, rather, as a contempo-rary adaptation to livelihood insecurity. This case study illustrates how prevailing concepts of "tradition," "culture," "victimhood," and "collective rights" in human rights theory obscure important structural factors that give rise to early marriage and deflect attention from effective policy ini-tiatives. This article responds to recent calls for a critical anthropology of human rights, one that not only pursues an ethnography of human rights practice but also uses its findings to reflect back on basic theoretical and practical dimensions of the human rights project (Goodale 2006, 2009a, 2009b).

Critical Thinking

1. In what respects are young Maasai girls such as Esther con-sidered to be "rescued?" What are the "prevailing binaries" that characterize this story?

2. How is it that Esther's father did not fit the commonly viewed stereotype of the traditional conservative pastoral father and, yet, decided to marry off Esther at the age of 14?

3. What are the key provisions of Kenya's Children Act? What are the implications of early marriage in this context?

4. Why does the author describe Enkop as having little agricultural potential and little infrastructure?

5. What are the three main channels through which rights discourses flow?

Article 2. Ethnographic Empathy and the Social Context of Rights: "Rescuing" Maasai Girls from Early Marriage

6. How does Esther's case reflect the prevailing structural binaries found in popular narratives? In what respects and why did most people embrace a hybrid variation infused with local meaning?

7. Why is pastoralism becoming increasingly difficult for the region of Enkop? How is it that marriage and the social networks are of continuing importance in this context?

8. Why are the ages of circumcision and first marriage among the Maasai decreasing?

9. Discuss the implications and challenges raised by the "ethnographic version" put forth by the author.

10. What does Esther's case identify as the root cause of early marriage?

11. What policy initiatives does the author suggest for eliminating the practice of early marriage?

From *American Anthropologist,* Vol. 113, Issue 4; December 2011, pp. 632–643. Copyright © 2011 by American Anthropological Association. Reprinted by permission.

Eating Christmas in the Kalahari

RICHARD BORSHAY LEE

The !Kung Bushmen's knowledge of Christmas is third-hand. The London Missionary Society brought the holiday to the southern Tswana tribes in the early nineteenth century. Later, native catechists spread the idea far and wide among the Bantu-speaking pastoralists, even in the remotest corners of the Kalahari Desert. The Bushmen's idea of the Christmas story, stripped to its essentials, is "praise the birth of white man's god-chief"; what keeps their interest in the holiday high is the Tswana-Herero custom of slaughtering an ox for his Bushmen neighbors as an annual goodwill gesture. Since the 1930s, part of the Bushmen's annual round of activities has included a December congregation at the cattle posts for trading, marriage brokering, and several days of trance-dance feasting at which the local Tswana headman is host.

As a social anthropologist working with !Kung Bushmen, I found that the Christmas ox custom suited my purposes. I had come to the Kalahari to study the hunting and gathering subsistence economy of the !Kung, and to accomplish this it was essential not to provide them with food, share my own food, or interfere in any way with their food-gathering activities. While liberal handouts of tobacco and medical supplies were appreciated, they were scarcely adequate to erase the glaring disparity in wealth between the anthropologist, who maintained a two-month inventory of canned goods, and the Bushmen, who rarely had a day's supply of food on hand. My approach, while paying off in terms of data, left me open to frequent accusations of stinginess and hard-heartedness. By their lights, I was a miser.

The Christmas ox was to be my way of saying thank you for the cooperation of the past year; and since it was to be our last Christmas in the field, I determined to slaughter the largest, meatiest ox that money could buy, insuring that the feast and trance-dance would be a success.

Through December I kept my eyes open at the wells as the cattle were brought down for watering. Several animals were offered, but none had quite the grossness that I had in mind. Then, ten days before the holiday, a Herero friend led an ox of astonishing size and mass up to our camp. It was solid black, stood five feet high at the shoulder, had a five-foot span of horns, and must have weighed 1,200 pounds on the hoof. Food consumption calculations are my specialty, and I quickly figured that bones and viscera aside, there was enough meat—at least four pounds—for every man, woman, and child of the 150 Bushmen in the vicinity of /ai/ai who were expected at the feast.

Having found the right animal at last, I paid the Herero £20 ($56) and asked him to keep the beast with his herd until Christmas day. The next morning word spread among the people that the big solid black one was the ox chosen by /ontah (my Bushman name; it means, roughly, "whitey") for the Christmas feast. That afternoon I received the first delegation. Ben!a, an outspoken sixty-year-old mother of five, came to the point slowly.

"Where were you planning to eat Christmas?"

"Right here at /ai/ai," I replied.

"Alone or with others?"

"I expect to invite all the people to eat Christmas with me."

"Eat what?"

"I have purchased Yehave's black ox, and I am going to slaughter and cook it."

"That's what we were told at the well but refused to believe it until we heard it from yourself."

"Well, it's the black one," I replied expansively, although wondering what she was driving at.

"Oh, no!" Ben!a groaned, turning to her group. "They were right." Turning back to me she asked, "Do you expect us to eat that bag of bones?"

"Bag of bones! It's the biggest ox at /ai/ai."

"Big, yes, but old. And thin. Everybody knows there's no meat on that old ox. What did you expect us to eat off it, the horns?"

Everybody chuckled at Ben!a's one-liner as they walked away, but all I could manage was a weak grin.

That evening it was the turn of the young men. They came to sit at our evening fire. /gaugo, about my age, spoke to me man-to-man.

"/ontah, you have always been square with us," he lied. "What has happened to change your heart? That sack of guts and bones of Yehave's will hardly feed one camp, let alone all the Bushmen around ai/ai." And he proceeded to enumerate the seven camps in the /ai/ai vicinity, family by family. "Perhaps you have forgotten that we are not few, but many. Or are you too blind to tell the difference between a proper cow and an old wreck? That ox is thin to the point of death."

"Look, you guys," I retorted, "that is a beautiful animal, and I'm sure you will eat it with pleasure at Christmas."

"Of course we will eat it; it's food. But it won't fill us up to the point where we will have enough strength to dance. We will eat and go home to bed with stomachs rumbling."

That night as we turned in, I asked my wife, Nancy: "What did you think of the black ox?"

"It looked enormous to me. Why?"

"Well, about eight different people have told me I got gypped; that the ox is nothing but bones."

"What's the angle?" Nancy asked. "Did they have a better one to sell?"

"No, they just said that it was going to be a grim Christmas because there won't be enough meat to go around. Maybe I'll get an independent judge to look at the beast in the morning."

Bright and early, Halingisi, a Tswana cattle owner, appeared at our camp. But before I could ask him to give me his opinion on Yehave's black ox, he gave me the eye signal that indicated a confidential chat. We left the camp and sat down.

"/ontah, I'm surprised at you: you've lived here for three years and still haven't learned anything about cattle."

"But what else can a person do but choose the biggest, strongest animal one can find?" I retorted.

"Look, just because an animal is big doesn't mean that it has plenty of meat on it. The black one was a beauty when it was younger, but now it is thin to the point of death."

"Well I've already bought it. What can I do at this stage?"

"Bought it already? I thought you were just considering it. Well, you'll have to kill it and serve it, I suppose. But don't expect much of a dance to follow."

My spirits dropped rapidly. I could believe that Ben!a and /gaugo just might be putting me on about the black ox, but Halingisi seemed to be an impartial critic. I went around that day feeling as though I had bought a lemon of a used car.

In the afternoon it was Tomazo's turn. Tomazo is a fine hunter, a top trance performer . . . and one of my most reliable informants. He approached the subject of the Christmas cow as part of my continuing Bushman education.

"My friend, the way it is with us Bushmen," he began, "is that we love meat. And even more than that, we love fat. When we hunt we always search for the fat ones, the ones dripping with layers of white fat: fat that turns into a clear, thick oil in the cooking pot, fat that slides down your gullet, fills your stomach and gives you a roaring diarrhea," he rhapsodized.

"So, feeling as we do," he continued, "it gives us pain to be served such a scrawny thing as Yehave's black ox. It is big, yes, and no doubt its giant bones are good for soup, but fat is what we really crave and so we will eat Christmas this year with a heavy heart."

The prospect of a gloomy Christmas now had me worried, so I asked Tomazo what I could do about it.

"Look for a fat one, a young one . . . smaller, but fat. Fat enough to make us //gom ('evacuate the bowels'), then we will be happy."

My suspicions were aroused when Tomazo said that he happened to know of a young, fat, barren cow that the owner was willing to part with. Was Tomazo working on commission, I wondered? But I dispelled this unworthy thought when we approached the Herero owner of the cow in question and found that he had decided not to sell.

The scrawny wreck of a Christmas ox now became the talk of the /ai/ai water hole and was the first news told to the outlying groups as they began to come in from the bush for the feast. What finally convinced me that real trouble might be brewing was the visit from u!au, an old conservative with a reputation for fierceness. His nickname meant spear and referred to an incident thirty years ago in which he had speared a man to death. He had an intense manner; fixing me with his eyes, he said in clipped tones:

"I have only just heard about the black ox today, or else I would have come here earlier. /ontah, do you honestly think you can serve meat like that to people and avoid a fight?" He paused, letting the implications sink in. "I don't mean fight you, /ontah; you are a white man. I mean a fight between Bushmen. There are many fierce ones here, and with such a small quantity of meat to distribute, how can you give everybody a fair share? Someone is sure to accuse another of taking too much or hogging all the choice pieces. Then you will see what happens when some go hungry while others eat."

The possibility of at least a serious argument struck me as all too real. I had witnessed the tension that surrounds the distribution of meat from a kudu or gemsbok kill, and had documented many arguments that sprang up from a real or imagined slight in meat distribution. The owners of a kill may spend up to two hours arranging and rearranging the piles of meat under the gaze of a circle of recipients before handing them out. And I also knew that the Christmas feast at /ai/ai would be bringing together groups that had feuded in the past.

Convinced now of the gravity of the situation, I went in earnest to search for a second cow; but all my inquiries failed to turn one up.

The Christmas feast was evidently going to be a disaster, and the incessant complaints about the meagerness of the ox had already taken the fun out of it for me. Moreover, I was getting bored with the wisecracks, and after losing my temper a few times, I resolved to serve the beast anyway. If the meat fell short, the hell with it. In the Bushmen idiom, I announced to all who would listen:

"I am a poor man and blind. If I have chosen one that is too old and too thin, we will eat it anyway and see if there is enough meat there to quiet the rumbling of our stomachs."

On hearing this speech, Ben!a offered me a rare word of comfort. "It's thin," she said philosophically, "but the bones will make a good soup."

At dawn Christmas morning, instinct told me to turn over the butchering and cooking to a friend and take off with Nancy to spend Christmas alone in the bush. But curiosity kept me from retreating. I wanted to see what such a scrawny ox looked like on butchering and if there *was* going to be a fight, I wanted to catch every word of it. Anthropologists are incurable that way.

The great beast was driven up to our dancing ground, and a shot in the forehead dropped it in its tracks. Then, freshly cut branches were heaped around the fallen carcass to receive the meat. Ten men volunteered to help with the cutting. I asked /gaugo to make the breast bone cut. This cut, which begins the

11

butchering process for most large game, offers easy access for removal of the viscera. But it also allows the hunter to spot-check the amount of fat on the animal. A fat game animal carries a white layer up to an inch thick on the chest, while in a thin one, the knife will quickly cut to bone. All eyes fixed on his hand as /gaugo, dwarfed by the great carcass, knelt to the breast. The first cut opened a pool of solid white in the black skin. The second and third cut widened and deepened the creamy white. Still no bone. It was pure fat; it must have been two inches thick.

"Hey /gau," I burst out, "that ox is loaded with fat. What's this about the ox being too thin to bother eating? Are you out of your mind?"

"Fat?" /gau shot back, "You call that fat? This wreck is thin, sick, dead!" And he broke out laughing. So did everyone else. They rolled on the ground, paralyzed with laughter. Everybody laughed except me; I was thinking.

I ran back to the tent and burst in just as Nancy was getting up. "Hey, the black ox. It's fat as hell! They were kidding about it being too thin to eat. It was a joke or something. A put-on. Everyone is really delighted with it!"

"Some joke," my wife replied. "It was so funny that you were ready to pack up and leave /ai/ai."

If it had indeed been a joke, it had been an extraordinarily convincing one, and tinged, I thought, with more than a touch of malice as many jokes are. Nevertheless, that it was a joke lifted my spirits considerably, and I returned to the butchering site where the shape of the ox was rapidly disappearing under the axes and knives of the butchers. The atmosphere had become festive. Grinning broadly, their arms covered with blood well past the elbow, men packed chunks of meat into the big cast-iron cooking pots, fifty pounds to the load, and muttered and chuckled all the while about the thinness and worthlessness of the animal and /ontah's poor judgment.

We danced and ate that ox two days and two nights; we cooked and distributed fourteen potfuls of meat and no one went home hungry and no fights broke out.

But the "joke" stayed in my mind. I had a growing feeling that something important had happened in my relationship with the Bushmen and that the clue lay in the meaning of the joke. Several days later, when most of the people had dispersed back to the bush camps, I raised the question with Hakekgose, a Tswana man who had grown up among the !Kung, married a !Kung girl, and who probably knew their culture better than any other non-Bushman.

"With us whites," I began, "Christmas is supposed to be the day of friendship and brotherly love. What I can't figure out is why the Bushmen went to such lengths to criticize and belittle the ox I had bought for the feast. The animal was perfectly good and their jokes and wisecracks practically ruined the holiday for me."

"So it really did bother you," said Hakekgose. "Well, that's the way they always talk. When I take my rifle and go hunting with them, if I miss, they laugh at me for the rest of the day. But even if I hit and bring one down, it's no better. To them, the kill is always too small or too old or too thin; and as we sit down on the kill site to cook and eat the liver, they keep grumbling, even

with their mouths full of meat. They say things like, 'Oh this is awful! What a worthless animal! Whatever made me think that this Tswana rascal could hunt!' "

"Is this the way outsiders are treated?" I asked.

"No, it is their custom; they talk that way to each other too. Go and ask them."

/gaugo had been one of the most enthusiastic in making me feel bad about the merit of the Christmas ox. I sought him out first.

"Why did you tell me the black ox was worthless, when you could see that it was loaded with fat and meat?"

"It is our way," he said smiling. "We always like to fool people about that. Say there is a Bushman who has been hunting. He must not come home and announce like a braggart, 'I have killed a big one in the bush!' He must first sit down in silence until I or someone else comes up to his fire and asks, 'What did you see today?' He replies quietly, 'Ah, I'm no good for hunting. I saw nothing at all [pause] just a little tiny one.' Then I smile to myself," /gaugo continued, "because I know he has killed something big."

"In the morning we make up a party of four or five people to cut up and carry the meat back to the camp. When we arrive at the kill we examine it and cry out, 'You mean to say you have dragged us all the way out here in order to make us cart home your pile of bones? Oh, if I had known it was this thin I wouldn't have come.' Another one pipes up, 'People, to think I gave up a nice day in the shade for this. At home we may be hungry but at least we have nice cool water to drink.' If the horns are big, someone says, 'Did you think that somehow you were going to boil down the horns for soup?'

"To all this you must respond in kind. 'I agree,' you say, 'this one is not worth the effort; let's just cook the liver for strength and leave the rest for the hyenas. It is not too late to hunt today and even a duiker or a steenbok would be better than this mess.'

"Then you set to work nevertheless; butcher the animal, carry the meat back to the camp and everyone eats," /gaugo concluded.

Things were beginning to make sense. Next, I went to Tomazo. He corroborated /gaugo's story of the obligatory insults over a kill and added a few details of his own.

"But," I asked, "why insult a man after he has gone to all that trouble to track and kill an animal and when he is going to share the meat with you so that your children will have something to eat?"

"Arrogance," was his cryptic answer.

"Arrogance?"

"Yes, when a young man kills much meat he comes to think of himself as a chief or a big man, and he thinks of the rest of us as his servants or inferiors. We can't accept this. We refuse one who boasts, for someday his pride will make him kill somebody. So we always speak of his meat as worthless. This way we cool his heart and make him gentle."

"But why didn't you tell me this before?" I asked Tomazo with some heat.

"Because you never asked me," said Tomazo, echoing the refrain that has come to haunt every field ethnographer.

The pieces now fell into place. I had known for a long time that in situations of social conflict with Bushmen I held all the cards. I was the only source of tobacco in a thousand square miles, and I was not incapable of cutting an individual off for non-cooperation. Though my boycott never lasted longer than a few days, it was an indication of my strength. People resented my presence at the water hole, yet simultaneously dreaded my leaving. In short I was a perfect target for the charge of arrogance and for the Bushmen tactic of enforcing humility.

I had been taught an object lesson by the Bushmen; it had come from an unexpected corner and had hurt me in a vulnerable area. For the big black ox was to be the one totally generous, unstinting act of my year at /ai/ai, and I was quite unprepared for the reaction I received.

As I read it, their message was this: There are no totally generous acts. All "acts" have an element of calculation. One black ox slaughtered at Christmas does not wipe out a year of careful manipulation of gifts given to serve your own ends. After all, to kill an animal and share the meat with people is really no more than Bushmen do for each other every day and with far less fanfare.

In the end, I had to admire how the Bushmen had played out the farce—collectively straight-faced to the end. Curiously, the episode reminded me of the *Good Soldier Schweik* and his marvelous encounters with authority. Like Schweik, the Bushmen had retained a thorough-going skepticism of good intentions. Was it this independence of spirit, I wondered, that had kept them culturally viable in the face of generations of contact with more powerful societies, both black and white? The thought that the Bushmen were alive and well in the Kalahari was strangely comforting. Perhaps, armed with that independence and with their superb knowledge of their environment, they might yet survive the future.

Critical Thinking

1. To what extent do the Bushmen typically celebrate Christmas?

2. Why did Lee wish to slaughter an ox for the Bushmen?

3. What was it about the Bushman ways of life and Lee's role as an anthropologist that led to their reactions to his generosity?

4. Why was the Bushman reaction "strangely comforting" to Lee in the final analysis?

RICHARD BORSHAY LEE is a full professor of anthropology at the University of Toronto. He has done extensive fieldwork in southern Africa, is coeditor of *Man the Hunter* (1968) and *Kalahari Hunter-Gatherers* (1976), and author of *The !Kung San: Men, Women, and Work in a Foraging Society.*

From *Natural History*, December 1969, pp. 14–22, 60–64. Copyright © 1969 by Natural History Magazine. Reprinted by permission.

Tricking and Tripping
Fieldwork on Prostitution in the Era of AIDS

CLAIRE E. STERK

Students often think of anthropological fieldwork as requiring travel to exotic tropical locations, but that is not necessarily the case. This reading is based on fieldwork in the United States—on the streets in New York City as well as Atlanta. Claire Sterk is an anthropologist who works in a school of public health and is primarily interested in issues of women's health, particularly as it relates to sexual behavior. In this selection, an introduction to a recent book by the same title, she describes the basic fieldwork methods she used to study these women and their communities. Like most cultural anthropologists, Sterk's primary goal was to describe "the life" of prostitution from the women's own point of view. To do this, she had to be patient, brave, sympathetic, trustworthy, curious, and nonjudgmental. You will notice these characteristics in this selection; for example, Sterk begins her book with a poem written by one of her informants. Fieldwork is a slow process, because it takes time to win people's confidence and to learn their language and way of seeing the world. In this regard, there are probably few differences between the work of a qualitative sociologist and that of a cultural anthropologist (although anthropologists would not use the term "deviant" to describe another society or a segment of their own society).

Throughout the world, HIV/AIDS is fast becoming a disease found particularly in poor women. Sex workers or prostitutes have often been blamed for AIDS, and they have been further stigmatized because of their profession. In reality, however, entry into prostitution is not a career choice; rather, these women and girls are themselves most often victims of circumstances such as violence and poverty. Public health officials want to know why sex workers do not always protect their health by making men wear condoms. To answer such questions, we must know more about the daily life of these women. The way to do that, the cultural anthropologist would say, is to ask and to listen.

As you read this selection, ask yourself the following questions:

- What happens when Sterk says, "I'm sorry for you" to one of her informants? Why?
- Why do you think fieldwork might be a difficult job?
- Do you think that the fact that Sterk grew up in Amsterdam, where prostitution is legal, affected her research?
- Which of the six themes of this work, described at the end of the article, do you think is most important?

One night in March of 1987 business was slow. I was hanging out on a stroll with a group of street prostitutes. After a few hours in a nearby diner/coffee shop, we were kicked out. The waitress felt bad, but she needed our table for some new customers. Four of us decided to sit in my car until the rain stopped. While three of us chatted about life, Piper wrote this poem. As soon as she read it to us, the conversation shifted to more serious topics—pimps, customers, cops, the many hassles of being a prostitute, to name a few. We decided that if I ever finished a book about prostitution, the book would start with her poem.

This book is about the women who work in the lower echelons of the prostitution world. They worked in the streets and other public settings as well as crack houses. Some of these women viewed themselves primarily as prostitutes, and a number of them used drugs to cope with the pressures of the life. Others identified themselves more as drug users, and their main reason for having sex for money or other goods was to support their own drug use and often the habit of their male partner. A small group of women interviewed for this book had left prostitution, and most of them were still struggling to integrate their past experiences as prostitutes in their current lives.

The stories told by the women who participated in this project revealed how pimps, customers, and others such as police officers and social and health service providers treated them as "fallen" women. However, their accounts also showed their strengths and the many strategies they developed to challenge these others. Circumstances, including their drug use, often forced them to sell sex, but they all resisted the notion that they might be selling themselves. Because they engaged in an illegal profession, these women had little status: their working conditions were poor, and their work was physically and mentally exhausting. Nevertheless, many women described the ways in which they gained a sense of control over their lives. For instance, they learned how to manipulate pimps, how to control the types of services and length of time bought by their customers, and how to select customers. While none of these schemes explicitly enhanced their working conditions, they did make the women feel stronger and better about themselves.

In this book, I present prostitution from the point of view of the women themselves. To understand their current lives, it was necessary to learn how they got started in the life, the various processes involved in their continued prostitution careers, the link between prostitution and drug use, the women's interactions with their pimps and customers, and the impact of the AIDS epidemic and increasing violence on their experiences. I also examined the implications for women. Although my goal was to present the women's thoughts, feelings, and actions in their own words, the final text is a sociological monograph compiled by me as the researcher. Some women are quoted more than others because I developed a closer relationship with them, because they were more able to verbalize and capture their circumstances, or simply because they were more outspoken.

The Sample

The data for this book are qualitative. The research was conducted during the last ten years in the New York City and Atlanta metropolitan areas. One main data source was participant observation on streets, in hotels and other settings known for prostitution activity, and in drug-use settings, especially those that allowed sex-for-drug exchanges. Another data source was in-depth, life-history interviews with 180 women ranging in age from 18 to 59 years, with an average age of 34. One in two women was African-American and one in three white; the remaining women were Latina. Three in four had completed high school, and among them almost two-thirds had one or more years of additional educational training. Thirty women had graduated from college.

Forty women worked as street prostitutes and did not use drugs. On average, they had been prostitutes for 11 years. Forty women began using drugs an average of three years after they began working as prostitutes, and the average time they had worked as prostitutes was nine years. Forty women used drugs an average of five years before they became prostitutes, and on the average they had worked as prostitutes for eight years. Another forty women began smoking crack and exchanging sex for crack almost simultaneously, with an average of four years in the life. Twenty women who were interviewed were ex-prostitutes.

Comments on Methodology

When I tell people about my research, the most frequent question I am asked is how I gained access to the women rather than what I learned from the research. For many, prostitution is an unusual topic of conversation, and many people have expressed surprise that I, as a woman, conducted the research. During my research some customers indeed thought I was a working woman, a fact that almost always amuses those who hear about my work. However, few people want to hear stories about the women's struggles and sadness. Sometimes they ask questions about the reasons why women become prostitutes. Most of the time, they are surprised when I tell them that the prostitutes as well as their customers represent all layers of society. Before presenting the findings, it seems important to discuss the research process, including gaining access to the women, developing relationships, interviewing, and then leaving the field.[1]

Locating Prostitutes and Gaining Entree

One of the first challenges I faced was to identify locations where street prostitution took place. Many of these women worked on strolls, streets where prostitution activity is concentrated, or in hotels known for prostitution activity. Others, such as the crack prostitutes, worked in less public settings such as a crack house that might be someone's apartment.

I often learned of well-known public places from professional experts, such as law enforcement officials and health care providers at emergency rooms and sexually transmitted disease clinics. I gained other insights from lay experts, including taxi drivers, bartenders, and community representatives such as members of neighborhood associations. The contacts universally mentioned some strolls as the places where many women worked, where the local police focused attention, or where residents had organized protests against prostitution in their neighborhoods.

As I began visiting various locales, I continued to learn about new settings. In one sense, I was developing ethnographic maps of street prostitution. After several visits to a specific area, I also was able to expand these maps by adding information about the general atmosphere on the stroll, general characteristics of the various people present, the ways in which the women and customers connected, and the overall flow of action. In addition, my visits allowed the regular actors to notice me.

I soon learned that being an unknown woman in an area known for prostitution may cause many people to notice you, even stare at you, but it fails to yield many verbal interactions. Most of the time when I tried to make eye contact with one of the women, she quickly averted her eyes. Pimps, on the other hand, would stare at me straight on and I ended up being the one to look away. Customers would stop, blow their horn, or wave me over, frequently yelling obscenities when I ignored them. I realized that gaining entree into the prostitution world was not going to be as easy as I imagined it. Although I lacked such training in any of my qualitative methods classes, I decided to move slowly and not force any interaction. The most I said during the initial weeks in a new area was limited to "how are you" or "hi." This strategy paid off during my first visits to one of the strolls in Brooklyn, New York. After several appearances, one of the women walked up to me and sarcastically asked if I was looking for something. She caught me off guard, and all the answers I had practiced did not seem to make sense. I mumbled something about just wanting to walk around. She did not like my answer, but she did like my accent. We ended up talking about the latter and she was especially excited when I told her I came from Amsterdam. One of her friends had gone to Europe with her boyfriend, who was in the military. She understood from her that prostitution and drugs were legal in the Netherlands. While explaining to her that some of her friend's impressions were incorrect, I was able to show off some of my knowledge about prostitution. I mentioned that I was interested in prostitution and wanted to write a book about it.

Despite the fascination with my background and intentions, the prostitute immediately put me through a Streetwalker 101 test, and apparently I passed. She told me to make sure to come back. By the time I left, I not only had my first conversation but also my first connection to the scene. Variations of this entry process occurred on the other strolls. The main lesson I learned in these early efforts was the importance of having some knowledge of the lives of the people I wanted to study, while at the same time refraining from presenting myself as an expert.

Qualitative researchers often refer to their initial connections as gatekeepers and key respondents. Throughout my fieldwork I learned that some key respondents are important in providing initial access, but they become less central as the research evolves. For example, one of the women who introduced me to her lover, who was also her pimp, was arrested and disappeared for months. Another entered drug treatment soon after she facilitated my access. Other key respondents provided access to only a segment of the players on a scene. For example, if a woman worked for a pimp, [she] was unlikely . . . to introduce me to women working for another pimp. On one stroll my initial contact was with a pimp whom nobody liked. By associating with him, I almost lost the opportunity to meet other pimps. Some key respondents were less connected than promised—for example, some of the women who worked the street to support their drug habit. Often their connections were more frequently with drug users and less so with prostitutes.

Key respondents tend to be individuals central to the local scene, such as, in this case, pimps and the more senior prostitutes. Their function as gatekeepers often is to protect the scene and to screen outsiders. Many times I had to prove that I was not an undercover police officer or a woman with ambitions to become a streetwalker. While I thought I had gained entree, I quickly learned that many insiders subsequently wondered about my motives and approached me with suspicion and distrust.

Another lesson involved the need to proceed cautiously with self-nominated key respondents. For example, one of the women presented herself as knowing everyone on the stroll. While she did know everyone, she was not a central figure. On the contrary, the other prostitutes viewed her as a failed streetwalker whose drug use caused her to act unprofessionally. By associating with me, she hoped to regain some of her status. For me, however, it meant limited access to the other women because I affiliated myself with a woman who was marginal to the scene. On another occasion, my main key respondent was a man who claimed to own three crack houses in the neighborhood. However, he had a negative reputation, and people accused him of cheating on others. My initial alliance with him delayed, and almost blocked, my access to others in the neighborhood. He intentionally tried to keep me from others on the scene, not because he would gain something from that transaction but because it made him feel powerful. When I told him I was going to hang out with some of the other people, he threatened me until one of the other dealers stepped in and told him to stay away. The two of them argued back and forth, and finally

I was free to go. Fortunately, the dealer who had spoken up for me was much more central and positively associated with the local scene. Finally, I am unsure if I would have had success in gaining entrance to the scene had I not been a woman.

Developing Relationships and Trust

The processes involved in developing relationships in research situations amplify those involved in developing relationships in general. Both parties need to get to know each other, become aware and accepting of each other's roles, and engage in a reciprocal relationship. Being supportive and providing practical assistance were the most visible and direct ways for me as the researcher to develop a relationship. Throughout the years, I have given countless rides, provided child care on numerous occasions, bought groceries, and listened for hours to stories that were unrelated to my initial research questions. Gradually, my role allowed me to become part of these women's lives and to build rapport with many of them.

Over time, many women also realized that I was uninterested in being a prostitute and that I genuinely was interested in learning as much as possible about their lives. Many felt flattered that someone wanted to learn from them and that they had knowledge to offer. Allowing women to tell their stories and engaging in a dialogue with them probably were the single most important techniques that allowed me to develop relationships with them. Had I only wanted to focus on the questions I had in mind, developing such relationships might have been more difficult.

At times, I was able to get to know a woman only after her pimp endorsed our contact. One of my scariest experiences occurred before I knew to work through the pimps, and one such man had some of his friends follow me on my way home one night. I will never know what plans they had in mind for me because I fortunately was able to escape with only a few bruises. Over a year later, the woman acknowledged that her pimp had gotten upset and told her he was going to teach me a lesson.

On other occasions, I first needed to be screened by owners and managers of crack houses before the research could continue. Interestingly, screenings always were done by a man even if the person who vouched for me was a man himself. While the women also were cautious, the ways in which they checked me out tended to be much more subtle. For example, one of them would tell me a story, indicating that it was a secret about another person on the stroll. Although I failed to realize this at the time, my field notes revealed that frequently after such a conversation, others would ask me questions about related topics. One woman later acknowledged that putting out such stories was a test to see if I would keep information confidential.

Learning more about the women and gaining a better understanding of their lives also raised many ethical questions. No textbook told me how to handle situations in which a pimp abused a woman, a customer forced a woman to engage in unwanted sex acts, a customer requested unprotected sex from a woman who knew she was HIV infected, or a boyfriend had realistic expectations regarding a woman's earnings to support his drug habit. I failed to know the proper response when asked to engage in illegal activities such as holding drugs or money a woman had stolen from a customer. In general, my response was to explain that I was there as a researcher. During those occasions when pressures became too severe, I decided to leave a scene. For example, I never returned to certain crack houses because pimps there continued to ask me to consider working for them.

Over time, I was fortunate to develop relationships with people who "watched my back." One pimp in particular intervened if he perceived other pimps, customers, or passersby harassing me. He also was the one who gave me my street name: Whitie (indicating my racial background) or Ms. Whitie for those who disrespected me. While this was my first street name, I subsequently had others. Being given a street name was a symbolic gesture of acceptance. Gradually, I developed an identity that allowed me to be both an insider and an outsider. While hanging out on the strolls and other gathering places, including crack houses, I had to deal with some of the same uncomfortable conditions as the prostitutes, such as cold or warm weather, lack of access to a rest room, refusals from owners for me to patronize a restaurant, and of course, harassment by customers and the police.

I participated in many informal conversations. Unless pushed to do so, I seldom divulged my opinions. I was more open with my feelings about situations and showed empathy. I learned quickly that providing an opinion can backfire. I agreed that one of the women was struggling a lot and stated that I felt sorry for her. While I meant to indicate my "genuine concern for her, she heard that I felt sorry for her because she was a failure. When she finally, after several weeks, talked with me again, I was able to explain to her that I was not judging her, but rather felt concerned for her. She remained cynical and many times asked me for favors to make up for my mistake. It took me months before I felt comfortable telling her that I felt I had done enough and that it was time to let go. However, if she was not ready, she needed to know that I would no longer go along. This was one of many occasions when I learned that although I wanted to facilitate my work as a researcher, that I wanted people to like and trust me, I also needed to set boundaries.

Rainy and slow nights often provided good opportunities for me to participate in conversations with groups of women. Popular topics included how to work safely, what to do about condom use, how to make more money. I often served as a health educator and a supplier of condoms, gels, vaginal douches, and other feminine products. Many women were very worried about the AIDS epidemic. However, they also were worried about how to use a condom when a customer refused to do so. They worried particularly about condom use when they needed money badly and, consequently, did not want to propose that the customer use one for fear of rejection. While some women became experts at "making" their customers use a condom—for example, "by hiding it in their mouth prior to beginning oral sex—others would carry condoms to please me but never pull one out. If a woman was HIV positive and I knew she failed to use a condom, I faced the ethical dilemma of challenging her or staying out of it.

Developing trusting relationships with crack prostitutes was more difficult. Crack houses were not the right environment for

informal conversations. Typically, the atmosphere was tense and everyone was suspicious of each other. The best times to talk with these women were when we bought groceries together, when I helped them clean their homes, or when we shared a meal. Often the women were very different when they were not high than they were when they were high or craving crack. In my conversations with them, I learned that while I might have observed their actions the night before, they themselves might not remember them. Once I realized this, I would be very careful to omit any detail unless I knew that the woman herself did remember the event.

In-Depth Interviews

All interviews were conducted in a private setting, including women's residences, my car or my office, a restaurant of the women's choice, or any other setting the women selected. I did not begin conducting official interviews until I developed relationships with the women. Acquiring written informed consent prior to the interview was problematic. It made me feel awkward. Here I was asking the women to sign a form after they had begun to trust me. However, often I felt more upset about this technicality than the women themselves. As soon as they realized that the form was something the university required, they seemed to understand. Often they laughed about the official statements, and some asked if I was sure the form was to protect them and not the school.[2] None of the women refused to sign the consent form, although some refused to sign it right away and asked to be interviewed later.

In some instances the consent procedures caused the women to expect a formal interview. Some of them were disappointed when they saw I only had a few structured questions about demographic characteristics, followed by a long list of open-ended questions. When this disappointment occurred, I reminded the women that I wanted to learn from them and that the best way to do so was by engaging in a dialogue rather than interrogating them. Only by letting the women identify their salient issues and the topics they wanted to address was I able to gain an insider's perspective. By being a careful listener and probing for additional information and explanation, I as the interviewer, together with the women, was able to uncover the complexities of their lives. In addition, the nature of the interview allowed me to ask questions about contradictions in a woman's story. For example, sometimes a woman would say that she always used a condom. However, later on in the conversation she would indicate that if she needed drugs she would never use one. By asking her to elaborate on this, I was able to begin developing insights into condom use by type of partner, type of sex acts, and social context.

The interviewer becomes much more a part of the interview when the conversations are in-depth than when a structured questionnaire is used. Because I was so integral to the process, the way the women viewed me may have biased their answers. On the one hand, this bias might be reduced because of the extent to which both parties already knew each other; on the other, a woman might fail to give her true opinion and reveal her actions if she knew that these went against the interviewer's opinion. I suspected that some women played down the ways in which their pimps manipulated them once they knew that I was not too fond of these men. However, some might have taken more time to explain the relationship with their pimp in order to "correct" my image.

My background, so different from that of these women, most likely affected the nature of the interviews. I occupied a higher socioeconomic status. I had a place to live and a job. In contrast to the nonwhite women, I came from a different racial background. While I don't know to what extent these differences played a role, I acknowledge that they must have had some effect on this research.

Leaving the Field

Leaving the field was not something that occurred after completion of the fieldwork, but an event that took place daily. Although I sometimes stayed on the strolls all night or hung out for several days, I always had a home to return to. I had a house with electricity, a warm shower, a comfortable bed, and a kitchen. My house sat on a street where I had no fear of being shot on my way there and where I did not find condoms or syringes on my doorstep.

During several stages of the study, I had access to a car, which I used to give the women rides or to run errands together. However, I will never forget the cold night when everyone on the street was freezing, and I left to go home. I turned up the heat in my car, and tears streamed down my cheeks. I appreciated the heat, but I felt more guilty about that luxury than ever before. I truly felt like an outsider, or maybe even more appropriate, a betrayer.

Throughout the years of fieldwork, there were a number of times when I left the scene temporarily. For example, when so many people were dying from AIDS, I was unable to ignore the devastating impact of this disease. I needed an emotional break.

Physically removing myself from the scene was common when I experienced difficulty remaining objective. Once I became too involved in a woman's life and almost adopted her and her family. Another time I felt a true hatred for a crack house owner and was unable to adhere to the rules of courteous interactions. Still another time, I got angry with a woman whose steady partner was HIV positive when she failed to ask him to use a condom when they had sex.

I also took temporary breaks from a particular scene by shifting settings and neighborhoods. For example, I would invest most of my time in women from a particular crack house for several weeks. Then I would shift to spending more time on one of the strolls, while making shorter and less frequent visits to the crack house. By shifting scenes, I was able to tell people why I was leaving and to remind all of us of my researcher role.

While I focused on leaving the field, I became interested in women who had left the life. It seemed important to have an understanding of their past and current circumstances. I knew some of them from the days when they were working, but identifying others was a challenge. There was no gathering place for ex-prostitutes. Informal networking, advertisements in local newspapers, and local clinics and community settings allowed

me to reach twenty of these women. Conducting interviews with them later in the data collection process prepared me to ask specific questions. I realized that I had learned enough about the life to know what to ask. Interviewing ex-prostitutes also prepared me for moving from the fieldwork to writing.

It is hard to determine exactly when I left the field. It seems like a process that never ends. Although I was more physically removed from the scene, I continued to be involved while analyzing the data and writing this book. I also created opportunities to go back, for example, by asking women to give me feedback on parts of the manuscript or at times when I experienced writer's block and my car seemed to automatically steer itself to one of the strolls. I also have developed other research projects in some of the same communities. For example, both a project on intergenerational drug use and a gender-specific intervention project to help women remain HIV negative have brought me back to the same population. Some of the women have become key respondents in these new projects, while others now are members of a research team. For example, Beth, one of the women who has left prostitution, works as an outreach worker on another project.

Six Themes in the Ethnography of Prostitution

The main intention of my work is to provide the reader with a perspective on street prostitution from the point of view of the women themselves. There are six fundamental aspects of the women's lives as prostitutes that must be considered. The first concerns the women's own explanations for their involvement in prostitution and their descriptions of the various circumstances that led them to become prostitutes. Their stories include justifications such as traumatic past experiences, especially sexual abuse, the lack of love they experienced as children, pressures by friends and pimps, the need for drugs, and most prominently, the economic forces that pushed them into the life. A number of women describe these justifications as excuses, as reflective explanations they have developed after becoming a prostitute.

The women describe the nature of their initial experiences, which often involved alienation from those outside the life. They also show the differences in the processes between women who work as prostitutes and use drugs and women who do not use drugs.

Although all these women work either on the street or in drug-use settings, their lives do differ. My second theme is a typology that captures these differences, looking at the women's prostitution versus drug-use identities. The typology distinguishes among (a) streetwalkers, women who work strolls and who do not use drugs; (b) hooked prostitutes, women who identify themselves mainly as prostitutes but who upon their entrance into the life also began using drugs; (c) prostituting addicts, women who view themselves mainly as drug users and who became prostitutes to support their drug habit; and (d) crack prostitutes, women who trade sex for crack.

This typology explains the differences in the women's strategies for soliciting customers, their screening of customers, pricing of sex acts, and bargaining for services. For example, the streetwalkers have the most bargaining power, while such power appears to be lacking among the crack prostitutes.

Few prostitutes work in a vacuum. The third theme is the role of pimps, a label that most women dislike and for which they prefer to substitute "old man" or "boyfriend." Among the pimps, one finds entrepreneur lovers, men who mainly employ streetwalkers and hooked prostitutes and sometimes prostituting addicts. Entrepreneur lovers engage in the life for business reasons. They treat the women as their employees or their property and view them primarily as an economic commodity. The more successful a woman is in earning them money, the more difficult it is for that woman to leave her entrepreneur pimp.

Most prostituting addicts and some hooked prostitutes work for a lover pimp, a man who is their steady partner but who also lives off their earnings. Typically, such pimps employ only one woman. The dynamics in the relationship between a prostitute and her lover pimp become more complex when both partners use drugs. Drugs often become the glue of the relationship.

For many crack prostitutes, their crack addiction serves as a pimp. Few plan to exchange sex for crack when they first begin using; often several weeks or months pass before a woman who barters sex for crack realizes that she is a prostitute.

Historically, society has blamed prostitutes for introducing sexually transmitted diseases into the general population. Similarly, it makes them scapegoats for the spread of HIV/AIDS. Yet their pimps and customers are not held accountable. The fourth theme in the anthropological study of prostitution is the impact of the AIDS epidemic on the women's lives. Although most are knowledgeable about HIV risk behaviors and the ways to reduce their risk, many misconceptions exist. The women describe the complexities of condom use, especially with steady partners but also with paying customers. Many women have mixed feelings about HIV testing, wondering how to cope with a positive test result while no cure is available. A few of the women already knew their HIV-infected status, and the discussion touches on their dilemmas as well.

The fifth theme is the violence and abuse that make common appearances in the women's lives. An ethnography of prostitution must allow the women to describe violence in their neighborhoods as well as violence in prostitution and drug-use settings. The most common violence they encounter is from customers. These men often assume that because they pay for sex they buy a woman. Apparently, casual customers pose more of a danger than those who are regulars. The types of abuse the women encounter are emotional, physical, and sexual. In addition to customers, pimps and boyfriends abuse the women. Finally, the women discuss harassment by law enforcement officers.

When I talked with the women, it often seemed that there were no opportunities to escape from the life. Yet the sixth and final theme must be the escape from prostitution. Women who have left prostitution can describe the process of their exit from prostitution. As ex-prostitutes they struggle with the stigma of their past, the challenges of developing a new identity, and the impact of their past on current intimate relationships. Those who were also drug users often view themselves as ex-prostitutes and recovering addicts, a perspective that seems to create a role conflict. Overall, most ex-prostitutes find that their past follows them like a bad hangover.

Notes

1. For more information about qualitative research methods, see, for example, Patricia Adler and Peter Adler, *Membership Roles in Field Research* (Newbury Park: Sage, 1987); Michael Agar, *The Professional Stranger* (New York: Academic Press, 1980) and *Speaking of Ethnography* (Beverly Hills: Sage, 1986); Howard Becker and Blanche Geer, "Participant Observation and Interviewing: A Comparison," *Human Organization* 16 (1957): 28–32; Norman Denzin, *Sociological Methods: A Sourcebook* (Chicago: Aldine, 1970); Barney Glaser and Anselm Strauss, *The Discovery of Grounded Theory: Strategies for Qualitative Research* (Chicago: Aldine, 1967); Y. Lincoln and E. Guba, *Naturalistic Inquiry* (Beverly Hills: Sage, 1985); John Lofland, "Analytic Ethnography: Features, Failings, and Futures," *Journal of Contemporary Ethnography* 24 (1996): 30–67; and James Spradley, *The Ethnographic Interview* (New York: Holt, Rinehart and Winston, 1979) and *Participant Observation* (New York: Holt, Rinehart and Winston, 1980).

2. For a more extensive discussion of informed consent procedures and related ethical issues, see Bruce L. Berg, *Qualitative Research Methods for the Social Sciences,* 3rd edition, Chapter 3: "Ethical Issues" (Boston: Allyn and Bacon, 1998).

Critical Thinking

1. How do prostitutes gain a sense of control over their lives?

2. How does the author describe the women in her study?

3. How does the author describe people's reactions when she tells them what her research is about?

4. How and where did she find places of prostitution?

5. What was the main lesson she learned in her early efforts?

6. How does she describe "key respondents?"

7. How did she manage to develop relationships with prostitutes? What was the single most important technique?

8. How did the author handle situations involving ethical questions?

9. Describe the author's interview techniques and the rationale behind them.

10. How did the author feel about being able to "leave the field" daily?

11. Under what circumstances would she leave a scene temporarily?

12. What explanations do the women themselves give for their involvement in prostitution?

13. What is the author's typology regarding prostitutes? What kinds of strategies are thereby explained? Which has the most bargaining power? Which has the least?

14. How does the author describe the different kinds of pimps?

15. Who is historically held responsible for the spread of HIV/AIDS? Who is not held responsible?

16. How does the author describe the violence and abuse suffered by prostitutes and who is likely to inflict it?

17. With what do ex-prostitutes come to struggle?

The September 11 Effect on Anthropology

LARA DEEB AND JESSICA WINEGAR

Conventional wisdom among scholars of the Middle East is that the September 11, 2001 attacks left behind a threatening professional environment. Graduate students and faculty alike speak of hostile infiltrators in their classrooms, inevitably bitter tenure battles and the self-censorship that both can produce. At the same time, in the aftermath of September 11 Middle East scholars anticipated that the perennially spotty job market might improve.

Our research for *Anthropology's Politics,* a book project under contract with Stanford University Press, thus far confirms that scholars have in fact gained new "opportunities" during the past decade, but with government agencies or NGOs rather than in academe, where tenure-track jobs (as in most fields) have become scarcer. Our data also shows that scholars employed at universities, particularly those without tenure, labor under greater surveillance and suspicion. While trepidation about this climate is general to Middle East anthropologists regardless of specialty, the vast majority of actual incidents have been related to scholars' analysis of the conflict in Israel-Palestine.

Time and time again, in our interviews with anthropologists of the Middle East, they describe their jobs as "a minefield." They may have problems explaining research on politically sensitive topics to their universities' institutional review boards; they may see their grant funding denied or withdrawn; they may encounter prejudice among colleagues on hiring and tenure committees; and they may experience conflict with students when presenting critical perspectives on the US-led "war on terror." Whether or not their difficulties were expressly tied to politics, faculty frequently linked their personal stories to the political climate. One person described the resulting fear as "knowing that people who fall on the wrong side can suffer in their careers."

Scholars are increasingly worried about losing access to field sites and control over the use of their work. The new "security" orientation of the study of the Middle East and Islam has led to more frequent invitations from government agencies, Washington think tanks and military subcontractors. These invitations often make anthropologists nervous, as they do not want to be identified with US Middle East policy or have their insights employed in its formulation.

But when it comes to tangibly negative effects on careers and academic freedom, Palestine—not the "war on terror"—is the enduring issue. "The word on the street" in graduate school, many anthropologists say, is that "if you work on Palestine you will never get a job," at least not in the United States. Indeed, Palestine frequently rose as a specter in anthropologists' job interviews in the 2000s. In the words of one Palestine scholar, "It's not what I said, it's the subject I work on. . . . People don't want to open themselves up to controversy—once the word Palestine is there, people say, 'Why do we want to make everyone upset?'" Even scholars who research other countries were often questioned about their politics on Palestine during campus visits, sometimes point blank.

Quantitatively, we have found that Palestine is the number-one cause of persecution of faculty in the classroom, despite anthropologists' assumption that everyone is at risk in the post-September 11 political climate. Many whose research does not focus on Palestine avoid it in their teaching, in part because they feel "on less sure ground," but also due to worries about classroom consequences. Well-publicized right-wing attacks—from inside and outside the discipline—foment this atmosphere of apprehension. On Campus Watch, the most robust of the conservative websites that collects reports on scholars of the Middle East, the vast majority of the articles about Middle East anthropology or anthropologists concern Israel-Palestine. The question of Palestine also dominates the websites Discover the Network and Students for Academic Freedom, both sponsored by right-wing activist David Horowitz. This focus is not a post-September 11 phenomenon, but a continuation of decades of concerted agitation against those speaking out about Palestinian rights. There does, however, seem to be a difference in the scale and organization of the attacks, which are facilitated by the Internet and other new media, and have been strengthened by the deeper Islamophobia of the post-September 11 era.

Nevertheless, there were in fact more job opportunities for Middle East anthropologists in the 2000s than in the preceding decade. Our quantitative analysis shows, however, that the increase paled in comparison to increases in fields such as history, political science and religious studies—presumably because those disciplines are thought to provide birds-eye views of the region or explanations for the September 11 events. At the same time, the US government has presumed that anthropology is able to provide on-the-ground information useful for counter-terrorism, and thus anthropologists are heavily recruited to staff "Human Terrain Systems" or other military projects that depend on local knowledge. The recruitment efforts have met with little success, as they run up against the anthropological Code of Ethics and anthropologists' political sensibilities, both of which prohibit such collaboration. The 2009 version of the Code of Ethics, currently under revision, clearly states that it is a set of guidelines for anthropologists rather than a binding document that adjudicates violations for its members. It states that "anthropological researchers must ensure that they do not harm the safety, dignity or privacy of the people with whom they work, conduct research or perform other professional activities, or who might reasonably be thought to be affected by their research." The vast majority of anthropologists understand providing information to the US military to contradict this tenet of the code.

September 11 affected scholarly life by pushing many scholars to speak publicly about the Middle East and Islam. In this regard, the "war on terror" is viewed as both opportunity and danger-filled obligation, an ambivalence perfectly captured in one anthropologist's phrase, "poisoned chalice." While a few resisted sipping from this cup, explaining that their scholarly work was not so conventionally political, most felt that they faced an ethical imperative to correct stereotypes and dispel misunderstandings—even if they became subject to slander and libel.

September 11 also shaped scholars' choices of field site and topic. Many anthropologists continue to shy away from Israel-Palestine. Some have begun to work on US military engagement in the region. Others have moved toward studies of Islam, although many anthropologists express concern that religion has come to stand in for the Middle East in the academy as it has in public discourse. It remains to be seen what impact the "Arab spring" might have on this trend.

In general, Middle East anthropologists share other Middle East scholars' sense that American institutions of higher education have become battlegrounds pitting defenders of academic freedom against defenders of various state policies, particularly those of Israel. The explosion of media outlets and the corporatization of universities in the 2000s have created a feeling that off-campus forces have more power today than in the past to shape scholarly discourse. Even scholars with tenure often find civic engagement unpleasant, not because they do not want to speak to the public, but because uninformed political opinion often trumps fact-based discussion in these forums. Those without tenure, especially those whose specialties or views generate controversy, have to fear for their job security as well. Those who call for eliminating tenure would do well to recognize that such a move might diminish the supply of in-depth knowledge of the Middle East to the American public.

Critical Thinking

1. What has been the conventional wisdom among scholars of the Middle East as a result of the September 11, 2001 attacks?

2. What did the authors' discover as a result of their research?

3. Why do anthropologists of the Middle East describe their jobs as "a minefield?" Why they are increasingly worried?

4. What is the "enduring issue" and why? Why is there a difference in the scale and organization of the attacks on anthropologists since September 11 even though this has been a decades-long issue?

5. How do the authors assess the job opportunities for Middle East anthropologists compared to other fields?

6. Why have recruitment efforts met with little success?

7. Why has the "war on terror" been viewed as both an opportunity and a danger-filled obligation?

8. How has September 11 shaped scholars' choices of field site and topic?

9. In what respects have American institutions of higher education become battlegrounds? What might be the result of eliminating tenure?

LARA DEEB, an editor of this magazine, teaches anthropology at Scripps College. **JESSICA WINEGAR** teaches anthropology at Northwestern University.

UNIT 2
Culture and Communication

Unit Selections

Learning Outcomes

After reading this Unit, you will be able to:

- Explain how language can restrict our thought processes.

- Describe the relationship between a people's language, culture, and interaction with their environment.

- How much influence does a brand name have in terms of selling a product and why?

- Explain how the "argument culture" has affected the way we conduct ourselves vis-à-vis others.

- Give examples of the ways in which communication is difficult in a cross-cultural situation.

- Explain how this section has enhanced your ability to communicate more effectively.

Student Website
www.mhhe.com/cls

Internet References

Center for Nonverbal Studies
www.library.kent.edu/resource.php?id=2800

Exploratorium Magazine: "The Evolution of Languages"
www.exploratorium.edu/exploring/language

Hypertext and Ethnography
www.umanitoba.ca/anthropology

International Communication Association
www.icahdq.org

Intute: Social Sciences
www.intute.ac.uk/socialsciences/cgi-bin/browse.pl?id=120052

Language and Culture
http://anthro.palomar.edu/language/default.htm

Language Extinction
www.colorado.edu/iec

Nonverbal Behavior
www.usal.es/~nonverbal/researchcenters.htm

Showcase Anthropology
www.anthropology.wisc.edu

Anthropologists are interested in all aspects of human behavior and how they interrelate. Language is a form of such behavior (albeit, primarily verbal behavior) and, therefore, worthy of study. Although it changes over time, language is culturally patterned and passed down from one generation to the next through learning, not instinct. In keeping with the idea that language is integral to human social interactions, it has long been recognized that human communication through language is, by its nature, different from the communication found among other animals. Central to this difference is the fact that humans communicate abstractly, with symbols that have meaning independent of the immediate sensory experiences of either the sender or the receiver of the message. Thus, for instance, humans are able to refer to the future and the past and not just the present.

Recent experiments have shown that anthropoid apes can be taught a small portion of Ameslan or American Sign Language. It must be remembered, however, that their very rudimentary ability has to be tapped by painstaking human effort, and that the degree of difference between apes and humans serves only to emphasize the peculiar need of humans for, and development of, language.

Just as the abstract quality of symbols lifts our thoughts beyond our immediate sense perceptions, so also it inhibits our ability to think about and convey the full meaning of our personal experience. No categorical term can do justice to its referents—the variety of forms to which the term refers. The degree to which this is an obstacle to clarity of thought and communication relates to the degree of abstraction involved in the symbols. The word "chair," for instance, would not present much difficulty, as it has objective referents. However, consider the trouble we have in thinking and communicating with words whose referents are not tied to immediate sense perception—words such as "freedom," "democracy," and "justice." Deborah Tannen's discussion of the "argument culture" (in "Fighting for Our Lives") is a prime example of this. At best, the likely result is *symbolic confusion:* an inability to think or communicate in objectively definable symbols. At worst, language may be used to purposefully obfuscate. As shown in "Famous Names: The World of Business" by John Colapinto, the power of words over thoughts can even be used to sell us something we did not even need or want.

A related issue has to do with the fact that languages differ as to what is relatively easy to express within the restrictions of their particular vocabularies and grammatical structure. (See "How Language Shapes Thought" by Lera Boroditsky.) Thus, although

© Brand X Pictures/PunchStock

a given language may not have enough words to cope with a new situation or a new field of activity, the typical solution is to invent words or to borrow them. In this way, it has been claimed that any language can be used to say anything. This point is challenged, however, by Laura Bohannan's attempt to convey the "true" meaning of Shakespeare's *Hamlet* to the West African Tiv (see "Shakespeare in the Bush"). Much of her task was devoted to finding the most appropriate words in the Tiv language to convey her Western thoughts. At least part of her failure was due to the fact that some of the words just don't exist in the native language, and her inventions were unacceptable to the Tiv.

In summary, the articles in this unit show how symbolic confusion may occur between individuals or groups; they illustrate the beauty and wonder inherent in this uniquely human form of communication we call "language," and they demonstrate the tremendous potential of recent research to enhance effective communication among all of us.

How Language Shapes Thought

The languages we speak affect our perceptions of the world.

LERA BORODITSKY

I am standing next to a five-year-old girl in Pormpuraaw, a small Aboriginal community on the western edge of Cape York in northern Australia. When I ask her to point north, she points precisely and without hesitation. My compass says she is right. Later, back in a lecture hall at Stanford University, I make the same request of an audience of distinguished scholars—winners of science medals and genius prizes. Some of them have come to this very room to hear lectures for more than 40 years. I ask them to close their eyes (so they don't cheat) and point north. Many refuse; they do not know the answer. Those who do point take a while to think about it and then aim in all possible directions. I have repeated this exercise at Harvard and Princeton and in Moscow, London and Beijing, always with the same results.

A five-year-old in one culture can do something with ease that eminent scientists in other cultures struggle with. This is a big difference in cognitive ability. What could explain it? The surprising answer, it turns out, may be language.

The notion that different languages may impart different cognitive skills goes back centuries. Since the 1930s it has become associated with American linguists Edward Sapir and Benjamin Lee Whorf, who studied how languages vary and proposed ways that speakers of different tongues may think differently. Although their ideas met with much excitement early on, there was one small problem: a near complete lack of evidence to support their claims. By the 1970s many scientists had become disenchanted with the Sapir-Whorf hypothesis, and it was all but abandoned as a new set of theories claiming that language and thought are universal muscled onto the scene. But now, decades later, a solid body of empirical evidence showing how languages shape thinking has finally emerged. The evidence overturns the long-standing dogma about universality and yields fascinating insights into the origins of knowledge and the construction of reality. The results have important implications for law, politics and education.

Under the Influence

Around the world people communicate with one another using a dazzling array of languages—7,000 or so all told—and each language requires very different things from its speakers. For example, suppose I want to tell you that I saw *Uncle Vanya* on 42nd Street. In Mian, a language spoken in Papua New Guinea, the verb I used would reveal whether the event happened just now, yesterday or in the distant past, whereas in Indonesian, the verb wouldn't even give away whether it had already happened or was still coming up. In Russian, the verb would reveal my gender. In Mandarin, I would have to specify whether the titular uncle is maternal or paternal and whether he is related by blood or marriage, because there are different words for all these different types of uncles and then some (he happens to be a mother's brother, as the Chinese translation clearly states). And in Pirahã, a language spoken in the Amazon, I couldn't say "42nd," because there are no words for exact numbers, just words for "few" and "many."

Languages differ from one another in innumerable ways, but just because people talk differently does not necessarily mean they think differently. How can we tell whether speakers of Mian, Russian, Indonesian, Mandarin or Pirahã actually end up attending to, remembering and reasoning about the world in different ways because of the languages they speak? Research in my lab and in many others has been uncovering how language shapes even the most fundamental dimensions of human experience: space, time, causality and relationships to others.

Let us return to Pormpuraaw. Unlike English, the Kuuk Thaayorre language spoken in Pormpuraaw does not use relative spatial terms such as left and right. Rather Kuuk Thaayorre speakers talk in terms of absolute cardinal directions (north, south, east, west, and so forth). Of course, in English we also use cardinal direction terms but only for large spatial scales. We would not say, for example, "They set the salad forks southeast of the dinner forks—the philistines!" But in Kuuk Thaayorre cardinal directions are used at all scales. This means one ends up saying things like "the cup is southeast of the plate" or "the boy standing to the south of Mary is my brother." In Pormpuraaw, one must always stay oriented, just to be able to speak properly.

Moreover, groundbreaking work conducted by Stephen C. Levinson of the Max Planck Institute for Psycholinguistics in Nijmegen, the Netherlands, and John B. Haviland of the

University of California, San Diego, over the past two decades has demonstrated that people who speak languages that rely on absolute directions are remarkably good at keeping track of where they are, even in unfamiliar landscapes or inside unfamiliar buildings. They do this better than folks who live in the same environments but do not speak such languages and in fact better than scientists thought humans ever could. The requirements of their languages enforce and train this cognitive prowess.

People who think differently about space are also likely to think differently about time. For example, my colleague Alice Gaby of the University of California, Berkeley, and I gave Kuuk Thaayorre speakers sets of pictures that showed temporal progressions—a man aging, a crocodile growing, a banana being eaten. We then asked them to arrange the shuffled photographs on the ground to indicate the correct temporal order.

We tested each person twice, each time facing in a different cardinal direction. English speakers given this task will arrange the cards so that time proceeds from left to right. Hebrew speakers will tend to lay out the cards from right to left. This shows that writing direction in a language influences how we organize time. The Kuuk Thaayorre, however, did not routinely arrange the cards from left to right or right to left. They arranged them from east to west. That is, when they were seated facing south, the cards went left to right. When they faced north, the cards went from right to left. When they faced east, the cards came toward the body, and so on. We never told anyone which direction they were facing—the Kuuk Thaayorre knew that already and spontaneously used this spatial orientation to construct their representations of time.

Representations of time vary in many other ways around the world. For example, English speakers consider the future to be "ahead" and the past "behind." In 2010 Lynden Miles of the University of Aberdeen in Scotland and his colleagues discovered that English speakers unconsciously sway their bodies forward when thinking about the future and back when thinking about the past. But in Aymara, a language spoken in the Andes, the past is said to be in front and the future behind. And the Aymara speakers' body language matches their way of talking: in 2006 Raphael Núñez of U.C.S.D. and Eve Sweetser of U.C. Berkeley found that Aymara gesture in front of them when talking about the past and behind them when discussing the future.

Remembering Whodunit

Speakers of different languages also differ in how they describe events and, as a result, how well they can remember who did what. All events, even split-second accidents, are complicated and require us to construe and interpret what happened. Take, for example, former vice president Dick Cheney's quail-hunting accident, in which he accidentally shot Harry Whittington. One could say that "Cheney shot Whittington" (wherein Cheney is the direct cause), or "Whittington got shot by Cheney" (distancing Cheney from the outcome), or "Whittington got peppered pretty good" (leaving Cheney out altogether). Cheney himself said "Ultimately I'm the guy who pulled the trigger

that fired the round that hit Harry," interposing a long chain of events between himself and the outcome. President George Bush's take—"he heard a bird flush, and he turned and pulled the trigger and saw his friend get wounded"—was an even more masterful exculpation, transforming Cheney from agent to mere witness in less than a sentence.

Speakers of different languages differ in how well they can remember who did what.

The American public is rarely impressed with such linguistic wiggling because nonagentive language sounds evasive in English, the province of guilt-shirking children and politicians. English speakers tend to phrase things in terms of people doing things, preferring transitive constructions like "John broke the vase" even for accidents. Speakers of Japanese or Spanish, in contrast, are less likely to mention the agent when describing an accidental event. In Spanish one might say *Se rompió el florero*," which translates to "the vase broke" or "the vase broke itself."

My student Caitlin M. Fausey and I have found that such linguistic differences influence how people construe what happened and have consequences for eyewitness memory. In our studies, published in 2010, speakers of English, Spanish and Japanese watched videos of two guys popping balloons, breaking eggs and spilling drinks either intentionally or accidentally. Later we gave them a surprise memory test. For each event they had witnessed, they had to say which guy did it, just like in a police line-up. Another group of English, Spanish and Japanese speakers described the same events. When we looked at the memory data, we found exactly the differences in eyewitness memory predicted by patterns in language. Speakers of all three languages described intentional events agentively, saying things such as "He popped the balloon," and all three groups remembered who did these intentional actions equally well. When it came to accidents, however, interesting differences emerged. Spanish and Japanese speakers were less likely to describe the accidents agentively than were English speakers, and they correspondingly remembered who did it less well than English speakers did. This was not because they had poorer memory overall—they remembered the agents of intentional events (for which their languages would naturally mention the agent) just as well as English speakers did.

Not only do languages influence what we remember, but the structures of languages can make it easier or harder for us to learn new things. For instance, because the number words in some languages reveal the underlying base-10 structure more transparently than do the number words in English (there are no troublesome teens like 11 or 13 in Mandarin, for instance), kids learning those languages are able to learn the base-10 insight sooner. And depending on how many syllables the number words have, it will be easier or harder to keep a phone number in mind or to do mental calculation. Language can even affect how quickly children figure out whether they are male or female. In 1983 Alexander Guiora of the University of Michigan at Ann Arbor compared three groups of kids growing up with Hebrew, English or Finnish as their native language. Hebrew marks gender prolifically (even the word "you" is different depending on gender), Finnish has no gender marking and English is somewhere in between. Accordingly, children growing up in a Hebrew-speaking environment figure out their own gender about a year earlier than Finnish-speaking children; English-speaking kids fall in the middle.

What Shapes What?

These are just some of the many fascinating findings of cross-linguistic differences in cognition. But how do we know whether differences in language create differences in thought, or the other way around? The answer, it turns out, is both—the way we think influences the way we speak, but the influence also goes the other way. The past decade has seen a host of ingenious demonstrations establishing that language indeed plays a causal role in shaping cognition. Studies have shown that changing how people talk changes how they think. Teaching people new color words, for instance, changes their ability to discriminate colors. And teaching people a new way of talking about time gives them a new way of thinking about it.

Another way to get at this question is to study people who are fluent in two languages. Studies have shown that bilinguals change how they see the world depending on which language they are speaking. Two sets of findings published in 2010 demonstrate that even something as fundamental as who you like and do not like depends on the language in which you are asked. The studies, one by Oludamini Ogunnaike and his colleagues at Harvard and another by Shai Danziger and his colleagues at Ben-Gurion University of the Negev in Israel, looked at Arabic-French bilinguals in Morocco, Spanish-English bilinguals in the U.S. and Arabic-Hebrew bilinguals in Israel, in each case testing the participants' implicit biases. For example, Arabic-Hebrew bilinguals were asked to quickly press buttons in response to words under various conditions. In one condition if they saw a Jewish name like "Yair" or a positive trait like "good" or "strong," they were instructed to press "M,"; if they saw an Arab name like "Ahmed" or a negative trait like "mean" or "weak," they were told to press "X." In another condition the pairing was reversed so that Jewish names and negative traits shared a response key, and Arab names and positive traits shared a response key. The researchers measured how quickly subjects were able to respond under the two conditions. This task has been widely used to measure involuntary or automatic biases—how naturally things such as positive traits and ethnic groups seem to go together in people's minds.

Surprisingly, the investigators found big shifts in these involuntary automatic biases in bilinguals depending on the language in which they were tested. The Arabic-Hebrew bilinguals, for their part, showed more positive implicit attitudes toward Jews when tested in Hebrew than when tested in Arabic.

People communicate using a multitude of languages that vary considerably in the information they convey.

Scholars have long wondered whether different languages might impart different cognitive abilities.

In recent years empirical evidence for this causal relation has emerged, indicating that one's mother tongue does indeed mold the way one thinks about many aspects of the world, including space and time.

The latest findings also hint that language is part and parcel of many more aspects of thought than scientists had previously realized.

Language also appears to be involved in many more aspects of our mental lives than scientists had previously supposed. People rely on language even when doing simple things like distinguishing patches of color, counting dots on a screen or orienting in a small room: my colleagues and I have found that limiting people's ability to access their language faculties fluently—by giving them a competing demanding verbal task such as repeating a news report, for instance—impairs their ability to perform these tasks. This means that the categories and distinctions that exist in particular languages are meddling in our mental lives very broadly. What researchers have been calling "thinking" this whole time actually appears to be a collection of both linguistic and nonlinguistic processes. As a result, there may not be a lot of adult human thinking where language does not play a role.

A hallmark feature of human intelligence is its adaptability, the ability to invent and rearrange conceptions of the world to suit changing goals and environments. One consequence of this flexibility is the great diversity of languages that have emerged around the globe. Each provides its own cognitive toolkit and encapsulates the knowledge and worldview developed over thousands of years within a culture. Each contains a way of perceiving, categorizing and making meaning in the world, an invaluable guidebook developed and honed by our ancestors. Research into how the languages we speak shape the way we think is helping scientists to unravel how we create knowledge and construct reality and how we got to be as smart and sophisticated as we are. And this insight, in turn, helps us understand the very essence of what makes us human.

More to Explore

Language Changes Implicit Associations between Ethnic Groups and Evaluation in Bilinguals. Shai Danziger and Robert Ward in *Psychological Science,* Vol. 21, No. 6, pages 799–800; June 2010.

Constructing Agency: The Role of Language. Caitlin M. Fausey et al. in *Frontiers in Cultural Psychology,* Vol. 1, Article 162. Published online October 15, 2010.

Remembrances of Times East: Absolute Spatial Representations of Time in an Australian Aboriginal Community. Lera Boroditsky and Alice Gaby in *Psychological Science,* Vol. 21, No. 11, pages 1635–1639; November 2010.

Critical Thinking

1. How is it that a 5-year-old in the Pormpuraaw community of northern Australia has a better sense of direction than many trained scientists in the United States?

2. Be familiar with the examples cited as to how people differ cross-culturally in terms of their perceptions of space and time.

3. What are some of the cultural differences in terms of how people describe events, especially in terms of agency?

4. What evidence is there that languages affect people's perceptions of color? How they learn? Who they like and don't like? That they need language in order to perform certain mental tasks?

LERA BORODITSKY is an assistant professor of cognitive psychology at Stanford University and editor in chief of *Frontiers in Cultural Psychology*. Her lab conducts research around the world, focusing on mental representation and the effects of language on cognition.

Famous Names: The World of Business

JOHN COLAPINTO

In the summer of 1998, a group of executives from a small technology startup called Research in Motion arrived at the California offices of Lexicon, a firm devoted to inventing names for products. The executives had brought with them the prototype for a new device, a two-way pager that could send and receive e-mail wirelessly. They could not agree on a name, but they had a few contenders: EasyMail, MegaMail, and ProMail.

"Everybody likes to name something 'Pro,'" Lexicon's founder and C.E.O., David Placek, told me dryly. Placek is a stocky man of fifty-eight whose unassuming presentation—blue blazer, shirt and tie, clipped blond hair—disguises an unpredictable imagination. He told the executives, "You guys are the underdog. You want to name it something that the big guys—A.T. & T., Southwestern Bell, California Bell—would never think of. You have to be distinctive, a little bold—or rebellious."

To begin the naming process, Placek and a few members of his staff interviewed commuters riding the ferry from San Francisco to Sausalito, where Lexicon's offices are situated, near the foot of the Golden Gate Bridge. They wanted to know how, in those early days of the digital revolution, people felt about the prospect of being able to receive e-mail everywhere. "When you said 'e-mail' to someone, it wasn't a joyous thing," Placek said. "The way I explained it to Research in Motion was 'Blood pressure goes up.'" Placek told the executives that the device needed a name that would soothe this stress response. MegaMail, with its connotations of an unstoppable avalanche of virtual messages, was definitely out.

Most projects at Lexicon start off with free-associated Mind Maps—large diagrams of words that spread out like dendrites from a central concept. A map of hundreds of words, generated at the pace of a brainstorming session, can take less than ten minutes to produce and can resemble a Cy Twombly scribble painting. The maps help to stake out linguistic territory, and to bring forth the deeper associations that a particular product evokes—"the words underneath the name," as Placek puts it. For the Research in Motion

device, he said, "we had teams working on 'things that are natural,' 'things that are fresh,' 'things that are fun.' At a certain point, we got into the area of 'things that are enjoyable.'" On a Mind Map, someone wrote "strawberry." Then someone wrote beside it, "Strawberry is too slow." Placek pronounced the word—"Str-a-a-a-w-w-berry"—drawing it out. "This technology is instantaneous," he said.

On the map, someone else wrote "blackberry." "I'd love to be able to say I saw it on the wall and said, 'Wham, this is it! I'm a genius!'" Placek told me. But the process by which a name is selected from hundreds of candidates can be arduous, and often comes down to a combination of instinct, abstract reasoning, and the client's idiosyncratic demands. "Blackberry" went onto a list of about forty potential names that Placek took to Research in Motion's offices, in Waterloo, Canada. In the next few weeks, he and the R.I.M. executives narrowed the list, and eventually talked themselves into the name Blackberry. Its strengths, they decided, were not limited to blood-pressure-lowering associations with fruit. The word "black" evoked the color of high-tech devices, and the gadget's small, oval keys looked like the drupelets of a blackberry.

Lexicon employs two in-house linguists and consults with seventy-seven others around the world, specialists in languages as diverse as Urdu, Tagalog, and Hindi—a critical resource, Placek says. They screen names for embarrassing associations. (The industry abounds in tales of cross-linguistic gaffes, like Creap coffee creamer from Japan, Bum potato chips from Spain, and the Chevy Nova—in Spanish, the "no go.") They also offer input on the unconscious resonance of particular sounds. In the mid-nineties, Lexicon funded a linguistic study whose results suggested that the sound of the letter "b" was one of the most "reliable" in any language—"whether you were in Poland or Paris or New York," Placek said. He mentioned this to the Research in Motion executives, and they decided to capitalize both "b"s: BlackBerry.

In January, 1999, the BlackBerry was launched. Despite heavy competition from the Droid and the iPhone, it remains one of the best-selling smart phones, with seventy million subscribers worldwide. Lexicon's most successful names—among them Pentium, for Intel; Swiffer, for Procter & Gamble; PowerBook, for Apple; Dasani, for Coca-Cola—have become immensely lucrative global brands, which collectively have brought in billions of dollars for their companies.

Of course, not all successful brand names are created by professionals. Larry Page and Sergey Brin came up with the name of their search engine by misspelling "googol," the word for the number one followed by a hundred zeros. The name Coca-Cola was devised by an accountant working for the drink's creator—he thought that the two "C"s would look good in advertisements. But such happy accidents are increasingly rare. Products are proliferating around the world, from automobiles to cleansers, drugs, and, especially, electronics. In 1980, there were fewer than ten thousand registered high-tech trademarks in the United States; now there are more than three hundred thousand. The ideal contemporary name works across languages, on search engines, and on Twitter and Facebook, all while displaying the ingenuity necessary to stand out—a difficult standard for business owners to meet without help.

Placek maintains that the best brand names, like poems, work by compressing into a single euphonious word an array of specific, resonant meanings and associations. But he prefers to emphasize the practical aspects of his work. "I've learned that if I use that with prospective clients— 'Hey, what we're creating here is a small poem'—you can see people sort of get concerned," he told me. "Like, 'This isn't really about art here. This is about getting things done.'"

Brand naming has existed for centuries. Italians made watermarks on paper in the twelve-hundreds. During the industrial revolution, companies sought to inspire consumer confidence with names borrowed from their owners' families: Singer sewing machines, Fuller brushes, Hoover vacuums—all names that are still in use. Before the First World War, there was a wave of abstract names ending in "o" (like Brillo and Brasso), followed, in the nineteen-twenties, by one of "ex" names: Pyrex, Cutex, Windex. But, according to Eric Yorkston, a marketing professor at Texas Christian University, modern brand naming—with its sophisticated focus groups and its linguistic and psychological analysis— began in the years after the Second World War, when the explosion of similar products from competing companies made imaginative naming an increasing necessity.

In 1957, the Ford Motor Company made an enormous investment in a newly engineered and designed mid-priced car. When Henry Ford introduced the first affordable automobile, a half century earlier, the lack of competition allowed him to name it, prosaically, the Model T (coming, as it did, after the Model S). Now, with the rise of G.M. and Chrysler, Ford was forced to take a different approach. It hired an advertising agency and asked its employees to generate potential names. (The list—more than eighteen thousand names in all— included Citation, Corsair, Pacer, and Ranger, which were scrupulously tested with focus groups and man-on-the-street interviews before being rejected.) Ford even wrote to the poet Marianne Moore, asking her to think up a name that would "convey, through association or other conjuration, some visceral feeling of elegance, fleetness, advanced features and design." Moore responded with a list of names that demonstrated a serene distance from the commercial marketplace: among them were Intelligent Bullet, Utopian Turtletop, Bullet Cloisone, Pastelogram, Mongoose Civique, and Andante con Moto.

Ultimately, Ford executives, unable to reach an agreement, reverted to nineteenth-century custom and named the car after Henry Ford's son Edsel. Launched with an unprecedented, fifty-million-dollar advertising and marketing campaign, the Edsel was one of the most spectacular business flops in history; the name has become synonymous with failure.

During the sixties and seventies, companies looking for brand names increasingly turned to Madison Avenue advertising agencies, with their professed expertise in the collective unconscious of the buying public. Snappy, "Mad Men"-style initialisms became popular: A.T. & T., 3M, I.B.M., G.M. With the mergers-and-acquisitions boom of the nineteen-eighties, brand names took on a new importance. "A lot of the value that was being paid for companies was for their brands," Kevin Lane Keller, a professor of marketing at Dartmouth College, says. "There was no other way to justify paying x billions of dollars for this company from just the physical plants, equipment, and everything else. It was intangible assets." In 1982, amid this new interest in brand naming, Placek launched Lexicon, which was among the first companies in the United States dedicated solely to the practice.

Placek grew up in Santa Rosa, California, where his father was a flooring contractor and his mother a homemaker. After graduating from U.C.L.A. with a political-science degree, he worked for the Senate Commerce Committee, researching solar energy. He liked Washington, but the job often involved little more than pouring water for senators. In 1976, he went to Missouri to become the press secretary for Governor Warren Hearnes in his run for the U.S. Senate. During the campaign, Placek said, he began to understand how words could make ideas salable—especially when those ideas were compressed into a brief, memorable phrase. "I learned the beauty of a well-written headline," he said, "and began to think that this was something I could do."

He returned to California, where he got a job in the San Francisco office of Foote, Cone & Belding, a prominent ad agency. As an account supervisor, he had a gift for communicating to creative teams the messages that clients wanted to convey about their products, and then running the intimate creative sessions that helped turn those messages into advertisements. He got his first experience of naming while working on the Levi's account. "Every denim line, spring and fall, had to have a moniker, usually just for the business-retail end of things," he says. He remembers a line of children's jeans for which his group, working with the manufacturer, dreamed up the name Little Levi's. "Beautiful little name," he said. "The alliteration. Things I didn't know about at the time. The 'L's working together. It was a good name by accident."

After six years, Placek was hired by an aggressive new agency called S & O, where he was put in charge of new-product development and naming. By then, he had become a devotee of the 1970 book "The Practice of Creativity," by George Prince, a former adman who, with the inventor and psychologist William J. J. Gordon, created an organization called Synectics, which ran workshops on how to increase creativity in small groups. The method stressed openness to ideas that seem irrelevant to the problem at hand; one of Gordon's maxims was "Trust things that are alien, and alienate things that are trusted." At the workshops, Placek said, he developed many of the techniques he employs at Lexicon. He guided teams on "excursions" that elicited creative responses by introducing unexpected stimuli, "maybe passing out sports magazines if we're naming a women's cosmetic." Placek's methods helped him excel at S & O, where he ran naming sessions for Taco Bell, Holiday Inn, and other major corporations. In 1982, after less than a year, he left to start Lexicon.

For almost a decade, the company relied on naming jobs subcontracted by other firms. In the mid-eighties, it came up with Outback, for a Subaru S.U.V. At the time, just about every new S.U.V. name carried associations with the American West: Scout, Cherokee, Wagoneer. Placek wanted to suggest ruggedness but avoid predictability. "I love Oscar Wilde's line that an idea that isn't dangerous is hardly worth calling an idea at all," he told me.

Lexicon's first big success came in the early nineties, when Apple hired Placek to name its first laptop. The new computer would replace the Macintosh Portable, a sixteen-pound behemoth not much smaller than a desktop computer, and Lexicon's brief was to devise a name that would overcome consumers' skepticism about Apple's ability to make a truly portable computer. "We were looking at those word units: 'port,' 'carry'—metaphors for things that are small," Placek said. "So 'book' was there." The notion of computing speed and performance was captured by the word "power." Lexicon combined the terms to come up with PowerBook. Placek says that some people at Apple thought the name boring. "My response was 'Yes, it is two common words put together, but there is no such thing as a PowerBook.'" The PowerBook was introduced in 1991 and became an immediate best-seller.

Placek maintains that an effective brand name can shape an entire industry. Until 1992, when Lexicon came up with the name Pentium for a computer chip made by Intel Corporation, microprocessors were identified by number, and for a long time were considered so fungible that manufacturers would share design specifications. "The salesman would tell you, 'This computer has a 286 processor, this one has a 386,'" Placek told me. "And you'd say, 'What's the difference?' And they'd say, 'It's faster.' But there's nothing special about those things." Intel's new microprocessor was the first one capable of running the video and graphics that were about to transform the home computer. The company's C.E.O., Andy Grove, wanted to make it stand out. He declined to share the specifications with other chipmakers, and, after finding that it was impossible to trademark a number, he decided that the new chip needed a name. His marketing team hired Lexicon.

Because the microprocessor is the brains of the computer, Placek decided that the name had to sound like a fundamental component of the machine. Lexicon looked to the periodic table of the elements and found titanium, which suggested scarcity, strength, and worth. Placek also had to consider Intel's marketing team, which had asked for a name that "sounded like an ingredient"—something that goes into the computer to enhance it. So Lexicon took note of sodium, an additive that enhances a dish. Using the phoneme that the words had in common, "ium," the company generated thousands of names. "I remember being in the office by myself on a Saturday morning and going over a list," Placek said. On it was the word "pentium." "The first thing I thought of was the Pentagon, and I thought, Huh, that's pretty interesting, because it's a shape." Then he remembered that "pente" means five in Greek. "I thought, Wait a minute—we're going from 486 to the fifth generation, the 586."

The name seemed promising, but Lexicon first had to determine whether it was original. Much of a naming company's daily business is scanning worldwide databases to make sure that a name does not impinge on an existing trademark. The law prohibits any names "close enough in sound, appearance, or meaning" to create "confusion"—wording vague enough to make companies leery of duplicating even a syllable of another brand name. Violations can be costly; in the nineties, Microsoft launched the Web browser Internet Explorer and was sued by a small company in the Midwest that had already used the name. Microsoft was obliged to pay five million dollars for the rights. More recently, the movie-rental service Netflix announced that it was renaming the DVD-by-mail part of its business Qwikster. In two days, its Web site received twenty-four thousand comments, many of them negative; critics pointed out that the name was indistinguishable from that of a former Amway enterprise, a chain of convenience stores, and a "hard-rockin' trio" from Montana.

Lexicon's lawyers found that Pentium bore few similarities to existing names. "We see 'ium' in things, but 'tium' is less occurring," Placek said. There remained the hurdle of convincing Intel to accept the name. "Clients typically drill down on 'I don't know, is that really supporting our positioning? Because that really means this, so I don't really know if it would work.'" One naysayer, Grove recalls, said that Pentium sounded "like a toothpaste."

In order to convince the company, Placek conducted focus groups and interviews in the U.S., Europe, and Asia, presenting subjects with a fictitious new car called the Porsche Pentium and asking them to describe it. "People around the world said, 'That's the premium line, that's the performance line,'" Placek noted. "We were probing: 'Who drives that?' 'Well,' people said, 'a person that's successful, educated.' We were able to communicate back to Intel that this name had a lot of what we call 'intrinsic value.'" In October, 1992, Grove announced the name on CNN. Despite skepticism in the computer-trade press, which predicted that "Pentium" would never catch on, the name quickly replaced the numbering system and became the centerpiece of Intel's global advertising campaign. Placek said, "Instead of saying, 'I'm thinking of an H.P. or a Dell—what's the difference?,' now consumers were saying, 'I want a Pentium computer.'"

"It was one of our great success stories," Grove told me. "According to our own internal research, in the late nineties Pentium was a more recognized brand name than Intel—which is actually a little scary."

Not everyone is convinced of the power of brand names. Bernd Schmitt, a marketing professor at Columbia Business School, points out that when a product is launched its name is only part of a multimillion-dollar marketing campaign that also involves advertising, research, and social media. "Would Amazon be just as successful if it was called Nile?" he says. "My guess would be yes, because the name is just a starting point for a brand. The most important branding decision is more about brand strategy, distribution channels—where are the customers you want to reach?" Furthermore, virtually any name can be made successful through the sheer ubiquity that a multimedia ad campaign provides. Grove told me that his executives chose Pentium from a group of finalists that included Razar and Intellec, and thought that they could "probably have made any of these names work by repetition and exposure." Schmitt concedes that a name can help grab attention, but the degree to which the name alone dictates a product's success has never been precisely determined. "We would need to do a lab or field experiment where we have various names on a single product," he says. "That's tough to do."

Yet it is difficult to imagine that "The Great Gatsby"—with its crisp, alliterative, lightly ironic title—would have fared as well under Fitzgerald's preferred name, "Trimalchio in West Egg," or that "Pride and Prejudice" would have flourished as "First Impressions." And, while field experiments of the sort that Schmitt suggests are impractical, businesspeople are often willing to take the importance of names on faith. After all, the Patagonian toothfish—a large, sharp-toothed codlike fish—became popular among diners after it was renamed the Chilean sea bass; likewise the slimehead, reborn as the orange roughy. A few years ago, Lexicon was hired to rename a dessert—small nubs of ice cream coated with chocolate—that Nestle was selling under the name Snack-a-Bites. Lexicon re-dubbed them Dibs, a play on the childhood expression "I've got dibs on that." The product was a hit.

Naming experts agree on several universals of great names. It's probably best to keep them short. (Dibs beats the longueurs of Snack-a-Bites.) Names that display a consonant-vowel-consonant pattern, like Gatorade, Lipitor, and Amazon, are often easiest to say, since these sorts of letter combinations are among the first that infants learn in any language. Pleasantness of sound—the use of alliteration and assonance—also plays a part. But Placek said that it can be dangerous to become too programmatic about what he calls "tactical" aspects of naming. The real goal, he says, is to determine what "story" a client wishes to tell about his product (it's faster, it's more powerful, it's easier to use) and then find a word that evokes it, without being predictable or even necessarily logical; straightforward labels do not worm their way into the consumer's subconscious, touching off the insecurity and acquisitiveness that provoke the impulse to buy. Not long ago, Lexicon was hired to name a new product for Colgate: a portable mini-toothbrush whose bristles contain a bead of breath-freshening liquid that users can safely swallow. Placek ruled out names with any suggestion of portability or miniaturization—too predictable. Instead, he wanted a word that merely evoked those qualities. Lexicon came up with Wisp, which satisfied the criteria of insubstantiality and lightness (not to mention shortness and euphony) and also suggested "whisper," something that the user might do with greater confidence if there were no particles of his dinner lodged in his teeth.

The very best brand names, Placek says, can help a company gain a near-monopoly. Kleenex and Xerox have not only become synonymous with the products they represent; they have replaced the actual names. Placek cites Google, iPod, and Amazon (none of them Lexicon names) as contemporary names that have come to define a product or service. "I'm not sure you could find an experienced marketing person who wouldn't say that these names made a difference," he said. As a young man at Foote, Cone & Belding, he was tutored by Mike Koelker and Chris Blum, who in the sixties and seventies created television commercials for Levi's jeans that helped make denim a symbol of the global youth culture. "They would talk to clients about using film to create what they described as 'a strategic alteration of reality,'" Placek said. "In a way, isn't that what Google or iPod or BlackBerry does? It takes reality and just alters it a little bit."

In the past fifteen years or so, naming has entered a kind of postmodern phase, venturing from descriptive, functional labels—Mop & Glo, Mr. Coffee, Cocoa Krispies—toward esoterica like Viagra and Dasani, in which the meaning yields only to deep textual analysis. (Dasani, which Lexicon devised for Coca-Cola's brand of bottled water, is supposed to convey health and purity through the root "sani.") Much of this comes from the growing role of linguistic professionals in naming products.

In the early nineties, Lexicon was naming a new cereal for General Mills, and Placek asked Will Leben, one of his freelance linguists, what he thought of the name Triples. Without hesitation, Leben said that the name would test best with focus groups around the idea of "crisp."

"I said, 'How do you know that?'" Placek recalls. "He said, 'Well, look at the sound trip. Look at the "p." Puh. Cris-puh. It's perfectly matched.' We went into focus groups and everybody said Triples would be best for crispness. So then I thought, O.K., there is more to this linguistics than just having people give us Greek and Latin names or Sanskrit." Placek invited Leben to become a full-time member of Lexicon's staff.

Leben, who had studied under Noam Chomsky at M.I.T., was an expert in Hausa, a West African language, and taught at Stanford University from 1972 until 2003. He took the job at Lexicon, he says, "because it opened up a whole new way to make linguistics useful." One of his first tasks was to do a study of what linguists call "sound symbolism"—the way sounds convey meaning independent of what a word actually signifies.

For the study, which was called Sounder, Leben asked test subjects a hundred and thirty-five questions—"Which car sounds faster: Tarin or Parin?," "Which sounds more luxurious?"—to tease out the associations evoked by individual letters and sounds. The results were dramatic, he says: Tarin sounded "faster" but "less luxurious" than Parin, because less work goes into pronouncing a "t," which uses only the tip of the tongue. The "p" sound uses the "massive articulators" of the lips, so it is "heavier, slower, and thus more luxurious." The "b" sound—a plosive, like "p," but with the vocal cords and the lungs engaged—sounded more luxurious still. "We checked four other world languages and got the same results," Leben says. "It works in Japanese, Polish, Spanish, and Dutch—these things are either very common or universal."

In 2001, Leben and another linguist completed a second study, called Sounder II, using five hundred subjects in the U.S., Europe, and Asia. "We were trying to get toward emotions," he says. By asking questions such as "Which sounds more happy, which more sad?," "Which more alive, which more lifeless?," and "Which more daring, which more insecure?," Lexicon isolated consonants—such as "c," "v," and "p"—that conveyed vigor, liveliness, and well-being.

The Sounder studies changed the way that Lexicon generates names. In the mid-nineties, the company was hired to name a new mop, developed by Procter & Gamble, that used disposable pads charged with static electricity to pick up dust and crumbs. Placek instructed his staff to avoid any reference to the word "mop" (which evokes drudgery), but the name still needed to suggest the act of cleaning. "So what are the actions?" Placek said to me. "You dust, you sweep, you swipe, you wash." The name also needed to convey ease and speed. From a list that included "swipe," "sweep," "swift," and "fast," Lexicon isolated various sound combinations, including sw, ft, sh. Then, Placek explained, "you just start building out names."

The process generated thousands of possibilities, and Leben particularly liked "swiffer." "'Swiff' is phonologically very close to 'sweep,'" he notes. "The two vowels are distinct, but 'i' and 'e' are pronounced close to one another in the vocal tract." "Swiff" also, of course, sounds like "swift"—the job will be over soon. The ending was also important, he says. "'Er' means it's something that performs an action"—and thus carries the suggestion that the Swiffer is doing the work, not you. The Swiffer, launched in 1999, has become a half-billion-dollar brand in fifteen countries; Procter & Gamble now uses the name for an array of cleaning products.

Placek is fond of pointing out to potential clients the difference in name recognition between the Swiffer and the knockoff Clorox product, the ReadyMop. But not every C.E.O. buys Lexicon's linguistic rationales. Talking to Intel's Andy Grove, I recounted Lexicon's analysis of the word "Pentium": "The 'p' and 't' at the beginning of the first two syllables are voiceless sounds," Leben had told me. "They're quick, they explode. But the consonants at the end of the syllables, the 'n' and the 'm,' they hum—mmm—the way you think a microprocessor should." Grove heard me out patiently. Then he said, "Lexicon is very lucky in not having presented this idea to me."

One morning in late March, Placek assembled six staff members in Lexicon's main work studio, a large room with a wall of windows looking out onto Richardson Bay. The team was beginning an "exploratory," an anticipatory exercise to create names with such great intrinsic value that they would suit products that did not yet exist. Today's project was car names. "What we're trying to do is get ahead of what car companies might be thinking when they come to us a year from now," Placek said. To make sure that the names did not infringe on any trademarks, Lexicon had posted on the wall some eight hundred and fifty existing car names, ranging from Gullwing to Veloster.

In the next three weeks, the team generated thousands of names, and then—with the aid of consumer focus groups and e-mail exchanges with linguists—selected a few keepers. (One focus group that I observed came up with Hawkbat, Bustang, and Killer Whale. Placek, watching the group through one-way glass, remarked, "This is why we don't get consumers to name things.")

Propped against a wall of the studio was the Mind Map that had got the process started. It was built around the notion that, in response to environmental concerns, rising gas prices, and the recession, the cars of the very near future will be smaller and more fuel-efficient. The nucleus term "natural transportation" was written in the center of a ten-foot-by-six-foot foam-core board. From it sprouted hundreds of scribbled words, covering the surface: "deep," "birds," "propagation," "wings," "butterflies," "stained glass," "arteries."

The team members were seated at cafe tables scattered at one end of the loftlike room. Placek shared a table with Marc Hershon, a senior staffer in his early fifties who has worked at Lexicon for fifteen years. Hershon, who is also a screenwriter and a teacher and performer of improvisational comedy, was dressed in creative-worker motley: goatee, black shirt, colorful tie. He told me, "Early in our process, it's a messy thing. You can't just go, 'I'm going to give you twenty-five great names, and I'm going to write them out right now.' There's a lot of pushing and shoving and playing around. Then you start shaving away all the stuff. And it's almost like creating a sculpture. The name is in here—let's get to it."

To the uninitiated viewer, the beginning of the exercise would be difficult to distinguish from chatting—a group of co-workers on their lunch break, idly chewing over a topic. But Placek was tactfully closing off unproductive lines of inquiry and clearing the way for ones that seemed to have promise. An hour into the session, as the team started to lose energy, he introduced a thought experiment: gasoline reaches eight dollars a gallon, and, rather than own cars, people buy memberships in a comprehensive transportation system.

"I think we should think about naming a brand, a platform—just like Swiffer is for all kinds of cleaning things," he said. "It should be a name that fits a small car, a rental city bike, and a shuttle bus, like a big van." He glanced at the Mind Map, where the word "wave" was written. "I'll use Wave," he said. "Wave is my transportation provider."

"It would be interesting to ask what people's threshold is for riding public transportation," Hershon said. "People don't like riding the bus, it's too crowded—"

"Germs," Placek said.

"Germs," Hershon agreed.

"I guess that's it," Placek went on. "How to create a name that would affect public transportation?"

"I was thinking of this whole idea of moving toward sustainability and recycled materials," Greg Alger, a linguist, said. "A lot of it is driven by a sense of responsibility. So I think a sort of responsibility direction might be worth pursuing."

"Can you give me an example?" Placek asked.

"Um," Alger said, glancing around the room. "Like an example of . . . ?" he said.

"Well, like, you're talking about a car brand—Pledge."

"Right!" Alger said. "Exactly! Something like that. I mean, take the Civic, for example."

"O.K.—perfect example," Placek said. "Even better."

"A sense of responsibility that people have to the environment," Alger said.

"Community Car," Placek mused. "The Eco car." He looked dissatisfied. "But Civic is a great name," he said—those vigorous "c"s and "v"s. "See how fast that is? And yet totally unexpected at the time."

Then Placek addressed the unthinkable: that car companies would get rid of names altogether. "It just becomes Honda's P-190: it gets a hundred and ninety miles to the gallon. Very practical, and it's a pledge to the world. Because gas is going up, no question about it. Peak oil—that's that term that says we're running out. And I think that's in 2030, something like that?"

"Sooner," a bearded staffer named Allen Kohlhepp said. He cited a recent WikiLeaks revelation. "Some documents showed that the Saudis are lying about the amount of oil they have," he said.

"I've got a name for a new car," someone said. "The Peak."

"Drive it till you run out," Hershon said.

"The Last Car You'll Ever Need," Kohlhepp said. "The Slimmo."

"The Peako," Placek replied.

33

Hershon, jotting on his iPad screen with a stylus, nodded and said, "I'm writing those down."

Does it matter what a product is called?

Critical Thinking

1. How did Lexicon come up with the name "BlackBerry"? In general, what kind of linguistic advice do they give?

2. In what ways must the ideal contemporary product name work? In what ways do the best brand names work?

3. How does modern band-naming differ from the past? Why have companies looking for brand names increasingly turned to Madison Avenue?

4. Why was the name, "PowerBook" chosen for Apple's first laptop?

5. How did Placek come up with the name "Pentium" for Intel's microprocessor?

6. Discuss the pros and cons regarding the importance of brand names.

7. What are the universals of great names, according to naming experts?

8. Describe the "postmodern" phase of product naming.

9. Using examples, discuss the importance of "sound symbolism."

10. What were the findings of the study, "Sounder II"? How did Lexicon come up with the name, "Swiffer," for Procter and Gamble's new mop?

11. Using cars as an example, how is Lexicon trying to "get ahead of the game"?

Fighting for Our Lives

Deborah Tannen, PhD

This is not another book about civility. "Civility" suggests a superficial, pinky-in-the-air veneer of politeness spread thin over human relations like a layer of marmalade over toast. This book is about a pervasive war-like atmosphere that makes us approach public dialogue, and just about anything we need to accomplish, as if it were a fight. It is a tendency in Western culture in general, and in the United States in particular, that has a long history and a deep, thick, and far-ranging root system. It has served us well in many ways but in recent years has become so exaggerated that it is getting in the way of solving our problems. Our spirits are corroded by living in an atmosphere of unrelenting contention—an argument culture.

The argument culture urges us to approach the world—and the people in it—in an adversarial frame of mind. It rests on the assumption that opposition is the best way to get anything done: The best way to discuss an idea is to set up a debate; the best way to cover news is to find spokespeople who express the most extreme, polarized views and present them as "both sides"; the best way to settle disputes is litigation that pits one party against the other; the best way to begin an essay is to attack someone; and the best way to show you're really thinking is to criticize.

Our public interactions have become more and more like having an argument with a spouse. Conflict can't be avoided in our public lives any more than we can avoid conflict with people we love. One of the great strengths of our society is that we can express these conflicts openly. But just as spouses have to learn ways of settling their differences without inflicting real damage on each other, so we, as a society, have to find constructive ways of resolving disputes and differences. Public discourse requires *making* an argument for a point of view, not *having* an argument—as in having a fight.

The war on drugs, the war on cancer, the battle of the sexes, politicians' turf battles—in the argument culture, war metaphors pervade our talk and shape our thinking. Nearly everything is framed as a battle or game in which winning or losing is the main concern. These all have their uses and their place, but they are not the only way—and often not the best way—to understand and approach our world. Conflict and opposition are as necessary as cooperation and agreement, but the scale is off balance, with conflict and opposition overweighted. In this book, I show how deeply entrenched the argument culture is, the forms it takes, and how it affects us every day—sometimes in useful ways, but often creating more problems than it solves, causing rather than avoiding damage. As a sociolinguist, a social scientist, I am trained to observe and explain language and its role in human relations, and that is my biggest job here. But I will also point toward other ways for us to talk to each other and get things done in our public lives.

The Battle of the Sexes

My interest in the topic of opposition in public discourse intensified in the years following the publication of *You Just Don't Understand,* my book about communication between women and men. In the first year I appeared on many television and radio shows and was interviewed for many print articles in newspapers and magazines. For the most part, that coverage was extremely fair, and I was—and remain—indebted to the many journalists who found my ideas interesting enough to make them known to viewers, listeners, and readers. But from time to time—more often than I expected—I encountered producers who insisted on setting up a television show as a fight (either between the host and me or between another guest and me) and print journalists who made multiple phone calls to my colleagues, trying to find someone who would criticize my work. This got me thinking about what kind of information comes across on shows and in articles that take this approach, compared to those that approach topics in other ways.

At the same time, my experience of the academic world that had long been my intellectual home began to change. For the most part, other scholars, like most journalists, were welcoming and respectful in their responses to my work, even if they disagreed on specific points or had alternative views to suggest. But about a year after *You Just Don't Understand* became a best-seller—the wheels of academia grind more slowly than those of the popular press—I began reading attacks on my work that completely misrepresented it. I had been in academia for over fifteen years by then, and had valued my interaction with other researchers as one of the greatest rewards of academic life. Why, I wondered, would someone represent me as having said things I had never said or as having failed to say things I had said?

The answer crystallized when I put the question to a writer who I felt had misrepresented my work: "Why do you need to make others wrong for you to be right?" Her response: "It's an argument!" Aha, I thought, that explains it. When you're having an argument with someone, your goal is not to listen and understand. Instead, you use every tactic you can think of—including distorting what your opponent just said—in order to win the argument.

Not only the level of attention *You Just Don't Understand* received but, even more, the subject of women and men, triggered the tendency to polarize. This tendency to stage a fight on television or in print was posited on the conviction that opposition leads to truth. Sometimes it does. But the trouble is, sometimes it doesn't. I was asked at the start of more than one talk show or print interview, "What is the most controversial thing about your book?" Opposition does not lead to truth when the most controversial thing is not the most important.

The conviction that opposition leads to truth can tempt not only members of the press but just about anyone seeking to attract an audience to frame discussions as a fight between irreconcilable opposites. Even the Smithsonian Institution, to celebrate its 150th anniversary, sponsored a series of talks billed as debates. They invited me to take part in one titled "The Battle of the Sexes." The organizer preempted my objection: "I know you won't be happy with this title, but we want to get people interested." This is one of many assumptions I question in this book: Is it necessary to frame an interchange as a battle to get people interested? And even if doing so succeeds in capturing attention, does it risk dampening interest in the long run, as audiences weary of the din and begin to hunger for more substance?

Thought-Provoking or Just Provocative?

In the spring of 1995, Horizons Theatre in Arlington, Virginia, produced two one-act plays I had written about family relationships. The director, wanting to contribute to the reconciliation between Blacks and Jews, mounted my plays in repertory with two one-act plays by an African American playwright, Caleen Sinnette Jennings. We had both written plays about three sisters that explored the ethnic identities of our families (Jewish for me, African-American for her) and the relationship between those identities and the American context in which we grew up. To stir interest in the plays and to explore the parallels between her work and mine, the theater planned a public dialogue between Jennings and me, to be held before the plays opened.

As production got under way, I attended the audition of actors for my plays. After the auditions ended, just before everyone headed home, the theater's public relations volunteer distributed copies of the flyer announcing the public

dialogue that she had readied for distribution. I was horrified. The flyer announced that Caleen and I would discuss "how past traumas create understanding and conflict between Blacks and Jews today." The flyer was trying to grab by the throat the issue that we wished to address indirectly. Yes, we were concerned with conflicts between Blacks and Jews, but neither of us is an authority on that conflict, and we had no intention of expounding on it. We hoped to do our part to ameliorate the conflict by focusing on commonalities. Our plays had many resonances between them. We wanted to talk about our work and let the resonances speak for themselves.

Fortunately, we were able to stop the flyers before they were distributed and devise new ones that promised something we could deliver: "a discussion of heritage, identity, and complex family relationships in African-American and Jewish-American culture as represented in their plays." Jennings noticed that the original flyer said the evening would be "provocative" and changed it to "thought-provoking." What a world of difference is implied in that small change: how much better to make people think, rather than simply to "provoke" them—as often as not, to anger.

It is easy to understand why conflict is so often highlighted: Writers of headlines or promotional copy want to catch attention and attract an audience. They are usually under time pressure, which lures them to established, conventionalized ways of expressing ideas in the absence of leisure to think up entirely new ones. The promise of controversy seems an easy and natural way to rouse interest. But serious consequences are often unintended: Stirring up animosities to get a rise out of people, though easy and "provocative," can open old wounds or create new ones that are hard to heal. This is one of many dangers inherent in the argument culture.

For the Sake of Argument

In the argument culture, criticism, attack, or opposition are the predominant if not the only ways of responding to people or ideas. I use the phrase "culture of critique" to capture this aspect. "Critique" in this sense is not a general term for analysis or interpretation but rather a synonym for criticism.

It is the *automatic* nature of this response that I am calling attention to—and calling into question. Sometimes passionate opposition, strong verbal attack, are appropriate and called for. No one knows this better than those who have lived under repressive regimes that forbid public opposition. The Yugoslavian-born poet Charles Simic is one. "There are moments in life," he writes, "when true invective is called for, when it becomes an absolute necessity, out of a deep sense of justice, to denounce, mock, vituperate, lash out, in the strongest possible language." I applaud and endorse this view. There are times when it is necessary and right to fight—to defend your country or yourself, to argue for right against wrong or against offensive or dangerous ideas or actions.

What I question is the ubiquity, the knee-jerk nature, of approaching almost any issue, problem, or public person in an adversarial way. One of the dangers of the habitual use of adversarial rhetoric is a kind of verbal inflation—a rhetorical boy who cried wolf: The legitimate, necessary denunciation is muted, even lost, in the general cacophony of oppositional shouting. What I question is using opposition to accomplish *every* goal, even those that do not require fighting but might also (or better) be accomplished by other means, such as exploring, expanding, discussing, investigating, and the exchanging of ideas suggested by the word "dialogue." I am questioning the assumption that *everything* is a matter of polarized opposites, the proverbial "two sides to every question" that we think embodies open-mindedness and expansive thinking.

In a word, the type of opposition I am questioning is what I call "agonism." I use this term, which derives from the Greek word for "contest," *agonia,* to mean an automatic warlike stance—not the literal opposition of fighting against an attacker or the unavoidable opposition that arises organically in response to conflicting ideas or actions. An agonistic response, to me, is a kind of programmed contentiousness—a prepatterned, unthinking use of fighting to accomplish goals that do not necessarily require it.

How Useful Are Fights?

Noticing that public discourse so often takes the form of heated arguments—of having a fight—made me ask how useful it is in our personal lives to settle differences by arguing. Given what I know about having arguments in private life, I had to conclude that it is, in many cases, not very useful.

In close relationships it is possible to find ways of arguing that result in better understanding and solving problems. But with most arguments, little is resolved, worked out, or achieved when two people get angrier and less rational by the minute. When you're having an argument with someone, you're usually not trying to understand what the other person is saying, or what in their experience leads them to say it. Instead, you're readying your response: listening for weaknesses in logic to leap on, points you can distort to make the other person look bad and yourself look good. Sometimes you know, on some back burner of your mind, that you're doing this—that there's a kernel of truth in what your adversary is saying and a bit of unfair twisting in what you're saying. Sometimes you do this because you're angry, but sometimes it's just the temptation to take aim at a point made along the way because it's an easy target.

Here's an example of how this happened in an argument between a couple who had been married for over fifty years. The husband wanted to join an HMO by signing over their Medicare benefits to save money. The wife objected because it would mean she could no longer see the doctor she knew and trusted. In arguing her point of view, she said, "I like Dr. B. He knows me, he's interested in me. He calls me by my first name." The husband parried the last point: "I don't

like that. He's much younger than we are. He shouldn't be calling us by first name." But the form of address Dr. B. uses was irrelevant. The wife was trying to communicate that she felt comfortable with the doctor she knew, that she had a relationship with him. His calling her by first name was just one of a list of details she was marshaling to explain her comfort with him. Picking on this one detail did not change her view—and did not address her concern. It was just a way to win the argument.

We all are guilty, at times, of seizing on irrelevant details, distorting someone else's position the better to oppose it, when we're arguing with those we're closest to. But we are rarely dependent on these fights as sources of information. The same tactics are common when public discourse is carried out on the model of personal fights. And the results are dangerous when listeners are looking to these interchanges to get needed information or practical results.

Fights have winners and losers. If you're fighting to win, the temptation is great to deny facts that support your opponent's views and to filter what you know, saying only what supports your side. In the extreme form, it encourages people to misrepresent or even to lie. We accept this risk because we believe we can tell when someone is lying. The problem is, we can't.

Paul Ekman, a psychologist at the University of California, San Francisco, studies lying. He set up experiments in which individuals were videotaped talking about their emotions, actions, or beliefs—some truthfully, some not. He has shown these videotapes to thousands of people, asking them to identify the liars and also to say how sure they were about their judgments. His findings are chilling: Most people performed not much better than chance, and those who did the worst had just as much confidence in their judgments as the few who were really able to detect lies. Intrigued by the implications of this research in various walks of life, Dr. Ekman repeated this experiment with groups of people whose jobs require them to sniff out lies: judges, lawyers, police, psychotherapists, and employees of the CIA, FBI, and ATF (Bureau of Alcohol, Tobacco, and Firearms). They were no better at detecting who was telling the truth than the rest of us. The only group that did significantly better were members of the U.S. Secret Service. This finding gives some comfort when it comes to the Secret Service but not much when it comes to every other facet of public life.

Two Sides to Every Question

Our determination to pursue truth by setting up a fight between two sides leads us to believe that every issue has two sides—no more, no less: If both sides are given a forum to confront each other, all the relevant information will emerge, and the best case will be made for each side. But opposition does not lead to truth when an issue is not composed of two opposing sides but is a crystal of many sides. Often the truth is in the complex middle, not the oversimplified extremes.

We love using the word "debate" as a way of representing issues: the abortion debate, the health care debate, the affirmative action debate—even "the great backpacking vs. car camping debate." The ubiquity of this word in itself shows our tendency to conceptualize issues in a way that predisposes public discussion to be polarized, framed as two opposing sides that give each other no ground. There are many problems with this approach. If you begin with the assumption that there *must* be an "other side," you may end up scouring the margins of science or the fringes of lunacy to find it. As a result, proven facts, such as what we know about how the earth and its inhabitants evolved, are set on a par with claims that are known to have no basis in fact, such as creationism.

The conviction that there are two sides to every story can prompt writers or producers to dig up an "other side," so kooks who state outright falsehoods are given a platform in public discourse. This accounts, in part, for the bizarre phenomenon of Holocaust denial. Deniers, as Emory University professor Deborah Lipstadt shows, have been successful in gaining television airtime and campus newspaper coverage by masquerading as "the other side" in a "debate."

Appearance in print or on television has a way of lending legitimacy, so baseless claims take on a mantle of possibility. Lipstadt shows how Holocaust deniers dispute established facts of history, and then reasonable spokespersons use their having been disputed as a basis for questioning known facts. The actor Robert Mitchum, for example, interviewed in *Esquire,* expressed doubt about the Holocaust. When the interviewer asked about the slaughter of six million Jews, Mitchum replied, "I don't know. People dispute that." Continual reference to "the other side" results in a pervasive conviction that everything has another side—with the result that people begin to doubt the existence of any facts at all.

The Expense of Time and Spirit

Lipstadt's book meticulously exposes the methods used by deniers to falsify the overwhelming historic evidence that the Holocaust occurred. That a scholar had to invest years of her professional life writing a book unraveling efforts to deny something that was about as well known and well documented as any historical fact has ever been—while those who personally experienced and witnessed it are still alive—is testament to another way that the argument culture limits our knowledge rather than expanding it. Talent and effort were wasted when individuals who have been unfairly attacked must spend years of their creative lives defending themselves rather than advancing their work. The entire society loses their creative efforts. This is what happened with scientist Robert Gallo.

Dr. Gallo is the American virologist who codiscovered the AIDS virus. He is also the one who developed the technique for studying T-cells, which made that discovery possible. And Gallo's work was seminal in developing the test to detect the AIDS virus in blood, the first and for a long time the only means known of stemming the tide of death from AIDS. But in 1989, Gallo became the object of a four-year investigation into allegations that he had stolen the AIDS virus from Luc Montagnier of the Pasteur Institute in Paris, who had independently identified the AIDS virus. Simultaneous investigations by the National Institutes of Health, the office of Michigan Congressman John Dingell, and the National Academy of Sciences barreled ahead long after Gallo and Montagnier settled the dispute to their mutual satisfaction. In 1993 the investigations concluded that Gallo had done nothing wrong. Nothing. But this exoneration cannot be considered a happy ending. Never mind the personal suffering of Gallo, who was reviled when he should have been heralded as a hero. Never mind that, in his words, "These were the most painful years and horrible years of my life." The dreadful, unconscionable result of the fruitless investigations is that Gallo had to spend four years fighting the accusations instead of fighting AIDS.

The investigations, according to journalist Nicholas Wade, were sparked by an article about Gallo written in the currently popular spirit of demonography: not to praise the person it features but to bury him—to show his weaknesses, his villainous side. The implication that Gallo has stolen the AIDS virus was created to fill a requirement of the discourse: In demonography, writers must find negative sides of their subjects to display for readers who enjoy seeing heroes transformed into villains. The suspicion led to investigations, and the investigations became a juggernaut that acquired a life of its own, fed by the enthusiasm for attack on public figures that is the culture of critique.

Metaphors: We Are What We Speak

Perhaps one reason suspicions of Robert Gallo were so zealously investigated is that the scenario of an ambitious scientist ready to do anything to defeat a rival appeals to our sense of story; it is the kind of narrative we are ready to believe. Culture, in a sense, is an environment of narratives that we hear repeatedly until they seem to make self-evident sense in explaining human behavior. Thinking of human interactions as battles is a metaphorical frame through which we learn to regard the world and the people in it.

All language uses metaphors to express ideas; some metaphoric words and expressions are novel, made up for the occasion, but more are calcified in the language. They are simply the way we think it is natural to express ideas. We don't think of them as metaphors. Someone who says, "Be careful: You aren't a cat, you don't have nine lives," is explicitly comparing you to a cat, because the cat is named in words. But what if someone says, "Don't pussyfoot around; get to the point"? There is no explicit comparison to a cat, but the comparison is there nonetheless, implied in the word "pussyfoot." This expression probably developed as a reference to the movement of a cat cautiously circling a suspicious object. I doubt that individuals using the word "pussyfoot" think consciously of cats. More often than not, we use expressions without thinking about their metaphoric implications. But that doesn't mean those implications are not influencing us.

At a meeting, a general discussion became so animated that a participant who wanted to comment prefaced his remark by saying, "I'd like to leap into the fray." Another participant called out, "Or share your thoughts." Everyone laughed. By suggesting a different phrasing, she called attention to what would probably have otherwise gone unnoticed: "Leap into the fray" characterized the lively discussion as a metaphorical battle.

Americans talk about almost everything as if it were a war. A book about the history of linguistics is called *The Linguistics Wars*. A magazine article about claims that science is not completely objective is titled "The Science Wars." One about breast cancer detection is "The Mammogram War"; about competition among caterers, "Party Wars"—and on and on in a potentially endless list. Politics, of course, is a prime candidate. One of innumerable possible examples, the headline of a story reporting that the Democratic National Convention nominated Bill Clinton to run for a second term declares, "DEMOCRATS SEND CLINTON INTO BATTLE FOR A 2ND TERM." But medicine is as frequent a candidate, as we talk about battling and conquering disease.

Headlines arc intentionally devised to attract attention, but we all use military or attack imagery in everyday expressions without thinking about it: "Take a shot at it," "I don't want to be shot down," "He went off half cocked," "That's half the battle." Why does it matter that our public discourse is filled with military metaphors? Aren't they just words? Why not talk about something that matters—like actions?

Because words matter. When we think we are using language, language is using us. As linguist Dwight Bolinger put it (employing a military metaphor), language is like a loaded gun: It can be fired intentionally, but it can wound or kill just as surely when fired accidentally. The terms in which we talk about something shape the way we think about it—and even what we see.

The power of words to shape perception has been proven by researchers in controlled experiments. Psychologist Elizabeth Loftus and John Palmer, for example, found that the terms in which people are asked to recall something affect what they recall. The researchers showed subjects a film of two cars colliding, then asked how fast the cars were going; one week later, they asked whether there had been any broken glass. Some subjects were asked, "About how fast were the cars going when they smashed into each other?" Those who read the question with the verb "smashed" estimated that the cars were going faster. They were also more likely to "remember" having seen broken glass. (There wasn't any.)

This is how language works. It invisibly molds our way of thinking about people, actions, and the world around us. Military metaphors train us to think about—and see—everything in terms of fighting, conflict, and war. This perspective then limits our imaginations when we consider what we can do about situations we would like to understand or change.

Even in science, common metaphors that are taken for granted influence how researchers think about natural phenomena. Evelyn Fox Keller describes a case in which acceptance of a metaphor led scientists to see something that was not there. A mathematical biologist, Keller outlines the fascinating behavior of cellular slime mold. This unique mold can take two completely different forms: It can exist as single-cell organisms, or the separate cells can come together to form multicellular aggregates. The puzzle facing scientists was: What triggers aggregation? In other words, what makes the single cells join together? Scientists focused their investigations by asking what entity issued the order to start aggregating. They first called this bosslike entity a "founder cell," and later a "pacemaker cell," even though no one had seen any evidence for the existence of such a cell. Proceeding nonetheless from the assumption that such a cell must exist, they ignored evidence to the contrary: For example, when the center of the aggregate is removed, other centers form.

Scientists studying slime mold did not examine the interrelationship between the cells and their environment, nor the interrelationship between the functional systems within each cell, because they were busy looking for the pacemaker cell, which, as eventually became evident, did not exist. Instead, under conditions of nutritional deprivation, each individual cell begins to feel the urge to merge with others to form the conglomerate. It is a reaction of the cells to their environment, not to the orders of a boss. Keller recounts this tale to illustrate her insight that we tend to view nature through our understanding of human relations as hierarchical. In her words, "We risk imposing on nature the very stories we like to hear." In other words, the conceptual metaphor of hierarchical governance made scientists "see" something—a pacemaker cell—that wasn't there.

Among the stories many Americans most like to hear are war stories. According to historian Michael Sherry, the American war movie developed during World War II and has been with us ever since. He shows that movies not explicitly about war were also war movies at heart, such as westerns with their good guy–bad guy battles settled with guns. *High Noon,* for example, which became a model for later westerns, was an allegory of the Second World War: The happy ending hinges on the pacifist taking up arms. We can also see this story line in contemporary adventure films: Think of *Star Wars,* with its stirring finale in which Han Solo, having professed no interest in or taste for battle, returns at the last moment to destroy the enemy and save the day. And precisely the same theme is found in a contemporary low-budget independent film, *Sling Blade,* in which a peace-loving retarded man becomes a hero at the end by murdering the man who has been tormenting the family he has come to love.

Put up Your Dukes

If war provides the metaphors through which we view the world and each other, we come to view others—and ourselves—as warriors in battle. Almost any human encounter can be framed as a fight between two opponents. Looking at it this way brings particular aspects of the event into focus and obscures others.

Framing interactions as fights affects not only the participants but also the viewers. At a performance, the audience, as well as the performers, can be transformed. This effect was noted by a reviewer in *The New York Times,* commenting on a musical event:

> **Showdown at Lincoln Center.** Jazz's ideological war of the last several years led to a pitched battle in August between John Lincoln Collier, the writer, and Wynton Marsalis, the trumpeter, in a debate at Lincoln Center. Mr. Marsalis demolished Mr. Collier, point after point after point, but what made the debate unpleasant was the crowd's blood lust; humiliation, not elucidation, was the desired end.

Military imagery pervades this account: the difference of opinions between Collier and Marsalis was an "ideological war," and the "debate" was a "pitched battle" in which Marsalis "demolished" Collier (not his arguments, but him). What the commentator regrets, however, is that the audience got swept up in the mood instigated by the way the debate was carried out: "the crowd's blood lust" for Collier's defeat.

This is one of the most dangerous aspects of regarding intellectual interchange as a fight. It contributes to an atmosphere of animosity that spreads like a fever. In a society that includes people who express their anger by shooting, the result of demonizing those with whom we disagree can be truly tragic.

But do audiences necessarily harbor within themselves a "blood lust," or is it stirred in them by the performances they are offered? Another arts event was set up as a debate between a playwright and a theater director. In this case, the metaphor through which the debate was viewed was not war but boxing—a sport that is in itself, like a debate, a metaphorical battle that pitches one side against the other in an all-out effort to win. A headline describing the event set the frame: "AND IN THIS CORNER . . . ," followed by the subhead "A Black Playwright and White Critic Duke It Out." The story then reports:

> the face-off between August Wilson, the most successful black playwright in the American theater, and Robert Brustein, longtime drama critic for *The New Republic* and artistic director of the American Repertory Theatre in Cambridge, Mass. These two heavyweights had been battling in print since last June. . . .
>
> Entering from opposite sides of the stage, the two men shook hands and came out fighting—or at least sparring.

Wilson, the article explains, had given a speech in which he opposed Black performers taking "white" roles in color-blind casting; Brustein had written a column disagreeing; and both followed up with further responses to each other.

According to the article, "The drama of the Wilson-Brustein confrontation lies in their mutual intransigence." No one would question that audiences crave drama. But is intransigence the most appealing source of drama? I happened to hear this debate broadcast on the radio. The line that triggered the loudest cheers from the audience was the final question put to the two men by the moderator, Anna Deavere Smith: "What did you each learn from the other in this debate?" The loud applause was evidence that the audience did not crave intransigence. They wanted to see another kind of drama: the drama of change—change that comes from genuinely listening to someone with a different point of view, not the transitory drama of two intransigent positions in stalemate.

To encourage the staging of more dramas of change and fewer of intransigence, we need new metaphors to supplement and complement the pervasive war and boxing match metaphors through which we take it for granted issues and events are best talked about and viewed.

Mud Splatters

Our fondness for the fight scenario leads us to frame many complex human interactions as a battle between two sides. This then shapes the way we understand what happened and how we regard the participants. One unfortunate result is that fights make a mess in which everyone is muddied. The person attacked is often deemed just as guilty as the attacker.

The injustice of this is clear if you think back to childhood. Many of us still harbor anger as we recall a time (or many times) a sibling or playmate started a fight—but both of us got blamed. Actions occur in a stream, each a response to what came before. Where you punctuate them can change their meaning just as you can change the meaning of a sentence by punctuating it in one place or another.

Like a parent despairing of trying to sort out which child started a fight, people often respond to those involved in a public dispute as if both were equally guilty. When champion figure skater Nancy Kerrigan was struck on the knee shortly before the 1994 Olympics in Norway and the then-husband of another champion skater, Tonya Harding, implicated his wife in planning the attack, the event was characterized as a fight between two skaters that obscured their differing roles. As both skaters headed for the Olympic competition, their potential meeting was described as a "long-anticipated figure-skating shootout." Two years later, the event was referred to not as "the attack on Nancy Kerrigan" but as "the rivalry surrounding Tonya Harding and Nancy Kerrigan."

By a similar process, the Senate Judiciary Committee hearings to consider the nomination of Clarence Thomas for Supreme Court justice at which Anita Hill was called to testify are regularly referred to as the "Hill-Thomas hearings," obscuring the very different roles played by Hill and Thomas. Although testimony by Anita Hill was the occasion for reopening the hearings, they were still the Clarence Thomas confirmation hearings: Their purpose was to evaluate Thomas's candidacy. Framing these hearings as a two-sides dispute between Hill and Thomas allowed the senators to focus their investigation on cross-examining Hill rather than seeking other sorts of evidence, for example by consulting experts on sexual harassment to ascertain whether Hill's account seemed plausible.

Slash-and-Burn Thinking

Approaching situations like warriors in battle leads to the assumption that intellectual inquiry, too, is a game of attack, counterattack, and self-defense. In this spirit, critical thinking is synonymous with criticizing. In many classrooms, students are encouraged to read someone's life work, then rip it to shreds. Though criticism is one form of critical thinking—and an essential one—so are integrating ideas from disparate fields and examining the context out of which ideas grew. Opposition does not lead to the whole truth when we ask only "What's wrong with this?" and never "What can we use from this in building a new theory, a new understanding?"

There are many ways that unrelenting criticism is destructive in itself. In innumerable small dramas mirroring what happened to Robert Gallo (but on a much more modest scale), our most creative thinkers can waste time and effort responding to critics motivated less by a genuine concern about weaknesses in their work than by a desire to find something to attack. All of society loses when creative people are discouraged from their pursuits by unfair criticism. (This is particularly likely to happen since, as Kay Redfield Jamison shows in her book *Touched with Fire,* many of those who are unusually creative are also unusually sensitive; their sensitivity often drives their creativity.)

If the criticism is unwarranted, many will say, you are free to argue against it, to defend yourself. But there are problems with this, too. Not only does self-defense take time and draw off energy that would better be spent on new creative work, but any move to defend yourself makes you appear, well, defensive. For example, when an author wrote a letter to the editor protesting a review he considered unfair, the reviewer (who is typically given the last word) turned the very fact that the author defended himself into a weapon with which to attack again. The reviewer's response began, "I haven't much time to waste on the kind of writer who squanders his talent drafting angry letters to reviewers."

The argument culture limits the information we get rather than broadening it in another way. When a certain kind of interaction is the norm, those who feel comfortable with that type of interaction are drawn to participate, and those who do not feel comfortable with it recoil and go elsewhere. If public discourse included a broad range of types, we would be making room for individuals with different temperaments to take part and contribute their perspectives and insights. But when debate, opposition, and fights overwhelmingly predominate, those who enjoy verbal sparring are likely to take part—by calling in to talk shows, writing letters to the editor or articles, becoming journalists—and those who cannot comfortably take part in oppositional discourse, or do not wish to, are likely to opt out.

This winnowing process is easy to see in apprenticeship programs such as acting school, law school, and graduate school. A woman who was identified in her university drama program as showing exceptional promise was encouraged to go to New York to study acting. Full of enthusiasm, she was accepted by a famous acting school where the teaching method entailed the teacher screaming at students, goading and insulting them as a way to bring out the best in them. This worked well with many of the students but not with her. Rather than rising to the occasion when attacked, she cringed, becoming less able to draw on her talent, not more. After a year, she dropped out. It could be that she simply didn't have what it took—but this will never be known, because the adversarial style of teaching did not allow her to show what talent she had.

Polarizing Complexity: Nature or Nurture?

Few issues come with two neat, and neatly opposed, sides. Again, I have seen this in the domain of gender. One common polarization is an opposition between two sources of differences between women and men: "culture," or "nurture," on one hand and "biology," or "nature," on the other.

Shortly after the publication of *You Just Don't Understand,* I was asked by a journalist what question I most often encountered about women's and men's conversational styles. I told her, "Whether the differences I describe are biological or cultural." The journalist laughed. Puzzled, I asked why this made her laugh. She explained that she had always been so certain that any significant differences are cultural rather than biological in origin that the question struck her as absurd. So I should not have been surprised when I read, in the article she wrote, that the two questions I am most frequently asked are "Why do women nag?" and "Why won't men ask for directions?" Her ideological certainty that the question I am most frequently asked was absurd led her to ignore my answer and get a fact wrong in her report of my experience.

Some people are convinced that any significant differences between men and women are entirely or overwhelmingly due to cultural influences—the way we treat girls and boys, and men's dominance of women in society. Others are convinced that any significant differences are entirely or overwhelmingly due to biology: the physical facts of female and male bodies, hormones, and reproductive functions. Many problems are caused by framing the question as a dichotomy: Are behaviors that pattern by sex biological or cultural? This polarization encourages those on one side to demonize those who take the other view, which leads in turn to misrepresenting the work of those who are assigned to the opposing camp. Finally, and most devastatingly, it prevents us from exploring the interaction of biological and cultural factors—factors that must, and can only, be understood together. By posing the question as either/or, we reinforce a false assumption that biological and cultural factors are separable and preclude the investigations that would help us understand their interrelationship. When a problem is posed in a way that polarizes, the solution is often obscured before the search is under way.

Who's Up? Who's Down?

Related to polarization is another aspect of the argument culture: our obsession with ratings and rankings. Magazines offer the 10, 50, or 100 best of everything: restaurants, mutual funds, hospitals, even judges. Newsmagazines tell us Who's up, Who's down, as in *Newsweek*'s "Conventional Wisdom Watch" and *Time*'s "Winners and Losers." Rankings and ratings pit restaurants, products, schools, and people against each other on a single scale, obscuring the myriad differences among them. Maybe a small Thai restaurant in one neighborhood can't really be compared to a pricey French one in another, any more than judges with a vast range of abilities and beliefs can be compared on a single scale. And timing can skew results: Ohio State University protested to *Time* magazine when its football team was ranked at the bottom of a scale because only 29 percent of the team graduated. The year before it would have ranked among the top six with 72 percent.

After a political debate, analysts comment not on what the candidates said but on the question "Who won?" After the president delivers an important speech, such as the State of the Union Address, expert commentators are asked to give it a grade. Like ranking, grading establishes a competition. The biggest problem with asking what grade the president's speech deserves, or who won and who lost a campaign debate, is what is not asked and is therefore not answered: What was said, and what is the significance of this for the country?

An Ethic of Aggression

In an argument culture aggressive tactics are valued for their own sake. For example, a woman called in to a talk show on which I was a guest to say, "When I'm in a place where a man is smoking, and there's a no-smoking sign, instead of saying to him 'You aren't allowed to smoke in here. Put that out,' I say, 'I'm awfully sorry, but I have asthma, so your smoking makes it hard for me to breathe. Would you mind terribly not smoking?' Whenever I say this, the man is extremely polite and solicitous, and he puts his cigarette out, and I say, 'Oh,

thank you, thank you!' as if he's done a wonderful thing for me. Why do I do that?"

I think this woman expected me to say that she needs assertiveness training to learn to confront smokers in a more aggressive manner. Instead, I told her that there was nothing wrong with her style of getting the man to stop smoking. She gave him a face-saving way of doing what she asked, one that allowed him to feel chivalrous rather than chastised. This is kind to him, but it is also kind to herself, since it is more likely to lead to the result she desires. If she tried to alter his behavior by reminding him of the rules, he might well rebel: "Who made you the enforcer? Mind your own business!" Indeed, who gives any of us the authority to set others straight when we think they're breaking rules?

Another caller disagreed with me, saying the first caller's style was "self-abasing" and there was no reason for her to use it. But I persisted: There is nothing necessarily destructive about conventional self-effacement. Human relations depend on the agreement to use such verbal conventions. I believe the mistake this caller was making—a mistake many of us make—was to confuse *ritual* self-effacement with the literal kind. All human relations require us to find ways to get what we want from others without seeming to dominate them. Allowing others to feel they are doing what you want for a reason less humiliating to them fulfills this need.

Thinking of yourself as the wronged party who is victimized by a lawbreaking boor makes it harder to see the value of this method. But suppose you are the person addicted to smoking who lights up (knowingly or not) in a no-smoking zone. Would you like strangers to yell at you to stop smoking, or would you rather be allowed to save face by being asked politely to stop in order to help them out? Or imagine yourself having broken a rule inadvertently (which is not to imply rules are broken only by mistake; it is only to say that sometimes they are). Would you like some stranger to swoop down on you and begin berating you, or would you rather be asked politely to comply?

As this example shows, conflicts can sometimes be resolved without confrontational tactics, but current conventional wisdom often devalues less confrontational tactics even if they work well, favoring more aggressive strategies even if they get less favorable results. It's as if we value a fight for its own sake, not for its effectiveness in resolving disputes.

This ethic shows up in many contexts. In a review of a contentious book, for example, a reviewer wrote, "Always provocative, sometimes infuriating, this collection reminds us that the purpose of art is not to confirm and coddle but to provoke and confront." This false dichotomy encapsulates the belief that if you are not provoking and confronting, then you are conforming and coddling—as if there weren't myriad other ways to question and learn. What about exploring, exposing, delving, analyzing, understanding, moving, connecting, integrating, illuminating . . . or any of innumerable verbs that capture other aspects of what art can do?

The Broader Picture

The increasingly adversarial spirit of our contemporary lives is fundamentally related to a phenomenon that has been much remarked upon in recent years: the breakdown of a sense of community. In this spirit, distinguished journalist and author Orville Schell points out that in his day journalists routinely based their writing on a sense of connection to their subjects—and that this sense of connection is missing from much that is written by journalists today. Quite the contrary, a spirit of demonography often prevails that has just the opposite effect: Far from encouraging us to feel connected to the subjects, it encourages us to feel critical, superior—and, as a result, distanced. The cumulative effect is that citizens feel more and more cut off from the people in public life they read about.

The argument culture dovetails with a general disconnection and breakdown of community in another way as well. Community norms and pressures exercise a restraint on the expression of hostility and destruction. Many cultures have rituals to channel and contain aggressive impulses, especially those of adolescent males. In just this spirit, at the 1996 Republican National Convention, both Colin Powell and Bob Dole talked about growing up in small communities where everyone knew who they were. This meant that many people would look out for them, but also that if they did something wrong, it would get back to their parents. Many Americans grew up in ethnic neighborhoods that worked the same way. If a young man stole something, committed vandalism, or broke a rule or law, it would be reported to his relatives, who would punish him or tell him how his actions were shaming the family. American culture today often lacks these brakes.

Community is a blend of connections and authority, and we are losing both. As Robert Bly shows in his book by that title, we now have a *Sibling Society:* Citizens are like squabbling siblings with no authority figures who can command enough respect to contain and channel their aggressive impulses. It is as if every day is a day with a substitute teacher who cannot control the class and maintain order.

The argument culture is both a product of and a contributor to this alienation, separating people, disconnecting them from each other and from those who are or might have been their leaders.

What Other Way Is There?

Philosopher John Dewey said, on his ninetieth birthday, "Democracy begins in conversation." I fear that it gets derailed in polarized debate.

In conversation we form the interpersonal ties that bind individuals together in personal relationships; in public discourse, we form similar ties on a larger scale, binding individuals into a community. In conversation, we exchange the many types of information we need to live our lives as members of a community. In public discourse, we exchange the information that citizens in a democracy need in order to decide how to vote. If public discourse provides entertainment first and foremost—and if entertainment is first and foremost watching fights—then citizens do not get the information they need to make meaningful use of their right to vote.

Of course it is the responsibility of intellectuals to explore potential weaknesses in others' arguments, and of journalists to represent serious opposition when it exists. But when opposition becomes the overwhelming avenue of inquiry—a formula that *requires* another side to be found or a criticism to be voiced; when the lust for opposition privileges extreme views and obscures complexity; when our eagerness to find weaknesses blinds us to strengths; when the atmosphere of animosity precludes respect and poisons our relations with one another; then the argument culture is doing more damage than good.

I offer this book not as a formal assault in the argument culture. That would be in the spirit of attack that I am questioning. It is an attempt to examine the argument culture—our use of attack, opposition, and debate in public discourse—to ask, What are its limits as well as its strengths? How has it served us well, but also how has it failed us? How is it related to culture and gender? What other options do we have?

I do not believe we should put aside the argument model of public discourse entirely, but we need to rethink whether this is the *only* way, or *always* the best way, to carry out our affairs. A step toward broadening our repertoires would be to pioneer reform by experimenting with metaphors other than sports and war, and with formats other than debate for framing the exchange of ideas. The change might be as simple as introducing a plural form. Instead of asking "What's the other side?" we might ask instead, "What are the other sides?" Instead of insisting on hearing "both sides," we might insist on hearing "all sides."

Another option is to expand our notion of "debate" to include more dialogue. This does not mean there can be no negativity, criticism, or disagreement. It simply means we can be more creative in our ways of managing all of these, which are inevitable and useful. In dialogue, each statement that one person makes is qualified by a statement made by someone else, until the series of statements and qualifications moves everyone closer to a fuller truth. Dialogue does not preclude negativity. Even saying "I agree" makes sense only against the background assumption that you might disagree. In dialogue, there is opposition, yes, but no head-on collision. Smashing heads does not open minds.

There are times when we need to disagree, criticize, oppose, and attack—to hold debates and view issues as polarized battles. Even cooperation, after all, is not the absence of conflict but a means of managing conflict. My goal is not a make-nice false veneer of agreement or a dangerous ignoring of true opposition. I'm questioning the *automatic* use of adversarial formats—the assumption that it's *always* best to address problems and issues by fighting over them. I'm hoping for a broader repertoire of ways to talk to each other and address issues vital to us.

Notes

Note: Sources referred to by short form are cited in full in the References.

[Numbers indicate page numbers of original document. Ed]

7. *"culture of critique"*: I first introduced this term in an op-ed essay, "The Triumph of the Yell," *The New York Times,* Jan. 14, 1994, p. A29.

7. *"There are moments"*: Charles Simic, "In Praise of Invective," *Harper's,* Aug. 1997, pp. 24, 26–27; the quote is from p. 26. The article is excerpted from *Orphan Factory* (Ann Arbor: University of Michigan Press, 1997). I am grateful to Amitai Etizioni for calling this article to my attention.

8. Both the term "agonism" and the phrase "programmed contentiousness" come from Walter Ong, *Fighting for Life.*

10. *"the great backpacking vs. car camping debate"*: Steven Hendrix, "Hatchback vs. Backpack," *The Washington Post Weekend,* Mar. 1, 1996, p. 6.

11. *creationism:* See, for example, Jessica Mathews, "Creationism Makes a Comeback," *The Washington Post,* Apr. 8, 1996, p. A21.

11. *"People dispute that"*: Lipstadt, *Denying the Holocaust,* p. 15. Lipstadt cites *Esquire,* Feb. 1983, for the interview with Mitchum.

12. *Gallo had to spend:* See Nicholas Wade, "Method and Madness: The Vindication of Robert Gallo," *The New York Times Magazine,* Dec. 26, 1993, p. 12, and Elaine Richman, "The Once and Future King," *The Sciences,* Nov.–Dec. 1996, pp. 12–15. The investigations of Gallo were among a series of overly zealous investigations of suspected scientific misconduct—all of which ended in the exoneration of the accused, but not before they had caused immense personal anguish and professional setbacks. Others similarly victimized were Gallo's colleague Mike Popovic, immunologist Thereza Imanishi-Kari, and her coauthor (not accused of wrongdoing but harmed as a result of his defense of her), Nobel Prize winner David Baltimore. On Popovic, see Malcolm Gladwell, "Science Friction," *The Washington Post Magazine,* Dec. 6, 1992, pp. 18–21, 49–51. On Imanishi-Kari and Baltimore, see *The New Yorker,* May 27, 1996, pp. 94–98ff.

14. *potentially endless list:* Randy Allen Harris, *The Linguistics Wars* (New York: Oxford University Press, 1993); "The Science Wars," *Newsweek,* Apr. 21, 1997, p. 54; "The Mammogram War," *Newsweek,* Feb. 24, 1997, p. 54; "Party Wars," *New York,* June 2, 1997, cover. The subhead of the latter reads, "In the battle to feed New York's elite, the top caterers are taking off their white gloves and sharpening their knives."

14. *"DEMOCRATS SEND CLINTON"*: *The New York Times,* Aug. 29, 1996, p. A1.

15. *"We risk imposing"*: Keller, *Reflections on Gender and Science,* p. 157. Another such case is explained by paleontologist Stephen Jay Gould in his book *Wonderful Life* about the Burgess shale—a spectacular deposit of 530-million-year-old fossils. In 1909, the first scientist to study these fossils missed the significance of the find, because he "shoehorned every last Burgess animal into a modern group, viewing the fauna collectively as a set of primitive or ancestral versions of later, improved forms" (p. 24). Years later, observers looked at the Burgess shale fossils with a fresh eye and saw a very different reality: a panoply of life forms, far more diverse and numerous than what exists today. The early scientists missed what was right before their eyes because, Gould shows, they proceeded from a metaphoric understanding of evolution as a linear march of progress from the ancient and primitive to the modern and complex, with humans the inevitable, most complex apex. Accepting the metaphor of "the cone of increasing diversity" prevented the early scientists from seeing what was really there.

16. *"Showdown at Lincoln Center"*: Peter Watrous, "The Year in the Arts: Pop & Jazz/1994," *The New York Times,* Dec. 25, 1994, sec. 2, p. 36.

17. *"the face-off between"*: Jack Kroll, "And in This Corner . . . ," *Newsweek,* Feb. 10, 1997, p. 65.

18. *a fight between two skaters:* Though Harding was demonized somewhat more as an unfeminine, boorish "Wicked Witch of the West" (George Vecsey, "Let's Begin the Legal Olympics," *The New York Times,* Feb. 13, 1994, sec. 8, p. 1.), Kerrigan was also demonized as cold and aloof, an "ice princess."

18. *"long-anticipated figure-skating shootout"*: Jere Longman, "Kerrigan Glides Through Compulsory Interviews," *The New York Times,* Feb. 13, 1994, sec. 8, p. 9.

18. *"the rivalry surrounding"*: Paul Farhi, "For NBC, Games Not Just for Guys; Network Tailors Its Coverage to Entice Women to Watch," *The Washington Post,* July 26, 1996, p. A1.

20. *"I haven't time"* *The Washington Post Book World,* June 16, 1996, p. 14.

21. *even judges: Washingtonian,* June 1996, ranked judges.

22. *Ohio State University protested:* Letter to the editor by Malcolm S. Baroway, Executive Director, University Communications, *Time,* Oct. 3, 1994, p. 14.

22. Overlaid on the talk show example is the gender issue: The woman who called wished she had the courage to stand up to a man and saw her habitual way of speaking as evidence of her insecurity. This interpretation is suggested by our assumptions about women and men. Many people, researchers included, start from the assumption that women are insecure, so ways they speak are scrutinized for evidence of insecurity. The result is often a failure to understand or appreciate women's styles on their own terms, so women are misinterpreted as defective men.

23. *"Always provocative, sometimes infuriating"*: Jill Nelson, "Fighting Words," review of Ishmael Reed, *Airing Dirty Laundry, The New York Times Book Review,* Feb. 13, 1994, p. 28.

24. *In this spirit:* John Krich, "To Teach Is Glorious: A Conversation with the New Dean of Cal's Journalism School," Orville Schell, *Express,* Aug. 23, 1996, pp. 1, 14–16, 18, 20–22. The remark is from p. 15.

24. *Many cultures have rituals:* See Schlegel and Barry, *Adolescence.*

25. *"Democracy begins in conversation" Dialogue on John Dewey,* Corliss Lamont, ed. (New York: Horizon Press, 1959), p. 88. Thanks to Pete Becker for this reference.

26. *In dialogue, there is:* This insight comes from Walter Ong, who writes, "There is opposition here but no head-on collision, which stops dialogue. (Of course, sometimes dialogue has to be stopped, but that is another story.)" (*Fighting for Life,* p. 32).

References

Gould, Stephen Jay. *Wonderful Life: The Burgess Shale and the Nature of History* (New York: W. W. Norton, 1989).

Keller, Evelyn Fox. *Reflections on Gender and Science* (New Haven: Yale University Press, 1985).

Krich, John. "To Teach Is Glorious: A Conversation with the New Dean of Cal's Journalism School, Orville Schell." *Express,* Aug. 23, 1996, pp. 1, 14–16, 18, 20–22.

Lipstadt, Deborah. *Denying the Holocaust: The Growing Assault on Truth and Memory* (New York: Free Press, 1993).

Ong, Walter J. *Fighting for Life: Contest, Sexuality, and Consciousness* (Ithaca, N.Y.: Cornell University Press, 1981).

Schlegel, Alice, and Herbert Barry III. *Adolescence: An Anthropological Inquiry* (New York: Free Press, 1991).

Critical Thinking

1. What is "the argument culture?" What should public discourse be, and not be?

2. How is the argument culture expressed in metaphors? How does the author see this as a problem?

3. How does the author describe "an argument?"

4. What conviction is behind the tendency to stage a fight? What is the problem with this idea? What assumption does the author challenge?

5. Why is conflict so often highlighted? Why is this dangerous?

6. What is the "culture of critique?" Are there times when passionate opposition is called for? What does the author question and why? What is "agonism" or an "agonistic response?"

7. Describe what happens when people have "an argument."

8. What did Paul Ekman's experiments show about the ability to detect lies?

9. What is the problem with the idea that "every issue has two sides?"

10. Describe the problem with assuming that there *must* be an "other side" and list the examples cited.

11. How can talent and effort be wasted by the argument culture?

12. How is people's thinking influenced by metaphors, especially the metaphor of war? Why is this a problem? How is the experiment by Loftus and Palmer relevant? In what ways are our imaginations limited by metaphors?

13. What is one of the "most dangerous aspects" of regarding intellectual interchange as a fight?

14. How does the argument culture:
    (a) limit the information we get rather than broadening it?
    (b) polarize issues?
    (c) lead to an obsession with ratings and rankings?
    (d) encourage aggressive tactics for their own sake?

15. In what ways is the argument culture related to a general disconnection and breakdown of community?

16. What alternatives to the argument culture does the author propose? What is her goal?

DEBORAH TANNEN is best known as the author of *You Just Don't Understand: Women and Men in Conversation,* which was on *The New York Times* bestseller list for nearly four years, including eight months as number one, and has been translated into twenty-four languages. Her book, *Talking from 9 to 5: Women and Men in the Workplace: Language, Sex, and Power,* was a *New York Times* Business bestseller. She has written for and been featured in *The New York Times, Newsweek, Time, USA Today, People,* and *The Washington Post.* Her many national television and radio appearances include *20/20, 48 Hours,* CBS *News,* ABC *World News Tonight,* and *Good Morning America.* She is one of only three University Professors at Georgetown University in Washington, D.C., where she is on the Linguistics Department faculty. *The Argument Culture* is her sixteenth book.

Deborah Tannen has also published short stories, essays, and poems. Her first play, *An Act of Devotion,* is included in *Best Short Plays 1993–1994.* It was produced, together with her play *Sisters,* by Horizons Theatre in Arlington, VA.

Shakespeare in the Bush

LAURA BOHANNAN

Just before I left Oxford for the Tiv in West Africa, conversation turned to the season at Stratford. "You Americans," said a friend, "often have difficulty with Shakespeare. He was, after all, a very English poet, and one can easily misinterpret the universal by misunderstanding the particular."

I protested that human nature is pretty much the same the whole world over; at least the general plot and motivation of the greater tragedies would always be clear—everywhere—although some details of custom might have to be explained and difficulties of translation might produce other slight changes. To end an argument we could not conclude, my friend gave me a copy of *Hamlet* to study in the African bush: it would, he hoped, lift my mind above its primitive surroundings, and possibly I might, by prolonged meditation, achieve the grace of correct interpretation.

It was my second field trip to that African tribe, and I thought myself ready to live in one of its remote sections—an area difficult to cross even on foot. I eventually settled on the hillock of a very knowledgeable old man, the head of a homestead of some hundred and forty people, all of whom were either his close relatives or their wives and children. Like the other elders of the vicinity, the old man spent most of his time performing ceremonies seldom seen these days in the more accessible parts of the tribe. I was delighted. Soon there would be three months of enforced isolation and leisure, between the harvest that takes place just before the rising of the swamps and the clearing of new farms when the water goes down. Then, I thought, they would have even more time to perform ceremonies and explain them to me.

I was quite mistaken. Most of the ceremonies demanded the presence of elders from several homesteads. As the swamps rose, the old men found it too difficult to walk from one homestead to the next, and the ceremonies gradually ceased. As the swamps rose even higher, all activities but one came to an end. The women brewed beer from maize and millet. Men, women, and children sat on their hillocks and drank it.

People began to drink at dawn. By midmorning the whole homestead was singing, dancing, and drumming. When it rained, people had to sit inside their huts: there they drank and sang or they drank and told stories. In any case, by noon or before, I either had to join the party or retire to my own hut and my books. "One does not discuss serious matters when there is beer. Come, drink with us." Since I lacked their capacity for the thick native beer, I spent more and more time with *Hamlet*. Before the end of the second month, grace descended on me. I was quite sure that *Hamlet* had only one possible interpretation, and that one universally obvious.

Early every morning, in the hope of having some serious talk before the beer party, I used to call on the old man at his reception hut—a circle of posts supporting a thatched roof above a low mud wall to keep out wind and rain. One day I crawled through the low doorway and found most of the men of the homestead sitting huddled in their ragged cloths on stools, low plank beds, and reclining chairs, warming themselves against the chill of the rain around a smoky fire. In the center were three pots of beer. The party had started.

The old man greeted me cordially. "Sit down and drink." I accepted a large calabash full of beer, poured some into a small drinking gourd, and tossed it down. Then I poured some more into the same gourd for the man second in seniority to my host before I handed my calabash over to a young man for further distribution. Important people shouldn't ladle beer themselves.

"It is better like this," the old man said, looking at me approvingly and plucking at the thatch that had caught in my hair. "You should sit and drink with us more often. Your servants tell me that when you are not with us, you sit inside your hut looking at a paper."

The old man was acquainted with four kinds of "papers": tax receipts, bride price receipts, court fee receipts, and letters. The messenger who brought him letters from the chief used them mainly as a badge of office, for he always knew what was in them and told the old man. Personal letters for the few who had relatives in the government or mission stations were kept until someone went to a large market where there was a letter writer and reader. Since my arrival, letters were brought to me to be read. A few men also brought me bride price receipts, privately, with requests to change the figures to a higher sum. I found moral arguments were of no avail, since in-laws are fair game, and the technical hazards of forgery difficult to explain to an illiterate people. I did not wish them to think me silly enough to look at any such papers for days on end, and I hastily explained that my "paper" was one of the "things of long ago" of my country.

"Ah," said the old man. "Tell us."

I protested that I was not a storyteller. Story telling is a skilled art among them; their standards are high, and the audiences critical—and vocal in their criticism. I protested in vain. This morning they wanted to hear a story while they drank. They threatened to tell me no more stories until I told them one of mine. Finally, the old man promised that no one would criticize my style "for we know you are struggling with our language." "But," put in one of the elders, "you must explain what we do not understand, as we do when we tell you our stories." Realizing that here was my chance to prove *Hamlet* universally intelligible, I agreed.

The old man handed me some more beer to help me on with my storytelling. Men filled their long wooden pipes and knocked coals from the fire to place in the pipe bowls; then, puffing contentedly, they sat back to listen. I began in the proper style, "Not yesterday, not yesterday, but long ago, a thing occurred. One night three men were keeping watch outside the homestead of the great chief, when suddenly they saw the former chief approach them."

"Why was he no longer their chief?"

"He was dead," I explained. "That is why they were troubled and afraid when they saw him."

"Impossible," began one of the elders, handing his pipe on to his neighbor, who interrupted, "Of course it wasn't the dead chief. It was an omen sent by a witch. Go on."

Slightly shaken, I continued. "One of these three was a man who knew things"—the closest translation for scholar, but unfortunately it also meant witch. The second elder looked triumphantly at the first. "So he spoke to the dead chief saying, 'Tell us what we must do so you may rest in your grave,' but the dead chief did not answer. He vanished, and they could see him no more. Then the man who knew things—his name was Horatio—said this event was the affair of the dead chief's son, Hamlet."

There was a general shaking of heads round the circle. "Had the dead chief no living brothers? Or was this son the chief?"

"No," I replied. "That is, he had one living brother who became the chief when the elder brother died."

The old men muttered: such omens were matters for chiefs and elders, not for youngsters; no good could come of going behind a chief's back; clearly Horatio was not a man who knew things.

"Yes, he was," I insisted, shooing a chicken away from my beer. "In our country the son is next to the father. The dead chief's younger brother had become the great chief. He had also married his elder brother's widow only about a month after the funeral."

"He did well," the old man beamed and announced to the others, "I told you that if we knew more about Europeans, we would find they really were very like us. In our country also," he added to me, "the younger brother marries the elder brother's widow and becomes the father of his children. Now, if your uncle, who married your widowed mother, is your father's full brother, then he will be a real father to you. Did Hamlet's father and uncle have one mother?"

His question barely penetrated my mind; I was too upset and thrown too far off balance by having one of the most important elements of *Hamlet* knocked straight out of the picture. Rather uncertainly I said that I thought they had the same mother, but I wasn't sure—the story didn't say. The old man told me severely that these genealogical details made all the difference and that when I got home I must ask the elders about it. He shouted out the door to one of his younger wives to bring his goatskin bag.

Determined to save what I could of the mother motif, I took a deep breath and began again. "The son, Hamlet, was very sad because his mother had married again so quickly. There was no need for her to do so, and it is our custom for a widow not to go to her next husband until she has mourned for two years."

"Two years is too long," objected the wife, who had appeared with the old man's battered goatskin bag. "Who will hoe your farms for you while you have no husband?"

"Hamlet," I retorted without thinking, "was old enough to hoe his mother's farms himself. There was no need for her to remarry." No one looked convinced. I gave up. "His mother and the great chief told Hamlet not to be sad, for the great chief himself would be a father to Hamlet. Furthermore, Hamlet would be the next chief: therefore he must stay to learn the things of a chief. Hamlet agreed to remain, and all the rest went off to drink beer."

While I paused, perplexed at how to render Hamlet's disgusted soliloquy to an audience convinced that Claudius and Gertrude had behaved in the best possible manner, one of the younger men asked me who had married the other wives of the dead chief.

"He had no other wives," I told him.

"But a chief must have many wives! How else can he brew beer and prepare food for all his guests?"

I said firmly that in our country even chiefs had only one wife, that they had servants to do their work, and that they paid them from tax money.

It was better, they returned, for a chief to have many wives and sons who would help him hoe his farms and feed his people; then everyone loved the chief who gave much and took nothing—taxes were a bad thing.

I agreed with the last comment, but for the rest fell back on their favorite way of fobbing off my questions: "That is the way it is done, so that is how we do it."

I decided to skip the soliloquy. Even if Claudius was here thought quite right to marry his brother's widow, there remained the poison motif, and I knew they would disapprove of fratricide. More hopefully I resumed, "That night Hamlet kept watch with the three who had seen his dead father. The dead chief again appeared, and although the others were afraid, Hamlet followed his dead father off to one side. When they were alone, Hamlet's dead father spoke."

"Omens can't talk!" The old man was emphatic.

"Hamlet's dead father wasn't an omen. Seeing him might have been an omen, but he was not." My audience looked as confused as I sounded. "It *was* Hamlet's dead father. It was a thing we call a 'ghost.'" I had to use the English word, for unlike many of the neighboring tribes, these people didn't believe in the survival after death of any individuating part of the personality.

"What is a 'ghost?' An omen?"

"No, a 'ghost' is someone who is dead but who walks around and can talk, and people can hear him and see him but not touch him."

They objected. "One can touch zombis."

"No, no! It was not a dead body the witches had animated to sacrifice and eat. No one else made Hamlet's dead father walk. He did it himself."

"Dead men can't walk," protested my audience as one man.

I was quite willing to compromise. "A 'ghost' is the dead man's shadow."

But again they objected. "Dead men cast no shadows."

"They do in my country," I snapped.

The old man quelled the babble of disbelief that arose immediately and told me with that insincere, but courteous, agreement one extends to the fancies of the young, ignorant, and superstitious, "No doubt in your country the dead can also walk without being zombis." From the depths of his bag he produced a withered fragment of kola nut, bit off one end to show it wasn't poisoned, and handed me the rest as a peace offering.

"Anyhow," I resumed, "Hamlet's dead father said that his own brother, the one who became chief, had poisoned him. He wanted Hamlet to avenge him. Hamlet believed this in his heart, for he did not like his father's brother." I took another swallow of beer. "In the country of the great chief, living in the same homestead, for it was a very large one, was an important elder who was often with the chief to advise and help him. His name was Polonius. Hamlet was courting his daughter, but her father and her brother . . . [I cast hastily about for some tribal analogy] warned her not to let Hamlet visit her when she was alone on her farm, for he would be a great chief and so could not marry her."

"Why not?" asked the wife, who had settled down on the edge of the old man's chair. He frowned at her for asking stupid questions and growled, "They lived in the same homestead."

"That was not the reason," I informed them. "Polonius was a stranger who lived in the homestead because he helped the chief, not because he was a relative."

"Then why couldn't Hamlet marry her?"

"He could have," I explained, "but Polonius didn't think he would. After all, Hamlet was a man of great importance who ought to marry a chief's daughter, for in his country a man could have only one wife. Polonius was afraid that if Hamlet made love to his daughter, then no one else would give a high price for her."

"That might be true," remarked one of the shrewder elders, "but a chief's son would give his mistress's father enough presents and patronage to more than make up the difference. Polonius sounds like a fool to me."

"Many people think he was," I agreed. "Meanwhile Polonius sent his son Laertes off to Paris to learn the things of that country, for it was the homestead of a very great chief indeed. Because he was afraid that Laertes might waste a lot of money on beer and women and gambling, or get into trouble by fighting, he sent one of his servants to Paris secretly, to spy out what Laertes was doing. One day Hamlet came upon Polonius's daughter Ophelia. He behaved so oddly he frightened her. Indeed"—I was fumbling for words to express the dubious quality of Hamlet's madness—"the chief and many others had also noticed that when Hamlet talked one could understand the words but not what they meant. Many people thought that he had become mad." My audience suddenly became much more attentive. "The great chief wanted to know what was wrong with Hamlet, so he sent for two of Hamlet's age mates [school friends would have taken long explanation] to talk to Hamlet and find out what troubled his heart. Hamlet, seeing that they had been bribed by the chief to betray him, told them nothing. Polonius, however, insisted that Hamlet was mad because he had been forbidden to see Ophelia, whom he loved."

"Why," inquired a bewildered voice, "should anyone bewitch Hamlet on that account?"

"Bewitch him?"

"Yes, only witchcraft can make anyone mad, unless, of course, one sees the beings that lurk in the forest."

I stopped being a storyteller, took out my notebook and demanded to be told more about these two causes of madness. Even while they spoke and I jotted notes, I tried to calculate the effect of this new factor on the plot. Hamlet had not been exposed to the beings that lurk in the forests. Only his relatives in the male line could bewitch him. Barring relatives not mentioned by Shakespeare, it had to be Claudius who was attempting to harm him. And, of course, it was.

For the moment I staved off questions by saying that the great chief also refused to believe that Hamlet was mad for the love of Ophelia and nothing else. "He was sure that something much more important was troubling Hamlet's heart."

"Now Hamlet's age mates," I continued, "had brought with them a famous storyteller. Hamlet decided to have this man tell the chief and all his homestead a story about a man who had poisoned his brother because he desired his brother's wife and wished to be chief himself. Hamlet was sure the great chief could not hear the story without making a sign if he was indeed guilty, and then he would discover whether his dead father had told him the truth."

The old man interrupted, with deep cunning, "Why should a father lie to his son?" he asked.

I hedged: "Hamlet wasn't sure that it really was his dead father." It was impossible to say anything, in that language, about devil-inspired visions.

"You mean," he said, "it actually was an omen, and he knew witches sometimes send false ones. Hamlet was a fool not to go to one skilled in reading omens and divining the truth in the first place. A man-who-sees-the-truth could have told him how his father died, if he really had been poisoned, and if there was witchcraft in it; then Hamlet could have called the elders to settle the matter."

The shrewd elder ventured to disagree. "Because his father's brother was a great chief, one-who-sees-the-truth might therefore have been afraid to tell it. I think it was for that reason that a friend of Hamlet's father—a witch and an elder—sent an omen so his friend's son would know. Was the omen true?"

"Yes," I said, abandoning ghosts and the devil; a witch-sent omen it would have to be. "It was true, for when the storyteller was telling his tale before all the homestead, the great chief rose in fear. Afraid that Hamlet knew his secret he planned to have him killed."

The stage set of the next bit presented some difficulties of translation. I began cautiously. "The great chief told Hamlet's mother to find out from her son what he knew. But because a woman's children are always first in her heart, he had the important elder Polonius hide behind a cloth that hung against the wall of Hamlet's mother's sleeping hut. Hamlet started to scold his mother for what she had done."

There was a shocked murmur from everyone. A man should never scold his mother.

"She called out in fear, and Polonius moved behind the cloth. Shouting, 'A rat!' Hamlet took his machete and slashed through the cloth." I paused for dramatic effect. "He had killed Polonius!"

The old men looked at each other in supreme disgust. "That Polonius truly was a fool and a man who knew nothing! What child would not know enough to shout, 'It's me!'" With a pang, I remembered that these people are ardent hunters, always armed with bow, arrow, and machete; at the first rustle in the grass an arrow is aimed and ready, and the hunter shouts "Game!" If no human voice answers immediately, the arrow speeds on its way. Like a good hunter Hamlet had shouted, "A rat!"

I rushed in to save Polonius's reputation. "Polonius did speak. Hamlet heard him. But he thought it was the chief and wished to kill him earlier that evening. . . ." I broke down, unable to describe to these pagans, who had no belief in individual afterlife, the difference between dying at one's prayers and dying "unhousell'd, disappointed, unaneled."

This time I had shocked my audience seriously. "For a man to raise his hand against his father's brother and the one who has become his father—that is a terrible thing. The elders ought to let such a man be bewitched."

I nibbled at my kola nut in some perplexity, then pointed out that after all the man had killed Hamlet's father.

"No," pronounced the old man, speaking less to me than to the young men sitting behind the elders. "If your father's brother has killed your father, you must appeal to your father's age mates; *they* may avenge him. No man may use violence against his senior relatives." Another thought struck him. "But if his father's brother had indeed been wicked enough to bewitch Hamlet and make him mad that would be a good story indeed, for it would be his fault that Hamlet, being mad, no longer had any sense and thus was ready to kill his father's brother."

There was a murmur of applause. *Hamlet* was again a good story to them, but it no longer seemed quite the same story to me. As I thought over the coming complications of plot and motive, I lost courage and decided to skim over dangerous ground quickly.

"The great chief," I went on, "was not sorry that Hamlet had killed Polonius. It gave him a reason to send Hamlet away, with his two treacherous mates, with letters to a chief of a far country, saying that Hamlet should be killed. But Hamlet changed the writing on their papers, so that the chief killed his age mates instead." I encountered a reproachful glare from one of the men whom I had told undetectable forgery was not merely immoral but beyond human skill. I looked the other way.

"Before Hamlet could return, Laertes came back for his father's funeral. The great chief told him Hamlet had killed Polonius. Laertes swore to kill Hamlet because of this, and because his sister Ophelia, hearing her father had been killed by the man she loved, went mad and drowned in the river."

"Have you already forgotten what we told you?" The old man was reproachful. "One cannot take vengeance on a madman; Hamlet killed Polonius in his madness. As for the girl, she not only went mad, she was drowned. Only witches can make people drown. Water itself can't hurt anything. It is merely something one drinks and bathes in."

I began to get cross. "If you don't like the story, I'll stop."

The old man made soothing noises and himself poured me some more beer. "You tell the story well, and we are listening. But it is clear that the elders of your country have never told you what the story really means. No, don't interrupt! We believe you when you say your marriage customs are different, or your clothes and weapons. But people are the same everywhere; therefore, there are always witches and it is we, the elders, who know how witches work. We told you it was the great chief who wished to kill Hamlet, and now your own words have proved us right. Who were Ophelia's male relatives?"

"There were only her father and her brother." *Hamlet* was clearly out of my hands.

"There must have been many more; this also you must ask of your elders when you get back to your country. From what you tell us, since Polonius was dead, it must have been Laertes who killed Ophelia, although I do not see the reason for it."

We had emptied one pot of beer, and the old men argued the point with slightly tipsy interest. Finally one of them demanded of me, "What did the servant of Polonius say on his return?"

With difficulty I recollected Reynaldo and his mission. "I don't think he did return before Polonius was killed."

"Listen," said the elder, "and I will tell you how it was and how your story will go, then you may tell me if I am right. Polonius knew his son would get into trouble, and so he did. He had many fines to pay for fighting, and debts from gambling. But he had only two ways of getting money quickly. One was to marry off his sister at once, but it is difficult to find a man who will marry a woman desired by the son of a chief. For if the chief's heir commits adultery with your wife, what can you do? Only a fool calls a case against a man who will someday be his judge. Therefore Laertes had to take the second way: he killed his sister by witchcraft, drowning her so he could secretly sell her body to the witches."

I raised an objection. "They found her body and buried it. Indeed Laertes jumped into the grave to see his sister once more—so, you see, the body was truly there. Hamlet, who had just come back, jumped in after him."

"What did I tell you?" The elder appealed to the others. "Laertes was up to no good with his sister's body. Hamlet prevented him, because the chief's heir, like a chief, does not wish any other man to grow rich and powerful. Laertes would be angry, because he would have killed his sister without benefit to himself. In our country he would try to kill Hamlet for that reason. Is this not what happened?"

"More or less," I admitted. "When the great chief found Hamlet was still alive, he encouraged Laertes to try to kill Hamlet and arranged a fight with machetes between them. In the fight both the young men were wounded to death. Hamlet's mother drank the poisoned beer that the chief meant for Hamlet in case he won the fight. When he saw his mother die of poison, Hamlet, dying, managed to kill his father's brother with his machete."

"You see, I was right!" exclaimed the elder.

"That was a very good story," added the old man, "and you told it with very few mistakes. There was just one more error, at the very end. The poison Hamlet's mother drank was obviously meant for the survivor of the fight, whichever it was. If Laertes had won, the great chief would have poisoned him, for no one would know that he arranged Hamlet's death. Then, too, he need not fear Laertes' witchcraft; it takes a strong heart to kill one's only sister by witchcraft.

"Sometime," concluded the old man, gathering his ragged toga about him, "you must tell us some more stories of your country. We, who are elders, will instruct you in their true meaning, so that when you return to your own land your elders will see that you have not been sitting in the bush, but among those who know things and who have taught you wisdom."

Critical Thinking

1. What attitude did Laura Bohannan have about cross-cultural translation of Shakespeare before visiting the Tiv?

2. What differences in custom and belief hampered her telling of "Hamlet" and how?

3. Was there a difference between Laura Bohannan and the Tiv in terms of what they got out of this experience? Explain.

LAURA BOHANNAN is a former professor of anthropology at the University of Illinois, at Chicago.

UNIT 3

The Organization of Society and Culture

Unit Selections

Learning Outcomes

After reading this Unit, you will be able to:

- Discuss the benefits of breastfeeding for child, mother, and society.

- Explain why marriage between cousins has been so common in the human past.

- Identify the traditional Inuit (Eskimo) practices that are important for their survival in the circumstances they live in and contrast them with the values professed by the society you live in.

- Discuss what contemporary hunter-collector societies teach us about the quality of life in the prehistoric past.

- Define the "Inuit paradox" and explain what we can learn from it with regard to modern-day eating practices.

- Explain the significance of "the gift" in traditional Hopi society.

- Discuss the economics, the politics, and the sociality of cell phone use in Nigeria.

Student Website
www.mhhe.com/cls

Internet References

Smithsonian Institution Website
  www.si.edu
Sociology Guy's Anthropology Links
  www.trinity.edu/~mkearl/anthro.html

Human beings do not interact with one another or think about their world in random fashion. They engage in structured and recurrent physical and mental activities. In this section, such patterns of behavior and thought—referred to here as the organization of society and culture—may be seen in a number of different contexts, from the mating preferences of hunter-gatherer bands (see "When Cousins Do More than Kiss"), or whether a mother breastfeeds her child (see "Breastfeeding and Culture") to the value the Hopi place on the gift as a symbol of social relations built on kinship and altruism (as discussed in "Ties That Bind") to the etiquette and protocol of cell phone use with friends and family ("Cell Phones, Sharing, and Social Status in an African Society").

Of special importance are the ways in which people make a living—in other words, the production, distribution, and consumption of goods and services. It is only by knowing the basic subsistence systems that we can hope to gain insight into other levels of social and cultural phenomena, for they are all inextricably bound together. Noting the various aspects of a sociocultural system in harmonious balance, however, does not imply an anthropological seal of approval. To understand infanticide (killing of the newborn) in the manner that it is practiced among some peoples is neither to condone nor condemn it. The adaptive patterns that have been in existence for a great length of time, such as many of the patterns of hunters and gatherers, probably owe their existence to their contributions to long-term human survival.

Anthropologists, however, are not content with the data derived from individual experience. On the contrary, personal descriptions must become the basis for sound anthropological theory. Otherwise, they remain meaningless, isolated relics of culture in the manner of museum pieces. In other words, while the articles in this unit are to some extent descriptive, they also serve to challenge both the academic and commonsense notions about why people behave and think the way they do. They remind us that assumptions are never really safe. As long as anthropologists are kept on their toes, the field as a whole will be better.

© PhotoLink/Getty Images

51

Breastfeeding and Culture

Kathryn Dettwyler

In a perfect world—one where child health and cognitive development were optimal—all children would be breastfed for as long as they wanted. As large-bodied, highly intelligent primates, that would be for a minimum of 2.5 years and as long as 6 or 7 years, or longer. In a perfect world, all mothers would know how to breastfeed and be supported in their efforts to do so by health care providers, spouses, friends, neighbors, co-workers, and the general beliefs of their culture.

Breastfeeding is, first and foremost, a way to provide protective immunities and health-promoting factors to children. Breast milk should be the primary source of nutrition for the first two years of life, complemented by appropriate solid foods around six months of age. Breast milk provides important immunities and nutrients, especially for growing brains, for as long as the child is breastfed. It is a source of physical and emotional comfort to a child, and for the mother it is the wellspring of the important mothering hormones, prolactin and oxytocin.

Ordinarily, childbirth is followed by breastfeeding, with its flood of prolactin, the "mothering hormone," and oxytocin, "the hormone of love." Both hormones elicit caretaking, affective, and protective behaviors by the mother towards her child. If the mother does not breastfeed, her body interprets this as "the baby died," and enters a state of hormonal grieving, preparing for a new attempt at reproduction. The mother, however, still has to cope with a newborn, and later a toddler, without the calming and nurturing influence of prolactin and oxytocin.

Like childbirth, however, breastfeeding is influenced by a variety of cultural beliefs, some directly related to breastfeeding itself, and others pertaining to a woman's role in society, to the proper relationship between mother and child, to the proper relationship between mother and father, and even to beliefs about breasts themselves.

One way of thinking about cultural influences on breastfeeding initiation and duration is based on the Demographic Transition, in which societies move from a pre-transition state of high birth and death rates, through a transitional stage of high birth but low death rates (resulting in rapid population growth), and eventually into a post-transition stage of low birth and death rates. Margaret Mead was the first to recognize an "Infant Feeding Transition." A culture begins in a pre-transition state of almost everyone breastfeeding for several years, then moves through a transitional stage of bottle-feeding. Three main forces conspire to move women away from breastfeeding: (1) the separation of their productive labor and their reproductive labor, as societies shift from subsistence-based economies to wage labor-based economies, and/or women are taken away from both productive and reproductive work to be their husband's social partners; (2) increasing confidence in the power of science to provide "better living through chemistry" coupled with decreasing confidence in the ability of women's bodies to function normally, and (3) the rise of commercial interests intent on making a profit by convincing women that breastfeeding is less

healthy, difficult, primitive, and/or shameful. The transition is initiated by women with more education and higher incomes turning to shorter and shorter durations of breastfeeding, and eventually only wet-nursing (in previous centuries) or bottle-feeding (in the 20th and 21st centuries) from birth.

As time goes by, women with less education and lower income levels emulate their social superiors and adopt bottle-feeding as well. By the time the last of the lower classes have adopted bottle-feeding as being "modern and scientific," the well-educated upper-class women are returning to breastfeeding, first for short periods, and then for increasing durations. They have moved on to the post-transition stage. The return to breastfeeding by well-educated upper-class women is fueled by several factors, including research during the last few decades clearly documenting the superiority of breastfeeding over formula in terms of maternal and child health and child cognitive development, feminism's insistence that women's reproductive powers are of great value, and a general backlash against the infant formula companies for promoting their products in unethical ways. Primarily, in the United States it has been well-educated middle- and upper-class women who have fought for legislation to protect the rights of mothers to breastfeed in public, and for better maternity care and on-site child care facilities.

In the late 1950s, anthropologist Margaret Mead urged researchers to: "Find out how we can get from the working class mothers who breastfeed to the upper middle class women who also breastfeed, without a generation of bottle feeders in between" (Raphael 1979). We still haven't figured out how to do this.

There are still a number of "pre-transition" cultures in the world, in which all women breastfeed each child for several years, but Western influence—particularly in the form of aggressive infant formula marketing strategies and the export of Western cultural beliefs about breasts as sex objects—is affecting even the remotest regions of the world. Korea, for example, is in the early stages of the transition from universal long-term breastfeeding to the adoption of bottles. Survey data reveal a decline in breastfeeding incidence and duration from the 1960s to the 1990s, led by upper-class, well-educated urban Korean women. China, likewise, has begun the transition to bottle-feeding, experiencing a rapid decline in the prevalence of breastfeeding in urban and periurban areas. Not surprisingly, China has been targeted by the infant formula companies as the next great market for their products.

Cuba is at the beginning of the infant feeding transition, with mothers of higher educational levels having the shortest duration of breastfeeding. Cuba seems to be well ahead of the United States in meeting established goals for maternal and child health through breastfeeding, with national strategies for supporting and promoting breastfeeding, including having all government hospitals participate in the World Health Organization's Baby-Friendly Hospital Initiative, and developing educational programs for day care centers and elementary and secondary schools to try to create a breastfeeding-friendly culture among both males and females from an early age. Cuba may be able to avoid a complete switch to bottle-feeding.

The Arabian Gulf countries (Bahrain, Kuwait, Oman, Qatar, Saudi Arabia, and the United Arab Emirates) are fully into the transitional phase, with middle- and upper-class women seldom breastfeeding, or only for a few weeks, and older women nursing longer than younger women. The influence of oil revenues on the lifestyles of these women, including the common employment of foreign housemaids and nannies, who bottle-feed the children, is fascinating and disturbing. The transition from full breastfeeding to almost full bottle-feeding has been particularly swift in this part of the world. "Westernized" hospital practices have been especially harmful, with hospital personnel and private clinics being used to promote the use of formula.

Australia, Canada, and the United States represent societies farthest along this "Infant Feeding Transition," with women of higher incomes and more education initiating breastfeeding in great numbers, and with increasing durations as well. This trend began in the 1970s, but was helped by the 1997 statement by the American Academy of Pediatrics that all children in the United States should be nursed for a minimum of one year (and thereafter as long as both mother and child wish), as well as by recent research showing that formula-fed children have lower IQs than their breastfed counterparts. In the United States, breastfeeding to the age of three years or beyond is becoming more and more common, as is breastfeeding siblings of different ages, known as "tandem nursing" (Dettwyler 2001). In the last decades, the biggest leaps in initiating breastfeeding in the United States have been among WIC clients (women, infants, and children), who tend to be poor and less well-educated, indicating a trickle-down effect of breastfeeding from the upper classes, as well as the success of WIC Peer Counselor training programs.

Exactly how a particular region responds to influence from the Western industrialized nations and from the multinational infant formula companies depends on many different social, political, and economic factors. This makes it difficult to predict how the infant feeding transition will look in a specific region, or how long the bottle-feeding stage will last.

Cultural beliefs affect breastfeeding in other ways as well. Among the Bambara of Mali, people believe that because breast milk is made from a woman's blood, the process of breastfeeding creates a special relationship between a child and the woman who breastfeeds that child, whether or not she is the child's biological mother. In addition, breastfeeding creates a bond among all of the children who nurse from the same woman, whether or not they are biological siblings.

Having milk-siblings expands one's kinship network, providing more people one can call on for help in times of need. However, these kinship ties also prohibit marriage between the related children. In order to reduce the impact on potential marriage partners, women try to breastfeed other women's children only if they would already be excluded as marriage partners. Thus, a woman might wet-nurse the children of her co-wives, the children of her husband's brothers, or her grandchildren, while avoiding breastfeeding the children of her best friend, who she hopes will grow up to marry her own children. Similar beliefs about the "milk tie" are found among people in Haiti, Papua New Guinea, the Balkans, Burma, and among the Badawin of Kuwait and Saudi Arabia. In cultures where everyone is breastfed, or where everyone is bottle-fed, one's identity does not hinge on how one was fed. But in cultures entering or leaving the transition, feeding practices can be very important to one's identity. In a culture just entering the transition, to be bottle-fed is to have high status and be wealthy and modern. In a culture entering the final stage, to be breastfed is to have high status and be wealthy and modern.

In a wide variety of cultures, males are breastfed longer than females, sometimes much longer. These practices are supported by a variety of cultural beliefs, including the ideas that earlier weaning for girls insures a much-desired earlier menopause (Taiwan), that boys must be nursed longer so they will be willing to take care of their aged parents (Ireland), and that breast milk is the conduit for machismo, something boys need, but girls do not (Ecuador). Additionally, a number of societies have noted that males are physiologically weaker than females, more prone to illness and early death, so mothers nurse their sons longer to help ensure their survival.

Cultural beliefs about birth can have a profound influence on the success or failure of breastfeeding. Breastfeeding works best when the mother and baby are un-drugged at delivery, when they are kept together after birth, when the baby is not washed, when the baby is fed at the first cue (long before crying), when breastfeeding occurs early and often, when free formula samples and other gifts are not given to the mother, and when all those who surround the mother are knowledgeable and supportive of breastfeeding. Where the culture of birthing meets most or all of these criteria, we find higher rates of breastfeeding as well as longer durations. The World Health Organization's Baby-Friendly Hospital Initiative provides both a blueprint for optimal breastfeeding conditions and references to support their recommendations.

Cultural beliefs about how often children should breastfeed can help or hinder the process. The composition of human milk, as well as studies of human populations where children are allowed to breastfeed on demand, suggests that the natural frequency of breastfeeding is several times an hour for a few minutes each time, rather than according to a schedule, with longer feedings separated by several hours. Infrequent feeding in the early days and weeks of breastfeeding can permanently affect a mother's milk supply. As control of breast milk production gradually shifts from primarily endocrine (prolactin) to primarily autocrine (based on breast fullness) during the first few months postpartum, women who have been nursing on a three- to four-hour schedule may find that they no longer have sufficient milk to meet their babies' needs. A simple strategy of unrestricted breastfeeding from birth onwards would prevent this supply problem.

Perhaps the most pernicious cultural belief affecting breastfeeding is the one found in the United States and a small number of other (mostly Western) cultures—the belief that women's breasts are naturally erotic. American culture is obsessed with the sexual nature of women's breasts and their role in attracting and keeping male attention, as well as their role in providing sexual pleasure. This is reflected by the "normal" circumstances under which breasts are exposed in the United States (*Playboy* centerfolds, low-cut evening gowns, bikinis), by the phenomenon of breast augmentation surgery, by the association of breasts with sexual pleasure, and by the reactions of some people when they see women breastfeeding (embarrassment, horror, disgust, disapproval). In fact, the cultural belief that breasts are intrinsically erotic is just that, a cultural belief of limited distribution—one that has devastating consequences for women who want to breastfeed their children.

The mammary glands play no role in sexual behavior in any species other than humans. Among humans, the cross-cultural evidence clearly shows that most cultures do not define the breasts as sex objects. Extensive cross-cultural research in the 1940s and 1950s, published by Ford and Beach, found that, of 190 cultures surveyed, only 13 viewed women's breasts as sexually attractive. Likewise, 13 cultures out of 190 involved women's breasts in sexual activity. Of these latter 13, only three are also listed among the 13 where breasts are considered sexually attractive.

In most cultures, breasts are viewed solely as functional body parts, used to feed children—similar to how the typical American male views women's elbows, as devices to bend arms. Thus, in most cultures, it doesn't matter whether they are covered or not, or how big they are; husbands do not feel jealous of their nursing children, and women are never accused of breastfeeding for their own sexual pleasure. In the United States, and increasingly where Western ideas about breasts as sex objects are taking hold, women find that they must be extremely discreet about where and how they breastfeed. They may get little support for breastfeeding, or even active resistance from jealous husbands; they may receive dirty looks or rude comments or be asked to go elsewhere (often the bathroom) to nurse. Still others are accused of sexually abusing their children for breastfeeding them longer than a year (Dettwyler 2001).

The evolution of cultural beliefs about breasts is difficult to pin down. Carolyn Latteier and Marilyn Yalom provide the most thorough research on the history of Western culture's obsession with breasts. The rise of both the infant formula industry and commercial pornography following World War II contributed to modern views of breasts as sex objects, rather than glands for producing milk for children.

Among health care providers themselves, a culture of denial about the health risks of formula contributes to the persistence of bottle-feeding. Many physicians view bottle-feeding as "almost as good" in spite of overwhelming research to the contrary. It is estimated that for every 1,000 deaths of infants in the United States, four of those deaths can be directly attributed to the use of infant formula. Additionally, children who are formula-fed have higher rates of many illnesses during childhood including diabetes, ear infections, gastrointestinal and upper respiratory infections, lymphoma, Sudden Infant Death Syndrome, and allergies. They continue to have higher rates of illnesses throughout life, including heart disease, some types of cancer, and multiple sclerosis. Children who are formula-fed likewise have lower average scores on intelligence tests and lower grades in school. Mothers who breastfeed their children, especially for longer durations, have lower rates of reproductive cancers (especially breast cancer), and lower rates of osteoporosis.

Unfortunately, obstetricians often view infant nutrition as the responsibility of the pediatrician, while the pediatrician claims that by the time the child is born, the mother has long since made up her mind about how she will feed her child. Many health care professionals say that they hesitate to discuss the dangers of formula for fear of "making women feel guilty." This is patronizing of parents and robs them of their chance to make an informed decision about this important area of child care.

In a perfect world, all cultural beliefs would support breastfeeding. The World Health Organization's Baby-Friendly Hospital Initiative and the Coalition for Improving Maternity Services' Mother-Friendly Childbirth Initiative are two attempts to clarify the best cultural practices for initiating breastfeeding. The Internet has also had a major impact on the culture of breastfeeding support. LactNet is an e-mail list for professionals who work in the lactation field. Kathleen Bruce and Kathleen Auerbach, both lactation consultants in the United States, began the list in March of 1995. It has grown to include more than 3,000 individuals from 38 countries who share ideas, beliefs, research studies, and clinical experience. Documents such as the Baby-Friendly Hospital Initiative and the Mother-Friendly Childbirth Initiative, and resources such as LactNet, are creating and sustaining a global culture of breastfeeding support.

Critical Thinking

1. Discuss the importance of breastfeeding for both mother and child.

2. What kinds of cultural factors influence breastfeeding?

3. Discuss the main forces that move women away from breastfeeding.

4. What factors have fueled the return to breastfeeding?

5. How has Western influence brought about bottle-feeding in countries that are undergoing a transition? Why might Cuba be an exception in this regard?

6. Why are the Arabian Gulf countries "fully into the transitional phase?"

7. Describe the "Infant Feeding Transition" and why it is occurring.

8. How do cultural beliefs affect breastfeeding?

9. Why are males breastfed more often than females?

10. What are some of the detrimental effects of not breastfeeding?

Additional Resources

For Internet links related to this chapter, please visit our website at www.mhhe.com/dettwyler

Ford, C. S.; and F. A. Beach. *Patterns of Sexual Behavior.* New York: Harper & Row, 1951.

Giuliani, Rudolph W. (Introduction) and the editors of LIFE Magazine. *One Nation: America Remembers September 11, 2001.* New York: Little Brown & Company, 2001.

Kear, Adrian, and Deborah Lynn Steinberg, eds. *Mourning Diana: Nation, Culture and the Performance of Grief.* New York: Routledge, 1999.

Latteier, C. *Breasts: The Women's Perspective on an American Obsession.* Binghamton, NY: Haworth Press, 1998.

Podolefsky, Aaron, and Peter J. Brown, eds. *Applying Anthropology: An Introductory Reader.* 7th ed. New York: McGraw-Hill Higher Education, 2002.

Raphael, D. "Margaret Mead—A Tribute." *The Lactation Review* 4, no. 1 (1979), pp. 1–3.

Simopoulos, A. P., J. E. Dutra de Oliveira, and I. D. Desai, eds. *Behavioral and Metabolic Aspects of Breastfeeding: International Trends. World Review of Nutrition and Dietetics, Volume 78.* Basel, Switzerland: S. Karger, 1995.

Stuart-Macadam, Patricia, and Katherine A. Dettwyler, eds. *Breastfeeding: Biocultural Perspectives.* New York: Aldine de Gruyter Publishers, 1995.

Walker, M. "A Fresh Look at the Hazards of Artificial Infant Feeding, II." 1998. Available from the International Lactation Consultants Association.

Yalom, M. *A History of the Breast.* New York: Random House, Inc., 1997.

When Cousins Do More than Kiss

Anthony Layng

Now that same-sex marriage increasingly is becoming acceptable in the U.S., might not incestuous marriage be next? Both have been condemned by legal sanctions and religious beliefs. However, since these are subject to change, what is to prevent first cousin marriage from gaining popularity?

While visiting recently with a group of my Catholic in-laws, the subject of incest came up. Actually, no one used the term "incest" but when my brother-in-law mentioned that he once dated his first cousin, others in the room clearly were shocked. After all, it says in the Bible that sex with close relatives, even some in-laws, is abhorrent to God. This reaction encouraged me to play anthropologist by pointing out that in some societies, the most preferred marriages are between first cousins. Predictably, someone asked, "What about inbreeding?" Since most Americans probably would ask the same question, here is my professorial answer

Incest taboos in practically all societies prohibit copulation between parent and child and, with a few rare exceptions, sex between siblings is not allowed. Beyond these relationships, there is very little international agreement concerning the extent to which incest taboos should apply to relatives outside one's nuclear family and, where marriage between certain cousins is the ideal, other cousins strictly may be off-limits. For instance, among the Trobriand Islanders of the South Pacific, a man is forbidden to have sex with the daughter of his mother's sister, and yet he is encouraged to marry a daughter of his mother's brother. Both are, of course, first cousins and equally close genetic relatives.

The scope of incest taboos varies widely from one society to another. Where descent is traced strictly through males, as among the Lakher of Southeast Asia, one cannot marry anyone within his or her clan or lineage, including many distant cousins. Likewise, many mairi lineal societies, like the inhabitants of Chuuk (Truk) in the central Pacific, frequently extend incest taboos to all matrilineal relatives. That means that a man cannot even marry his mother's mother's mother's sister's daughter's daughter's daughter's daughter—a third cousin once removed. In China, traditionally, people with the same surname are discouraged from marrying even when there was no indication of common kinship. In some states in the U.S., it used to be illegal for in-laws to marry, especially for a man to marry his stepdaughter. Clearly, this did not represent any concern about inbreeding.

Another interesting variable regarding incest taboos has to do with the fact that some societies permit certain exceptions. Historically, royal siblings in Egypt, Hawaii, and Peru were expected to marry each other to produce an heir, thus preventing dilution of royal blood. The Tonga of East Africa sometimes encouraged an esteemed hunter to have sexual intercourse with his daughter prior to stalking lions.

Given the fact that many tribal societies have westernized their incest taboos as a result of Christian missionary influence, illustrating how flexible they can be, we must ask: If incest taboos are instinctual as so many believe, why do they vary so from one society to another, and why are they so subject to change over time? Yet, first we have to ask: How did incest taboos get started? The Australian Tiwi of Bathurst Island are a particularly interesting case. To them, a child was considered unrelated to his or her mother's husband. Daddy was seen as playing only a mechanical role in inducing pregnancy, making it possible for some family ancestor to complete spiritual conception. A man's children, strictly speaking, were not considered to be his offspring. Nevertheless, the mother's husband was not allowed to have sex with her daughters. If this prohibition is not based on genetic considerations, how do we explain it?

In most societies, violations of incest taboos do occur, as in our own country. For every case of father-daughter or brother-sister incest that is brought to the attention of authorities, there must be many that go unreported. After all, shame and guilt can be strong motives to remain silent. Believing that you either have been a perpetrator of sin or a victim of a sinful act, especially when the participants are immediate family members, makes most of us disinclined to go public.

Given the variability of the range of these taboos and the fact that exceptions are made in some places, the numerous illegal cases of incest involving parents, siblings, and cousins, and those societies where conception was considered to be caused by dead ancestors, it seems unlikely that humans have some sort of instinct regarding inbreeding. Also, it is not probable that genetic closeness is the major concern here. After all, the children of your father's brother and the children of your mother's brother share the same amount of common genes with you but in tribal societies, seldom are considered equally close relatives.

We all have heard the stories of European royal cousins who perpetuated a high incidence of hemophilia in their offspring. Yet, just as unfortunate genetic propensities can show up more readily when people marry close relatives, desirable propensities can be encouraged in the same way. Understandably, given the emotionally charged nature of this subject we have had little opportunity to learn much about the biological consequences of incest. It is interesting to note that among chimpanzees, our closest living nonhuman relatives, mother-son copulation has been observed, although the mothers usually protest.

In this country, we are encouraged to focus on assumed deleterious genetic abnormalities, believing that it is this concern that initially gave rise to incest taboos and the laws enacted to prohibit inbreeding. However, it seems quite possible that American incest taboos essentially are a case of retaining ancient tribal beliefs.

Let us consider a nonbiological explanation for how incest taboos got started. Unlike what it says in the Bible about our earliest ancestors being farmers, they actually lived in small, vulnerable hunter-gatherer bands that needed to form alliances with others to ensure their survival. To the extent that marriage between siblings and some close cousins was discouraged, many of the young men would have to seek mates from outside their band. Incest taboos would have served them well in this regard, encouraging kinship ties among bands. This greatly facilitated cooperation and exchanges of food and information regarding where and how to hunt and gather. In regions where food scarcity was severe from time to time, bands that maintained incest taboos had an advantage because of the cooperation fostered by kinship affiliation with other bands. Members could call on kin in other bands who were likely to share whatever food they had.

Where incest was not prohibited, there were fewer kin ties among bands, so assistance and practical knowledge from others would be less available. Survival was more hazardous under these circumstances because starvation was more likely. Such bands produced fewer children who reached adulthood and reproduced, giving rise, over thousands of years, to incest taboos becoming a cultural universal.

In this age of computers and a global economy, what utility do moral restrictions on sex with close relatives have now? Perhaps we hold on to incest taboos today not merely because of Bible lore or the fact that we favor some degree of eugenics, but because they still benefit us socially. After all, in spite of the prevalence of in-law jokes, having an extensive network of relatives continues to be quite useful when we need a favor, such as help in acquiring a job or a stock tip. Given the importance of such benefits, it is not unsuitable that we continue to act as if incest is harmful biologically to our society. If the only reason we had in mind for avoiding sex with first cousins and siblings was sociological, it is unlikely that most of us would consider that such avoidance was absolutely imperative. At the very least, we would be more inclined to question such restrictions, and copulation and even marriage of close relatives would be far more common than it is now, resulting in less extensive kinship networks. On the other hand, the assumed genetic role played by incest perpetuates the belief that incest is forbidden by God and, therefore, sinful. Such thinking is very helpful in ensuring that we keep the benefits of having in-laws that can expand the number of persons we can look to for assistance.

Since incest taboos are so ancient and continue today very much as they did in the past having near unanimity regarding their moral necessity, it seems safe to assume that they still serve some practical need. As in our tribal past, incest taboos may have far more to do with maintaining a pragmatic and orderly society than with presumed deleterious effects on our genes.

Critical Thinking

1. What evidence is there that the incest taboos vary widely from one society to another?

2. What examples are there that some societies even provide exceptions to their own incest taboos?

3. Why does it seem unlikely that humans have an instinct regarding inbreeding? Why does genetic closeness not seem to be a concern?

4. What social benefits derive from the incest taboo?

5. Why is it still important that humans think that there would be dangerous biological consequences of incest?

ANTHONY LAYNG is professor emeritus of anthropology at Elmira (N. Y.) College.

The Inuit Paradox

How can people who gorge on fat and rarely see a vegetable be healthier than we are?

PATRICIA GADSBY

Patricia Cochran, an Inupiat from Northwestern Alaska, is talking about the native foods of her childhood: "We pretty much had a subsistence way of life. Our food supply was right outside our front door. We did our hunting and foraging on the Seward Peninsula and along the Bering Sea."

"Our meat was seal and walrus, marine mammals that live in cold water and have lots of fat. We used seal oil for our cooking and as a dipping sauce for food. We had moose, caribou, and reindeer. We hunted ducks, geese, and little land birds like quail, called ptarmigan. We caught crab and lots of fish—salmon, whitefish, tomcod, pike, and char. Our fish were cooked, dried, smoked, or frozen. We ate frozen raw whitefish, sliced thin. The elders liked stinkfish, fish buried in seal bags or cans in the tundra and left to ferment. And fermented seal flipper, they liked that too."

Cochran's family also received shipments of whale meat from kin living farther north, near Barrow. Beluga was one she liked; raw muktuk, which is whale skin with its underlying blubber, she definitely did not. "To me it has a chew-on-a-tire consistency," she says, "but to many people it's a mainstay." In the short subarctic summers, the family searched for roots and greens and, best of all from a child's point of view, wild blueberries, crowberries, or salmonberries, which her aunts would mix with whipped fat to make a special treat called *akutuq*—in colloquial English, Eskimo ice cream.

Now Cochran directs the Alaska Native Science Commission, which promotes research on native cultures and the health and environmental issues that affect them. She sits at her keyboard in Anchorage, a bustling city offering fare from Taco Bell to French cuisine. But at home Cochran keeps a freezer filled with fish, seal, walrus, reindeer, and whale meat, sent by her family up north, and she and her husband fish and go berry picking—"sometimes a challenge in Anchorage," she adds, laughing. "I eat fifty-fifty," she explains, half traditional, half regular American.

No one, not even residents of the northernmost villages on Earth, eats an entirely traditional northern diet anymore. Even the groups we came to know as Eskimo—which include the Inupiat and the Yupiks of Alaska, the Canadian Inuit and Inuvialuit, Inuit Greenlanders, and the Siberian Yupiks—have probably seen more changes in their diet in a lifetime than their ancestors did over thousands of years. The closer people live to towns and the more access they have to stores and cash-paying jobs, the more likely they are to have westernized their eating. And with westernization, at least on the North American continent, comes processed foods and cheap carbohydrates—Crisco, Tang, soda, cookies, chips, pizza, fries. "The young and urbanized," says Harriet Kuhnlein, director of the Centre for Indigenous Peoples' Nutrition and Environment at McGill University in Montreal, "are increasingly into fast food." So much so that type 2 diabetes, obesity, and other diseases of Western civilization are becoming causes for concern there too.

Today, when diet books top the best-seller list and nobody seems sure of what to eat to stay healthy, it's surprising to learn how well the Eskimo did on a high-protein, high-fat diet. Shaped by glacial temperatures, stark landscapes, and protracted winters, the traditional Eskimo diet had little in the way of plant food, no agricultural or dairy products, and was unusually low in carbohydrates. Mostly people subsisted on what they hunted and fished. Inland dwellers took advantage of caribou feeding on tundra mosses, lichens, and plants too tough for humans to stomach (though predigested vegetation in the animals' paunches became dinner as well). Coastal people exploited the sea. The main nutritional challenge was avoiding starvation in late winter if primary meat sources became too scarce or lean.

These foods hardly make up the "balanced" diet most of us grew up with, and they look nothing like the mix of grains, fruits, vegetables, meat, eggs, and dairy we're accustomed to seeing in conventional food pyramid diagrams. How could such a diet possibly be adequate? How did people get along on little else but fat and animal protein?

The diet of the Far North shows that there are no essential foods—only essential nutrients.

What the diet of the Far North illustrates, says Harold Draper, a biochemist and expert in Eskimo nutrition, is that there are no essential foods—only essential nutrients. And humans can get those nutrients from diverse and eye-opening sources.

One might, for instance, imagine gross vitamin deficiencies arising from a diet with scarcely any fruits and vegetables. What furnishes vitamin A, vital for eyes and bones? We derive much of ours from colorful plant foods, constructing it from pigmented plant precursors called carotenoids (as in carrots). But vitamin A, which is oil soluble, is also plentiful in the oils of cold-water fishes and sea mammals, as well as in the animals' livers, where fat is processed. These dietary staples also provide vitamin D, another oil-soluble vitamin needed for bones. Those of us living in temperate and tropical climates, on the other hand, usually make vitamin D indirectly by exposing skin to strong sun—hardly an option in the Arctic winter—and by consuming fortified cow's milk, to which the indigenous northern groups had little access until recent decades and often don't tolerate all that well.

As for vitamin C, the source in the Eskimo diet was long a mystery. Most animals can synthesize their own vitamin C, or ascorbic acid, in their livers, but humans are among the exceptions, along with other primates and oddballs like guinea pigs and bats. If we don't ingest enough of it, we fall apart from scurvy, a gruesome connective-tissue disease. In the United States today we can get ample supplies from orange juice, citrus fruits, and fresh vegetables. But vitamin C oxidizes with time; getting enough from a ship's provisions was tricky for early 18th- and 19th-century voyagers to the polar regions. Scurvy—joint pain, rotting gums, leaky blood vessels, physical and mental degeneration—plagued European and U.S. expeditions even in the 20th century. However, Arctic peoples living on fresh fish and meat were free of the disease.

Impressed, the explorer Vilhjalmur Stefansson adopted an Eskimo-style diet for five years during the two Arctic expeditions he led between 1908 and 1918. "The thing to do is to find your antiscorbutics where you are," he wrote. "Pick them up as you go." In 1928, to convince skeptics, he and a young colleague spent a year on an Americanized version of the diet under medical supervision at Bellevue Hospital in New York City. The pair ate steaks, chops, organ meats like brain and liver, poultry, fish, and fat with gusto. "If you have some fresh meat in your diet every day and don't overcook it," Stefansson declared triumphantly, "there will be enough C from that source alone to prevent scurvy."

In fact, all it takes to ward off scurvy is a daily dose of 10 milligrams, says Karen Fediuk, a consulting dietitian and former graduate student of Harriet Kuhnlein's who did her master's thesis on vitamin C. (That's far less than the U.S. recommended daily allowance of 75 to 90 milligrams—75 for women, 90 for men.) Native foods easily supply those 10 milligrams of scurvy prevention, especially when organ meats—preferably raw—are on the menu. For a study published with Kuhnlein in 2002, Fediuk compared the vitamin C content of 100-gram (3.55-ounce) samples of foods eaten by Inuit women living in the Canadian Arctic: Raw caribou liver supplied almost 24 milligrams, seal brain close to 15 milligrams, and raw kelp more than 28 milligrams. Still higher levels were found in whale skin and muktuk.

As you might guess from its antiscorbutic role, vitamin C is crucial for the synthesis of connective tissue, including the matrix of skin. "Wherever collagen's made, you can expect vitamin C," says Kuhnlein. Thick skinned, chewy, and collagen rich, raw muktuk can serve up an impressive 36 milligrams in a 100-gram piece, according to Fediuk's analyses. "Weight for weight, it's as good as orange juice," she says. Traditional Inuit practices like freezing meat and fish and frequently eating them raw, she notes, conserve vitamin C, which is easily cooked off and lost in food processing.

Hunter-gatherer diets like those eaten by these northern groups and other traditional diets based on nomadic herding or subsistence farming are among the older approaches to human eating. Some of these eating plans might seem strange to us—diets centered around milk, meat, and blood among the East African pastoralists, enthusiastic tuber eating by the Quechua living in the High Andes, the staple use of the mongongo nut in the southern African !Kung—but all proved resourceful adaptations to particular eco-niches. No people, though, may have been forced to push the nutritional envelope further than those living at Earth's frozen extremes. The unusual makeup of the far-northern diet led Loren Cordain, a professor of evolutionary nutrition at Colorado State University at Fort Collins, to make an intriguing observation.

Four years ago, Cordain reviewed the macronutrient content (protein, carbohydrates, fat) in the diets of 229 hunter-gatherer groups listed in a series of journal articles collectively known as the Ethnographic Atlas. These are some of the oldest surviving human diets. In general, hunter-gatherers tend to eat more animal protein than we do in our standard Western diet, with its reliance on agriculture and carbohydrates derived from grains and starchy plants. Lowest of all in carbohydrate, and highest in combined fat and protein, are the diets of peoples living in the Far North, where they make up for fewer plant foods with extra fish. What's equally striking, though, says Cordain, is that these meat-and-fish diets also exhibit a natural "protein ceiling." Protein accounts for no more than 35 to 40 percent of their total calories, which suggests to him that's all the protein humans can comfortably handle.

Wild-animal fats are different from other fats. Farm animals typically have lots of highly saturated fat.

This ceiling, Cordain thinks, could be imposed by the way we process protein for energy. The simplest, fastest way to make energy is to convert carbohydrates into glucose, our body's primary fuel. But if the body is out of carbs, it can burn fat, or if necessary, break down protein. The name given to the convoluted business of making glucose from protein is gluconeogenesis. It takes place in the liver, uses a dizzying slew of enzymes, and creates nitrogen waste that has to be converted into urea and disposed of through the kidneys. On a truly traditional diet, says Draper, recalling his studies in the 1970s, Arctic people had plenty of protein but little carbohydrate, so they often relied on gluconeogenesis. Not only did they have bigger livers to handle the additional work but their urine volumes were also typically larger to get rid of the extra urea. Nonetheless, there appears to be a limit on how much protein the human liver can safely cope with: Too much overwhelms the liver's waste-disposal system, leading to protein poisoning—nausea, diarrhea, wasting, and death.

Whatever the metabolic reason for this syndrome, says John Speth, an archaeologist at the University of Michigan's Museum of Anthropology, plenty of evidence shows that hunters through the ages avoided protein excesses, discarding fat-depleted animals even when food was scarce. Early pioneers and trappers in North America encountered what looks like a similar affliction, sometimes referred to as rabbit starvation because rabbit meat is notoriously lean. Forced to subsist on fat-deficient meat, the men would gorge themselves, yet wither away. Protein can't be the sole source of energy for humans, concludes Cordain. Anyone eating a meaty diet that is low in carbohydrates must have fat as well.

Stefansson had arrived at this conclusion, too, while living among the Copper Eskimo. He recalled how he and his Eskimo companions had become quite ill after weeks of eating "caribou so skinny that there was no appreciable fat behind the eyes or in the marrow." Later he agreed to repeat the miserable experience at Bellevue Hospital, for science's sake, and for a while ate nothing but defatted meat. "The symptoms brought on at Bellevue by an incomplete meat diet [lean without fat] were exactly the same as in the Arctic . . . diarrhea and a feeling of general baffling discomfort," he wrote. He was restored with a fat fix but "had lost considerable weight." For the remainder of his year on meat, Stefansson tucked into his rations of chops and steaks with fat intact. "A normal meat diet is not a high-protein diet," he pronounced. "We were really getting three-quarters of our calories from fat." (Fat is more than twice as calorie dense as protein or carbohydrate, but even so, that's a lot of lard. A typical U.S diet provides about 35 percent of its calories from fat.)

Stefansson dropped 10 pounds on his meat-and-fat regimen and remarked on its "slenderizing" aspect, so perhaps it's no surprise he's been co-opted as a posthumous poster boy for Atkins-type diets. No discussion about diet these days can avoid Atkins. Even some researchers interviewed for this article couldn't resist referring to the Inuit way of eating as the "original Atkins." "Superficially, at a macronutrient level, the two diets certainly look similar," allows Samuel Klein, a nutrition researcher at Washington University in St. Louis, who's attempting to study how Atkins stacks up against conventional weight-loss diets. Like the Inuit diet, Atkins is low in carbohydrates and very high in fat. But numerous researchers, including Klein, point out that there are profound differences between the two diets, beginning with the type of meat and fat eaten.

Fats have been demonized in the United States, says Eric Dewailly, a professor of preventive medicine at Laval University in Quebec. But all fats are not created equal. This lies at the heart of a paradox—the Inuit paradox, if you will. In the Nunavik villages in northern Quebec, adults over 40 get almost half their calories from native foods, says Dewailly, and they don't die of heart attacks at nearly the same rates as other Canadians or Americans. Their cardiac death rate is about half of ours, he says. As someone who looks for links between diet and cardiovascular health, he's intrigued by that reduced risk. Because the traditional Inuit diet is "so restricted," he says, it's easier to study than the famously heart-healthy Mediterranean diet, with its cornucopia of vegetables, fruits, grains, herbs, spices, olive oil, and red wine.

A key difference in the typical Nunavik Inuit's diet is that more than 50 percent of the calories in Inuit native foods come from fats. Much more important, the fats come from wild animals.

Wild-animal fats are different from both farm-animal fats and processed fats, says Dewailly. Farm animals, cooped up and stuffed with agricultural grains (carbohydrates) typically have lots of solid, highly saturated fat. Much of our processed food is also riddled with solid fats, or so-called trans fats, such as the reengineered vegetable oils and shortenings cached in baked goods and snacks. "A lot of the packaged food on supermarket shelves contains them. So do commercial french fries," Dewailly adds.

Trans fats are polyunsaturated vegetable oils tricked up to make them more solid at room temperature. Manufacturers do this by hydrogenating the oils—adding extra hydrogen atoms to their molecular structures—which "twists" their shapes. Dewailly makes twisting sound less like a chemical transformation than a perversion, an act of public-health sabotage: "These man-made fats are dangerous, even worse for the heart than saturated fats." They not only lower high-density lipoprotein cholesterol (HDL, the "good" cholesterol) but they also raise low-density lipoprotein cholesterol (LDL, the "bad" cholesterol) and triglycerides, he says. In the process, trans fats set the stage for heart attacks because they lead to the increase of fatty buildup in artery walls.

Wild animals that range freely and eat what nature intended, says Dewailly, have fat that is far more healthful. Less of their fat is saturated, and more of it is in the monounsaturated form (like olive oil). What's more, cold-water fishes and sea mammals are particularly rich in polyunsaturated fats called n-3 fatty acids or omega-3 fatty acids. These fats appear to benefit the heart and vascular system. But the polyunsaturated fats in most Americans' diets are the omega-6 fatty acids supplied by vegetable oils. By contrast, whale blubber consists of 70 percent monounsaturated fat and close to 30 percent omega-3s, says Dewailly.

Dieting is the price we pay for too little exercise and too much mass-produced food.

Omega-3s evidently help raise HDL cholesterol, lower triglycerides, and are known for anticlotting effects. (Ethnographers have remarked on an Eskimo propensity for nosebleeds.) These fatty acids are believed to protect the heart from life-threatening arrhythmias that can lead to sudden cardiac death. And like a "natural aspirin," adds Dewailly, omega-3 polyunsaturated fats help put a damper on runaway inflammatory processes, which play a part in atherosclerosis, arthritis, diabetes, and other so-called diseases of civilization.

You can be sure, however, that Atkins devotees aren't routinely eating seal and whale blubber. Besides the acquired taste problem, their commerce is extremely restricted in the United States by the Marine Mammal Protection Act, says Bruce Holub, a nutritional biochemist in the department of human biology and nutritional sciences at the University of Guelph in Ontario.

"In heartland America it's probable they're not eating in an Eskimo-like way," says Gary Foster, clinical director of the Weight and Eating Disorders Program at the Pennsylvania School of Medicine. Foster, who describes himself as open-minded about Atkins, says he'd nonetheless worry if people saw the diet as a green light to eat all the butter and bacon—saturated fats—they want. Just before rumors surfaced that Robert Atkins had heart and weight problems when he died, Atkins officials themselves were stressing saturated fat should account for no more than 20 percent of dieters' calories. This seems to be a clear retreat from the diet's original don't-count-the-calories approach to bacon and butter and its happy exhortations to "plow into those prime ribs." Furthermore, 20 percent of calories from saturated fats is *double* what most nutritionists advise. Before plowing into those prime ribs, readers of a recent edition of the *Dr. Atkins' New Diet Revolution* are urged to take omega-3 pills to help protect their hearts. "If you watch carefully," says Holub wryly, "you'll see many popular U.S. diets have quietly added omega-3 pills, in the form of fish oil or flaxseed capsules, as supplements."

Needless to say, the subsistence diets of the Far North are not "dieting." Dieting is the price we pay for too little exercise and too much mass-produced food. Northern diets were a way of life in places too cold for agriculture, where food, whether hunted, fished, or foraged, could not be taken for granted. They were about keeping weight on.

This is not to say that people in the Far North were fat: Subsistence living requires exercise—hard physical work. Indeed, among the good reasons for native people to maintain their old way of eating, as far as it's possible today, is that it provides a hedge against obesity, type 2 diabetes, and heart disease. Unfortunately, no place on Earth is immune to the spreading taint of growth and development. The very well-being of the northern food chain is coming under threat from global warming, land development, and industrial pollutants in the marine environment. "I'm a pragmatist," says Cochran, whose organization is involved in pollution monitoring and disseminating food-safety information to native villages. "Global warming we don't have control over. But we can, for example, do cleanups of military sites in Alaska or of communication cables leaching lead into fish-spawning areas. We can help communities make informed food choices. A young woman of childbearing age may choose not to eat certain organ meats that concentrate contaminants. As individuals, we do have options. And eating our salmon and our seal is still a heck of a better option than pulling something processed that's full of additives off a store shelf."

Not often in our industrial society do we hear someone speak so familiarly about "our" food animals. We don't talk of "our pig" and "our beef." We've lost that creature feeling, that sense of kinship with food sources. "You're taught to think in boxes," says Cochran. "In our culture the connectivity between humans, animals, plants, the land they live on, and the air they share is ingrained in us from birth.

"You truthfully can't separate the way we get our food from the way we live," she says. "How we get our food is intrinsic to our culture. It's how we pass on our values and knowledge to the young. When you go out with your aunts and uncles to hunt or to gather, you learn to smell the air, watch the wind, understand the way the ice moves, know the land. You get to know where to pick which plant and what animal to take."

"It's part, too, of your development as a person. You share food with your community. You show respect to your elders by offering them the first catch. You give thanks to the animal that gave up its life for your sustenance. So you get all the physical activity of harvesting your own food, all the social activity of sharing and preparing it, and all the spiritual aspects as well," says Cochran. "You certainly don't get all that, do you, when you buy prepackaged food from a store."

"That's why some of us here in Anchorage are working to protect what's ours, so that others can continue to live back home in the villages," she adds. "Because if we don't take care of our food, it won't be there for us in the future. And if we lose our foods, we lose who we are." The word Inupiat means "the real people." "That's who we are," says Cochran.

Critical Thinking

1. What kinds of diseases are on the increase among the Inuit and why?

2. How does their traditional high-protein, high-fat diet compare with the "balanced diet" most of us grew up with? What does this mean, according to Harold Draper?

3. What are the contrasting sources of vitamins A, D, and C between our diet and the diet of the Inuit? What is the advantage of eating meat and fish raw?

4. What is a "protein ceiling?" How did hunter-gatherers cope with this problem?

5. Where do the more healthful fats (monounsaturated and omega-3 fatty acids) come from? What are their benefits?

6. Why is it that Atkins-dieters are not really eating in an "Eskimo-like way?"

7. What are the differences between the subsistence diets of the Far North and "dieting?"

8. Were people of the Far North fat? Why not? In what ways did the old way of eating protect them?

9. How is the northern food chain threatened?

10. In what sense is there a kinship with food sources in the Far North that our industrial societies do not have? Why is it also a part of one's development as a person?

From *Discover*, October 2004, pp. 48, 50, 52, 54. Copyright © 2004 by Patricia Gadsby. Reprinted by permission of the author.

Ties That Bind

Hopi gift culture and its first encounter with the United States.

PETER M. WHITELEY

In 1852, shortly after the United States had nominally annexed Hopi country, in northern Arizona, the Hopi people arranged for a diplomatic packet to reach President Millard Fillmore at the White House. Part message and part magical gift, the packet was delivered by a delegation of five prominent men from another Pueblo tribe, the Tewas of Tesuque Pueblo in New Mexico, who wanted to gain legal protection from Anglo and Hispanic settlers who were encroaching on their lands. The delegation traveled for nearly three months, on horseback, steamboat, and train, from Santa Fe to Washington, D.C., more than 2,600 miles away. The five men spoke fluent Spanish, the dominant European language of the region at the time—which made them ideally suited to convey the gift packet and its message to the president.

At the time, no U.S. government official had visited the Hopi (and few would do so before the 1890s). Their "unique diplomatic pacquet," in the words of the nineteenth-century ethnologist Henry Rowe Schoolcraft, offered "friendship and intercommunication . . . opening, symbolically, a road from the Moqui [Hopi] country to Washington." The packet was in two parts. The first part comprised two *pahos,* or prayer-sticks, at either end of a long cotton cord, dyed for part of its length. Separating the dyed from the undyed part of the cord were six varicolored feathers, knotted into a bunch. The *pahos* "represent the Moqui [Hopi] people and the President [respectively]," Schoolcraft wrote; "the cord is the road which separates them; the [bunch of feathers] tied to the cord is the meeting point."

As well as encoding a message, the *pahos* were an offering of a kind that Hopi deities such as Taawa, the Sun god, traditionally like to receive. By giving the president *pahos* worthy of the Sun, the Hopi signaled their expectation that he would reciprocate. Just as the Sun, on receiving the appropriate offerings, would send rain clouds for sustaining life and growth, so, too, the president would send protection for Hopi lives and lands—in this instance, protection from assaults by neighboring tribes such as the Navajo.

The second part of the packet comprised a cornstalk cigarette filled with tobacco ("to be smoked by the president") and a small cornhusk package that enclosed honey-soaked cornmeal. According to the Tesuque delegation, the honey-meal package was "a charm to call down rain from heaven." When the president smoked the cigarette, he would exhale clouds of smoke, which would sympathetically attract the clouds of the sky. Then, when he chewed the cornmeal and spat the wild honey on ground that needed rain, the Tesuque statement concluded, "the Moquis assure him that it [the rain] will come."

In sum, the packet was three things at once: message, offering, and gift of magical power. In conveying those elements, the Hopi sought to open diplomatic relations with the U.S.

But their intent appears to have been lost on their recipient. As so often happens when two cultures make contact, deep misunderstandings can arise: What does a gift mean? What, if anything, does the gift giver expect in return? Do the giver and the recipient both assign the same value to the gift? In twenty-five years of ethnographic fieldwork with the Hopi, it has been my goal to learn something of their history and culture. Recently I turned my attention to certain important events, such as the Millard Fillmore episode, that might shed light on how Hopi society changed as the U.S. developed. In that context Hopi gift giving and the ways it functions as a pillar of Hopi social organization have been central to my studies. One lesson of my work shines through: When nations exchange gifts, all the parties would do best to keep in mind the old adage, "It's the thought that counts."

Given the differences between Hopi and Western traditions and culture, perhaps it is not surprising that the Hopi idea of "gift" is only loosely equivalent to the Western one. In 1852 the Hopi people were still little affected by outside populations, and Hopi land use spread across much of northern Arizona and even into southern Utah. At that time, the Hopi lifestyle was traditional, based on farming, foraging, and some pastoralism. Even today, important elements of the subsistence economy persist, though wage labor and small business provide supplemental income.

The Hopi typically divide their work according to gender. Work done by men (such as farming and harvesting of crops) is perceived as a gift to the women; work done by women (such as gardening, gathering of piñon nuts, grasses, wild fruits, berries, and the like) is perceived as a gift to the men. Women also own and manage the distribution of their household's goods and crops. In fact, Hopi women control most of the material economic life, whereas Hopi men largely control the ritual and spiritual aspects.

The Hopi take part in an elaborate cycle of religious ceremonies, to which a range of specialized offices and privileges is attached. But individuals gain those distinctive social positions not through material wealth but rather through gender and kinship relations, which are ordered in a matrilineal manner. In fact, clan heads and chiefs of religious societies are typically worse off materially than the average member of the clan. Hopi leaders are supposed to be materially poor, and a wealthy individual is often criticized as *qahopi,* un-Hopi, for failing to share. Wealth and status among the Hopi is thus phrased in ritual terms: a poor person is one without ceremonial prerogatives, not one without money. So averse are the Hopi to material accumulation that in May 2004, for the second time, they voted against casino gambling, despite substantial poverty on the reservation.

Does such a primacy of value placed on ceremonial roles explain the evanescent nature of the gift given to President Fillmore? In what world of meaning did the packet represent great value? Indeed, what's in a gift?

Anthropologists have been making hay of that last question ever since 1925, when the French anthropologist Marcel Mauss published his groundbreaking *Essai sur le Don* (translated into English as "The Gift"). Mauss convincingly argued that in small-scale societies (10,000 or fewer persons) gifts are "total social facts." What he meant is that, in gift- or barter-based social systems, divisions of social life into discrete domains—such as economy, politics, law, or religion—are meaningless; each sphere interpenetrates and overlaps the others.

As in strict barter, an exchange in Hopi culture that begins by making a gift to someone does not involve money, but it does require reciprocity. Thus goods, services, or knowledge "given" to an individual or a group are answered with something of equivalent value. "Gifts" develop an interconnectedness between Hopi individuals in a way that outright purchases cannot. Furthermore, the Hopi offer gifts in a much broader range of circumstances than people in Western cultures do, and the value of those gifts extends to the religious realm, tying individuals and groups to each other and to the realm of the spirits.

Probably the key to understanding a gift-based system such as that of the Hopi is to recognize that such systems are built on kinship. "Kinship"—the godzilla that has driven multitudes of college students screaming from anthropology 101—is, in this regard at least, straightforward. It means simply that the great majority of human social activity is framed in terms of reciprocal family ties. Where all personal relationships are cast within the "kinship idiom" there are no members of the society who are not kin to me, nor I to them.

Kinship terms encode behavioral expectations as well as familial role. As anthropologists never tire of saying, such terms are primarily social, not biological: obviously if I call fifteen women "mother," as the average Hopi can do, I do not assume that each woman physically gave birth to me. But my "mothers" all have rights and duties in relation to me. And, reciprocally, I have duties and rights with respect to them: in fact, their duties are my rights, and my duties are their rights in the relationship. That is what reciprocity is all about. You give me food, I plant your cornfield, to give a crude example. But, in a kinship society, such a basic structure of mutual expectations forms the foundation for an entire apparatus of courtesy and manners, deference and respect, familiarity or distance. Those expectations are concretely expressed by gifts—spontaneous and planned, routine and special, trivial and grand. Gifts are thus communications in a language of social belonging.

So averse are the Hopi to material accumulation that in May 2004 they voted against casino gambling.

So-called gift economies entail a certain kind of sociality, or sense of what it means to belong to a community. In such an economy, one gives a gift to mark social relations built on kinship and altruism, but without the expectation of direct repayment. According to some arguments, gifts are also given to foster a sense of community, as well as sustainable interrelations with the local environment. In fact, in some respects the giver still "owns" some part of the gift, and it is the intangible connection between the two parties, mediated by the gift, that forms the basis of interpersonal relationships.

In contrast, in exchange economies, commodities dominate social interchange. Competitive markets, governed by the profit motive, connect buyer and seller, and social relations are characterized by individualism. A gift, once given, belongs entirely to the recipient; only when the item given has sentimental value does it keep the bond between giver and recipient alive.

That is not to say the Hopi did not engage in the more impersonal, "Western" forms of material exchange. In the Hopi language, as in English, several words describe how an item is transferred from one person to another: *maqa* ("to give"); *hùuya* ("to barter or trade"); and *tu'i* ("to buy"). Those words all antedate the arrival of Europeans—and anthropological classifications. Barter and purchase, as well as gifts, have all long been present in Hopi life. Furthermore, gift exchange in the West can also function as it does among the Hopi, as part of kinship obligations or ordinary social life.

What is distinctive about Hopi custom is the fact that the gift economy is responsible for the great majority of exchanges. Furthermore, there is no such thing as a free gift. The strong interpersonal bonds created by a gift make giving almost de rigueur at ceremonial events. Gifts, particularly gifts of food or utensils, are transmitted during ceremonies of personal milestones (at a birth or a marriage), as well as at public gatherings.

For example, at the annual so-called basket dances, girls and women distribute a variety of objects they have collected for the occasion. The dances illustrate the Hopi lack of acquisitiveness. The women form a semicircle and dance and sing; after each song two girls fling gifts into the crowd of men assembled outside the circle. Among the gifts are valuable baskets and buckskins, though inexpensive utensils and manufactured items are also popular. Each man zealously grabs for the flying objects, and if two men happen to catch the same item, both wrestle with the object, often until it has been totally destroyed.

Although gift giving has been a pillar of Hopi society, trade has also flourished in Hopi towns since prehistory, with a network that extended from the Great Plains to the Pacific Coast, and from the Great Basin, centered on present-day Nevada and Utah, to the Valley of Mexico. Manufactured goods, raw materials, and gems drove the trade, supplemented by exotic items such as parrots. The Hopis were producers as well, manufacturing large quantities of cotton cloth and ceramics for the trade. To this day, interhousehold trade and barter, especially for items of traditional manufacture for ceremonial use (such as basketry, bows, cloth, moccasins, pottery, and rattles), remain vigorous.

For hundreds of years, at least, the Hopi traded with the Rio Grande Pueblos to acquire turquoise, *heishi* (shell necklaces), and buckskins; one long string of *heishi,* for instance, was worth two Hopi woven cotton mantas. Similarly, songs, dances, and other ritual elements were often exchanged for an agreed-upon equivalent.

The high value the Hopi placed on the items they acquired by trade correlate, in many respects, with the value Europeans placed on them. Silver, for instance, had high value among both Westerners and Native Americans as money and as jewelry. *Siiva,* the Hopi word both for "money" and for "silver jewelry" was borrowed directly from the English word "silver." Paper money itself was often treated the way traditional resources were: older Hopi men bundled it and stored it in trunks, stacked by denomination.

It was not until the 1890s, however, that silver jewelry began to be produced by the Hopi. A man named Sikyatala learned silversmithing from a Zuni man, and his craftsmanship quickly made silver jewelry into treasured adornments. Those among the Hopi who cared for it too much, though, were criticized for vanity; one nickname, Siisiva ("[wearing] a lot of silver"), characterized a fop.

Some jewels, such as turquoise, traditionally had a sacred value, beyond adornment. Even today, flakes of turquoise are occasionally offered to the spirits in religious ceremonies. Turquoise and shell necklaces appear in many ritual settings, frequently adorning the costumes of *katsinas* (ceremonial figures) and performers in the social dances.

How much the Hopi value turquoise becomes apparent toward the close of a ritual enactment known as the Clown Ceremony. The "clowns"—more than mere entertainers—represent unbridled human impulses. Warrior *katsinas* arrive to punish the clowns for licentious behavior and teach them good Hopi behavior: modest and quiet in conduct, careful and decorous in speech, abstemious and sharing about food, and unselfish about other things. The clowns fail miserably (and hilariously) at their lessons. Eventually the warrior chief presents an ultimatum: stop flaunting chaos or die. The clown chief then offers him a turquoise necklace as a "mortgage" on the clowns' lives. The warrior chief accepts, the clowns receive a lesser punishment, and community life goes on—not with perfection, but with a human mixture of the virtuous and the flawed.

In Hopi tradition, the first clan among the Hopi, and the one that supplied the *kikmongwi,* or village chief, was Bear. When other clans arrived, their leaders approached the *kikmongw*i to request entry into the village. He asked what they had to contribute, such as a beneficial ceremony. So challenged, each clan performed its ceremony, and if successful, say, in producing rain, its members were invited to live in the village, assigned an area for housing, and granted agricultural lands to work in the valley below. In return, the clan agreed to perform its ceremony, as part of a cycle of ceremonies throughout the year, and to intermarry with the other clans of the community, a practice called exogamous marriage. In that way, the Snake clan brought the Snake Dance, the Badger clan introduced principal katsina ceremonies, and the Fire clan brought the Warriors' society to the Hopi village. The villages thus came to be made up of mutually interdependent clans.

One of the essential principles expressed here, and the very cornerstone of Hopi society and sociality, is the exchange of mutually beneficial gifts—ceremonies for land, people in exogamous marriage—and the relationships reconfigured by those exchanges. And the same model is extended to the supernatural world: the gods must be propitiated with offerings of ritual gifts, and thus reminded of their dependence upon and obligations to mortal people.

The items sent to President Fillmore conform to the archetypal Hopi offering. Seeking to incorporate the president into the Hopi world, the appropriate strategy was to give him valuable presents that sought something in return, and to make sure he understood what that meant. Addressing him with prayer-sticks the way they might address the Sun father, the delegation sought to engage him within the gifting and kinship idiom. The instructions delivered with the packet—even across a succession of translations—spoke clearly of the Hopi intent. As with the turquoise mortgage of the *katsina* clowns, the idea of reciprocity is central. If the president wants more of, say, rain-magic, he must give back: he must receive the gift and its political proposal, and provide something in return.

Alas, the magico-religious sensibility of the Hopi worldview and the offer of serial reciprocity clashed with Manifest Destiny and the assimilationist ideology of Fillmore's presidency. Historical records make it clear that he did not smoke the cigarette, nor chew nor spit the honey-meal, and, so far as we know, he sent no formal reply. None of the objects has survived.

What the five men of the Tesuque delegation received no doubt perplexed them as much as the packet they delivered perplexed the president: Each man was given a Millard Fillmore peace medal, a Western-style business suit, and a daguerreotype portrait (all now lost, as well). They also got a tour of standard destinations in Washington, including the Patent Office and the Smithsonian Institution, where they were introduced to the "wonders of electricity," according to a contemporary newspaper account in the *Daily National Intelligencer.* In their meeting with Fillmore they heard the president say he "hoped the Great Spirit would bless and sustain them till they again returned to the bosom of their families."

Certainly Fillmore expressed the goodwill of the U.S. toward the Pueblos in general and to the Tesuque party in particular—who, in all probability, conveyed that sentiment to the Hopi. But the dissonance between gift and exchange economies helps explain why the Hopis did not achieve their goals. (The U.S. did not protect the Hopi from intrusions by the Navajo or by anyone else.)

The Hopi sought to embrace the president in their own sphere of sociality and mutuality—to extend kinship to him. But in a social system like the president's, where gifts are not total social facts, the political belongs in a separate domain from the religious or the economic, and kinship is secondary. The gift of a jeweled sword, for instance, might have impressed Fillmore more, but for the Hopi, its strictly symbolic value—as an item for display, but with no political, religious, or social value—would not have ensured a return, a social connection built on mutual exchange. More, by Hopi standards, presenting such a gift might have seemed inhospitable and materialistic, indeed, undiplomatic and even selfish. Thus does understanding fail between nations.

Critical Thinking

1. What was the intent of the diplomatic packet sent to President Millard Fillmore by the Hopi?

2. Describe Hopi lifestyle and attitudes toward material wealth.

3. What is the significance of a "gift" in Hopi culture?

4. In what sense is Hopi kinship social, not biological?

5. What is the difference between a gift economy and an exchange economy? How does the "gift" differ in these two contexts?

6. What are the distinctive qualities of gifts in Hopi culture?

7. Although the Hopi do trade, what indications are there that exchanges are primarily ceremonial and are conducted as gifts?

8. Why did the Hopi not achieve their goal of reciprocity with President Fillmore?

From *Natural History*, November 2004, pp. 26–31. Copyright © 2004 by Natural History Magazine. Reprinted by permission.

Cell Phones, Sharing, and Social Status in an African Society

Daniel Jordan Smith

Contemporary processes of globalization have stimulated many anthropologists to begin asking new research questions. One important area of innovative research pertains to the global spread of technology and its influence on local people, practices, values, and behaviors. Globalization involves the worldwide transfer of technology, capital, industry, people, and cultural ideas. It has made the world a smaller place, but it has also increased social inequalities across the "digital divide."

In the twentieth century, radio and television played powerful roles in creating linkages between previously disconnected areas of the world. Without a doubt, new mass media brought the signs, symbols, images, and cultural values of the industrialized "First World" to people and communities in poorer "Third World" regions. The globalization of technology is not a top-down, unidirectional process. New technologies create new ways in which small groups of people can shape the ideas, values, political opinions, and even the actions of large groups of people within a particular town, district, country, or world region.

Recent technological developments are influencing people and communities in new ways, raising new research questions for anthropologists. One such development is the Internet, although on a global scale fewer people have access to that technology than the topic of this selection: cell phones. Like radio and television before them, cell phones create new and unprecedented opportunities for communication across distances. As this selection vividly demonstrates, the ways in which people use cell phones are powerfully influenced by local ideas, values, customs, and practices. In other words, global processes always take place within local contexts. Both the symbolic meaning and the social rules for using cell phones change in different cultural contexts.

Introduction

On July 19, 2004, the popular BBC Africa Service morning news program, *Network Africa,* carried a curious story from its Nigeria correspondent. He described a recent epidemic of rumors circulating in the country, purporting that anyone who answered calls on their cellular telephones originating from several specific numbers risked madness, and even death. I had heard a similar story in the previous few days from dozens of friends and acquaintances in and around the towns of Owerri and Umuahia in southeastern Nigeria, where I was conducting research. Ironically, cell phone usage around the country surged in the wake of the rumors, as people phoned and sent text messages to friends and relatives, warning them of the "killer numbers."

Once the popular rumors circulated widely, Nigerian newspapers carried stories printing some of the suspected numbers and incorporating quotations from citizens who allegedly witnessed the effects of these sinister calls (Akinsuyi 2004). But the newspapers also published statements from spokespersons for the country's major mobile telephone service providers, denying that such killer numbers existed (Ikhemuemhe 2004). Further, they published interviews with government authorities and university scientists disputing the technological feasibility of transmitting witchcraft through cell phones. Radio call-in programs and television talk shows buzzed with debate about the story, mesmerizing the nation for the better part of two weeks. Eventually, popular attention faded, as it had with regard to a previous rumor suggesting that men who carried cell phones in their pockets or strapped them to their belts risked becoming infertile.

The rumors that mobile phones might be implicated in infertility, madness, and murder are a testament to how dramatically this new technology has affected Nigeria. A few elite Nigerians had access to older cellular telephone technologies beginning in the 1990s, but the number of such phones was minuscule. The introduction of the Global System for Mobile Communications (GSM) technology to Nigeria in 2001 and the liberalization of Nigeria's previously government-controlled telecommunications industry transformed cell phones from an extreme rarity into an everyday technology to which literally millions of ordinary citizens have access. When GSM technology was first introduced in Nigeria, the country had only approximately 500,000 landlines for over 100 million people (Obadare 2004), a number which had not increased significantly in many years. By the end of 2004, less than four years after the first GSM cellular phones and services went on sale to the Nigerian public, the country had over seven million subscribers (Mobile Africa 2005), with some recent estimates putting the number of mobile phones users in Nigeria at over eleven million (PANA 2005).

In addition, millions more people without their own phones were provided easy access to cell phone service, as individual cell phone owners became small-scale entrepreneurs, converting their personal phones into informal businesses. By the time the BBC story was broadcast, thousands of call centers, most with just one or two phones and a single attendant, dotted Nigeria's landscape. Every major city and many small towns are now connected, and countless rural and urban communities that have no running water and little or no electricity service are integrated into the country's vast and expanding mobile telephone network.

Cell phones have produced dramatic changes in communication in Nigeria, with many positive effects. Mobile phones have been integrated into long-standing patterns of social relationship, enabling Nigerians separated by great distances to continue to interact based on expectations of sharing and reciprocity. But just as important, they have become symbols of social status. Nigerians assert and express modern identities by purchasing, using, and publicly displaying the latest consumer commodities. Mastery of the new phone technology is a marker of being middle class, educated, and urban. Yet the reality is that cell phones represent a level of economic achievement that is out of reach to most Nigerians. The majority of new cell phone consumers experience the costs of usage as exorbitant, reinforcing the sense that middle-class status remains elusive. Thus, while the burgeoning popularity of cell phones in Nigeria, and throughout sub-Saharan Africa, represents the aspirations of ordinary people for better lives, this new technology exposes the pronounced and enduring nature of social inequality.

Cell Phone Economics

Owning and using a cell phone in Nigeria requires three primary investments: (1) buying a phone; (2) accessing service from one of the country's four major providers through the purchase of a SIM (Subscriber Identity Module) card that is installed in the back of the phone to connect it to the service network; and (3) procuring "recharge cards," through which call time is paid for by loading a unique pin number each time one wants to add credit to an individual account. While the phone and the SIM card are onetime acquisitions, access to service depends on the regular purchase of the recharge cards to load call time as previously purchased amounts are exhausted.

In 2005, new phones are available in Nigeria for as little as 6,000 naira (approximately forty-five U.S. dollars), and as much as 60,000 naira (over U.S. $450), depending on the brand, the model, and the complexity of features offered on the phone. The price of SIM cards declined dramatically in the past several years, to about five to ten dollars, with companies sometimes offering free SIM cards as part of periodic marketing campaigns. The vast majority of customers use the "pay as you go" recharge card system.

Most crucial from the perspective of ordinary Nigerians is the cost of calls themselves. As with every other feature of cell phone service, the cost of calls has declined significantly over the four years since GSM service was introduced. But the price of calls per minute and per second (a choice between these rates is now available to most consumers) is still expensive, relative to both Nigerians' purchasing power and the cost of cell phone service in other countries (Obadare 2004). Importantly, although incoming calls are free, every outgoing call is charged—there are no free minutes per month or at night and on weekends, though lower rates apply in off-peak hours. Further, recharge cards expire. Credit not utilized within a specified period of time is forever lost. For example, ten dollars of credit would typically need to be used within about two weeks.

Initially, when GSM cell phone service was first introduced, domestic calls cost approximately fifty naira (thirty-seven U.S. cents) per minute. Recently, the cost has declined to about twenty-five naira (nineteen cents) per minute, with the precise amount depending upon the volume of calls per month, whether the call is in or out of network, the time of day, and so on. Each of the country's four main service providers (Glomobile, Mtel, MTN, and Vmobile) offers a diverse range of service packages and special deals, but most consumers cannot afford to make enough calls to qualify for the plans that offer the cheapest calling rates. Indeed, an entire discourse of complaint about the high cost of cell phone calls has emerged in Nigeria (Obadare 2004). Popular reaction to the economics of personal cell phone use has generated a new lexicon and a growing repertoire of behaviors designed to mitigate the financial burdens of cell phone ownership.

"The Fire That Consumes Money"

In southeastern Nigeria, where I work, and where the predominant language is Igbo, the vernacular name for a cell phone is *oku na iri ego,* which translates literally as "the fire that consumes money." This popular local name reflects ordinary citizens' frustrations with the perceived exorbitant costs of cell phone calls. New linguistic turns of phrase and innovative social practices that have evolved with the proliferation of cell phone technology build on people's aggravation over the strain of cell phone ownership, but they also indicate the degree to which cell phone culture has taken root in everyday life.

Nigerians have adapted their cell phone usage to suit their economic circumstances, and some aspects of the service plans offered by the country's main providers are clearly designed to attract and keep customers who cannot afford to make a high volume of phone calls. For example, the Short Messaging Systems (SMS), through which customers can send "text messages," is extremely popular in Nigeria and typically costs only fifteen naira (about ten U.S. cents) per message. Text messages must be limited in size, usually no more than 160 characters. Text messaging is particularly popular with younger customers and it has generated its own lexicon of abbreviations, an economy of language that has also become part of Nigeria's youth culture, as it has in other settings (for literature on text messaging generally see Fox 2001; Dooring 2002; and Sylvia and Hady 2004).

Text messaging has become a common way for Nigerians who cannot afford regular phone calls to communicate using the new technology. But for older people, and even among young folks, using text messages too frequently without also calling can be interpreted as sign of unwillingness to spend money on a particular relationship—reflecting either stinginess or a lack of deep concern about the relationship or both. As a consequence, although text messaging is extremely popular, people are careful not to rely on it too exclusively, lest they become objects of criticism. In times of economic hardship, the willingness to spend money on a phone call is evidence of interest or commitment to a relationship, whether it is a friendship, a family tie, a business partnership, or a romance. The consequences of the microeconomics of cell phone use reflect the importance and the complexity of how issues of wealth, inequality, and status are negotiated in human relationships.

"Flash Me, I Flash You"

Other common practices besides text messaging illustrate the economics and micropolitics of cell phone behavior, and the importance of these behaviors in navigating issues of inequality in social relationships. For example, a major consequence of the fact that many cell phone owners cannot afford to maintain credit on a regular basis is the innovation of what Nigerians call "flashing." To "flash" someone means to call the recipient's line and allow the phone to ring just once, so that the incoming number is displayed to the recipient, but the caller hangs up before the recipient answers. This way, the recipient knows the number of the person trying to reach him or her, and hopefully has enough credit to call back. Flashing is possible because one can make a call without paying for it as long as no one picks up. Under the prevailing plans in Nigeria, it is possible to receive incoming calls even when one does not have any credit.

From my experience observing scores of friends and acquaintances receiving flashes, whether or not the recipient of the flash could identify the caller from the incoming number was not necessarily a good predictor of a callback. Sometimes knowledge of the identity of the incoming caller created the incentive to call back immediately, perhaps out of obligation, affection, or some prior awareness about the reason for the call. Conversely, on other occasions, knowledge of the identity of the caller had the opposite effect, the attitude being that anyone who had something important to communicate would find a way to pay for a call, even if only for a minute or two. People often refused to call back after a flash out of suspicion that the caller wanted the recipient to bear the cost of the conversation. Nevertheless, unidentified flashes often sparked curiosity, and people frequently responded to them.

Given that countless Nigerians who own cell phones are often in a position where credit is exhausted or very low, and therefore very precious, flashing can sometimes become a comical exchange in which no one wants to bear the costs of a call. In the Pidgin English that is often the lingua franca in Nigeria, people expressed the phenomenon of reciprocal flashing, in which no one was willing to pay for a call, with the phrase "flash me, I flash you." Mostly in good humor, friends frequently suspected each other of trying to transfer and defray the costs of communication through flashing. As a consequence, people sometimes tried to answer their phones before the end of the first ring, engaging the call before the flasher could hang up. This practice was particularly common when someone flashed more than once, giving the recipient time to prepare for a quick answer. Over the past couple of years I witnessed numerous comic scenes where people plotted to "catch" flashers before they could hang up, making them pay for the connection.

Sharing Credit: Inequality and Sociality

Of course most people who communicate by telephone eventually see each other in person, and past episodes of flashing are often topics of discussion. A typical face-to-face conversation about flashing might include a query by the flasher as to why the recipient did not call back, followed by an admission (or assertion) by the recipient that he or she did not have any credit. The recipient, in turn, may accuse the flasher of having credit and being unwilling to use it. These mostly good-natured conversations reproduce some of the complexity of how people in Nigeria navigate the social representation of wealth more generally. On the one hand, using and sharing one's cell phone liberally are clear signals of wealth, and, like many kinds of conspicuous consumption in Nigeria, seemingly carefree cell phone usage can be rewarded with recognition and prestige. On the other hand, in Nigeria's current economic climate, in which most people are struggling to make ends meet, a strong ethos prevails in which even the relatively affluent portray themselves as just getting by, particularly among people who are otherwise their peers.

These contradictory dimensions of people's public representations of wealth play out constantly in the arena of cell phone socioeconomics. For those who really are struggling, claiming one has no credit can be a strategy for protecting a precious and dwindling resource. Conversely, using one's cell phone generously even when one cannot actually afford it can be a way of portraying or maintaining social status that is threatened by economic hardship. For those who are better off, claiming not to have credit can be a form of humility, representing oneself as just as much of a victim of Nigeria's unjust political economy as one's peers. But the balance can be precarious. Humility can easily be interpreted as stinginess if a wealthy person persists too long in feigning hardship. However, acting too carefree can be seen as ostentatious or arrogant. Ultimately, affluent people are meant to demonstrate and share their prosperity, but in ways that do not humiliate their peers. The proliferation of cell phones has created a very prominent sphere in which the micropolitics of social inequality in Nigeria are enacted (for other examples see Barber 1995; Cornwall 2002; and Smith 2004).

Although Nigerians' cell phone-related social behaviors illustrate the importance of economics in how people manage their phone usage, including strategizing about the social representation of one's wealth, it would be a mistake to emphasize only the economic dimensions of Nigeria's emerging cell phone culture and its associated behavior. A good deal of cell phone-related behavior requires a social rather than an economic interpretation.

Perhaps the most striking example is the way that Nigerians conceptualize cell phone credit. Clearly, everyone who uses cell phones knows how much phone calls cost, and people are aware of the exact amounts in which recharge cards are sold. Further, as the discussion above regarding the phenomenon of flashing suggests, there is a considerable degree of conscious jockeying with regard to sharing and spending one's credit. However, to a remarkable extent, Nigerians seem to think of cell phone credit in much different terms than they think of money. Once money is transformed into cell phone credit through the purchase and loading of recharge cards, cell phone credit becomes much more like food or drink than money, in the sense that people feel more entitled to share in it without the strict incursion of a debt that would be the case if one asked to borrow money. As with food or drink, there is a strong social expectation that cell phone credit should be shared if one has it.

My awareness of the difference between Nigerian and Western (or at least American) sensibilities in this matter was driven home to me by the experience of an American student who worked as my summer research assistant. She lived with a Nigerian family and found them amazingly hospitable and generous, to the point where they refused to allow her to pay rent or contribute to the household budget for food. She felt guilty about this, knowing the family's limited means, and we devised ways that she could contribute without offending her hosts. But when it came to the student's cell phone, the situation was quite the opposite. She had acquired a cell phone mainly so that her parents could call her at any time from the United States. Over the course of the summer, she found that people in the household had no compunctions about asking if she had credit, and, if she did, they had no hesitation in asking to use her phone to make calls. One young woman in the household asked to use her phone so often that the student finally became exasperated and reported it to me. She could not understand how the same family that was so generous and so unwilling to accept her money could expect to use her cell phone in ways that, from her perspective, seemed so insensitive.

Conceived of as a consumable commodity, cell phone credit was easily incorporated into long-standing traditions of sharing, gift giving, and reciprocity, in which people are expected and often genuinely desire to share without incurring the equivalent of a monetary debt. Of course money too is highly implicated in social relationships, and it can be gifted and shared as well as borrowed, lent, or spent, but it was clear from my student's experience, and from numerous similar interactions that I have since participated in and observed, that cell phone credit is transformed into a medium of social exchange that is much different from money once it is loaded into a phone. Nigerians routinely ask their friends and family, and even acquaintances of less intimacy, whether or not they have credit, in ways they would rarely, if ever, ask so openly about money.

The politics of sharing cell phone credit is nonetheless complicated, both because forms of nonmonetary sharing and reciprocity have their own moral economy, with numerous unspoken rules and expectations, and because cell phone credit is, in fact, in some ways more like money than are consumable commodities like food or drink. Even in the sharing of food and drink, in which Nigerians, like people in many societies, are extremely generous and social, there are expectations of generalized reciprocity (Bearman 1997). Although one does not incur a quantifiable debt by sharing someone's food, if, over time, one only takes and never gives, this will be recognized and admonished in some way. Similarly, with the sharing of cell phone credit, someone asking to make calls on another's phone cannot expect indefinite cooperation if favors are not eventually reciprocated.

However, cell phone credit is still more like money than is a beer or a plate of cooked meat. Although ordinary Nigerians have obviously participated in the conversion of cell phone credit from money into a commodity that carries a more social definition, this transformation is not complete. People routinely lied to their friends about their credit, and I observed countless instances in which people were "caught" misrepresenting their credit. At a club in Nigeria where I play tennis, men would commonly pick up a person's phone while he was on the court to check how much credit was available. Someone caught underreporting his credit would almost certainly have to relent and share his phone. Through such actions people contribute to the demonetization of cell phone credit. But this demonetization did not occur without ambivalence. Indeed, the social expectation that one must share phone credit contributed further to the notion that cell phones are a "fire that consumes money."

As these anecdotes suggest, sociality is at least as important a dynamic in Nigerian social life as inequality, and not just in terms of sharing, but also with regard to the importance of regularly greeting and communicating with people in one's social network. The preeminent value of sociality has greatly influenced cell phone usage, in ways that have significant economic implications, even if economic calculations are not always foremost in the minds of cell phone users. Although much of what I have described above demonstrates that Nigerians are highly conscious of the economics of cell phone use and deeply aware of the social implications of cell phone behavior, it is also true that people's penchant for regular communication for purely social purposes means that people make many calls just to say hello and to be in touch. To have a phone and not use it to reach out to family and friends is similar to the idea of living alone or preferring solitude and privacy to social interaction. For most Nigerians it is not only unconscionable, it is unthinkable (Uchendu 1965). As a consequence, although many Nigerians rightly extol the virtues of the country's new cell phone services for promoting business and facilitating a more effective and productive commercial sector, my observations suggest that the vast majority of ordinary customers use a good deal of their credit making calls that are the cellular telephone version of a friendly visit. All this suggests that while cell phone technology has sparked some changes in social life, in many ways the new technology has also adapted to and been incorporated into longer-standing behavioral customs.

"Glo with Pride:" Cell Phones as Status Symbols

As I sat down in the parlor of my friend's house in the south-eastern town of Owerri, her twenty-three-year-old son, Uzoma, inquired whether I owned a cell phone. I said I did, and he asked to see it. After a quick inspection of my very simple and obviously low-end Motorola phone, Uzoma declared dismissively: "This phone doesn't fit you." He meant that a person of my status should have a fancier and more expensive phone, preferably the type currently most popular in Nigeria, where the face flips open, the phone has numerous elaborate technical features, and the screen looks like a computer LCD. I defended my simple phone, but I was not surprised at Uzoma's evaluation. I had encountered this reaction to my phone many times before in a society where cell phones have become important markers of social status.[1]

The relatively educated, mostly urban, and at least marginally economically successful Nigerians who own the majority of the country's more than ten million cell phones are acutely aware of the status distinctions conferred by different models. People are constantly noting the quality of their peers' phones, openly conveying approval or disapproval in ways that consciously connect cell phones to social status. Even where people cannot afford to upgrade their phones, the quality of one's cell phone cover and the type and number of accessories owned can be the subject of more fine-grained attempts to assert both status and fashion. Indeed, as status symbols, the cell phones operate at the cusp between economics and fashion, marking both financial position and sense of style. Uzoma assumed I could afford a more expensive phone, so he concluded that I was either too cheap to own a phone fit for a man of my means or too fashion-challenged to know that my phone was a disgrace.

In a huge country like Nigeria, where many people migrate from their villages of origin to cities and towns in search of education, employment, and economic advancement (Geschiere and Gugler 1998; Gugler 2002), the advent of cell phones in a context where landlines served less than 1 percent of the population has revolutionized communication between family and friends separated by long distances. It is little wonder that so many people want cell phones, or that people who can barely afford some of the basic necessities of everyday life make extraordinary efforts to acquire one. But aside from the practical advantages of cell phone ownership, there is no doubt that cell phones have become an important form of symbolic capital, and that the social status conferred by owning a cell phone is a major motivation for many people (Bourdieu 1984). The cell phone companies cultivate and exploit the symbolic dimensions of cell phone ownership in their advertising, and the pressure of seeing peers enjoy the benefits and social recognition of cell phone ownership induces ever larger numbers of consumers to take the leap.

Whereas just ten years ago, before the advent of GSM technology in Nigeria, cell phones were the exclusive province of the superelite, by 2004 many Nigerians who were not wealthy enough to own their own houses and could not afford to buy a used car were able to acquire the latest marker of modernity. The transition from an elite exoticism to an almost essential accessory for an aspiring middle class happened remarkably fast. Just two years ago, Umuahia, a small city of less than 200,000 that is the capital of Abia State, had not yet been linked to the network of any of the four main service providers. However, for those who really wanted cell phone service, a regional company called Baudex provided a mostly effective but very expensive service.

At the social club where I frequently played tennis, a playground for the town's elite, approximately fifteen to twenty men owned these Baudex phones in the summer of 2003. To call further attention to the status they displayed by owning and sporting these expensive phones, the owners formed a club within the club. They called themselves "*Ofo* United." "*Ofo*" refers to a mystical staff that is the emblem of traditional authority in Igbo society, a symbol that implies supernatural backing. "United" presumably refers to the name of famous football teams, most notably the world-famous Manchester United, but also to teams in Nigeria that use "United" in their names. The members of *Ofo* United sometimes further separated themselves from other members of the larger club, sharing a roasted goat and several cartons of beer, greeting each other saying "*Ofo* United," and brandishing their phones like some sort of secret society symbol. Just a year later, all this changed dramatically, as both MTN and Glomobile had established full service in Umuahia. By the time I left Nigeria in December of 2004, literally every member of the tennis club had a phone, as did the club's receptionists, one of the bar girls, and some of the kitchen staff. *Ofo* United was no more.

As cell phones have come within the reach of more ordinary citizens, their availability has only intensified the status competition associated with the new technology. Just as the poorest Nigerians have for many years worn watches that do not keep time in order to appear better off than they are, one now sees many young people carrying cell phones that are just shells—though being exposed in such a deception is worse than having no phone at all. Because so many people can aspire to having a cell phone, the distinctions noticed with regard to brands, models, and accessories have become even more fine-grained. Many wealthier people now own multiple phones, with one line for each provider, and they carry them wherever they go. Having a cell phone is no longer so distinctive, but having two or three is still notable. Similarly, making calls to friends or relatives in London or New York, seemingly without a care about the higher cost, can still impress one's peers. In late 2004, camera phones were just hitting the Nigerian market, and I have no doubt they will be all the rage in a very short time.

Conclusion

Although it is impossible to pinpoint the origin of the "killer numbers" rumors described at the start of this article, I suggest that their currency and appeal were related to popular discontents about the role of cell phones in highlighting and sometimes aggravating social inequality. Some speculated that the rumors were the work of one provider trying to undermine the business of another (the killer numbers were first associated with the phone numbers of one company, though, in time, it spread to them all). Others argued that the rumors were a form of consumer revenge, with the allegations meant to damage the reputation and profits of companies toward which customers felt increasing anger. Still others suggested that the rumors were started by some among the vast majority of Nigerians who still cannot afford to own cell phones, in order to strike fear into those who were intimidating their economic inferiors with their ostentatious use of this flashy new technology. More important than these theories about origin is the speed with which the rumors spread and the extent to which they captured popular imagination. The fascination they generated reflects the fact that, as happy as most Nigerians are for their newfound access to a modern communications technology, ordinary citizens remain extremely discontented over the extent of inequality in their society. The new technology is being interpreted, to a large extent, in relation to these discontents.

Note

1. In 2000, the *New York Times* published an article suggesting the importance of cell phones not only for displaying social status generally, but for the attraction of mates. The newspaper account drew on an article in the journal *Human Nature,* entitled "Mobile Phones as Lekking Devices among Human Males" (Lycett and Dunbar 2000). Regardless of whether one finds a sociobiological argument convincing, the association of cell phones with social status seems to strike a chord across many societies.

References

Akinsuyi, Yemi. 2004. Anxiety Over 'Satanic' GSM Phone Numbers. *This Day* (Nigeria), July 23.

Barber, Karin. 1995. Money, Self-Realization, and the Person Yoruba Texts. In *Money Matters: Instability, Values and Social Payments in the Modern History of West African Communities,* ed. J. Guyer, 205–224. Portsmouth, NH: Heinemann.

Bearman, Peter. 1997. Generalized Exchange. *American Journal of Sociology* 102(5): 1383–1415.

Bourdieu, Pierre. 1984. *Distinction: A Social Critique of the Judgement of Taste.* Translated by Richard Nice. Cambridge: Harvard University Press.

Cornwall, Andrea. 2002. Spending Power: Love, Money, and the Reconfiguration of Gender Relations in Ado-Odo, Southwestern Nigeria. *American Ethnologist* 29(4): 963–980.

Dooring, Nicolas. 2002. 'Kurzm-wird-gesendet'—Abbreviations and Acronyms in SMS Communication (Short-Message-Service). *Muttersparche.*

Fox, Barry. 2001. No 2MORO for Text Messaging Lingo. *New Scientist* 171(2298): 24.

Geschiere, Peter, and Josef Gugler. 1998. The Urban-Rural Connection: Changing Issues of Belonging and Identification. *Africa* 68(3): 309–319.

Gugler, Josef. 2002. The Son of a Hawk Does Not Remain Abroad: The Urban-Rural Connection in Africa. *African Studies Review* 45(1): 21–41.

Ikhemuemhe, Godfrey. 2004. The Killer Phone Rumour—Operators Cry Foul. *Vanguard* (Nigeria), July 26, 2004.

Lycett, John, and Robin Dunbar. 2000. Mobile Phones as Lekking Devices among Human Males. *Human Nature* 11(1): 93–104.

Mobile Africa. 2005. Cellular/Mobile Phone Networks in Africa, www.mobileafrica.net/mobile-phone-networks-in-africa.php. (Accessed June 7, 2005).

Obadare, Ebenezer. 2004. "The Great GSM (cell phone) Boycott: Civil Society, Big Business and the State in Nigeria." Dark Roast Occasional Paper Series, No. 18. Cape Town: South Africa: Isandla Institute.

PANA (Pan African News Agency). 2005. Nigeria's Phone Subscriber Base Hits 12 Million. *PanAfrican News Agency Daily Newswire,* May 4.

Smith, Daniel Jordan. 2004. Burials and Belonging in Nigeria: Rural-Urban Relations and Social Inequality in a Contemporary African Ritual. *American Anthropologist* 106(3): 569–579.

Sylvia, K. N., and S. W. Hady. 2004. Communication Pattern with SMS: Short Message Service and MMS: Multimedia Message Service as a Trend of Conduct of Modern Teenagers. *International Journal of Psychology* 39(5–6): 289.

Uchendu, Victor. 1965. *The Igbo of Southeast Nigeria.* Fort Worth, TX: Holt, Reinhart, Winston.

Critical Thinking

1. How and why does cell phone use touch upon wealth, inequality, and status in Nigeria? How are these issues reflected in the vernacular name, "the fire that eats money" and in the use of text messaging? In "flashing"?

2. Describe the economic dimensions of cell phone use and sharing.

3. How do Nigerians think about cell phone credit in different terms than they think of money?

4. In what sense is cell phone use a reflection of sociality?

5. In what respects can cell phones be seen as status symbols in Nigeria?

UNIT 4

Other Families, Other Ways

Unit Selections

Learning Outcomes

After reading this Unit, you will be able to:

- Explain why marriage was an early and vitally important human invention.

- Discuss why "fraternal polyandry" is socially acceptable in Tibet but not in our society.

- Describe how the ecological conditions and social arrangements of a society may lead to the selective neglect of children and passive infanticide.

- List the pros and cons of arranged marriages versus love marriages.

- Determine whether the stability of Japanese marriages implies compatibility and contentment.

Student Website

www.mhhe.com/cls

Internet References

Kinship and Social Organization
    www.umanitoba.ca/anthropology
Sex and Marriage
    http://anthro.palomar.edu/marriage/default.htm
Wedding Traditions and Customs
    http://worldweddingtraditions.com

Because most people in small-scale societies of the past spent their whole lives within a local area, it is understandable that their primary interactions—economic, religious, and otherwise—were with their relatives. It also makes sense that, through marriage customs, they strengthened those kinship relationships that clearly defined their mutual rights and obligations. (See "The Invention of Marriage" by Stephanie Coontz.) More recently, the family structure has been surprisingly flexible and adaptive, as witnessed in the essays "When Brothers Share a Wife: Among Tibetans, the Good Life Relegates Many Women to Spinsterhood" by Melvyn Goldstein and "Arranging a Marriage in India" by Serena Nanda.

For these reasons, anthropologists have looked upon family and kinship as the key mechanisms for transmitting culture from one generation to the next. Social changes may have been slow to take place throughout the world, but as social horizons have widened, family relationships and community alliances are increasingly based upon new principles. Even as birth rates have increased, kinship networks have diminished in size and strength. As people have increasingly become involved with others as coworkers in a market economy, our associations depend more and more upon factors such as personal aptitudes, educational backgrounds, and job opportunities. Yet the family still exists. Except for some rather unusual exceptions, the family is small, but still functions in its age-old nurturing and protective role, even under conditions where there is little affection (see "Who Needs Love!: In Japan, Many Couples Don't" by Nicholas Kristof) or under conditions of extreme poverty and a high infant mortality rate (see "Death without Weeping" by Nancy Scheper-Hughes). Beyond the immediate family, the situation is in a state of flux. Certain ethnic groups, especially those in poverty, still have a need for the broader network and in some ways seem to be reformulating those ties.

We do not know where the changes described in this section will lead us and which ones will ultimately prevail. One thing is certain: Anthropologists will be there to document the trends, because the discipline of anthropology has had to change as well. One important feature of the essays in this section is the growing interest of anthropologists in the study of complex societies where old theoretical perspectives are inadequate. The current trends, however, do not necessarily depict

© Santokh Kochar/Getty Images

the decline of the kinship unit. The large family network is still the best guarantee of individual survival and well-being in an urban setting.

The Invention of Marriage

STEPHANIE COONTZ

Marriage is a social invention, unique to humans. Of the hundreds of theories, stories, and fables explaining its origins, my favorite is a Blackfoot Indian tale recorded in 1911. I love this story not because I think it's any "truer" than the others but because it makes such a wonderful change from the equally fanciful theories most of us were taught in high school and college during the 1950s and 1960s. Before marriage was invented, according to the Piegan, or Blackfoot Indians:

> The men and women of the ancient Piegans did not live about together in the beginning. The women . . . made buffalo corrals. Their lodges were fine. . . . They tanned the buffalo-hides, those were their robes. They would cut the meat in slices. In summer they picked berries. They used those in winter. Their lodges all were fine inside. And their things were just as fine. . . . Now, the men were . . . very poor. . . . They had no lodges. They wore raw-hides. . . . They did not know, how they should make lodges. They did not know, how they should tan the buffalo-hides. They did not know, too, how they should cut dried meat, how they should sew their clothes.[1]

In the Blackfoot legend, it was the men, not the women, who needed marriage. Hungry and cold, the men followed the women and found out where they lived. Then they gathered on a nearby hill and waited patiently until the women decided to choose husbands and allow them into their lodges. The female chief selected her mate first, and the rest of the women followed suit.

This is only a folktale, of course, but it is no further off the mark than the story that some anthropologists and sociobiologists have told for years. Before marriage was invented, according to an Anglo-American anthropological theory,

> The men hunted wild animals and feasted on their meat. Their brains became very large because they had to cooperate with each other in the hunt. They stood upright, made tools, built fires, and invented language. Their cave art was very fine. . . . But the women were very poor. They were tied down by childbearing, and they did not know how to get food for themselves or their babies. They did not know how to protect themselves from predators. They did not know, too, how to make tools, produce art, and build lodges or campfires to keep themselves warm.

In this story, as in the Blackfoot tale, the invention of marriage supplies the happy ending for the hapless sex. Here, however, women were the weaker gender. They initiated marriage by offering to trade sex for protection and food. Instead of the men waiting patiently on the hill for the women to pick their mates, the men got to pick the women, and the strongest, most powerful males got first choice. Then the men set their women up by the hearth to protect them from predators and from rival males.

The story that marriage was invented for the protection of women is still the most widespread myth about the origins of marriage. According to the protective or provider theory of marriage, women and infants in early human societies could not survive without men to bring them the meat of woolly mammoths and protect them from marauding saber-toothed tigers and from other men seeking to abduct them. But males were willing to protect and provide only for their "own" females and offspring they had good reason to believe were theirs, so a woman needed to find and hold on to a strong, aggressive mate.

One way a woman could hold a mate was to offer him exclusive and frequent sex in return for food and protection. According to the theory, that is why women lost the estrus cycle that is common to other mammals, in which females come into heat only at periodic intervals. Human females became sexually available year-round, so they were able to draw men into long-term relationships. In anthropologist Robin Fox's telling of this story, "The females could easily trade on the male's tendency to want to monopolize (or at least think he was monopolizing) the females for mating purposes, and say, in effect 'okay, you get the monopoly . . . and we get the meat.'"[2]

The male willingness to trade meat for sex (with the females throwing in whatever nuts and berries they'd gathered to sweeten the deal) was, according to Fox, "the root of truly human society." Proponents of this protective theory of marriage claim that the nuclear family, based on a sexual division of labor between the male hunter and the female hearth keeper, was the most important unit of survival and protection in the Stone Age.

People in the mid-twentieth century found this story persuasive because it closely resembled the male breadwinner/female homemaker family to which they were accustomed. The male breadwinner model of marriage, as we shall see later, was a late and relatively short-lived way of organizing gender roles and dividing work in human history. But in the 1950s, 1960s, and 1970s most people believed it was the natural and "traditional" family form.

In 1975, sociobiologist E. O. Wilson drew a direct line from the male hunter marriages that he imagined had prevailed on the African savanna at the dawn of human history to the marriages he observed in the jungle of Wall Street: "During the day the women and children remain in the residential area while the men forage for game or its symbolic equivalent in the form of money."[3] The protective theory is still periodically recycled to explain why women are supposedly attracted to powerful, dominant men, while men seek younger women who will be good breeders and hearth keepers.

But since the 1970s other researchers have poked holes in the protective theory of marriage. Some denied that male dominance and female dependence came to us from our primate ancestors. Among baboons, they pointed out, a female who pairs up with a male does not get more access to food than females outside such a relationship. Among chimpanzees, most food sharing occurs between mothers and their offspring, not between male and female sexual partners. Adult female chimps give food to other females (even unrelated ones) just as often as males give food to females, and female chimps are often more protective of other females than males are. A female chimp who wants food from a male may make sexual overtures, or a male chimp who has meat to spare may use it as a bargaining chip. But males cannot control the sexual behavior of the estrus females. And when members of the group, male or female, want food from a female, they hold or play with her infant, in effect offering babysitting for handouts.[4]

Studies of actual human hunting and gathering societies also threw doubt on the male provider theory. In such societies, women's foraging, not men's hunting, usually contributes the bulk of the group's food. The only exceptions to this rule are Eskimo and other herding or hunting peoples in areas where extremely hostile climates make foraging for plants difficult.[5]

Nor are women in foraging societies tied down by child rearing. One anthropologist, working with an African hunter-gatherer society during the 1960s, calculated that an adult woman typically walked about twelve miles a day gathering food, and brought home anywhere from fifteen to thirty-three pounds. A woman with a child under two covered the same amount of ground and brought back the same amount of food while she carried her child in a sling, allowing the child to nurse as the woman did her foraging. In many societies women also participate in hunting, whether as members of communal hunting parties, as individual hunters, or even in all-female hunting groups.

Today most paleontologists reject the notion that early human societies were organized around dominant male hunters providing for their nuclear families. For one thing, in the early phases of hominid and human evolution, hunting big game was less important for group survival than were gathering plants, bird eggs, edible insects, and shellfish, trapping the occasional small animal, and scavenging the meat of large animals that had died of natural causes.

When early humans began to hunt large animals, they did so by driving animals over cliffs or into swamps. These activities involved the whole group, women as well as men. That is what happens in the surrounds conducted by modern-day foragers, where the entire band encircles the game and gradually herds it into a trap.[6]

We cannot know for sure how the earliest hominids and humans organized their reproduction and family lives. But there are three general schools of thought on the subject. Some researchers believe that early humans lived in female-centered groups made up of mothers, sisters, and their young, accompanied by temporary male companions. Younger males, they suggest, left the group when they reached mating age. Other scholars argue that the needs of defense would have encouraged the formation of groups based on male kin, in which fathers, brothers, and sons, along with their female mates, stayed together. In this view, the female offspring rather than males left the group at puberty. A third group of researchers theorizes that hominid groups were organized around one male mating with several females and traveling with them and their offspring. [7]

But none of these three theories, not even the male with his harem, suggests that an individual male provided for "his" females and children or that the male-female pair was the fundamental unit of economic survival and cooperation. No one could have survived very long in the Paleolithic world if individual nuclear families had had to take primary responsibility for all food production, defense, child rearing, and elder care.[8]

A division of labor between males and females certainly developed fairly early and was reinforced when groups developed weapons effective enough to kill moving animals from a distance. Such weapons made it possible for small groups to hunt solitary, fast-moving animals. Hunting with projectile weapons became the domain of men, partly because it was hard for women to chase swift game while they were nursing. So wherever humans organized small hunting parties that left the main camp, they were likely to be all or mostly male. However, this did not make women dependent upon their individual mates.

Women, keeping their children near, were more likely to specialize in gathering and processing plants and shellfish, manufacturing clothing, trapping small animals, and making digging or cooking implements. This gender specialization led to greater interdependence between males and females. As these productive techniques became more complicated, people had to invest more time in teaching them to children, providing an incentive for couples to stay together for longer stretches.

Having a flexible, gender-based division of labor within a mated pair was an important tool for human survival. One partner, typically the female, could concentrate on the surer thing, finding food through foraging or digging. The other partner could try for a windfall, hunting for food that would be plentiful and filling if it could be caught. Yet this division of labor did not make nuclear families self-sufficient. Collective hunting and gathering remained vital to survival.[9]

Couples in the Paleolithic world would never have fantasized about running off by themselves to their own little retreats in the forest. No Stone Age lovers would have imagined in their wildest dreams that they could or should be "everything" to each other. That way lay death.

Until about twelve thousand years ago, say archaeologists Colin Renfrew and Paul Bahn, nearly all human societies were comprised of bands of mobile hunter-gatherers who moved seasonally between different sleeping camps and work sites, depending on the weather and food supply. Humans lived in these band-level societies and small, semipermanent hamlets far longer than the few millennia they have lived in more complex villages, cities, states, and empires.[10]

Reconstructions by archaeologists suggest that bands were made up of anywhere from a handful to as many as a hundred people, but commonly numbered around two dozen. Bands lived off the land, using simple tools to process a wide range of animals and plants for food, medicines, clothing, and fuel. They typically moved back and forth over a home territory until resources were depleted or other environmental changes spurred them to move on. Periodically they might travel longer distances to find valued raw materials and take advantage of seasonal game or fish runs.[11]

Sometimes the band would break down into individual family groups that foraged alone. But the archaeological record shows that families regularly came back to a main camp, or hooked up with a new one, for protection and to cooperate in communal hunts. Regional networks of camps routinely came together at water holes or to collectively exploit fish runs or seasonally abundant plants. During those times, dances, festivals, and other rituals took place, building connections between families and bands that were dispersed for much of the year. On such occasions, people might seek mates—or change them—from within the larger groups.

No one suggests that prehistoric bands existed in utopian harmony. But social interactions were governed by the overwhelming need to pool and share resources. The band's mobility made it impractical for people to accumulate significant surpluses, which would have to be lugged from place to place. In the absence of money and nonperishable wealth, the main currency in nomadic foraging societies would have been favors given and owed. Sharing beyond the immediate family or local group was a rudimentary form of banking. It allowed people to accumulate personal credit or goodwill that could be drawn on later.[12]

Using computer simulations and mathematical calculations to compare the outcome of different ways of organizing the production and consumption of food, economic anthropologist Bruce Winterhalder has established the decisive importance of prehistoric sharing. His calculations show that because the results of hunting and gathering varied on a daily basis, the surest way for individuals to minimize the risk of not having enough to eat on a bad day was not to save what they gathered or killed on good days for later use by their "own" nuclear family, but to pool and divide the whole harvest among the entire group every day.[13]

With few exceptions, hunting and gathering societies throughout history have emphasized sharing and reciprocity.

Band-level societies put extraordinary time and energy into establishing norms of sharing. People who share gain status, while individuals who refuse to share are shunned and ostracized. Ethnographer Lorna Marshall reports that for the Dobe !Kung Bushmen of the Kalahari Desert in Africa, "the idea of eating alone and not sharing is shocking. . . . It makes them shriek with uneasy laughter." They think that "lions could do that, not men." In seventeenth-century America, William Penn marveled that the Indians always redistributed the gifts or trade goods that European settlers brought, rather than keep them for their own families. "Wealth circulateth like the Blood," he wrote. "All parts partake."[14]

Many simple hunting and gathering societies place so much emphasis on sharing that a person who kills an animal gets no more of its meat than do his companions. A review of twenty-five hunting and gathering societies found that in only three did the hunter get the largest share of his kill. In most, the hunter was obliged to share the meat equally with other camp members, and in a few he got less than he distributed to others. Anthropologist Polly Wiessner observes that these customs create total interdependence among families: "[T]he hunter spends his life hunting for others, and others spend their lives hunting for him."[15]

The idea that in prehistoric times a man would spend his life hunting only for the benefit of his own wife and children, who were dependent solely upon his hunting prowess for survival, is simply projection of 1950s marital norms onto the past. The male/female pair was a good way to organize sexual companionship, share child rearing, and divide daily work. A man who was a skilled hunter might have been an attractive mate, as would have been a woman who was skilled at foraging or making cooking implements, but marrying a good hunter was not the main way that a woman and her children got access to food and protection.

Marriage was certainly an early and a vitally important human invention. One of its crucial functions in the Paleolithic era was its ability to forge networks of cooperation beyond the immediate family group or local band. Bands needed to establish friendly relations with others so they could travel more freely and safely in pursuit of game, fish, plants, and water holes or move as the seasons changed. Archaeologist Brian Hayden argues that hunter-gatherers of the past used a combination of five strategies to create such ties with other groups and to defuse tensions: frequent informal visits, interband sharing, gift giving, periodic large gatherings for ritual occasions, and the establishment of marriage and kinship ties.[16]

All these customs built goodwill and established social networks beyond a single camp or a group of families. But using marriage to create new ties of kinship was an especially powerful way of binding groups together because it produced children who had relatives in both camps. The Maori of New Zealand say that "a gift connection may be severed, but not so a human link."[17]

However, a kin group that sent its daughters or sons to other groups as marriage partners also needed to make sure that it received spouses in return. Moreover, to create lasting links among groups, the exchange of spouses had to be renewed in later generations.

Sometimes such marriage exchanges would be very direct and immediate, a sister from one group being exchanged for a sister from the other. The exchange need not occur simultaneously, as long as the obligation to pay back one person with another was acknowledged. In other cases, spouses were not exchanged directly. Instead several lineages or clans would be linked in a pattern in which the sisters always married in one direction around the circle while the brothers always married in the opposite one. Lineage A would send its sisters and daughters as wives to lineage B, which sent wives to C, which sent them to A. As practiced among one present-day hunter-gatherer group, the Murngin of Australia, the circle of wife exchange takes seven generations to complete.[18]

Some people believe that from the very beginning, marriage alliances led to strict controls over a young person's choice of mates, especially a woman's. Among the Aborigines of Australia, one of the few places where hunter-gatherer societies lived completely untouched by contact with other societies for thousands of years, marriages were traditionally arranged when girls were still in their childhood and were strictly controlled by elders. Because of the scarcity of food and water in that harsh environment and the need to travel over long distances to ensure survival, Aboriginal elders had to ensure that their community's children were distributed in ways that gave the community family connections to the land and resources wherever they traveled. No rebellion against this system was tolerated.[19]

But the Indians of northeastern North America, who also lived for thousands of years in a "pristine" setting similar to the environment in which many of our Stone Age ancestors operated, traditionally took a very different approach toward marriage, divorce, and sexual activity from that of the Australian Aborigines. Among the Chippewyan people of Canada, the main function of marriage was also to build far-flung personal networks that gave people access to hunting, natural resources, or water holes in other regions. But in this more forgiving environment, individuals tended to make their own marital choices, and no one interfered if a couple decided to part.[20]

Nevertheless, many people argue that marriage originated as a way of exchanging women. Marriage alliances, the eminent anthropologist Claude Lévi-Strauss declared, were "not established between men and women, but between men by means of women." Women were merely the vehicle for establishing this relationship.[21]

In the 1970s several feminist researchers built on this idea to turn the protective theory of marriage on its head. They suggested that marriage originated not to protect women but to oppress them. These researchers argued that because women probably played a leading role in the invention of agriculture through their experimentation with plants and food preservation, and because women were certainly responsible for the physical reproduction of the group, the origins of marriage lay not in the efforts of women to attract protectors and providers but in the efforts of men to control the productive and reproductive powers of women for their own private benefit.[22]

According to this oppressive theory, men coerced women into marriage, often using abduction, gang rape, or wife beating to enforce their will. Brothers essentially traded their sisters for wives. Fathers gained power in the community by passing their daughters out to young men, who gave the fathers gifts and services in return. Rich men accumulated many wives, who worked for them and bore more daughters who could be exchanged to place other men in their debt.

Like the protective theory of marriage, the oppressive theory still has defenders. Philosopher Iris Marion Young maintains that the historical function of marriage was "to use women as a means of forging alliances among men and perpetuating their 'line.'" Even today, Young says, marriage is "the cornerstone of patriarchal power." Christine Delphy and Diana Leonard argue that marriage is one of the primary ways that "men benefit from, and exploit, the work of women."[23]

In today's political climate, in which men's power over their wives and daughters has greatly diminished, it is tempting to write off the oppressive theory of marriage as a product of 1970s feminist excesses. But there is strong historical evidence that in many societies marriage was indeed a way that men put women's labor to their private use. We can watch this process develop as recently as the eighteenth and nineteenth centuries among the Plains Indians.

In the Blackfoot legend about the origins of marriage, the men got dried meat and berries, warm robes, soft moccasins, and fine lodges only after the women chose to take them as husbands. In real life, men began to accumulate buffalo hides, large lodges, and other "fine" things, including, often, more than one wife, in a process that involved far less female choice.

Before the Europeans introduced the horse to the western United States, the Blackfoot and other Plains Indians hunted buffalo on foot, using surrounds. The entire group—men, women, and children—took part in driving the animals into traps or over cliffs. The men clubbed the buffalo to death, and the women dried the meat and tanned the hides. Although the men took on the more risky, up-close killing tasks, the work was evenly divided, and it was episodic; a good hunt could provide meat and clothes for a long time.[24]

But once Europeans introduced the horse, the gun, and the fur trade to North America, everything changed. Indian men were able to hunt buffalo individually. They had both the opportunity and incentive to kill more buffalo than they needed for their own subsistence because they could trade their surplus to whites for personal gain. This hugely increased the number of hides to be tanned and the amount of meat to be dried. The most successful hunters could now kill far more buffalo than one wife could process, and having more wives suddenly meant having more wealth. Richer men began to accumulate wives by offering horses to girls' fathers.

The expansion of the trade in buffalo hides brought a sharp increase in the number of wives per hunter. It also caused the age of marriage for women to drop to preadolescence, and it greatly multiplied social restrictions upon wives. According to nineteenth-century observers, the practice of keeping multiple wives was most common among groups that traded with the fur companies, and in these groups women's labor was much more intensive. These tribes too were more likely to practice forms of punishment such as cutting off a woman's nose for adultery.[25]

There are many other examples of societies in which men have exchanged women without consulting them and in which husbands have used the labor of their wives and children to produce surpluses that increased the men's prestige and power. It is also true that many more societies exchange women in marriage than exchange men, and there are some disadvantages to being the sex that moves after marriage. But in small-scale societies these disadvantages were not necessarily severe. Women could return home to their parents or call on their brothers for protection. Furthermore, in some societies men were the ones who moved at marriage. In these cases, one could just as easily argue that men were being exchanged by women.

In a current example, the Minangkabau of Indonesia, where marriage perpetuates the female line, refer to a husband as "the borrowed man." In traditional Hopi Indian marriages, a woman's kin made "a ceremonial presentation of cornmeal to the groom's household, conceptualized by the Hopi as 'paying for him.'" There is evidence that marriage systems in which men rather than women were circulated may have been more common in kinship societies of the distant past than in those observed over the past several hundred years.[26]

Even in cultures where women move at marriage, there has always been a huge variation in how much male dominance accompanies this arrangement. There are also enough exceptions to the practice of controlling women through marriage to call the oppressive theory into question. In the early eighteenth century a French baron, traveling among hunting and gathering peoples in what is now Canada, was scandalized to find that native parents believed "their Daughters have the command of their own Bodies and may dispose of their Persons as they think fit; they being at liberty to do what they please."[27]

In many hunting and gathering and simple horticultural societies, parents are likely to arrange a first marriage. They may even force a woman into a match. However, in most societies without extensive private property, marriages tend to be fragile, and women whose families have arranged their marriages frequently leave their husbands or run off with lovers without suffering any reprisals.[28]

I do not believe, then, that marriage was invented to oppress women any more than it was invented to protect them. In most cases, marriage probably originated as an informal way of organizing sexual companionship, child rearing, and the daily tasks of life. It became more formal and more permanent as groups began to exchange spouses over larger distances. There was nothing inherent in the institution of marriage that protected women and children from violence or produced the fair and loving relationships that many modern couples aspire to. But there was also nothing inherent in the institution of marriage, as there was, say, in slavery, that required one group to subordinate another. The effect of marriage on people's individual lives has always depended on its functions in economic and social life, functions that have changed immensely over time.

It is likely that our Stone Age ancestors varied in their behaviors just as do the hunting and gathering societies observed in more recent times. But in early human societies, marriage was primarily a way to extend cooperative relations and circulate people and resources beyond the local group. When people married into new groups, it turned strangers into relatives and enemies into allies.

That changed, however, as societies developed surpluses and became more sedentary, populous, and complex.[29] As kin groups began to assert permanent rights over territory and resources, some families amassed more goods and power than others. When that happened, the wealthier families lost interest in sharing resources, pooling labor, or developing alliances with poorer families. Gradually marriage exchanges became a way of consolidating resources rather than creating a circle of reciprocal obligations and connections.

With the growth of inequality in society, the definition of an acceptable marriage narrowed. Wealthy kin groups refused to marry with poorer ones and disavowed any children born to couples whose marriage they hadn't authorized. This shift constituted a revolution in marriage that was to shape people's lives for thousands of years. Whereas marriage had once been a way of expanding the number of cooperating groups, it now became a way for powerful kin groups to accumulate both people and property.

The Transformation of Marriage in Ancient Societies

Wherever this evolution from foraging bands to sedentary agriculturalists occurred, it was accompanied by a tendency to funnel cooperation and sharing exclusively through family ties and kinship obligations and to abandon more informal ways of pooling or sharing resources. In the American Southwest we can trace this transition through changes in architectural patterns. Originally surplus grains were stored in communal spaces in open, visible parts of the village. Later, storage rooms were enclosed within individual residences and could be entered only from the rooms where the family or household actually lived. Surpluses had become capital to be closely guarded, with access restricted to family members.[30]

As some kin groups became richer than others, they sought ways to enhance their own status and to differentiate themselves from "lesser" families. Excavations of ancient living sites throughout the world show growing disparities in the size and quality of dwellings, as well as in the richness of the objects buried with people.

Greater economic differentiation reshaped the rules of marriage. A kin group or lineage with greater social status and material resources could demand a higher "price" for handing over one of its children in marriage. Within the leading lineages, young men often had to borrow from their seniors in order to marry, increasing the control of elders over junior men as well as over women. A lineage that couldn't pay top prices for spouses had to drop out of the highest rungs of the marriage exchange system. Sometimes a poorer lineage would forgo the bridewealth a groom's family traditionally paid and give its daughters away as secondary wives or concubines to the leading lineages, in order to forge even a second-class connection with a leading family. But in other cases, lower-status kin groups were not allowed to intermarry with those of higher status under any circumstances.[31]

As dominant kin groups became more wealthy and powerful, they married in more restricted circles. Sometimes they even turned away from exogamy (the practice of marrying out of the group) and engaged in endogamy (marriage with close kin), in order to preserve and consolidate their property and kin members.[32] The more resources were at stake in marriage alliances, the more the relatives had an interest in whom their kin married, whether a marriage lasted, and whether a second marriage, which might produce new heirs to complicate the transmission of property, could be contracted if the first one ended.

In many ancient agricultural societies, if an heir was already in place and the birth of another child would complicate inheritance and succession, a woman might be forced to remain single and celibate after her husband's death. In a few cultures the ideal was for a widow to kill herself after her husband died.[33] More often, the surviving spouse was required to marry another member of the deceased's family in order to perpetuate the alliance between the two kin groups.

In India, early law codes provided that a widow with no son had to marry her husband's brother, in order to produce a male child to carry on his lineage. The Old Testament mentions several examples of the same custom. Indeed, it seems to have been preferred practice among the ancient Hebrews. A man who refused to marry his brother's widow had to go through a public ceremony of halizah, or "unshoeing." This passage from the Torah shows how intense the social pressure was against making such a choice: "Then shall his brother's wife come unto him in the presence of the elders, and loose his shoe from off his foot, and spit in his face, and shall answer and say, so shall it be done unto that man that will not build up his brother's house. And his name shall be called in Israel the house of him that hath his shoe loosed."[34]

As marriage became the primary vehicle for transmitting status and property, both men and women faced greater restrictions on their behavior. Men, like women, could be forced to marry women chosen by their parents. But because women could bear a child with an "impure" bloodline, introducing a "foreign interest" into a family, their sexual behavior tended to be more strictly supervised, and females were subject to severe penalties for adultery or premarital sex. The laws and moral codes of ancient states exhorted men to watch carefully over their wives "lest the seed of others be sown on your soil."[35]

Distinctions between legitimate and illegitimate children became sharper in all the early states. Children born into unauthorized liaisons could not inherit land, titles, or citizenship rights and so in many cases were effectively condemned to slavery or starvation.

The subordination of wives in the ancient world was exacerbated by the invention of the plow. Use of the plow diminished the value of women's agricultural labor, because plowing requires greater strength than women were believed to have and is less compatible with child care than gardening with a hoe. Husbands began to demand dowries instead of giving bridewealth for wives, and daughters were devalued to the point that families sometimes resorted to female infanticide. The spread of warfare that accompanied the emergence of early states also pushed women farther down in the hierarchy.[36]

As societies became more complex and differentiated, upper classes sometimes displayed their wealth by adopting standards of beauty or behavior that effectively hobbled women. Restrictive clothing, heavy jewelry, or exceedingly long fingernails, for example, made a public statement that the family had slaves to do the work once done by wives and daughters. By the second millennium B.C. the practice of secluding women in special quarters had become widespread in the Middle East. This was done not just to guard their chastity but to signify that a family had so much wealth that its women did not even have to leave the home.

Much later, in China, binding the feet of young girls became a symbol of prestige. Upper-class girls had their feet bound so tightly that the small bones broke and the feet were permanently bowed over, making it excruciatingly painful to walk.[37]

In many societies, elaborate ideologies of purity grew up around the women of the highest-ranking classes. A man who courted a high-ranking woman outside regular channels faced harsh sanctions or even death, while women who stepped out of their assigned places in the marriage market were severely punished.

Assyrian laws from the twelfth and eleventh centuries B.C. guarded women's premarital virginity and condemned to death married women who committed adultery. Married women were required to wear veils, but concubines were forbidden to do so. A man who wanted to raise the status of his concubine and make her his wife could have her veiled. But a woman who veiled herself without the authority of a propertied husband was to be flogged fifty times, have tar poured over her head, and have her ears cut off.[38]

Women's bodies came to be regarded as the properties of their fathers and husbands. Assyrian law declared: "A man may flog his wife, pluck her hair, strike her and mutilate her ears. There is no guilt." The Old Testament suggests that a bride whose virginity was not intact could be stoned to death.[39]

Centuries later in China, Confucius defined a wife as "someone who submits to another." A wife, according to Confucian philosophy, had to follow "the rule of the three obediences: while at home she obeys her father, after marriage she obeys her husband, after he dies she obeys her son."[40]

But men too faced new controls over their personal behavior. If a woman could no longer choose her mate, this also meant that a man could not court a wife on his own initiative but needed to win her father's permission. And in many states, the confinement of wives to household activities "freed" their husbands to be drafted into the army or dragooned into backbreaking labor on huge public works projects.[41]

By the time we have written records of the civilizations that arose in the ancient world, marriage had become the way most wealth and land changed hands. Marriage was also the main vehicle by which leading families expanded their social networks and political influence. It even sealed military alliances and peace treaties.

With so much at stake, it is hardly surprising that marriage became a hotbed of political intrigue. Families and individuals developed elaborate strategies to create unions that furthered their interests and to block marriages that might benefit their rivals. Elites jockeyed to acquire powerful in-laws. If, after they had agreed to seal a match, a better one presented itself, they maneuvered (and sometimes murdered) to get out of the old one.

Commoners could no longer hope to exchange marriage partners with the elites. At best they might hope to have one of their children marry up. Even this became more difficult as intricate distinctions were created between the rights of primary wives, secondary wives, and concubines. Formal rules detailed what kinds of marriage could and could not produce legitimate heirs. In some places authorities prohibited lower-class groups from marrying at all or made it illegal for individuals from different social classes to wed each other.

The right to decide who could marry whom had become an extremely valuable political and economic weapon and remained so for thousands of years. From the Middle Eastern kingdoms that arose three thousand years before the birth of Christ to the European ones fifteen hundred years later, factions of the ruling circles fought over who had the right to legitimize marriages or authorize divorces. These battles often changed the course of history.

For millennia, the maneuvering of families, governing authorities, and social elites prevailed over the individual desires of young people when it came to selecting or rejecting marriage partners. It was only two hundred years ago that men and women began to wrest control over the right to marry from the hands of parents, church, and state. And only in the last hundred years have women had the independence to make their marital choices without having to bow to economic need and social pressure.

Have we come full circle during the past two centuries, as the power of kin, community, and state to arrange, prohibit, and interfere in marriages has waned? Legal scholar Harry Willekins argues that in most modern industrial societies, marriages are contracted and dissolved in ways that have more in common with the habits of some egalitarian band-level societies than the elaborate rules that governed marriage in more complex societies over the past 5,000 years.[42] In many contemporary societies, there is growing acceptance of premarital sex, divorce, and remarriage, along with an erosion of sharp distinctions between cohabitation and marriage and between "legitimate" and out-of-wedlock births.

Some people note this resemblance between modern family relations and the informal sexual and marital norms of many band-level societies and worry that we are throwing away the advantages of civilization. They hope to reinstitutionalize marriage as the main mechanism that regulates sexuality, legitimizes children, organizes the division of labor between men and women, and redistributes resources to dependents. But the last century of social change makes this highly unlikely. Yet if it is unrealistic to believe we can reimpose older social controls over marriage, it is also naive to think we can effortlessly revive the fluid interpersonal relationships that characterized simpler cultures. In hunting and gathering bands and egalitarian horticultural communities, unstable marriages did not lead to the impoverishment of women or children as they often do today. Unmarried women participated in the work of the group and were entitled to a fair share, while children and other dependents were protected by strong customs that mandated sharing beyond the nuclear family.

This is not the case today, especially in societies such as the United States, where welfare provisions are less extensive than in Western Europe. Today's winner-take-all global economy may have its strong points, but the practice of pooling resources and sharing with the weak is not one of them. The question of how we organize our personal rights and obligations now that our older constraints are gone is another aspect of the contemporary marriage crisis.

Critical Thinking

1. Explain why the story that marriage was invented for the protection of women was such a persuasive theory in the mid-twentieth century. In what ways have researchers poked holes in this theory?

2. What have been the three general schools of thought on how the earliest hominids and humans organized their reproduction and family lives?

3. How does the author characterize early hunter-gatherer societies and their gender-based division of labor and why?

4. What were such societies like, according to reconstructions by archaeologists?

5. Discuss the importance of prehistoric sharing. How is this contrary to the 1950s marital norms?

6. Why was marriage "an early and a vitally important human invention"?

7. According to archaeologist Brian Hayden, what were the five strategies used to create ties with groups and to defuse tensions?

8. Be familiar with some of the means by which marriage became an especially powerful way of binding groups together.

9. Discuss the "oppressive theory" as to the origin of marriage and the evidence provided by the author to contradict it.

10. How did the development of surpluses and a more sedentary life-style change the function of marriage?

11. How did greater economic differentiation reshape the rules of marriage, inheritance and sexual behavior?

12. How was the subordination of wives in the ancient world exacerbated by the invention of the plow?

13. How is it that, as societies became more complex and differentiated, upper classes sometimes displayed their wealth by adopting standards of beauty or behavior that effectively hobbled women? What kinds of controls did men face?

14. In what ways did marriage become a "hotbed of political intrigue"?

15. Now that women have achieved some degree of economic independence and there is a degree of resemblance in family relations between ourselves and band-level societies, have we come full circle? Explain.

From *Marriage: A History,* Viking, 2005, pp. 1–13. Copyright © 2005 by Penguin Group (USA) Inc. Reprinted by permission.

When Brothers Share a Wife

Among Tibetans, the Good Life Relegates Many Women to Spinsterhood

MELVYN C. GOLDSTEIN

Eager to reach home, Dorje drives his yaks hard over the 17,000-foot mountain pass, stopping only once to rest. He and his two older brothers, Pema and Sonam, are jointly marrying a woman from the next village in a few weeks, and he has to help with the preparations.

Dorje, Pema, and Sonam are Tibetans living in Limi, a 200-square-mile area in the northwest corner of Nepal, across the border from Tibet. The form of marriage they are about to enter—fraternal polyandry in anthropological parlance—is one of the world's rarest forms of marriage but is not uncommon in Tibetan society, where it has been practiced from time immemorial. For many Tibetan social strata, it traditionally represented the ideal form of marriage and family.

The mechanics of fraternal polyandry are simple. Two, three, four, or more brothers jointly take a wife, who leaves her home to come and live with them. Traditionally, marriage was arranged by parents, with children, particularly females, having little or no say. This is changing somewhat nowadays, but it is still unusual for children to marry without their parents' consent. Marriage ceremonies vary by income and region and range from all the brothers sitting together as grooms to only the eldest one formally doing so. The age of the brothers plays an important role in determining this: very young brothers almost never participate in actual marriage ceremonies, although they typically join the marriage when they reach their mid-teens.

The eldest brother is normally dominant in terms of authority, that is, in managing the household, but all the brothers share the work and participate as sexual partners. Tibetan males and females do not find the sexual aspect of sharing a spouse the least bit unusual, repulsive, or scandalous, and the norm is for the wife to treat all the brothers the same.

Offspring are treated similarly. There is no attempt to link children biologically to particular brothers, and a brother shows no favoritism toward his child even if he knows he is the real father because, for example, his other brothers were away at the time the wife became pregnant. The children,

in turn, consider all of the brothers as their fathers and treat them equally, even if they also know who is their real father. In some regions children use the term "father" for the eldest brother and "father's brother" for the others, while in other areas they call all the brothers by one term, modifying this by the use of "elder" and "younger."

Unlike our own society, where monogamy is the only form of marriage permitted, Tibetan society allows a variety of marriage types, including monogamy, fraternal polyandry, and polygyny. Fraternal polyandry and monogamy are the most common forms of marriage, while polygyny typically occurs in cases where the first wife is barren. The widespread practice of fraternal polyandry, therefore, is not the outcome of a law requiring brothers to marry jointly. There is choice, and in fact, divorce traditionally was relatively simple in Tibetan society. If a brother in a polyandrous marriage became dissatisfied and wanted to separate, he simply left the main house and set up his own household. In such cases, all the children stayed in the main household with the remaining brother(s), even if the departing brother was known to be the real father of one or more of the children.

The Tibetans' own explanation for choosing fraternal polyandry is materialistic. For example, when I asked Dorje why he decided to marry with his two brothers rather than take his own wife, he thought for a moment, then said it prevented the division of his family's farm (and animals) and thus facilitated all of them achieving a higher standard of living. And when I later asked Dorje's bride whether it wasn't difficult for her to cope with three brothers as husbands, she laughed and echoed the rationale of avoiding fragmentation of the family and land, adding that she expected to be better off economically, since she would have three husbands working for her and her children.

Exotic as it may seem to Westerners, Tibetan fraternal polyandry is thus in many ways analogous to the way primogeniture functioned in nineteenth-century England. Primogeniture dictated that the eldest son inherited the family estate, while younger sons had to leave home and seek their

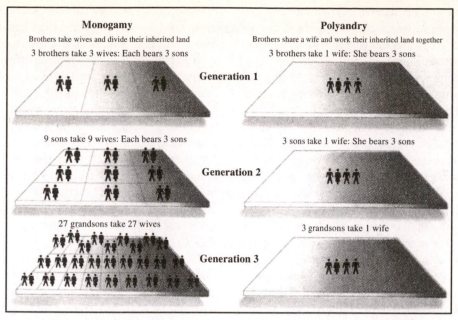

Monogamy	Polyandry
Brothers take wives and divide their inherited land	Brothers share a wife and work their inherited land together
3 brothers take 3 wives: Each bears 3 sons	3 brothers take 1 wife: She bears 3 sons

Generation 1

9 sons take 9 wives: Each bears 3 sons	3 sons take 1 wife: She bears 3 sons

Generation 2

27 grandsons take 27 wives	3 grandsons take 1 wife

Generation 3

Joe LeMonnier

Family Planning in Tibet   An economic rationale for fraternal polyandry is outlined in the diagram, which emphasizes only the male offspring in each generation. If every wife is assumed to bear three sons, a family splitting up into monogamous households would rapidly multiply and fragment the family land. In this case, a rule of inheritance, such as primogeniture, could retain the family land intact, but only at the cost of creating many landless male offspring. In contrast, the family practicing fraternal polyandry maintains a steady ratio of persons to land.

own employment—for example, in the military or the clergy. Primogeniture maintained family estates intact over generations by permitting only one heir per generation. Fraternal polyandry also accomplishes this but does so by keeping all the brothers together with just one wife so that there is only one *set* of heirs per generation.

While Tibetans believe that in this way fraternal polyandry reduces the risk of family fission, monogamous marriages among brothers need not necessarily precipitate the division of the family estate: brothers could continue to live together, and the family land could continue to be worked jointly. When I asked Tibetans about this, however, they invariably responded that such joint families are unstable because each wife is primarily oriented to her own children and interested in their success and well-being over that of the children of the other wives. For example, if the youngest brother's wife had three sons while the eldest brother's wife had only one daughter, the wife of the youngest brother might begin to demand more resources for her children since, as males, they represent the future of the family. Thus, the children from different wives in the same generation are competing sets of heirs, and this makes such families inherently unstable. Tibetans perceive that conflict will spread from the wives to their husbands and consider this likely to cause family fission. Consequently, it is almost never done.

Although Tibetans see an economic advantage to fraternal polyandry, they do not value the sharing of a wife as an end in itself. On the contrary, they articulate a number of problems inherent in the practice. For example, because authority is customarily exercised by the eldest brother, his younger male siblings have to subordinate themselves with little hope of changing their status within the family. When these younger brothers are aggressive and individualistic, tensions and difficulties often occur despite there being only one set of heirs.

In addition, tension and conflict may arise in polyandrous families because of sexual favoritism. The bride normally sleeps with the eldest brother, and the two have the responsibility to see to it that the other males have opportunities for sexual access. Since the Tibetan subsistence economy requires males to travel a lot, the temporary absence of one or more brothers facilitates this, but there are also other rotation practices. The cultural ideal unambiguously calls for the wife to show equal affection and sexuality to each of the brothers (and vice versa), but deviations from this ideal occur, especially when there is a sizable difference in age between the partners in the marriage.

Dorje's family represents just such a potential situation. He is fifteen years old and his two older brothers are twenty-five and twenty-two years old. The new bride is twenty-three years old, eight years Dorje's senior. Sometimes such a bride finds the youngest husband immature and adolescent and does not treat him with equal affection; alternatively, she may find his youth attractive and lavish special attention on him. Apart from that consideration, when a younger male like Dorje grows up, he may consider his wife "ancient" and

81

prefer the company of a woman his own age or younger. Consequently, although men and women do not find the idea of sharing a bride or bridegroom repulsive, individual likes and dislikes can cause familial discord.

Two reasons have commonly been offered for the perpetuation of fraternal polyandry in Tibet: that Tibetans practice female infanticide and therefore have to marry polyandrously, owing to a shortage of females; and that Tibet, lying at extremely high altitudes, is so barren and bleak that Tibetans would starve without resort to this mechanism. A Jesuit who lived in Tibet during the eighteenth century articulated this second view: "One reason for this most odious custom is the sterility of the soil, and the small amount of land that can be cultivated owing to the lack of water. The crops may suffice if the brothers all live together, but if they form separate families they would be reduced to beggary."

Both explanations are wrong, however. Not only has there never been institutionalized female infanticide in Tibet, but Tibetan society gives females considerable rights, including inheriting the family estate in the absence of brothers. In such cases, the woman takes a bridegroom who comes to live in her family and adopts her family's name and identity. Moreover, there is no demographic evidence of a shortage of females. In Limi, for example, there were (in 1974) sixty females and fifty-three males in the fifteen- to thirty-five-year age category, and many adult females were unmarried.

The second reason is also incorrect. The climate in Tibet is extremely harsh, and ecological factors do play a major role perpetuating polyandry, but polyandry is not a means of preventing starvation. It is characteristic, not of the poorest segments of the society, but rather of the peasant landowning families.

In the old society, the landless poor could not realistically aspire to prosperity, but they did not fear starvation. There was a persistent labor shortage throughout Tibet, and very poor families with little or no land and few animals could subsist through agricultural labor, tenant farming, craft occupations such as carpentry, or by working as servants. Although the per person family income could increase somewhat if brothers married polyandrously and pooled their wages, in the absence of inheritable land, the advantage of fraternal polyandry was not generally sufficient to prevent them from setting up their own households. A more skilled or energetic younger brother could do as well or better alone, since he would completely control his income and would not have to share it with his siblings. Consequently, while there was and is some polyandry among the poor, it is much less frequent and more prone to result in divorce and family fission.

An alternative reason for the persistence of fraternal polyandry is that it reduces population growth (and thereby reduces the pressure on resources) by relegating some females to lifetime spinsterhood. Fraternal polyandrous marriages in Limi (in 1974) averaged 2.35 men per woman, and not surprisingly, 31 percent of the females of child-bearing age (twenty to forty-nine) were unmarried. These spinsters either continued to live at home, set up their own households, or worked as servants for other families. They could also become Buddhist nuns. Being unmarried is not synonymous with exclusion from the reproductive pool. Discreet extramarital relationships are tolerated, and actually half of the adult unmarried women in Limi had one or more children. They raised these children as single mothers, working for wages or weaving cloth and blankets for sale. As a group, however, the unmarried woman had far fewer off-spring than the married women, averaging only 0.7 children per woman, compared with 3.3 for married women, whether polyandrous, monogamous, or polygynous. While polyandry helps regulate population, this function of polyandry is not consciously perceived by Tibetans and is not the reason they consistently choose it.

If neither a shortage of females nor the fear of starvation perpetuates fraternal polyandry, what motivates brothers, particularly younger brothers, to opt for this system of marriage? From the perspective of the younger brother in a land-holding family, the main incentive is the attainment or maintenance of the good life. With polyandry, he can expect a more secure and higher standard of living, with access not only to this family's land and animals but also to its inherited collection of clothes, jewelry, rugs, saddles, and horses. In addition, he will experience less work pressure and much greater security because all responsibility does not fall on one "father." For Tibetan brothers, the question is whether to trade off the greater personal freedom inherent in monogamy for the real or potential economic security, affluence, and social prestige associated with life in a larger, labor-rich polyandrous family.

A brother thinking of separating from his polyandrous marriage and taking his own wife would face various disadvantages. Although in the majority of Tibetan regions all brothers theoretically have rights to their family's estate, in reality Tibetans are reluctant to divide their land into small fragments. Generally, a younger brother who insists on leaving the family will receive only a small plot of land, if that. Because of its power and wealth, the rest of the family usually can block any attempt of the younger brother to increase his share of land through litigation. Moreover, a younger brother may not even get a house and cannot expect to receive much above the minimum in terms of movable possessions, such as furniture, pots, and pans. Thus, a brother contemplating going it on his own must plan on achieving economic security and the good life not through inheritance but through his own work.

The obvious solution for younger brothers—creating new fields from virgin land—is generally not a feasible option. Most Tibetan populations live at high altitudes (above 12,000 feet), where arable land is extremely scarce. For example, in Dorje's village, agriculture ranges only from about 12,900 feet, the lowest point in the area, to 13,300 feet. Above that altitude, early frost and snow destroy the staple barley crop. Furthermore, because of the low rainfall caused by the Himalayan rain shadow, many areas in Tibet and northern Nepal that are within the appropriate altitude range for agriculture have no reliable sources of irrigation. In the end, although there is plenty of unused land in such areas, most of it is either too high or too arid.

Even where unused land capable of being farmed exists, clearing the land and building the substantial terraces necessary for irrigation constitute a great undertaking. Each plot has to be completely dug out to a depth of two to two and half feet so that the large rocks and boulders can be removed. At best, a man might be able to bring a few new fields under cultivation in the first years after separating from his brothers, but he could not expect to acquire substantial amounts of arable land this way.

In addition, because of the limited farmland, the Tibetan subsistence economy characteristically includes a strong emphasis on animal husbandry. Tibetan farmers regularly maintain cattle, yaks, goats, and sheep, grazing them in the areas too high for agriculture. These herds produce wool, milk, cheese, butter, meat, and skins. To obtain these resources, however, shepherds must accompany the animals on a daily basis. When first setting up a monogamous household, a younger brother like Dorje would find it difficult to both farm and manage animals.

In traditional Tibetan society, there was an even more critical factor that operated to perpetuate fraternal polyandry—a form of hereditary servitude somewhat analogous to serfdom in Europe. Peasants were tied to large estates held by aristocrats, monasteries, and the Lhasa government. They were allowed the use of some farmland to produce their own subsistence but were required to provide taxes in kind and corvée (free labor) to their lords. The corvée was a substantial hardship, since a peasant household was in many cases required to furnish the lord with one laborer daily for most of the year and more on specific occasions such as the harvest. This enforced labor, along with the lack of new land and ecological pressure to pursue both agriculture and animal husbandry, made polyandrous families particularly beneficial. The polyandrous family allowed an internal division of adult labor, maximizing economic advantage. For example, while the wife worked the family fields, one brother could perform the lord's corvée, another could look after the animals, and a third could engage in trade.

Although social scientists often discount other people's explanations of why they do things, in the case of Tibetan fraternal polyandry, such explanations are very close to the truth. The custom, however, is very sensitive to changes in its political and economic milieu and, not surprisingly, is in decline in most Tibetan areas. Made less important by the elimination of the traditional serf-based economy, it is disparaged by the dominant non-Tibetan leaders of India, China, and Nepal. New opportunities for economic and social mobility in these countries, such as the tourist trade and government employment, are also eroding the rationale for polyandry, and so it may vanish within the next generation.

Author's Note

The Revival of Fraternal Polyandry in Tibet: Old Solutions for New Problems

In spite of my observation at the end of this article—that political and economic changes were eroding the rationality for fraternal polyandry—there has been a remarkable revival of polyandry in the Tibet Autonomous Region.

After the failed Tibetan Uprising in 1959, the Chinese government acted to end the traditional land-holding system and replace it with communes in which individual commune members worked under a set of managers. Fraternal polyandry ended, as families had no land to conserve and farm.

The rise to power of Deng Xiaoping in 1978 changed China radically. China now opened its doors to the West and adopted Western-style market economics complete with the reintroduction of the profit motive and individual wealth seeking. In rural Tibet, this resulted in communes closing in 1980–81, with each commune member receiving an equal share of the commune's land regardless of age or sex. Thus, if each person received 1 acre, a family of 6 received 6 acres, on which it now managed to maximize production and income. However, families actually held this land as a long-term lease from the government so land could not be bought or sold. Consequently, as children were born and the size of families grew, land per capita began to decrease. At the same time, as sons reached the age of marriage, it was obvious that if families with several sons allowed each to marry and set up nuclear families, the land the family received from the commune would decline dramatically, and with no way to buy more land, each of the family units would have difficulty growing enough grain for subsistence. Families, therefore, as in the old society, began to utilize traditional fraternal polyandry to keep their sons together at marriage to conserve the family's land intact across generations.

A second factor underlying the widespread revival of fraternal polyandry concerned its concentration of male labor in the family. However, in the new socioeconomic environment, this has not been used to fulfill corvée labor obligations to one's lord (as mentioned in the article), but rather to increase family income by sending surplus labor (one or more of the set of siblings) to "go for income," i.e., to go outside the village as migrant laborers to earn cash income working for part of the year in cities or on rural construction projects. By the time of my last stint of fieldwork in rural Tibet in 2009, this had become the largest source of rural family income.

Fraternal polyandry has therefore undergone an unexpected revival in Tibet because its traditional functions of conserving land intact across generations and concentrating male labor in the family has offered families in the new economic system old solutions to new problems. Rapidly changing socioeconomic conditions, therefore, do not necessarily erode traditional cultural practices. They can, as in this case, revive and sustain them as well.

Critical Thinking

1. What is "fraternal polyandry"? How is it arranged?

2. How do marriage ceremonies vary? When do younger brothers typically join the marriage?

3. How are authority, work, and sex dealt with?

4. Describe the relationship between fathers and children. How is family structure reflected in kinship terminology?

5. What types of marriage are allowed in Tibetan society? Which are the most common? When does polygyny typically occur? Is fraternal polyandry a matter of law or choice? What happens if a brother is dissatisfied? What about his children?

6. How do the Tibetans explain fraternal polyandry? How is this analogous to primogeniture in 19th century England?

7. Why does it seem that monogamous marriages among brothers in the same household would not work?

8. What kinds of problems occur with fraternal polyandry that make it less than ideal?

9. What two reasons have been commonly offered for the perpetuation of fraternal polyandry in Tibet and how does the author refute these?

10. What percentage of women remain unmarried in Tibetan society? What happens to them? To what extent does polyandry thereby limit population growth? Are the Tibetans aware of this effect?

11. Why would a younger brother accept such a marriage form?

12. How is the polyandrous family more adaptive to the system of hereditary servitude in traditional Tibet?

13. Why is the custom of fraternal polyandry in decline?

14. Explain the disappearence and subsequent revival of fraternal polyandry in Tibet.

MELVYN C. GOLDSTEIN, now a professor of anthropology at Case Western Reserve University in Cleveland, has been interested in the Tibetan practice of fraternal polyandry (several brothers marrying one wife) since he was a graduate student in the 1960s.

From *Natural History,* March 1987, pp. 39–48. Copyright © 1987 by Natural History Magazine. Reprinted by permission.

Author's note: An original essay written for this volume. Copyright © 2011 by Melvin C. Goldstein. Used by permission.

Death without Weeping

Has poverty ravaged mother love in the shantytowns of Brazil?

NANCY SCHEPER-HUGHES

I have seen death without weeping,
The destiny of the Northeast is death,
Cattle they kill,
To the people they do something worse
  —Anonymous Brazilian singer (1965)

"Why do the church bells ring so often?" I asked Nailza de Arruda soon after I moved into a corner of her tiny mud-walled hut near the top of the shantytown called the Alto do Cruzeiro (Crucifix Hill). I was then a Peace Corps volunteer and community development/health worker. It was the dry and blazing hot summer of 1965, the months following the military coup in Brazil, and save for the rusty, clanging bells of N. S. das Dores Church, an eerie quiet had settled over the market town that I call Bom Jesus da Mata. Beneath the quiet, however, there was chaos and panic. "It's nothing," replied Nailza, "just another little angel gone to heaven."

Nailza had sent more than her share of little angels to heaven, and sometimes at night I could hear her engaged in a muffled but passionate discourse with one of them, two-year-old Joana. Joana's photograph, taken as she lay propped up in her tiny cardboard coffin, her eyes open, hung on a wall next to one of Nailza and Ze Antonio taken on the day they eloped.

Nailza could barely remember the other infants and babies who came and went in close succession. Most had died unnamed and were hastily baptized in their coffins. Few lived more than a month or two. Only Joana, properly baptized in church at the close of her first year and placed under the protection of a powerful saint, Joan of Arc, had been expected to live. And Nailza had dangerously allowed herself to love the little girl.

In addressing the dead child, Nailza's voice would range from tearful imploring to angry recrimination: "Why did you leave me? Was your patron saint so greedy that she could not allow me one child on this earth?" Ze Antonio advised me to ignore Nailza's odd behavior, which he understood as a kind of madness that, like the birth and death of children, came and went. Indeed, the premature birth of a stillborn son some months later "cured" Nailza of her "inappropriate" grief, and the day came when she removed Joana's photo and carefully packed it away.

More than fifteen years elapsed before I returned to the Alto do Cruzeiro, and it was anthropology that provided the vehicle of my return. Since 1982 I have returned several times in order to pursue a problem that first attracted my attention in the 1960s. My involvement with the people of the Alto do Cruzeiro now spans a quarter of a century and three generations of parenting in a community where mothers and daughters are often simultaneously pregnant.

The Alto do Cruzeiro is one of three shantytowns surrounding the large market town of Bom Jesus in the sugar plantation zone of Pernambuco in Northeast Brazil, one of the many zones of neglect that have emerged in the shadow of the now tarnished economic miracle of Brazil. For the women and children of the Alto do Cruzeiro the only miracle is that some of them have managed to stay alive at all.

The Northeast is a region of vast proportions (approximately twice the size of Texas) and of equally vast social and developmental problems. The nine states that make up the region are the poorest in the country and are representative of the Third World within a dynamic and rapidly industrializing nation. Despite waves of migrations from the interior to the teeming shantytowns of coastal cities, the majority still live in rural areas on farms and ranches, sugar plantations and mills.

Life expectancy in the Northeast is only forty years, largely because of the appallingly high rate of infant and child mortality. Approximately one million children in Brazil under the age of five die each year. The children of the Northeast, especially those born in shantytowns on the periphery of urban life, are at a very high risk of death. In these areas, children are born without the traditional protection of breast-feeding, subsistence gardens, stable marriages, and multiple adult caretakers that exists in the interior. In the hillside shantytowns that spring up around cities or, in this case, interior market towns, marriages are brittle, single parenting is the norm, and women are frequently forced into the shadow economy of domestic work in the homes of the rich or into unprotected and oftentimes "scab" wage labor on the surrounding sugar plantations, where they clear land for planting and weed for a pittance, sometimes less than a dollar a day. The women of the Alto may not bring their babies with them into the homes of the wealthy, where the often-sick infants are considered sources of contamination, and they cannot carry the little ones to the riverbanks where they wash clothes because the river is heavily infested with schistosomes and other deadly parasites. Nor can they carry their young children to the plantations, which are often several miles away. At wages of a dollar a day, the women of the Alto cannot hire baby sitters. Older children who are not in school will sometimes serve as somewhat indifferent caretakers. But any child not in school is also expected to find wage work. In most cases, babies are simply left at home alone, the door securely fastened. And so many also die alone and unattended.

Bom Jesus da Mata, centrally located in the plantation zone of Pernambuco, is within commuting distance of several sugar plantations and mills. Consequently, Bom Jesus has been a magnet for rural workers forced off their small subsistence plots by large landowners wanting to use every available piece of land for sugar cultivation. Initially, the rural migrants to Bom Jesus were squatters who were given tacit approval by the mayor to put up temporary straw huts on each of the three hills overlooking the town. The Alto do Cruzeiro is the oldest, the largest, and the poorest of the shantytowns. Over the past three decades many of the original migrants have become permanent residents, and the primitive and temporary straw huts have been replaced by small homes (usually of two rooms) made of wattle and daub, sometimes covered with plaster. The more affluent residents use bricks and tiles. In most Alto homes, dangerous kerosene lamps have been replaced by light bulbs. The once tattered rural garb, often fashioned from used sugar sacking, has likewise been replaced by store-bought clothes, often castoffs from a wealthy *patrão* (boss). The trappings are modern, but the hunger, sickness, and death that they conceal are traditional, deeply rooted in a history of feudalism, exploitation, and institutionalized dependency.

My research agenda never wavered. The questions I addressed first crystalized during a veritable "die-off" of Alto babies during a severe drought in 1965. The food and water shortages and the political and economic chaos occasioned by the military coup were reflected in the handwritten entries of births and deaths in the dusty, yellowed pages of the ledger books kept at the public registry office in Bom Jesus. More than 350 babies died in the Alto during 1965 alone—this from a shantytown population of little more than 5,000. But that wasn't what surprised me. There were reasons enough for the deaths in the miserable conditions of shantytown life. What puzzled me was the seeming indifference of Alto women to the death of their infants, and their willingness to attribute to their own tiny offspring an aversion to life that made their death seem wholly natural, indeed all but anticipated.

Although I found that it was possible, and hardly difficult, to rescue infants and toddlers from death by diarrhea and dehydration with a simple sugar, salt, and water solution (even bottled Coca-Cola worked fine), it was more difficult to enlist a mother herself in the rescue of a child she perceived as ill-fated for life or better off dead, or to convince her to take back into her threatened and besieged home a baby she had already come to think of as an angel rather than as a son or daughter.

I learned that the high expectancy of death, and the ability to face child death with stoicism and equanimity, produced patterns of nurturing that differentiated between those infants thought of as thrivers and survivors and those thought of as born already "wanting to die." The survivors were nurtured, while stigmatized, doomed infants were left to die, as mothers say, *a mingua,* "of neglect." Mothers stepped back and allowed nature to take its course. This pattern, which I call mortal selective neglect, is called passive infanticide by anthropologist Marvin Harris. The Alto situation, although culturally specific in the form that it takes, is not unique to Third World shantytown communities and may have its correlates in our own impoverished urban communities in some cases of "failure to thrive" infants.

I use as an example the story of Zezinho, the thirteen-month-old toddler of one of my neighbors, Lourdes. I became involved with Zezinho when I was called in to help Lourdes in the delivery of another child, this one a fair and robust little tyke with a lusty cry. I noted that while Lourdes showed great interest in the newborn, she totally ignored Zezinho who, wasted and severely malnourished, was curled up in a fetal position on a piece of urine- and feces-soaked cardboard placed under his mother's hammock. Eyes open and vacant, mouth slack, the little boy seemed doomed.

When I carried Zezinho up to the community day-care center at the top of the hill, the Alto women who took turns caring for one another's children (in order to free themselves for part-time work in the cane fields or washing clothes) laughed at my efforts to save Ze, agreeing with Lourdes that here was a baby without a ghost of a chance. Leave him alone, they cautioned. It makes no sense to fight with death. But I did do battle with Ze, and after several weeks of force-feeding (malnourished babies lose their interest in food), Ze began to succumb to my ministrations. He acquired some flesh across his taut chest bones, learned to sit up, and even tried to smile. When he seemed well enough, I returned him to Lourdes in her miserable scrap-material lean-to, but not without guilt about what I had done. I wondered whether returning Ze was at all fair to Lourdes and to his little brother. But I was busy and washed my hands of the matter. And Lourdes did seem more interested in Ze now that he was looking more human.

When I returned in 1982, there was Lourdes among the women who formed my sample of Alto mothers—still struggling to put together some semblance of life for a now grown Ze and her five other surviving children. Much was made of my reunion with Ze in 1982, and everyone enjoyed retelling the story of Ze's rescue and of how his mother had given him up for dead. Ze would laugh the loudest when told how I had had to force-feed him like a fiesta turkey. There was no hint of guilt on the part of Lourdes and no resentment on the part of Ze. In fact, when questioned in private as to who was the best friend he ever had in life, Ze took a long drag on his cigarette and answered without a trace of irony, "Why my mother, of course." "But of course," I replied.

Part of learning how to mother in the Alto do Cruzeiro is learning when to let go of a child who shows that it "wants" to die or that it has no "knack" or no "taste" for life. Another part is learning when it is safe to let oneself love a child. Frequent child death remains a powerful shaper of maternal thinking and practice. In the absence of firm expectation that a child will survive, mother love as we conceptualize it (whether in popular terms or in the psychobiological notion of maternal bonding) is attenuated and delayed with consequences for infant survival. In an environment already precarious to young life, the emotional detachment of mothers toward some of their babies contributes even further to the spiral of high mortality—high fertility in a kind of macabre lock-step dance of death.

The average woman of the Alto experiences 9.5 pregnancies, 3.5 child deaths, and 1.5 stillbirths. Seventy percent of all child deaths in the Alto occur in the first six months of life, and 82 percent by the end of the first year. Of all deaths in the community each year, about 45 percent are of children under the age of five.

Women of the Alto distinguish between child deaths understood as natural (caused by diarrhea and communicable diseases) and those resulting from sorcery, the evil eye, or other magical or supernatural afflictions. They also recognize a large category of infant deaths seen as fated and inevitable. These hopeless cases are classified by mothers under the folk terminology "child sickness" or "child attack." Women say that there are at least fourteen different types of hopeless child sickness, but most can be subsumed under two categories—chronic and acute. The chronic cases refer to infants who are born small and wasted. They are deathly pale, mothers say, as well as weak and passive. They demonstrate no vital force, no liveliness. They do not suck vigorously; they hardly cry. Such babies can be this way at birth or they can be born sound but soon show no resistance, no "fight" against the common crises of infancy: diarrhea, respiratory infections, tropical fevers.

The acute cases are those doomed infants who die suddenly and violently. They are taken by stealth overnight, often following convulsions that bring on head banging, shaking, grimacing, and shrieking. Women say it is horrible to look at such a baby. If the infant begins to foam at the mouth or gnash its teeth or go rigid with its eyes turned back inside its head, there is absolutely no hope. The infant is "put aside"—left alone—often on the floor in a back room, and allowed to die. These symptoms (which accompany high fevers, dehydration, third-stage malnutrition, and encephalitis) are equated by Alto women with madness, epilepsy, and worst of all, rabies, which is greatly feared and highly stigmatized.

Most of the infants presented to me as suffering from chronic child sickness were tiny, wasted famine victims, while those labeled as victims of acute child attack seemed to be infants suffering from the deliriums of high fever or the convulsions that can accompany electrolyte imbalance in dehydrated babies.

Local midwives and traditional healers, praying women, as they are called, advise Alto women on when to allow a baby to die. One midwife explained: "If I can see that a baby was born unfortuitously, I tell the mother that she need not wash the infant or give it a cleansing tea. I tell her just to dust the infant with baby powder and wait for it to die." Allowing nature to take its course is not seen as sinful by these often very devout Catholic women. Rather, it is understood as cooperating with God's plan.

Often I have been asked how consciously women of the Alto behave in this regard. I would have to say that consciousness is always shifting between allowed and disallowed levels of awareness. For example, I was awakened early one morning in 1987 by two neighborhood children who had been sent to fetch me to a hastily organized wake for a two-month-old infant whose mother I had unsuccessfully urged to breast-feed. The infant was being sustained on sugar water, which the mother referred to as *soro* (serum), using a medical term for the infant's starvation regime in light of his chronic diarrhea. I had cautioned the mother that an infant could not live on *soro* forever.

The two girls urged me to console the young mother by telling her that it was "too bad" that her infant was so weak that Jesus had to take him. They were coaching me in proper Alto etiquette. I agreed, of course, but asked, "And what do *you* think?" Xoxa, the eleven-year-old, looked down at her dusty flip-flops and blurted out, "Oh, Dona Nanci, that baby never got enough to eat, but you must never say that!" And so the death of hungry babies remains one of the best kept secrets of life in Bom Jesus da Mata.

Most victims are waked quickly and with a minimum of ceremony. No tears are shed, and the neighborhood children form a tiny procession, carrying the baby to the town graveyard where it will join a multitude of others. Although a few fresh flowers may be scattered over the tiny grave, no stone or wooden cross will mark the place, and the same spot will be reused within a few months' time. The mother will never visit the grave, which soon becomes an anonymous one.

What, then, can be said of these women? What emotions, what sentiments motivate them? How are they able to do what, in fact, must be done? What does mother love mean in this inhospitable context? Are grief, mourning, and melancholia present, although deeply repressed? If so, where shall we look for them? And if not, how are we to understand the moral visions and moral sensibilities that guide their actions?

I have been criticized more than once for presenting an unflattering portrait of poor Brazilian women, women who are, after all, themselves the victims of severe social and institutional neglect. I have described these women as allowing some of their children to die, as if this were an unnatural and inhuman act rather than, as I would assert, the way any one of us might act, reasonably and rationally, under similarly desperate conditions. Perhaps I have not emphasized enough the real pathogens in this environment of high risk: poverty, deprivation, sexism, chronic hunger, and economic exploitation. If mother love is, as many psychologists and some feminists believe, a seemingly natural and universal maternal script, what does it mean to women for whom scarcity, loss, sickness, and deprivation have made that love frantic and robbed them of their grief, seeming to turn their hearts to stone?

Throughout much of human history—as in a great deal of the impoverished Third World today—women have had to give birth and to nurture children under ecological conditions and social arrangements hostile to child survival, as well as to their own well-being. Under circumstances of high childhood mortality, patterns of selective neglect and passive infanticide may be seen as active survival strategies.

They also seem to be fairly common practices historically and across cultures. In societies characterized by high childhood mortality and by a correspondingly high (replacement) fertility, cultural practices of infant and child care tend to be organized primarily around survival goals. But what this means is a pragmatic recognition that not all of one's children can be expected to live. The nervousness about child survival in areas of northeast Brazil, northern India, or Bangladesh, where a 30 percent or 40 percent mortality rate in the first years of life is common, can lead to forms of delayed attachment and a casual or benign neglect that serves to weed out the worst bets so as to enhance the life chances of healthier siblings, including those yet to be born. Practices similar to those that I am describing have been recorded for parts of Africa, India, and Central America.

Life in the Alto do Cruzeiro resembles nothing so much as a battlefield or an emergency room in an overcrowded inner-city public hospital. Consequently, mortality is guided by a kind of "life-boat ethics," the morality of triage. The seemingly studied indifference toward the suffering of some of their infants, conveyed in such sayings as "little critters have no feelings," is understandable in light of these women's obligation to carry on with their reproductive and nurturing lives.

In their slowness to anthropomorphize and personalize their infants, everything is mobilized so as to prevent maternal over-attachment and, therefore, grief at death. The bereaved mother is told not to cry, that her tears will dampen the wings of her little angel so that she cannot fly up to her heavenly home. Grief at the death of an angel is not only inappropriate, it is a symptom of madness and of a profound lack of faith.

Infant death becomes routine in an environment in which death is anticipated and bets are hedged. While the routinization of death in the context of shantytown life is not hard to understand, and quite possible to empathize with, its routinization in the formal institutions of public life in Bom Jesus is not as easy to accept uncritically. Here the social production of indifference takes on a different, even a malevolent, cast.

In a society where triplicates of every form are required for the most banal events (registering a car, for example), the registration of infant and child death is informal, incomplete, and rapid. It requires no documentation, takes less than five minutes, and demands no witnesses other than office clerks. No questions are asked concerning the circumstances of the death, and the cause of death is left blank, unquestioned and unexamined. A neighbor, grandmother, older sibling, or common-law husband may register the death. Since most infants die at home, there is no question of a medical record.

From the registry office, the parent proceeds to the town hall, where the mayor will give him or her a voucher for a free baby coffin. The full-time municipal coffinmaker cannot tell you exactly how many baby coffins are dispatched each week. It varies, he says, with the seasons. There are more needed during the drought months and during the big festivals of Carnaval and Christmas and São Joao's Day because people are too busy, he supposes, to take their babies to the clinic. Record keeping is sloppy.

Similarly, there is a failure on the part of city-employed doctors working at two free clinics to recognize the malnutrition of babies who are weighed, measured, and immunized without comment and as if they were not, in fact, anemic, stunted, fussy, and irritated starvation babies. At best the mothers are told to pick up free vitamins or a health "tonic" at the municipal chambers. At worst, clinic personnel will give tranquilizers and sleeping pills to quiet the hungry cries of "sick-to-death" Alto babies.

The church, too, contributes to the routinization of, and indifference toward, child death. Traditionally, the local Catholic church taught patience and resignation to domestic tragedies that were said to reveal the imponderable workings of God's will. If an infant died suddenly, it was because a particular saint had claimed the child. The infant would be an angel in the service of his or her heavenly patron. It would be wrong, a sign of a lack of faith, to weep for a child with such good fortune. The infant funeral was, in the past, an event celebrated with joy. Today, however, under the new regime of "liberation theology," the bells of N. S. das Dores parish church no longer peal for the death of Alto babies, and no priest accompanies the procession of angels to the cemetery where their bodies are disposed of casually and without ceremony. Children bury children in Bom Jesus da Mata. In this most Catholic of communities, the coffin is handed to the disabled and irritable municipal gravedigger, who often chides the children for one reason or another. It may be that the coffin is larger than expected and the gravedigger can find no appropriate space. The children do not wait for the gravedigger to complete his task. No prayers are recited and no sign of the cross made as the tiny coffin goes into its shallow grave.

When I asked the local priest, Padre Marcos, about the lack of church ceremony surrounding infant and childhood death today in Bom Jesus, he replied; "In the old days, child death was richly celebrated. But those were the baroque customs of a conservative church that wallowed in death and misery. The new church is a church of hope and joy. We no longer celebrate the death of child angels. We try to tell mothers that Jesus doesn't want all the dead babies they send him." Similarly, the new church has changed its baptismal customs, now often refusing to baptize dying babies brought to the back door of a church or rectory. The mothers are scolded by the church attendants and told to go home and take care of their sick babies. Baptism, they are told, is for the living; it is not to be confused with the sacrament of extreme unction, which is the anointing of the dying. And so it appears to the women of the Alto that even the church has turned away from them, denying the traditional comfort of folk Catholicism.

The contemporary Catholic church is caught in the clutches of a double bind. The new theology of liberation imagines a kingdom of God on earth based on justice and equality, a world without hunger, sickness, or childhood mortality. At the same time, the church has not changed its official position on sexuality and reproduction, including its sanctions against birth control, abortion, and sterilization. The padre of Bom Jesus da Mata recognizes this contradiction intuitively, although he shies away from discussions on the topic, saying that he prefers to leave questions of family planning to the discretion and the "good consciences" of his impoverished parishioners. But this, of course, sidesteps the extent to which those good consciences have been shaped by traditional church teachings in Bom Jesus, especially by his recent predecessors. Hence, we can begin to see that the seeming indifference of Alto mothers toward the death of some of their infants is but a pale reflection of the official indifference of church and state to the plight of poor women and children.

Nonetheless, the women of Bom Jesus are survivors. One woman, Biu, told me her life history, returning again and again to the themes of child death, her first husband's suicide, abandonment by her father and later by her second husband, and all the other losses and disappointments she had suffered in her long forty-five years. She concluded with great force, reflecting on the days of Carnaval '88 that were fast approaching:

> No, Dona Nanci, I won't cry, and I won't waste my life thinking about it from morning to night. . . . Can I argue with God for the state that I'm in? No! And so I'll dance and I'll jump and I'll play Carnaval! And yes, I'll laugh and people will wonder at a *pobre* like me who can have such a good time.

And no one did blame Biu for dancing in the streets during the four days of Carnaval—not even on Ash Wednesday, the day following Carnaval '88 when we all assembled hurriedly to assist in the burial of Mercea, Biu's beloved *casula*, her last-born daughter who had died at home of pneumonia during the festivities. The rest of the family barely had time to change out of their costumes. Severino, the child's uncle and godfather, sprinkled holy water over the little angel while he prayed: "Mercea, I don't know whether you were called, taken, or thrown out of this world. But look down at us from your heavenly home with tenderness, with pity, and with mercy." So be it.

Author's Note

Many students write to me after reading this article asking whether the situation has changed in the Alto do Cruzeiro. Is life better or worse for mothers and newborn babies? One of the advantages of traditional, long-term ethnographic research is that one gets to see history in the making. I began my engagements with the people of the Alto in 1964 at the start of twenty years of military rule, a ruthless political-economic regime that produced widespread impoverishment among those excluded populations living in deep urban slums (favelas) and in peripheral rural communities. The scarcities and insecurities of that era contributed to the death of infants and small babies. By the time I completed my study of mother love and child death in the early 1990s, Brazil was well on its way to democratization which ushered in many important changes, most notably a free, public, national health care system (SUS) which guaranteed poor women adequate pre-natal care, hospital delivery, and basic maternal infant care during the first years of life. The decade of the 1990s witnessed in Brazil what population experts call the demographic or epidemiologic transition. Both births and infant deaths declined, radically transforming the way newborns were perceived and received by Alto mothers. The old stance of maternal "watchful waiting" that was accompanied by maternal "de-selections" of those infants viewed as having no "taste" or "talent" for life, was replaced by a maternal ethos of "holding on" and "holding dear" each infant now seen as potentially capable of survival.

Today, young women of the Alto can expect to give birth to three or fewer infants and to see all of them live to adolescence. Many factors came together in producing this crucial reproductive transition. The new teachings of liberation theology did eventually dislodge a baroque folk Catholicism that saw God and the saints as "authorizing" infant death by "calling" the infants to themselves. Women began to think of themselves as capable of deciding how many pregnancies they would have. The ready availability of over or "under" the counter drug, Cytotec, an effective but risky "morning after" pill, provided an easy means of birth spacing that had not existed before. President Fernando Henrique Cardoso (1995–2003) fortified the national health care system (Serviço Único de Saúde) with a program of local "health agents," "barefoot doctors," who visit poor households door to door, identifying those at risk and rescuing a great many vulnerable infants, toddlers, and old people from premature death. President "Lula's" program supporting monthly stipends (called student grants) to poor women who keep their children in primary school, made children into valuable household "workers" and literacy increased for both the children and their mothers who often studied (surreptitiously) alongside their children as they completed their homework. Women's literacy is the best predictor of lowered birth rates and reduced infant mortality. The primary cause of the decline in infant mortality on the Alto do Cruzeiro, however, was the result of a "simple" municipal program, the installation of water pipes reaching almost all the homes in the shantytown with sufficient and clean water. Water = life! It is amazing to observe how "culture," "beliefs," "maternal sentiments," and infant and child care practices are transformed, even revolutionized, following basic changes in the material conditions and therefore the possibilities of everyday life. Motherhood is not only a social and a cultural construction but a constellation of embodied practices responding to the requirements and limitations of the political economy that determines the food people eat or don't eat, the water they drink or don't drink, the shoes they wear or don't wear, the books they read or cannot read, the homes made of mud and sticks or of brick and tiles.

There are other new problems faced by the people of the Alto do Cruzeiro today. Since the publication of "Death without Weeping," drugs and gangs have made their ugly mark on the community, as have new disease epidemics. The community was devastated by a cholera epidemic that carried away hundreds of residents, needlessly. Death squads and "extermination groups" have grown and spread so that by the first decade of 2000 the extermination groups and their hit men (and women) became, for all practical purposes, law and order (or disorder) and the shadow "government" of the municipality—its legal, executive, and judicial branches combined. These new features of antisocial life in "Bom Jesus da Mata" (the municipio of Timbauba, its real name) take some of the pleasure away, as one now sees the young boys of the Alto do Cruzeiro who survived that dangerous first year of life only to be cut down by bullets and knives at the age of 15 or 17 by local gangs, "strong men," bandidos, and local police in almost equal measure. The favorite son of one of my closest and dearest key informants, Biu, was killed by that death squad in 2000 and Biu herself died, so unfairly, in 2004 of drug resistant tuberculosis, wasting, and ovarian cancer. On my last visit to the Alto do Cruzeiro, a few months before she died, Biu was thin as a rail but cheerful and upbeat. It pleased her to know that many students from all over frequently asked about her and wished her well. I took Biu to the local clinics and then to a public hospital in Recife. It was obviously too late for Biu and I grieved deeply her loss and the realization that health agents, activists, and visitadoras (as I had been) can catch certain problems, but community workers and anthropologists are not physicians, and sometimes our job, though not nearly adequate, nor even "good enough" is what it is, an attempt to listen, to record as accurately as we can, and to hold dear our fieldwork friends, and to do our best to keep their lives and their stories alive.

Critical Thinking

1. How is the poverty of the Brazilian Northeast reflected in its life expectancy and infant and child mortality?

2. What traditional protections are absent for the children?

3. How does the author characterize marriage and the lives of women and their children?

4. Under what circumstances have people come to Bom Jesus?

5. What puzzled the author about the death of infants? How was it possible to rescue their children and yet difficult to enlist the mothers' help?

6. Describe "mortal selective neglect" (or "passive infanticide").

7. Describe the case of "Ze" as it illustrates the author's later points.

8. What must one learn to be a mother?

9. Why is "allowing nature to take its course" not seen as sinful?

10. What is "one of the best kept secrets of life"?

11. How does the author explain the mothers' "delayed attachment" and "benign neglect"?

12. How is infant death "routinized" with respect to official records and medical care? How has the church contributed to this indifference? What changes have occurred under "liberation theology"?

13. How is the church caught in a "double bind"?

14. Describe the "reproductive transition" for the women of the Alto and why it came about.

15. What new problems face the people of the Alto?

NANCY SCHEPER-HUGHES is a professor in the Department of Anthropology at the University of California, Berkeley. She has written *Death Without Weeping: Violence of Everyday Life in Brazil* (1992).

From *Natural History*, October 1989, pp. 8, 10, 12, 14, 16. Copyright © 1989 by Nancy Scheper-Hughes. Reprinted by permission.

Author's note: An original essay written for this volume. Copyright © 2011 by Nancy Scheper-Hughes. Used by permission.

Arranging a Marriage in India

SERENA NANDA

Sister and doctor brother-in-law invite correspondence from North Indian professionals only, for a beautiful, talented, sophisticated, intelligent sister, 5'3", slim, M.A. in textile design, father a senior civil officer. Would prefer immigrant doctors, between 26–29 years. Reply with full details and returnable photo. A well-settled uncle invites matrimonial correspondence from slim, fair, educated South Indian girl, for his nephew, 25 years, smart, M.B.A., green card holder, 5'6". Full particulars with returnable photo appreciated.

—*Matrimonial Advertisements,*
India Abroad

In India, almost all marriages are arranged. Even among the educated middle classes in modern, urban India, marriage is as much a concern of the families as it is of the individuals. So customary is the practice of arranged marriage that there is a special name for a marriage which is not arranged: It is called a "love match."

On my first field trip to India, I met many young men and women whose parents were in the process of "getting them married." In many cases, the bride and groom would not meet each other before the marriage. At most they might meet for a brief conversation, and this meeting would take place only after their parents had decided that the match was suitable. Parents do not compel their children to marry a person who either marriage partner finds objectionable. But only after one match is refused will another be sought.

As a young American woman in India for the first time, I found this custom of arranged marriage oppressive. How could any intelligent young person agree to such a marriage without great reluctance? It was contrary to everything I believed about the importance of romantic love as the only basis of a happy marriage. It also clashed with my strongly held notions that the choice of such an intimate and permanent relationship could be made only by the individuals involved. Had anyone tried to arrange my marriage, I would have been defiant and rebellious!

At the first opportunity, I began, with more curiosity than tact, to question the young people I met on how they felt about this practice. Sita, one of my young informants, was a college graduate with a degree in political science. She had been waiting for over a year while her parents were arranging a match for her. I found it difficult to accept the docile manner in which this well-educated young woman awaited the outcome of a process that would result in her spending the rest of her life with a man she hardly knew, a virtual stranger, picked out by her parents.

"How can you go along with this?" I asked her, in frustration and distress. "Don't you care who you marry?"

"Of course I care," she answered." This is why I must let my parents choose a boy for me. My marriage is too important to be arranged by such an inexperienced person as myself. In such matters, it is better to have my parents' guidance."

I had learned that young men and women in India do not date and have very little social life involving members of the opposite sex. Although I could not disagree with Sita's reasoning, I continued to pursue the subject.

Young men and women do not date and have very little social life involving members of the opposite sex.

"But how can you marry the first man you have ever met? Not only have you missed the fun of meeting a lot of different people, but you have not given yourself the chance to know who is the right man for you."

"Meeting with a lot of different people doesn't sound like any fun at all," Sita answered. "One hears that in America the girls are spending all their time worrying about whether they will meet a man and get married. Here we have the chance to enjoy our life and let our parents do this work and worrying for us."

She had me there. The high anxiety of the competition to "be popular" with the opposite sex certainly was the most prominent feature of life as an American teenager in the late fifties. The endless worrying about the rules that governed our behavior and about our popularity ratings sapped both our self-esteem and our enjoyment of adolescence. I reflected that absence of this competition in India most certainly may have contributed to the self-confidence and natural charm of so many of the young women I met.

And yet, the idea of marrying a perfect stranger, whom one did not know and did not "love," so offended my American ideas of individualism and romanticism, that I persisted with my objections.

"I still can't imagine it," I said. "How can you agree to marry a man you hardly know?"

"But of course he will be known. My parents would never arrange a marriage for me without knowing all about the boy's family background. Naturally we will not rely only on what the family tells us. We will check the particulars out ourselves. No one will want their daughter to marry into a family that is not good. All these things we will know beforehand."

Impatiently, I responded, "Sita, I don't mean know the family, I mean, know the man. How can you marry someone you don't know personally and don't love? How can you think of spending your life with someone you may not even like?"

"If he is a good man, why should I not like him?" she said. "With you people, you know the boy so well before you marry, where will be the fun to get married? There will be no mystery and no romance. Here we have the whole of our married life to get to know and love our husband. This way is better, is it not?"

Her response made further sense, and I began to have second thoughts on the matter. Indeed, during months of meeting many intelligent young Indian people, both male and female, who had the same ideas as Sita, I saw arranged marriages in a different light. I also saw the importance of the family in Indian life and realized that a couple who took their marriage into their own hands was taking a big risk, particularly if their families were irreconcilably opposed to the match. In a country where every important resource in life—a job, a house, a social circle—is gained through family connections, it seemed foolhardy to cut oneself off from a supportive social network and depend solely on one person for happiness and success.

Six years later I returned to India to again do fieldwork, this time among the middle class in Bombay, a modern, sophisticated city. From the experience of my earlier visit, I decided to include a study of arranged marriages in my project. By this time I had met many Indian couples whose marriages had been arranged and who seemed very happy. Particularly in contrast to the fate of many of my married friends in the United States who were already in the process of divorce, the positive aspects of arranged marriages appeared to me to outweigh the negatives. In fact, I thought I might even participate in arranging a marriage myself. I had been fairly successful in the United States in "fixing up" many of my friends, and I was confident that my matchmaking skills could be easily applied to this new situation, once I learned the basic rules. "After all," I thought, "how complicated can it be? People want pretty much the same things in a marriage whether it is in India or America."

An opportunity presented itself almost immediately. A friend from my previous Indian trip was in the process of arranging for the marriage of her eldest son. In India there is a perceived shortage of "good boys," and since my friend's family was eminently respectable and the boy himself personable, well educated, and nice looking, I was sure that by the end of my year's fieldwork, we would have found a match.

The basic rule seems to be that a family's reputation is most important. It is understood that matches would be arranged only within the same caste and general social class, although some crossing of subcastes is permissible if the class positions of the bride's and groom's families are similar. Although dowry is now prohibited by law in India, extensive gift exchanges took place with every marriage. Even when the boy's family do not "make demands," every girl's family nevertheless feels the obligation to give the traditional gifts, to the girl, to the boy, and to the boy's family. Particularly when the couple would be living in the joint family—that is, with the boy's parents and his married brothers and their families, as well as with unmarried siblings—which is still very common even among the urban, upper-middle class in India, the girls' parents are anxious to establish smooth relations between their family and that of the boy. Offering the proper gifts, even when not called "dowry," is often an important factor in influencing the relationship between the bride's and groom's families and perhaps, also, the treatment of the bride in her new home.

In a society where divorce is still a scandal and where, in fact, the divorce rate is exceedingly low, an arranged marriage is the beginning of a lifetime relationship not just between the bride and groom but between their families as well.

In a society where divorce is still a scandal and where, in fact, the divorce rate is exceedingly low, an arranged marriage is the beginning of a lifetime relationship not just between the bride and groom but between their families as well. Thus, while a girl's looks are important, her character is even more so, for she is being judged as a prospective daughter-in-law as much as a prospective bride. Where she would be living in a joint family, as was the case with my friend, the girls's ability to get along harmoniously in a family is perhaps the single most important quality in assessing her suitability.

My friend is a highly esteemed wife, mother, and daughter-in-law. She is religious, soft-spoken, modest, and deferential. She rarely gossips and never quarrels, two qualities highly desirable in a woman. A family that has the reputation for gossip and conflict among its womenfolk will not find it easy to get good wives for their sons. Parents will not want to send their daughter to a house in which there is conflict.

My friend's family were originally from North India. They had lived in Bombay, where her husband owned a business, for forty years. The family had delayed in seeking a match for their eldest son because he had been an Air Force pilot for several years, stationed in such remote places that it had seemed fruitless to try to find a girl who would be willing to accompany him. In their social class, a military career, despite its economic security, has little prestige and is considered a drawback in finding a suitable bride. Many families would not allow their daughters

Even today, almost all marriages in India are arranged. It is believed that parents are much more effective at deciding whom their daughters should marry.

to marry a man in an occupation so potentially dangerous and which requires so much moving around.

The son had recently left the military and joined his father's business. Since he was a college graduate, modern, and well traveled, from such a good family, and, I thought, quite handsome, it seemed to me that he, or rather his family, was in a position to pick and choose. I said as much to my friend.

While she agreed that there were many advantages on their side, she also said, "We must keep in mind that my son is both short and dark; these are drawbacks in finding the right match." While the boy's height had not escaped my notice, "dark" seemed to me inaccurate; I would have called him "wheat" colored perhaps, and in any case, I did not realize that color would be a consideration. I discovered, however, that while a boy's skin color is a less important consideration than a girl's, it is still a factor.

An important source of contacts in trying to arrange her son's marriage was my friend's social club in Bombay. Many of the women had daughters of the right age, and some had already expressed an interest in my friend's son. I was most enthusiastic about the possibilities of one particular family who had five daughters, all of whom were pretty, demure, and well educated. Their mother had told my friend, "You can have your pick for your son, whichever one of my daughters appeals to you most."

I saw a match in sight. "Surely," I said to my friend, "we will find one there. Let's go visit and make our choice." But my friend held back; she did not seem to share my enthusiasm, for reasons I could not then fathom.

When I kept pressing for an explanation of her reluctance, she admitted, "See, Serena, here is the problem. The family has so many daughters, how will they be able to provide nicely for any of them? We are not making any demands, but still, with so many daughters to marry off, one wonders whether she will even be able to make a proper wedding. Since this is our eldest son, it's best if we marry him to a girl who is the only daughter, then the wedding will truly be a gala affair." I argued that surely the quality of the girls themselves made up for any deficiency in the elaborateness of the wedding. My friend admitted this point but still seemed reluctant to proceed.

"Is there something else," I asked her, "some factor I have missed?" "Well," she finally said, "there is one other thing. They have one daughter already married and living in Bombay. The mother is always complaining to me that the girl's in-laws don't let her visit her own family often enough. So it makes me wonder, will she be that kind of mother who always wants her daughter at her own home? This will prevent the girl from adjusting to our house. It is not a good thing." And so, this family of five daughters was dropped as a possibility.

Somewhat disappointed, I nevertheless respected my friend's reasoning and geared up for the next prospect. This was also the daughter of a woman in my friend's social club. There was clear interest in this family and I could see why. The family's reputation was excellent; in fact, they came from a subcaste slightly higher than my friend's own. The girl, who was an only daughter, was pretty and well educated and had a brother studying in the United States. Yet, after expressing an interest to me in this family, all talk of them suddenly died down and the search began elsewhere.

"What happened to that girl as a prospect?" I asked one day. "You never mention her any more. She is so pretty and so educated, what did you find wrong?"

"She is too educated. We've decided against it. My husband's father saw the girl on the bus the other day and thought her forward. A girl who 'roams about' the city by herself is not the girl for our family." My disappointment this time was even greater, as I thought the son would have liked the girl very much. But then I thought, my friend is right, a girl who is going to live in a joint family cannot be too independent or she will make life miserable for everyone. I also learned that if the family of the girl has even a slightly higher social status than the family of the boy, the bride may think herself too good for them, and this too will cause problems. Later my friend admitted to me that this had been an important factor in her decision not to pursue the match.

The next candidate was the daughter of a client of my friend's husband. When the client learned that the family was looking for a match for their son, he said, "Look no further, we have a daughter." This man then invited my friends to dinner to see the girl. He had already seen their son at the office and decided that "he liked the boy." We all went together for tea, rather than dinner—it was less of a commitment—and while we were there, the girl's mother showed us around the house. The girl was studying for her exams and was briefly introduced to us.

After we left, I was anxious to hear my friend's opinion. While her husband liked the family very much and was impressed with his client's business accomplishments and reputation, the wife didn't like the girl's looks. "She is short, no doubt, which is an important plus point, but she is also fat and wears glasses." My friend obviously thought she could do better for her son and asked her husband to make his excuses to his client by saying that they had decided to postpone the boy's marriage indefinitely.

By this time almost six months had passed and I was becoming impatient. What I had thought would be an easy matter to arrange was turning out to be quite complicated. I began to believe that between my friend's desire for a girl who was modest enough to fit into her joint family, yet attractive and educated enough to be an acceptable partner for her son, she would not find anyone suitable. My friend laughed at my impatience: "Don't be so much in a hurry," she said. "You Americans want everything done so quickly. You get married quickly and then just as quickly get divorced. Here we take marriage more seriously. We must take all the factors into account. It is not enough for us to learn by our mistakes. This is too serious a business. If a mistake is made we have not only ruined the life of our son or daughter, but we have spoiled the reputation of our family as well. And that will make it much harder for their brothers and sisters to get married. So we must be very careful."

If a mistake is made we have not only ruined the life of our son or daughter, but we have spoiled the reputation of our family as well.

What she said was true and I promised myself to be more patient, though it was not easy. I had really hoped and expected that the match would be made before my year in India was up. But it was not to be. When I left India my friend seemed no further along in finding a suitable match for her son than when I had arrived.

Two years later, I returned to India and still my friend had not found a girl for her son. By this time, he was close to thirty, and I think she was a little worried. Since she knew I had friends all over India, and I was going to be there for a year, she asked me to "help her in this work" and keep an eye out for someone suitable. I was flattered that my judgment was respected, but knowing now how complicated the process was, I had lost my earlier confidence as a matchmaker. Nevertheless, I promised that I would try.

It was almost at the end of my year's stay in India that I met a family with a marriageable daughter whom I felt might be a good possibility for my friend's son. The girl's father was related to a good friend of mine and by coincidence came from the same village as my friend's husband. This new family had a successful business in a medium-sized city in central India and were from the same sub-caste as my friend. The daughter was pretty and chic; in fact, she had studied fashion design in college. Her parents would not allow her to go off by herself to any of the major cities in India where she could make a career, but they had compromised with her wish to work by allowing her to run a small dress-making boutique from their home. In spite of her desire to have a career, the daughter was both modest and home-loving and had had a traditional, sheltered upbringing. She had only one other sister, already married, and a brother who was in his father's business.

I mentioned the possibility of a match with my friend's son. The girl's parents were most interested. Although their daughter was not eager to marry just yet, the idea of living in Bombay—a sophisticated, extremely fashion-conscious city where she could continue her education in clothing design—was a great inducement. I gave the girl's father my friend's address and suggested that when they went to Bombay on some business or whatever, they look up the boy's family.

Returning to Bombay on my way to New York, I told my friend of this newly discovered possibility. She seemed to feel there was potential but, in spite of my urging, would not make any moves herself. She rather preferred to wait for the girl's family to call upon them. I hoped something would come of this introduction, though by now I had learned to rein in my optimism.

A year later I received a letter from my friend. The family had indeed come to visit Bombay, and their daughter and my

Appendix
Further Reflections on Arranged Marriage . . .

This essay was written from the point of view of a family seeking a daughter-in-law. Arranged marriage looks somewhat different from the point of view of the bride and her family. Arranged marriage continues to be preferred, even among the more educated, Westernized sections of the Indian population. Many young women from these families still go along, more or less willingly, with the practice, and also with the specific choices of their families. Young women do get excited about the prospects of their marriage, but there is also ambivalence and increasing uncertainty, as the bride contemplates leaving the comfort and familiarity of her own home, where as a "temporary guest" she had often been indulged, to live among strangers. Even in the best situation she will now come under the close scrutiny of her husband's family. How she dresses, how she behaves, how she gets along with others, where she goes, how she spends her time, her domestic abilities—all of this and much more—will be observed and commented on by a whole new set of relations. Her interaction with her family of birth will be monitored and curtailed considerably. Not only will she leave their home, but with increasing geographic mobility, she may also live very far from them, perhaps even on another continent. Too much expression of her fondness for her own family, or her desire to visit them, may be interpreted as an inability to adjust to her new family, and may become a source of conflict. In an arranged marriage the burden of adjustment is clearly heavier for a woman than for a man. And that is in the best of situations.

In less happy circumstances, the bride may be a target of resentment and hostility from her husband's family, particularly her mother-in-law or her husband's unmarried sisters, for whom she is now a source of competition for the affection, loyalty, and economic resources of their son or brother. If she is psychologically, or even physically abused, her options are limited, as returning to her parents' home, or divorce, are still very stigmatized. For most Indians, marriage and motherhood are still considered the only suitable roles for a woman, even for those who have careers, and few women can comfortably contemplate remaining unmarried. Most families still consider "marrying off" their daughters as a compelling religious duty and social necessity. This increases a bride's sense of obligation to make the marriage a success, at whatever cost to her own personal happiness.

The vulnerability of a new bride may also be intensified by the issue of dowry, which although illegal, has become a more pressing issue in the consumer conscious society of contemporary urban India. In many cases, where a groom's family is not satisfied with the amount of dowry a bride brings to her marriage, the young bride will be constantly harassed to get her parents to give more. In extreme cases, the bride may even be murdered, and the murder disguised as an accident or suicide. This also offers the husband's family an opportunity to arrange another match for him, thus bringing in another dowry. This phenomena, called dowry death, calls attention not just to the "evils of dowry" but also to larger issues of the powerlessness of women as well.

Serena Nanda
March 1998

---

friend's daughter, who were near in age, had become very good friends. During that year, the two girls had frequently visited each other. I thought things looked promising.

Last week I received an invitation to a wedding: My friend's son and the girl were getting married. Since I had found the match, my presence was particularly requested at the wedding. I was thrilled. Success at last! As I prepared to leave for India, I began thinking, "Now, my friend's younger son, who do I know who has a nice girl for him . . .?"

Critical Thinking

1. To what extent are marriages arranged in India? How do middle class families in modern urban India feel about marriage? What is a "love match?"

2. How does the author describe the process of the parents' "getting them married" (with regard to young men and women)? Why did the author find this "oppressive?"

3. Describe the arguments and counter-arguments regarding arranged marriages as revealed in the verbal exchanges between the author and Sita.

4. In what sense did the author see arranged marriage as successful in contrast to marriage in the United States?

5. Why was the author so sure that a match could be made quickly for her friend's son?

6. What factors must be taken into account in arranging a marriage?

7. Why was the friend's son originally not considered a good match? What happened that would change his prospects? What drawbacks remained?

8. Describe the "problems" that arose with regard to the various "prospects" as well as the positive factors involved in the final match.

Edited by Philip R. DeVita.

From *Stumbling Toward Truth: Anthropologists at Work*, Waveland Press, 2000, pp. 196–204. Copyright © 2000 by Serena Nanda. Reprinted by permission of the author. The author has also written *The Gift of a Bride: A Tale of Anthropology, Matrimony, and Murder* (with Joan Gregg). New York: Altamira/Rowman 2009.

Article 19

Who Needs Love!
In Japan, Many Couples Don't

NICHOLAS D. KRISTOF

Yuri Uemura sat on the straw tatami mat of her living room and chatted cheerfully about her 40-year marriage to a man whom, she mused, she never particularly liked.

"There was never any love between me and my husband," she said blithely, recalling how he used to beat her. "But, well, we survived."

A 72-year-old midwife, her face as weathered as an old baseball and etched with a thousand seams, Mrs. Uemura said that her husband had never told her that he liked her, never complimented her on a meal, never told her "thank you," never held her hand, never given her a present, never shown her affection in any way. He never calls her by her name, but summons her with the equivalent of a grunt or a "Hey, you."

"Even with animals, the males cooperate to bring the females some food," Mrs. Uemura said sadly, noting the contrast to her own marriage. "When I see that, it brings tears to my eyes."

In short, the Uemuras have a marriage that is as durable as it is unhappy, one couple's tribute to the Japanese sanctity of family.

The divorce rate in Japan is at a record high but still less than half that of the United States, and Japan arguably has one of the strongest family structures in the industrialized world. As the United States and Europe fret about the disintegration of the traditional family, most Japanese families remain as solid as the small red table on which Mrs. Uemura rested her tea.

It does not seem that Japanese families survive because husbands and wives love each other more than American couples, but rather because they perhaps love each other less.

A study published last year by the Population Council, an international nonprofit group based in New York, suggested that the traditional two-parent household is on the wane not only in America but throughout most of the world. There was one prominent exception: Japan.

In Japan, for example, only 1.1 percent of births are to unwed mothers—virtually unchanged from 25 years ago. In the United States, the figure is 30.1 percent and rising rapidly.

Yet if one comes to a little Japanese town like Omiya to learn the secrets of the Japanese family, the people are not as happy as the statistics.

"I haven't lived for myself," Mrs. Uemura said, with a touch of melancholy, "but for my kids, and for my family, and for society."

Mrs. Uemura's marriage does not seem exceptional in Japan, whether in the big cities or here in Omiya. The people of Omiya, a community of 5,700 nestled in the rain-drenched hills of the Kii Peninsula in Mie Prefecture, nearly 200 miles southwest of Tokyo, have spoken periodically to a reporter about various aspects of their daily lives. On this visit they talked about their families.

Survival Secrets, Often the Couples Expect Little

Osamums Torida furrowed his brow and looked perplexed when he was asked if he loved his wife of 33 years.

"Yeah, so-so, I guess," said Mr. Torida, a cattle farmer. "She's like air or water. You couldn't live without it, but most of the time, you're not conscious of its existence."

The secret to the survival of the marriage, Mr. Torida acknowledged, was not mutual passion.

"Sure, we had fights about our work," he explained as he stood beside his barn. "But we were preoccupied by work and our debts, so we had no time to fool around."

That is a common theme in Omiya. It does not seem that Japanese families survive because husbands and wives love each other more than American couples, but rather because they perhaps love each other less.

"I think love marriages are more fragile than arranged marriages," said Tomika Kusukawa, 49, who married her high-school sweetheart and now runs a car repair shop with him. "In love marriages, when something happens or if the couple falls out of love, they split up."

If there is a secret to the strength of the Japanese family it consists of three ingredients: low expectations, patience, and shame.

96

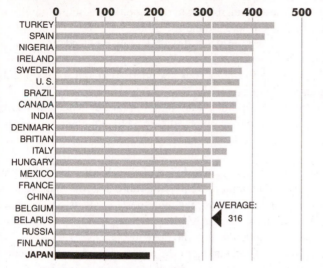

GETTING ALONG

Matchmaker, Matchmaker

How countries compare on an index of compatibility of spouses, based on answers to questions about politics, sex, social issues, religion and ethics, from a survey by the Dentsu Research Institute and Leisure Development Center in Japan. A score of 500 would indicate perfect compatibility.

Country	
TURKEY	
SPAIN	
NIGERIA	
IRELAND	
SWEDEN	
U.S.	
BRAZIL	
CANADA	
INDIA	
DENMARK	
BRITIAN	
ITALY	
HUNGARY	
MEXICO	
FRANCE	
CHINA	
BELGIUM	AVERAGE: 316
BELARUS	
RUSSIA	
FINLAND	
JAPAN	

The advantage of marriages based on low expectations is that they have built in shock absorbers. If the couple discover that they have nothing in common, that they do not even like each other, then that is not so much a reason for divorce as it is par for the course.

Even the discovery that one's spouse is having an affair is often not as traumatic in a Japanese marriage as it is in the West. A little sexual infidelity on the part of a man (though not on the part of his wife) was traditionally tolerated, so long as he did not become so besotted as to pay his mistress more than he could afford.

Tsuzuya Fukuyama, who runs a convenience store and will mark her 50th wedding anniversary this year, toasted her hands on an electric heater in the front of the store and declared that a woman would be wrong to get angry if her husband had an affair.

The durability of the Japanese family is particularly wondrous because couples are, by international standards, exceptionally incompatible.

"It's never just one side that's at fault," Mrs. Fukuyama said sternly. "Maybe the husband had an affair because his wife wasn't so hot herself. So she should look at her own faults."

Mrs. Fukuyama's daughter came to her a few years ago, suspecting that her husband was having an affair and asking what to do.

"I told her, 'Once you left this house, you can only come back if you divorce; if you're not prepared to get a divorce, then you'd better be patient,'" Mrs. Fukuyama recalled. "And so she was patient. And then she got pregnant and had a kid, and now they're close again."

The word that Mrs. Fukuyama used for patience is "gaman," a term that comes up whenever marriage is discussed in Japan. It means toughing it out, enduring hardship, and many Japanese regard gaman with pride as a national trait.

Many people complain that younger folks divorce because they do not have enough gaman, and the frequency with which the term is used suggests a rather bleak understanding of marriage.

"I didn't know my husband very well when we married, and afterward we used to get into bitter fights," said Yoshiko Hirowaki, 56, a store owner. "But then we had children, and I got very busy with the kids and with this shop. Time passed."

Now Mrs. Hirowaki has been married 34 years, and she complains about young people who do not stick to their vows.

"In the old days, wives had more gaman," she said. "Now kids just don't have enough gaman."

The durability of the Japanese family is particularly wondrous because couples are, by international standards, exceptionally incompatible.

One survey asked married men and their wives in 37 countries how they felt about politics, sex, religion, ethics and social issues. Japanese couples ranked dead last in compatibility of views, by a huge margin. Indeed, another survey found that if they were doing it over again, only about one-third of Japanese would marry the same person.

A national survey found that 30 percent of fathers spend less than 15 minutes a day on weekends talking with or playing with their children.

Incompatibility might not matter so much, however, because Japanese husbands and wives spend very little time talking to each other.

"I kind of feel there's nothing new to say to her," said Masayuki Ogita, an egg farmer, explaining his reticence.

In a small town like Omiya, couples usually have dinner together, but in Japanese cities there are many "7-11 husbands," so called because they leave at 7 A.M. and return after 11 P.M.

Masahiko Kondo now lives in Omiya, working in the chamber of commerce, but he used to be a salesman in several big cities. He would leave for work each morning at 7, and about four nights a week would go out for after-work drinking or mahjongg sessions with buddies.

"I only saw my baby on Saturdays or Sundays," said Mr. Kondo, a lanky good-natured man of 37. "But in fact, I really enjoyed that life. It didn't bother me that I never spent time with my kid on weekdays."

Mr. Kondo's wife, Keiko, had her own life, spent with her child and the wives of other workaholic husbands.

"We had birthday parties, but they were with the kids and the mothers," she remembers. "No fathers ever came."

A national survey found that 30 percent of fathers spend less than 15 minutes a day on weekdays talking with or playing with their children. Among eighth graders, 51 percent reported that they never spoke with their fathers on weekdays.

Traditionally, many companies were reluctant to promote employees who had divorced or who had major problems at home.

As a result, the figures in Japan for single-parent households can be deceptive. The father is often more a theoretical presence than a homework-helping reality.

Still, younger people sometimes want to see the spouses in daylight, and a result is a gradual change in focus of lives from work to family. Two decades ago, nearly half of young people said in surveys that they wanted their fathers to put priority on work rather than family. Now only one-quarter say that.

Social Pressures
Shame Is Keeping Bonds in Place

For those who find themselves desperately unhappy, one source of pressure to keep plugging is shame.

"If you divorce, you lose face in society," said Tatsumi Kinoshita, a tea farmer. "People say, 'His wife escaped.' So folks remain married because they hate to be gossiped about."

Shame is a powerful social sanction in Japan, and it is not just a matter of gossip. Traditionally, many companies were reluctant to promote employees who had divorced or who had major problems at home.

"If you divorce, it weakens your position at work," said Akihiko Kanda, 27, who works in a local government office. "Your bosses won't give you such good ratings, and it'll always be a negative factor."

The idea, Mr. Kanda noted, is that if an employee cannot manage his own life properly, he should not be entrusted with important corporate matters.

Financial sanctions are also a major disincentive for divorce. The mother gets the children in three-quarters of divorces, but most mothers in Japan do not have careers and have few financial resources. Fathers pay child support in only 15 percent of all divorces with children, partly because women often hesitate to go to court to demand payments and partly because men often fail to pay even when the court orders it.

"The main reason for lack of divorce is that women can't support themselves," said Mizuko Kanda, a 51-year-old housewife. "My friends complain about their husbands and say that they'd divorce if they could, but they can't afford to."

The result of these social and economic pressures is clear.

Even in Japan, there are about 24 divorces for every 100 marriages, but that compares with 32 in France, and 42 in England, and 55 in the United States.

The Outlook
Change Creeps in, Imperiling Family

But society is changing in Japan, and it is an open question whether these changes will undermine the traditional family as they have elsewhere around the globe.

The nuclear family has already largely replaced the extended family in Japan, and shame is eroding as a sanction. Haruko Okumura, for example, runs a kindergarten and speaks openly about her divorce.

"My Mom was uneasy about it, but I never had an inferiority complex about being divorced," said Mrs. Okumura, as dozens of children played in the next room. "And people accepted me easily."

Mrs. Okumura sees evidence of the changes in family patterns every day: fathers are playing more of a role in the kindergarten. At Christmas parties and sports contests, fathers have started to show up along with mothers. And Mrs. Okumura believes that divorce is on the upswing.

"If there's a weakening of the economic and social pressures to stay married," she said, "surely divorce rates will soar."

Already divorce rates are rising, approximately doubling over the last 25 years. But couples are very reluctant to divorce when they have children, and so single-parent households account for exactly the same proportion today as in 1965.

Shinsuke Kawaguchi, a young tea farmer, is one of the men for whom life is changing. Americans are not likely to be impressed by Mr. Kawaguchi's open-mindedness, but he is.

"I take good care of my wife," he said. "I may not say 'I love you,' but I do hold her hand. And I might say, after she makes dinner, 'This tastes good.'"

"Of course," Mr. Kawaguchi quickly added, "I wouldn't say that unless I'd just done something really bad."

Even Mrs. Uemura, the elderly woman whose husband used to beat her, said that her husband was treating her better.

"The other day, he tried to pour me a cup of tea," Mrs. Uemura recalled excitedly. "It was a big change. I told all my friends."

Critical Thinking

1. How does the author describe the marriage of Yuri Uemura?
2. How does the current Japanese divorce rate compare with the past and with that of the United States?
3. What are the statistics regarding unwed mothers?
4. In what sense are love marriages more fragile than arranged marriages?
5. What three ingredients add to the strength of Japanese marriages?
6. How do low expectations strengthen Japanese marriages?
7. Why is an affair "not as traumatic?"
8. What is "gaman" and how important is it to the Japanese?

9. To what extent are Japanese couples incompatible? What is the measure of this? Why does it not seem to matter much?

10. How much time do Japanese fathers spend with their children? What trend does the author see in this regard?

11. What are the social pressures working against divorce?

12. What changes does the author see with regard to the nuclear family versus the extended family and with regard to shame as a social sanction?

13. What changes are occurring with regard to the role of the father?

14. Are divorce rates rising? Under what specific circumstances?

From *The New York Times*, February 11, 1996, pp. 1, 12. Copyright © 1996 by The New York Times Company. Reprinted by permission via PARS International.

UNIT 5
Gender and Status

Unit Selections

Learning Outcomes

After reading this Unit, you will be able to:

- Explain how the institution of marriage is changing today and in what ways it is moving "forward to the past."

- Define *berdache* and explain how it highlights the ways in which different societies accommodate atypical individuals.

- Describe the transgender hijra of India in terms of their traditional social and religious roles and with respect to the challenge they represent to the binary sex/gender notions of the West.

- Explain how and why perceptions of feminine beauty vary from culture to culture.

- Describe the social forces that have contributed to the increasing death rate of females in Asia.

- Discuss the increase in the international marriage trade and how it is affecting the nations involved.

- Explain why there is a rising number of dowry deaths in India.

- Discuss the social forces at work in "honor killing" in Jordan and how it can be a tragedy not only for the victim, but also for the family and even the murderer.

- Discuss the notion that women are the "invisible gravity" of society and how the female amputees of Angola are making the economy work for them.

Student Website
www.mhhe.com/cls

Internet References

Heal Africa
www.healafrica.org

It's Time: African Women Join Hands against Domestic Violence
www.itstimeafrica.org/index.html

Reflections on Sinai Bedouin Women
www.sherryart.com/women/bedouin.html

Women Watch
www.un.org/womenwatch/about

The feminist movement in the United States has had a significant impact upon the development of anthropology. Feminists have rightly charged that anthropologists have tended to gloss over the lives of women in studies of society and culture. In part this is because, until recent times, most anthropologists have been men. The result has been an undue emphasis on male activities as well as male perspectives in descriptions of particular societies.

These charges, however, have proven to be a firm corrective. In the last few decades, anthropologists have studied women and, more particularly, the division of labor based on gender and its relation to biology, as well as to social and political status. In addition, these changes in emphasis have been accompanied by an increase in the number of women in the field.

Feminist anthropologists have critically attacked many of the established anthropological beliefs. They have shown, for example, that field studies of nonhuman primates, which were often used to demonstrate the evolutionary basis of male dominance, distorted the actual evolutionary record by focusing primarily on baboons. (Male baboons are especially dominant and aggressive.) Other, less-quoted primate studies show how dominance and aggression are highly situational phenomena, sensitive to ecological variation. Feminist anthropologists have also shown that the subsistence contribution of women was likewise ignored by anthropologists. A classic case is that of the !Kung, a hunting and gathering group in southern Africa, where women provide the bulk of the foodstuffs, including most of the available protein, and who, not coincidentally, enjoy a more egalitarian relationship than usual with men. Thus, since political control is a matter of cultural variation, male authority is not biologically predetermined. There are many cultures in which some men may play a more feminine or, at least, asexual role, as described in "The Berdache Tradition" and "The Hijras: An Alternative Gender in India." In fact, as Gregory M. Herek explains in "Sexual Orientation Differences," the gender categories employed in any given culture such as ours may be inadequate to do justice to the actual diversity that exists and, as we see in "Where Fat Is a Mark of Beauty," gender relationships are deeply embedded in social experience.

Lest we think that gender issues are primarily academic, we need only consider the articles, "Murder in Amman" by Rana

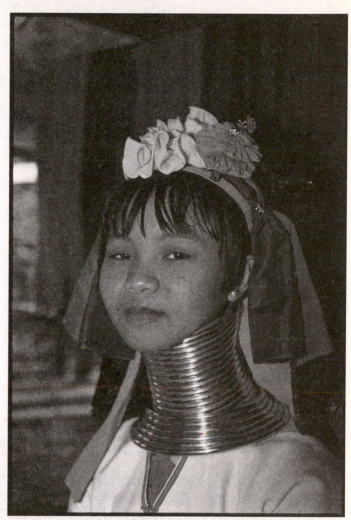

Husseini, "Missing Girls" by Michelle Goldberg, and "The Untold Stories of the Amputees" by Carolyn Nordstrom to realize that gender equality in this world is still a distant dream.

The New Monogamy: Forward to the Past

An author and anthropologist looks at the future of love.

HELEN FISHER

Marriage has changed more in the past 100 years than it has in the past 10,000, and it could change more in the next 20 years than in the last 100. We are rapidly shedding traditions that emerged with the Agricultural Revolution and returning to patterns of sex, romance, and attachment that evolved on the grasslands of Africa millions of years ago.

Let's look at virginity at marriage, arranged marriages, the concept that men should be the sole family breadwinners, the credo that a woman's place is in the home, the double standard for adultery, and the concepts of "honor thy husband" and "til death do us part." These beliefs are vanishing. Instead, children are expressing their sexuality. "Hooking up" (the new term for a onenight stand) is becoming commonplace, along with living together, bearing children out of wedlock, womenheaded households, interracial marriages, homosexual weddings, commuter marriages between individuals who live apart, childless marriages, betrothals between older women and younger men, and small families.

Our concept of infidelity is changing. Some married couples agree to have brief sexual encounters when they travel separately; others sustain long-term adulterous relationships with the approval of a spouse. Even our concept of divorce is shifting. Divorce used to be considered a sign of failure; today it is often deemed the first step toward true happiness.

These trends aren't new. Anthropologists have many clues to life among our forebears; the dead do speak. A million years ago, children were most likely experimenting with sex and love by age six. Teens lived together, in relationships known as "trial marriages." Men and women chose their partners for themselves. Many were unfaithful-a propensity common in all 42 extant cultures I have examined. When our forebears found themselves in an unhappy partnership, these ancients walked out. A million years ago, anthropologists suspect, most men and women had two or three longterm partners across their lifetimes. All these primordial habits are returning.

But the most profound trend forward to the past is the rise of what sociologists call the companionate, symmetrical, or peer marriage: marriage between equals. Women in much of the world are regaining the economic power they enjoyed for millennia. Ancestral women left camp almost daily to gather fruits, nuts, and vegetables, returning with 60% to 80% of the evening meal. In the hunting and gathering societies of our past, women worked outside the home; the double-income family was the rule, and women were just as economically, sexually, and socially powerful as men. Today, we are returning to this lifeway, leaving in the "dustbin of history" the traditional, male-headed, patriarchal family-the bastion of agrarian society.

This massive change will challenge many of our social traditions, institutions, and policies in the next 20 years. Perhaps we will see wedding licenses with an expiration date. Companies may have to reconsider how they distribute pension benefits. Words like marriage, family, adultery, and divorce are likely to take on a variety of meanings. We may invent some new kinship terms. Who pays for dinner will shift. Matriliny may become common as more children trace their descent through their mother.

All sorts of industries are already booming as spin-offs of our tendencies to marry later, then divorce and remarry. Among these are Internet dating services, marital mediators, artists who airbrush faces out of family albums, divorce support groups, couples therapists, and self-improvement books. As behavioral geneticists begin to pinpoint the biology of such seemingly amorphous traits as curiosity, cautiousness, political orientation, and religiosity, the rich may soon create designer babies.

For every trend there is a countertrend, of course. Religious traditions are impeding the rise of women in some societies. In countries where there are far more men than women, due to female infanticide, women are likely to become coveted-and cloistered. The aging world population may cling to outmoded social values, and population surges and declines will affect our attitudes toward family life.

Adding to this mix will be everything we are learning about the biology of relationships. We now know that kissing a long-term partner reduces cortisol, the stress hormone. Certain genes in the vasopressin system predispose men to make less-stable partnerships. My colleagues and I have discovered that the feeling of romantic love is associated with the brain's dopamine system-the system for wanting. Moreover, we have found that romantic rejection activates brain regions associated with profound addiction. Scientists even know some of the payoffs of "hooking up." Casual sex can trigger the brain systems for romantic love and/or feelings of deep attachment. In a study led by anthropologist Justin Garcia, some 50% of men and women reported that they initiated a hook up in order to trigger a longer partnership; indeed, almost a third of them succeeded.

What will we do with all these data? One forward-thinking company has begun to bottle what our forebears would have called "love magic." They sell Liquid Trust, a perfume that contains oxytocin, the natural brain chemical that, when sniffed, triggers feelings of trust and attachment.

We are living in a sea of social and technological currents that are likely to reshape our family lives. But much will remain the same. To bond is human. The drives to fall in love and form an attachment to a mate are deeply embedded in the human brain. Indeed, in a study I just completed on 2,171 individuals (1,198 men, 973 women) at the Internet dating site Chemistry .com, 84% of participants said they wanted to marry at some point. They will. Today, 84% of Americans wed by age 40-albeit making different kinds of marriages. Moreover, with the expansion of the roles of both women and men, with the new medical aids to sex and romance (such as Viagra and estrogen replacement), with our longer life spans, and with the growing social acceptance of alternative ways to bond, I believe we now have the time and tools to make more-fulfilling partnerships than at any time in human evolution. The time to love is now.

Critical Thinking

1. How is marriage changing? In what ways is it moving "forward to the past?"

2. How are so many of our social traditions, institutions, and policies being challenged?

3. What kinds of industries are booming as a result?

4. What have been the countertrends?

5. How is the "biology of relationships" adding to the mix?

6. Why is there much that will remain the same?

7. Why does the author claim that more fulfilling partnerships are possible?

Helen Fisher is a research professor in biological anthroplogy at Rutgers University and chief scientific advisor of Chemistry.com. Her most recent book is *Why We Love: The Nature and Chemistry of Love* (Henry Holt, 2010).

Originally published in the Vol. 44, No. 6, November/December 2010, pp. 26–28 issue of *The Futurist*. Copyright © 2010 by World Future Society, Bethesda, MD. Used with permission. www.wfs.org.

The Berdache Tradition

WALTER L. WILLIAMS

Because it is such a powerful force in the world today, the Western Judeo-Christian tradition is often accepted as the arbiter of "natural" behavior of humans. If Europeans and their descendant nations of North America accept something as normal, then anything different is seen as abnormal. Such a view ignores the great diversity of human existence.

This is the case of the study of gender. How many genders are there? To a modern Anglo-American, nothing might seem more definite than the answer that there are two: men and women. But not all societies around the world agree with Western culture's view that all humans are either women or men. The commonly accepted notion of "the opposite sex," based on anatomy, is itself an artifact of our society's rigid sex roles.

Among many cultures, there have existed different alternatives to "man" or "woman." An alternative role in many American Indian societies is referred to by anthropologists as *berdache*. . . . The role varied from one Native American culture to another, which is a reflection of the vast diversity of aboriginal New World societies. Small bands of hunter-gatherers existed in some areas, with advanced civilizations of farming peoples in other areas. With hundreds of different languages, economies, religions, and social patterns existing in North America alone, every generalization about a cultural tradition must acknowledge many exceptions.

This diversity is true for the berdache tradition as well, and must be kept in mind. My statements should be read as being specific to a particular culture, with generalizations being treated as loose patterns that might not apply to peoples even in nearby areas.

Briefly, a berdache can be defined as a morphological male who does not fill a society's standard man's role, who has a non-masculine character. This type of person is often stereotyped as effeminate, but a more accurate characterization is androgyny. Such a person has a clearly recognized and accepted social status, often based on a secure place in the tribal mythology. Berdaches have special ceremonial roles in many Native American religions, and important economic roles in their families. They will do at least some women's work, and mix together much of the behavior, dress, and social roles of women and men. Berdaches gain social prestige by their spiritual, intellectual, or craftwork/artistic contributions, and by their reputation for hard work and generosity. They serve a mediating function between women and men, precisely because their character is seen as distinct from either sex. They are not seen as men, yet they are not seen as women either. They occupy an alternative gender role that is a mixture of diverse elements.

In their erotic behavior berdaches also generally (but not always) take a nonmasculine role, either being asexual or becoming the passive partner in sex with men. In some cultures the berdache might become a wife to a man. This male-male sexual behavior became the focus of an attack on berdaches as "sodomites" by the Europeans who, early on, came into contact with them. From the first Spanish conquistadors to the Western frontiersmen and the Christian missionaries and government officials, Western culture has had a considerable impact on the berdache tradition. In the last two decades, the most recent impact on the tradition is the adaptation of a modern Western gay identity.

To Western eyes berdachism is a complex and puzzling phenomenon, mixing and redefining the very concepts of what is considered male and female. In a culture with only two recognized genders, such individuals are gender nonconformist, abnormal, deviant. But to American Indians, the institution of another gender role means that berdaches are not deviant—indeed, they do conform to the requirements of a custom in which their culture tells them they fit. Berdachism is a way for society to recognize and assimilate some atypical individuals without imposing a change on them or stigmatizing them as deviant. This cultural institution confirms their legitimacy for what they are.

Societies often bestow power upon that which does not neatly fit into the usual. Since no cultural system can explain everything, a common way that many cultures deal with these inconsistencies is to imbue them with negative power, as taboo, pollution, witchcraft, or sin. That which is not understood is seen as a threat. But an alternative method of dealing with such things, or people, is to take them out of the realm of threat and to sanctify them.[1] The berdaches' role as mediator is thus not just between women and men, but also between the physical and the spiritual. American Indian cultures have taken what Western culture calls negative, and made it a positive; they have successfully utilized the different skills and insights of a class of people that Western culture has stigmatized and whose spiritual powers have been wasted.

Many Native Americans also understood that gender roles have to do with more than just biological sex. The standard

Western view that one's sex is always a certainty, and that one's gender identity and sex role always conform to one's morphological sex is a view that dies hard. Western thought is typified by such dichotomies of groups perceived to be mutually exclusive: male and female, black and white, right and wrong, good and evil. Clearly, the world is not so simple; such clear divisions are not always realistic. Most American Indian world-views generally are much more accepting of the ambiguities of life. Acceptance of gender variation in the berdache tradition is typical of many native cultures' approach to life in general.

Overall, these are generalizations based on those Native American societies that had an accepted role for berdaches. Not all cultures recognized such a respected status. Berdachism in aboriginal North America was most established among tribes in four areas: first, the Prairie and western Great Lakes, the northern and central Great Plains, and the lower Mississippi Valley; second, Florida and the Caribbean; third, the Southwest, the Great Basin, and California; and fourth, scattered areas of the Northwest, western Canada, and Alaska. For some reason it is not noticeable in eastern North America, with the exception of its southern rim. . . .

American Indian Religions

Native American religions offered an explanation for human diversity by their creation stories. In some tribal religions, the Great Spiritual Being is conceived as neither male nor female but as a combination of both. Among the Kamia of the Southwest, for example, the bearer of plant seeds and the introducer of Kamia culture was a man-woman spirit named Warharmi.[2] A key episode of the Zuni creation story involves a battle between the kachina spirits of the agricultural Zunis and the enemy hunter spirits. Every four years an elaborate ceremony commemorates this myth. In the story a kachina spirit called *ko'lhamana* was captured by the enemy spirits and transformed in the process. This transformed spirit became a mediator between the two sides, using his peacemaking skills to merge the differing lifestyles of hunters and farmers. In the ceremony, a dramatic reenactment of the myth, the part of the transformed *ko'lhamana* spirit, is performed by a berdache.[3] The Zuni word for berdache is *lhamana*, denoting its closeness to the spiritual mediator who brought hunting and farming together.[4] The moral of this story is that the berdache was created by the deities for a special purpose, and that this creation led to the improvement of society. The continual reenactment of this story provides a justification for the Zuni berdache in each generation.

In contrast to this, the lack of spiritual justification in a creation myth could denote a lack of tolerance for gender variation. The Pimas, unlike most of their Southwestern neighbors, did not respect a berdache status. *Wi-kovat*, their derogatory word, means "like a girl," but it does not signify a recognized social role. Pima mythology reflects this lack of acceptance, in a folk tale that explains male androgyny as due to Papago witchcraft. Knowing that the Papagos respected berdaches, the Pimas blamed such an occurrence on an alien influence.[5] While the Pimas' condemnatory attitude is unusual, it does point out the importance of spiritual explanations for the acceptance of gender variance in a culture.

Other Native American creation stories stand in sharp contrast to the Pima explanation. A good example is the account of the Navajos, which presents women and men as equals. The Navajo origin tale is told as a story of five worlds. The first people were First Man and First Woman, who were created equally and at the same time. The first two worlds that they lived in were bleak and unhappy, so they escaped to the third world. In the third world lived two twins, Turquoise Boy and White Shell Girl, who were the first berdaches. In the Navajo language the world for berdache is *nadle,* which means "changing one" or "one who is transformed." It is applied to hermaphrodites—those who are born with the genitals of both male and female—and also to "those who pretend to be *nadle,*" who take on a social role that is distinct from either men or women.[6]

In the third world, First Man and First Woman began farming, with the help of the changing twins. One of the twins noticed some clay and, holding it in the palm of his/her hand, shaped it into the first pottery bowl. Then he/she formed a plate, a water dipper, and a pipe. The second twin observed some reeds and began to weave them, making the first basket. Together they shaped axes and grinding stones from rocks, and hoes from bone. All these new inventions made the people very happy.[7]

The message of this story is that humans are dependent for many good things on the inventiveness of *nadle*. Such individuals were present from the earliest eras of human existence, and their presence was never questioned. They were part of the natural order of the universe, with a special contribution to make.

Later on in the Navajo creation story, White Shell Girl entered the moon and became the Moon Bearer. Turquoise Boy, however, remained with the people. When First Man realized that Turquoise Boy could do all manner of women's work as well as women, all the men left the women and crossed a big river. The men hunted and planted crops. Turquoise Boy ground the corn, cooked the food, and weaved cloth for the men. Four years passed with the women and men separated, and the men were happy with the *nadle*. Later, however the women wanted to learn how to grind corn from the *nadle,* and both the men and women had decided that it was not good to continue living separately. So the women crossed the river and the people were reunited.[8]

They continued living happily in the third world, until one day a great flood began. The people ran to the highest mountaintop, but the water kept rising and they all feared they would be drowned. But just in time, the ever-inventive Turquoise Boy found a large reed. They climbed upward inside the tall hollow reed, and came out at the top into the fourth world. From there, White Shell Girl brought another reed, and they climbed again to the fifth world, which is the present world of the Navajos.[9]

These stories suggest that the very survival of humanity is dependent on the inventiveness of berdaches. With such a mythological belief system, it is no wonder that the Navajos held *nadle* in high regard. The concept of the *nadle* is well formulated in the creation story. As children were educated by these stories, and all Navajos believed in them, the high status accorded to gender variation was passed down from generation to generation. Such stories also provided instruction for *nadle* themselves to live by. A spiritual explanation guaranteed a special place for a person who was considered different but not deviant.

For American Indians, the important explanations of the world are spiritual ones. In their view, there is a deeper reality than the here-and-now. The real essence or wisdom occurs when one finally gives up trying to explain events in terms of "logic" and "reality." Many confusing aspects of existence can better be explained by actions of a multiplicity of spirits. Instead of a concept of a single god, there is an awareness of "that which we do not understand." In Lakota religion, for example, the term *Wakan Tanka* is often translated as "god." But a more proper translation, according to the medicine people who taught me, is "The Great Mystery."[10]

While rationality can explain much, there are limits to human capabilities of understanding. The English language is structured to account for cause and effect. For example, English speakers say, "It is raining," with the implication that there is a cause "it" that leads to rain. Many Indian languages, on the other hand, merely note what is most accurately translated as "raining" as an observable fact. Such an approach brings a freedom to stop worrying about causes of things, and merely to relax and accept that our human insights can go only so far. By not taking ourselves too seriously, or overinflating human importance, we can get beyond the logical world.

The emphasis of American Indian religions, then, is on the spiritual nature of all things. To understand the physical world, one must appreciate the underlying spiritual essence. Then one can begin to see that the physical is only a faint shadow, a partial reflection, of a supernatural and extrarational world. By the Indian view, everything that exists is spiritual. Every object—plants, rocks, water, air, the moon, animals, humans, the earth itself—has a spirit. The spirit of one thing (including a human) is not superior to the spirit of any other. Such a view promotes a sophisticated ecological awareness of the place that humans have in the larger environment. The function of religion is not to try to condemn or to change what exists, but to accept the realities of the world and to appreciate their contributions to life. Everything that exists has a purpose.[11]

One of the basic tenets of American Indian religion is the notion that everything in the universe is related. Nevertheless, things that exist are often seen as having a counterpart: sky and earth, plant and animal, water and fire. In all of these polarities, there exist mediators. The role of the mediator is to hold the polarities together, to keep the world from disintegrating. Polarities exist within human society also. The most important category within Indian society is gender. The notions of Woman and Man underlie much of social interaction and are comparable to the other major polarities. Women, with their nurtural qualities, are associated with the earth, while men are associated with the sky. Women gatherers and farmers deal with plants (of the earth), while men hunters deal with animals.

The mediator between the polarities of woman and man, in the American Indian religious explanation, is a being that combines the elements of both genders. This might be a combination in a physical sense, as in the case of hermaphrodites.

Many Native American religions accept this phenomenon in the same way that they accept other variations from the norm. But more important is their acceptance of the idea that gender can be combined in ways other than physical hermaphroditism. The physical aspects of a thing or a person, after all, are not nearly as important as its spirit. American Indians use the concept of a person's *spirit* in the way that other Americans use the concept of a person's *character*. Consequently, physical hermaphroditism is not necessary for the idea of gender mixing. A person's character, their spiritual essence, is the crucial thing.

The Berdache's Spirit

Individuals who are physically normal might have the spirit of the other sex, might range somewhere between the two sexes, or might have a spirit that is distinct from either women or men. Whatever category they fall into, they are seen as being different from men. They are accepted spiritually as "Not Man." Whichever option is chosen, Indian religions offer spiritual explanations. Among the Arapahos of the Plains, berdaches are called *haxu'xan* and are seen to be that way as a result of a supernatural gift from birds or animals. Arapaho mythology recounts the story of Nih'a'ca, the first *haxu'xan*. He pretended to be a woman and married the mountain lion, a symbol for masculinity. The myth, as recorded by ethnographer Alfred Kroeber about 1900, recounted that "These people had the natural desire to become women, and as they grew up gradually became women. They gave up the desires of men. They were married to men. They had miraculous power and could do supernatural things. For instance, it was one of them that first made an intoxicant from rainwater."[12] Besides the theme of inventiveness, similar to the Navajo creation story, the berdache role is seen as a product of a "natural desire." Berdaches "gradually became women," which underscores the notion of woman as a social category rather than as a fixed biological entity. Physical biological sex is less important in gender classification than a person's desire—one's spirit.

They myths contain no prescriptions for trying to change berdaches who are acting out their desires of the heart. Like many other cultures' myths, the Zuni origin myths simply sanction the idea that gender can be transformed independently of biological sex.[13] Indeed, myths warn of dire consequences when interference with such a transformation is attempted. Prince Alexander Maximilian of the German state of Wied, traveling in the northern Plains in the 1830s, heard a myth about a warrior who once tried to force a berdache to avoid women's clothing. The berdache resisted, and the warrior shot him with an arrow. Immediately the berdache disappeared, and the warrior saw only a pile of stones with his arrow in them. Since then, the story concluded, no intelligent person would try to coerce a berdache.[14] Making the point even more directly, a Mandan myth told of an Indian who tried to force *mihdake* (berdaches) to give up their distinctive dress and status, which led the spirits to punish many people with death. After that, no Mandans interfered with berdaches.[15]

With this kind of attitude, reinforced by myth and history, the aboriginal view accepts human diversity. The creation story of the Mohave of the Colorado River Valley speaks of a time when people were not sexually differentiated. From this perspective, it is easy to accept that certain individuals might combine elements of masculinity and femininity.[16] A respected Mohave elder, speaking in the 1930s, stated this viewpoint simply: "From the very beginning of the world it was meant that there should be [berdaches], just as it was instituted that there should be shamans. They were intended for that purpose."[17]

This elder also explained that a child's tendencies to become a berdache are apparent early, by about age nine to twelve, before the child reaches puberty: "That is the time when young persons become initiated into the functions of their sex. . . . None but young people will become berdaches as a rule."[18] Many tribes have a public ceremony that acknowledges the acceptance of berdache status. A Mohave shaman related the ceremony for his tribe: "When the child was about ten years old his relatives would begin discussing his strange ways. Some of them disliked it, but the more intelligent began envisaging an initiation ceremony." The relatives prepare for the ceremony without letting the boy know of it. It is meant to take him by surprise, to be both an initiation and a test of his true inclinations. People from various settlements are invited to attend. The family wants the community to see it and become accustomed to accepting the boy as an *alyha*.

On the day of the ceremony, the shaman explained, the boy is led into a circle: "If the boy showed a willingness to remain standing in the circle, exposed to the public eye, it was almost certain that he would go through with the ceremony. The singer, hidden behind the crowd, began singing the songs. As soon as the sound reached the boy he began to dance as women do." If the boy is unwilling to assume *alyha* status, he would refuse to dance. But if his character—his spirit—is *alyha*, "the song goes right to his heart and he will dance with much intensity. He cannot help it. After the fourth song he is proclaimed." After the ceremony, the boy is carefully bathed and receives a woman's skirt. He is then led back to the dance ground, dressed as an *alyha*, and announces his new feminine name to the crowd. After that he would resent being called by his old male name.[19]

Among the Yuman tribes of the Southwest, the transformation is marked by a social gathering, in which the berdache prepares a meal for the friends of the family.[20] Ethnographer Ruth Underhill, doing fieldwork among the Papago Indians in the early 1930s, wrote that berdaches were common among the Papago Indians, and were usually publicly acknowledged in childhood. She recounted that a boy's parents would test him if they noticed that he preferred female pursuits. The regular pattern, mentioned by many of Underhill's Papago informants, was to build a small brush enclosure. Inside the enclosure they placed a man's bow and arrows, and also a woman's basket. At the appointed time the boy was brought to the enclosure as the adults watched from outside. The boy was told to go inside the circle of brush. Once he was inside, the adults "set fire to the enclosure. They watched what he took with him as he ran out and if it was the basketry materials, they reconciled themselves to his being a berdache."[21]

What is important to recognize in all of these practices is that the assumption of a berdache role was not forced on the boy by

others. While adults might have their suspicions, it was only when the child made the proper move that he was considered a berdache. By doing woman's dancing, preparing a meal, or taking the woman's basket he was making an important symbolic gesture. Indian children were not stupid, and they knew the implications of these ceremonies beforehand. A boy in the enclosure could have left without taking anything, or could have taken both the man's and the woman's tools. With the community standing by watching, he was well aware that his choice would mark his assumption of berdache status. Rather than being seen as an involuntary test of his reflexes, this ceremony may be interpreted as a definite statement by the child to take on the berdache role.

Indians do not see the assumption of berdache status, however, as a free will choice on the part of the boy. People felt that the boy was acting out his basic character. The Lakota shaman Lame Deer explained:

> They were not like other men, but the Great Spirit made them *winktes* and we accepted them as such. . . . We think that if a woman has two little ones growing inside her, if she is going to have twins, sometimes instead of giving birth to two babies they have formed up in her womb into just one, into a half-man/half-woman kind of being. . . . To us a man is what nature, or his dreams, make him. We accept him for what he wants to be. That's up to him.[22]

While most of the sources indicate that once a person becomes a berdache it is a lifelong status, directions from the spirits determine everything. In at least one documented case, concerning a nineteenth-century Klamath berdache named Lele'ks, he later had a supernatural experience that led him to leave the berdache role. At that time Lele'ks began dressing and acting like a man, then married women, and eventually became one of the most famous Klamath chiefs.[23] What is important is that both in assuming berdache status and in leaving it, supernatural dictate is the determining factor.

Dreams and Visions

Many tribes see the berdache role as signifying an individual's proclivities as a dreamer and a visionary. . . .

Among the northern Plains and related Great Lakes tribes, the idea of supernatural dictate through dreaming—the vision quest—had its highest development. The goal of the vision quest is to try to get beyond the rational world by sensory deprivation and fasting. By depriving one's body of nourishment, the brain could escape from logical thought and connect with the higher reality of the supernatural. The person doing the quest simply sits and waits for a vision. But a vision might not come easily; the person might have to wait for days.

The best way that I can describe the process is to refer to my own vision quest, which I experienced when I was living on a Lakota reservation in 1982. After a long series of prayers and blessings, the shaman who had prepared me for the ceremony took me out to an isolated area where a sweat lodge had been set up for my quest. As I walked to the spot, I worried that I might not be able to stand it. Would I be overcome by hunger?

Could I tolerate the thirst? What would I do if I had to go to the toilet? The shaman told me not to worry, that a whole group of holy people would be praying and singing for me while I was on my quest.

He had me remove my clothes, symbolizing my disconnection from the material would, and crawl into the sweat lodge. Before he left me I asked him, "What do I think about?" He said, "Do not think. Just pray for spiritual guidance." After a prayer he closed the flap tightly and I was left in total darkness. I still do not understand what happened to me during my vision quest, but during the day and a half that I was out there, I never once felt hungry or thirsty or the need to go to the toilet. What happened was an intensely personal experience that I cannot and do not wish to explain, a process of being that cannot be described in rational terms.

When the shaman came to get me at the end of my time, I actually resented having to end it. He did not need to ask if my vision quest was successful. He knew that it was even before seeing me, he explained, because he saw an eagle circling over me while I underwent the quest. He helped interpret the signs I had seen, then after more prayers and singing he led me back to the others. I felt relieved, cleansed, joyful, and serene. I had been through an experience that will be a part of my memories always.

If a vision quest could have such an effect on a person not even raised in Indian society, imagine its impact on a boy who from his earliest years had been waiting for the day when he could seek his vision. Gaining his spiritual power from his first vision, it would tell him what role to take in adult life. The vision might instruct him that he is going to be a great hunter, a craftsman, a warrior, or a shaman. Or it might tell him that he will be a berdache. Among the Lakotas, or Sioux, there are several symbols for various types of visions. A person becomes *wakan* (a sacred person) if she or he dreams of a bear, a wolf, thunder, a buffalo, a white buffalo calf, or Double Woman. Each dream results in a different gift, whether it is the power to cure illness or wounds, a promise of good hunting, or the exalted role of a *heyoka* (doing things backward).

A white buffalo calf is believed to be a berdache. If a person has a dream of the sacred Double Woman, this means that she or he will have the power to seduce men. Males who have a vision of Double Woman are presented with female tools. Taking such tools means that the male will become a berdache. The Lakota word *winkte* is composed of *win,* "woman," and *kte,* "would become."[24] A contemporary Lakota berdache explains, "To become a *winkte,* you have a medicine man put you up on the hill, to search for your vision. "You can become a *winkte* if you truly are by nature. You see a vision of the White Buffalo Calf Pipe. Sometimes it varies. A vision is like a scene in a movie."[25] Another way to become a *winkte* is to have a vision given by a *winkte* from the past.[26] . . .

By interpreting the result of the vision as being the work of a spirit, the vision quest frees the person from feeling responsible for his transformation. The person might even claim that the change was done against his will and without his control. Such a claim does not suggest a negative attitude about berdache status, because it is common for people to claim reluctance to fulfill their spiritual duty no matter what vision appears to them. Becoming any kind of sacred person involves taking on various social responsibilities and burdens.[27] . . .

A story was told among the Lakotas in the 1880s of a boy who tried to resist following his vision from Double Woman. But according to Lakota informants "few men succeed in this effort after having taken the strap in the dream." Having rebelled against the instructions given him by the Moon Being, he committed suicide.[28] The moral of that story is that one should not resist spiritual guidance, because it will lead only to grief. In another case, an Omaha young man told of being addressed by a spirit as "daughter," whereupon he discovered that he was unconsciously using feminine styles of speech. He tried to use male speech patterns, but could not. As a result of this vision, when he returned to his people he resolved himself to dress as a woman.[29] Such stories function to justify personal peculiarities as due to a fate over which the individual has no control.

Despite the usual pattern in Indian societies of using ridicule to enforce conformity, receiving instructions from a vision inhibits others from trying to change the berdache. Ritual explanation provides a way out. It also excuses the community from worrying about the cause of that person's difference, or the feeling that it is society's duty to try to change him.[30] Native American religions, above all else, encourage a basic respect for nature. If nature makes a person different, many Indians conclude, a mere human should not undertake to counter this spiritual dictate. Someone who is "unusual" can be accommodated without being stigmatized as "abnormal." Berdachism is thus not alien or threatening; it is a reflection of spirituality.

Notes

1. Mary Douglas, *Purity and Danger* (Baltimore: Penguin, 1966), p. 52. I am grateful to Theda Perdue for convincing me that Douglas's ideas apply to berdachism. For an application of Douglas's thesis to berdaches, see James Thayer, "The Berdache of the Northern Plains: A Socioreligious Perspective," *Journal of Anthropological Research 36* (1980): 292–93.

2. E. W. Gifford, "The Kamia of Imperial Valley," *Bureau of American Ethnology Bulletin 97* (1931): 12.

3. By using present tense verbs in this text, I am not implying that such activities are necessarily continuing today. I sometimes use the present tense in the "ethnographic present," unless I use the past tense when I am referring to something that has not continued. Past tense implies that all such practices have disappeared. In the absence of fieldwork to prove such disappearance, I am not prepared to make that assumption, on the historic changes in the berdache tradition.

4. Elsie Clews Parsons, "The Zuni La' Mana," *American Anthropologist 18* (1916): 521; Matilda Coxe Stevenson, "Zuni Indians," *Bureau of American Ethnology Annual Report 23* (1903): 37; Franklin Cushing, "Zuni Creation Myths," *Bureau of American Ethnology Annual Report 13* (1894): 401–3. Will Roscoe clarified this origin story for me.

5. W. W. Hill, "Note on the Pima Berdache," *American Anthropologist 40* (1938): 339.

6. Aileen O'Bryan, "The Dine': Origin Myths of the Navaho Indians," *Bureau of American Ethnology Bulletin 163* (1956): 5;

W. W. Hill, "The Status of the Hermaphrodite and Transvestite in Navaho Culture," *American Anthropologist 37* (1935): 273.

7. Martha S. Link, *The Pollen Path: A Collection of Navajo Myths* (Stanford: Stanford University Press, 1956).

8 O'Bryan, "Dine'," pp. 5, 7, 9–10.

9. Ibid.

10. Lakota informants, July 1982. See also William Powers, *Oglala Religion* (Lincoln: University of Nebraska Press, 1977).

11. For this admittedly generalized overview of American Indian religious values, I am indebted to traditionalist informants of many tribes, but especially those of the Lakotas. For a discussion of native religions see Dennis Tedlock, *Finding the Center* (New York: Dial Press, 1972); Ruth Underhill, *Red Man's Religion* (Chicago: University of Chicago Press, 1965); and Elsi Clews Parsons, *Pueblo Indian Religion* (Chicago: University of Chicago Press, 1939).

12. Alfred Kroeber, "The Arapaho," *Bulletin of the American Museum of Natural History 18* (1902–7): 19.

13. Parsons, "Zuni La' Mana," p. 525.

14. Alexander Maximilian, *Travels in the interior of North America, 1832–1834,* vol. 22 of *Early Western Travels,* ed. Reuben Gold Thwaites, 32 vols. (Cleveland: A. H. Clark, 1906), pp. 283–84, 354. Maximilian was quoted in German in the early homosexual rights book by Ferdinand Karsch-Haack, *Das Gleichgeschlechtliche Leben der Naturvölker* (The same-sex life of nature peoples) (Munich: Verlag von Ernst Reinhardt, 1911; reprinted New York: Arno Press, 1975), pp. 314, 564.

15. Oscar Koch, *Der Indianishe Eros* (Berlin: Verlag Continent, 1925), p. 61.

16. George Devereux, "Institutionalized Homosexuality of the Mohave Indians," *Human Biology 9* (1937): 509.

17. Ibid., p. 501

18. Ibid.

19. Ibid., pp. 508–9.

20. C. Daryll Forde, "Ethnography of the Yuma Indians," *University of California Publications in American Archaeology and Ethnology 28* (1931): 157.

21. Ruth Underhill, *Social Organization of the Papago Indians* (New York: Columbia University Press, 1938), p. 186. This story is also mentioned in Ruth Underhill, ed., *The Autobiography of a Papago Woman* (Menasha, Wisc.: American Anthropological Association, 1936), p. 39.

22. John Fire and Richard Erdoes, *Lame Deer, Seeker of Visions* (New York: Simon and Schuster, 1972), pp. 117, 149.

23. Theodore Stern, *The Klamath Tribe: A People and Their Reservation* (Seattle: University of Washington Press, 1965), pp. 20, 24; Theodore Stern, "Some Sources of Variability in Klamath Mythology," *Journal of American Folklore 69* (1956): 242ff; Leshe Spier, *Klamath Ethnography* (Berkeley: University of California Press, 1930), p. 52.

24. Clark Wissler, "Societies and Ceremonial Associations in the Oglala Division of the Teton Dakota," *Anthoropological Papers of the American Museum of Natural History 11,* pt. 1 (1916): 92; Powers, *Oglala Religion,* pp. 57–59.

25. Ronnie Loud Hawk, Lakota informant 4, July 1982.

26. Terry Calling Eagle, Lakota informant 5, July 1982.

27. James S. Thayer, "The Berdache of the Northern Plains: A Socioreligious Perspective," *Journal of Anthropological Research 36* (1980): 289.

28. Fletcher, "Elk Mystery," p. 281.

29. Alice Fletcher and Francis La Flesche, "The Omaha Tribe," *Bureau of American Ethnology Annual Report 27* (1905–6): 132.

30. Harriet Whitehead offers a valuable discussion of this element of the vision quest in "The Bow and the Burden Strap: A New Look at Institutionalized Homosexuality in Native North America," in *Sexual Meanings,* ed. Sherry Ortner and Harriet Whitehead (Cambridge: Cambridge University Press, 1981), pp. 99–102. See also Erikson, "Childhood," p. 329.

Critical Thinking

1. What is a berdache? What special roles have berdaches played in Native American societies?

2. What kinds of erotic behavior have they exhibited?

3. How have Europeans and American Indians differed in their treatment of the berdaches? How does the author explain these two different approaches?

4. How does the author contrast Western thought with Native American views regarding gender?

5. Why do Native Americans explain things in spiritual terms rather than "logic" and "reality?"

6. What is the emphasis of American Indian religions? What is the function of such religion?

7. What is one of the most basic tenets of American Indian religion? What kinds of polarities exist? Why are mediators necessary?

8. What is the most important category within Indian society? How do men and women differ?

9. Describe some of the Native American beliefs regarding the berdache.

The Hijras: An Alternative Gentle in India

The Hijras: An Alternative Gender in India

SERENA NANDA

My first encounter with the hijras was in 1971. While walking on Churchgate in Bombay with an Indian friend one day, we were confronted by two persons in female clothing, who stood before us, blocking our passage. They clapped their hands in a peculiar manner and then put out their upturned palms in the traditional Indian gesture of a request for alms. My friend hurriedly dropped a few rupees into the outstretched palms in front of us, and pulled me along at a quick pace, almost shoving me in front of her. Startled at her abrupt reaction, I took another look at the two people who had intercepted us. It was only then that I realized that they were not females at all, but men, dressed in women's clothing. Now curious, I asked my friend who these people were and why she had reacted so strongly to their presence, but she just shook her head and would not answer me. Sensing her discomfort, I let the subject drop but raised it with other friends at a later time. In this way I found out a little about the hijras, and became determined to learn more.

For the next 10 years my professional interests as an anthropologist centered on culture and gender roles. As part of my interest in sexual variation I read what little I could find on the hijras, asking my Indian friends and relatives about them, and extending this interest through several field trips over the next twenty years. I learned that the hijras, described as neither men nor women, performed on auspicious occasions such as births and marriages, where they are believed to have the power to confer blessings of fertility; from some male acquaintances I discovered that hijras may also be prostitutes. Hijras were called eunuchs, but also said to be born intersexed, a contradiction I could not untangle. I realized that without talking with hijras themselves, I could not distinguish fact from fiction, myth from reality.

In 1981 I lived in India for a year with my family and decided to learn more about the hijras. During this time I met and interviewed many hijras in several of the major cities in North and South India. I spent days with them in their homes, attended their performances, met their husbands and customers, and also members of their families, and formed some good friendships among them. As a result of one of these friendships, I was made a ritual younger sister to a hijra guru. I also visited the temple of Bahuchara Mataji, the special deity of the hijras, located close to Ahmadabad. In addition, I spoke at length with doctors and social scientists in India who had personal knowledge of individual hijras or had written about them. All of these investigators were males, however, and I think being a woman gave me a great advantage in getting to know individual hijras in a more personal, and therefore, deeper way.

While hijras are regarded as deviant, and even bizarre, perhaps, in Indian society, in my hundreds of conversations with them, I was most forcibly struck by them as individuals who share in our common humanity. Like human beings everywhere, hijras are both shaped by their culture and the role they play in society, but are also individuals who vary in their emotions, behavior, and outlook on life. Some hijras were outgoing, flirtatious, and jolly, and loved to dress up, perform, and have their photos taken. They met the difficulties of their lives with a good sense of humor, which they often turned on themselves. Kamladevi was one of these: she was a favorite friend of mine because she was so amusing and she spoke fluent English, having graduated from a convent high school. She was a great gossip and imitated her hijra friends and elders in funny and very insightful ways. In telling a story of how she and several other hijra prostitutes were picked up by the police one evening, she captured to perfection the intimidating attitude of the police, the arrogance of the magistrate, and the combination of innocence and boldness she had used in telling them off. Like many hijra prostitutes, Kamladevi worked very hard under the watchful and demanding eye of the hijra "madam" who swallowed most of her earnings. Although she made a fair living as a prostitute, Kamladevi always spent more than she had as she could not resist buying saris and jewelry. But in spite of her poverty, and ill health as well, she always had an eye for the humorous side of things.

Other hijras I knew were very serious and even shy. They saw their life as a fate "written on their forehead," and accepted with resignation whatever insults or abuses were meted out to them. They worked all day, every day, at whatever they did to earn a living, whether begging alms from shops, or serving in bathhouses, or at various domestic chores within their households, which included cooking, cleaning, or small tasks such as grinding spices, which they did for outsiders to earn a few extra rupees. These hijras had few interests or social contacts, some even relatively isolated within the hijra community itself. Hijras who earned a living performing at marriages and childbirths were the elite of their community. Although they also worked very hard, they were better rewarded financially and gained status within the hijra community for earning a living in this traditional manner, rather than practicing prostitution or eking out a living begging for alms. Kavita, for example, one of the hijra performers I knew well, was determined to sing and dance whenever she got the opportunity. She not only performed at marriages and childbirths, but also in more contemporary settings, such as "stag parties" and college functions. Her energy in dancing for hours at a time, as well as her ability to "keep her cool" in the face of the teasing and rowdiness of large crowds of men was a well deserved source of pride to her.

While younger hijras are often playful and sometimes even outrageously bold in public, hijra elders, or gurus, as they are called, most often maintain a great degree of dignity. They, like other middle aged and elderly Indian women, tend to wear simple clothing and little jewelry, though what they wear is often real gold. They are modest in their manner, and also, like many middle class housewives, do not "roam about" but stay close to home, supervising the households of which they are in charge. Hijra gurus are also the ones who are most familiar with their place in India, which is rooted both in Hindu mythology, which incorporates many transgender figures, and in Islam, with its tradition of eunuchs who served at the courts of kings (Nanda 1999). Most gurus I met were happy to share this information with me, as it is the basis of their power and respect in Indian society.

But whatever their personality, their age, or social status within the hijra community, I almost always found a very courteous, and even hospitable reception among the hijras I visited. Occasionally hijras in the largest cities were hostile or even aggressive, an attitude undoubtedly fostered by the abuse or prurient curiosity they sometimes receive from the larger society, including foreigners. Given the many reasons hijras have to resent outsiders, I was overcome by the welcome I received, and the several close relationships that I formed. But even when courteous and hospitable, not all the hijras I met were interested in being interviewed. Some hijras would reveal nothing about their lives before they joined the community, while others were more forthcoming.

My interviews convince me, however, that the common belief in India that all hijras are born intersexed (hermaphrodites) and are taken away from their parents and brought into the hijra community as infants, is not correct. Most hijras are physically normal men, whose effeminacy, sometimes accompanied by an interest in homosexual activity, led them to seek out the hijra community in their late childhood or adolescence. Their childhood effeminacy, expressed in a wish to wear girl's clothing and imitate girl's behavior was the source of ridicule or abuse by their peers and family and the only solution appeared to be that of leaving their families and joining up with the hijras. While many hijras subsequently lose all contact with their families, others maintain a connection; they may occasionally visit their parents or siblings or these family members may visit them.

Rukhmini was a hijra whose break with her family was permanent and complete. She came from a middle class family and her father was a high ranking police officer. In spite of the many attempts of her father and brothers to prevent her, she persisted

in acting and dressing as a girl. When it became known to her father that Rukhmini had had sexual relations with the gardener's son, he almost killed her by holding her head down in a barrel of water and beating her with his cross belt. "My mother cried tears of blood," she said. After this incident, Rukhmini ran away from her home and never returned.

In Sushila's case, she lived at home until her late teens, in relative peace with her family, until one night an elder brother falsely accused her of stealing some money from him. In his anger he told her to "use your own money that you get from selling your anus." She was more outraged at the false accusation of theft than the insult about her homosexuality and then and there left her home to join a hijra commune in a nearby city. Sushila keeps in touch with her family, and sends them gifts on the occasion of her brothers' and sisters' marriage. Meera, a hijra guru, joined the hijra community from a different and less typical route. She had grown up with the desires to be like a female, but followed the conventions of society by having her family arrange her marriage. She was married for over twenty years, and the father of several children, before she "upped one day and joined the hijras." She, too, keeps track of her family and occasionally sends them money when they need it.

As physically normal men, Kavita, Kamladevi, Rukhmini, Sushila, Rekha, and Meera were required to undergo an "operation" which removed their male genitals and transformed them into hijras. This operation, called "nirvana" or rebirth, is a religious ritual for hijras which positions them as ascetics, whose creative powers derive from their rejecting and thus transcending normal sexuality. This role connects them to Shiva, the great Hindu deity, who through his asceticism was given powers to create by Lord Brahma. The operation also identifies hijras with their special goddess and gives them the power to confer blessings of fertility, and equally, curse those who resist their demand for alms. For the small percentage of hijras who are born intersexed, no such operation is necessary. Salima, for example, a hijra from Bombay, told me that from a very early age she had "an organ that was very small." Her mother thought it would grow as she grew older, but when this did not happen her mother took her to many doctors, all to no avail. When Salima was about ten years old, a doctor told her mother, "nothing can be done, your child is neither a man nor a woman," and so Salima's mother gave her to a household of hijras who lived nearby. Salima lived with this group very happily and reported that they treated her with great kindness when she was a child.

But whatever their former lives had been, whether they had joined the hijras voluntarily, or been given to the community in despair by their parents, once an individual joins the community, they become subject to its rules and must adapt to its restrictions. This is not easy. In return for the emotional and economic security provided by the hijra community, an individual must give up some freedom, although probably not more than a young woman gives up when she becomes a bride living in a joint family. Unlike similar persons in the United States, who primarily live and work on their own, the hijras, shaped as they are by Indian culture in spite of their deviance, seem to prefer, like most Indians, to live in groups.

The Hijra Community

The hijra community in India has the qualities of both a religious cult and a caste and takes its customs, social organization and history from both Hinduism and Islam (Nanda 1999; Reddy 2005). Hijras find great pride in citing their identification with many of the great male figures of Hindu mythology who take on female forms in various situations. Familiar to all Hindus is Arjun's disguise as a eunuch in the Mahabharata and Shiva's form as Ardhanarisvara, half man/half woman, just two examples of powerful males in Hindu culture who act or dress as women or who partake of feminine qualities.

Many Hindu festivals include male transgenderism, like the one in south India that attracts thousands of hijras from all over India. This festival is based on a story of a king, who, in order to avert defeat in a war, promised to sacrifice his eldest son to the Gods, asking only that he first be allowed to arrange his son's marriage. Because no woman could be found who would marry a man about to be sacrificed, Lord Krishna came to earth as a woman to marry the King's son and the king won the battle, as the gods had promised. For the festival, men dress as women and go through a marriage ceremony with the deity. The priest performs the marriage, tying on the traditional wedding necklace. The next day the deity is carried to a burial ground and all of those who have "married" him remove their wedding necklaces, cry and beat their breasts, break their bangles, and remove the flowers from their hair, as a widow does in mourning. Hijra participation in this ritual affirms their identification with Krishna, one of the most important Indian deities.

The identification of males with female deities, expressed by the hijras through their cross dressing and emasculation, is a traditional part of Hinduism. This identification reinforces the legitimacy of the hijras as devotees of the Mother Goddess and vehicles of her power, which they use to confer blessings of fertility and prosperity at the births and weddings where they perform. The importance of the mother goddess in India is thus critical to understanding the role of the hijras. Hijra devotion to the goddess, Bahucharaji, a version of the Mother Goddess, closely identified with Durga, is central to their community. Bahucharaji's temple, near Ahmedabad, always has several hijra attendants present who bless visitors and tell them the stories of the powers of the goddess, which has specific references to transgenderism. It is in the name of the goddess that the hijras undergo their emasculation operation, which to them is a ritual of rebirth, transforming them from men to hijras.

Hindu, Muslim, and even Christian hijras revere the goddess, while at the same time embracing elements of Islamic culture. The Indian tradition among both Hindus and Muslims of seeking blessings from saint-like figures whose personal power and charisma supersedes their ascribed religion permits the hijras to find some respect in both these religious communities. In pre-independence India, for example, Muslim rulers gave land grants and special rights to hijras in their kingdoms. And while the hijra role is definitely rooted in early Hinduism, the use of eunuchs in the Mughal courts also strengthened its emergence as a distinct sub-culture. The incorporation of both Hinduism and Islam in the hijras' identity and community is characteristic of the power of Indian culture to incorporate seeming contradictions and paradoxes, into itself, including gender ambiguity, variation, and contradictions (O'Flaherty 1980).

As a caste (jati), or community (quam), hijras have a highly structured social organization whose dominant feature is a hierarchical relationship between the elders, or gurus, and the juniors, or chelas (the guru/chela relationship models itself on the teacher/disciple relationships which are an important feature of Hinduism). Each hijra joins the community under the sponsorship of a guru, and the guru-chela relationship ideally lasts a lifetime. Chelas of the same guru consider themselves "sisters" and adopt fictive kinship relations, such as "aunty" and "grandmother" with hijra elders. As chelas get older, they may become gurus by recruiting chelas for themselves. This process both offers scope for social mobility within the hijra community and also helps maintain the community over time. Hijra social organization, particularly in the guru-chela relationship, thus attempts to substitute for the family life which hijras have abandoned: the guru offers protection, care, and security to the chela and receives in return obedience, loyalty, and a portion of their earnings. Another important advantage of belonging to the hijra community is that it provides a haven when a hijra becomes aged or ill, and can no longer work. A hijra guru with many chelas will be well taken care of, but even a hijra with no chelas will be taken care of by the members of her community.

The typical effective working group of hijras is a communal household, consisting of 5–15 people, headed by a guru. The household members contribute part or all of their earnings to the household and share household chores. In return they get a roof over their heads, food, protection from the police for those who engage in prostitution, and a place from which to carry on their business. Most importantly, as all of the work hijras do, whether begging, entertaining, or prostitution, is strictly divided up among all the hijra households in a city, joining a hijra commune is practically the only way a hijra can get work. The hijra household is thus both an economic and a residential unit, as well as a family-like group which provides emotional satisfaction and a network of social relationships.

Living in a hijra household puts many restrictions on behavior. Just as an Indian bride must make adjustments to her in-laws when she moves into a joint family, so a new hijra must make many accommodations to her new "family" in a hijra commune. Kumari, an independent sort of person, who, with her guru's permission, eventually moved out to her own place, told me that "living with the hijras was very difficult. There were so many jobs to do . . . like cooking and housework. After coming home from a whole day of dancing, I then had to cook and do other chores. If I did the household chores during the day, I wouldn't have time to go out and the whole day would be lost. Gurus are very strict. If you don't keep your hair covered with your sari, if you don't cook properly, if the house is not spotlessly clean, for all these things they give you trouble. You can't just throw your dirty clothes down anywhere, you have to hang them up. If you don't serve food on the proper dishes, they will shout, 'What, are you a man that you cannot do these things properly!' I got tired of all that and so asked my guru permission to live on my own."

But even for hijras like Kumari, who prefer to live on their own, the idea of living as a hijra without the support of a guru is unthinkable. "You can never be without a guru," says Kumari, "anymore than you people (non-hijras) can be without a mother. Just as a daughter is known by her mother, so we are known by our guru. To belong to the hijra community, to live in a sari like this, you must have a guru; otherwise you will have no respect in society."

An individual can only join the hijra community under the sponsorship of a guru, and as a member of her guru's "house" (gharana). The "houses" into which the hijra community is divided are similar to symbolic descent groups, like clans or lineages. Although there are few meaningful distinctions between these "houses," each has its own founder and history. Hijras say the "houses" are like several brothers from the same mother, or two countries, like England and America, which have a common origin. A hijra remains in the "house" of her guru even if she moves her residence to some other household or even some other city. When a hijra dies, it is the elders of her "house," rather than her household, who arrange for her funeral; and a guru will pass her property to chelas belonging to her "house" when she dies.

Each "house" has a naik, or chief and it is the naiks who get together locally, and also nationally, to decide on major policy issues for the hijra community, or to celebrate some event within the community, such as the death anniversary of a famous guru. At the local level, it is the naiks who get together in a jamaat (meeting of the elders) to resolve conflict among hijra individuals or households within a city or region.

One of the most important tasks of the jamaat is to make sure that hijras do not violate the rules of their community. Honesty is one of the unshakable hijra norms. Hijras frequently change their residence, both within and between cities, and a hijra who has been found guilty of stealing someone's property will not be accepted in any hijra household. Without a household, a hijra will find herself without friends, and more important, without access to work. In respectable hijra households, individuals are expected to behave with some propriety, and hijras who drink heavily, or who are quarrelsome, or cannot control their aggression, will find themselves out on the street. The punishment for misbehavior varies with the crime: in some cases fines are levied; in more serious cases a hijra's hair will be cut as a way of stigmatizing her within the community, as hijras are obliged to wear their hair long, like women. For the most serious offenses, such as abusing or assaulting one's guru, a hijra may be cast out of the community altogether and have to pay a very heavy fine to re-enter.

This had happened to Rehka. Rehka had been in the hijra community for the last 15 years, earning her keep by playing the dholak (drum) which always accompanies hijra performances. Several years ago, provoked in an argument over men and money, Rehka insulted her guru and struck her. A meeting of the naiks determined that she should be cast out of the hijra community. From living very comfortably and with her future secure, Rehka now found herself, literally, on the street. Her sister chelas would no longer talk to her, not even, she said, "give me a drink of water." There was no place within walking distance she could work that was not already part of another hijra group's territory. If she tried to perform or even beg, she would be chased away by other hijras. With no money, and no work, Rehka took up residence on the street, earning a few rupees caring for some neighbor's children, or sometimes walking miles to a suburb to beg for alms. When it rained she slept under a bus. Living in the open, her clothes became tattered, her appearance and her health deteriorated and she was constantly insulted by neighborhood rowdies. It was a vicious cycle: Rekha was cast out of the community until she could raise the substantial fine of over 1000 rupees that the naiks determined as the price of her re-entry into the community and apart from the community it was hopeless to even think of earning that sum, never mind saving it. Rehka's transformation was not lost on the hijras in her city. For all who knew her, it acted as a powerful incentive to maintain their own obedience and loyalty to their gurus.

The most important conflicts that naiks resolve are those that occur when the rigid territorial allotment of work within a city is violated. Naiks reach agreement about which hijra groups may work—whether begging alms from shop owners or in traditional performances—in particular areas of a city. When a hijra group finds others encroaching on their assigned territory, there may be arguments or even fist fights, and the naiks must negotiate new allotments of territory or maintain traditional boundaries. Because hijras can hardly go to the police or courts to settle their disputes—nor would they wish to give up such power to outsiders—disputes are settled within the community.

The hijras today are an example of a highly successful cultural adaptation. Their structured social organization, which imitates both a family and a caste, the use of the guru/chela relationship as a recruitment strategy, their willingness to move into new economic niches, and the effective control over economic rights exercised within the community, provide hijras with both the flexibility and control needed to succeed in today's complex and highly competitive society. In the face of dwindling opportunities for their traditional performances, prostitution, always a lucrative profession, has expanded. Hijras now bless girl infants as well as boys; they have become tax collectors, and have successfully run for political office. In politics, hijras have largely succeeded by emphasizing that their ascetic role as neither man nor woman, with no families to support, which they contrast to the widespread nepotism and corruption engaged in by so many Indian politicians (Reddy 2003).

Hijras have also successfully weathered the attempts of the Indian government to outlaw their emasculation operation, which serves as the definitive symbol of their identity. Indeed, they have become politically organized and have petitioned various state governments to grant them, as members of the "sexually marginalized," rights to jobs, marriage, legal recognition as a third gender and to consider sending a hijra into space as part of India's space program (Reddy 2010:140).

Gender Variation in Other Cultures

The assumption by a man of a woman's character, sex/gender role and identity in a spiritual or religious context, and even as a means of salvation, which has long been part of the Hindu tradition, is found in many other cultural traditions as well

(Herdt 1996), particularly in Southeast Asia (Peletz 2009). In many great agricultural civilizations of the ancient world, arising around 10,000 years ago, Mother Goddess cults were prominent. Some of these goddesses were attended by a priesthood that included men who acted and dressed as women, either specifically during religious rituals, or permanently, while other cults involved male priests who castrated themselves while in ecstasy, in a gesture of renunciation and identification with her, very similar to the hijra nirvana ritual. The numerous images of Hermaphroditus (from which the English term hermaphrodite derives) found in Greek mythology and statuary, make it clear that androgyny and sex-change also had special meaning for the ancient Greeks.

By the end of the 4th century, B.C.E., however, cultural diffusion, through the spread of Christianity and later, in the 8th century C.E. through the spread of Islam, led to the dominance of male deities. By the 8th century C.E., mother goddess worship had virtually disappeared (India is one of the few places where it remained culturally central), and with it, of course, the sexually ambiguous priesthoods. Still later, European colonialism began to have its effect in repressing sexual and gender diversity in the New World as well as the old. The British, for example, outlawed the land grants to hijras in India, which had been awarded in various princely states, and repressed the many transgender roles in Southeast Asia (Peletz 2009), while the 19th century American occupation of Hawai'i, led to the decline of the indigenous role of the mahu (Matzner 2001).

In the mid-20th century, the European medical model, which pathologized gender diversity and homosexuality, spread throughout Asia, and had a particularly negative impact in Thailand. The kathoey, a third gender, mentioned in ancient Buddhist scriptures and tolerated by society, as well as homosexuality, came to be viewed as "social problems," and were subject to both attempted "treatment" and repression (Jackson 1999; Costa and Matzner 2007). The contemporary global spread of fundamental Islam has also affected Islamic states such as Malaysia and Indonesia, whose previous casual toleration of indigenous transgender roles and male same-sex relationships, is now replaced by increasing public surveillance; in Indonesia a ban on the transsexual operation is being proposed.

At the same time, in recent decades, there has been a countercurrent to the decline of gender diversity, as the effects of ethnography, international human rights, the internet, and global media have sent information and images all over the world. Transgender beauty contests, long practiced in the Philippines—and based on American images of beauty rooted in the American occupation of the turn of the 20th century—have proliferated throughout Asia and the Pacific (Johnson 1997; Besnier 2011). In Indonesia, the waria, an indigenous transgender role, has become a symbol of nationalism and warias dominate beauty salons which prepare brides for traditional Indonesian weddings (Boellstorff 2005). The diffusion of a global gay identity, which is now associated with many different transgender roles throughout Asia, is spread by the media and by internet-based solidarity, even as it is transformed in local cultures in a variety of ways. Similarly, many international NGOs have set up HIV/AIDS clinics throughout Asia and Africa, which form a nexus of homosexual and transgender relationships, although in fact, AIDS in Asia and Africa is spread more by heterosexual than by same-sex relationships. Global migration, too, has been an important source of cultural diffusion, bringing for example, large numbers of transgendered Filipinos to Israel, where they dominate in the care of the aged (Heymann 2006). These globalizing dimensions of sex/gender diversity, have also affected the United States.

Sex/Gender Diversity and Change in the United States

One of the most important roles of anthropology is to increase our awareness of our own culture by reflecting on the cultures of others; as the famous anthropologist, Claude Levi-Strauss said, ethnography makes an important contribution to an ongoing critique of Western culture. The descriptions of sex/gender diversity in other cultures provokes us to re-examine the nature and assumptions of our own sex/gender system; the cultural basis of its categories; the relations between sex, sexuality, gender, and other aspects of culture; and the ways in which this impacts on individuals with alternative sex/gender identities who engage in diverse sexual practices (Nanda 2000).

Until the late 20th century, the binary Western concept of sex and gender—male and female—as well as condemnation of homosexuality, described in the book of Genesis, left no room for alternative sex/gender identities or varied sexual practices. The emergence of medical technology which enabled sex reassignment surgery both reflected and intensified this dichotomy. For an individual whose gender identity or sexual relationships were in conflict with his or her biological sex, the sex change operation provided one way out of the dilemma. Transsexuals in American culture were defined as "biologically normal persons of one sex convinced that they were members of the *opposite* sex" (Stoller, cited in Kessler and McKenna, 1978:115). The aim of sex reassignment surgery and the psychological and medical treatments (such as hormone therapy) that were required to accompany it, was the transformation of an individual from their natal sex into the sex with which they identified. An important aspect of the treatment required the individual to demonstrate to psychological and medical professionals that the individual was committed to, and was able to, make this transition.

This construction of the transsexual was consistent with the binary American sex/gender system and was supported in the larger culture by permitting various legal changes as part of a revised life story (Bolin 1988). Unlike alternative sex/gender figures in other cultures, however, transsexuals were viewed as a source of cultural anxiety, pathology, and a social problem; at best, as figures of scorn or pity. While the gay liberation movement in the United States helped our society become more humane and egalitarian in its response to sex and gender variations, our culture has not yet been able to incorporate the wide tolerance or spiritual roles for gender difference and ambiguity that traditionally existed in India and in other societies.

Even with emerging cultural and indeed legal supports of the construct of the transsexual as someone who crosses over completely to the "opposite" sex, this concept was not—and is not today—wholly accepted in our society. In a 2002 legal case in which a transsexual claimed the estate of her deceased spouse, the Kansas Supreme Court stated that both science and the courts are divided on whether transsexuals are more appropriately defined in terms of their birth sex status or their post-operative sex/gender status [*In re Marshall G. Gardiner, deceased.* (2002), in Norgren and Nanda 2006]. The Court held that, while "through surgery and hormones, a transsexual can be made to look like a woman . . . the sex assignment surgery does not create the sexual organs of a woman." The Court further held that while the plaintiff (a male to female transsexual) "wants and believes herself to be a woman [and] . . . has made every conceivable effort to make herself a female . . . her female anatomy, however, is still all man-made. The body [the plaintiff] inhabits is a male body in all aspects other than what the physicians have supplied . . . From that the Court has to conclude, that . . . as a matter of law [the plaintiff] is a male."

In spite of American resistance to changing concepts of sex and gender, illustrated by the legal decision cited above, the increasing awareness of the sex/gender systems of other cultures has led to a change in our own society. Within the last three decades America's rigid binary cultural boundaries—nature/culture, male/female, homosexual/heterosexual—have become blurred. Transgenderism is now a recognized cultural category, one that transcends the historical American "incorrigible proposition" that tells us that sex and gender are ascribed and permanent.

Transgenderism today incorporates a variety of subjective experiences, identities, and sexual practices that range widely over a sex/gender continuum, from androgynous to transsexual (Valentine 2007). Increasingly, persons defining themselves as transpeople see transgenderism as a way "out of the constraints imposed by a dichotomous sex/gender system [with the aim] . . . not to mandate anything, but to . . . be able to play with the categories, . . . to challenge the reductionism and essentialism that has accompanied these [binary] categories for so many millennia" (Ducat 2006: 48). In spite of the many differences among individuals experiencing transgender identities, one repeated theme of the transgender movement is that gender and sex categories are improperly imposed by society and its "sexual identity gatekeepers," referring here to the gender identity professionals who accepted and furthered the binary system of American sex/gender roles (Bolin 1996: 447). The transgendered are challenging and stretching the boundaries of the American system of sex/gender binary oppositions, and renouncing the American definition of gender as dependent on a consistency of genitals, body type, identity, role behaviors, sexual orientation, and sexual practice. Contemporary transgender communities include a continuum of people, from those who wish to undergo sex reassignment surgery, to those who wish to live their lives androgynously (Winter 2006). The previous split between transsexuals who viewed surgery as the only authentic expression of a feminine nature, as opposed to "part time" gender crossers who did not wish to have sex reassignment surgery, has to some extent been reconciled by

the emergence of a transgender community which attempts to validate a whole range of gender roles and identities. As one transperson expressed it, " . . . you no longer have to fit into a box . . . it is okay to be transgendered. You can now lay anywhere on the spectrum from non-gendered to full transsexual" (Bolin 1996: 475). Transpeople are trying not so much to do away with maleness and femaleness as to de-naturalize them, that is, take away their privileged status in relation to all other possible combinations of behaviors, roles, and identities. The point for some transpeople is that gender categories should be something that individuals can construct for themselves, through self-reflection and observation (Cromwell 1997).

The dynamism of the contemporary transgender movement, which includes both transgender activists and mental health professionals, was recently acknowledged in a proposal by the New York City Board of Health to allow people to alter the sex on their birth certificate even if they have not had sex-change surgery (Cave 2006: A1). While this proposal, which emphasized the importance of separating anatomy from gender identity, ultimately failed, New York City has adopted other measures aimed at blurring the lines of gender identification. It has, for example, allowed beds in homeless shelters to be distributed according to appearance, applying equally to post-operative transsexuals, cross-dressers, and persons perceived to be androgynous. A Metropolitan Transit Authority policy also allows people to define their own gender when deciding whether to use men's or women's bathrooms. These new, even radical, policies are just one of the many aspects of the current transgender movement. Other aims of this movement are the redefining of gender diversity as a naturally occurring phenomenon rather than a psychological disorder; dismantling gender stereotypes, and reducing harassment and discrimination against those who do not wish to conform to current sex/gender norms (Brown 2006: A1). As Sam Winter, director of the Transgender Asia website suggests, although treating gender disorders as a mental illness, as in the United States, is useful for Western transsexuals in obtaining medical services, it extracts too high a price in substantially contributing to transphobia. For contemporary transpeople he says, "transgender is one aspect of human diversity. . . . It is a difference, not a disorder . . . If we can speak to any gender identity disorder at all, it is in the inability of many societies to accept the particular gender identity difference we call transgender" (Winter, accessed 2006).

A core American cultural pattern which places a high value on the "authentic self"—on integrating the inner person with external actions—is central to the current transgender movement, as well as to contemporary gay activism. This core American cultural value is not universal, which makes it easier for sex/gender diversity to exist in other societies. In Thailand, for example, little value is attached to acknowledging or displaying one's private sexual orientation in public. In Thailand, how one acts is more important than how one feels. Leading a "double life" is a generally accepted feature of Thai culture, not necessarily equated with duplicity or deception as in the United States. Thus, "coming out" as a homosexual in Thailand brings shame or "loss of face" both to the individual and to the family without the compensation of expressing one's "true self" so valued in the United States. Similar values also hold in Indonesia (Wieringa 2008). In Malaysia, too, the Islamic emphasis on marriage and family takes precedence over asserting one's individuality and agency, as required in the process of "coming out" (Peletz 2009). Martin Manalansan, in his ethnography of transgendered Philippine migrants in New York, makes a similar point, quoting a "bakla" informant: "The Americans are different, darling. Coming out is their drama. When I studied at [a New England college] the queens had nothing better to talk about than coming out . . . the whites, my God, shedding tears, leaving the families. The stories are always so sad" (2003).

This contrast between cultural values, as they affect homosexuals and transgender people in Thailand, Malaysia and the Philippines, and those in the United States, casts a revealing perspective on the demand for repeal of "Don't Ask, Don't Tell," the shortsighted, politically motivated policy that banned openly gay men and women from the American military. That policy, which burdened the individual with the necessity of hiding his or her "true self" is quite simply incompatible with American culture and is now in the process of being repealed.

Unlike transsexualism, which reinforces the binary American sex/gender system, transgenderism is culturally subversive: it calls into question the rightness of binary sex/gender categories. It also provides a wider range of individual possibilities for those who experience distress by trying to conform to exclusively binary sex/gender categories, including sexual practices. The American transgender movement has been empowered by knowledge about alternative sex/gender systems throughout the world. Some of these sex/gender systems have offered American transpeople a source of meaning, and especially spiritual meaning, that they do not find in the binary, transphobic culture that is still dominant within the United States. As the West becomes more aware of alternatives and variations in gender roles in other cultures, both past and present, it can also perhaps become more accommodating of those individuals who do not fit into their traditionally prescribed—and limited—sex/gender categories.

References

Besnier, N. 2011. *On the edge of the global: Modern anxieties in a Pacific Island nation.* Stanford, CA: Stanford University Press.

Boelstorff, T. 2005. *The gay archipelago: Sexuality and nation in Indonesia.* Princeton, NJ: Princeton University Press.

Bolin, A. 1988. *In search of Eve: Transsexual rites of passage.* South Hadley, MA: Bergin and Garvey.

Bolin A. 1996. "Transcending and transgendering: Male-to-female transsexuals, dichotomy and diversity." In G. Herdt (Ed.), *Third sex third gender: Beyond sexual dimorphism in culture and history* (pp. 447–485). New York: Zone Books.

Brown, P.L. 2006. "Supporting boys or girls when the line isn't clear." *The New York Times,* December 2, p. A1.

Cave, D. 2006. "New York plans to make gender personal choice." *The New York Times,* November 7, p. A1.

Costa, L. and Andrew Matzner, A. 2007. *Male bodies, women's souls: Personal narratives of Thailand's transgendered youth.* Binghamton, NY: Haworth Press.

Cromwell, J. 1977. "Traditions of gender diversity and sexualities: A female-to-male transgendered perspective." In S. Jacobs,

W. Thomas, and S. Lang (Eds.). *Two spirit people: Native American gender identity, sexuality, and spirituality.* Urbana, IL: University of Illinois Press.

Ducat, S. 2006. "Slipping into something more comfortable: Towards a liberated continuum of gender." *LiP,* Summer, pp. 46–61.

Herdt, G. 1996. *Third sex third gender: Beyond sexual dimorphism in culture and history.* New York: Zone Books.

Heymann, T. 2006. *Paper Dolls.* (film). Strand Releasing.

Jackson, P. 1999. *Lady boys, tom boys, rentboys: Male and female homosexualities in contemporary Thailand.* Binghamton, NY: Haworth Press.

Johnson, M. 1997. *Beauty and power: Transgendering and cultural transformation in the Southern Philippines.* New York: Berg.

Kessler, S.J., and W. McKenna. 1978. *Gender: An ethnomethodological approach.* New York: Wiley.

Manalansan, M. 2003. *Global divas: Filipino gay men in the diaspora.* Durham, NC: Duke University Press.

Matzner, A. 2001. *'O au no keia: Voices from Hawai'i's Mahu and transgender community.'* Philadelphia: XLibris.

Nanda, S. 1999. *Neither man nor woman: the hijras of India.* 2nd. Ed. Belmont, CA: Wadsworth.

Nanda, S. 2000. *Gender diversity: crosscultural variations.* Prospect Heights, IL: Waveland.

Norgren, J. and S. Nanda. 2006. *American cultural pluralism and law.* Westport, CN: Praeger.

O'Flaherty, W.D. 1980. *Women, androgynies, and other mythical beasts.* Chicago: University of Chicago Press.

Peletz, M. 2009. *Gender pluralism: southeast asia since early modern times.* NY: Routledge.

Reddy, G. 2003. "'Men' who would be kings: celibacy, emasculation and reproduction of hijras in contemporary Indian politics. *Social Research,* 70, no. 1:163–198.

Reddy, G. 2005. *With respect to sex: negotiating hijra identity in South India.* Chicago: University of Chicago Press.

Reddy, G. 2010. "Crossing "Lines" of difference: Transnational Movements and Sexual Subjectivities In Hyderabad, India." In Diane P. Mines and Sarah Lamb (Eds.), *Everyday life in south Asia,* 2nd. Ed. Bloomington, IN: University of Indiana Press.

Valentine, D. 2007. *Imagining transgender: An ethnography of a category.* Durham, NC: Duke University Press.

Wieringa, S. 2008. "If there is no feeling . . . The Dilemma between Silence and Coming Out in a Working Class Butch/Femme Community in Jakarta." In Mark B. Padilla, Jennifer S. Hirsch, Miguel Munoz-Laboy, Robert E. Sember, and Richard G. Parker (Eds.), *Love and globalization: Transformations of intimacy in the contemporary world.* Nashville, TN: University of Vanderbilt Press, pp. 70–90.

Winter, S. 2006. "Transphobia: A price worth paying for gender identity disorder? Retrieved from http://web.hku.hk/~ sjwinter/Transgender ASIA/index.htm.

Critical Thinking

1. Be aware of the various social roles played by the hijra and how individuals become part of a hijra community.

2. What is the significance of the operation known as "nirvana"?

3. Be familiar with the hijra community in terms of its religious and caste qualities.

4. Be familiar with the hijra household in terms of its structure and rules.

5. What kinds of tasks are carried out by the "naiks" and the "jamaat"?

6. In what respects are the hijras an example of a highly successful cultural adaptation?

7. What evidence is there of gender variation throughout history? How did cultural diffusion and colonialism suppress it? How and why have there been countercurrents to such suppression?

8. What is meant by the American notion of a "binary sex and gender"? How has this been reinforced by medical technology?

9. What kinds of changes did the "transgender movement" bring about?

10. How and why is "coming out" treated differently in the United States and Thailand?

11. Why is "transgenderism" more subversive than "transsexualism"?

SERENA NANDA is Professor Emeritus, Anthropology, at John Jay College, City University of New York. Many thanks to Joan Gregg, Mary Winslow, Cory Harris, and Barry Kass for their encouragement and suggestions.

Adapted for use in *Annual Editions*, 2011, from an article in *Manushi*, vol. 72, 1992. Copyright © 2011 by Serena Nanda. Reprinted by permission of Serena Nanda.

Where Fat Is a Mark of Beauty

In a rite of passage, some Nigerian girls spend months gaining weight and learning customs in a special room. "To be called a 'slim princess' is an abuse," says a defender of the practice.

ANN M. SIMMONS

Margaret Bassey Ene currently has one mission in life: gaining weight.

The Nigerian teenager has spent every day since early June in a "fattening room" specially set aside in her father's mud-and-thatch house. Most of her waking hours are spent eating bowl after bowl of rice, yams, plantains, beans and *gari,* a porridge-like mixture of dried cassava and water.

After three more months of starchy diet and forced inactivity, Margaret will be ready to reenter society bearing the traditional mark of female beauty among her Efik people: fat.

In contrast to many Western cultures where thin is in, many culture-conscious people in the Efik and other communities in Nigeria's southeastern Cross River state hail a woman's rotundity as a sign of good health, prosperity and allure.

The fattening room is at the center of a centuries-old rite of passage from maidenhood to womanhood. The months spent in pursuit of poundage are supplemented by daily visits from elderly matrons who impart tips on how to be a successful wife and mother. Nowadays, though, girls who are not yet marriage-bound do a tour in the rooms purely as a coming-of-age ceremony. And sometimes, nursing mothers return to the rooms to put on more weight.

"The fattening room is like a kind of school where the girl is taught about motherhood," said Sylvester Odey, director of the Cultural Center Board in Calabar, capital of Cross River state. "Your daily routine is to sleep, eat and grow fat."

Like many traditional African customs, the fattening room is facing relentless pressure from Western influences. Health campaigns linking excess fat to heart disease and other illnesses are changing the eating habits of many Nigerians, and urban dwellers are opting out of the time-consuming process.

Effiong Okon Etim, an Efik village chief in the district of Akpabuyo, said some families cannot afford to constantly feed a daughter for more than a few months. That compares with a stay of up to two years, as was common earlier this century, he said.

But the practice continues partly because "people might laugh at you because you didn't have money to allow your child to pass through the rite of passage," Etim said. What's more, many believe an unfattened girl will be sickly or unable to bear children.

Etim, 65, put his two daughters in a fattening room together when they were 12 and 15 years old, but some girls undergo the process as early as age 7, after undergoing the controversial practice of genital excision.

Bigger Is Better, According to Custom

As for how fat is fat enough, there is no set standard. But the unwritten rule is the bigger the better, said Mkoyo Edet, Etim's sister.

"Beauty is in the weight," said Edet, a woman in her 50s who spent three months in a fattening room when she was 7. "To be called a 'slim princess' is an abuse. The girl is fed constantly whether she likes it or not."

In Margaret's family, there was never any question that she would enter the fattening room.

"We inherited it from our forefathers; it is one of the heritages we must continue," said Edet Essien Okon, 25, Margaret's stepfather and a language and linguistics graduate of the University of Calabar. "It's a good thing to do; it's an initiation rite."

His wife, Nkoyo Effiong, 27, agreed: "As a woman, I feel it is proper for me to put my daughter in there, so she can be educated."

Effiong, a mother of five, spent four months in a fattening room at the age of 10.

Margaret, an attractive girl with a cheerful smile and hair plaited in fluffy bumps, needs only six months in the fattening room because she was already naturally plump, her stepfather said.

During the process, she is treated as a goddess, but the days are monotonous. To amuse herself, Margaret has only an instrument made out of a soda bottle with a hole in it, which she taps on her hand to play traditional tunes.

Still, the 16-year-old says she is enjoying the highly ritualized fattening practice.

"I'm very happy about this," she said, her belly already distended over the waist of her loincloth. "I enjoy the food, except for *gari.*"

Day in, day out, Margaret must sit cross-legged on a special stool inside the secluded fattening room. When it is time to eat, she sits on the floor on a large, dried plantain leaf, which also serves as her bed. She washes down the mounds of food with huge pots of water and takes traditional medicine made from leaves and herbs to ensure proper digestion.

As part of the rite, Margaret's face is decorated with a white, claylike chalk.

"You have to prepare the child so that if a man sees her, she will be attractive," Chief Etim said.

Tufts of palm leaf fiber, braided and dyed red, are hung around Margaret's neck and tied like bangles around her wrists and ankles. They are adjusted as she grows.

Typically, Margaret would receive body massages using the white chalk powder mixed with heavy red palm oil. But the teen said her parents believe the skin-softening, blood-stimulating massages might cause her to expand further than necessary.

Margaret is barred from doing her usual chores or any other strenuous physical activities. And she is forbidden to receive visitors, save for the half a dozen matrons who school Margaret in the etiquette of the Efik clan.

They teach her such basics as how to sit, walk and talk in front of her husband. And they impart wisdom about cleaning, sewing, child care and cooking—Efik women are known throughout Nigeria for their chicken pepper soup, pounded yams and other culinary creations.

"They advise me to keep calm and quiet, to eat the *gari,* and not to have many boyfriends so that I avoid unwanted pregnancy," Margaret said of her matron teachers. "They say that unless you have passed through this, you will not be a full-grown woman."

What little exercise Margaret gets comes in dance lessons. The matrons teach her the traditional *ekombi,* which she will be expected to perform before an audience on the day she emerges from seclusion—usually on the girl's wedding day, Etim said.

But Okon said his aim is to prepare his stepdaughter for the future, not to marry her off immediately. Efik girls receive more education than girls in most parts of Nigeria, and Okon hopes Margaret will return to school and embark on a career as a seamstress before getting married.

Weddings Also Steeped in Tradition

Once she does wed, Margaret will probably honor southeastern Nigeria's rich marriage tradition. It begins with a letter from the family of the groom to the family of the bride, explaining that "our son has seen a flower, a jewel, or something beautiful in your family, that we are interested in," said Josephine Effah-Chukwuma, program officer for women and children at the Constitutional Rights Project, a law-oriented nongovernmental organization based in the Nigerian commercial capital of Lagos.

If the girl and her family consent, a meeting is arranged. The groom and his relatives arrive with alcoholic beverages, soft drinks and native brews, and the bride's parents provide the food. The would-be bride's name is never uttered, and the couple are not allowed to speak, but if all goes well, a date is set for handing over the dowry. On that occasion, the bride's parents receive about $30 as a token of appreciation for their care of the young woman. "If you make the groom pay too much, it is like selling your daughter," Effah-Chukwuma said. Then, more drinks are served, and the engagement is official.

On the day of the wedding, the bride sits on a specially built wooden throne, covered by an extravagantly decorated canopy. Maidens surround her as relatives bestow gifts such as pots, pans, brooms, plates, glasses, table covers—everything she will need to start her new home. During the festivities, the bride changes clothes three times.

The high point is the performance of the *ekombi,* in which the bride twists and twirls, shielded by maidens and resisting the advances of her husband. It is his task to break through the ring and claim his bride.

Traditionalists are glad that some wedding customs are thriving despite the onslaught of modernity.

Traditional weddings are much more prevalent in southeastern Nigeria than so-called white weddings, introduced by colonialists and conducted in a church or registry office.

"In order to be considered married, you have to be married in the traditional way," said Maureen Okon, a woman of the Qua ethnic group who wed seven years ago but skipped the fattening room because she did not want to sacrifice the time. "Tradition identifies a people. It is important to keep up a culture. There is quite a bit of beauty in Efik and Qua marriages."

Critical Thinking

1. How do the Efik contrast with many Western cultures with respect to a woman's "rotundity?"

2. What was the traditional role of the fattening room? What purpose does it serve today?

3. What kind of pressure does the fattening room face today? Why does the practice continue today?

4. What is the unwritten rule about "how fat?"

5. How does the author describe the fattening room experience? What exercise does Margaret get and why?

Missing Girls

Michelle Goldberg

Fatehgarh Sahib, a district in the northern India state of Punjab, is rich in rupees and poor in girls. Called the breadbasket of India, Punjab's wealth is built on agriculture; flat fields of ripe, gold wheat stretch out from straight, smooth highways, plowed by giant tractors driven by turbaned Sikh farmers. Unlike in southern India, women have little role in agriculture here, which is one of several reasons that so many in Punjab see them as a useless investment, one better avoided altogether.

India, like other Asian countries, has long had a pronounced son preference, which has translated into a population with more males than females. Punjab is one of several Indian states with a history of female infanticide that shocked the British colonialists, who found entire villages without a single girl.[1] The British banned female infanticide in 1870—almost a hundred years after they discovered the practice—yet more subtle forms of discrimination and neglect continued to cull India's population of girls, who were, and still are, fed less than boys and given less medical care.

"The actual murder of little girls has in a great measure ceased, but it has been replaced in some tribes by a degree of carelessness hardly less criminal," one observer wrote toward the end of the 1800s. "It is found in some districts that, when fever is prevalent, girls' deaths, especially in the first three years of life, so largely exceed those of males that it is impossible not to believe that but small attempts are made to save the girls, and in many places deaths caused by disease of the lungs or malnutrition suggest the same conclusion."[2]

The care deficit has never been eliminated, but it seemed to have been improving throughout the twentieth century, and in India in the 1950s and 1960s there were almost as many female children as male.[3] Even Punjab saw a sustained increase in girls relative to boys. That's why the publication of India's 2001 census came as such a painful shock. Girls and women were living longer thanks to increased medical care, but the sex ratio had nonetheless gone seriously askew.* In seventy districts, the ratio of girls to boys had declined by more than 50 points in the previous decade.[4] With 798 female children for every thousand males, Punjab had the worst sex ratio in India, and Fatehgarh Sahib, with a sex ratio of 766, was the worst district in Punjab.

The decline was overwhelmingly due to the epidemic spread of sex-selective abortion, which most people in India refer to as "female feticide." Sex determination tests first appeared in India in the 1970s through the use of amniocentesis and chorionic villus sampling, both relatively invasive procedures that had to be done by a doctor. It wasn't until ultrasound, which spread throughout the country in the 1990s, that sex determination became easy and accessible. According to a 2006 study by *The Lancet,* a conservative estimate is that there are half a million sex-selective abortions in India each year.[5]

"Ultrasound really came as a WMD," said Puneet Bedi, a Delhi gynecologist who is one of the country's most vocal activists against sex selection. "Parts of India where there is no drinking water or flush toilets, you can find ultrasound. They have no electricity—they carry their own car batteries." Ultrasound can only detect sex at around four months, meaning sex-selective abortions are usually late-term abortions, a more complicated, dangerous procedure than early abortions. It doesn't matter: Some women go through them over and over again, sacrificing their bodies for a boy.

General Electric, which dominates India's ultrasound market in concert with the Indian company Wipro, provided cheap credit to help practitioners buy the machines. "The present marketing strategy of GE-WIPRO to target smaller towns is a matter of concern," wrote Sabu George, a leading anti–sex selection activist.

Once a private practitioner in a small town buys a machine then there is great pressure on other doctors to buy. Multiple machines where there is little demand for legitimate prenatal care increases competition, reduces scan rates and motivates abuses like fetal sex determination so that clinics can recover their investment. . . . At the global level, it is imperative that those concerned with human rights expose the transnational corporations involved in marketing ultrasound machines for these purposes.[6]

But the bitter problem of the missing girls cannot simply be laid at the door of even the most callous corporate behemoth. The sins of capitalism may exacerbate it, but behind it

---

*Sex ratio can be defined in several different ways. Internationally, most use the number of boys per 100 or 1,000 girls, which means that discrimination results in high sex ratios. But Indians tend to use the number of girls per 1,000 boys, so that areas of discrimination against girls are said to have low sex ratios.

are fantastically complex hierarchies of the world's most multifarious country, where feudalism and technocapitalism, extreme superstition and hypermodernity, purdah and professional women all coexist. Even as it highlights the desperate need for women's empowerment, sex-selective abortion sometimes looks, in a bizarre way, like a symptom of it. For reproductive rights advocates the whole issue has a looking-glass quality to it. It is a moral labyrinth that leads everyone but absolutists to sometimes uncomfortable and contradictory positions.

"You're going to get multiple opinions on everything on this," said Ena Singh, UNFPA's assistant representative in India and a particularly impassioned combatant against sex-selective abortion. (The day I met her a major Punjabi pop star, Rabbi Shergill, surprised her in her office; she had convinced him to make sex selection the theme of a new music video, which was about to debut on Indian TV.)

You're going to get multiple opinions on terminology; you're going to get multiple opinions on policy; you're going to get multiple opinions about rights, choice, gender, the way the law should be framed, the way it should be implemented, who should be implementing it. Because this issue is so fundamental, it's so deep, it impacts everything. It's about men and women—about every aspect of that relationship. It's about existence; it's about marriage; it's about love; it's about sex; it's about children; it's about globalization; it's about economics; it's about rights; it's about norms; it's about the media; it's about crime; it's about medicine; it's about medical ethics; it's about dowry; it's about property; and a hundred other things. Tell me what this is not about!

According to Amarjit Singh, a thirty-one-year-old family planning fieldworker from Fatehgarh Sahib, ultrasound exploded throughout his area in 1994. "Even remote villages knew about it," he said. Infamous advertisements went up across the region: "Spend 500 Rupees today and save 500,000 Rupees later." The numbers were a reference to the sometimes crushing cost of dowry, the main reason Indians give for the misery that commonly greets the birth of girls. Amarjit* remembers salesmen traveling to Punjabi villages touting the wonders of the new innovations. The same year India passed a law banning sex-determination tests for the purpose of sex-selective abortion, but it was widely ignored. "Everything was practiced very openly," said Amarjit.

A tall man with an easy smile and a shadow of a beard, Amarjit donates some of his time to the Voluntary Health Association of Punjab, the primary NGO addressing sex-selective abortion in that state. Like most of the district's residents he's a Sikh, though he long ago cut his hair and stopped wearing a turban except on special occasions. Sikhs have the worst sex ratio of all the groups in India, and the worst among the Sikhs are the Jat Sikhs, the land-owning caste that Amarjit belongs to.

He recalled an old chant he heard from relatives. Decades before he was born, when infanticide was committed openly, it was sung by those killing girl babies.

Eat the jaggery

Spin the cotton

You should not come

Send your brother

Today Amarjit is as active an opponent of sex selection as one is likely to find in Fatehgarh Sahib. He has allied himself with Manmohan Sharma, the founder of the Voluntary Health Association of Punjab, a frail, ardently committed social scientist who has dedicated the last fifteen years to combating his state's inequities, particularly those arising from sex discrimination. Amarjit insists that the mind-set that values men over women must be wiped out. And yet, less than twenty minutes after we first met, he explained to me why, in certain cases, he supports "female feticide."

"Supposing somebody has three, four, five girl children. In that case I think it's right that they plan a female feticide," he said. "You cannot change the idea of that woman who has three daughters. She keeps producing children in hopes of producing a son. So I think in such a situation it is acceptable. Sometimes in hopes of a son they produce too many girl children. They have no proper nutrition, education, or security. In that situation, it is very painful. Girls will be maltreated. They will not get good husbands."

The problem of sex-selective abortion is not, of course, limited to India. Across Asia it is reshaping the population in unprecedented ways. In most populations around 105 boys are born for every 100 girls. Male infants are weaker and more susceptible to illness, leading ratios to even out over time. The arrival of sex-selection technology has profoundly disrupted this equilibrium. According to the UNFPA, in 2005 six Asian countries reported imbalances of more than 108 male children for every 100 females: India, South Korea, Georgia, Azerbaijan, China, and Armenia. In China and India the situation has clearly deteriorated since the 1980s. "The fact that the child sex ratio has unexpectedly increased is going to influence the entire population over the coming decades: the entire population will gradually grow increasingly more masculine in their make-up, as the new generations born after the 1980s grow older," demographer Christophe Z. Guilmoto wrote of Asia.[7]

Immigration, meanwhile, has brought sex selection to the United States, Britain, and Canada, where advertisements for sex determination have appeared in newspapers aimed at the Indian diaspora.[8] A 2008 article in the *Proceedings of the National Academy of Sciences* documented skewed sex ratios among the children of Chinese, Korean, and Indian parents in the United States. "Using the 2000 U.S. Census, we find that the sex ratio

---

*Because so many Sikh men have the last name "Singh," and Sikh women the last name "Kaur," when dealing with groups, I'm going to refer to people by their first names to avoid confusion.

of the oldest child to be normal, but that of subsequent children to be heavily male if there was no previous son," it said.[9]

But the problem of the missing girls has been especially confounding in India, one of the two countries in the world where it is most prevalent. In the other, China, widespread sex selection is happening in the context of government compulsion. That makes the solution easy enough to see: End the one-child policy. India's situation is more complicated. It would be comforting to think that sex-selective abortion there is the product of poverty-driven desperation, of a kind of backwardness that could be remedied by development and education. Comforting, but wrong. In fact, while sex-selective abortion is sometimes motivated by economic need, other times it's the product of a twisted kind of consumerism.

It is widely practiced by India's emerging middle class, those with enough money and education to skirt the law and take advantage of technology. They fully embrace the two-child ideal that India's government—with outside help—pushed for decades, but only on the condition that they have at least one son. In a modernizing but still rigidly patriarchal society, boys hold out the prospect of a lifetime of economic security for their parents, while girls, who will join the household of their in-laws, are widely seen as simply a drain on expenses.

Female education is a remedy for almost every form of discrimination against girls—except this one. Indeed, in much of India higher rates of female literacy are correlated with higher rates of sex-selective abortion. This contrasts with China, where urbanites and those with higher education have the most normal sex ratios—despite the fact that the one-child policy is enforced more strictly in the cities.[10]

The posh, leafy suburbs of South Delhi, full of gracious homes occupied by professional couples with multiple servants, have sex ratios well under 900 girls for every 1,000 boys.[11] Bedi, a specialist in fetal medicine—and the father of two girls—has his practice there, in an elite neighborhood called Haus Kauz. He is a bearish man with a gray mustache, a Sikh from a caste, ironically, famous for female infanticide. A copy of the Dalai Lama's poem "A Precious Human Life" hangs on the wall of his office. On his desktop is one of his anti-sex selection PowerPoint presentations, which begins with a quote from Malcolm X: "It isn't that time is running out—time has run out!"

"This whole myth of somehow the poor women being forced to undergo sex determination and abortion is the biggest bullshit," said Bedi. "Seventy percent of the women who come to me [asking for sex determination], their husbands or their families don't even know that they're coming. The first demand for female feticide comes from the mother herself."

Bedi's patients, of course, are hardly representative of Indian women. They represent the richest sliver of Indian society: As he himself says, no one else can afford him. If the problem of sex-selective abortion were confined to people like them, it would barely show up in censuses. Still, the fact that even such privileged women seek out sex selection says much about how entrenched the preference for sons is throughout Indian society.

Given that Bedi is a high-profile crusader against sex selection, it seems strange that any of his patients would ask him for help in finding out the sex of their fetuses. That they do

is evidence of how much cynicism and corruption surrounds efforts to ban the practice. According to Bedi, most doctors who declaim against sex selection in public profit from it in private, a view I heard echoed by doctors in Punjab as well. He speaks about sex-selective abortion in the shrillest possible terms, calling it a genocide, a holocaust. Still, some women assume that he must not really mean it, that for the right price he'll help them avoid the burden of girls.

Bedi exudes a poignant mix of urgency and fatalism; he believes that everything possible must be done to stop sex-selective abortion, and that none of his activism is having any impact at all. In the last fifteen years, he said, he has talked two women out of aborting female fetuses, one of whom was pregnant after a long period of infertility. Both of them come to see him every year or two to castigate him for ruining their lives. They come, he said, to "remind me what a mistake they made because they listened to me, while everybody in their peer group has sons, [women] who were also my patients but had gone to better doctors later and got sons and abortions, while they had not."

These women are not cowering victims, he insisted. They "are women like you, like my wife and my sister. Empowered, with big cars, big houses, and the best possible college degrees."

There are several reasons for the counterintuitive connection between prosperity, education, and sex discrimination. Wealthier communities in India's northwest—precisely those who can most afford decent schools for their children—have always been the most averse to the birth of daughters. Members of the urban middle class want smaller families than poor people in the countryside, leaving less room for girls. Those with at least some education are better able to navigate the medical system, especially now that sex-determination tests have become illegal.

Most of all, though, more prosperous families are rejecting daughters because of the toxic, exponential growth of dowries. Dowry has been illegal in India since 1961, but that law is hardly enforced. In theory, dowry is a gift parents give to a daughter to ensure her future security; because she won't inherit any of her parents' property, it represents her share of their wealth. As it's practiced, though, dowry is a kind of tribute paid to the family of the groom. In much of northern India it's not a one-time gift, either: A girl's parents are expected to offer a continuous flow of presents to her husband's family, and to be somewhat abject before them. "In the power relations between the bride's and groom's families, the former always have to give in and put up with any humiliation, indignity, and oblique or direct insults on the part of the latter," wrote Indian sociologist Tulsi Patel.[12]

In recent years, with India suddenly awash in consumerist bounty, dowry demands have exploded, turning the whole thing into a materialistic free-for-all. In the high-caste communities where dowry had long been established, demands became inflated. At the same time, the custom took hold in places where it had never existed before as the upwardly mobile tried to imitate those further up the caste and class hierarchy.[13]

Historically, female infanticide was practiced mostly by the upper castes in India's highly conservative, Pakistan-bordering northern and northwestern plains, which stretch from Gujarat to Punjab, and that is where the problem of sex-selective abortion is most acute. Dowry is out of control in the region. "We have a developing society, and so much consumerism," said Nirupama Dutt, editor of the Punjabi edition of the *Sunday Indian,* a national newsmagazine. "It's so important to have the modern gadgets, ostentatious weddings." Her cousin, she said, from "a slightly backward rural area," considers the minimum acceptable dowry to include a television, a motorcycle, a refrigerator, and a washing machine, as well as quantities of gold. "This is the done thing," said Dutt. "Newspapers advertise package deals. And among the landlords, the Jats, a car is a must."

Exorbitant demands have been spreading from the north to the rest of the country, and as they have, sex-selective abortion has made inroads in parts of India where female infanticide had been unknown. A slight female deficit even appeared among children in the southernmost state of Kerala, where matriarchal traditions and leftist government combined to create a relative idyll of gender equality, with a female literacy rate of almost 90 percent, compared to less than 50 percent in India as a whole.

When dowry demands continue after marriage, a woman can become a kind of hostage in her in-laws' home, tormented, beaten, and even killed if enough money isn't forthcoming. In a not atypical story from May 2008, the *Times of India* reported that twenty-four-year-old Astha Jain was found hanging in her South Delhi home on her one-year wedding anniversary, her suicide note saying she could no longer bear her husband's family's dowry harassment. The in-laws owned a steel factory; her parents owned a paper business. According to her parents, they had already spent a crore—10 million rupees, or a quarter million dollars—during her wedding, and had given a Mercedes to the groom, Amit Jain, and gold rings to every member of the wedding party. In order to placate Amit's parents, they had handed over another 35 lakh, or $86,500, a few months before Astha's death. Their "greed could not be satisfied," said one of her relatives.[14]

On a searingly hot spring day in 2008, Amarjit Singh took me to one of the Fatehgarh Sahib villages where he worked. The people who live there are far from the rarefied realm of the Jains or of Bedi's patients, but the upper-caste Sikhs' section of the village has nearly as many modern conveniences as an American suburb. The houses are two stories high, with satellite dishes and designer water tanks shaped like birds or soccer balls perched on top. Behind the gates are courtyards big enough to park cars and John Deere tractors. Here, said Amarjit, there aren't more than 400 girls for every 1,000 boys. "The numbers look better because of Muslims and migrants," he said, both groups that have higher birthrates and more females.

Harpreet Singh, a lean, attractive man in white kurta pajamas and an orange turban, shared his late father's house with his brother, Narpreet. Each of them had one son. Harpreet, whose boy was six years old, planned to stop while he was ahead.

"The money that I earn is not enough to raise a girl child," he said. "I have already got one son, so I don't want any second child at all." Another boy would create his own problems, forcing Harpreet to split his share of his father's land in two. If dowries keep growing as they have been, meanwhile, he estimated he'd have to spend at least 15 lakh—1.5 million rupees, or $37,000—by the time any daughter of his would marry. With one boy he feels assured that his family line will continue and his wealth won't be dispersed.

"I know my district is famous for having the least number of girl children," he said. He worries, sometimes, about where his son will find a bride. But no one wanted to spend their own fortune providing wives for Punjab's boys: As the famous Punjabi saying goes, "Raising a daughter is like watering your neighbor's garden." If anything, Harpreet thought that increasing competition for women made it all the more imperative that he invest everything in his only boy. With so few girls, he said, "the time will come when the girls will be choosers in marriage. So in most cases the girls will choose the richer families to be married into. So those who are financially weaker, they will not get brides. That will be a very big crisis in our society."

Faced with such economic fears, he found official attempts to change attitudes wholly unconvincing. Like elsewhere in India, when people in the village have sons, they decorate their houses and hand out sweets. Usually, there is no celebration for a girl. Lately, people connected to the government and NGOs had been distributing sweets for daughters as well, which Harpreet saw as insincere "showing off." Deep down, he insisted, they're as desperate for boys as everyone else.

A short walk down a brick lane led us to the home of Balwant Singh, a milk seller and practitioner of ayurvedic medicine, and his wife, Gurjit Kaur. They had two daughters, twenty and twenty-two, and a five-year-old son. "I am very happy that I have two girls," Balwant insisted. "Clinton has only one daughter, but I have two daughters." Both girls were studying: The eldest, Ranbir, was working on a master's degree in commerce, and the younger, Satvir, was getting a BA in ayurvedic medicine, like her father.

In the curio case in the small sitting room, though, along with the birds made of seashells, the stuffed dog, and the yellow fabric flowers, there were no photos of Ranbir or Satvir. There were only pictures of little Inderbir, a boisterous boy who ran around the room soaking up attention as his sisters sat decorously to the side or went back and forth to the kitchen with drinks.

"Those people who have only girls in a family, the neighbors think that family is useless," said Gurjit, forty-four. "I'm thankful to God that I have a son."

Balwant's sister, Charanjit, and her husband, Harpreet, a young policeman in a light blue turban, were visiting that day with their only son. They were silent as their relatives and I talked about sex selection until, suddenly, Harpreet's indignation boiled over. He burst out, speaking Punjabi, "Take a look at Muslim families in other states—they have got nine children, twelve children. Take a look at the girls in this family. One is studying ayurveda, one is preparing for her MBA. These are smaller families, and we are planning them rather well, we think. Whatever is being practiced here, take a look at how we have controlled the population growth."

Harpreet continued in a rapid soliloquy: "I am a Jat Sikh. I feel bad that people are always blaming us for killing our girl children. We love all our children—we love our boy children, and also we love our girl children. But through this thing, we have controlled our population in such a way that—take a look at our families—we don't have the kind of poverty that exists in other parts of the country, where they have five children, six children, seven children. They cannot even feed their children, forget about their education." His son, he said, is studying in the top school in the area. "If I had five children, I couldn't afford to keep him in the best school."

Harpreet's wife was sterilized, and as a government employee, he was rewarded for her operation. Policemen like him who have two children or fewer, and foreclose the possibility of having any more, get an extra five hundred rupees, or twelve dollars, every month. Thus, Harpreet was incensed that his community's highly successful mode of population control is now under attack.

"The government took such big trouble during Sanjay Gandhi's time to do all these things," Harpreet continued, exasperated. "But we are naturally doing it! We are not being coerced, we are not being forced. So what's the problem?"

For all his passion Harpreet spoke elliptically, avoiding any actual mention of sex-selective abortion, instead calling it "this thing." Only once, during a particularly heated moment, did he use the phrase *kudi maar,* which means girl killer.

India's government has spent the last half century trying to persuade, cajole, and sometimes coerce its population into having smaller families, and they have largely succeeded. In 2005 the country's total fertility rate averaged 2.9 children per woman, down more than 17 percent in just the last decade. Women in India's cities average only 2.1 children each. The decline has been felt even among poor people in remote areas. In rural Rajasthan, for example, the total fertility rate dropped from 4.7 in the mid 1990s to 4.0 ten years later.[15]

Son preference, though, has remained unchanged. "Since the desired family size has come down to two or three—two in many cases—they still want *at least* one if not more sons," said Saroj Pachauri, Asia region director of the Population Council. "That's where the distortions are occurring."

Population control, divorced from an appreciable increase in women's status, replaced one demographic problem with another. "Some things are so ironic when you look back," Pachauri said sadly, recalling her long history in India's population movement. "We did this with such good intentions, and it backfired on us."

A grandmotherly woman with a gentle face, bobbed hair, and a fashionably understated *salwar kameez,* Pachauri has been involved in the movement since the early 1970s; in many ways, its history is her own. She worked at the Ford Foundation's India office when Adrienne Germain was representing Ford in Bangladesh; like Germain she struggled to make population

programs more responsive to women's rights. "I am absolutely convinced that unless you address the underlying gender problem, you will get nowhere," she said.

Yet India's population programs never did this before Cairo, when the focus was on reducing fertility at all costs. While the central government has become much more sensitive since then, some state governments continue to employ punitive targets and quotas, barring people with more than two children from local political office and denying them maternity benefits. Among India's elite there continues to be near unanimity about the necessity of population control. (As recently as 2003, India's Supreme Court characterized "the torrential increase in the population" as "more dangerous than a hydrogen bomb.")

It's impossible to say how much of India's fertility decline is due to state policy and how much to increasing wealth, urbanization, and decreasing agricultural plot sizes in the countryside. But the government has almost certainly played a partial role, suggesting that a colossal official mobilization can over time help change social norms. Had the campaign, with all its resources, focused on women's rights from the start, India's success in addressing overpopulation may not have come so much at girls' expense.

Despite the small recent decline in its child sex ratio, Kerala remains a model of what's possible. Until 1971, Kerala had the highest population growth rate in India, with an average of 4.1 children per woman. By 1992, enormous investments in women's education, freely available family planning, and comprehensive health care had led to India's lowest infant mortality rate, all helping to push fertility down to 1.8 children per woman without coercion or, at the time, a decrease in the proportion of girls to boys.[16] Kerala's women still both outlive and outnumber its men, although unless current trends are halted, their demographic superiority may not last.[17]

As early as the 1970s some predicted—approvingly—that sex selection could be a tool for limiting population. In May 1975, when amniocentesis was first being used for prenatal diagnoses in India, a group of Indian doctors published a report in the journal *Indian Pediatrics* that mentioned the potential of the new method for population control. "In India, cultural and economical factors make the parents desire a son, and in many instances the couple keeps on reproducing just to have a son," they wrote. "Prenatal determination of sex would put an end to this unnecessary fecundity. There is of course the tendency to abort the fetus if it is female. This may not be acceptable to persons in the West, but in our patients this plan of action was followed in seven of eight patients who had the test carried out primarily for the determination of sex of the fetus."[18]

After protests from women's groups, the government of India banned sex tests in public hospitals in 1976. Within a few years, though, private clinics offering sex determination appeared. In the mid 1980s a study commissioned by anti-sex-selection activists found that 84 percent of gynecologists in Bombay were performing amniocentesis for sex determination. "A majority of the doctors thought the sex-determination tests were a humane service for women who did not want any more daughters, and some even felt that they could be an important family planning device for our country," the activists wrote.[19] At one city hospital, of 8,000 abortions following amniocentesis, 7,999 were of female fetuses.[20]

Through the efforts of feminist organizers, the state of Maharashtra, where Bombay is located, outlawed sex-determination tests in 1988, and the central government followed suit in 1994. But sex-selective abortion was too popular to control. Most people are willing to leave their first child up to chance, but after one or two daughters they take matters into their own hands. "[I]t is with regards to later pregnancies among sonless couples that SRB [sex-ratio at birth] values tend to surge," wrote Guilmoto. "Parents want to avoid the 'worst-case' scenario—i.e., a family without a son."[21] Following the 2001 census the government made the anti-sex-selection law more stringent, and as a result prices went up, but other than that there was little evidence that people were being deterred.

Although feminists have taken a leading role in India's anti-sex-selection campaign, it's a supremely tricky issue for those who care deeply about abortion rights. Women's rights activists with experience in Western countries worry that the language of the campaign is shading into the idiom of the Western antiabortion movement. "Murder in the Womb" was the title of a six-part exposé aired on the national news channel *Sahara Samay*. Educational posters, produced by the government and by local NGOs, show swords and daggers pointed at fetuses. The almost universal use of the term "female feticide" or, in Hindi, *kanya bhronn hatya,* which literally means "the killing of young girls," begs the question of why feticide in general is OK.

Abortion up to twenty weeks was legalized in India in 1971 as part of the country's attempt to control population growth. It was never about women's rights. The Medical Termination of Pregnancy Act allows abortion for a wide range of reasons, including failure of contraception, but it is the doctor, not the woman, who has the right to decide whether an abortion is warranted. Unlike the legalization of abortion in the United States, the MTP Act wasn't associated with any sort of social upheaval or disruption in gender roles—premarital sex remained as taboo as ever, and notions of wifely obedience as deeply engrained. That's likely why it passed without controversy, and why India has never had a serious antiabortion movement.

Yet while abortion is legal, unsafe abortion remains a major problem; in many places safe services either aren't available or aren't known, leading millions of women to seek abortions from traditional midwives and unqualified quacks. Research in the mid-1990s showed botched abortions were responsible for 13 percent of India's staggeringly high maternal mortality rate.[22]

Most abortions in India are for unwanted pregnancies, not sex selection.[23] Still, with the campaign against sex-selective abortion injecting the idea of fetal rights into the public conversation as never before, there was reason to fear that efforts to expand access to safe abortion would be hurt. "The biggest danger, which is the one we're dealing with right now, is that the anti-sex-selection campaigns not turn into antiabortion campaigns," said Gita Sen, the longtime women's rights activist and Cairo lobby veteran.

Dr. Sharad Iyengar and his wife, Dr. Kirti Iyengar, run an NGO called Action Research and Training for Health in the poor desert state of Rajasthan. They provide child immunizations, family planning, and prenatal care and safe delivery, running two friendly and basic but clean clinics that are open twenty-four hours a day for people in the surrounding villages. Thanks to a scheme meant to reduce India's maternal mortality, women are paid cash to have their babies in government hospitals, but some of the poor women ARTH serves would rather forgo that money and instead pay a nominal fee to ARTH to deliver at their centers, where they're treated with care and dignity.

Safe abortion is an important part of ARTH's work; health volunteers in the villages steer women away from the quacks, who are known as "Bengali doctors," and rotating gynecologists perform both manual vacuum aspiration and medical abortions at its clinics. These services are crucial. On a scorching April day in 2008 I visited a village where ARTH works, in a hilly, marble-mining area in Rajasthan's south. A small group of illiterate women, dressed brightly and wearing big, beaded nose rings and tarnished silver ankle bracelets, sat on the dusty ground around an ARTH employee using a specially designed picture book to teach them about reproductive and child health. One woman quickly volunteered that before ARTH local women used to seek abortions from a nearby practitioner "who gave some tablets and used some instruments." There was a lot of pain and bleeding, but they wouldn't tell anyone or go to the hospital. A young woman in a green sari—a teenager, or a little older—added that her mother died after taking some abortifacient plants given by a local *dai,* or midwife.

According to Sharad Iyengar, the campaign against sex-selective abortion has had a chilling effect on legitimate abortion providers in Rajasthan. "There is stigmatization of abortion. A lot of providers have become averse to providing abortion services," he said. "Some gynecologists are now against abortions. Those who do it, do it quietly—they're not ready to talk about it. The public health dimensions of unsafe abortion never were on the agenda."

Elsewhere in India enterprising local officials tackled the problem of sex selection by targeting women who had had abortions. Krishan Kumar, deputy commissioner of the Nawanshahr district of Punjab, made national news for his success in combating sex-selective abortion. Partly, he did it through an impressive crackdown on illegal ultrasound operations and unscrupulous doctors. One gynecologist arrested during his reign, back at work after Kumar was transferred, told me with obvious self-pity that Kumar had been a "dictator." The gynecologist remained unapologetic: Anyone with a daughter should be allowed sex determination for her next pregnancy, he insisted, adding, "In no situation should there be a third child."

But Kumar also humiliated many women, organizing groups of volunteers to stage loud, public mourning ceremonies outside the homes of women thought to have had sex-selective abortions. "Two days ago when news came that an unborn girl had been murdered in her mother Manjit Kaur's womb, hundreds of villagers wearing white assembled outside Manjit Kaur's house and took out a 'funeral procession,'" reported the *Times of India,* noting that "sadness was writ large in the eyes of Manjit, who is already a mother of a three-year-old daughter."[24]

Feminists have been understandably alarmed. They've struggled against the phrase "female feticide," but it is used so widely that even the UNFPA sometimes employs it, prioritizing effective grassroots communication over global abortion politics. Worse, in local efforts, "female" is sometimes dropped. Official campaigns against "feticide" are especially problematic, given that many rural Indians are already unaware that abortion is legal.[25]

Some campaigners dismiss anxieties about abortion rights as a Western projection, noting that India has never had a real antiabortion movement. "Please understand, in this country there was no pro-life, pro-choice debate," said Bedi. "Nobody has ever fought for fetal rights. The medical profession has not. The ethicists have not. The temples and the gurudawaras have not. So to say that any voice against [sex-selective abortion] will give vent to the prolifers and hence restrict the reproductive choice of a woman is ridiculous."

Perhaps. But India *does* have pronatalist Hindu rightists, who have urged women to have more sons for the sake of communal demographic strength. The secretary of the Vishwa Hindu Parishad, a hard-line Hindu nationalist group, encouraged every Hindu woman to become an *Ashtaputra,* or mother of eight sons. The leader of the Rashtriya Swayamsevak Sangh, the VHP's parent organization, called on Hindu women to produce at least three sons each to ensure that Hindus do not become outnumbered by Muslims.[26]

With increasing efforts afoot to enlist religious figures in the fight against sex selection, some fear that they'll start attacking abortion rather than the preference for sons. "One of India's biggest pluses in being able to hold up women's reproductive rights around abortion has always been that the religious dimension has never been very strong," said Sen. "That doesn't mean that with the Hindu fundamentalists running riot all over the country, some crackpot doesn't pick that up."

Sex selection poses an additional challenge to women's rights activists, one that's philosophical rather than tactical. To confront the issue of sex-selective abortion as a feminist is to see the world in much the same way pro-lifers do, at least for a moment. It's to look in horror at a culture where potential life is tossed away in the quest for economic advancement and status, debasing all involved. It's to see some choices as illegitimate.

The American antiabortion movement has relished pointing out the contradiction. "It is perhaps obvious why sex-selective abortion is an embarrassment to feminism: while the preference for sons is deeply rooted in history, the other factors, such as reduced family size and cultural acceptance of abortion, are central pillars of feminist thought," wrote Douglas A. Sylva of the Catholic Family and Human Rights Institute in the *Weekly Standard.* "Since at least the 1995 Beijing Women's Conference, feminist champions have argued that international 'gender justice' could only be established if women possessed the reproductive rights necessary to reduce their family sizes, thereby liberating them for higher education and successful careers." It is never pleasant, he continued, "to admit that one's revolutionaries have begun to devour their own."[27]

There is indeed an inconsistency between believing in absolute reproductive choice and in wanting to outlaw abortions performed for the "wrong" reason. That's why American feminists tend to see domestic attempts to ban sex selection as threats to *Roe v. Wade.* Indian feminists, though, have never prioritized the concept of choice the way Westerners do, in part because whatever choices Indian women face are so constrained. Women's rights activists in India fight against the "choice" of families to pay dowry to marry their daughters off, and to both practice and glorify *sati,* in which living widows burn with their husbands on their funeral pyres.

"My own view is that the question of reproductive rights is much bigger than the question of just reproductive choice," said Sen. "The language of choice, while it's very useful in holding up individual rights, often misses that behind the way in which people make choices are a lot of social pressures, forces, relationships, and so on." A woman's choice to have a sex-selective abortion, said Sen, "may reflect the fact that she has very few rights."

This approach doesn't jibe with the debate about abortion in the United States, where rights and choice are seen as synonymous, and where feminists are constantly defending the right of women to make reproductive decisions unencumbered by others' beliefs about what is best for them or for society. But it is not, obviously, the job of Indian feminists to map their politics onto the ideological topography of the West. There may be no overarching philosophy that can reconcile the two stances, except perhaps for solidarity between groups of women working in vastly different contexts.

Distorted sex ratios pose a concrete threat to Indian women that goes beyond the disturbing demonstration of how little they are esteemed. Some have suggested, based on crude economic logic, that the deficit in women would raise their value. On the ground, this has not been the case. Already in northern India shortages of women have led to increases in sexual violence and trafficking for both marriage and prostitution. Though dowry has persisted unabated, men who can't find wives have begun importing poor women from the country's south and east, who then find themselves isolated in an alien culture where they don't even speak the language and may be treated as little more than chattel.

Parts of Haryana, which borders Punjab and has India's second-worst sex ratio, have witnessed a return of polyandry, in which one woman is shared among several brothers. In February 2006, Tripala Kurmari, an eighteen-year-old girl from one of India's minority tribes, was murdered there. "The tribal girl was brought to Haryana by an agent who promised to get her a job," wrote Gita Aravamudan, author of the book *Disappearing Daughters: The Tragedy of Female Foeticide.* "She was 'married' to Ajmer Singh who desperately wanted a male heir. However, soon after her marriage she found she was expected to sleep with all his brothers. When she refused, he killed her. The murder of Tripala Kumari gave a gruesome face to a form of sexual exploitation which has become increasingly popular in the women-starved states of Punjab and Haryana."[28] And this was before the hardest-hit generation in those states reached adulthood.

Sexual violence, meanwhile, reinforced some families' motives for rejecting daughters in the first place. The investment of family honor in girls' sexual purity, and the terror of losing it, long played a role in northern India's tradition of infanticide. As Amarjit Singh explained, "The Afghan plunderers on horseback used to come to Punjab to plunder and rob this area. They picked up beautiful women." People thought it was "better to kill the girls before they are picked up, raped, and taken away." In the twenty-first century there are no more invading hordes from the north and west, but the constant vigilance required to keep girls safe from violation is one reason people say they don't want them in the first place.

Declining sex ratios curtail female freedom in additional ways as well. Guilmoto speculated that the increased demand for women to serve as wives and mothers will cut off other opportunities. "The reduced number of women in these areas would have an interesting corollary, in that women's roles as wife, daughter-in-law or mother would become more essential to society," he wrote. "The enhancement of this traditional family role will, however, come at the expense of other life trajectories, such as remaining single or a career-oriented strategy. Indeed, if new incentives towards early marriage and childbearing are offered to women, this could lead to their temporary or permanent withdrawal from the workforce."[29] Evidence from societies with highly uneven sex ratios bear him out; in such places women have lower levels of literacy and labor force participation, and higher rates of suicide, than in countries where the numbers of men and women are more even.[30]

It's not just women whose futures are imperiled. Countries with millions of alienated, unmarriageable men are likely to be both more internally insecure and externally belligerent. In their book *Bare Branches: The Security Implications of Asia's Surplus Male Population,* political scientists Valerie M. Hudson and Andrea M. den Boer show how historically, in areas where men have outnumbered women due to widespread female infanticide, superfluous single men have played a violently destabilizing role. To channel their aggression governments have sometimes embarked on campaigns of expansion, threatening nearby countries.

"The evidence suggests that high-sex-ratio societies, especially those with unequal resource distribution and generalized resource scarcity, breed chronic violence and persistent social disorder and corruption," they concluded. "Indeed, bare branches in high-sex-ratio societies contribute to this disruption on a larger scale than might be possible in societies with lower sex ratios."[31]

Hudson and den Boer adopt the term "bare branches" from nineteenth-century China, where surplus bachelors formed criminal gangs that eventually coalesced into rebel militias. Like India, China has a long history of female infanticide, practiced for many of the same reasons. Women's status, thought to be relatively high during the Shang and Zhou dynasties (1766–1122 B.C. and 1122–221 B.C.) fell during the Qin and Han eras (221–206 B.C. and 206 B.C.–A.D. 220) as arranged marriages, female seclusion, and the cult of chastity became institutionalized.[32] As in India, dowries portended financial ruin for parents of daughters, and a mania for virginity made the killing of girls seem less shameful than the threat of premarital sex. Hudson and den Boer quote a scholar from the time of the Song dynasty (960–1279) who claimed, "[T]o starve to death is a very minor matter, but to lose one's chastity is a major matter."[33]

In the first half of the nineteenth century, Hudson and den Boer write, the Huai-pei region of northeast China had a series of natural disasters. The resulting poverty led to an increase in female infanticide and a sex ratio of around 129 men for every 100 women. Polygamy and concubinage, they write, further decreased the supply of wives. Thus, many poor men were unable to settle down and achieve the status of respectable adults; instead, they built a kind of antisocial subculture based on crime and martial arts. Eventually, the small bands of bandits started to organize on a larger scale to try to overthrow the Qing dynasty in the Nien Rebellion.

"The Nien Rebellion," write Hudson and den Boer, "is an example of how exaggerated offspring sex selection can threaten the stability of entire regions, and even great empires."[34]

Beyond questions of demographics and geopolitics, India's epidemic of sex-selective abortion—and, more generally, its pathological mania for sons—victimizes individual women. It is way too simple to claim that all women who abort female fetuses are forced into it, but despite the experiences of Puneet Bedi and his elite patients, for some coercion is very real.

"In Gujarat, women do not decide whether they will have male children or female children," said Ila Pathak, secretary of the Ahmedabad Women's Action Group, a feminist organization based in Gajarat's largest city. "To be frank, she is never consulted whether she will go to bed with the man. So there is no freedom of decision."

Prosperous Gujarat, birthplace of Jawaharlal Nehru and cradle of India's independence struggle, is famous in more recent years for right-wing Hindu progroms against Muslims. While Punjab has agriculture, Gujarat has trade and industry; the Gujarati businessman is a national stereotype. Like elsewhere in India, its wealth is inverse to its tolerance for girls. The state's sex ratio is 883 girls for every 1,000 boys. In Ahmedabad, it is 836. Pathak, a white-haired, soft-spoken, retired English professor, has studied violence against women in Gujarat extensively, spending several years combing through police records to produce a systematic analysis of domestic violence cases and of the circumstances surrounding women's deaths. "In Gujarat, so many women die or commit suicide because they give birth to daughters," she said. "Husbands torturing wives because of the birth of a daughter is not unique."

At around 8:00 P.M. one evening in May 2007, two confused, terrified women, Sunita Rajput and her cowife, Kajal, appeared with their daughters at the Kasturba Gandhi Memorial Trust, a shelter for abused women on the outskirts of Ahmedabad. They could barely walk and had to be helped from the gate. Both were covered with welts from beatings with a belt. Sunita needed a blood transfusion. They had just escaped from their husband, Rajesh Rajput, seller of ayurvedic remedies, a sadist who had forced the women to have eight abortions between them because they hadn't produced a boy.

When I met Sunita a year later she was in her late twenties. Her huge obsidian eyes, perfect almonds fringed by thick lashes, were still shadowed and often blank, and she often broke into tears as she spoke. She found it too painful to recount much of her past in detail, so Pratima Pandya, the shelter's director, told her story instead.

Sunita, who has a seventh-grade education, had married Rajesh ten years earlier, and after a year her first daughter, Anjali, was born. A year and a half later there was another girl, Kashish. It is the sperm that determines whether a baby will be male or female, but Rajesh blamed his wife, and, furious at his failure to have a son, he would beat Sunita terribly. His mother blamed Sunita as well, and after the first two daughters, she and Rajesh arranged for ultrasound tests followed by abortions for each of Sunita's next four pregnancies.

Each time she went, Sunita recalled with an angry little laugh, there was a sign outside announcing, as per the law, that the clinics did not perform sex-determination tests. "They should be stopped, they should not exist," she said. It should have been obvious to the doctors, she said, that she was there under duress: "Of course no mother wants to kill her baby. Of course Rajesh took me there forcibly."

The next two times Sunita was pregnant, Rajesh, assuming she was incapable of having sons, didn't even take her for ultrasound—he just brought her for abortions. Meanwhile, flouting Hindu law, he married another woman, Kajal, hoping that she could give him a son. At first he installed Kajal in his brother's house, not bringing her home until she was seven months pregnant. He treated her decently until she too gave birth to a girl. Rajesh didn't go to the hospital to see the newborn, and when Kajal brought her home, he held her up by one leg and started hitting her. Together, the two women rushed at him, fighting to save the girl's life. From then on he would torture the two of them together—beating them daily, driving nails into their fingers and ears, even forcing them to drink his urine. They weren't allowed any contact with the outside world. Kajal would eventually have two abortions as well. As Rajesh's persecution increased, Sunita stopped eating. They started to go mad.

The torments Sunita and Kajal faced, said Pandya, exceed anything she's seen in her many years at the shelter. It is not unusual, though, for abuse to escalate following the birth of a girl. "Almost for twenty years I have been working in this field," she said. "If a boy is born, [a woman's] position in the family becomes consolidated. If a girl is born, she has to face the usual torture."

Finally, when Sunita was pregnant for the ninth time, the two women made their escape together. Neither had any idea where to go—Kajal was an orphan and Sunita's family was too poor to help her. Fleeing their village, they got in a rickshaw and asked to go to the nearest town. They were sobbing, and the rickshaw driver asked what was wrong. They told him their story. Fortunately, he'd heard of the Kasturba Gandhi Trust, and he brought them there.

In addition to medical treatment, Pandya called the police and got the women legal representation. Rajesh was arrested and jailed, and two clinics where Sunita had undergone ultrasounds had their registrations suspended. Meanwhile, the story hit the local media. A young woman named Usha, who had been raped and branded with hot metal by cousins of the mentally retarded man she'd been married to, read about it in *Chitralekha*, a popular magazine. It inspired her to run away, too; today she shares a room with Sunita and her children at the shelter. At least one other woman also fled to Kasturba Gandhi after seeing Sunita's story.

Usha may have been moved by Sunita's strength, but Sunita feels anything but powerful. Several months after arriving at the shelter she gave birth, in a cosmic irony, to a boy, whom she named Dharmik. In jail Rajesh read about Dharmik in the paper and began sending letters to the shelter, demanding that Sunita and his son be returned to him and promising that he would no longer torture her now that she's succeeded in producing a male heir.

To Sunita's horror, Rajesh was released from jail pending the outcome of the trial, which, given India's glacial legal system, could take years. Hoping to pressure her, he beat up her father and brother. "Bring back Sunita to me," he told them. "I want my son back." As long as he's free she lives in terror that he will try to take Dharmik. Compounding her shock, Kajal, restless at the shelter, returned to Rajesh, assuming the more legitimate role of his only wife. (According to Pandya, a momentarily solicitous Rajesh, hoping to stop Kajal from testifying against him, promised to put the house, now partly in Sunita's name, in Kajal's instead.) "They are in that home," said Sunita, "and I am in an orphanage."

Sunita never leaves Kasturba Gandhi except for medical and legal appointments. She's learning handicrafts—embroidery and beading—but can't imagine how she'll ever support herself independently. The day we met she was sitting in one of the shelter's airy cement common rooms, which is half open to the leafy compound outside. Other residents were sifting wheat for chapatis. Eyes downcast, she rocked Dharmik in a rustic cradle; her lovely daughters, saucer-eyed and solemn, were perched protectively beside her.

She had only one wish: She wanted Rajesh back in jail. Please, she implored, wasn't there something I could do? "I don't want anything but that Rajesh should be punished." She started crying. "I don't have an identity!" she said, repeating it over and over, "I don't have an identity!" Her only hope was in the sleeping six-month-old. "When Dharmik grows up," she said, "I will have someone to cling to."

In the end, as long as women lack an identity without a husband or a son, sex-selective abortion will continue to deform India's—and Asia's—demographics. That's why what is happening in India is more complicated than modernization gone awry. Rather, social modernization has proven unable to catch up with technological progress. Indian society is reforming, slowly and incrementally. The very fact that Sunita escaped her hellish home, said Pandya, is evidence of a small shift. Twenty years ago, "she would have committed suicide," Pandya said. "That Sunita came here, it is a sign of seeking freedom." Gradually, she insisted, women are moving beyond utter dependence on men. Due to increased education, she said, "twenty, twenty-five percent of women who have faced such torture are trying their best to get out, the way Sunita or Usha did."

If you look hard you can see such faintly hopeful signs everywhere. Dutt, the editor of the *Sunday Indian,* comes from a family with an infanticidal history. Of her grandfather's sisters just one survived; an elderly female member of her great-grandfather's family put the others to sleep with overdoses of opium. Just two generations later she chose to remain single and to adopt a baby girl.

Some believe only a boy can light his parents' funeral pyres; indeed, that's said to be one of the many reasons Hindus are so desperate for sons. "Now girls are doing it," said Dutt. "I lit my mother's funeral pyre." Dutt, a large woman with a sweet smile, was wearing a royal blue *salwar kameez;* as she spoke, her teenage daughter, wearing jeans, did homework at the kitchen table. They seem more a remarkable exception than the edge of an emerging trend, but they are there nonetheless, in one of the most hostile parts of the country. There has been "slow change," said Dutt. "There has been a lot of change from the late nineteenth century until now. When I was born my mother distributed sweets. She was bored of having sons—I had six brothers. I opted to adopt a girl child. So there are exceptions like that, and slow change, but it is very, very rare."

The coming of sex-selection technology overtook this sluggish process, amplifying all the country's atavisms. Skewed gender ratios are the terrible result of one kind of progress. The ultimate solution will have to be progress of another kind. "Culture and tradition is not a monolith," said Bedi. "It is not permanent. It changes. For example, twenty years ago it was ridiculous to see a girl from a small town from [the state of] Utter Pradesh to come to Delhi, live on her own, and earn money, because the money she earned was a pittance. Now she works in a call center and earns ten times more than her father, and it is acceptable. Social acceptability follows economic compulsions." He is fulsomely cynical about the "awareness campaigns" and street plays put on by many NGOs. But, he said, "if people realize after two hundred years that those who have two daughters have a better quality of life than those who have two sons, then it will obviously change."

South Korea, the first Asian country to begin to reverse the trend of sex selection, offers a hopeful example that such change needn't take two hundred years. To be sure, South Koreans continue to have more boys than girls, but the ratio of male to female births has been declining since the 1990s. Interestingly, it has been falling in tandem with the total fertility rate, the opposite of the usual pattern, in which the desire for fewer children leaves less space for daughters.[35]

"Until a few years ago, South Korea appeared to epitomize the pattern of rising sex ratios despite rapid development—with dramatic increases in levels of education, industrialization, and urbanization, as well as in women's education and participation in the formal labor force," researchers Woojin Chung and Monica Das Gupta wrote in a 2007 World Bank paper. "By the mid-1990s, South Korea was officially included as a member of the developed countries' club, the [Organization for Economic Co-operation and Development]. Yet sex ratios at birth rose steeply during this period."[36]

It was the same paradox now seen in India. As Chung and Das Gupta point out, "This flew in the face of over a century of social science theory," which had always posited that modernization lessened the pull of tradition and made status dependent on individual achievement rather than immutable identity. It also seemed to challenge the idea that increased education and female employment reduce gender inequalities within households.[37]

The operative word is "seemed." Chung and Das Gupta make an important distinction "between the *intensity* of son preference felt by people, and its actual *manifestation* on the ground in sex ratios," and they show that the two can actually move in opposite directions. When new technology makes sex selection accessible, sex ratios can get worse even as attitudes are getting more progressive. "Moreover," they write, "since educated women are typically better able to access and implement these new technologies, studies can even appear to suggest that gender outcomes for children are worsened by development, and even by improvements in the position of women."

This is a distortion, though, caused by a lag between social change and technological advancement. In fact, the number of South Korean women who said they "must have a son" fell slowly between 1985 and 1991, and then precipitously after that. Son preference, Chung and Das Gupta found, "declines with increasing socio-economic status, lower parental control, younger birth cohort, and older age at marriage." Less intense desire for boys is significantly correlated with living in cities, especially big ones.[38] It took a few years for behavior to catch up with beliefs, but eventually the new values snowballed through the population.

Interestingly, these changes took place despite the fact that until very recently South Korean government policy purposely worked to prop up patriarchy. (Abortion, in fact, is highly restricted in South Korea, though safe illgal terminations, performed by doctors, are widely available.) Thus, Chung and Das Gupta speculate that change could come to China and India even before they reach Korea's level of modernization. "It is notable that in China and India, public policies have sought to lead changes in social norms, whereas in South Korea public policies sought to *prevent* changes in social norms," they write. "Without these countervailing public policies, son preference may have declined in South Korea before it reached such high levels of development. This offers hope that in China and India, public policies will accelerate the process of change such that son preference may decline before they reach South Korea's levels of development."[39]

Despite such cause for optimism, though, to experts and activists in India the crisis is too acute to wait for an evolution in gender norms. Besides, as Sen pointed out, the Indian case is complicated by dowry. Had outsize dowry demands not proliferated across southern India, perhaps that region, more socially progressive than the north, might have seen something akin to the South Korean phenomenon, she said. As it is, though, sex selection can't be effectively tackled without taking on the system that turns women into financial liabilities—an epochal challenge, one that will require something close to a revolution in deeply rooted ideas about marriage and family. Dowry, said Sen, was a major issue for the women's movement in the 1980s, but it proved so implacable that dispiritedness set in. But no matter the difficulty, such efforts have to be revived, both for their own sake and for there to be any hope of righting the country's gender balance. "I think this is a nexus that has to be dealt with together," she said.

With masculinization out of control, almost everyone sees the need for more immediate intervention. "I think it's a struggle over the long haul, but some sort of tough and salutary short-term punishments for doctors who provide the service wouldn't hurt," said Sen. Some in the government clearly agree. In April 2008 the Health minister, responding to "shockingly low" conviction rates, called for tough new measures against sex determination practitioners, including longer jail terms, higher fines, and special public prosecutors to handle cases. "Launching the country's biggest ever campaign against the 'inhuman and uncivilised practise' of female feticide, Prime Minister Manmohan Singh . . . said no nation, society or community could hold its head high and claim to be part of a civilised world if it condoned the practice of discriminating against women," reported the *Times of India*.[40]

It remains to be seen whether this time the law will be enforced with more zeal than in the past. While most experts welcome such a move, few believe it will be nearly enough. Already technology is one step ahead. Though illegal, in vitro fertilization clinics offer sex selection without abortion to those who can afford it. Meanwhile, some Western companies are marketing at-home tests with names like Pink or Blue over the Internet for a few hundred dollars. Women using them send a drop of blood to the companies' laboratories, which claim they can tell the sex of the fetus a mere six or seven weeks after conception by analyzing fetal DNA in the mother's bloodstream. The Indian government has talked about blocking access to the companies' Web sites, an idea that only underscores how powerless it is to stem the adoption of new innovations by a free people hungry for them.[41]

There will be no easy answer. Once again India is faced with the specter of demographic catastrophe, and once again the only sustainable solution lies in making a massive commitment to women's rights. Doing what needs to be done would be controversial, socially disruptive, and extraordinarily difficult politically. As disparate as India's cultures are, most of them are bound up with female submission. Any threat to that order would arouse the rage of those who see the self-abnegation of women as the essence of virtue and the guarantee of group identity. Like any democracy, India will probably find it easier to slouch toward disaster than to infuriate the defenders of patriarchy. Ultimately, though, unless the country finds a way to break through the encrustations of centuries of misogyny, its democracy itself could be in danger from an unmanageable excess of men.

Notes

1. Barbara D. Miller, *The Endangered Sex* (Ithaca, NY: Cornell University Press, 1981), pp. 50–51.

2. Ibid., p. 58.

3. Christophe Z. Guilmoto, "Characteristics of Sex-Ratio Imbalance in India, and Future Scenarios," United Nations Population Fund. Presented at the Fourth Asia Pacific Conference on Reproductive and Sexual Health and Rights. Hyderabad, India, October 29–31, 2007.

4. United Nations Population Fund, *Missing: Mapping the Adverse Child Sex Ratio in India,* November 2003.

5. Prabhat Jha, Rajesh Kumar, Priya Vasa, Neeraj Dhingra, Deva Thiruchelvam, and Rahim Moineddin, "Low Male-to-Female Sex Ratio of Children Born in India: National Survey of 1.1 Million Households," *The Lancet,* vol. 367, iss. 9506 (January 21, 2006), pp. 211–18.

6. Sabu George, "Sex Selection/Determination in India: Contemporary Developments," *Reproductive Health Matters,* vol. 10, no. 19, *Abortion: Women Decide* (special issue, May 2002), pp. 190–92.

7. Christophe Z. Guilmoto, "Sex-ratio Imbalance in Asia: Trends, Consequences and Policy Responses," United Nations Population Fund. Available at the UNFPA website, www.unfpa.org

8. "Vernacular Dailies Pulling NRIs Back Home for Sex Tests," *Times of India,* August 19, 2007.

9. Douglas Almond and Lena Edlund, "Son-Biased Sex Ratios in the 2000 United States Census," Proceedings of the National Academy of Science, March 31, 2008.

10. Valerie M. Hudson and Andrea M. den Boer, *Bare Branches: The Security Implications of Asia's Surplus Male Population* (Cambridge, MA: MIT Press, 2004), pp. 164–67.

11. *Missing: Mapping the Adverse Child Sex Ratio in India.*

12. Tulsi Patel, "The Mindset Behind Eliminating the Female Foetus," in *Sex-Selective Abortion in India: Gender Society and New Reproductive Technology,* Tulsi Patel, ed. (New Delhi: Sage Publications, 2007), p. 170.

13. Ibid., pp. 161–62, 170–71.

14. "Dowry 'Kills' Her on 1st Anniversary," *Times of India.* May 1, 2008.

15. "Sample Registration System Statistic Report 2005," Office of the Registrar General, India.

16. Data available on the Kerala government website, www.kerala.org

17. Ibid.

18. Ishwar C. Verma, Rose Joseph, Kusum Verma, Kamal Buckshee, and O. P. Ghai, "Prenatal Diagnosis of Genetic Disorders," *Indian Pediatrics* (May 1975).

19. Forum Against Sex Determination and Sex Pre-selection, "Using Technology, Choosing Sex, the Campaign Against

Sex Determination and the Question of Choice," *Development Dialogue,* vol. 1, no. 2 (1992), pp. 91–102.

20. John Ward Anderson and Molly Moore, "Born Oppressed: Women in the Developing World Face Cradle-to-Grave Discrimination, Poverty," *Washington Post,* February 14, 1993.

21. Guilmoto, "Characteristics of Sex-Ratio Imbalance in India."

22. Ravi Duggal and Vimala Ramachandran, "The Abortion Assessment Project—India: Key Findings and Recommendations," *Reproductive Health Matters,* vol. 12, no. 24, Supplement: Abortion Law, Policy, and Practice in Transition (November 2004), pp. 122–29.

23. Ibid.

24. "Punjab Village Cries for Unborn Girls," *Times of India,* January 19, 2006.

25. According to the World Health Organization, a survey in the state of Madhya Pradesh showed that 49 percent of women thought abortion was illegal, and 36 percent did not know its legal status. *Unsafe Abortion: Global and Regional Estimates of the Incidence of Unsafe Abortion and Associated Mortality in 2003,* World Health Organization, 2007. Available at the WHO website, www.who.int

26. Manisha Gupte, "Declining Sex Ratio. The Two Child Norm, and Women's Status," in *Coercion Versus Empowerment: Perspectives from the Peoples Tribunal on India's Coercive Population Policies and Two-Child Norm,* Shruti Pandey, Abhijit Das, Shravanti Reddy, and Binamrata Rani, eds. (New Delhi: Human Rights Law Network, 2006), p. 55. See also, "Defeat Because Hindutva Agenda Abandoned: VHP," *Times of India,* October 17, 2004.

27. Douglas A. Sylva, "The Lost Girls," *Weekly Standard,* March 21, 2007.

28. Gita Aravamudan, "Who Killed the Girls?" *Deccan Herald,* August 5, 2007.

29. Guilmoto, "Sex-Ratio Imbalance in Asia."

30. Scott J. South and Katherine Trent, "Sex Ratios and Women's Roles: A Cross-National Analysis," *American Journal of Sociology,* vol. 93, no. 5 (March 1988).

31. Hudson and den Boer, *Bare Branches,* p. 261.

32. Ibid., pp. 134–36.

33. Ibid., p. 140.

34. Ibid., pp. 208–11.

35. Woojin Chung and Monica Das Gupta, "Why Is Son Preference Declining in South Korea? The Role of Development and Public Policy, and the Implications for China and India," Policy Research Working Paper, the World Bank Development Research Group, Human Development and Public Services Team (October 2007).

36. Ibid.

37. Ibid.

38. Ibid.

39. Ibid.

40. *Times of India,* "Save the Girl Child, Says Manmohan Singh," April 29, 2008.

41. Maria Cheng, "Next Test Tells Fetus Sex After 6 Weeks," Associated Press, May 15, 2007; "Easy Availability of Gender ID Kits on Net a Threat: Minister," Indo-Asian News Service, March 15, 2008.

Critical Thinking

1. Why were there historically fewer females in the Indian state of Punjab? Why, after decades of improvement, was there another decline in females shown in the 2001 census?

2. What is the relationship between prosperity, education and sex discrimination in India?

3. Why is the dowry becoming more characteristic of the upwardly mobile, whereas traditionally it was practiced by the upper castes?

4. Why has India never had an anti-abortion movement? What is the dilemma faced by women's rights activitst with regard to abortion in India?

5. How have distorted sex ratios posed a threat to Indian women beyond the disturbing demonstration of how little they are esteemed? How might this exacerbate the problems for society as a whole?

6. How are women being victimized as individuals?

7. What does the author mean by pointing out that social modernization has proven unable to catch up with technological progress?

8. How does South Korea serve as a hopeful sign that the changes do not have to take two hundred years?

9. Why does the author claim that a sustainable solution to the problems of women in India requires a massive commitment to women's rights?

The Bride

Mara Hvistendahl

It is a truth universally acknowledged, that a single man in possession of a good fortune, must be in want of a wife.

—Jane Austen, *Pride and Prejudice*

Please don't treat your brides like goods.

—Malaysian chinese association public
services and complaint bureau
director datuk michael chong,
addressing men with vietnamese wives[1]

Cheng Ching-huang and Nguyen Thi Mai Chau got engaged the same week they met. That was fast for both of them, but it couldn't have happened any other way. Cheng had to catch a flight back to Taiwan, and Nguyen, who had been brought to Cheng's Ho Chi Minh City hotel by an acquaintance who dabbled in matchmaking, was awaited in her village, where it would have been better not to return than to return unattached. There was no time for courtship, and had there been time romance probably would have eluded them.

They didn't speak the same language, and they had little in common. Cheng had grown up in Taiwan during an era of prosperity. A simple man, a fruit farmer, he was nonetheless educated, keenly interested in the world outside his village, and relatively well-off at age thirty-one, a quality outwardly evident in his fleshy, generously nourished physique. Nguyen was Vietnamese, twenty, and petite. The ninth of ten children in a poor family from rural Vinh Long province, she had left school at fourteen to work as a maid. Few qualities bound her and Cheng, and in their case opposites most definitely did not attract. When she first laid eyes on Cheng, Nguyen thought, "He's so fat!" Cheng, meanwhile, fixated on the fact that the woman before him looked like a scared girl. He worried he'd have to teach her everything about life.

He asked for her hand in marriage anyway. A few years earlier, Cheng had resigned himself to the idea that he would never marry. His older brother, who farmed the family plot in the hills outside Taichung with him, had remained a bachelor, as had many men of his age throughout Taiwan who had the bad luck of being born at a time when Taiwanese were aborting female fetuses by the thousands. All told, Cheng's generation had nearly three-quarters of a million more men than women—a substantial gap in a country with only a few million working age adults.[2] To make matters worse, gender roles had changed. Not only were Taiwanese women scarce, but they chased jobs rather than family now, fleeing rural areas after high school for cities like Taipei in search of university degrees and good careers. Cheng knew it had become difficult to convince a modern Taiwanese woman to live on a farm. Then his sister suggested he find a wife in Vietnam.

Vietnamese women willing to wed strange men they had never met and move to strange lands they had never visited tended to come from remote villages in the Mekong Delta reachable only by boat. Their parents expected money in exchange for their daughters, and the negotiation process could prove complicated. But by 1999, when Cheng first looked into it, enough Taiwanese men had already married Vietnamese villagers that networks had sprouted, with the wives who arrived first serving as matchmakers for their husbands' single friends. A few enterprising women had started agencies that simplified the process by offering all-inclusive trips to Vietnam. For a mere $10,000, a man could buy a flight to Ho Chi Minh City, hotel, meals, transportation, and a wife. Cheng decided to give it a try.

Marriage had only recently occurred to Nguyen too, who thought she had a few more years of single life ahead of her. After the maid job didn't last, she spent several years jumping from one profession to the next, working at a shoe factory assembling high heels and later at a coffee shop near Ho Chi Minh City, always sending some of her earnings to her family. She was at the coffee shop when her mother sent word that she was sick, summoning Nguyen back to their village. When the young woman arrived she found her mother in fine health but with a mind fixated on one thing: it was time for her youngest daughter to *really* help the family.

Nguyen knew what that meant. A few women in her village had married Taiwanese men, and the money and gifts those marriages had brought in raised their families' standing and wealth to such a degree that locals had taken to talking about the Taiwanese Dream.[3] Beyond that everything got a little hazy, though. Nguyen had no idea what life in Taiwan was like. She knew the names of only a few of the countries outside Vietnam's borders, and her encounters with Taiwanese men extended to a few barked comments from her boss at the shoe factory. But she was an obedient daughter, and she agreed to her mother's plan.

The next thing she knew, she was at a dreary Ho Chi Minh City airport hotel, clutching the bouquet of flowers the matchmaker had instructed her to buy (she wondered why she should be the one to give flowers but was too shy to ask) as she waited with other women for an evening flight from Taipei to land.

Finally the men arrived. The matchmaker introduced the couple, and then Nguyen stood before Cheng silently, her eyes averted, and waited. "So?" the matchmaker asked him after he had had a few minutes to stare. "Will you marry her?"

They wedded in Nguyen's village, and Cheng brought Nguyen back to his farm near Taiwan's western coast, in the rolling hills outside Taichung, When they reached his driveway, she looked out the car window to see persimmon trees marching up the hills in orderly rows, their trunks held rigid by metal bars. Her parents, like Cheng, farmed fruit, and at first there was that to latch onto: in some ways, raising persimmons in Taiwan was not so different from growing longans in Vietnam. But in Taiwan a farm was a lonely place-mechanized, organized, and mostly devoid of people—and Nguyen struggled until she got word that a Vietnamese wife who had arrived before her had set up a small café in the area. With time more local men bought the brides who had eluded them, the houses surrounding Cheng's farm filled with Vietnamese women, and life got better for Nguyen. She had two children, a girl and a boy. She learned to make chicken in the Taiwanese style, to flavor noodles to Cheng's likings and finally to speak Mandarin. In this way the years passed.

Eleven years after they married, I find the couple sitting on overturned buckets in their storehouse, boxing persimmons. Nguyen has full lips and small wrinkles at the corners of her eyes. She is wearing a coral mock turtleneck and dangly silver earrings, and next to Cheng, who is clad in a black and red leather bomber jacket that accentuates his stocky figure, she looks slight. Her personality is also smaller, and at first only Cheng talks, reflecting on their marriage as he slips the fiery orange fruits into protective Styrofoam sheaths. "We fell in love *after* we got married," Cheng declares happily, chuckling. "And we're still falling in love." Nguyen says nothing. A few minutes later, as if in silent reply, she raises herself from the bucket, strolls over to her husband, and carefully removes a fleck of Styrofoam from his right eyebrow.

I spend the day with them, and by the time I leave it is clear to me that the marriage has improved Cheng's life. Relatives say he was always fun-loving and personable, but it is easy to believe that his outgoing personality blossomed after finding a wife, with the benefits that brought: two sweet children, a companion on the farm, a kitchen fragrant with rich broths and spices. The marriage also expanded Cheng's horizons. He has returned to Vietnam a few times with his wife to visit Nguyen's family, and he enjoys drinking rice wine with her father and uncles. He speaks only a few words of Vietnamese, but he finds his inability to communicate oddly freeing. "In Vietnam I can give my brain a rest," he says. After lunch he shows me to his family's den, where he puts on a home movie he filmed on a recent visit. The television fills with garishly colored houses, men on Honda Dream motorcycles, and children running alongside muddy, swollen rivers. Over the top of these images comes Cheng's voice, narrating in enthusiastic Mandarin.

Vietnam is an adventure for him, and no doubt that means something to his wife, whose eyes light up as she watches her country reel by on film. But when I ask if she misses Vietnam she dodges the question. "We go back there to have fun and see my father and mother," she says unsentimentally. "But after we're finished having fun we come back." She doesn't know much about the demographics that brought her to Taiwan, but she has determined staying is her fate. "I don't want to live there," she says. "Life is better here. That's how it is."

There are women like Nguyen everywhere there has been sex selective abortion for any extended period of time. Scholars call them marriage migrants; locals simply say foreign wives; you might think of them as bought brides. In wealthier countries like Taiwan, South Korea, and Singapore—the first nations to develop skewed sex ratio imbalances—the trade in women is now an entrenched industry negotiated by established agencies. A Singaporean man seeking a wife can choose from among J & N Viet-Bride Match-Making Agencies, First Overseas International Matchmaker, and Ideal Marriage Centre.[4] In South Korea there is Interwedding, which offers brides from a smattering of poorer Asian countries.[5] In Taiwan, Lotus 2000 specializes in Vietnamese women.

Typically the search starts online, where men browse photos of the various agencies' merchandise—often full-body shots showing thin, demure near-girls balancing in high heels on bare cement floors. Enough men follow through on their searches that the broker business is booming. In 2003, one-third of all marriages in Taiwan were between a local and a foreign spouse, the vast majority of them between local men and foreign women.[6] In South Korea over a thousand international marriage agencies have registered with the government.[7] Marriages to foreigners accounted for nearly 11 percent of all 2008 weddings in that country.[8] The rate was even higher in rural areas, where 40 percent of Korean farmers and fishermen who married that year wed foreigners.[9] Weddings between wealthy Asian men and women from poor neighboring countries are so common that the phenomenon has inspired movies (South Korea's *Wedding Campaign),* popular books (Taiwan's *Don't Call Me a Foreign Bride),* and dating programs (in one Taiwanese show, bachelors try their hand at winning a Vietnamese bride for free).[10]

When the numbers of marriageable males and females diverge significantly in a society, demographers say there is a "marriage squeeze." The dynamics of a marriage squeeze may sound intuitive, and to a degree they are: men have trouble finding wives when women are scarce. But various factors can also cause a squeeze to snowball. For the first generation in which men outnumber women, surplus men often marry younger women, meaning that the shortage of females does not really affect them. A few years down the line, though, as younger men come of age, things get tricky. Since the men in this new cohort have to compete with both older men and men their own age, they feel the shortage of women acutely. The surplus, as Christophe Guilmoto put it to me in Paris, "piles up," and many men in the second generation are left unmarried.

If a country's fertility rate dropped over the same period in which parents selected for boys (as has happened in both Taiwan and South Korea), the squeeze is intensified. Since fewer people in each successive generation translate into fewer young women, later crops of bachelors have an even harder time finding wives.

For men not inclined to be with women in the first place, of course, a marriage squeeze may not be so bad. In much of the developing world, gay and bisexual men come under significant pressure to marry women. As it becomes more common for men to remain unmarried, the marital arm-twisting may decrease, saving some men from living out lies. (For lesbian women, on the other hand, the gender imbalance has the opposite effect. When potential wives are scarce, women are pushed into marrying and having children, whether they want to or not.)[11]

Demographer Zhu Chuzhu, who has been writing about China's sex ratio imbalance since the 1980s, says gay rights groups have lately taken an interest in her work. At a conference on gender issues in Beijing in 2009, she recalls, a male activist approached her to critique a presentation she had just given. "You only focus on heterosexual relationships," the activist said. "But gay people aren't interested in those. So the imbalance may not be as serious as you all say."[12] In South Korea scholars speculated about a link between a surplus of men and an increase in male homosexual activity early on, and today in Mehsana, a high sex ratio district in northwest India, newspaper reports say the death of women has sparked demand for male prostitutes.[13] "I get at least eight to ten calls each month from [men in] Mehsana who pick me up from Ahmedabad," the *Times of India* quoted a male sex worker as saying. "We check into guest houses on the Ahmedabad-Mehsana highway."[14]

But most Asian men do want to marry. As the region develops rural weddings have become extravagant affairs; in China today they often entail hired sedans and white horses. The people I met in Suining were so fascinated by marriage that it sometimes seemed they didn't talk about anything else.[15] "If you don't get married," one bachelor told me, "you're like a child."

Vietnam is one of the most popular sources of women for desperate East Asian men. But wealthy bachelors also buy brides from Thailand, the Philippines, Uzbekistan, Russia, Malaysia, North Korea, and mainland China. Some of the sending countries have—or once had—women to spare. In some cases, war and regional conflicts killed many males. (In the Mekong Delta, the Vietnam War did the trick. "The Americans played a role in this," demographer Wen-shan Yang told me when I met him in Taipei to talk about Taiwanese men buying wives from Vietnam.) In other cases, a large proportion of adult men are working abroad. But the surplus of women is quickly drying up as surplus men from other countries come of age. The Caucasus countries, the Balkans, and, to a lesser degree, India, are all due for a very large marriage squeeze in the next two decades.* And some countries that send women abroad, like China and Vietnam, now have sex ratio imbalances of their own.

By 2013, one in ten Chinese men will lack a female counterpart. By the late 2020s, a projected one in five men will be surplus. According to one estimate, marriageable women will remain scarce until 2045, leaving around 15 percent of men lacking potential wives.[16] In another calculation, the number of Chinese surplus men in their twenties will soon outstrip the entire female population of Taiwan.[17] A similar scenario will play out across Asia. Between 15 and 20 percent of men in northwestern India will be surplus by 2020, a significant change in a society where until now the proportion of men who remain bachelors has hovered around 1 percent.[18] Scholars haven't yet begun to calculate the effect the sex ratio imbalance will have on marriage rates in Armenia, Albania, and Georgia. But high levels of female migration in the region could make the fate of boys there even bleaker.**

Some Chinese bachelors are following the example of Korean and Taiwanese bachelors in seeking wives in Vietnam. But most men in China and India can't afford to go abroad to find women. Instead, they seek wives from impoverished regions within their own borders. At a 2003 Congressional-Executive Commission on China forum on women's rights, historian and gender studies professor Christina Gilmartin said the number of domestic marriage migrants in China—largely poor peasants' daughters who marry men in wealthier areas—had reached 4 million. The figure is bound to increase, Gilmartin added, as the sex ratio imbalance worsens.[19]

Where scholars don't monitor the flow of women across regions and borders, it can be tracked by comparing the sex ratio at birth of a particular area with its adult sex ratio twenty or thirty years later—by counting how many girls are born in the area and then plotting that figure against how many remain or are added to the population as a generation grows up. The results are startling. Trouble spots like northwest India and eastern China, where baby girls are in short supply, have much more normal sex ratios among marriage-age adults. That disparity is made possible by a massive trade in girls and adult women.[20]

To a degree, East Asia's marriage agencies are like American mail-order bride services, playing to the desire of some men for feminine and subservient wives. Vietnamese women, the agencies' marketing materials claim, care about family. They listen to their husbands. They are "traditional." Graeme Hugo, an Australian geographer and migration scholar at the University of Adelaide who has studied the trade, says many of the Asian men who use agencies approach the process with chauvinistic ideas about the kind of woman they want. "They're looking for a very different type of partner, one who is less questioning and more submissive," he says.[21]

But unlike American companies, which tend to exoticize foreign women, the Taiwanese and Korean companies emphasize the Vietnamese brides' sameness. The websites give the sense that they serve men who are simply longing for a woman—any woman, but particularly the girl next door. "As I run an agency for Vietnamese brides," writes a Taiwanese broker on the site

---

*Indian men are relatively better off because the country's fertility rate is higher.
**While it was once men who left for Western Europe or the United States in search of wage work, today women go in larger numbers, drawn in part by the demands of aging industrialized countries for more nurses and caretakers.

www.vietnambride.tw, "people often ask me: Vietnamese brides, mainland Chinese brides, Russian brides, Ukrainian brides—which are best? If you ask me this question, I'll answer you this way: I think Vietnamese brides, mainland Chinese brides, Russian brides, Ukrainian brides, and other foreign brides are all bad! Taiwanese brides are the best!"[22] But, the broker continues, if you can't find a Taiwanese wife, Vietnam is a good option, and to that end she is here to help.

Vietnam is a popular source of women in part because—unlike Thailand, Cambodia, or the Philippines—it shares some traditions with its East Asian neighbors. A long history of Chinese influence has left the Vietnamese with a Confucian hierarchy, a similar approach to ancestor worship and lineage, and a mostly patriarchal family structure. Cheng Ching-huang, the Taiwanese farmer, can tick off a list of these similarities: both Taiwanese and Vietnamese worship at Buddhist temples, both place family altars in their homes, and both celebrate the lunar new year. Men like him are not seeking exoticism. They just want wives.*

Another difference between West and East when it comes to marrying foreign women is that in Asia the import of brides is encouraged by governments intent on bringing up sluggish birth rates.[23] One South Korean province briefly sponsored trips to Vietnam, covering men's expenses as they went in search of women, and the national government now endorses the trade in other ways, recently setting aside around $23 million for adaptation programs for new brides.[24] Most of these programs focus on assimilating the women to Korean culture: foreign brides can take courses in which they learn to speak Korean, deal with in-laws, and make kimchi. Korean roadways, meanwhile, are dotted with advertisements for marriage agencies that declare

A VIETNAMESE DAUGHTER-IN-LAW OBEYS.

and

FAST AND SUCCESSFUL MARRIAGE WITH FILIPINO, CAMBODIAN, AND VIETNAMESE WOMEN.[25]

The Taiwanese government has made a greater effort to safeguard the rights of Vietnamese women. Newly matched couples seeking marriage permits are required to undergo a course in Ho Chi Minh City outlining Taiwanese law on everything from domestic violence to inheritance.[26] But the government focuses on regulating the process, not stopping it, so that brides arriving in Taiwan can obtain the 130-page *Handbook of Living Information for Foreign Spouses in Taiwan,* which is conveniently printed in Vietnamese, Thai, Burmese, Cambodian, and Indonesian.[27]

And this is just the beginning. Taiwan and South Korea are small countries, and the impact they can have on the balance of sexes in a country like Vietnam is limited. As the Chinese and Indian economies take off and men in those countries make enough money to look abroad for wives, the repercussions will be grave. Already interest in marriage agencies has been piqued in China by Internet testimonials from men like Dai Wensheng, who bought a wife from Vietnam in 2009. "Most women I met in Vietnam are traditional, low maintenance, and quietly charming,"

Dai wrote on a forum a few months after settling with his new bride in the city of Nanjing. "My Vietnamese wife takes care of the laundry, cooking, and cleaning, and even peels the shells off shrimp for me. For the first time, I feel loved and spoiled."[28]

Doo-Sub Kim, a migration scholar in Seoul specialized in Asia's marriage trade, told me the resettlement of poorer Asian women in South Korea, Taiwan, and Singapore could augur a massive scramble for females elsewhere on the continent. This is just the tip of the iceberg, he says: "In the next twenty-five years, if the situation we have here [in Korea] continues in China, there's going to be a huge migration from Southeast Asian countries to the mainland. It's going to be total chaos."

Despite the rising number of bought brides and other evidence to the contrary, some scholars stubbornly maintain the laws of supply and demand apply to gender—that the value of women rises as their ranks thin. "As children become adults in cohorts with a high ratio of boys [to girls]," wrote economist Gary Becker and theorist Richard Posner in 2009, "the advantage of girls and women increases since they are scarcer." (Economists are particularly prone to this mode of thinking.) In a society with a sex ratio imbalance, the scholars continue, it is men, and not women, who find themselves at a disadvantage: as "the value of girls as wives and girlfriends, and in other ways, rises because they are scarcer . . . the value of boys as husbands and boyfriends tends to fall."[29]

This assessment is true only in the crudest sense. For women born into high sex ratio areas, scarcity can give them more bargaining power when it comes time to marry. In wealthy cities in eastern China, men now complain that women won't marry a suitor unless he has a house, a car, and a good job.[30] But attracting a high bride-price is not the same as gaining more autonomy, and the increased value experienced by the eastern Chinese woman occurs only on the most basic level, since the real test of equality is not what material goods a woman can ask a man to deliver but how she can expect him to treat her after marriage. A groom in a high sex ratio area may be kind and appreciative of his new wife, or he may fixate on the amount of capital he amassed in order to attract her and watch her like a hawk out of fear she will leave him. No majority group has ever aspired to become a minority under the illusion that a decrease in numbers will somehow lead the group's members to be more valued by the rest of society, and so it is with women. And in the case of women born into poor areas where they are likely to be bought, an imbalance often makes life considerably worse.

Asia's imported brides typically arrive in their new countries unable to speak their husband's language and dependent on the men for money and immigration status. Almost always they are younger, with the age gap frequently extending to fifteen to twenty years.[31] Youth is important because the women are expected to produce babies, but they are also chosen on looks, and sometimes on more archaic qualities. The Singaporean agency Life Partner Matchmaker medically examines its Vietnamese brides to ensure they are virgins. (Other agencies, warns founder Janson Ong in a

---

*Similarly, Korean men often seek ethnically similar wives in Uzbekistan and mainland China, both of which have Korean minorities.

video posted on the agency's website, simply teach women how to fake it.)[32] Since these are not what most marriage counselors would describe as the ingredients of a lasting relationship, the women have their work cut out for them.

Of the bought brides I met in Taiwan, South Korea, and China, only Nguyen Thi Mai Chau seemed to have achieved anything approaching contentment, and even hers was fleeting: two weeks after my visit Cheng Ching-huang suffered a heart attack while out tending his persimmon trees. He died soon after. In the months that followed, his family chipped in to help Nguyen make ends meet. Still, money became so tight that she had to relinquish the farmland Cheng had rented and apply for assistance from the Taiwanese government, which sets aside funds for foreign women whose husbands pass away as part of its support program for bought brides. There was no question, it seemed, of Nguyen returning with her children to Vietnam.

Most foreign brides live a life closer to that of Do Thi Nguyet, a thirty-four-year-old woman with a heart-shaped face, neatly permed hair, and a deep scar slicing across her nose. I meet Nguyet in the small eatery she runs outside Taipei, in an area that is rapidly becoming the city's Little Vietnam. She sets down the knife with which she has been chopping vegetables to talk to me, wiping her hands on a red apron and taking a seat at a greasy folding table. Around us, customers are slurping noodles, chatting away in Vietnamese, and silently tending babies. All but one are women.

I ask Nguyet how she came to live in Taiwan, thinking it a good warm-up question.

She bursts into tears.

Over a decade ago, Nguyet left her village in the Mekong Delta to marry a Taiwanese man fourteen years her senior. When she arrived in Taiwan her dreams of sending money home to her parents were quickly shattered. She discovered her new husband was an abusive philanderer with no job, an alcohol problem, and domineering live-in parents who treated her like a servant. But there were few other options available to her, and so she stayed. As the years rolled by, she gave her husband two children, raised them to adolescence, and even arranged for her older sister to journey from Vietnam to marry her husband's brother.

After her sister arrived, she finally worked up the courage to leave. The two women divorced their husbands on the same day, moved into a rented house, and opened a café with their meager savings. In the legal battle that followed, Nguyet's husband won custody of their children. But the children continued to run to her to be fed and clothed, and now here she is, a single immigrant mother of two, serving up bowls of noodles to make ends meet. I ask Nguyet what she would say to Vietnamese women from her village who are contemplating marrying Taiwanese men, and she replies without hesitation. "I would tell them not to do it," she says. "Taiwan is good. But the men who want to marry Vietnamese women are not."

Later I learn of more extreme cases and realize that Nguyet is fortunate, in a twisted way, in that her ex-husband at least allowed her to get a divorce. In Seoul I stop by the Korean Women Migrants Human Rights Center, an NGO set up by feminists to empower foreign brides. The center operates a shelter for women who are victims of domestic violence. All twelve spots are full, and activist Yeong Sug-heo tells me she has to turn away women in need of help. One-fourth of foreign wives in Korea report feeling physically threatened by their husbands.[33]

Even so, Yeong says only a fraction of abused women ever visit centers like hers. Many have mothers-in-law who won't let them out of the house, she says: "They paid a lot of money to get the women, so they trap them and keep them from going out." Occasionally wife abuse escalates into a headline-grabbing incident. In the summer of 2010, twenty-year-old Vietnamese Thach Thi Hoang Ngoc was stabbed to death by her forty-seven-year-old husband just eight days after she arrived in South Korea.[34]

In Taiwan, meanwhile, Vietnamese Catholic priest Peter Hung ministers to suffering brides in the industrial city of Taoyuan, arranging legal representation for runaways and sheltering them in the building attached to his church. "There are so many problems," Hung tells me when I meet him at his shelter, which he calls the Vietnamese Migrant Workers and Brides Office, one Sunday afternoon. He talks about a woman whose Taiwanese mother-in-law forced her to watch pornography in the belief it would help her produce a baby, of a woman married to a mentally ill man, of a woman who has herself gone crazy.* We talk in a small office on the second floor of the shelter while in the next room a handful of escaped women gather around a karaoke machine, singing to a backdrop of tinny synchronizer beats. The incongruously joyous music wafts through the thin office door. "So many problems," Hung continues. "But I think the most serious one is that the concept of marriage for these Taiwanese isn't marriage. It is buying and selling." Indeed, in 2004 three Vietnamese women were listed for sale, at the bargain price of $5,400 each, on Taiwan's, eBay.[35]

Even the harshest critics of the marriage trade are quick to point out that it is reshaping Asia's homogeneous societies in interesting ways. In South Korea and Taiwan, the children born to mixed marriages pose a powerful challenge to a prevailing concept of nationality that is deeply linked to race. Once, biracial children of American servicemen stationed in Korea were ostracized. Now international marriages happen with such frequency—and produce, on average, more children than marriages between two Koreans—that exclusion is not an option. In India, meanwhile, interregional marriage is breaking down the caste hierarchy. "Now because of [female] scarcity you see marrying outside of caste," says Sharada Srinivasan, the feminist sociologist I met in Christophe Guilmoto's living room. "Some of these barriers that go back a long time are beginning to weaken, and in some cases women are being married without dowries. So there might be some good coming out of this."

Women who migrate as brides also manage to send money home. Either at the wedding or in the months following it, Vietnamese families typically receive $1,000 to $2,000 in exchange for their daughters.[36] This is only a fraction of what men pay to

---

*Another case reported by the Taiwanese press involved a man who tortured his wife for seven months, binding her hands with duct tape, shooting rubber bands at her eyelids, and cutting her with a small knife.

agencies, but on later visits home a woman may bring as much as $10,000—nearly ten times Vietnam's per capita income—in gifts.[37] That amount has surprised many of the scholars who study the trade, and efforts to understand exactly what happens after men marry foreign women have yielded unexpected discoveries. In some cases, new brides convince their husbands to periodically fork over cash as a sort of guarantee of a harmonious marriage. In others, women earn money themselves by taking low-paid work upon arrival in Korea or Taiwan. "It's wrong to depict all of these women as victims," says Hugo, the Australian geographer who studies marriage migration. "It's clear that some of them become empowered at the destination."

To an extent, the increased earning potential of Vietnamese women who marry abroad has raised their status within their families. Because they furnish the cash that pays for remodeling projects, new appliances, and their brothers' weddings, overseas daughters are often consulted on important decisions.[38] But at the end of the day a Vietnamese bride is still mostly a medium for transferring money. Her value has risen, but again only crudely, benefiting her husband, her marriage broker, and her parents—everyone but herself.

Before he passed away, Cheng Ching-huang told me he recognized his marriage put his wife in a difficult situation. Vietnamese parents, he said, are typically more concerned about accruing appliances than they are about their daughters' happiness. "When you go back, they just look at how much money you're bringing," he said. "They don't care whether or not you're good to your wife."

To Lena Edlund, the Columbia University economist who uncovered evidence of sex selective abortion among Asian Americans, that makes intuitive sense. She finds economists who apply supply-and-demand logic to women maddening. "Okay, the value of a woman goes up" as the total number of women decreases, she says. "But does that mean that she will enjoy higher status? Not necessarily. Because she might be sold by her parents, or she might be kidnapped. So it's a bit of a paradox, but the more valuable women become, the higher the risk that they might get deprived of that value. Somebody might try to capture it."

Supply-and-demand reasoning also ignores the roles women are expected to play in high sex ratio societies. In Taiwan, South Korea, and other areas where females are scarce, women are coveted as wives, mothers, caregivers, housekeepers, and sex partners; when men list the qualities they hope to find in a Vietnamese wife, they do not mention intellect or a sense of humor or a desire to build an equal partnership. Historically, high sex ratio societies have exceptionally low rates of literacy and female workforce participation, and today's skewed societies maintain an emphasis on traditional gender roles.[39] Women who conform to those roles are valued, while those who buck expectations—by choosing to become lawyers or scientists, to remain unmarried, or to not have children—are perceived as threatening.

L ife on Tan Loc is regulated by the monsoon. The rain starts like clockwork every morning around 11:00 and pounds down long enough to fill the island's motor paths and swell the river that encircles it to capacity. In the hours that follow locals wait for the water to recede.

Afternoons are languorous, with the island finally waking up again at dusk. The weather is a stark reminder that one's fate is tied to the land, that to be born into a Mekong village is to have your future circumscribed by your origins. Perhaps that is why so many women leave to marry foreign men—why a decade or so into the marriage trade, Tan Loc is also known as Taiwan Island.[40]

I travel to Tan Loc on a motor scooter driven by Ms. Ha, a moonlighting middle-aged tour guide who accosted me in the lobby of my hotel, handing me a card that read, "Mekong Delta experience: People in the street pretending to be my brother or sister lie." A contact had inquired about a trip to Tan Loc on my behalf, but local officials apparently wary of the coverage the trade in brides was getting had sent back word that I was not welcome on the island, and that if I came they would know. So I invented a weak alibi and set out instead as a tourist. (Before departing, Ms. Ha and I mapped out a route to a stork sanctuary, one of the area's few tourist attractions, that conveniently passed through Tan Loc.)

Forty percent of people in Can Tho province live in poverty, and I expected to find the ride depressing.[41] Instead Ms. Ha's motor scooter traverses clean villages dotted with brightly colored houses and lush, thriving gardens. When after an hour on the road we arrive at Tan Loc, it turns out to be the nicest village of all—its motor path newly paved, its houses freshly painted and tiled, their courtyards swept clean and guarded by shiny stainless steel gates. In the surrounding villages, the gardens were mostly practical plots filled with cucumbers, green beans, and eggplants. On Tan Loc, they are decorative accents bursting with colorful flowers.

Local women started marrying Taiwanese men in the late 1990s, and by the turn of the millennium the outward flow of women had begun to change the island's fabric. As newlywed brides remitted payments to the parents who had sold them, Western Union set up a branch on Tan Loc, and from that point on money flowed in easily. It is customary in this part of Vietnam to carve the year a house is built into the doorframe, and the structures erected after the island's women started marrying foreigners—the houses whose frames read 2001 and 2004 and 2007—are outrageous things painted baby blue or mint green or bubblegum pink and sometimes all three and topped with Spanish tile roofs holding humongous television antennas. (Families in the Tan Loc area who have sent women abroad are more likely to own televisions—along with radios, motor scooters, cell phones, and air conditioners—than families with no women overseas.)[42] A few buildings have overgrown their foundations, yielding a sort of architecture on steroids.

Small one-story houses built earlier, meanwhile, have mushroomed into three-story towers outfitted with fake brick exteriors, tile patios, and appendages galore—porches, decks, balconies. Still others are works in progress, their exteriors crisscrossed with scaffolding and their yards strewn with paint cans. Several front doors are adorned with bright red cardboard cutout "double happiness" characters—signals of recent weddings.

But the story of Tan Loc is not entirely rosy. Before leaving for the island, I met Xoan Nguyen, a sociologist at Vietnam National University, at a coffee shop in Ho Chi Minh City. A thin, bubbly woman clad in a flouncy shirt, jeans, and flip-flops that reveal silver toenails, Nguyen focuses, unlike most scholars who study the marriage trade, on its impact on Vietnam. In her fieldwork, she catalogs overlooked details: the traits shared by women who marry foreigners, how much money they send back after they leave, and how many get divorced. (This last figure is striking, she says, but you wouldn't know it from looking at the demographic makeup of a place like Tan Loc. A large number of women return to Vietnam but only stay long enough to find a new foreign husband.)

Nguyen also looks at the effect the bride exodus has on local men. "A lot of ladies already have boyfriends, but the boyfriends are poor, so they leave them to find some Korean or Taiwanese men," she says. In 2005 she coauthored a study that found in some Mekong districts as many as half of recent weddings were between local women and Taiwanese men.[43] "The men who are left behind have no chance to find partners," she continues. "It's very sad."

During my day on Tan Loc I meet no women over thirty. The island is, however, filled with young men and boys. Before we leave, Ms. Ha and I stop at an open-air café near the ferry for some noodles. The café's customer base is exclusively male, and as we wait for our food I count over a dozen young men in various iterations of boredom: men drinking tea, men napping in the hammock, men playing billiards at a table whose green felt has worn down to a colorless nub.

After a while the loungers come together from their corners of the café and gather around a folding table, where the younger ones watch as the older ones begin a game of poker. They play for cigarettes, the action punctuated by dramatic gasps and fists pounding on the table and exclamations Ms. Ha translates as "Oh my god!" One of the bystanders wears a white T-shirt adorned with a sketch of a naked woman in profile. The caption reads, "What Men Want."

In Vietnam, as in China, even marriage between two locals typically involves a bride-price to the bride's family. But such payments never rivaled the amount of money that changes hands in marriages to foreigners—until recently, when competition started driving bride-price up. Should the men in the café succeed in finding women to marry, saving up enough money to secure the deal will be a challenge: parents of local young women now require suitors to furnish as much as twice the amount of goods they once did.[44] In 2007 Tran Giang Linh, a researcher at the Institute for Social Development Studies in Hanoi, surveyed hundreds of households in the Tan Loc area. "Almost all young pretty local women [have] already married abroad," one single man told her. "We—poor men—really have difficulty in getting married. Many of my friends had to find wives in . . . other proximate communes. I am also thinking about [doing] that."[45]

To make matters worse, Vietnam's own sex ratio imbalance means that by 2040 an additional 4.3 million men, mainly in the northern part of the country, will be unable to find wives.[46] Since most Vietnamese men can't afford to buy women from overseas, the imbalance will further increase pressure on the Mekong region to supply women.

The struggles of men in Tan Loc suggest one of the ugliest features of the trade in brides: the people who select for boys are not the same ones who have to watch their sons grow old alone. Just as globalization allows consumers to buy cheap goods without considering the toll those goods take on the workers who produce them, so too does it allow parents to ignore the impact of their actions by hiding away the unsavory after-math of sex selective abortion in places like Tan Loc. Wealthy parents in Taiwan and South Korea make decisions, while poor families in Vietnam feel their effects.

The Vietnamese government has not been entirely passive in the face of its women leaving, and officials have tried to staunch the flow of women to neighboring countries. After 2000, when more than 220 women were found crammed into seven rooms at a business hotel in downtown Ho Chi Minh City, where they were being held by brokers as they awaited selection by foreign men, the Hanoi government cracked down on the marriage trade.[47] State-run newspapers ran features debunking the Taiwan Dream. "Taiwan Disillusionment," the headlines called it.[48] In 2002 the government outlawed matchmaking agencies.[49]

But sociologist Nguyen says the crackdown simply had the effect of pushing the trade underground. After leaving their villages, women now gather in Cholon, Ho Chi Minh's Chinatown, where they are held in grimy back alley motels, packed six or more to a room, to await inspection by Taiwanese and Korean men. Waiting is not merely unpleasant. It is also a liability, for in some agency deals men have to cover the lodging fees of their new wives, making a woman who has sat on the shelf for weeks costly. A second consequence of the crackdown has been to propel the trade in women to the poorest corners of the earth. According to a 2008 International Organization for Migration report, the Asian marriage trade is now expanding into Cambodia.[50] The sex ratio imbalance has spawned a matrimonial race to the bottom.

When sex selective abortion arrives in the Mekong region, meanwhile, some scholars believe it will carry a twist: locals will select for girls. "Daughters nowadays are more preferable than sons because daughters can marry abroad and help families economically," a villager told Tran Giang Linh, the researcher who surveyed locals on the trade in women.[51] "Many people . . . feel unfortunate that they do not have daughters at marriageable ages," a middle-aged resident informed Nguyen in a focus group she conducted in An Giang province.*[52]

If the surveyed parents make good on these desires, Vietnam's sex ratio at birth will become more balanced—but the child populations of other, still poorer countries could start to skew female. As sex selection technology becomes cheaper, more sophisticated, and more widely available, and as the number of boys born to the world's upper and middle classes increases, predicts Lena Edlund in one paper, the poor will sense an opportunity: to select for daughters who can then be sold to wealthier families. "[T]he greatest danger associated with prenatal sex determination," she writes, "is the propagation of a female underclass."[53] In this scenario, we are left with a reality in which gender divides along income and class lines, and women go from not being born to being born into poverty.

---

*Similarly, in parts of Asia where large numbers of women go into sex work, parents tell researchers they celebrate the births of girls. In the 2001 book *Sex Slaves,* Louise Brown writes of rural Nepal: "[T]he birth of a daughter here is no longer a cause for lament. Sex work has given them a market value."

Critical Thinking

1. What were the circumstances that brought Cheng Ching-huang and Nguyen Thi Mai Chau together in marriage?

2. In what ways has the trade in women become and "entrenched industry?"

3. Explain the "marriage squeeze" and how it can snowball.

4. Why have some of the "sending countries" had "women to spare?" What is happening to their sex ratios?

5. How are East Asia's marriage agencies similar and yet different from American mail-order bride services? Why is Vietnam a popular source for brides in East Asia?

6. How does the author assess the claim that the laws of supply and demand affect gender preference?

7. How is the marriage trade re-shaping what were once Asia's homogeneous societies?

8. What seems to be ignored by the supply-and-demand logic regarding the status of women?

9. What effect is the marriage trade having on the men of the Tan Loc and of Vietnam in general?

10. What is one of the "ugliest features of the trade in brides?"

11. How might sex selective abortion "carry a twist?"

Rising Number of Dowry Deaths in India

Amanda Hitchcock

May 27: Young Housewife Burnt Alive for Dowry

Lucknow: For nineteen-year-old Rinki the dream of a happily married life was never to be. Barely a month after her marriage, she was allegedly tortured and then set ablaze by her in-laws for dowry in Indiranagar in the small hours of Saturday. Daughter of late Gyan Chand, a fish contractor who expired a year ago, Rinki was married to Anil on April 19 . . . However, soon after the marriage, Balakram [Anil's father] demanded a colour television instead of a black and white one and a motorcycle as well. When Rinki's mother failed to meet their demands, the teenage housewife was subjected to severe physical torture, allegedly by her husband and mother-in-law . . . On Saturday morning she [her mother] was informed that Rinki was charred to death when a kerosene lamp accidentally fell on her and her clothes caught fire. However, prima-facie it appeared that the victim was first attacked as her teeth were found broken. Injuries were also apparent on her wrist and chest.

June 7: Woman Ends Life Due to Dowry Harassment

Haveri: Dowry harassment claimed yet another life here recently. Jyoti, daughter of Chandrashekhar Byadagi, married to Ajjappa Siddappa Kaginelle in Guttal village (Haveri taluk) had taken her life after being allegedly harassed by her husband Ajjappa, mother-in-law Kotravva, sister-in-law Nagavva and father-in-law Siddappa for more dowry, the police said. Police said that the harassment compelled her to consume poison. . . . The Guttal police have arrested her husband and father-in-law.

June 7: Body Found Floating

Haveri: The police said that a woman's body was found floating in a well at Tilawalli (Hanagal taluk) near here. . . . The deceased has been identified as Akhilabanu Yadawad (26). The police said that Akhilabanu was married to Abdul Razaksab Yadawad five years ago. In spite of dowry being given, her husband and his family tortured her to bring some more dowry. Her

father, Abdulrope Pyati in his complaint, alleged that she was killed by them. Her husband and his two brothers have been arrested, the police added.

These three chilling reports from *The Times of India* are typical of the many accounts of dowry-related deaths that take place in the country every year. One cannot help but be struck by the offhand way in which a young woman's life and death is summed up, matter of factly, without any undue cause for alarm or probing of the causes. It is much as one would report a traffic accident or the death of a cancer patient—tragic certainly, but such things are to be expected.

The character of the articles points to the fact that the harassment, beating and in some cases murder of women over dowry is both common and commonly ignored or even tacitly condoned in official circles—by the police, the courts, politicians and media. These crimes are not isolated to particular groups, social strata, geographical regions or even religions. Moreover, they appear to be on the rise.

According to an article in *Time* magazine, deaths in India related to dowry demands have increase 15-fold since the mid-1980s from 400 a year to around 5,800 a year by the middle of the 1990s. Some commentators claim that the rising number simply indicates that more cases are being reported as a result of increased activity of women's organisations. Others, however, insist that the incidence of dowry-related deaths has increased.

An accurate picture is difficult to obtain, as statistics are varied and contradictory. In 1995, the National Crime Bureau of the Government of India reported about 6,000 dowry deaths every year. A more recent police report stated that dowry deaths had risen by 170 percent in the decade to 1997. All of these official figures are considered to be gross understatements of the real situation. Unofficial estimates cited in a 1999 article by Himendra Thakur "Are our sisters and daughters for sale?" put the number of deaths at 25,000 women a year, with many more left maimed and scarred as a result of attempts on their lives.

Some of the reasons for the under-reporting are obvious. As in other countries, women are reluctant to report threats and abuse to the police for fear of retaliation against themselves and their families. But in India there is an added disincentive. Any attempt to seek police involvement in disputes over dowry transactions may result in members of the woman's own family being subject to criminal proceedings and potentially imprisoned. Moreover, police action is unlikely to stop the demands for dowry payments.

The anti-dowry laws in India were enacted in 1961 but both parties to the dowry—the families of the husband and wife—are criminalised. The laws themselves have done nothing to halt dowry transactions and the violence that is often associated with them. Police and the courts are notorious for turning a blind eye to cases of violence against women and dowry associated deaths. It was not until 1983 that domestic violence became punishable by law.

Many of the victims are burnt to death—they are doused in kerosene and set light to. Routinely the in-laws claim that what happened was simply an accident. The kerosene stoves used in many poorer households are dangerous. When evidence of foul play is too obvious to ignore, the story changes to suicide—the wife, it is said, could not adjust to new family life and subsequently killed herself.

Research done in the late 1990s by Vimochana, a women's group in the southern city of Bangalore, revealed that many deaths are quickly written off by police. The police record of interview with the dying woman—often taken with her husband and relatives present—is often the sole consideration in determining whether an investigation should proceed or not. As Vimochana was able to demonstrate, what a victim will say in a state of shock and under threat from her husband's relatives will often change markedly in later interviews.

Of the 1,133 cases of "unnatural deaths" of women in Bangalore in 1997, only 157 were treated as murder while 546 were categorised as "suicides" and 430 as "accidents". But as Vimochana activist V. Gowramma explained: "We found that of 550 cases reported between January and September 1997, 71 percent were closed as 'kitchen/cooking accidents' and 'stove-bursts' after investigations under section 174 of the Code of Criminal Procedures." The fact that a large proportion of the victims were daughters-in-law was either ignored or treated as a coincidence by police.

Figures cited in *Frontline* indicate what can be expected in court, even in cases where murder charges are laid. In August 1998, there were 1,600 cases pending in the only special court in Bangalore dealing with allegations of violence against women. In the same year three new courts were set up to deal with the large backlog but cases were still expected to take six to seven years to complete. Prosecution rates are low. *Frontline* reported the results of one court: "Of the 730 cases pending in his court at the end of 1998, 58 resulted in acquittals and only 11 in convictions. At the end of June 1999, out of 381 cases pending, 51 resulted in acquittals and only eight in convictions."

Marriage as a Financial Transaction

Young married women are particularly vulnerable. By custom they go to live in the house of their husband's family following the wedding. The marriage is frequently arranged, often in response to advertisements in newspapers. Issues of status, caste and religion may come into the decision, but money is nevertheless central to the transactions between the families of the bride and groom.

The wife is often seen as a servant, or if she works, a source of income, but has no special relationship with the members of her new household and therefore no base of support. Some 40 percent of women are married before the legal age of 18. Illiteracy among women is high, in some rural areas up to 63 percent. As a result they are isolated and often in no position to assert themselves.

Demands for dowry can go on for years. Religious ceremonies and the birth of children often become the occasions for further requests for money or goods. The inability of the bride's family to comply with these demands often leads to the daughter-in-law being treated as a pariah and subject to abuse. In the worst cases, wives are simply killed to make way for a new financial transaction—that is, another marriage.

A recent survey of 10,000 Indian women conducted by India's Health Ministry found that more than half of those interviewed considered violence to be a normal part of married life—the most common cause being the failure to perform domestic duties up to the expectations of their husband's family.

The underlying causes for violence connected to dowry are undoubtedly complex. While the dowry has roots in traditional Indian society, the reasons for prevalence of dowry-associated deaths have comparatively recent origins.

Traditionally a dowry entitled a woman to be a full member of the husband's family and allowed her to enter the marital home with her own wealth. It was seen as a substitute for inheritance, offering some security to the wife. But under the pressures of cash economy introduced under British colonial rule, the dowry like many of the structures of pre-capitalist India was profoundly transformed.

Historian Veena Oldenburg in an essay entitled "Dowry Murders in India: A Preliminary Examination of the Historical Evidence" commented that the old customs of dowry had been perverted "from a strongly spun safety net twist into a deadly noose". Under the burden of heavy land taxes, peasant families were inevitably compelled to find cash where they could or lose their land. As a result the dowry increasingly came to be seen as a vital source of income for the husband's family.

Oldenburg explains: "The will to obtain large dowries from the family of daughters-in-law, to demand more in cash, gold and other liquid assets, becomes vivid after leafing through pages of official reports that dutifully record the effects of indebtedness, foreclosures, barren plots and cattle dying for lack of fodder. The voluntary aspects of dowry, its meaning as a mark of love for the daughter, gradually evaporates. Dowry becomes dreaded payments on demand that accompany and follow the marriage of a daughter."

What Oldenburg explains about the impact of money relations on dowry is underscored by the fact that dowry did not wither away in India in the 20th century but took on new forms. Dowry and dowry-related violence is not confined to rural areas or to the poor, or even just to adherents of the Hindu religion. Under the impact of capitalism, the old custom has been transformed into a vital source of income for families desperate to meet pressing social needs.

A number of studies have shown that the lower ranks of the middle class are particularly prone. According to the Institute of Development and Communication, "The quantum of dowry exchange may still be greater among the middle classes, but 85 percent of dowry death and 80 percent of dowry harassment occurs in the middle and lower stratas." Statistics produced by Vimochana in Bangalore show that 90 percent of the cases of dowry violence involve women from poorer families, who are unable to meet dowry demands.

There is a definite market in India for brides and grooms. Newspapers are filled with pages of women seeking husbands and men advertising their eligibility and social prowess, usually using their caste as a bargaining chip. A "good" marriage is often seen by the wife's family as a means to advance up the social ladder. But the catch is that there is a price to be paid in the form of a dowry. If for any reason that dowry arrangements cannot be met then it is the young woman who suffers.

One critic, Annuppa Caleekal, commented on the rising levels of dowry, particularly during the last decade. "The price of the Indian groom astronomically increased and was based on his qualifications, profession and income. Doctors, charted accountants and engineers even prior to graduation develop the divine right to expect a 'fat' dowry as they become the most sought after cream of the graduating and educated dowry league."

The other side of the dowry equation is that daughters are inevitably regarded as an unwelcome burden, compounding the already oppressed position of women in Indian society. There is a high incidence of gender-based abortions—almost two million female babies a year. One article noted the particularly crass billboard advertisements in Bombay encouraging pregnant women to spend 500 rupees on a gender test to "save" a potential 50,000 rupees on dowry in the future. According to the UN Population Fund report for the year 2000, female infanticide has also increased dramatically over the past decade and infant mortality rates are 40 percent higher for girl babies than boys.

Critics of the dowry system point to the fact that the situation has worsened in the 1990s. As the Indian economy has been opened up for international investment, the gulf between rich and poor widened and so did the economic uncertainty facing the majority of people including the relatively well-off. It was a recipe for sharp tensions that have led to the worsening of a number of social problems.

One commentator Zenia Wadhwani noted: "At a time when India is enjoying unprecedented economic advances and boasts the world's fastest growing middle class, the country is also experiencing a dramatic escalation in reported dowry deaths and bride burnings. Hindu tradition has been transformed as a means to escaping poverty, augmenting one's wealth or acquiring the modern conveniences that are now advertised daily on television."

Domestic violence against women is certainly not isolated to India. The official rate of domestic violence is significantly lower than in the US, for example, where, according to UN statistics, a woman is battered somewhere in the country on average once every 15 seconds. In all countries this violence is bound up with a mixture of cultural backwardness that relegates women to an inferior status combined with the tensions produced by the pressures of growing economic uncertainty and want.

In India, however, where capitalism has fashioned out of the traditions of dowry a particularly naked nexus between marriage and money, and where the stresses of everyday life are being heightened by widening social polarisation, the violence takes correspondingly brutal and grotesque forms.

Critical Thinking

1. What is implied by the character of the three articles cited, according to the author?
2. Why are the number of dowry deaths in India under-reported?
3. What are the typical explanations for why a woman might be burned to death?
4. Why are so many such deaths quickly written off by the police?
5. Why are young married women in such a vulnerable situation?
6. Why does the dowry system lead to their abuse?
7. How did the dowry function traditionally? How and why has it been transformed? In what segment of society are women most vulnerable?
8. What have been the consequences with respect to gender-based abortion and female infant mortality rates?

Murder in Amman

RANA HUSSEINI

In summer the temperature in Jordan soars to the unpleasantly high thirties. Across the sweltering capital, those of Amman's citizens who were fortunate enough not to have to make their living on the teeming streets hid away from the sun in the city's many coffee shops.

It was 31 May 1994, the day that Kifaya's mother, uncles and brothers had decided she would die.

In the built-up part of the conservative old city, Kifaya sat, tied to a chair in the kitchen of her family home. The sweets that her older brother, Khalid, had bought earlier to persuade her that everything was all right lay untouched on the counter.

Kifaya's crime was to have allowed herself to be raped by her other brother, Mohammad. She had then been forced by her family secretly to abort his child and had been made to marry a man thirty-four years her senior, whom she had divorced after six miserable months.

She had shamed her family. There was only one solution.

Khalid held a glass to Kifaya's lips, and told her to drink some water. He asked her to recite verses from the Quran and picked up a knife. Kifaya begged for mercy. Outside, the neighbours listened but did nothing as she started to scream.

• • •

'You're a professional,' I muttered to myself. 'Don't worry, you'll know what to say when you get there. Just stay focused, stay focused.'

It was 1 June 1994. I turned off Amman's busy commuter highway and drove upwards with mounting apprehension towards one of the most impoverished areas of the city.

Jordan's capital, home to two million souls, is always congested, but nowhere more so than in the poorest parts of the city. There's no rail or metro system, and in old Amman, the narrow streets cannot hope to cope with freight trucks, buses and cars.

As I sat behind an ancient truck that coughed exhaust fumes at my battered rust-bucket of a car, I recited the words I'd read in the paper for the umpteenth time that morning. 'Thirty-two-year-old man kills sixteen-year-old sister in Hashemi Shamali. Surrenders to police. Investigations underway.'

I don't know how many times I saw similar four-line stories spread all over the Arabic press. Something told me that I needed to investigate these stories. As a twenty-six-year-old crime journalist, I was still somewhat uncertain of myself. I had

been working for *The Jordan Times,* the only English-language daily in Jordan, for just nine months.

Journalism had become a career choice almost by accident. My father, a civil engineer, and my mother, a librarian, both supported my dreams of studying Public Relations and Advertising at a US university and so when I won a place at Oklahoma City University in 1987 they were only too happy for me to go.

This was around the time of the first Palestinian uprising, and a reporter called Corky Huffin asked me to write about the intifada (although I hold Jordanian nationality, I am originally Palestinian). I wrote the article and it was published. Corky then asked me to join the university's newspaper since they always needed reporters, so I did and loved it. I wrote about women's sports as I was an athlete myself (I played basketball for Jordan's national team) and then switched majors, focusing on journalism.

During the final semester I worked for the weekly *Oklahoma Gazette,* where I wrote about social issues; I learned how people can make a difference and help each other and how journalism helps them to do this. By the time I returned to Jordan, I knew I wanted to focus on women's issues but had no idea what I was about to get into.

As I drove deeper into the poor neighbourhood, the buildings became shabbier; the road narrowed and the streets soon became jammed with cars forced to a honking crawl as pedestrians spilled from the crowded pavements.

I stopped the car and rolled down the window. A young man was striding purposefully down the road towards me. I called out to him: 'Have you heard about a young girl who's been murdered?'

'Who hasn't?' he replied, pointing back in the direction he'd come. 'Round the corner, close to Omar's barbershop, you'll find her family's house; she was killed there.'

It seemed as though everyone knew. This was, after all, a very crowded neighbourhood where everybody knew everyone else's business. A real-life murder was a sure attention-getter in the absence of other distractions like movie theatres, parks or libraries.

'Do you know why they killed her?' I asked.

He was already walking away. 'Because her brother raped her,' he said casually.

Assuming I'd misheard him (who kills rape victims?), I soon found Omar's barbershop and parked my car. As I got out, a loose paving slab wobbled under the sneakers I'd decided to wear in case I had to run away—I was about to stick my nose in some very private business. My non-traditional baggy T-shirt and loose-fitting jeans also helped me feel more comfortable, although I stuck out like a sore thumb in this conservative part of town.

I pushed the front door halfway open; the smell of stale cigarettes and hair grease overwhelmed me. Through the haze, I saw there were two empty chairs to my left. A fat man, who I assumed was the proprietor from the way he straddled the chair, faced me. Two skinny middle-aged men were slouched on a brown hole-ridden sofa to his left. They were all smoking.

'Assalamu Alaikum,' I said.

'Wa Alaikum Assalam,' they chorused.

'A young girl was murdered around here, have you heard about this?'

At this the two men looked at each other and both sat up. 'Yes,' one of the skinnier ones said. 'Who told you?' he asked, suspiciously.

'It was in the paper this morning.' I pulled out the page I had torn from the newspaper and showed it to them while I remained on the doorstep.

'It's *already* made the papers?' This development was apparently unwelcome. The barber took a drag of his cigarette and asked, 'Who are you and why do you want to know?'

I declared confidently that I was a crime reporter working for *The Jordan Times*. Inside I was a bag of nerves. Media coverage only serves to keep any 'scandal' committed by the victim of the so-called honour crime alive, which is why so few reporters—in fact, no reporters whatsoever—investigated honour killings.

They didn't respond, so I stepped through the door and sat on the sofa next to the two men. Hoping to win their confidence and encourage them to speak to me about the murder, I chatted with them casually about my job, my education in the USA, journalism, the country and politics.

Our chat revealed that the two men on the couch were her uncles. 'Kifaya was not a good girl,' one of them said, as if killing a 'bad girl' was acceptable.

Kifaya. Suddenly, my story had a name.

I stayed and we talked some more. Every now and again I asked why Kifaya had been killed, until one of the uncles said, 'She was raped by Mohammad, her brother. That's why she was killed.'

I straightened my back, and placed my notebook on my lap, not sure what to say next.

Eventually I said, 'Why was she punished and not her brother? Why didn't Kifaya's family discipline him instead?'

One of the uncles looked worried. 'Do you think we killed the wrong person?'

Her other uncle answered quickly, 'Relax. We did the right thing.'

I struggled to contain my fury. It was as if they were speaking about a sheep. These men were part of the conspiracy. Her

body not yet cold, yet here they were—on a sofa in a barbershop chatting with the owner and smoking cigarettes.

'She seduced her brother. She tarnished the family's honour and deserved to die,' the skinnier uncle declared.

I sighed at his stupidity. Jordanian society blames women for everything: for being raped, for being harassed on the streets, for philandering husbands, for husbands who divorce them, for bearing a child of the wrong gender—the list is endless.

'But why would she choose to sleep with her brother? If she wanted to sleep with a man, surely, she would not choose to sleep with her brother.'

Instead of answering my question, the barber stood up and said, 'Why do you care for such a story?'

'Why are you dressed like this?' one of the uncles asked, pulling an expression of disgust at my jeans and T-shirt.

'Why are you in our neighbourhood?' the other continued. 'You do not belong here. You have become westernized in America. You forget where you are now.'

I was clearly 'not a good girl'. I thanked them and quickly left.

Outside, I looked at the houses stacked haphazardly on top of and overlapping each other. Kifaya's wasn't hard to find. Even the kids playing in the street could point me to the three-storey house situated at the end of the road. I looked at it with pain in my heart.

'Why did they kill you?' I asked myself. 'You were only sixteen.'

I headed towards her neighbours; a shabby house where a newly-wed couple lived. They offered me tea and told me what they saw.

They had heard Kifaya scream and beg for mercy. They had seen her brother Khalid standing outside his house holding the bloodstained knife and shouting, 'I have cleansed my family's honour.'

His family was waiting to congratulate him.

Khalid then went to the nearest police station and turned himself in, claiming to have killed Kifaya to cleanse the honour of his family.

I arrived back at the newspaper offices frustrated and exhausted. I needed to exorcize this experience from my system by telling my story to my editor, Jennifer Hamarneh. Jennifer had arrived at *The Jordan Times* a couple of years before me. She was a tough editor and would often get mad when I made mistakes. But she taught me so much; though at times it was tough, I took on board what she was telling me in a positive way; I certainly didn't make the same mistake twice.

'I don't want Kifaya's murder to be just another crime story; I want so-called honour killings to become a national issue.'

Jennifer looked at me like she was weighing me up. 'Tell the story, we'll make space for it.'

I think Jennifer knew then that Kifaya's story was going to change my life for good. In order to maintain objectivity, I had to suppress my great anger and sadness as I wrote, hoping that someone important, that any of our readers, would read it and would feel inspired to take action.

The following day my story appeared on page three with a headline that read: 'Victim of incestuous rape killed by second brother'.

The next morning George Hawatmeh, my former editor-in-chief, took a call from a Jordanian woman, who described herself as an intellectual who worked in an official position. George was also a strong believer in the fight against so-called honour crimes and was immediately thrilled at the thought that the caller was also outraged at this appalling murder and wanted to voice her objection. Perhaps she wanted to use her influential post to exert some pressure on the government to help prosecute all those involved in Kifaya's murder.

But his hopes were immediately dashed. She shouted down the phone at George: 'You should stop Rana Husseini from reporting these crimes because they do not exist in Jordan! This does not happen in our society!'

Luckily, George and Jennifer disagreed and supported me when I told them I wanted to become the voice of these women whose lives have been wiped out and every record of their existence destroyed by their family. I would expose each and every murder I heard about.

I didn't realize then quite how busy I was going to be.

Interview with a Killer

As I began to write more and more about honour killings, with the support of opinion writers and my editors, so our postbags began to swell. The readers of *The Jordan Times* are mostly the affluent English-speaking minority, many of whom were already aware of violence against women, but remained apathetic until we started reporting the cases in depth.

At the start of each week I'd arrive at work to find my own inbox filled with threatening letters. A typical one said, 'If you don't stop reporting these murders, I will send someone to visit you at your home or workplace.'

Another memorable warning read: 'I'm going to clean my hunting rifle; it's the season for hunting coloured birds.' Oddly enough, far from deterring me, threats like these made me all the more determined to carry on. I had found my life's mission.

As well as the threats, our postbags also began to fill with letters of support from readers, expressing their anger and outrage about the killing of innocent women and the leniency shown to killers for murder in the first degree.

But even some supporters, friends and colleagues were discouraging, and argued that we were wasting our time with a lost cause. 'No one will listen to you,' one friend told me. 'Nothing ever changes in this country.' Many urged me instead to write about politics because it was 'more rewarding' and because achieving social change was next to impossible.

I listened, but simply followed my heart and my conscience. These women needed a voice. They were lost souls, buried without ceremony in unmarked graves; it was as if they'd never existed. People needed to know that they had lived, loved and died in the cruellest manner possible. They needed to know who had murdered them and why their killers had gone unpunished.

I first met Sarhan in 1999, when CNN decided to film a documentary about so-called honour crimes in Jordan and approached me to be part of it. The programme makers wanted to interview prisoners who had killed their female relatives to

cleanse their family honour, or who were in prison awaiting a court verdict.

I agreed immediately. Back then it was almost impossible for a Jordanian reporter to be allowed to interview prisoners at all. This restriction, however, did not apply to the majority of foreign media representatives who were welcome to film inside prisons and interview any inmate they wanted. The double standards towards the two different media bodies still apply on occasion in other bureaucratic institutions around the country.

It was decided that the shoot was to take place at the Jweideh Correctional and Rehabilitation Centre, home to over a thousand men waiting to be tried for crimes ranging from robbery to first-degree murder.

After going through several security checks, the CNN crew and I were ushered into a small, windowless room filled with half-a-dozen prison guards and officials in civilian clothes. The crew began setting up their equipment and adjusting their cameras. I was directed to sit on a chair. The guards kept eyeing me, wondering what was so special about me that CNN wanted me on their programme.

A few minutes later, a well-built man in his late twenties entered the room, accompanied by several guards who seated him opposite me.

One of the prison officials said, 'This is Sarhan, he killed his sister to cleanse his honour.'

Oddly, Sarhan had a wide smile on his face, apparently welcoming the attention.

His sister, Yasmin, had been raped by her brother-in-law. Knowing full well the consequences of such a crime, she had turned herself in to the police, rather than risk the wrath of her family.

Sarhan headed to the police station the following day and tried to bail out his sister. His request was refused; the police thought he might kill her because she had lost her virginity.

Sarhan went to a friend's house and stayed there for a couple of days. When he returned home, he found his sister in the living room. Without uttering a word he shot her four times with an unlicensed gun and turned himself in.

The minute we made eye contact, I felt rage beginning to boil inside me. I tried hard to suppress it; I wanted to remain professional. I didn't want to get emotionally involved, not now.

'I killed her because she was no longer a virgin,' he told me. 'She made a mistake, willingly or not. It is better that one person dies than the whole family of shame and disgrace. It is like a box of apples. If you have one rotten apple would you keep it or get rid of it? I just got rid of it.'

When I challenged Sarhan by pointing out that his act contradicted the teachings of Islam and was punishable by God, he said, 'I know that killing my sister is against Islam and it angered God, but I had to do what I had to do and I will answer to God when the time comes.'

He added: 'People refused to talk with us. They told us to go cleanse our honour; then we were allowed to talk with them. Death is the only solution to end disgrace . . . Even if we had wed my sister society would not stop talking. They only stopped talking when she is dead.'

The story didn't end there. A few weeks later I was covering a high-profile case of a Jordanian teenager who killed his entire family because, he said, of the pressure they were putting on him to pass his school exams.

I was at court when I noticed a familiar face among the crowd. It was Sarhan! I could not even guess why he was a free man after such a short time in prison.

I found a seat next to him on the bench. He flashed the same smile he gave me during our interview. When the court adjourned for a ten-minute break, I was able to exchange a few words with him.

'What are you doing here? Who wants to be back in the courtroom where he was tried?' I asked him. He told me proudly that he had returned to offer support to a defendant with whom he had struck up a friendship during his incarceration.

I asked him how he ended up receiving such a lenient penalty when the facts of his sister's case were clear; it was a premeditated murder. Sarhan explained he took the advice of one of the officials who questioned him after he had turned himself in. Sarhan told the investigator in his initial testimony that he decided to kill his sister after learning that she was no longer a virgin. He said he asked his family to bail her out and that he waited for them to bring her home, which they did. The minute she walked in, he shot her to death.

The investigator informed him that if he insisted on this version then he might face life imprisonment and advised him to change his story to say he was taken by surprise by his sister's rape and the loss of her virginity, in order to get the lightest sentence possible. His lawyer gave him the same advice when the case was about to be heard in court.

Sarhan's confession meant that his father was an accomplice—a fact that was nowhere to be found in the verdict or in the charge sheet.

'I took the stand and told the judges that I had to kill my sister, because if I did not kill her, it would have been like killing more than a thousand men from my tribe.'

I told him this was impossible. How could a court accept such an argument?

After the court session had finished, I followed Sarhan outside. Again, I asked him why he killed her. Again, I pointed out that she had been raped. She was not at fault. He repeated what he had already told me; that she had to die because she had lost her virginity.

He said that he sat with his father, his mother, his uncles and around eight hundred men of his tribe and they had reached this consensus together. 'If I hadn't killed her, people would look down on me. Once she was raped, she was no longer a girl. My only alternative was to kill her. Death is the only way to erase shame.'

He also told me that his family and relatives visited him in prison to congratulate him on the act. Nevertheless, he did indicate that he was not entirely comfortable with what he'd done and told me he'd been 'forced' to kill his sister, whom he grew up with and loved deeply.

'I know my sister was killed unjustly but what can I do? This is how society thinks. Nobody really wants to kill his own sister,' he said.

I asked him why Yasmin's rapist was neither similarly punished nor questioned by his family. Sarhan said his brother-in-law had vanished. He insisted that if he found him he would kill him as well.

During the course of our conversation, I asked Sarhan how long his sentence was.

'One month for possession of an unregistered firearm and six months for the misdemeanour.'

I sat in shock. Misdemeanour?!

Sarhan had pleaded guilty to manslaughter and possessing an unlicensed gun during the trial, but the court decided that he did in fact 'benefit from a reduction in penalty because he committed his crime in a fit of fury.'

'Sarhan lost his temper and killed his sister in a moment of extreme rage after learning she was no longer a virgin. This was proven by the medical report,' the court verdict said. The court considered the girl's loss of her virginity a crime—even though it was clearly recorded by the court that she was raped. This lenience was made possible by Article 98 of the Penal Code which permits those acting in a 'fit of fury' to benefit from reduced penalties.

I couldn't understand the verdict. I immediately sought out one of the tribunal's three judges. Many judges had already heard of me and I had managed to build up relationships with some of them, and so one of them agreed to an interview. I had to be extremely careful about how I discussed any issue with the members of the judiciary; as a rule, no doubting, blaming or questioning was allowed. Judges were and still are considered to be among the most respected authorities in the kingdom. It was going to be extremely difficult for me to hold my tongue.

The judge was welcoming, and ordered us some mint tea. As soon as it had been poured I took a deep breath and started the interview. 'How do you explain that Sarhan received only six months when the case clearly does not qualify under the fit of fury clause as stipulated in Article 98 of the Penal Code? The girl was raped and it was not her fault,' I said. Yasmin had turned herself in to the police for protection. Before the authorities released her, her father signed a guarantee that she would not be harmed. Obviously—to me, at least—the 'fit of fury' argument should not apply in the court's consideration of the case, since, plainly, the murder was planned and coldly executed.

The judge took a sip of mint tea. 'The rape happened within the family, so it was clearly a family affair. Sarhan killed his sister after family encouragement, so this murder was a product of our culture.'

'But what about Yasmin? Who should then defend her? She was also a victim. Was her life worth nothing?'

The judge looked at me and said nothing. For a fleeting second, I felt that my argument had had an impact on him. But it was time for me to leave; the judge told me he was a busy man. I had pushed too hard.

Inam Asha, a social worker and activist who had seen Yasmin at the police station, offered me further details. The head of the station told her about the interrogation that took place. Yasmin had arrived at the station with her brother-in-law, the rapist, and he had asked her to claim that someone else raped her to cover up his crime. Yasmin tried to obey but because she was scared she kept getting the story wrong. Finally, after one of the interrogators slapped her across the face, she collapsed and told the truth.

My courtroom encounter with Sarhan was not the last. He was repeatedly interviewed by many local and international media agencies, some of which I worked for as a mediator. On one occasion, after Sarhan had finished an interview, I asked him if he regretted what he had done. He said that the murder had ruined his life. Today, he said, no woman wants to marry him. He had tried to seek the hand of eleven women in marriage, but they all refused, including a cousin whose father had encouraged him to kill his sister.

'They all refused for fear that I might kill them or my daughters one day. But if I were put in the same situation again I would kill my sister and any other sister who goes through the same thing. This is our society, this is how we are brought up and it will never change.'

He nostalgically told me he was treated as a hero in prison. 'All the men who were with me for the same reason in prison were treated as heroes by everybody.' Once he was back in the real world, he was ignored and felt worthless.

Sarhan kept telling me how much he loved his sister, even though he ended her life. 'She was so close to me. She was the one who resembled me the most. I had to kill her, I had no other choice. This is what our society wants. It is better to sacrifice one soul than to sacrifice my whole family.'

But he insisted his sibling died unjustly. 'I am sure of that fact. No one wants to be the one to kill his sister, but traditions and society inflict things on us that we really do not want to do. If society would not have shunned us after her rape, we would not have killed her and instead locked her inside the house until she died or someone married her.'

Sarhan's family's promises of rewarding him and helping him out for killing his sister were never fulfilled. He has been unable to find regular work and instead does odd jobs every now and then.

In one of our most recent interviews, he told me, 'To be honest with you, Rana, I am scared to have female children because society is harsh and I have a feeling that I might want to bury my female daughter because this is what I would feel is right . . . I wish my other sister would get married quickly because women are a source of concern. If something goes wrong, they do not pay the price; we do.'

He also acknowledged that his lenient punishment would encourage him and other males to murder again in the name of honour.

'If the state amends the law to execute men who kill their female relatives or lock us behind bars for good, I do not think that any family would venture and push her male relative to kill. No family wants to see its male relative executed or locked up for good.'

His final comment to me was, 'I hope that the situation will change because I alone cannot change or fix things in my society. My whole society has to change.'

Even Khalid, who admitted to murdering Kifaya, received a lenient sentence of seven-and-a-half years and was released

for good behaviour two years early. I only found out by accident when I returned to the scene of the crime to try and speak to Kifaya's father. They weren't there but the neighbours told me that Khalid was living on the first floor of their three-storey building. Feelings of anger and excitement flowed through my veins as I climbed the stairs and knocked on his door.

The door opened slowly and a short, tired-looking man in his mid-thirties asked me who I was. He invited me into the tiny one-room flat. Inside, he had mattresses spread out on the floor and so I chose a small one and sat on it. Khalid called his wife and asked her to make us some tea.

I started by asking him about his days in prison. 'All my cellmates sympathized with me and treated me as a champion. All the men who were in the prison for killing their sisters or female relatives were treated as champions.'

He told me he realized that what he did was against the Sharia (Islamic law), 'but society is stronger than me or religion. I had to kill her to preserve the family's honour. Society imposes rules on us and I did it to please society. No one was talking to me in the street. We live in a backward society that imposes backward ideas on our lives.'

He also told me bitterly that he suffered even though he was treated as a hero in prison. 'It was a tough experience that I had to go through. I have four children that I have been deprived of being with for over five years and now I am trying to compensate for these lost years.'

'Do you regret killing your sister and if you were put in the same situation again would you kill her?'

His answer was similar to many I would hear from killers I interviewed over the coming years.

'No, I do not regret killing Kifaya. But if I went back in time, I would not kill my sister. I would tie her up like a sheep in the house until she either died or someone married her. I have wasted enough of my life in prison and I would not repeat the same mistake.'

His words made me realize that Khalid was, like his sister, but to a lesser extent, a victim of his own society; a victim of ancient and unfair traditions that turned a normal human being into a killer.

Three years after Kifaya's murder, I found her father. I had been planning to do a follow-up story on her family but hadn't held out much hope of finding them in the same area. I knocked on the door and it was opened slowly, revealing a white-haired and sad-faced man in his mid-fifties. He invited us in, confirming in a sorrowful voice, 'Yes, I am her father'.

He ushered us into the sparsely furnished living room. A small coffee table was surrounded by mattresses where we sat. Kifaya's father called one of his daughters and asked her to make us tea.

'I am against what they did,' he told me. 'I would never have allowed anyone to kill my daughter, no matter what. Damn them for taking such a decision.'

At the time of the murder, he was working in the USA. 'I immediately returned to Jordan when I heard that my daughter had been killed. I could not believe it. I did not expect them to kill her. They did it because they were jealous of me living and working in the US.' He laughed bitterly and told me, 'You should see the kind of life I had in the US they were so envious of. I worked the dirty jobs that most immigrants take—as a garbage collector, a mechanic, a grass-cutter.'

I felt his bitterness as he talked. He told me that his wife, Kifaya's mother, died of cancer six months after her daughter's murder.

'Kifaya's mother had a hand in her death,' he added.

I was startled. 'What do you mean?' I asked him quickly.

'Her mother helped plot her murder along with her uncles,' he explained.

I screamed, 'But why?' He couldn't give me an answer. I thought that maybe she had no choice because they might have killed her as well had she not helped.

One of Kifaya's sisters offered me a small glass of tea. Her two siblings sat quietly next to their father. I asked him about Mohammad, the brother who raped Kifaya. 'Let him rot in prison. I have no sympathy for him. I do not want to see him ever again in my life.'

I then asked for his permission to discuss Kifaya's murder with his three daughters. The eldest sister, who was fifteen at the time of the murder, said Kifaya did not deserve to be killed and Mohammad was to blame for all the misery they had endured since her death.

The middle-aged sister, who was thirteen at the time, was undecided; she did not know what to think. The youngest sister, twelve at the time of the murder, was the most critical of her sister's actions. She blamed Kifaya for everything that had since gone wrong and accused her of destroying the stability of their family. She told me Kifaya had ruined her father and that both brothers were in jail because of her.

I asked the older sister if they had a photo of Kifaya. I just wanted to see her face and see what she looked like. I wanted to read her features, to try and get to know her, to establish her identity.

'We don't have any photos of Kifaya. Her uncles burned them all.'

It was as if she had never existed.

Critical Thinking

1. From the perspective of Kifaya's family, why was she murdered? For what kinds of things do Jordanian women get blamed? Why was the author considered to be clearly "not a good girl"?

2. How did Sarhan justify the murder of his sister?

3. Why was leniency granted to Sarhan who murdered his sister, Yasmin? Why does Sarhan say that the murder "ruined his life"? How and why does he think the "whole society has to change"?

4. What were the real reasons for Kifaya's murder, according to the father?

The Untold Story of the Amputees

Carolyn Nordstrom

Un-Armed

The truckers quietly moved their diamonds out and loudly moved their beer and commodities into town. The Gov'nor shipped his tomatoes abroad without worrying about how quietly or noisily he worked. The shopkeeper and the street child went about their business, holding down the town's center of commercial gravity. Amid this swirl of activity, other groups of people were redefining the economic landscapes of the country and its worldwide links in ways rarely recognized in business analyses.

These latter business ventures—challenging established notions of legality and nationality, of the divides between civil society, NGOs, and development—are best summed up for me in the example of a group of women amputees I met in Mulequc.

The story starts, not with these women, but with the belief that land mines are a military weapon. The mythology of land mines, which is sold along with the mines themselves, is that these explosives deter soldiers and protect sensitive sites. But the truth is that the most common victims are average civilians looking for food, water, and work. From country to country across the world's militarized; zones the same statistics emerge: children playing or going to school, women doing their daily chores, and men engaged in nonmilitary work are those most likely to step on the little metal and plastic units that blow off bits of humanity.

Many people's lives are defined not by whether war continues or peace emerges, but by a chance encounter with violence. A woman who loses her family to attack or a limb to a land mine, finds herself struggling to survive in war and peace alike. These tragedies can happen at the acme of war or long after a peace accord has been signed. In either instance, staying alive suddenly becomes far more tenuous.

Look at me, *the woman said,* I am incomplete for this world. I have no leg, not much of an arm. My heart is strong, and my spirit good. But heart and spirit don't carry water from the river for drinking or firewood for cooking; heart and spirit don't go out and put seeds in the field, get water to irrigate my crops, tend them, and then harvest them. Have you ever tried to do these things with one leg and arm? I have no husband; he left. If I don't do these things, I starve and die. There are no wheelchairs out here, no way to get them even if there were. If I have to crawl to carry water, I crawl.

She spits in disgust. This they call war? I won't get into that. There are thousands of us like me around here. But we are going to make a difference.

But Not Defenseless

The group of amputees, around Muleque began to congregate, to pool resources, and to help one another. An Irish INGO provided support: seeds and tools, a workshop, and other critical help. The first time I met the women, they had come from far and wide to attend a meeting and seed distribution at their center in town. Walking the long kilometers was the only means of travel they had—a tough ordeal for people who have lost limbs to explosions. The range and barbarity of the land mines available on the world's market was visible in the wounds the women carried. Some had barely the remnants of a leg. Others were missing arms. Some were scarred from face to torso by the shards of metal packed into shrapnel mines. A crutch was generally an impossible luxury; neither the crutches nor the money to buy them were available.

At the center, the women showed me a play they were working on—they had decided to use theater to educate people about land mines. They enacted despair and hope, support and a will to live. They sang of the difficulties of no longer fitting the ideal of a woman—whole in body, capable in limbs, desirable in womanhood—and of the families and men who had stayed to help, and those who had abandoned them; of the suffering and sanguinity entailed in creating a new kind of community of women, with and without families, helping each other. The performance didn't shy away from raw emotions or painful truths. But there was one topic that was left unspoken. Either a person is in the know, or isn't; and thus the knowledge is best left unsaid.

Coming Back from the Dead: Informal Economies and Formal Development

These women had developed survival skills: they cleared farmland and planted crops, built places to live, and established market and barter systems to gain essentials. These are the "informal economies" that governments and INGOs reckon keep the poor alive and the basics of a society intact. This is what the International Labor Organization deems small-scale, low-tech, low-income. But the women had larger plans. They didn't want to eke out the rest of their days hobbling to tiny fields, raising just enough food to keep body and soul together until a drought ended their hopes. They wanted the option to buy prostheses, build decent homes, go into business, and gain the kinds of power that could buy permits and sock away money to cushion them against life's unexpected upheavals.

The Muleque women had several money-making enterprises in mind. They operated what women throughout Southern Africa depend on: a self-run informal banking system. Women who know each other form a group based on stability, trust, and economics. Each month, all the members of the group put a predetermined amount of money into a communal pot, and one woman gets the entire pot that month. The next month the next woman on the rotation gains the entire amount, and so on, throughout the membership cycle. There are no laws or mechanisms to ensure that a member doesn't take her turn to get all the money and then leave the group. That these women's banks are so widespread and enduring is a testimony to the systems of trust and allegiance that can underscore informal economic networks.

With the proceeds of their banking investments, the women amputees were beginning to reap profits: some had been successful at farming and had surplus food. Some began to link into the secondhand clothing industry. And some had plans to begin producing small items to sell, from crafts to business components.

The trick, of course, is to broaden our markets, *they explained*. Oh, we can sell here. But this is a limited market. We will reach a certain volume and then that's it. We won't grow. We need to be able to sell our products to larger cities. We need to be able to reach Luanda, the capital, We have things that people across the border could use. With these connections, we can really make a go of it.

But as to how they could reach these markets, they remained silent. These were devastatingly poor women, women for whom many days went by when they couldn't scrape together enough to eat. Their impaired mobility made the normally difficult task of walking and trying to hitch rides across the country seemingly impossible. As women, they didn't have the networks of access that men who work in government, transport, or mining and industry have—networks where a friend who is making a flight or a truck run might let him bring his products along. To find the money to pay for such "help" was a distant dream.

The women's silence wasn't due to lack of ideas, but discretion. The story unfolded only when I sat talking to a local coordinator for an INGO working with the amputees. This woman, whom I'll call "Leli," had lived her whole life in the Muleque area and knew it well. She wasn't sure why she had escaped stepping on a mine or stopping a bullet, but she threw herself into helping these women and her community tirelessly. She was a font of enthusiasm, hard work, and dedicated vision. Leli and the hundreds of thousands like her who work beyond the pale of CNN and the *Times* of London give lie to tossed-off statements by Westerners that humanitarian aid produces complacent and dependent populations. I spoke to Leli in the small mud-walled room where she worked. She leaned across the rickety wooden table that served as her desk, taking my hand periodically as if to envelop me in the vitality of her work:

These are the women who are not supposed to make it—the women who fall off the margins. How does a woman make it in this kind of life. . . . a life where a healthy woman with all her limbs finds it hard. There are few precedents for women breaking out of traditional roles and forging new communities of all-women support So these land-mine victims are sort of expected to fall off the map. But they don't.

They start up farming and making small things they can barter for essentials. And then they start up with the ideas. They have talked with every trader who comes through here, and they know the markets in the next big city, in Luanda, across the border in Congo. They know what is available, what is desirable, and what the prices are. They have tailored their enterprises and products to suit these markets. And they are ready to sell. All they need is transport.

They have come to me to ask if I can take their goods on a flight to Luanda. They know that because I work with the INGO, I have access to flights and cargo rights. They know these flights are safe. And they know they can trust me. They have offered to cut me in on the business for this. I think it's an excellent idea. I am proud of the women. In truth, these INGO flights bring in seeds and tools to keep these women alive. But this is sheer subsistence. They give only enough to keep people alive. They live at the minimum. There is no real way in this scheme to improve, to grow, to gain some prosperity. If the INGO closes shop and moves, these people are left at the margins.

To use my rights as a worker for an INGO, to carry these women's products to the capital, this is development. Now these women, have a real chance. I am really moved by what they are doing, they are succeeding where no one expects them to. I'm glad to be a part of it Now women in my hometown may actually make it.

The women's ambition to group together, form banking and entrepreneurial systems, and move from local and subsistence to inter/national profit making is part of a larger ethos. It is neither haphazard nor reactionary; it follows a carefully crafted plan of development. It is not that the women just want to create a new market for their goods. The market is not the goal, but the means to expanding one's business, one's options, and one's opportunities.

Domingas's Story: From Rags to Riches

After speaking widi Leli, I grew increasingly curious about women, survival, and the intricacies of enterprise. At a UN program office for health and education, I spoke with Domingas, the only local woman on staff. Domingas exuded the same vibrant concern for her work and her people as Leli did. Both had seen the worst of war and poverty: Leli in the broken bodies left behind, Domingas in seven-day work weeks dedicated to broken families, communities, and economies.

"How do women and societies on the brink of existence make it?" I asked. It is one and the same thing, *she said with a smile.*

Women, Domingas explained, are the invisible center of gravity of the society. Gravity, because while men move more fluidly, women *are* families, in times when men are there and when they are not. As such, they forge the basic links of society: producing food, daily necessities, communal networks, market systems. Where families are centered, infrastructure, health, education, and trade emerge. Invisibly, because women's role in this is generally overlooked.

If women don't make it, families crumble and communities collapse. And perhaps, she added, economies collapse too; one could argue that the foundations of the economy spin out from here. "Let me give you an example" Domingas said:

No one starts out in this place with anything. Well, if you're a woman that's for sure. They start out below the bottom. They carry water for a penny. You see these poor, hungry women in rags carrying a beaten-up old bucket of water for someone, and you think, "There goes a person all of life has forgotten, a person who will live and die carrying that bucket."

But it is not so. She struggles down the road with a plan. When she scrapes together a few pennies, she will begin to make and sell charcoal.

Domingas grabbed a piece of paper and a pencil and began to draw on it. Her formal "professional in an interview with a stranger" demeanor relaxed into informality; she pushed up her shirt sleeves and hiked a foot up on the rung of her chair as she began to draw, and then stopped to chew thoughtfully on her pencil: "Did I," she wanted to know, "really want to understand the whole thing, the way the economy really worked?" She emphasized the word *really*. Her enthusiasm for her work, and her ideas, was contagious. I remember thinking even a stone would say yes to her question. She began her description, outlining it in a flow chart on paper as she explained it in words:

OK, here's the sequence:

1. You begin with carrying water, or some such hard labor.

2. And then move on to making a product to sell at a little "marketplace"—a patch of swept dirt by the roadside or a spot on the ground in the local open market. Maybe you go out and collect wood and make charcoal, or find food, herbal medicines, whatever, in the bush to sell.

3. You scrape together some few pennies. Enough to get by. Enough to join in a women's informal bank.

4. When your turn comes for the whole banking pot, you invest in a bit of farmland and begin harvesting produce to sell. Bananas, for example. Bananas open the door for you to actually make some money. You start selling in the local markets, reinvesting everything you can to grow. You check out what they are desperate for in the next country. In the places where the "tourist agencies" fly to. And you begin to plan for that trip.

5. You work the markets, trading and selling, bartering and speculating, to get the dollars to pay for that flight to the neighboring country. One hundred bucks per person per flight, 90 cents a kilo for cargo.

"You know the prices?" I asked.

You're missing the point if you ask this. Of course I know the prices. Everyone knows the prices. The bent-over woman in rags carrying that bucket of water knows the prices. This is where we live our lives. It is the stuff of survival.

6. And then you make the trip into the next country.

"Do you worry about visas, permits, taxes?"

Domingas seemed surprised by my question. The system was so well known that the question seemed irrelevant.

This has nothing to do with that kind of economy. This is informal. Daily life. It works because it is not formal. Entire infrastructures work on this.

7. In the neighboring country, you use the profits of your sales to buy what people need and will spend money for at home. Then you fly back home, sell, and continue the cycle, growing at each turn.

8. At some point, you begin to see real wealth. You build a decent house. You buy a car, hire a driver. You begin to put money into your community, provide jobs, develop the place. You give out goods for poor kids to sell in the streets so they can put together enough money at the end of the day to buy some food to eat. You care about schools and clinics for your kids. Your banking group really carries some weight now.

9. Your horizons expand, and you begin to make flights on commercial airlines to Europe to buy more expensive items to sell to those with real money in your community and country. Often, you bring back suitcases of goods and sell them out of your house.

10. And finally, you purchase a boutique and set up a formal business. You begin to pay some formal taxes. You invest in better education and social development for your country and your home region. But you don't give up your networks. You work them all. You send your children to private schools. And you make your own decisions: you have boyfriends, no husband. Like the Gov'nor's girlfriends who run their own businesses under his "protection."

OK, only the lucky make it all the way down this line, *Domingas added.* But people do. It is how we make the system work. How women make it.

Domingas leaned back in her chair and took a deep breath, saying she could use a cup of coffee. As we strolled over to the rustic kitchen in the UN office to make coffee, she confided that she didn't normally take time out of her demanding workday to talk to outsiders. "But this needs to be told." Like Leli, she cared deeply about finding solutions. While we were making coffee we ruminated over the process Domingas had just outlined. I asked her if it was only at the end of this, at point 10, that any of these transactions moved into the formal economy. "Of course," she replied. Points 1 through 9 are invisible to all formal economic reckoning.

Coffee in hand, we walked out to sit on the front stoop of the building. As we looked out over the town—the muddy dirt roads carrying nameless dreams, the women wrapped in bright African cloth hauling heavy burdens on their heads and in their hearts, the children trotting along at their sides—Domingas finished her explanation:

A huge economy forms the foundations of this country, and much of it runs along these lines—along what people call "informal." Consider: $250 billion of imports comes into this country through the informal economy yearly. Those are UN estimates. What does this say about determining economies? About the way people work? About the impact of women?

And the truth is, while the world talks about diamonds and oil, food and clothing are the real profits. These are where the biggest gains are. Remember: along that line of development from carrying water to a boutique, the leap in profits, the juncture where one can finally move from subsistence to capital ventures, is here—it is food and clothing that builds the houses, buys the cars, and launches the businesses.

Pictures of women who have stepped on land mines and lost limbs—women eking out a subsistence living by farming a small plot of land with a hoe and a crutch—are used worldwide to elicit outrage at perfidious weapons, sympathy for the victims, and money for the organizations helping them. The bananas, or charcoal, they sell constitute another stereotypic image of Africa: women on the margins of the economy offering a small homegrown harvest in neatly arranged piles on a mat in a local open-air market. Their earnings are counted up in single-digit figures; their impact left largely uncalculated because of indifference.

Why their stories, their earnings, their networks, and their contributions to development are not added up becomes an interesting question when we take the UN estimate that $250 billion in informal import earnings is made yearly in the country. The $1 million a day in unauthorized diamond earnings in this country pales in comparison. So too does the $1 billion a year lost from oil profits. Indeed, $250 billion rivals the entire GDPs of the countries of this region of the world.

It would seem the amputee women, and all the women working diligently to earn the money to support their families, are central to the economy. Where, then, are the margins?

And where do we place development? Illicit oil and diamond revenues can be easily channeled into foreign bank accounts and businesses, offering little to help this nation. But in the most basic sense, the work of these women is developing the country. Survival follows their footsteps; infrastructure settles in the imprints they make. They move food, clothing, household and industrial goods, and energy supplies. They set up local and international transport routes, and forge markets across borders and countries.

What they do may be deemed informal and even illegal. It is here that the very notion of "extra-state" becomes most interesting: it would seem that real profits, and real development, are to be found in the places economic analysts are not looking. Perhaps we don't look because we would have to reassess our most fundamental—and cherished—ideas about power, and about the morality and the legality of economics and development.

Critical Thinking

1. What is the mythology of land mines? What is the truth about them?

2. Why is it that many people's lives are not simply defined by whether or not there is peace?

3. What are some of the difficulties facing the amputees?

4. Discuss the importance of the "informal economy" and the self-run banking system of the women of Muleque.

5. How were the women able to "give lie" to the idea that humanitarian aid produces complacent and dependent populations?

6. Discuss the notion that women are the "invisible gravity" of society and its implications for society as a whole.

7. How must women really make the economy work for them, according to Domingas?

8. What is the value of the informal economy and where are the "real profits?" How does this compare with the illegal earnings in diamonds and oil?

9. Why are working women central to the economy? Why are economic analysts not looking there?

UNIT 6

Religion, Belief, and Ritual

Unit Selections

Learning Outcomes

After reading this Unit, you will be able to:

- Determine how we can best identify shamans and shamanic traditions apart from our own assumptions, stereotypes, desires, and expectations about them.

- Explain how beliefs about the supernatural contribute to a sense of personal security, individual responsibility, and social harmony.

- Describe the basic tenets of Islam and explain whether they really clash with Western values.

- Discuss how voodoo has become an important form of social control in rural Haiti.

- Discuss the role of rituals and taboos in our modern industrial society.

Student Website

www.mhhe.com/cls

Internet References

Anthropology Resources Page
www.usd.edu/anth
Apologetics Index
www.apologeticsindex.org/site/index-c
Magic and Religion
http://anthro.palomar.edu/religion/default.htm
Yahoo: Society and Culture: Death
http://dir.yahoo.com/Society_and_Culture/Death_and_Dying

The anthropological interest in religion, belief, and ritual is not concerned with the scientific validity of such phenomena but rather with the way in which people relate various concepts of the supernatural to their everyday lives. From this practical perspective, some anthropologists have found that some traditional spiritual healing is just as helpful in the treatment of illness, as is modern medicine; that voodoo is a form of social control (as in "The Secrets of Haiti's Living Dead"); and that mystical beliefs and rituals are not absent from the modern world. "Body Ritual among the Nacirema" reveals that even our daily routines have mystic overtones. In other words, the writings in this unit show religion, belief, and ritual in relationship to practical human affairs. The placing of belief systems in social context thus helps to not only counter popular stereotypes, but also serves to promote a greater understanding of and appreciation for other viewpoints (see "Understanding Islam").

Every society is composed of feeling, thinking, and acting human beings who, at one time or another, are either conforming to or altering the social order into which they were born. As described in "The Adaptive Value of Religious Ritual," religion is an ideological framework that gives special legitimacy and validity to human experience within any given sociocultural system. In this way, monogamy as a marriage form, or monarchy as a political form, ceases to be simply one of many alternative ways in which a society can be organized, but becomes, for the believer, the only legitimate way. Religion considers certain human values and activities as sacred and inviolable. It is this mythic function that helps explain the strong ideological attachments that some people have, regardless of the scientific merits of their points of view.

While, under some conditions, religion may in fact be "the opiate of the masses," under other conditions such a belief system may be a rallying point for social and economic protest.

© Royalty-Free/CORBIS

A contemporary example of the former might be the "Moonies" (members of the Unification Church founded by Sun Myung Moon), while a good example of the latter is the role of the Black Church in the American Civil Rights movement, along with the prominence of religious figures such as Martin Luther King Jr. and Jesse Jackson. A word of caution must be set forth concerning attempts to understand belief systems of other cultures. At times, the prevailing attitude seems to be, "What I believe in is religion, and what you believe in is superstition." While anthropologists generally do not subscribe to this view, some tend to explain such behavior as incomprehensible and impractical without considering its full meaning and function within its cultural context. The articles in this unit should serve as a strong warning concerning the pitfalls of that approach.

Shamanisms
Past and Present

DAVID KOZAK

For centuries, the exotic and romantic image and story line of the shaman as a religious virtuoso who takes magical, hallucinatory flights into the supernatural world, learning from or skirmishing with animal spirits and human ghosts, capturing and returning lost souls, and dwelling in a nether world of trance and ecstacy, has dominated both the scholarly and popular imaginations. The shaman has been perceived and represented as the prototypic, primordial religious practitioner who has direct contact with the supernatural, nonordinary realm of the phantasmic, a perception that has led to the widespread assumption that this is the central defining characteristic of this specialist. Along these lines, the shaman is viewed by some—in the past and in the present—as representative of a person who pursues an "authentic" religious experience and who consider shamanism as an "authentic" religious system when compared to various "inauthentic" institutionalized world religions. This often exotic and romantic image of shamans and shamanisms misrepresents or at least it misunderstands them. And importantly, if not ironically, to understand shamans and shamanisms we must look to ourselves and the stories we have told and continue to tell about them.

The study of shamans and shamanisms has been plagued with a number of conceptual problems. At root is the ethnographic-based difficulty in creating a satisfactory standardized definition. This is because, on the one hand, shamanisms are highly diverse, culturally and historically relative phenomena, encompassing a vast array of social behaviors and beliefs. On the other hand, it is possible to identify shared or perhaps core shamanic phenomena. Yet, to pin a tidy label and definition on what shamanism is, is to risk the social scientific sin of overly particularizing or generalizing a constellation of behaviors and beliefs. Another problem relates to how the shaman's psychological and phenomenological status has taken precedence in the literature. Central to this precedence is the interest in what is today called Altered States of Consciousness (ASC), the affective, inspirational, emotional, and ecstatic states experienced by many shamans. This emphasis is problematic because it largely ignores the very real problems of social history that place each shamanism in context and the individual culture history that drives the transformations that all individual shamanisms experience. While ASC is certainly important, it is debatable that it should be taken as an unproblematic feature of shamanisms. Finally, and related to the emphasis on ASC and shaman phenomenology, is that it has contributed to a line of self-help, self-actualization "New Age," neo-shamanism literature that often bears surprisingly little resemblance to what the ethnographic record tells us of indigenous forms of shamanism.

In this essay I propose to work backwards in that I will begin with a general discussion of the difficulties with the conflation of scholarly and popular writings and perceptions of shamanisms in the present. I then move toward providing a rough working definition and general description of shamanism. How anthropologists and other scholars explain shamanism is outlined prior to my offering three ethnographic (particularistic) case studies. I trust that the case-study approach that focuses on cultural particulars will demonstrate the difficulties inherent in defining the generalities of this subject matter. Moreover, my selection of case studies is intended to juxtapose the so-called "classical" Siberian shamanism with how colonialism, global capitalization, and Christian missionization have differentially affected Tohono O'odham and Putumayo shamanisms. This essay is not intended to be comprehensive—a perhaps impossible task. However, refer to Jane M. Atkinson and Joan B. Townsend for excellent literature reviews and discussions of the relevant issues.[1] Here I offer a more modest goal: to provide the reader a basis for exploring and learning more about this most important religious phenomenon.

The Stories We Tell

Shamans and shamanic traditions continue to captivate both the scholarly and popular consciousness. This captivation has run and continues to run the gamut of admiration to condemnation, acceptance to persecution, emulation to fear. While it may sound strange, shamans and shamanisms as we know them are in part the rhetorical inventions of the Western intellectual and popular cultural imaginations. Oftentimes the stories that outsiders to shamanic traditions tell about them are based less in empirical reality than in the storyteller's own assumptions, stereotypes, desires and expectations about what they themselves want from the exotic "other." The inaccuracies in these stories have less to do with cultural secrecy or of shamans intentionally misleading anthropologists than with the author's failure to appropriately document the phenomena. Perhaps such ill-informed storytelling is innocuous enough, but it is frequently the case that such storytelling serves political, cultural, social, "racial," even personal ends, from the usurping of sacred cultural traditions for personal needs at one end of a continuum to outright state-level political repression, domination, and oppression at the other end. Moreover, shamanism has served as a multivocal symbol for social, political, and religious purposes of the West. For instance, in the past, animistic religions were viewed by late nineteenth-century social evolutionists (e.g., E.B. Tylor, Sir James Frazer) as occupying an inferior or impoverished level of religious evolution and achievement, far behind the assumed superiority of monotheism found in the "civilized" West. Juxtaposed to this unfavorable view, shamanism is today frequently adopted by people who are unhappy with institutionalized and patriarchal Christianity. In the United States, the "New Age," neo-shamanism, and self-actualization movements make much use of shamanic (tribal) symbolism and ideas, taken largely out of context, in order to cobble together a personal religious belief system and ritual practice that satisfies the individual's needs. Whether historically or contemporarily, shamanism is often uncritically evoked as either impoverished as a pagan and archaic religious expression or exalted as the solution to contemporary human ecological, existential, and personal crises.

Anthropologists early recognized the importance of shamanism in human religious history and cultures and have formulated various explanations and interpretations. The explanatory and interpretive stories that anthropologists tell include evolutionary, functional, structural, psychological, Marxist, cultural, and political-economic strategies. And while the emphasis of shamanistic research has been on the shaman as healer, as bridge between this and other worlds, as individual, as an evolutionary type, a more recent trend has emerged with an emphasis on the role of the shaman and shamanisms as parts of larger political, historical, and economic contexts in the burgeoning global political economy. Various anthropologists have rightly criticized the emphasis that had been placed on such things as the distinctions made between the so-called "classical" shamans of Siberia and all others, the affective and hallucinatory states that shamans experience, the abnormal personality traits supposedly exhibited by individual shamans, and so on. The emphasis has also been on the universal characteristics shared by shamans and shamanistic systems. In response to the bulk of the literature, some anthropologists have gone so far as to say that "shamanism" is an invented and contentious category of disparate items, ripped out of context, artificially if artfully associated and all of it dreamed up in the West with little basis in reality.[2]

As indicated, anthropologists are not the only ones who find shamanisms of interest. In fact, the scholarly and the popular images merge with shamanism. Today there is a burgeoning popular, nonacademic and practitioner-based interest in shamans, and particularly in their altered states of consciousness, and ultimately in self-help and self-actualization as grounded frequently in Jungian psychology. And while the self-actualization approach is largely denigrated by anthropologists as opportunistic, superficial, and self-serving in its treatment of shamanism, it was originally anthropologists who promoted, if indirectly, the current popularity. It is reasonable to say that the current popular and self-help interest of the neo-shamanism, New Age, and self-actualization movements stem from the publications of anthropologists Carlos Casteñada, Ake Hultkrantz, and Michael Harner, and the religious historian Mircea Eliade.[3] There is a distinct romanticizing and exoticizing of shamanism in their publications which appeals to a consumer group who feels that their lives as members of Western industrial societies are vacuous and that institutional forms of religion are inauthentic. In this literature, whether stated implicitly or not, shamanism offers what is believed to be an authentic method for establishing a relation between the individual and the natural and supernatural worlds.

The overarching rhetorical strategy used by the aforementioned authors is what I call the "shaman-as-hero" archetype, as the striving, seeking, brave, self-assured individual (the image is usually male). With not a little irony, this shaman-as-hero is transformed by such speculations and interpretations into the quintessential laissez faire "self-made man," the rugged individualist-equivalent of the non-Western, "primitive" world. In other words, the shaman becomes imbued with the idealistic Western characteristics of hyper-individualism in order to better correspond to the lives of people who wish to use shamanism for their own psychic and spiritual needs, rather than for understanding the shaman on his or her own cultural terms. The shaman-as-hero archetype and hero rhetoric, as rugged individualist, thus become acceptable and appropriable. But in this process, the shaman becomes yet another commodity for consumer culture. Herein lies the crux of the storytelling quandary.

The shaman has been used to tell stories distinctly not of the shaman's making. Rather, the stories often tell as much if not more about the tellers of scholarly or popular culture stories. All such characterizations are deeply flawed as they neglect to account for the social context in which all shamans are a part. Shamanism is nothing, after all, if not a community-centered activity. What lacks in much of the literature on shamanisms is an appreciation for the social, political, historical, gendered, and economic contexts that shamans participate in. The struggles of shamans with other shamans, with other villagers, and with outside forces have significantly modified their cultures and religious practices. And the danger of representing the shaman as the rugged individual hero and archetype is that shamanism is trivialized, reduced to a caricature, and is literally eviscerated of its social meaning and context. This trivilization, of course, serves an important storytelling purpose: It affords outsiders easy access to the complex traditions of shamanism without forcing them to understand the intricacies of context or to become part of a community where shamanism is only a fraction of a much larger social and cultural whole. Importantly, it allows the storyteller's imagination to conjure and speculate freely; shamanism as aesthetics rather than science. But this is ideally not what the anthropological study of shamans and shamanisms is about. Rather, anthropologists wish to understand and perhaps partly explain some of the phenomena associated with this compelling and important social role and religious practice. Anthropological understanding is gained up close, through fieldwork observation and participation, through learning the language of the shaman's community, and distinctly not from a "safe" distance where insight derives from one's own imaginative flights of fancy or creative speculation.

Defining Shamanisms

Defining shamans and shamanisms is not an easy task. In fact, shamanism is truly many things to many people. For myself, I would prefer to avoid making categorical or definitional statements altogether. Yet it is reasonably possible to make a few general statements about shamans and shamanisms. Realize, however, that generalizations on this subject are tentative and any claim must be viewed and evaluated in the context of ethnographic data.

Let us begin by saying that a shaman is a ritualist who is able to divine, predict, and effect future outcomes, provide medical care, who is believed to have direct access to the supernatural, phantasmic realm, and who gains his or her powers and abilities by being tutored by spirits including deceased ancestors. Shamans are frequently skilled orators or singers. The social role of the shaman is often the only or one of only a few distinct social roles available in the culture. This general definition of the shaman shares characteristics with other ritualists known variously as medicine man, medium, spirit or faith healer, priest, oracle, witch doctor, among others.

Origins of shamanism. For many anthropologists today the origins of shamanism is a moot question because it must remain largely conjectural reconstruction and is ultimately unprovable. Despite this, hypothesizing and research continue. Siberian and Arctic shamanism is considered by some to be the original source and prototypic form of shamanism in the world. The word "shaman" was originally derived from the Tungus (a central Siberian tribe) word *saman,* with the English word shaman

being derived from the German noun *der schaman.* Others argue that Tungus shamanism was itself influenced by Buddhism. For this latter suggestion a linguistic affiliation has been explored with the Sanskrit word *sramana,* which translates as "one who practices austerities." Siberian origin also relates to the Bering Straights land bridge hypothesis which explains the peopling of the New World. This hypothesis is widely accepted by archaeologists and argues that the ancestors of today's Native Americans migrated from Northern Asia to North America, bringing their religious and shamanic practices with them. This diaspora hypothesis is based on linguistic and physiological data and partly on the similar, cross culturally shared shamanic practices which indicate a common heritage.[4]

Ancient rock art has produced some of the more intriguing sources of data and interpretation regarding the origins question. Several researchers suggest that some rock art styles are actually the renderings of the shaman's altered states of consciousness and of the shamanic cosmos dating to as long ago as 8,000 to 25,000 years. Rock art data suggesting paleolithic origins derive from Lascaux cave paintings in France, southern Africa, and the British Isles and are based on neurologically based entoptic phenomenon. Entoptic phenomena are those visual phenomena that people see while experiencing various altered states of consciousness, visual phenomena that are argued to follow distinctive pan-human patterns and forms. It is claimed that these visual forms and patterns were then chiseled or painted on stone and were used as sacred mnemonic and didactic devices. Moreover, it is argued that shamanistic power came to reside in the shaman's ability to control such altered states and visions and the creation of sacred images.[5]

While it is not possible to know the absolute origins of shamanism, interesting research and hypothesizing continue to be accomplished. The assumption that Siberian shamanism is prototypical and diffused outward, as with all origin theories, must be viewed with a healthy skepticism. The fact that cultures change, adapting and culling beliefs and practices, in myriad patterns, it becomes impossible to pinpoint the genesis of the shamanic science and art.

Where shamanisms are found. Shamans and shamanisms are found throughout North and South America, Siberia, parts of Asia, Polynesia, and Africa, virtually throughout the entire world. The ethnographic record reveals that shamanisms are related to a variety of levels of social structure. Gatherer-hunter, egalitarian populations like the San of southern Africa are the most likely to possess a shamanistic system. Yet, pastoralists like the Tungus of Siberia or the Somali of northeastern Africa and agriculturalists like the Pima of southern Arizona also have shamanic traditions. Recent studies of highly stratified, state-level systems of governing, as in Korea, have also documented the presence of shamanistic systems. Therefore, much of where we find shamanisms depends on how shamans are defined. Gatherer-hunter populations are largely egalitarian with minor status differentiation who subsist on a diet characterized by feast-and-famine food availability which radically fluctuates throughout the yearly cycle. The shaman's role in an often tenuous subsistence setting, for example, is that of mediator between his or her village and the environment where they live and the spirit forces that control food and water availability. The shaman divines to locate game animals and to diagnose and cure spirit sicknesses, soul loss, and sorcery malevolence. Spirit-caused sicknesses are frequently the result of human inattention to or disrespect for the spirit and natural worlds.

Shamanic cosmos. The cosmos is frequently, though not always, divided into a series of horizontally stacked layers, three or more. Humans occupy a middle earth level that is loosely demarcated by permeable boundaries by upper and lower spirit worlds. The upper and lower worlds are nonphysical in character and accessible only through spiritual means. The various levels are linked and readily accessible to shamans. The spirit worlds are sources of power for human benefit. A version of "balance" between these worlds is the desired state and it is the shaman whose job it is to maintain this balance. Imbalances are manifested in humans as illnesses, or in the lack of game animals, or in natural disasters. As in the human world, so too in the spirit world, there is an emphasis on reciprocity with the spirits who inhabit the supernatural realm. A shaman's job is to keep the spirits happy or at least mollified and fellow villagers healthy. The afterlife locality is conceived of as either an improved version of the human community or an ill-defined place. It is usually not a location of punishment or reward for a person's actions in life. The concept of sin seems to be absent. Spirits, including human ghosts or ancestors, may be malevolent, benevolent, both, or benign. In any case, spirits have a significant impact on the human community.

A shaman's training. Direct contact with spirits is a universal feature of the shaman's practice. A shaman's contact with spirits makes the power from the other nonearthly cosmos layers accessible to a larger community of people in the middle earth level. A shaman is taught this power by a spirit(s) and the teaching consists of learning songs, chants, speeches, ritual techniques, and in the construction and use of shaman's tools such as a drum or other musical instruments, clothing, smoke, feathers, rattles, and crystals. A shaman ideally uses this supernatural knowledge and power to aid his or her community members' health and well-being, although shamans are also able to use this power to harm other humans. Frequently, a shaman has the ability for soul flight, or at the very least the shaman is capable of making nocturnal journeys as guided by spirit tutelaries.

A shaman may inherit his or her abilities or be selected by spirits to accept this important social responsibility. A person may be approached by spirits as a child or at any time in one's life for that matter. Often, the selection occurs during an acute or trying period in a person's life such as psychological stress, physical illness, accident, or a "near death" experience. A person often has the choice of accepting or rejecting a spirit's advances, and the shaman role. If a person accepts a spirit's advances, the spirit(s) will tutor their pupil in the shamanic sciences during nocturnal dreams or in hallucinatory or trance-induced states. A shaman's training is a lifelong process and a shaman's abilities and effectiveness may wax and wane over a lifetime.

States of consciousness. The literature is crowded with discussions of the shaman's altered state of consciousness, Shamanic State of Consciousness (SSC), magic flight, trance, hallucinatory, inspirational, and ecstatic abilities. Made famous by Mircea Eliade, the shaman's ecstacy has come largely to define—as discussed above—much of what we think of as quintessentially shamanic. Altered states of consciousness are either induced with hallucinogenic plants, including fungi, or with nonhallucinogenic alcoholic drinks, tobacco smoke, hyperventilation, meditation, and rhythmic drumming. It is not the altered state per se that is important but rather the communication that the altered state facilitates between spirit-animal and shaman or shaman and the lost soul that he or she searches for. As mentioned above, the altered state is also a time when the shaman is tutored by spirits.

Sacramental actions. Blowing, sucking, singing, massaging, spitting, smudging, painting, chanting, touching, fanning, seeing, and sprinkling water, ashes, and corn meal are all sacramental actions used by shamans as taught to them by spirit tutelaries. By sacramental I mean how a shaman uses his soul, augmented by the soul(s) of his spirit helpers or tutelaries and tools (i.e., feathers, water, smoke, peyote, or other hallucinogens) to positively affect the soul of a patient and/or of an entire community. The sacramental act of blowing, for instance, may come in the form of singing songs to patients, reciting chants to spirits, or even of blowing cigarette smoke over a patient to illuminate embedded sickness or discover the location of sorcery objects. A sacrament's performative intent is to improve the living condition of a person or of a community through sacredly endowed actions: blessings made physically manifest for all to see. A shaman's sacramental actions are always for good; in comparison, sorcery could be classified as an antisacramental act.

Shamanic discourses. The verbalizations of shamans provide a rich avenue for understanding shamanism. Songs, chants, narratives, and verbal explanations given by shamans are ways to examine the internal and cultural dimensions and perceptions held by practitioners themselves. This area of research is perhaps the most challenging for an anthropologist as it demands the researcher to possess a firm grasp of the shaman's own language.[6] Text transcription and translation become central in this work and interpretations and explanations of a single or a few key words may be the foundation for an entire study. A rich corpus of song and chant texts has revealed the art of various shamanisms, but also the meaning and centrality of shamanic discourses in the work of healing or divining.

Empirical observations. Since the social evolutionist E.B. Tylor's time (late 1800s), some anthropologists have argued that religious beliefs and practices are ultimately based in people's systematic observations of the sentient world around them. Empirical observations of the physical world serve as a template for their ultimate conceptions of the soul, human body, the sacred, and the role of religious belief in human affairs. Furthermore, people are also astute observers of human-animal and human-plant interactions. As such, the empirical observations and experiments that people conduct in their natural world serve as the basis for their public and private religious lives.

Explaining Shamanisms

Anthropologists use various theoretical orientations to understand and explain the shamanism phenomenon. I will briefly discuss two general orientations: the psychological-physiological and the political-economic. This brief discussion lumps together general tendencies and the two theoretical categories could be divided in other ways.

Psychology and physiology. The belief that shamans are mentally ill, who suffer from neuroses, psychoses, or schizophrenia, has roots in the eighteenth century. During that time shamanic practices competed, if indirectly, with the ascendancy of rationalist principles being developed with the scientific revolution. At the time, inspirationally or mythically based ways of knowing were being systematically discredited as irrational and as nonsense. The shaman as crazy person penetrated well into the twentieth century with anthropologists such as A.L. Kroeber, Ralph Linton, and A.F.C. Wallace. These anthropologists, using one or another psychoanalytic theory, concluded that the shaman and potential shamans suffer from a number of severe mental or physical complaints. Kroeber went so far as to say that so-called primitive cultures not only condoned but exalted psychotic behavior, that the shaman's claim to see and deal with spirits was nothing other than a delusional psychopathology. The mental illness theory of the shaman persisted until the 1960s when counter-arguments mounted against this unfortunate interpretation. By the late 1960s shaman's behaviors were considered psychologically normal. And as Jane M. Atkinson has pointed out, the change of attitude that occurred in the 1960s toward shamanic psychology and behavior was affected by changing notions of consciousness in general spurred on by hallucinogenic-modified consciousness in particular and the effectiveness of shamanism as psychotherapy in general.[7]

The continued interest in the psychic states of shamans, anthropologists, and other behavioralist researchers, wishing to ground their work on a scientific footing, developed their research around the concept of altered states of consciousness or shamanic states of consciousness. The emphasis of this research is on the phenomenological experience of the practitioner, the cross-culturally shared trance-state characteristics, and more recently an interest in the neurophysiological bases of ASC. Of note in this regard are studies related to the role of endorphins and other chemicals released in the brain during rituals. More recently is an interest in what Michael Winkelman calls "neurognostic structures" of the psyche. He argues that shamanism is a biologically based transpersonal mode of consciousness.[8] It is suggested that the capacity for shamanic behavior—that is, trance and vision flights—is a biologically based memory device of sorts, a shamanistic

equivalent of a Chomskyan "deep structure" of linguistic ability or a Jungian "archetype" of collective consciousness, whereby shamanic behavior is a hard-wired and universal human characteristic and is evidenced in the similarities shared by shamans in vastly different cultures.

Politics, economics, and history. Complementing the biological- and psychological-based explanations for shamanism is a recent interest in the political, historical, and economic factors related to shamans, cultures with shamanic systems, and how these relate to state-level and global capitalist structures of power and institutionalized religions. This interest area reflects a general trend in anthropology that emphasizes historical and political economic factors.

Foremost in this approach is an appreciation for how shamanisms have been affected by various state, economic, and institutionalized religious structures. Due to the impacts of colonialism and neo-colonialism, the historical and political economic approach takes for granted that much of what we know of as shamanism today is the result of contact and change initiated by institutions stemming from the West. The implication is that to understand shamanism we must also understand how the structures of power have been manifested at the local level. Thus, much of the published work stemming from this general orientation takes change as inevitable, that shamanic-oriented cultures have been victimized, and that the search for pristine and "authentic" versions of shamanisms is fallacious and naïve. In response to the psychological-physiological approaches, to understand shaman psychology, ASC, and ritual actions, the researcher must be rigorous in defining the social, political, and economic context(s) in which individual shamanisms are expressed. Thus, this general approach emphasizes the social rather than the individual, the historical rather than the immediate, the cultural rather than the psychological, and the relations of power rather than altered states.[9]

The primary drawback to this general political economy orientation is that it may sacrifice the richness of local-level interpretations and individualistic articulations for its emphasis on structure, history, and power relations. Real people are often lost in a maze of political and economic and historic factors that seemingly override the agency of individual actors.

In sum, the theories that anthropologists use to explain or interpret shamanisms are of necessity incomplete. This is because human experience is far more complex and rich than our abstractions of it. Thus, our theories are ways to assist our comprehension of a culturally rich realm of humanness and each theory tends to privilege partial elements of that richness.

Three Case Studies

Ethnographic description, the product of intensive fieldwork conducted by an anthropologist who lives for an extended time with the people being studied, is crucial to the work of sociocultural anthropologists. The ethnographic method is perhaps the superior way for understanding shamanisms and it also offers the potential for a critical appraisal and reevaluation of past storytelling inaccuracies and excesses regarding the study of shamanisms around the world. Because the fieldwork experience demands that the anthropologist live among and participate in the subject's community life and have a familiarity with the host culture's language, the anthropological perspective holds out promise for a nuanced understanding and documentation to be found in this religious-medicinal practice. It is also a valuable source for critiquing the frequently problematic categories, analyses, and assumptions made by outside observers of shamanic phenomena. To illustrate this point and present a fragment of the diversity of shamanisms found in the world today, and to demonstrate its range of applicability, I here offer three case studies of shamanism in Northern Asia, North America, and South America. The case studies reveal that shamanisms are a complex interweaving of cultural practices, gifted individual practitioners, political economic issues, and ASC. They reveal how shamanisms change, how they are influenced by the institutionalized religions like Christianity, and by global capitalism and social change. Each case study demonstrates in its own way how the category of a generalized shamanism is a theoretical oversimplification at best and that shamanisms undergo change and modification to fit the needs of a people.

Siberian Shamanisms

Siberian shamanism is often referred to as the "classical" form that used to exist. Mircea Eliade made Siberian shamanism famous and identified it by their exotic and mystical rituals and costumes, hallucinations, trances, the mastering of spirits, and cosmic travels. Since Eliade's work, many shamanisms have been evaluated and compared with it. As Caroline Humphrey[10] has pointed out, Eliade's characterization is seriously flawed as it lacks social and historical context. Moreover, she criticizes Eliade's representations for effectively crystallizing the current belief in the context-free view of shamanism as a mysterious and purely inspirational phenomenon. In order to offer a context to Siberian shamanism I draw extensively from the research of Roberte Hamayon.[11]

According to Hamayon there are two primary types of Siberian shamanism: hunting and pastoral. Each corresponds to distinct social organizational forms, economic, and political characteristics. Siberian "hunting shamanism" is present in tribal, noncentralized, forest-dwelling societies like the Chugchee. Hunting shamanism is characteristic of the form Eliade spoke of in his writings. "Pastoral shamanism" as found among the Tungus is characterized by people who are patrilineal and patrilocal, who domesticate livestock, and live in regions that border the forest and steppe regions. A potential third type, what Hamayon calls "peripheral shamanism," is only marginally identifiable as shamanism as it is related to state formation and how the traditional shaman's

role and power were usurped by Lamaist Buddhist lamas and through the decentralization and feminization of the shaman's role in Siberian shamanic societies. With state formation, institutional religion gains power and pushes traditional inspirational religious practices and beliefs to the margins of society where women may become shamans as men become Buddhist lamas. In many ways state or institutionalized religion delegitimizes shamanism.

The fundamental element of "hunting shamanism" is that spirits of animal species are contacted directly by a shaman who makes compacts with them in order to supply humans with good luck at hunting. The divinely inspired and experienced shaman-spirit compacts assure food availability for human consumption. This compact is not conceived as one-sided in that while animal spirits supply humans with food through hunting successes, the other half of the compact is that humans will eventually supply the spirits with human flesh and blood. Such is the source and cause of much human sickness and death. The task, however, is for the shaman to limit the amount of human sickness and death while maximizing the amount of animal flesh available for human consumption. A shaman's success at this depends on another kind of compact: that of his ritual marriage to the daughter of the game spirit (an elk or reindeer spirit).

The exchanges and compacts established between spirit-animals and humans make them trading partners in an ongoing economic and social relationship. The relationship is a form of generalized reciprocity where the exchanges are never equally balanced and immediate in return. Rather, delayed and nonequivalent exchanges keep the relationship alive and in need of continual tinkering by the shaman and spirit(s). To balance out their reciprocity would mean an end to their relationship. Thus, a shaman's power resides in his ability to maintain this reciprocity. His authority in the human community, therefore, stems from his usefulness to his peers, in the shaman's ability to secure a plentiful supply of game animals while minimizing sickness and death.

The human-animal compacts—of food and marriage—serve as the model of social organization. The dualistic spirit-human relationship is replicated in human-animal relations and in the human kinship system of moieties or clan subdivisions. Here, too, in the human world of marriage alliances, society is predicated on compacts between moieties just as the shaman makes compacts with the animal-spirit world.

Reliance on the domestication of animals (pastoralism) presents a second type of Siberian shamanism and is related to alterations in inheritance patterns which are linked to changes in social organization which is in turn linked to a transformation in conceptions of the supernatural. With "pastoral shamanism," no longer does food flow directly from compacts made in the supernatural world but it instead derives from various locations in the observable environment where grazing and herding occur. For the Tungus, pasturage is associated with patrilineal descent groups (in this case, clan segments), and nearby mountains become the locations where ancestors reside after death. Patrilocal residence becomes important and land or pasture inheritance follows the male line. Sickness is no longer caused by animal spirits but is associated with transgressions of patrilineal kinship rules and by one's ancestral spirits. Pastoral shamans do not make compacts with spirit animals, nor do they ritually marry the daughter of the game spirit as food comes from other sources. Here the shaman's role changes in that it is entrusted with ensuring the fertility of both the domesticated animals and human villagers. Pastoralist shamans are related to tribal mythology where the shaman is synonymous with the tribal founder.

Here we see that even the classic Siberian shamanism takes several forms. Importantly, the forms are related to the mode of subsistence, social organization, residence patterns, and whether the shaman has intimate contact with animal spirits or deceased ancestor spirits who participate with the shaman in ongoing reciprocal exchanges.

Tohono O'odham Christian-Shamanism

The Tohono O'odham (formerly known as Papago) of southern Arizona and northern Sonora, Mexico, were gatherer-hunters and horticulturalists until the early part of the twentieth century.[12] This form of shamanism is comparable to the hunting shamanism of Siberia. Their subsistence strategy made the best of an existence in the heart of the Sonoran Desert where scarce and unpredictable rainfall made growing corn, beans, and squash very tenuous. Despite this, O'odham subsistence practices emphasized the importance of rain and crop production. In fact, O'odham ritual life—both individual and public—centered around moisture. The public ritual of the annual rain ceremony focused the community's religious sentiments on securing adequate moisture for plant, animal, and human consumption.

Village well-being was symbolized by sufficient rainfall, and the village shaman was in part responsible for securing it. Shamans worked together to sing for, divine, and encourage the rains to fall. They directed the annual rain festivities by overseeing the production of a mildly intoxicating wine brewed from the syrup of saguaro cactus fruits. During the rain dance ceremony, shamans from various villages gave speeches and sang songs to attract the rain clouds from the "rain houses" positioned at the cardinal directions. The proper execution of the ceremony secured the ultimate fertility of the natural and human worlds.

The other central role of O'odham shamans was to diagnose a series of sicknesses unique to the O'odham people. Until the middle of the twentieth century it was thought in O'odham cosmology and medical theory that there were approximately 50 "staying sicknesses" (only O'odham contract them) that were caused by the spirit protectors of various animal-persons (e.g., deer, badger, coyote), insect-persons (e.g., fly, butterfly), natural phenomena-persons (e.g., wind, lightning), humans (e.g., ghosts, prostitutes),

plant-persons (e.g., peyote, jimson weed), reptile-persons (e.g., rattle snake, chuckwalla), and bird-persons (e.g., eagle, owl, swallow) species. Being sickened is the result of a human's impropriety or disrespect toward or transgression on the integrity of the spirit species. The person does not know the moment that sickness is contracted, but once symptoms emerge, the person consults a shaman for diagnosis. Once diagnosed, which can take a quick or a protracted form, the person is instructed to have the appropriate curing songs sung for them.

A shaman's ability to diagnose, and to cure, derives from spirit helpers who tutor the shaman during nighttime dreams. Thus spirits both cause sicknesses and provide the means for their cure. This tutoring takes the form of learning songs that are authored and sung by the spirit species to the shaman who memorizes them verbatim. The songs are densely meaningful, haiku-like poems that tell brief stories of experiences that the shaman has had with the spirit, present images of a landscape, or are statements about the quirkiness of the spirit itself.

This version of O'odham shamanism has been modified during the past three hundred years of contact with Spanish, then Mexican, and finally with American colonizers and Catholic missionaries. Catholicism has made significant inroads in O'odham religious culture since their early contact with the Jesuit priest Eusebio Kino in the late 1690s. Catholicism continues to be a strong element of O'odham identity. Another significant source of change came with the introduction of cattle into the U.S. Southwest regional economy. The external influences of Catholicism and cattle capitalism prompted changes in O'odham shamanism in several ways. First, shamans gained power from Christian deities as spirit tutelaries, primarily the saints, but Jesus and God also, just as they did from the traditional spirit-beings. As the O'odham adopted Catholic public rituals and theological beliefs, and as they began to adopt saints for village patrons and for individuals, people began to be sickened by these Christian spirits in a manner similar to that described above. Saint sickness became an illness diagnosed and treated by shamans.

Second, the O'odham also began, by the late 1880s, to be sickened by the instruments of frontier capitalism—cattle and horses (known collectively as devil sickness). O'odham readily adopted a cowboy lifestyle and are still cattle ranchers to this day. Here too O'odham shamans became charged with the responsibility of contending with the new contagions. Today, devil sickness is thought by some O'odham to be the most commonly diagnosed staying sickness.

Saint and devil sicknesses in the O'odham theory of sickness and cure represent what I call Christian-shamanism. Not only do shamans continue to use the traditional tools of tobacco smoke, eagle and owl feathers, and crystals to augment their power in diagnostic sessions, but many shamans also use saints' images, a Christian cross, and holy water. Perhaps more telling is the fact that the Christian deities (spirits) also come to shamans in the same manner as the traditional spirits—in dreams, singing and tutoring their human pupils in the diagnostic healing art and science.

Christian-shamanism can be understood as a manifestation of significant political, religious, and economic changes that affected this culture. For the O'odham, shamanism has been effectively used to attend to and ameliorate the changes conceived in the three-hundred-year plus period of colonization and missionization. Some might conclude that the O'odham shamanic system as described has been "corrupted" or "polluted" by the Christian influence. I do not think so, nor do I think that most O'odham think so either. In many ways, the O'odham are merely using all that is available to them to make their lives better and healthier.

Shamanism, Terror, and the Putumayo of Colombia

By the turn of the twentieth century, in the industrializing West, the demand for rubber expanded quickly. Far from the crowded cities of London, Los Angeles, Chicago, and Paris, the Putumayo Indians of the sparsely populated lowland Amazonian jungles of southern Colombia were being forcibly incorporated into the Industrial Revolution as rubber tree tappers. This incorporation was often violent and terrifying. To coerce work out of this recalcitrant labor force, the Putumayo Indians were subjected to systematic torture, murder, and sexual abuses. This troubling period in Putumayo and Colombian social history continues to haunt and permeate the present in the form of *mal aire* (evil wind)[13] and in the shamanistic beliefs and practices that heal it. Current shamanic practice can be partly understood as an attempt to ameliorate the unquiet souls of the violently tortured and murdered Putumayo Indians of the southern Amazon jungle.[14]

Michael Taussig argues in his provocative book *Shamanism, Colonialism, and the Wild Man* that contemporary *yagé* (a hallucinogenic drink) shamanism in southern Colombia is an effort to heal the tortured memories of the violently killed Putumayo Indians. Sorcery and evil air are the two sicknesses that shamans currently treat. It is the latter that stems directly from rubber tapping and Christianization. Currently, both Indians and non-Indians of the region view the ancient ones, called the Huitoto (ancestral Putumayo), as sorcerers, demonic, and evil. Huitoto means "the people from below"— below the ground and below in the jungles. They were the people conquered during the Spanish conquest, people who were labeled and viewed by Europeans as evil, devil worshipping idolaters since Spanish times. The ideology of the Spanish was that they were violent, sorcerers, cannibals, and thus fearsome. This ideologically charged characterization persisted until the time of rubber exploration and production. The image of the savage other and of the wild, primordial jungles struck fear in the hearts of the rubber plantation managers. The managers saw Indian conspiracies and treachery everywhere. In their zeal to extract rubber and labor, company managers hired and trained gangs to carry out retribution stemming from their fears of the "savage" Putumayo. Rumors of the atrocities committed by the rubber companies led to an investigation and the eventual publication of Sir Roger Casement's revealing report in 1912 which substantiated the rumors' veracity.

The violent memories created in the colonial, and later the capitalist, contexts revisioned the shamanism of the region. Sickness was now thought to be caused by the evil airs emanating from below in the jungles, from the rotting evil ancestors (savages) buried beneath the ground. This miasmatic theory is perpetuated by locals, native and nonnative alike.

In this context, according to Taussig, Putumayo shamanism is above all else a healing of history, a healing of the excesses of Christian ideology and capitalist extraction. It is as if the former set the stage for the latter. Hence, for the Putumayo, shamanism is the method through which people attend to the horrific memories embedded in the history of the region. It is as if it is history-as-sorcery that today's Putumayo shamans strive to cure.

The three examples come nowhere near exhausting the possible ethnographic variation that continues to exist in the world today. Research into questions of history, global economy, and exploitation add to an already rich anthropological literature on the shaman's ASC, personality, and phenomenological characteristics. It is through a continued documentation of local expressions of shamanism, juxtaposed to macrolevel processes, that our understanding will be improved in this most dynamic arena of human spirituality.

Conclusion

The interest and study of shamanism has a long and often checkered history. Shamanism storytellings are varied and continue to be tightly bound to the defining culture's attitude toward indigenous peoples and their cultural practices. In the 1990s shamanisms have not only been tolerated but they have also been exulted as the true, authentic religious expression worthy of emulation. As discussed, this admiration has not always been the preferred story. Yet, this admiration, while meant with the best of intentions, must also be seen as potentially problematic, as it is yet another way people use shamanism in other than their intended contexts. And whether shamanisms are exalted or denigrated, both are equally stereotypic responses. It is my suspicion that shamans and shamanisms will continue to serve the rhetorical needs of members of Western or other dominant societies. It appears that the need for people to tell stories about other people remains strong. It also appears to matter not that the stories are only loosely, at best, based in empirical reality. And as I began this essay, it is important to remember that the stories we tell about others may say more about ourselves than about those of whom we supposedly tell the stories.

Notes

1. The combined reviews of Jane Monnig Atkinson, "Shamanisms Today," *Annual Review of Anthropology* 21:307–330, 1992, and Joan B. Townsend, "Shamanism," in Stephan Glazier, ed., *Anthropology of Religion: A Handbook* (Westport, CT: Greenwood Press, 1997), offer a wide-ranging and thorough overview of the subjects. One book by religious studies scholar Margaret Stutley, *Shamanism: An Introduction* (London: Routledge, 2003) provides general descriptive materials of shamanism throughout the world.

2. Perhaps most strident in this regard is Michael Taussig, who argues in "The Nervous System: Homesickness and Dada," *Stanford Humanities Review* 1(1):44–81, 1989, that shamanism is a "made-up," "artful reification of disparate practices" that are the creations of academic programs such as religious studies and anthropology. Much earlier, Clifford Geertz in "Religion as a Cultural System," in Michael Banton, ed., *Anthropological Approaches to the Study of Religion* (London: Tavistock, 1966), came to the same conclusion as Taussig. What Taussig and Geertz criticize are the overly large generalizations and characterizations that anthropologists and others have made of shamanisms, and, particularly for Taussig, how such characterizations reflect Western notions of religiosity. More recently, anthropologist Alice Kehoe takes up this critical stance in *Shamans and Religion: An Anthropological Exploration in Critical Thinking* (Prospect Heights, IL: Waveland Press, 2000).

3. Among the most influential of both anthropology and popular interest in shamanism are Eliade's *Shamanism: Archaic Techniques of Ecstacy* (Princeton, NJ: Princeton University Press, 1964); Casteñada's *The Teachings of Don Juan: A Yaqui Way of Knowledge* (New York: Ballantine Books, 1968); Harner's *Hallucinogens and Shamanism* (Oxford: Oxford University Press, 1973); and Hultkrantz's various articles on the subject: "An Ecological Approach to Religion," *Ethos* 31:131–150, 1966; "Spirit Lodge: A North American Shamanistic Seance," in Carl-Martin Edsman, ed., *Studies in Shamanism* (Stockholm: Almqvist and Wiksell, 1967); and "A Definition of Shamanism," *Temenos* 9:25–37, 1973. Of these works, it is perhaps the first two that have had the longest and most profound impact on shamanic studies in general and popular consciousness in particular.

4. Alice Kehoe in "Primal Gaia," in J. Clifton, ed., *The Invented Indian* (Somerset, NJ: Transaction Press, 1990); Michael Winkelman in "Shamans and Other 'Magico-Religious' Healers," *Ethos* 18(3):308–352, 1990; Ake Hultkrantz in "Ecological and Phenomenological Aspects of Shamanism, in L. Backman and A. Hultkrantz, eds. *Studies in Lapp Shamanism* (Stockholm: Almquivst and Wiksell, 1978); J.D. Lewis-Williams and T. Dowson in "The Signs of All Times," *Current Anthropology* 29(2):201–245, 1988; and Peter Furst in "The Roots and Continuities of Shamanism," in A. Brodzky, R. Daneswich, and N. Johnson, eds., *Stones, Bones, and Skin* (Toronto: Society for Art Publications, 1977), offer various perspectives of the paleolithic origins question. In general, origins are traced to the Siberian and Arctic shamanisms and are considered the "classic" form. Yet others such as Sergei Shirokogoroff in *Psychomental Complex of the Tungus* (London: Kegan Paul, Trench, Trubner and Company, 1935) and Mircea Eliade in *Shamanism: Archaic Techniques of Ecstacy* (Princeton, NJ: Princeton University Press, 1964), postulate that Buddhist Lamaism drastically modified Tungus shamanism. Thus, one version of origins suggests that shamanisms have a Tibetan source.

5. J.D. Lewis-Williams's name is synonymous with the work on entoptic phenomena. His works *Believing and Seeing* (New York: Academic Press, 1981) and "Cognitive and Optical Illusions in San Rock Art," *Current Anthropology* 27:171–178,

1986 are exemplary in this regard. See also his collaboration with T.A. Dowson, "The Signs of All Times," 1988, and "On Vision and Power in the Neolithic," *Current Anthropology* 34:55–65, 1993.

6. *Piman Shamanism and Staying Sickness* by Donald Bahr, Juan Gregorio, David Lopez, and Albert Alvarez (Tucson: University of Arizona Press, 1974) stands out as one of the first and is still one of the finest discussions between a shaman, Gregorio, an anthropologist, Donald Bahr, and two native speaker-translators, Lopez and Alvarez. Bahr has also written on shamanic song texts in "A Grey and Fervent Shamanism," *Journal of the Society of the Americas,* 67:7–26, 1991. Other collaborative and innovative work has been completed by Larry Evers and Felipe Molina in *Yaqui Deer Songs* (Tucson: University of Arizona Press, 1987), Jane Monnig Atkinson's *Wana Shamanship* (Berkeley: University of California Press, 1989), Anna Siikala's "Two Types of Shamanizing and Categories of Shamanistic Songs," in L. Honko and V. Voigt, eds., *Akademiai Kiado* (Budapest, 1980), and in B. Walraven's *Muga: The Songs of Korean Shamanism* (Dordredt: ICG Printing, 1985). A general beautifully illustrated guide to Native American Indian shamanism is Norman Bancroft Hunt, *Shamanism in North America* (Buffalo, NY: Firefly Books, 2003).

7. For arguments against the mentally ill shaman stereotype, see Alfred Kroeber, *The Nature of Culture* (Chicago: University of Chicago Press, 1952); L.B. Boyer, "Shamans: To Set the Record Straight," *American Anthropologist* 71(2):307–309, 1969; D. Handelman, "Shamanizing on an Empty Stomach," *American Anthropologist* 70(2):353–356, 1968; and George Murdock, "Tenino Shamanism," *Ethnology* 4:165–171, 1965, among others.

8. The desire to empirically ground the study of shamanic consciousness has led to this interesting version of a biopsychological approach. For a general discussion of this hypothesis, see C. Laughlin, J. McManus, and E. d'Aquili, *Brain, Symbol and Experience: Toward a Neurophenomenology of Consciousness* (New York: Columbia University Press, 1992) and Michael Winkelman, "Trance States: A Theoretical Model and Cross-Cultural Analysis," *Ethos* 14(2):174–203, 1986, and "Altered States of Consciousness and Religious Behavior," in S. Glazier, ed., *Anthropology of Religion* (Westport, CT: Greenwood Press, 1997).

9. A few recent examples of this work include Michael Taussig's *Shamanism, Colonialism, and the Wild Man* (Chicago: University of Chicago Press, 1987); N. Thomas and C. Humphrey's edited volume *Shamanism, History, and the State* (Ann Arbor: University of Michigan Press, 1994); and Atkinson's book cited in Endnote 6.

10. Refer to C. Humphrey's "Shamanic Practices and the State in Northern Asia," in Nicholas Thomas and Carolyn Humphrey, eds., *Shamanism, History and the State* (Ann Arbor: University of Michigan Press, 1994).

11. This section on Siberian shamanism draws heavily from the two works of R. Hamayon: *La Chasse à l'âme: Esquisse d'une Theorie du Chamanisme Siberien* (Société d'ethnologie Nanterre, 1990) and "Shamanism in Siberia," in N. Thomas and C. Humphrey, eds., *Shamanism, History, and the State* (Ann Arbor: University of Michigan Press, 1994). Her research and writing are exemplary for placing shamanism into a nuanced format rather than reifying much of what is assumed to be true about Siberian shamanism. See also Caroline Humphrey's, "Shamanic Practices and the State in Northern Asia," in N. Thomas and C. Humphrey, eds., *Shamanism, History, and the State* (Ann Arbor: University of Michigan Press, 1994).

12. This section on Tohono O'odham shamanism is based on my own research in various communities on the Sells Reservation

and on several published monographs. See Ruth Underhill's classic, *Papago Indian Religion* (New York: Columbia University Press, 1946) and the collaborative work *Piman Shamanism and Staying Sickness* by Donald Bahr, Juan Gregorio, David Lopez, and Albert Alvarez (Tucson: University of Arizona Press, 1974). For a detailed treatment of a single staying sickness, see my *Devil Sickness and Devil Songs: Tohono O'odham Poetics* (Washington, DC: Smithsonian Institution Press, 1999).

13. Mal aire is a widespread "folk" illness found throughout parts of North and South America as well as in parts of Europe. Evil air sickness in the New World is thought by most observers to be an import from the Old World.

14. This case study relies on the intriguing and ingenious work of M. Taussig, "History as Sorcery," *Representations* 7:87–109, 1984, and *Shamanism, Colonialism, and the Wild Man* (Chicago: University of Chicago Press, 1987).

Critical Thinking

1. What are the conceptual problems that have plagued the study of shamans and shamanism?

2. To what ends has the inaccurate "storytelling" about shamanism been used in the past?

3. In what sense have the scholarly and the popular images of shamanism merged?

4. How does the author explain the "shaman-as-hero" archetype?

5. In what sense are all such characterizations "deeply flawed?" Explain.

6. What is the danger of such trivialization? How does this contradict what the anthropological study of shamanism is all about?

7. How does the author define shamanism?

8. What have been the most prominent hypotheses about the origins of shamanism? Why must this remain speculative?

9. Where are shamanisms found?

10. Describe the "shamanic cosmos."

11. How do shamans typically acquire their ability to contact the spirit world?

12. How does the author characterize the sacramental actions of the shaman?

13. Why were shamans characterized as mentally ill until recently? How and why did this view change?

14. How does the author describe and explain the differences between "hunting shamanism" and "pastoral shamanism" in Siberia?

15. What was the role of shamans among the gatherer-hunters and horticulturalist Tohono O'odham people? What is "Christians-hamanism?"

16. In what sense does Putumayo shamanism represent a "healing of history?"

17. Why is it that "the stories we tell about others may say more about ourselves?"

The Adaptive Value of Religious Ritual

Rituals promote group cohesion by requiring members to engage in behavior that is too costly to fake.

RICHARD SOSIS

I was 15 years old the first time I went to Jerusalem's Old City and visited the 2,000-year-old remains of the Second Temple, known as the Western Wall. It may have foreshadowed my future life as an anthropologist, but on my first glimpse of the ancient stones I was more taken by the people standing at the foot of the structure than by the wall itself. Women stood in the open sun, facing the Wall in solemn worship, wearing long-sleeved shirts, head coverings and heavy skirts that scraped the ground. Men in their thick beards, long black coats and fur hats also seemed oblivious to the summer heat as they swayed fervently and sang praises to God. I turned to a friend, "Why would anyone in their right mind dress for a New England winter only to spend the afternoon praying in the desert heat?" At the time I thought there was no rational explanation and decided that my fellow religious brethren might well be mad.

Of course, "strange" behavior is not unique to ultraorthodox Jews. Many religious acts appear peculiar to the outsider. Pious adherents the world over physically differentiate themselves from others: Moonies shave their heads, Jain monks of India wear contraptions on their heads and feet to avoid killing insects, and clergy almost everywhere dress in outfits that distinguish them from the rest of society. Many peoples also engage in some form of surgical alteration. Australian aborigines perform a ritual operation on adolescent boys in which a bone or a stone is inserted into the penis through an incision in the urethra. Jews and Muslims submit their sons to circumcision, and in some Muslim societies daughters are also subject to circumcision or other forms of genital mutilation. Groups as diverse as the Nuer of Sudan and the Iatmul of New Guinea force their adolescents to undergo ritual scarification. Initiation ceremonies, otherwise known as rites of passage, are often brutal. Among Native Americans, Apache boys were forced to bathe in icy water, Luiseno initiates were required to lie motionless while being bitten by hordes of ants, and Tukuna girls had their hair plucked out.

How can we begin to understand such behavior? If human beings are rational creatures, then why do we spend so much time, energy and resources on acts that can be so painful or, at the very least, uncomfortable? Archaeologists tell us that our species has engaged in ritual behavior for at least 100,000 years, and every known culture practices some form of religion. It even survives covertly in those cultures where governments have attempted to eliminate spiritual practices. And, despite the unparalleled triumph of scientific rationalism in the 20th century, religion continued to flourish. In the United States a steady 40 percent of the population attended church regularly throughout the century. A belief in God (about 96 percent), the afterlife (about 72 percent), heaven (about 72 percent) and hell (about 58 percent) remained substantial and remarkably constant. Why do religious beliefs, practices and institutions continue to be an essential component of human social life?

Such questions have intrigued me for years. Initially my training in anthropology did not provide an answer. Indeed, my studies only increased my bewilderment. I received my training in a subfield known as human behavioral ecology, which studies the adaptive design of behavior with attention to its ecological setting. Behavioral ecologists assume that natural selection has shaped the human nervous system to respond successfully to varying ecological circumstances. All organisms must balance trade-offs: Time spent doing one thing prevents them from pursuing other activities that can enhance their survival or reproductive success. Animals that maximize the rate at which they acquire resources, such as food and mates, can maximize the number of descendants, which is exactly what the game of natural selection is all about.

Behavioral ecologists assume that natural selection has designed our decision-making mechanisms to optimize the rate at which human beings accrue resources under diverse ecological conditions—a basic prediction of *optimal foraging theory*. Optimality models offer predictions of the "perfectly adapted" behavioral response, given a set of environmental constraints. Of course, a perfect fit with the environment is almost never achieved because organisms rarely have perfect information and because environments are always changing. Nevertheless, this assumption has provided a powerful framework to analyze a variety of decisions, and most research (largely conducted among foraging populations) has shown that our species broadly conforms to these expectations.

If our species is designed to optimize the rate at which we extract energy from the environment, why would we engage in religious behavior that seems so counterproductive? Indeed, some religious practices, such as ritual sacrifices, are a conspicuous display of wasted resources. Anthropologists can explain why foragers regularly share their food with others in the group, but why would anyone share their food with a dead ancestor by burning it to ashes on an altar? A common response to this question is that people believe in the efficacy of the rituals and the tenets of the faith that give meaning to the ceremonies. But this response merely begs the question. We must really ask why natural selection has favored a psychology that believes in the supernatural and engages in the costly manifestations of those beliefs.

Ritual Sacrifice

Behavioral ecologists have only recently begun to consider the curiosities of religious activities, so at first I had to search other disciplines to understand these practices. The scholarly literature suggested that I wasn't the only one who believed that intense religious behavior was a sign of madness. Some of the greatest minds of the past two centuries, such as Marx and Freud, supported my thesis. And the early anthropological theorists also held that spiritual beliefs were indicative of a primitive and simple mind. In the 19th century, Edward B. Tylor, often noted as one of the founding fathers of anthropology, maintained that religion arose out of a misunderstanding among "primitives" that dreams are real. He argued that dreams about deceased ancestors might have led the primitives to believe that spirits can survive death.

Eventually the discipline of anthropology matured, and its practitioners moved beyond the equation that "primitive equals irrational." Instead, they began to seek functional explanations of religion. Most prominent among these early 20th-century theorists was the Polish-born anthropologist Bronislaw Malinowski. He argued that religion arose out of "the real tragedies of human life, out of the conflict between human plans and realities." Although religion may serve to allay our fears of death, and provide comfort from our incessant search for answers, Malinowski's thesis did not seem to explain the origin of rituals. Standing in the midday desert sun in several layers of black clothing seems more like a recipe for increasing anxiety than treating it. The classical anthropologists didn't have the right answers to my questions. I needed to look elsewhere.

Fortunately, a new generation of anthropologists has begun to provide some explanations. It turns out that the strangeness of religious practices and their inherent costs are actually the critical features that contribute to the success of religion as a universal cultural strategy and why natural selection has favored such behavior in the human lineage. To understand this unexpected benefit we need to recognize the adaptive problem that ritual behavior solves. William Irons, a behavioral ecologist at Northwestern University, has suggested that the universal dilemma is the promotion of cooperation within a community. Irons argues that the primary adaptive benefit of religion is its ability to facilitate cooperation within a group—while hunting, sharing food, defending against attacks and waging war—all critical activities in our evolutionary history. But, as Irons points out, although everyone is better off if everybody cooperates, this ideal is often very difficult to coordinate and achieve. The problem is that an individual is even better off if everyone else does the cooperating, while he or she remains at home enjoying an afternoon siesta. Cooperation requires social mechanisms that prevent individuals from free riding on the efforts of others. Irons argues that religion is such a mechanism.

The key is that religious rituals are a form of communication, which anthropologists have long maintained. They borrowed this insight from ethologists who observed that many species engage in patterned behavior, which they referred to as "ritual." Ethologists recognized that ritualistic behaviors served as a form of communication between members of the same species, and often between members of different species. For example, the males of many avian species engage in courtship rituals—such as bowing, head wagging, wing waving and hopping (among many other gestures)—to signal their amorous intents before a prospective mate. And, of course, the vibration of a rattlesnake's tail is a powerful threat display to other species that enter its personal space.

Irons's insight is that religious activities signal commitment to other members of the group. By engaging in the ritual, the member effectively says, "I identify with the group and I believe in what the group stands for." Through its ability to signal commitment, religious behavior can overcome the problem of free riders and promote cooperation within the group. It does so because trust lies at the heart of the problem: A member must assure everyone that he or she will participate in acquiring food or in defending the group. Of course, hunters and warriors may make promises—"you have my word, I'll show up tomorrow"—but unless the trust is already established such statements are not believable.

It turns out that there is a robust way to secure trust. Israeli biologist Amotz Zahavi observes that it is often in the best interest of an animal to send a dishonest signal—perhaps to fake its size, speed, strength, health or beauty. The only signal that can be believed is one that is too costly to fake, which he referred to as a "handicap." Zahavi argues that natural selection has favored the evolution of handicaps. For example, when a springbok antelope spots a predator it often *stots*—it jumps up and down. This extraordinary behavior puzzled biologists for years: Why would an antelope waste precious energy that could be used to escape the predator? And why would the animal make itself more visible to something that wants to eat it? The reason is that the springbok is displaying its quality to the predator—its ability to escape, effectively saying, "Don't bother chasing me. Look how strong my legs are, you won't be able to catch me." The only reason a predator believes the springbok is because the signal is too costly to fake. An antelope that is not quick enough to escape cannot imitate the signal because it is not strong enough to repeatedly jump to a certain height. Thus, a display can provide honest information if the signals are so costly to perform that lower quality organisms cannot benefit by imitating the signal.

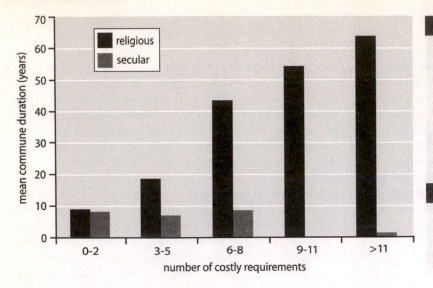

behaviors that are constrained

consumption of:
coffee, alcohol, tobacco, meat, other foods or beverages

use and ownership of:
photographs, jewelry, certain technology, other material items

activities:
monogamous marriage, gambling, communication with the outside, living as a nuclear family, maintaining rights to biological children

behaviors that are required

trial period for membership, surrender of material belongings, learn a body of knowledge, endure public sessions of criticism, certain clothing styles, certain hairstyles, fasting

In much the same way, religious behavior is also a costly signal. By donning several layers of clothing and standing out in the midday sun, ultraorthodox Jewish men are signaling to others: "Hey! Look, I'm a *haredi* Jew. If you are also a member of this group you can trust me because why else would I be dressed like this? No one would do this *unless* they believed in the teachings of ultraorthodox Judaism and were fully committed to its ideals and goals." The quality that these men are signaling is their level of commitment to a specific religious group.

Adherence to a set of religious beliefs entails a host of ritual obligations and expected behaviors. Although there may be physical or psychological benefits associated with some ritual practices, the significant time, energy and financial costs involved serve as effective deterrents for anyone who does not believe in the teachings of a particular religion. There is no incentive for nonbelievers to join or remain in a religious group, because the costs of maintaining membership—such as praying three times a day, eating only kosher food, donating a certain part of your income to charity and so on—are simply too high.

Those who engage in the suite of ritual requirements imposed by a religious group can be trusted to believe sincerely in the doctrines of their respective religious communities. As a result of increased levels of trust and commitment among group members, religious groups minimize costly monitoring mechanisms that are otherwise necessary to overcome free-rider problems that typically plague communal pursuits. Hence, the adaptive benefit of ritual behavior is its ability to promote and maintain cooperation, a challenge that our ancestors presumably faced throughout our evolutionary history.

Benefits of Membership

One prediction of the "costly signaling theory of ritual" is that groups that impose the greatest demands on their members will elicit the highest levels of devotion and commitment. Only committed members will be willing to dress and behave in ways that differ from the rest of society. Groups that maintain more-committed members can also offer more because it's easier for them to attain their collective goals than groups whose members

are less committed. This may explain a paradox in the religious marketplace: Churches that require the most of their adherents are experiencing rapid rates of growth. For example, the Church of Jesus Christ of Latter-day Saints (Mormons), Seventh-day Adventists and Jehovah's Witnesses, who respectively abstain from caffeine, meat and blood transfusions (among other things), have been growing at exceptional rates. In contrast, liberal Protestant denominations such as the Episcopalians, Methodists and Presbyterians have been steadily losing members.

Economist Lawrence Iannaccone, of George Mason University, has also noted that the most demanding groups also have the greatest number of committed members. He found that the more distinct a religious group was—how much the group's lifestyle differed from mainstream America—the higher its attendance rates at services. Sociologists Roger Finke and Rodney Stark, of Penn State and the University of Washington, respectively, have argued that when the Second Vatican Council in 1962 repealed many of the Catholic Church's prohibitions and reduced the level of strictness in the church, it initiated a decline in church attendance among American Catholics and reduced the enrollments in seminaries. Indeed, in the late 1950s almost 75 percent of American Catholics were attending Mass weekly, but since the Vatican's actions there has been a steady decline to the current rate of about 45 percent.

The costly signaling theory of ritual also predicts that greater commitment will translate into greater cooperation within groups. My colleague Eric Bressler, a graduate student at McMaster University, and I addressed this question by looking at data from the records of 19th-century communes. All communes face an inherent problem of promoting and sustaining cooperation because individuals can free ride on the efforts of others. Because cooperation is key to a commune's survival, we employed commune longevity as a measure of cooperation. Compared to their secular counterparts, the religious communes did indeed demand more of their members, including such behavior as celibacy, the surrender of all material possessions and vegetarianism. Communes that demanded more of their members survived longer, overcoming the fundamental challenges of cooperation. By placing greater demands on their

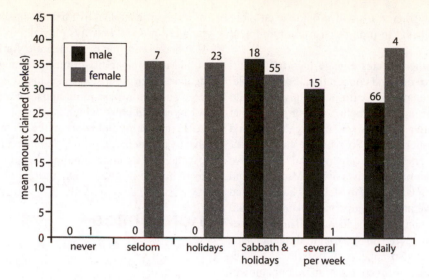

members, they were presumably able to elicit greater belief in and commitment toward the community's common ideology and goals.

I also wanted to evaluate the costly signaling theory of ritual within modern communal societies. The kibbutzim I had visited in Israel as a teenager provided an ideal opportunity to examine these hypotheses. For most of their 100-year history, these communal societies have lived by the dictum, "From each according to his abilities, to each according to his needs." The majority of the more than 270 kibbutzim are secular (and often ideologically antireligious); fewer than 20 are religiously oriented. Because of a massive economic failure—a collective debt of more than $4 billion—the kibbutzim are now moving in the direction of increased privatization and reduced communality. When news of the extraordinary debt surfaced in the late 1980s, it went largely unnoticed that the religious kibbutzim were financially stable. In the words of the Religious Kibbutz Movement Federation, "the economic position of the religious kibbutzim is sound, and they remain uninvolved in the economic crisis."

The success of the religious kibbutzim is especially remarkable given that many of their rituals inhibit economic productivity. For example, Jewish law does not permit Jews to milk cows on the Sabbath. Although rabbinic rulings now permit milking by kibbutz members to prevent the cows from suffering, in the early years none of this milk was used commercially. There are also significant constraints imposed by Jewish law on agricultural productivity. Fruits are not allowed to be eaten for the first few years of the tree's life, agricultural fields must lie fallow every seven years, and the corners of fields can never be harvested—they must be left for society's poor. Although these constraints appear detrimental to productivity, the costly signaling theory of ritual suggests that they may actually be the key to the economic success of the religious kibbutzim.

I decided to study this issue with economist Bradley Ruffle of Israel's Ben Gurion University. We developed a game to determine whether there were differences in how the members of secular and religious kibbutzim cooperated with each other. The game involves two members from the same kibbutz who remain anonymous to each other. Each member is told there

are 100 shekels in an envelope to which both members have access. Each participant decides how many shekels to withdraw and keep. If the sum of both requests exceeds 100 shekels, both members receive no money and the game is over. However, if the requests are less than or equal to 100 shekels, the money remaining in the envelope is increased by 50 percent and divided evenly among the participants. Each member also keeps the original amount he or she requested. The game is an example of a common-pool resource dilemma in which publicly accessible goods are no longer available once they are consumed. Since the goods are available to more than one person, the maintenance of the resources requires individual self-restraint; in other words, cooperation.

After we controlled for a number of variables, including the age and size of the kibbutz and the amount of privatization, we found not only that religious kibbutzniks were more cooperative with each other than secular kibbutzniks, but that male religious kibbutz members were also significantly more cooperative than female members. Among secular kibbutzniks we found no sex differences at all. This result is understandable if we appreciate the types of rituals and demands imposed on religious Jews. Although there are a variety of requirements that are imposed equally on males and females, such as keeping kosher and refraining from work on the Sabbath, male rituals are largely performed in public, whereas female rituals are generally pursued privately. Indeed, none of the three major requirements imposed exclusively on women—attending a ritual bath, separating a portion of dough when baking bread and lighting Shabbat and holiday candles—are publicly performed. They are not rituals that signal commitment to a wider group; instead they appear to signal commitment to the family. Men, however, engage in highly visible rituals, most notably public prayer, which they are expected to perform three times a day. Among male religious kibbutz members, synagogue attendance is positively correlated with cooperative behavior. There is no similar correlation among females. This is not surprising given that women are not required to attend services, and so their presence does not signal commitment to the group. Here the costly signaling theory of ritual provides a unique explanation of these findings. We expect that further work will provide even more insight into the ability of ritual to promote trust, commitment and cooperation.

We know that many other species engage in ritual behaviors that appear to enhance trust and cooperation. For example, anthropologists John Watanabe of Dartmouth University and Barbara Smuts at the University of Michigan have shown that greetings between male olive baboons serve to signal trust and commitment between former rivals. So why are human rituals often cloaked in mystery and the supernatural? Cognitive anthropologists Scott Atran of the University of Michigan and Pascal Boyer at Washington University in St. Louis have pointed out that the counterintuitive nature of supernatural concepts are more easily remembered than mundane ideas, which facilitates their cultural transmission. Belief in supernatural agents such as gods, spirits and ghosts also appears to be critical to religion's ability to promote long-term cooperation. In our study of 19th-century communes, Eric Bressler and I found that the strong positive relationship between the number of costly requirements imposed on members and commune longevity only held for religious communes, not secular ones. We were surprised by this result because secular groups such as militaries and fraternities appear to successfully employ costly rituals to maintain cooperation. Cultural ecologist Roy Rappaport explained, however, that although religious and secular rituals can both promote cooperation, religious rituals ironically generate greater belief and commitment because they sanctify unfalsifiable statements that are beyond the possibility of examination. Since statements containing supernatural elements, such as "Jesus is the son of God," cannot be proved or disproved, believers verify them "emotionally." In contrast to religious propositions, the kibbutz's guiding dictum, taken from Karl Marx, is not beyond question; it can be evaluated by living according to its directives by distributing labor and resources appropriately. Indeed, as the economic situation on the kibbutzim has worsened, this fundamental proposition of kibbutz life has been challenged and is now disregarded by many who are pushing their communities to accept differential pay scales. The ability of religious rituals to evoke emotional experiences that can be associated with enduring supernatural concepts and symbols differentiates them from both animal and secular rituals and lies at the heart of their efficiency in promoting and maintaining long-term group cooperation and commitment.

Evolutionary research on religious behavior is in its infancy, and many questions remain to be addressed. The costly signaling theory of ritual appears to provide some answers, and, of course, it has given me a better understanding of the questions I asked as a teenager. The real value of the costly signaling theory of ritual will be determined by its ability to explain religious phenomena across societies. Most of us, including ultraorthodox Jews, are not living in communes. Nevertheless, contemporary religious congregations that demand much of their members are able to achieve a close-knit social community—an impressive accomplishment in today's individualistic world.

Religion has probably always served to enhance the union of its practitioners; unfortunately, there is also a dark side to this unity. If the intragroup solidarity that religion promotes is one of its significant adaptive benefits, then from its beginning religion has probably always played a role in intergroup conflicts. In other words, one of the benefits for individuals of intragroup solidarity is the ability of unified groups to defend and compete against other groups. This seems to be as true today as it ever was, and is nowhere more apparent than the region I visited as a 15-year-old boy—which is where I am as I write these words. As I conduct my fieldwork in the center of this war zone, I hope that by appreciating the depth of the religious need in the human psyche, and by understanding this powerful adaptation, we can learn how to promote cooperation rather than conflict.

References

Atran, S. 2002. *In Gods We Trust*. New York: Oxford University Press.

Iannaccone, L. 1992. Sacrifice and stigma: Reducing free-riding in cults, communes, and other collectives. *Journal of Political Economy* 100:271–291.

Iannaccone, L. 1994. Why strict churches are strong. *American Journal of Sociology* 99:1180–1211.

Irons, W. 2001. Religion as a hard-to-fake sign of commitment. In *Evolution and the Capacity for Commitment*, ed. R. Nesse, pp. 292–309. New York: Russell Sage Foundation.

Rappaport, R. 1999. *Ritual and Religion in the Making of Humanity*. Cambridge: Cambridge University Press.

Sosis, R. 2003. Why aren't we all Hutterites? Costly signaling theory and religious behavior. *Human Nature* 14:91–127.

Sosis, R., and C. Alcorta. 2003. Signaling, solidarity, and the sacred: The evolution of religious behavior. *Evolutionary Anthropology* 12:264–274.

Sosis, R., and E. Bressler. 2003. Cooperation and commune longevity: A test of the costly signaling theory of religion. *Cross-Cultural Research* 37:211–239.

Sosis, R., and B. Ruffle. 2003. Religious ritual and cooperation: Testing for a relationship on Israeli religious and secular kibbutzim. *Current Anthropology* 44:713–722.

Zahavi, A., and A. Zahavi. 1997. *The Handicap Principle*. New York: Oxford University Press.

Critical Thinking

1. What is the universal dilemma with regard to cooperation in a community, according to William Irons?

2. In what sense is religious ritual a form of communication?

3. What is the only kind of signal that can be believed? How does the example of the springbok antelope illustrate the point?

4. Why is there no incentive for nonbelievers to join or remain in a religious group? Are there costly monitoring mechanisms? Explain.

5. What is the relationship between demands upon members and levels of devotion and commitment? What paradox does this explain?

6. What groups have the most committed members?

7. What was observed among American Catholics once the Vatican Council reduced the level of strictness in the church?

8. Which 19th century communes survived long and why?

9. Which kibbutzim survived better and why? What constraints existed among the religious kibbutzim and what effect did they have?

10. Describe the overall results of the game experiment with regard to religious versus secular kibbutzim and men versus women.

11. Why are religious rituals more successful at promoting belief than are secular rituals?

12. What is the "dark side" to the unity provided by religious intragroup solidarity?

RICHARD SOSIS is an assistant professor of anthropology at the University of Connecticut. His research interests include the evolution of cooperation, utopian societies and the behavioral ecology of religion. Address: Department of Anthropology, U-2176, University of Connecticut, Storrs, CT 06269–2176. Internet: richard.sosis@uconn.edu

Understanding Islam

KENNETH JOST

Is Islam Compatible with Western Values?

With more than 1 billion adherents, Islam is the world's second-largest religion after Christianity. Within its mainstream traditions, Islam teaches piety, virtue and tolerance. Ever since the Sept. 11, 2001, terrorist attacks in the United States, however, many Americans have associated Islam with the fundamentalist groups that preach violence against the West and regard "moderate" Muslims as heretics. Mainstream Muslims and religious scholars say Islam is wrongly blamed for the violence and intolerance of a few. But some critics say Muslims have not done enough to oppose terrorism and violence. They also contend that Islam's emphasis on a strong relationship between religion and the state is at odds with Western views of secularism and pluralism. Some Muslims are calling for a more progressive form of Islam. But radical Islamist views are attracting a growing number of young Muslims in the Islamic world and in Europe.

Overview

Aishah Azmi was dressed all in black, her face veiled by a *niqab* that revealed only her brown eyes through a narrow slit.

"Muslim women who wear the veil are not aliens," the 24-year-old suspended bilingual teaching assistant told reporters in Leeds, England, on Oct. 19. "Integration [of Muslims into British society] requires people like me to be in the workplace so that people can see that we are not to be feared or mistrusted."

But school officials defended their decision to suspend Azmi for refusing to remove her veil in class with a male teacher, saying it interfered with her ability to communicate with her students—most of them Muslims and, like Azmi, British Asians.

"The school and the local authority had to balance the rights of the children to receive the best quality education possible and Mrs. Azmi's desire to express her cultural beliefs," said local Education Minister Jim Dodds.

Although an employment tribunal rejected Azmi's discrimination and harassment claims, it said the school council had handled her complaint poorly and awarded her 1,100 British pounds—about $2,300.

Azmi's widely discussed case has become part of a wrenching debate in predominantly Christian England over relations with the country's growing Muslim population.

In September, a little more than a year after subway and bus bombings in London claimed 55 lives, a government minister called on Muslim parents to do more to steer their children away from violence and terrorism. Then, in October, a leaked report being prepared by the interfaith adviser of the Church of England complained that what he called the government's policy of "privileged attention" toward Muslims had backfired and was creating increased "disaffection and separation."

The simmering controversy grew even hotter after Jack Straw, leader of the House of Commons and former foreign secretary under Prime Minister Tony Blair, called full-face veils "a visible statement of separation and difference" that promotes separatism between Muslims and non-Muslims. Straw, whose constituency in northwestern England includes an estimated 25 percent Muslim population aired the comments in a local newspaper column.

Hamid Qureshi, chairman of the Lancashire Council of Mosques, called Straw's remarks "blatant Muslim-bashing."

"Muslims feel they are on center stage, and everybody is Muslim-bashing," says Anjum Anwar, the council's director of education. "They feel very sensitive."

Britain's estimated 1.5 million Muslims—comprising mostly Pakistani or Indian immigrants and their British-born children—are only a tiny fraction of Islam's estimated 1.2 billion adherents worldwide. But the tensions surfacing in the face-veil debate exemplify the increasingly strained relations between the predominantly Christian West and the Muslim world.

The world's two largest religions—Christianity has some 2 billion adherents—have had a difficult relationship at least since the time of the European Crusades against Muslim rulers, or caliphs, almost 1,000 years ago. Mutual suspicion and hostility have intensified since recent terrorist attacks around the world by militant Islamic groups and President George W. Bush proclaimed a worldwide "war on terror" in response to the Sept. 11, 2001, attacks in the United States.

Bush, who stumbled early on by referring to a "crusade" against terrorism, has tried many times since then to dispel perceptions of any official hostility toward Islam or Muslims generally. In Britain, Blair's government has carried on a 40-year-old policy of "multiculturalism" aimed at promoting cohesion among the country's various communities, Muslims in particular.

Despite those efforts, widespread distrust of Islam and Muslims prevails on both sides of the Atlantic. In a recent poll in the United States, 45 percent of those surveyed said they had an unfavorable view of Islam—a higher percentage than registered in a similar poll four years earlier.

British Muslim leaders also say they feel increasingly hostile anti-Muslim sentiments from the general public and government officials. "Muslims are very fearful, frustrated, upset, angry," says Asghar Bukhari, a spokesman for the Muslim Public Affairs Committee in London. "It's been almost like a mental assault on the Muslim psyche here."

As the face-veil debate illustrates, the distrust stems in part from an array of differences between today's Christianity and Islam as variously practiced in the so-called Muslim world, including the growing Muslim diaspora in Europe and North America.

In broad terms, Islam generally regards religion as a more pervasive presence in daily life and a more important source for civil law than contemporary Christianity, according to the British author Paul Grieve, who wrote a comprehensive guide to Islam after studying Islamic history and thought for more than three years. "Islam is a system of rules for all aspects of life," Grieve writes, while Western liberalism limits regulation of personal behavior. In contrast to the secular nation-states of the West, he explains, Islam views the ideal Muslim society as a universal community—such as the *ummah* established by the Prophet Muhammed in the seventh century.

Those theological and cultural differences are reflected, Grieve says, in Westerners' widespread view of Muslims as narrow-minded and extremist. Many Muslims correspondingly view Westerners as decadent and immoral.

The differences also can be seen in the debates over the role Islam plays in motivating terrorist violence by Islamic extremist groups such as al Qaeda and the objections raised by Muslims to what they consider unflattering and unfair descriptions of Islam in the West.

Muslim leaders generally deny responsibility for the violence committed by Islamic terrorists, including the 9/11 terrorist attacks in the United States and subsequent attacks in Indonesia, Spain and England. "Muslim organizations have done more than ever before in trying to advance community cohesion," Anwar says. They also deny any intention to deny freedom of expression, even though Muslims worldwide denounced a Danish cartoonist's satirical portrayal of Muhammad and Pope Benedict XVI's citation of a medieval Christian emperor's description of Islam as a violent religion.

For many Westerners, however, Islam is associated with radical Muslims—known as Islamists—who either advocate or appear to condone violence and who take to the streets to protest unfavorable depictions of Islam. "A lot of traditional or moderate Islam is inert," says Paul Marshall, a senior fellow at Freedom House's Center for Religious Freedom in Washington. "Many of the people who disagree with radicals don't have a developed position. They keep their heads down."

Meanwhile, many Muslims and non-Muslims alike despair at Islam's sometimes fratricidal intrafaith disputes. Islam split within the first decades of its founding in the seventh century into the Sunni and Shiite (Shia) branches. The Sunni-Shiite conflict helps drive the escalating insurgency in Iraq three years after the U.S.-led invasion ousted Saddam Hussein, a Sunni who pursued generally secularist policies. "A real geopolitical fracturing has taken place in the Muslim world since the end of the colonial era," says Reza Aslan, an Iranian-born Shiite Muslim now a U.S. citizen and author of the book *No god but God*.

The tensions between Islam and the West are on the rise as Islam is surging around the world, growing at an annual rate of about 7 percent. John Voll associate director of the Prince Alwaleed bin Talal Centre for Christian-Muslim Understanding at Georgetown University, notes that the growth is due largely to conversions, not the high birth rates that are driving Hinduism's faster growth.

Moreover, Voll says, Muslims are growing more assertive. "There has been an increase in intensity and an increase in strength in the way Muslims view their place in the world and their place in society," he says.

Teaching assistant Azmi's insistence on wearing the *niqab* exemplifies the new face of Islam in parts of the West. But her choice is not shared by all, or even, most of her fellow Muslim women. "I don't see why she needs to wear it," says Anwar. "She's teaching young children under 11." (Azmi says she wears it because she works with a male classroom teacher.)

Muslim experts generally agree the Koran does not require veils, only modest dress. Observant Muslim women generally comply with the admonition with a head scarf and loose-fitting attire. In particularly conservative cultures, such as Afghanistan under Taliban rule, women cover their entire bodies, including their eyes.

Still, despite the varying practices, many Muslim groups see a disconnect between the West's self-proclaimed tolerance and its pressure on Muslims to conform. "It's a Muslim woman's right to dress as she feels appropriate, given her religious views," says Ibrahim Hooper, director of communications for the Council on American-Islamic Relations in Washington. "But then when somebody actually makes a choice, they're asked not to do that."

Indeed, in Hamtramck, Mich., a judge recently came under fire for throwing out a small-claims case because the Muslim plaintiff refused to remove her full-face veil.

As the debates continue, here are some of the questions being considered:

Is Islam a Religion That Promotes Violence?

Within hours of the London subway and bus bombings on July 7, 2005, the head of the Muslim World League condemned the attacks as un-Islamic. "The heavenly religions, notably Islam, advocate peace and security," said Abdallah al-Turki, secretary-general of the Saudi-funded organization based in Mecca.

The league's statement echoed any number of similar denunciations of Islamist-motivated terrorist attacks issued since 9/11 by Muslims in the United States and around the world. Yet many non-Muslim public officials, commentators, experts and others say Muslims have not done enough to speak out against terrorism committed in the name of their religion.

"Mainstream Muslims have not stepped up to the plate, by and large," says Angel Rabasa, a senior fellow at the Rand Corp., a California think tank, and lead author of a U.S. Air Force-sponsored study, *The Muslim World after 9/11*.

Muslim organizations voice indignant frustration in disputing the accusation. "We can always do more," says Hooper. "The problem is that it never seems to be enough. But that doesn't keep us from trying."

Many Americans, in fact, believe Islam actually encourages violence among its adherents. A CBS poll in April 2006 found that 46 percent of those surveyed believe Islam encourages violence more than other religions. A comparable poll four years earlier registered a lower figure: 32 percent.

Those perceptions are sometimes inflamed by U.S. evangelical leaders. Harsh comments about Islam have come from religious leaders like Franklin Graham, Jerry Falwell, Pat Robertson and Jerry Vines, the former president of the Southern Baptist Convention. Graham called Islam "a very evil and wicked religion," and Vines called Muhammad, Islam's founder and prophet, a "demon-possessed pedophile." Falwell, on the CBS news magazine "60 Minutes" in October 2002, declared, "I think Muhammad was a terrorist."

Mainstream Muslims insist Islam is a peaceful religion and that terrorist organizations distort its tenets and teachings in justifying attacks against the West or other Muslims. But Islamic doctrine and history sometimes seem to justify the use of violence in propagating or defending the faith. The dispute revolves around the meaning of *jihad,* an Arabic word used in the Koran and derived from a root meaning "to strive" or "to make an effort for." Muslim scholars can point to verses in the Koran that depict *jihad* merely as a personal, spiritual struggle and to others that describe *jihad* as encompassing either self-defense or conquest against non-believers.

Georgetown historian Voll notes that, in contrast to Christianity, Islam achieved military success during Muhammad's life and expanded into a major world empire within decades afterward. That history "reinforces the idea that militancy and violence can, in fact, be part of the theologically legitimate plan of the Muslim believer," says Voll.

"Islam, like all religions, has its historical share of violence," acknowledges Stephen Schwartz, an adult convert to Islam and executive director of the Center for Islamic Pluralism in Washington. "But there's no reason to single out Islam."

Modern-day jihadists pack their public manifestos with Koranic citations and writings of Islamic theologians to portray themselves as warriors for Allah and defenders of true Islam. But Voll and others stress that the vast majority of Muslims do not subscribe to their views. "You have a highly visible minority that represents a theologically extreme position in the Muslim world," Voll says.

In particular, writes Seyyed Hossein Nasr, a professor of Islamic studies at George Washington University, Islamic law prohibits the use of force against women, children or civilians—even during war. "Inflicting injuries outside of this context," he writes, "is completely forbidden by Islamic law."

Rabasa says, however, that Muslims who disapprove of terrorism have not said enough or done enough to mobilize opposition to terrorist attacks. "Muslims see themselves as part of a community and are reluctant to criticize radical Muslims," he says.

In addition, many Muslims are simply intimidated from speaking out, he explains. "Radicals are not reluctant to use violence and the threat of violence," he says. Liberal and moderate Muslims are known to receive death threats on their cell phones, even in relatively peaceful Muslim countries such as Indonesia.

Voll also notes that Islamic radicals have simply outorganized the moderates. "There is no moderate organization that even begins to resemble some of the radical organizations that have developed," he says.

In Britain, Bukhari of the Muslim Public Affairs Committee criticizes Muslim leaders themselves for failing to channel young people opposed to Britain's pro-U.S. foreign policy into non-violent political action. "Children who could have been peaceful react to that foreign policy in a way that they themselves become criminals," he says.

The Council on American-Islamic Relations' Hooper details several anti-terrorism pronouncements and drives issued following the London bombings by various Muslim groups and leaders in Britain and in the United States, including *fatwas,* or legal opinions, rejecting terrorism and extremism.

For his part, Omid Safi, an associate professor of Islamic studies at the University of North Carolina in Chapel Hill, points out that virtually every Muslim organization in the United States issued condemnations of violence almost immediately after the 9/11 terrorist attacks.

"How long must we keep answering this question?" Safi asks in exasperation. But he concedes a few moments later that the issue is more than perception. "Muslims must come to terms with our demons," he says, "and one of those demons is violence."

Is Islam Compatible with Secular, Pluralistic Societies?

In 2003, Germany's famed Deutsche Oper staged an avant-garde remake of Mozart's opera "Idomeneo," which dramatizes the composer's criticism of organized religion, with a scene depicting the severed heads of Muhammad, Jesus, Buddha and Poseidon. That production was mounted without incident, but the company dropped plans to restage it in November 2006 after police warned of a possible violent backlash from Muslim fundamentalists.

The cancellation prompted protests from German officials and artistic-freedom advocates in Europe and in the United States, who saw the move as appeasement toward terrorists. Wolfgang Bornsen, a spokesman for conservative Chancellor Angela Merkel, said the cancellation was "a signal" to other artistic companies to avoid any works critical of Islam.

The debate continued even after plans were discussed to mount the production after all—with enhanced security and the blessing of German Muslim leaders. "We live in Europe, where democracy was based on criticizing religion," remarked Philippe Val, editor of the French satirical magazine *Charlie Hebdo.* "If we lose the right to criticize or attack religions in our free countries . . . we are doomed."

As with the issue of violence, Islam's doctrines and history can be viewed as pointing both ways on questions of pluralism and tolerance. "There are a great many passages [in the Koran] that support a pluralistic interpretation of Islam," says the Rand Corp.'s Rabasa. "But you also find a great many that would support an intolerant interpretation."

"Intellectual pluralism is traditional Islam," says Schwartz at the Center for Islamic Pluralism. An oft-quoted verse from the Koran specifically prohibits compulsion in religion, he says. Voll and other historians agree that Muslim countries generally tolerated Christians and Jews, though they were often subject to special taxes or other restrictions.

"Islam is the only major religious system that has built-in protections for minorities," says Hooper at the Council on American-Islamic Relations. "You don't see the kind of persecutions of minorities that we often saw in Europe for hundreds of years. Many members of the Jewish community fled to find safety within the Muslim world."

Even so, Islam's view of religion and politics as inseparable creates difficult issues. Outside the Arab world, most Muslims live in practicing democracies with fair to good human-rights records. But some Muslim countries—Arab and non-Arab—have either adopted or been urged to adopt provisions of Islamic law—*sharia*—that are antithetical to modern ideas of human rights, such as limiting women's rights and prescribing stoning or amputations as criminal penalties.

Muslims participating in a society as a minority population face different issues, according to author Grieve. "Islam is difficult to accommodate in a determinedly secular Western society where almost all views are equally respected, and none is seen as either right or wrong," he writes.

The tensions played out in a number of controversies in recent years were provoked by unflattering depictions of Islam in Europe. A Danish cartoonist's satirical view of Muhammad provoked worldwide protests from Muslim leaders and groups after they were publicized in early 2006. Scattered violence resulted in property damage and more than 30 deaths.

Somewhat similarly, Pope Benedict XVI drew sharp criticism after a Sept. 12, 2006, lecture quoting a medieval Christian emperor's description of Islam as "evil and inhuman." Along with verbal denunciations, protesters in Basra, Iraq, burned an effigy of the pope. Within a week, he disclaimed the remarks and apologized.

Freedom House's Marshall says such controversies, as well as the cancellation of the opera in Berlin, strengthens radical Muslim elements. "Bending to more radical demands marginalizes the voices of moderate Muslims and hands over leadership to the radicals," he says.

Many Muslims in European countries, however, view the controversies—including the current debate over the veil in England—as evidence of pervasive hostility from the non-Muslim majorities. "There is a growing hatred of Muslims in Britain, and anybody who bashes Muslims can only get brownie points," says Bukhari of the Muslim Public Affairs Committee.

"These are not friendly times for Western Muslims," says Safi, at the University of North Carolina. "Whenever people

Basic Tenets of Islam

Islam is the youngest of the world's three major monotheistic religions. Like the other two, Judaism and Christianity, Islam (the word means both "peace" and "submission") holds there is but one God (Allah). Muslims believe God sent a number of prophets to teach mankind how to live according to His law. Muslims consider Jesus, Moses and Abraham as prophets of God and hold the Prophet Muhammad as his final and most sacred messenger. Many accounts found in Islam's sacred book, the Koran (Qur'an), are also found in sacred writings of Jews and Christians.

There are five basic pillars of Islam:

- Creed—Belief in God and Muhammad as his Prophet.
- Almsgiving—Giving money to charity is considered a sacred duty.
- Fasting—From dawn to dusk during the month of Ramadan.
- Prayer—Five daily prayers must be given facing Mecca, Islam's holiest city.
- Pilgrimage—All Muslims must make a baff to Mecca at least once during their lifetime, if they are physically able.

find themselves under assault, opening their arms and opening their hearts is difficult."

Does Islam Need a "Reformation"?

If Pakistan's Punjab University expected a chorus of approval when it decided to launch a master's program in musicology in fall 2006, it was in for a surprise. At the Lahore campus, the conservative Islamic Assembly of Students, known as I.J.T., rose up in protest.

Handbills accused school authorities of forsaking Islamic ideological teachings in favor of "the so-called enlightened moderation" dictated by "foreign masters." Undeterred, administrators opened the program for enrollment in September. When fewer students applied than expected, they blamed the poor response in part on the I.J.T. campaign.

The episode reflects how Islam today is evolving differently in the West and in some parts of the Muslim world. Many Muslim writers and scholars in the United States and Europe are calling for Islam to adapt to modern times by, for example, embracing pluralism and gender equality. Introducing a collection of essays by "progressive" Muslims, the University of North Carolina's Safi says the movement seeks to "start swimming through the rising waters of Islam and modernity, to strive for justice in the midst of society."

In much of the Muslim world, however, Islam is growing—in numbers and intensity—on the strength of literal interpretations of the Koran and exclusivist attitudes toward the non-Muslim world. "In the Muslim world in general, more extreme or reactionary forms of Islam are getting stronger—in Africa, Asia and the Middle East," says Freedom House's Marshall, who has previously worked on issues pertaining to persecution of Christians around the world.

Islamist groups such as I.J.T. talk about "reforming" or "purifying" Islam and adopting Islamic law as the primary or exclusive source of civil law. In fact, one version of reformed Islam—Wahhabism[1] or the currently preferred term Salafism—espouses a literalistic reading of the Koran and a puritanical stance toward such modern practices as listening to music or watching television. It has been instituted in Saudi Arabia and has advanced worldwide because of financial backing from the oil-rich kingdom and its appeal to new generations of Muslims.

"The Salafi movement is a fringe," says the Rand Corp.'s Rabasa. "But it's growing because it's dynamic and revolutionary, whereas traditional Islam tends to be conservative. It has this appeal to young people looking for identity."

But the Center for Islamic Pluralism's Schwartz, an outspoken critic of Salafism, says many Muslims are rejecting it because of its tendency to view other branches of Islam as apostasy. "People are getting sick of this," he says. "They're tired of the social conflict and upheaval."

Voll at the Center for Christian-Muslim Understanding also says some Muslim legal scholars are disputing literalistic readings of *sharia* by contending that the Islamic law cited as divinely ordained is actually "a human construct subject to revision."

Some Western commentators refer to a "reformation" in calling for a more liberal form of Islam. Nicholas D. Kristof, a *New York Times* columnist who focuses on global human-rights issues, sees "hopeful rumblings . . . of steps toward a Muslim Reformation," especially on issues of gender equality. He notes that feminist Muslim scholars are reinterpreting passages in the Koran that other Muslims cite in justifying restrictions on women, such as the Saudi ban on women driving.

Safi says he avoids the term reformation because it has been adopted by Salafists and also because it suggests a need to break from traditional Islam. He says "progressive" Muslims return to the Prophet's vision of the common humanity of all human beings and seek "to hold Muslim societies accountable for justice and pluralism."

Rabasa also says reformation is historically inappropriate as a goal for liberal or progressive Muslims. "What is needed is not an Islamic reformation but an Islamic enlightenment," says Rabasa. The West's liberal tradition, he notes, was produced not by the Reformation but by the Enlightenment—the 18th-century movement that used reason to search for objective truth.

Whatever terms are used, the clash between different visions of Islam will be less susceptible to resolution than analogous disputes within most branches of Christianity because Islam lacks any recognized hierarchical structure. Islam has no pope or governing council. Instead, each believer is regarded as having a direct relationship with God, or Allah, with no ecclesiastical intermediary.

"In the face of contemporary Islam, there is absolutely the sense of an authority vacuum," says Safi. Islam's future, he adds, "is a question that can only be answered by Muslims."

Note

1. Wahhabism originated in the Arabian peninsula in the late 1700s from the teachings of Arabian theologian Muhammand ibn Abd al Wahhab (1703–1792).

Critical Thinking

1. What are the main points of contention regarding the strained relationship between the Christian West and Muslim world?

2. Does Islam encourage violence? Explain.

3. Is Islam compatible with secular, pluralistic societies? Explain.

4. Does Islam need a "Reformation"? Explain.

The Secrets of Haiti's Living Dead

A Harvard botanist investigates mystic potions, voodoo rites, and the making of zombies.

Gino Del Guercio

Five years ago, a man walked into l'Estère, a village in central Haiti, approached a peasant woman named Angelina Narcisse, and identified himself as her brother Clairvius. If he had not introduced himself using a boyhood nickname and mentioned facts only intimate family members knew, she would not have believed him. Because, eighteen years earlier, Angelina had stood in a small cemetery north of her village and watched as her brother Clairvius was buried.

The man told Angelina he remembered that night well. He knew when he was lowered into his grave, because he was fully conscious, although he could not speak or move. As the earth was thrown over his coffin, he felt as if he were floating over the grave. The scar on his right cheek, he said, was caused by a nail driven through his casket.

The night he was buried, he told Angelina, a voodoo priest raised him from the grave. He was beaten with a sisal whip and carried off to a sugar plantation in northern Haiti where, with other zombies, he was forced to work as a slave. Only with the death of the zombie master were they able to escape, and Narcisse eventually returned home.

Legend has it that zombies are the living dead, raised from their graves and animated by malevolent voodoo sorcerers, usually for some evil purpose. Most Haitians believe in zombies, and Narcisse's claim is not unique. At about the time he reappeared, in 1980, two women turned up in other villages saying they were zombies. In the same year, in northern Haiti, the local peasants claimed to have found a group of zombies wandering aimlessly in the fields.

But Narcisse's case was different in one crucial respect; it was documented. His death had been recorded by doctors at the American-directed Schweitzer Hospital in Deschapelles. On April 30, 1962, hospital records show, Narcisse walked into the hospital's emergency room spitting up blood. He was feverish and full of aches. His doctors could not diagnose his illness, and his symptoms grew steadily worse. Three days after he entered the hospital, according to the records, he died. The attending physicians, an American among them, signed his death certificate. His body was placed in cold storage for twenty hours, and then he was buried. He said he remembered hearing his doctors pronounce him dead while his sister wept at his bedside.

At the Centre de Psychiatrie et Neurologie in Port-au-Prince, Dr. Lamarque Douyon, a Haitian-born, Canadian-trained psychiatrist, has been systematically investigating all reports of zombies since 1961. Though convinced zombies were real, he had been unable to find a scientific explanation for the phenomenon. He did not believe zombies were people raised from the dead, but that did not make them any less interesting. He speculated that victims were only made to *look* dead, probably by means of a drug that dramatically slowed metabolism. The victim was buried, dug up within a few hours, and somehow reawakened.

The Narcisse case provided Douyon with evidence strong enough to warrant a request for assistance from colleagues in New York. Douyon wanted to find an ethnobotanist, a traditional-medicines expert, who could track down the zombie potion he was sure existed. Aware of the medical potential of a drug that could dramatically lower metabolism, a group organized by the late Dr. Nathan Kline—a New York psychiatrist and pioneer in the field of psychopharmacology—raised the funds necessary to send someone to investigate.

The search for that someone led to the Harvard Botanical Museum, one of the world's foremost institutes of ethnobiology. Its director, Richard Evans Schultes, Jeffrey professor of biology, had spent thirteen years in the tropics studying native medicines. Some of his best-known work is the investigation of curare, the substance used by the nomadic people of the Amazon to poison their darts. Refined into a powerful muscle relaxant called D-tubocurarine, it is now an essential component of the anesthesia used during almost all surgery.

Schultes would have been a natural for the Haitian investigation, but he was too busy. He recommended another Harvard ethnobotanist for the assignment, Wade Davis, a 28-year-old Canadian pursuing a doctorate in biology.

Davis grew up in the tall pine forests of British Columbia and entered Harvard in 1971, influenced by a *Life* magazine story on the student strike of 1969. Before Harvard, the only Americans he had known were draft dodgers, who seemed very exotic. "I used to fight forest fires with them," Davis says. "Like everybody else, I thought America was where it was at. And I wanted to go to Harvard because of that *Life* article. When I got there, I realized it wasn't quite what I had in mind."

Davis took a course from Schultes, and when he decided to go to South America to study plants, he approached his professor for guidance. "He was an extraordinary figure," Davis remembers. "He was a man who had done it all. He had lived alone for years in the Amazon." Schultes sent Davis to the rain forest with two letters of introduction and two pieces of advice: wear a pith helmet and try ayahuasca, a powerful hallucinogenic vine. During that expedition and others, Davis proved himself an "outstanding field man," says his mentor. Now, in early 1982, Schultes called him into his office and asked if he had plans for spring break.

"I always took to Schultes's assignments like a plant takes to water," says Davis, tall and blond, with inquisitive blue eyes. "Whatever Schultes told me to do, I did. His letters of introduction opened up a whole world." This time the world was Haiti.

Davis knew nothing about the Caribbean island—and nothing about African traditions, which serve as Haiti's cultural basis. He certainly did not believe in zombies. "I thought it was a lark," he says now.

Davis landed in Haiti a week after his conversation with Schultes, armed with a hypothesis about how the zombie drug—if it existed—might be made. Setting out to explore, he discovered a country materially impoverished, but rich in culture and mystery. He was impressed by the cohesion of Haitian society; he found none of the crime, social disorder, and rampant drug and alcohol abuse so common in many of the other Caribbean islands. The cultural wealth and cohesion, he believes, spring from the country's turbulent history.

During the French occupation of the late eighteenth century, 370,000 African-born slaves were imported to Haiti between 1780 and 1790. In 1791, the black population launched one of the few successful slave revolts in history, forming secret societies and overcoming first the French plantation owners and then a detachment of troops from Napoleon's army, sent to quell the revolt. For the next hundred years Haiti was the only independent black republic in the Caribbean, populated by people who did not forget their African heritage. "You can almost argue that Haiti is more African than Africa," Davis says. "When the west coast of Africa was being disrupted by colonialism and the slave trade, Haiti was essentially left alone. The amalgam of beliefs in Haiti is unique, but it's very, very African."

Davis discovered that the vast majority of Haitian peasants practice voodoo, a sophisticated religion with African roots. Says Davis, "It was immediately obvious that the stereotypes of voodoo weren't true. Going around the countryside, I found clues to a whole complex social world." Vodounists believe they communicate directly with, indeed are often possessed by, the many spirits who populate the everyday world. Vodoun society is a system of education, law, and medicine; it embodies a code of ethics that regulates social behavior. In rural areas, secret vodoun societies, much like those found on the west coast of Africa, are as much or more in control of everyday life as the Haitian government.

Although most outsiders dismissed the zombie phenomenon as folklore, some early investigators, convinced of its reality, tried to find a scientific explanation. The few who sought a zombie drug failed. Nathan Kline, who helped finance Davis's expedition, had searched unsuccessfully, as had Lamarque Douyon, the Haitian psychiatrist. Zora Neale Hurston, an American black woman, may have come closest. An anthropological pioneer, she went to Haiti in the thirties, studied vodoun society, and wrote a book on the subject, *Tell My Horse,* first published in 1938. She knew about the secret societies and was convinced zombies were real, but if a power existed, she too failed to obtain it.

Davis obtained a sample in a few weeks.

He arrived in Haiti with the names of several contacts. A BBC reporter familiar with the Narcisse case had suggested he talk with Marcel Pierre. Pierre owned the Eagle Bar, a bordello in the city of Saint Marc. He was also a voodoo sorcerer and had supplied the BBC with a physiologically active powder of unknown ingredients. Davis found him willing to negotiate. He told Pierre he was a representative of "powerful but anonymous interests in New York," willing to pay generously for the priest's services, provided no questions were asked. Pierre agreed to be helpful for what Davis will only say was a "sizable sum." Davis spent a day watching Pierre gather the ingredients—including human bones—and grind them together with mortar and pestle. However, from his knowledge of poison, Davis knew immediately that nothing in the formula could produce the powerful effects of zombification.

Three weeks later, Davis went back to the Eagle Bar, where he found Pierre sitting with three associates. Davis challenged him. He called him a charlatan. Enraged, the priest gave him a second vial, claiming that this was the real poison. Davis pretended to pour the powder into his palm and rub it into his skin. "You're a dead man," Pierre told him, and he might have been, because this powder proved to be genuine. But, as the substance had not actually touched him, Davis was able to maintain his bravado, and Pierre was impressed. He agreed to make the poison and show Davis how it was done.

The powder, which Davis keeps in a small vial, looks like dry black dirt. It contains parts of toads, sea worms, lizards, tarantulas, and human bones. (To obtain the last ingredient, he and Pierre unearthed a child's grave on a nocturnal trip to the cemetery.) The poison is rubbed into the victim's skin. Within hours he begins to feel nauseated and has difficulty breathing. A pins-and-needles sensation afflicts his arms and legs, then progresses to the whole body. The subject becomes paralyzed; his lips turn blue for lack of oxygen. Quickly—sometimes within six hours—his metabolism is lowered to a level almost indistinguishable from death.

As Davis discovered, making the poison is an inexact science. Ingredients varied in the five samples he eventually acquired, although the active agents were always the same. And the poison came with no guarantee. Davis speculates that sometimes instead of merely paralyzing the victim, the compound kills him. Sometimes the victim suffocates in the coffin before he can be resurrected. But clearly the potion works well enough often enough to make zombies more than a figment of Haitian imagination.

Analysis of the powder produced another surprise. "When I went down to Haiti originally," says Davis, "my hypothesis was that the formula would contain *concombre zombi,* the 'zombie's cucumber,' which is a *Datura* plant. I thought somehow *Datura*

Richard Schultes

His students continue his tradition of pursuing botanical research in the likeliest of unlikely places.

Richard Evans Schultes, Jeffrey professor of biology emeritus, has two homes, and they could not be more different. The first is Cambridge, where he served as director of the Harvard Botanical Museum from 1970 until last year, when he became director emeritus. During his tenure he interested generations of students in the exotic botany of the Amazon rain forest. His impact on the field through his own research is worldwide. The scholarly ethnobotanist with steel-rimmed glasses, bald head, and white lab coat is as much a part of the Botanical Museum as the thousands of plant specimens and botanical texts on the museum shelves.

In his austere office is a picture of a crew-cut, younger man stripped to the waist, his arms decorated with tribal paint. This is Schultes's other persona. Starting in 1941, he spent thirteen years in the rain forests of South America, living with the Indians and studying the plants they use for medicinal and spiritual purposes.

Schultes is concerned that many of the people he has studied are giving up traditional ways. "The people of so-called primitive societies are becoming civilized and losing all their forefathers' knowledge of plant lore," he says. "We'll be losing the tremendous amounts of knowledge they've gained over thousands of years. We're interested in the practical aspects with the hope that new medicines and other things can be developed for our own civilization."

Schultes's exploits are legendary in the biology department. Once, while gathering South American plant specimens hundreds of miles from civilization, he contracted beri-beri. For forty days he fought creeping paralysis and overwhelming fatigue as he paddled back to a doctor. "It was an extraordinary feat of endurance," says disciple Wade Davis. "He is really one of the last nineteenth-century naturalists."

Hallucinogenic plants are one of Schultes's primary interests. As a Harvard undergraduate in the thirties, he lived with Oklahoma's Kiowa Indians to observe their use of plants. He participated in their peyote ceremonies and wrote his thesis on the hallucinogenic cactus. He has also studied other hallucinogens, such as morning glory seeds, sacred mushrooms, and ayahuasca, a South American vision vine. Schultes's work has led to the development of anesthetics made from curare and alternative sources of natural rubber.

Schultes's main concern these days is the scientific potential of plants in the rapidly disappearing Amazon jungle. "If chemists are going to get material on 80,000 species and then analyze them, they'll never finish the job before the jungle is gone," he says. "The short cut is to find out what the [native] people have learned about the plant properties during many years of living in the very rich flora."

—G.D.G.

was used in putting people down." *Datura* is a powerful psychoactive plant, found in West Africa as well as other tropical areas and used there in ritual as well as criminal activities. Davis had found *Datura* growing in Haiti. Its popular name suggested the plant was used in creating zombies.

But, says Davis, "there were a lot of problems with the *Datura* hypothesis. Partly it was a question of how the drug was administered. *Datura* would create a stupor in huge doses, but it just wouldn't produce the kind of immobility that was key. These people had to appear dead, and there aren't many drugs that will do that."

One of the ingredients Pierre included in the second formula was a dried fish, a species of puffer or blowfish, common to most parts of the world. It gets its name from its ability to fill itself with water and swell to several times its normal size when threatened by predators. Many of these fish contain a powerful poison known as tetrodotoxin. One of the most powerful nonprotein poisons known to man, tetrodotoxin turned up in every sample of zombie powder that Davis acquired.

Numerous well-documented accounts of puffer fish poisoning exist, but the most famous accounts come from the Orient, where *fugu* fish, a species of puffer, is considered a delicacy. In Japan, special chefs are licensed to prepare *fugu*. The chef removes enough poison to make the fish nonlethal, yet enough remains to create exhilarating physiological effects—tingles up and down the spine, mild prickling of the tongue and lips,

euphoria. Several dozen Japanese die each year, having bitten off more than they should have.

"When I got hold of the formula and saw it was the *fugu* fish, that suddenly threw open the whole Japanese literature," says Davis. Case histories of *fugu* poisoning read like accounts of zombification. Victims remain conscious but unable to speak or move. A man who had "died" after eating *fugu* recovered seven days later in the morgue. Several summers ago, another Japanese poisoned by *fugu* revived after he was nailed into his coffin. "Almost all of Narcisse's symptoms correlated. Even strange things such as the fact that he said he was conscious and could hear himself pronounced dead. Stuff that I thought had to be magic, that seemed crazy. But, in fact, that is what people who get *fugu*-fish poisoning experience."

Davis was certain he had solved the mystery. But far from being the end of his investigation, identifying the poison was, in fact, its starting point. "The drug alone didn't make zombies," he explains. "Japanese victims of puffer-fish poisoning don't become zombies, they become poison victims. All the drug could do was set someone up for a whole series of psychological pressures that would be rooted in the culture. I wanted to know why zombification was going on," he says.

He sought a cultural answer, an explanation rooted in the structure and beliefs of Haitian society. Was zombification simply a random criminal activity? He thought not. He had discovered that Clairvius Narcisse and "Ti Femme," a second victim he interviewed, were village pariahs. Ti Femme was regarded as a thief. Narcisse had abandoned his children and deprived his brother of land that was rightfully his. Equally suggestive, Narcisse claimed that his aggrieved brother had sold him to a *bokor,* a voodoo priest who dealt in black magic; he made cryptic reference to having been tried and found guilty by the "masters of the land."

Gathering poisons from various parts of the country, Davis had come into direct contact with the vodoun secret societies. Returning to the anthropological literature on Haiti and pursuing his contacts with informants, Davis came to understand the social matrix within which zombies were created.

Davis's investigations uncovered the importance of the secret societies. These groups trace their origins to the bands of escaped slaves that organized the revolt against the French in the late eighteenth century. Open to both men and women, the societies control specific territories of the country. Their meetings take place at night, and in many rural parts of Haiti the drums and wild celebrations that characterize the gatherings can be heard for miles.

Davis believes the secret societies are responsible for policing their communities, and the threat of zombification is one way they maintain order. Says Davis, "Zombification has a material basis, but it also has a societal logic." To the uninitiated, the practice may appear a random criminal activity, but in rural vodoun society, it is exactly the opposite—a sanction imposed by recognized authorities, a form of capital punishment. For rural Haitians, zombification is an even more severe punishment than death, because it deprives the subject of his most valued possessions: his free will and independence.

The vodounists believe that when a person dies, his spirit splits into several different parts. If a priest is powerful enough, the spiritual aspect that controls a person's character and individuality, known as *ti bon ange,* the "good little angel," can be captured and the corporeal aspect, deprived of its will, held as a slave.

From studying the medical literature on tetrodotoxin poisoning, Davis discovered that if a victim survives the first few hours of the poisoning, he is likely to recover fully from the ordeal. The subject simply revives spontaneously. But zombies remain without will, in a trance-like state, a condition vodounists attribute to the power of the priest. Davis thinks it possible that the psychological trauma of zombification may be augmented by *Datura* or some other drug; he thinks zombies may be fed a *Datura* paste that accentuates their disorientation. Still, he puts the material basis of zombification in perspective: "Tetrodotoxin and *Datura* are only templates on which cultural forces and beliefs may be amplified a thousand times."

Davis has not been able to discover how prevalent zombification is in Haiti. "How many zombies there are is not the question," he says. He compares it to capital punishment in the United States: "It doesn't really matter how many people are electrocuted, as long as it's a possibility." As a sanction in Haiti, the fear is not of zombies, it's of becoming one.

Davis attributes his success in solving the zombie mystery to his approach. He went to Haiti with an open mind and

immersed himself in the culture. "My intuition unhindered by biases served me well," he says. "I didn't make any judgments." He combined this attitude with what he had learned earlier from his experiences in the Amazon. "Schultes's lesson is to go and live with the Indians as an Indian." Davis was able to participate in the vodoun society to a surprising degree, eventually even penetrating one of the Bizango societies and dancing in their nocturnal rituals. His appreciation of Haitian culture is apparent. "Everybody asks me how did a white person get this information? To ask the question means you don't understand Haitians—they don't judge you by the color of your skin."

As a result of the exotic nature of his discoveries, Davis has gained a certain notoriety. He plans to complete his dissertation soon, but he has already finished writing a popular account of his adventures. To be published in January by Simon and Schuster, it is called *The Serpent and the Rainbow,* after the serpent that vodounists believe created the earth and the rainbow spirit it married. Film rights have already been optioned; in October Davis went back to Haiti with a screenwriter. But Davis takes the notoriety in stride. "All this attention is funny," he says. "For years, not just me, but all Schultes's students have had extraordinary adventures in the line of work. The adventure is not the end point, it's just along the way of getting the data. At the Botanical Museum, Schultes created a world unto itself. We didn't think we were doing anything above the ordinary. I still don't think we do. And you know," he adds, "the Haiti episode does not begin to compare to what others have accomplished—particularly Schultes himself."

Critical Thinking

1. What were the circumstances of Clairvius Narcisse's disappearance for eighteen years and what makes this case of "zombification" unique?

2. Describe and explain the cohesion of Haitian society.

3. Describe voodoo and its place in Haitian society.

4. How is the poison used and what are its effects on the victim? Why does it come with no guarantee?

5. What is the one ingredient which turns up in all of the formulas and where does it come from? How and why is this poison used in Japan? What effects have been observed there?

6. What is the "cultural answer" to the zombie mystery? Describe the secret societies and their importance in maintaining order.

7. Why is zombification seen as a punishment more severe than death?

8. How do the priests continue their control over the individual after the effects of tetrodotoxin have worn off, according to Davis?

9. Is it important that there be a lot of zombies in Haiti for social control to be achieved?

GINO DEL GUERCIO is a national science writer for United Press International.

Body Ritual among the Nacirema

HORACE MINER

The anthropologist has become so familiar with the diversity of ways in which different peoples behave in similar situations that he is not apt to be surprised by even the most exotic customs. In fact, if all of the logically possible combinations of behavior have not been found somewhere in the world, he is apt to suspect that they must be present in some yet undescribed tribe. This point has, in fact, been expressed with respect to clan organization by Murdock (1949: 71). In this light, the magical beliefs and practices of the Nacirema present such unusual aspects that it seems desirable to describe them as an example of the extremes to which human behavior can go.

Professor Linton first brought the ritual of the Nacirema to the attention of anthropologists twenty years ago (1936: 326), but the culture of this people is still very poorly understood. They are a North American group living in the territory between the Canadian Cree, the Yaqui and Tarahumare of Mexico, and the Carib and Arawak of the Antilles. Little is known of their origin, though tradition states that they came from the east. According to Nacirema mythology, their nation was originated by a culture hero, Notgnishaw, who is otherwise known for two great feats of strength—the throwing of a piece of wampum across the river Pa-To-Mac and the chopping down of a cherry tree in which the Spirit of Truth resided.

Nacirema culture is characterized by a highly developed market economy which has evolved in a rich natural habitat. While much of the people's time is devoted to economic pursuits, a large part of the fruits of these labors and a considerable portion of the day are spent in ritual activity. The focus of this activity is the human body, the appearance and health of which loom as a dominant concern in the ethos of the people. While such a concern is certainly not unusual, its ceremonial aspects and associated philosophy are unique.

The fundamental belief underlying the whole system appears to be that the human body is ugly and that its natural tendency is to debility and disease. Incarcerated in such a body, man's only hope is to avert these characteristics through the use of the powerful influences of ritual and ceremony. Every household has one or more shrines devoted to this purpose. The more powerful individuals in the society have several shrines in their houses and, in fact, the opulence of a house is often referred to in terms of the number of such ritual centers it possesses. Most houses are of wattle and daub construction, but the shrine rooms of the more wealthy are walled with stone. Poorer families imitate the rich by applying pottery plaques to their shrine walls.

While each family has at least one such shrine, the rituals associated with it are not family ceremonies but are private and secret. The rites are normally only discussed with children, and then only during the period when they are being initiated into these mysteries. I was able, however, to establish sufficient rapport with the natives to examine these shrines and to have the rituals described to me.

The focal point of the shrine is a box or chest which is built into the wall. In this chest are kept the many charms and magical potions without which no native believes he could live. These preparations are secured from a variety of specialized practitioners. The most powerful of these are the medicine men, whose assistance must be rewarded with substantial gifts. However, the medicine men do not provide the curative potions for their clients, but decide what the ingredients should be and then write them down in an ancient and secret language. This writing is understood only by the medicine men and by the herbalists who, for another gift, provide the required charm.

The charm is not disposed of after it has served its purpose, but is placed in the charm-box of the household shrine. As these magical materials are specific for certain ills, and the real or imagined maladies of the people are many, the charm-box is usually full to overflowing. The magical packets are so numerous that people forget what their purposes were and fear to use them again. While the natives are very vague on this point, we can only assume that the idea in retaining all the old magical materials is that their presence in the charm-box, before which the body rituals are conducted, will in some way protect the worshipper.

Beneath the charm-box is a small font. Each day every member of the family, in succession, enters the shrine room, bows his head before the charm-box, mingles different sorts of holy water in the font, and proceeds with a brief rite of ablution. The holy waters are secured from the Water Temple of the community, where the priests conduct elaborate ceremonies to make the liquid ritually pure.

In the hierarchy of magical practitioners, and below the medicine men in prestige, are specialists whose designation is best translated "holy-mouth-men." The Nacirema have an almost pathological horror and fascination with the mouth, the condition of which is believed to have a supernatural influence on all social relationships. Were it not for the rituals of the mouth, they believe that their teeth would fall out, their gums bleed, their jaws shrink, their friends desert them, and their lovers reject them. (They also believe that a strong relationship exists between oral and moral characteristics. For example, there is a ritual ablution of the mouth for children which is supposed to improve their moral fiber.)

The daily body ritual performed by everyone includes a mouth-rite. Despite the fact that these people are so punctilious about care of the mouth, this rite involves a practice which strikes the uninitiated stranger as revolting. It was reported to me that the ritual consists of inserting a small bundle of hog hairs into the mouth, along with certain magical powders, and then moving the bundle in a highly formalized series of gestures.

In addition to the private mouth-rite, the people seek out a holy-mouth-man once or twice a year. These practitioners have an impressive set of paraphernalia, consisting of a variety of augers, awls, probes, and prods. The use of these objects in the exorcism of the evils of the mouth involves almost unbelievable ritual torture of the client. The holy-mouth-man opens the client's mouth and, using the above mentioned tools, enlarges any holes which decay may have created in the teeth. Magical materials are put into these holes. If there are no naturally occurring holes in the teeth, large sections of one or more teeth are gouged out so that the supernatural substance can be applied. In the client's view, the purpose of these ministrations is to arrest decay and to draw friends. The extremely sacred and traditional character of the rite is evident in the fact that the natives return to the holy-mouth-men year after year, despite the fact that their teeth continue to decay.

It is to be hoped that, when a thorough study of the Nacirema is made, there will be a careful inquiry into the personality structure of these people. One has but to watch the gleam in the eye of a holy-mouth-man, as he jabs an awl into an exposed nerve, to suspect that a certain amount of sadism is involved. If this can be established, a very interesting pattern emerges, for most of the population shows definite masochistic tendencies. It was to these that Professor Linton referred in discussing a distinctive part of the daily body ritual which is performed only by men. This part of the rite involves scraping and lacerating the surface of the face with a sharp instrument. Special women's rites are performed only four times during each lunar month, but what they lack in frequency is made up in barbarity. As part of this ceremony, women bake their heads in small ovens for about an hour. The theoretically interesting point is that what seems to be a preponderantly masochistic people have developed sadistic specialists.

The medicine men have an imposing temple, or *latipso,* in every community of any size. The more elaborate ceremonies required to treat very sick patients can only be performed at this temple. These ceremonies involve not only the thaumaturge but a permanent group of vestal maidens who move sedately about the temple chambers in distinctive costume and headdress.

The *latipso* ceremonies are so harsh that it is phenomenal that a fair proportion of the really sick natives who enter the temple ever recover. Small children whose indoctrination is still incomplete have been known to resist attempts to take them to the temple because "that is where you go to die." Despite this fact, sick adults are not only willing but eager to undergo the protracted ritual purification, if they can afford to do so. No matter how ill the supplicant or how grave the emergency, the guardians of many temples will not admit a client if he cannot give a rich gift to the custodian. Even after one has gained admission and survived the ceremonies, the guardians will not permit the neophyte to leave until he makes still another gift.

The supplicant entering the temple is first stripped of all his or her clothes. In every-day life the Nacirema avoids exposure of his body and its natural functions. Bathing and excretory acts are performed only in the secrecy of the household shrine, where they are ritualized as part of the body-rites. Psychological shock results from the fact that body secrecy is suddenly lost upon entry into the *latipso.* A man, whose own wife has never seen him in an excretory act, suddenly finds himself naked and assisted by a vestal maiden while he performs his natural functions into a sacred vessel. This sort of ceremonial treatment is necessitated by the fact that the excreta are used by a diviner to ascertain the course and nature of the client's sickness. Female clients, on the other hand, find their naked bodies are subjected to the scrutiny, manipulation, and prodding of the medicine men.

Few supplicants in the temple are well enough to do anything but lie on their hard beds. The daily ceremonies, like the rites of the holy-mouth-men, involve discomfort and torture. With ritual precision, the vestals awaken their miserable charges each dawn and roll them about on their beds of pain while performing ablutions, in the formal movements of which the maidens are highly trained. At other times they insert magic wands in the supplicant's mouth or force him to eat substances which are supposed to be healing. From time to time the medicine men come to their clients and jab magically treated needles into their flesh. The fact that these temple ceremonies may not cure, and may even kill the neophyte, in no way decreases the people's faith in the medicine men.

There remains one other kind of practitioner, known as a "listener." This witch-doctor has the power to exorcise the devils that lodge in the heads of people who have been bewitched. The Nacirema believe that parents bewitch their own children. Mothers are particularly suspected of putting a curse on children while teaching them the secret body rituals. The counter-magic of the witch-doctor is unusual in its lack of ritual. The patient simply tells the "listener" all his troubles and fears, beginning with the earliest difficulties he can remember. The memory displayed by the Nacirema in these exorcism sessions is truly remarkable. It is not uncommon for the patient to bemoan the rejection he felt upon being weaned as a babe, and a few individuals even see their troubles going back to the traumatic effects of their own birth.

In conclusion, mention must be made of certain practices which have their base in native esthetics but which depend upon the pervasive aversion to the natural body and its functions. There are ritual fasts to make fat people thin and ceremonial feasts to make thin people fat. Still other rites are used to make women's breasts large if they are small, and smaller if they are large. General dissatisfaction with breast shape is symbolized in the fact that the ideal form is virtually outside the range of human variation. A few women afflicted with almost inhuman hypermammary development are so idolized that they make a handsome living by simply going from village to village and permitting the natives to stare at them for a fee.

Reference has already been made to the fact that excretory functions are ritualized, routinized, and relegated to secrecy. Natural reproductive functions are similarly distorted. Intercourse is taboo as a topic and scheduled as an act. Efforts are made to avoid pregnancy by the use of magical materials or by limiting intercourse to certain phases of the moon. Conception is actually very infrequent. When pregnant, women dress so as to hide their condition. Parturition takes place in secret, without friends or relatives to assist, and the majority of women do not nurse their infants.

Our review of the ritual life of the Nacirema has certainly shown them to be a magic-ridden people. It is hard to understand how they have managed to exist so long under the burdens which they have imposed upon themselves. But even such exotic customs as these take on real meaning when they are viewed with the insight provided by Malinowski when he wrote (1948:70):

Looking from far and above, from our high places of safety in the developed civilization, it is easy to see all the crudity and irrelevance of magic. But without its power

and guidance early man could not have mastered his practical difficulties as he has done, nor could man have advanced to the higher stages of civilization.

References

Linton, Ralph. 1936. *The Study of Man.* New York, D. Appleton-Century Co.

Malinowski, Bronislaw. 1948. *Magic, Science, and Religion.* Glencoe, The Free Press.

Murdock, George P. 1949. *Social Structure.* New York, The Macmillan Co.

Critical Thinking

1. What is "Nacirema" spelled backwards? Where are they actually located on a map? Who are they, really?

2. Why do the customs of the Nacirema seem so bizarre when they are written about in anthropological style?

3. Having read the article, do you view American culture any differently than you did before? If so, how?

4. Has this article helped you to view other cultures differently? If so, how?

5. If this article has distorted the picture of American culture, how difficult is it for all of us, anthropologists included, to render objective descriptions of other cultures?

From *American Anthropologist*, by Horace Miner, June 1956, pp. 503–507.

UNIT 7
Sociocultural Change

Unit Selections

Learning Outcomes

After reading this Unit you will be able to:

- Define a subsistence system and discuss the effects of colonialism on former subsistence-oriented socioeconomic systems.

- Explain how the production of cash crops inevitably leads to class distinctions and poverty.

- Explain how globalization is undermining local conceptions of self and modes of healing.

- Discuss the biological and social circumstances of disease transmission from animals to humans.

- Explain why we should care about the loss of several thousand human cultures within the next generation.

- Determine if wealth and power are distributed fairly across the world.

- Show how exploitation of indigenous people has persisted in Africa even after political independence.

- Explain how climate change has affected Siberian villagers and why we should be concerned.

- Discuss if it is possible for the world's indigenous people to make their way into the modern world without losing sight of who they are.

- Define what is meant by the *demographic transition* and discuss the role it has played in world population growth.

Student Website
www.mhhe.com/cls

Internet References

Association for Political and Legal Anthropology
www.aaanet.org/apla/index.htm
Human Rights and Humanitarian Assistance
www.etown.edu/vl/humrts.html
The Indigenous Rights Movement in the Pacific
www.inmotionmagazine.com/pacific.html
Murray Research Center
www.radcliffe.edu/murray_redirect/index.php
RomNews Network—Online

www.romnews.com/community/index.php
Small Planet Institute
www.smallplanet.org/food
WWW Virtual Library: Indigenous Studies
www.cwis.org

The origins of academic anthropology lie in the colonial and imperial ventures of the past five hundred years. During this period, many people of the world were brought into a relationship with Europe and the United States that was usually exploitative and often socially and culturally disruptive. For over a century, anthropologists have witnessed this process, and the transformations that have taken place in those social and cultural systems brought under the umbrella of a world economic order. Early anthropological studies—even those widely regarded as pure research—directly or indirectly served colonial interests. Many anthropologists certainly believed that they were extending the benefits of Western technology and society, while preserving the cultural rights of those people whom they studied. But representatives of poor nations challenge this view and are far less generous in describing the past role of the anthropologist. Most contemporary anthropologists, however, have a deep moral commitment to defending the legal, political, and economic rights of the people with whom they work.

When anthropologists discuss social change, they usually mean the change brought about in pre-industrial societies through longstanding interaction with the nation-states of the industrialized world. In early anthropology, contact between the West and the remainder of the world was characterized by the terms *acculturation* and *culture contact*. These terms were used to describe the diffusion of cultural traits between the developed and the less-developed countries. Often this was analyzed as a one-way process, in which cultures of the less-developed world were seen, for better or worse, as receptacles for Western cultural traits. Nowadays, many anthropologists believe that the diffusion of cultural traits across social, political, and economic boundaries was emphasized at the expense of the real issues of dominance, subordination, and dependence that characterized the colonial experience. Just as important, many anthropologists recognize that the present-day forms of cultural, economic, and political interaction between the developed and the so-called underdeveloped world are best characterized as neocolonial. Most of the authors represented in this unit take the perspective that anthropology should be critical as well as descriptive. They raise questions about cultural contact and subsequent economic and social disruption.

In keeping with the notion that the negative impact of the West on traditional cultures began with colonial domination, this unit opens with "Why Can't People Feed Themselves?" Continuing

© The McGraw-Hill Companies, Inc./Barry Barker, photographer

with "The Arrow of Disease," "The Americanization of Mental Illness," and "The Price of Progress," and "The Tractor Invasion," we see that "progress" for the West has often meant poverty, hunger, disease, and death for traditional peoples.

None of this is to say that indigenous peoples can or even should be left entirely alone to live in isolation from the rest of the world. A much more sensible, as well as more practical, approach would involve some degree of self-determination and considerably more respect for their cultures.

Of course, traditional peoples are not the only losers in the process of technological "progress" and cultural destruction. In "We are Going Underwater," we find that the very same climate change negatively affecting Siberian villagers should be taken as a warning for what may be in store for the rest of us. The more we deprive the traditional stewards (the Indigenous peoples) of their land, the greater the loss in overall biodiversity. In "Population Seven Billion," we see how unchecked population growth may result in making the planet less inhabitable for everyone.

Finally, all of humanity stands to suffer as resources dwindle and as a vast store of human knowledge—embodied in tribal subsistence practices, language, medicine, and folklore—is obliterated, in a manner not unlike the burning of the library of Alexandria 1,600 years ago (see "Last of Their Kind"). We can only hope that it is not too late to save what is left.

Why Can't People Feed Themselves?

FRANCES MOORE LAPPÉ AND JOSEPH COLLINS

Question: You have said that the hunger problem is not the result of overpopulation. But you have not yet answered the most basic and simple question of all: Why can't people feed themselves? As Senator Daniel P. Moynihan put it bluntly, when addressing himself to the Third World, "Food growing is the first thing you do when you come down out of the trees. The question is, how come the United States can grow food and you can't?"

Our Response: In the very first speech I, Frances, ever gave after writing *Diet for a Small Planet,* I tried to take my audience along the path that I had taken in attempting to understand why so many are hungry in this world. Here is the gist of that talk that was, in truth, a turning point in my life:

When I started I saw a world divided into two parts: a *minority* of nations that had "taken off" through their agricultural and industrial revolutions to reach a level of unparalleled material abundance and a *majority* that remained behind in a primitive, traditional, undeveloped state. This lagging behind of the majority of the world's peoples must be due, I thought, to some internal deficiency or even to several of them. It seemed obvious that the underdeveloped countries must be deficient in natural resources—particularly good land and climate—and in cultural development, including modern attitudes conducive to work and progress.

But when looking for the historical roots of the predicament, I learned that my picture of these two separate worlds was quite false. My two separate worlds were really just different sides of the same coin. One side was on top largely because the other side was on the bottom. Could this be true? How were these separate worlds related?

Colonialism appeared to me to be the link. Colonialism destroyed the cultural patterns of production and exchange by which traditional societies in "underdeveloped" countries previously had met the needs of the people. Many precolonial social structures, while dominated by exploitative elites, had evolved a system of mutual obligations among the classes that helped to ensure at least a minimal diet for all. A friend of mine once said: "Precolonial village existence in subsistence agriculture was a limited life indeed, but it's certainly not Calcutta." The misery of starvation in the streets of Calcutta can only be

understood as the end-point of a long historical process—one that has destroyed a traditional social system.

"Underdeveloped," instead of being an adjective that evokes the picture of a static society, became for me a verb (to "underdevelop") meaning the *process* by which the minority of the world has transformed—indeed often robbed and degraded—the majority.

That was in 1972. I clearly recall my thoughts on my return home. I had stated publicly for the first time a world view that had taken me years of study to grasp. The sense of relief was tremendous. For me the breakthrough lay in realizing that today's "hunger crisis" could not be described in static, descriptive terms. Hunger and underdevelopment must always be thought of as a *process.*

To answer the question "why hunger?" it is counterproductive to simply *describe* the conditions in an underdeveloped country today. For these conditions, whether they be the degree of malnutrition, the levels of agricultural production, or even the country's ecological endowment, are not static factors—they are not "givens." They are rather the *results* of an ongoing historical process. As we dug ever deeper into that historical process for the preparation of this book, we began to discover the existence of scarcity-creating mechanisms that we had only vaguely intuited before.

We have gotten great satisfaction from probing into the past since we recognized it is the only way to approach a solution to hunger today. We have come to see that it is the *force* creating the condition, not the condition itself, that must be the target of change. Otherwise we might change the condition today, only to find tomorrow that it has been recreated—with a vengeance.

Asking the question "Why can't people feed themselves?" carries a sense of bewilderment that there are so many people in the world not able to feed themselves adequately. What astonished us, however, is that there are not *more* people in the world who are hungry—considering the weight of the centuries of effort by the few to undermine the capacity of the majority to feed themselves. No, we are not crying "conspiracy!" If these forces were entirely conspiratorial, they would be easier to detect and many more people would by now have risen up to resist. We are talking about something more subtle and insidious; a heritage of a colonial order in which people with the advantage of considerable power sought their own self-interest, often arrogantly believing they were acting in the interest of the people whose lives they were destroying.

The Colonial Mind

The colonizer viewed agriculture in the subjugated lands as primitive and backward. Yet such a view contrasts sharply with documents from the colonial period now coming to light. For example, A. J. Voelker, a British agricultural scientist assigned to India during the 1890s wrote:

> Nowhere would one find better instances of keeping land scrupulously clean from weeds, of ingenuity in device of water-raising appliances, of knowledge of soils and their capabilities, as well as of the exact time to sow and reap, as one would find in Indian agriculture. It is wonderful too, how much is known of rotation, the system of "mixed crops" and of fallowing. . . . I, at least, have never seen a more perfect picture of cultivation.[1]

None the less, viewing the agriculture of the vanquished as primitive and backward reinforced the colonizer's rationale for destroying it. To the colonizers of Africa, Asia, and Latin America, agriculture became merely a means to extract wealth— much as gold from a mine—on behalf of the colonizing power. Agriculture was no longer seen as a source of food for the local population, nor even as their livelihood. Indeed the English economist John Stuart Mill reasoned that colonies should not be thought of as civilizations or countries at all but as "agricultural establishments" whose sole purpose was to supply the "larger community to which they belong." The colonized society's agriculture was only a subdivision of the agricultural system of the metropolitan country. As Mill acknowledged, "Our West India colonies, for example, cannot be regarded as countries. . . . The West Indies are the place where England *finds it convenient* to carry on the production of sugar, coffee and a few other tropical commodities."[2]

Prior to European intervention, Africans practiced a diversified agriculture that included the introduction of new food plants of Asian or American origin. But colonial rule simplified this diversified production to single cash crops—often to the exclusion of staple foods—and in the process sowed the seeds of famine.[3] Rice farming once had been common in Gambia. But with colonial rule so much of the best land was taken over by peanuts (grown for the European market) that rice had to be imported to counter the mounting prospect of famine. Northern Ghana, once famous for its yams and other foodstuffs, was forced to concentrate solely on cocoa. Most of the Gold Coast thus became dependent on cocoa. Liberia was turned into a virtual plantation subsidiary of Firestone Tire and Rubber. Food production in Dahomey and southeast Nigeria was all but abandoned in favor of palm oil; Tanganyika (now Tanzania) was forced to focus on sisal and Uganda on cotton.

The same happened in Indochina. About the time of the American Civil War the French decided that the Mekong Delta in Vietnam would be ideal for producing rice for export. Through a production system based on enriching the large landowners, Vietnam became the world's third largest exporter of rice by the 1930s; yet many landless Vietnamese went hungry.[4]

Rather than helping the peasants, colonialism's public works programs only reinforced export crop production. British irrigation works built in nineteenth-century India did help increase production, but the expansion was for spring export crops at the expense of millets and legumes grown in the fall as the basic local food crops.

Because people living on the land do not easily go against their natural and adaptive drive to grow food for themselves, colonial powers had to force the production of cash crops. The first strategy was to use physical or economic force to get the local population to grow cash crops instead of food on their own plots and then turn them over to the colonizer for export. The second strategy was the direct takeover of the land by large-scale plantations growing crops for export.

Forced Peasant Production

As Walter Rodney recounts in *How Europe Underdeveloped Africa,* cash crops were often grown literally under threat of guns and whips.[5] One visitor to the Sahel commented in 1928: "Cotton is an artificial crop and one the value of which is not entirely clear to the natives . . . " He wryly noted the "enforced enthusiasm with which the natives . . . have thrown themselves into . . . planting cotton."[6] The forced cultivation of cotton was a major grievance leading to the Maji Maji wars in Tanzania (then Tanganyika) and behind the nationalist revolt in Angola as late as 1960.[7]

Although raw force was used, taxation was the preferred colonial technique to force Africans to grow cash crops. The colonial administrations simply levied taxes on cattle, land, houses, and even the people themselves. Since the tax had to be paid in the coin of the realm, the peasants had either to grow crops to sell or to work on the plantations or in the mines of the Europeans.[8] Taxation was both an effective tool to "stimulate" cash cropping and a source of revenue that the colonial bureaucracy needed to enforce the system. To expand their production of export crops to pay the mounting taxes, peasant producers were forced to neglect the farming of food crops. In 1830, the Dutch administration in Java made the peasants an offer they could not refuse; if they would grow government-owned export crops on one fifth of their land, the Dutch would remit their land taxes.[9] If they refused and thus could not pay the taxes, they lost their land.

Marketing boards emerged in Africa in the 1930s as another technique for getting the profit from cash crop production by native producers into the hands of the colonial government and international firms. Purchases by the marketing boards were well below the world market price. Peanuts bought by the boards from peasant cultivators in West Africa were sold in Britain for more than *seven times* what the peasants received.[10]

The marketing board concept was born with the "cocoa hold-up" in the Gold Coast in 1937. Small cocoa farmers refused to sell to the large cocoa concerns like United Africa Company (a subsidiary of the Anglo-Dutch firm, Unilever—which we know as Lever Brothers) and Cadbury until they got a higher price. When the British government stepped in and agreed to buy the cocoa directly in place of the big business concerns, the smallholders must have thought they had scored at least a minor victory. But had they really? The following year the British formally set up the West African Cocoa Control Board. Theoretically, its purpose was to pay the peasants a reasonable price for their crops. In practice, however, the board, as sole purchaser, was able to hold down the prices paid the peasants for their crops when the world prices were rising. Rodney sums up the real "victory":

> None of the benefits went to Africans, but rather to the British government itself and to the private companies. . . . Big companies like the United African Company and John Holt were given . . . quotas to fulfill on behalf of the boards. As agents of the government, they were no longer exposed to direct attack, and their profits were secure.[11]

These marketing boards, set up for most export crops, were actually controlled by the companies. The chairman of the Cocoa Board was none other than John Cadbury of Cadbury Brothers (ever had a Cadbury chocolate bar?) who was part of a buying pool exploiting West African cocoa farmers.

The marketing boards funneled part of the profits from the exploitation of peasant producers indirectly into the royal treasury. While the Cocoa Board sold to the British Food Ministry at low prices, the ministry upped the price for British manufacturers, thus netting a profit as high as 11 million pounds in some years.[12]

These marketing boards of Africa were only the institutionalized rendition of what is the essence of colonialism—the extraction of wealth. While profits continued to accrue to foreign interests and local elites, prices received by those actually growing the commodities remained low.

Plantations

A second approach was direct takeover of the land either by the colonizing government or by private foreign interests. Previously self-provisioning farmers were forced to cultivate the plantation fields through either enslavement or economic coercion.

After the conquest of the Kandyan Kingdom (in present day Sri Lanka), in 1815, the British designated all the vast central part of the island as crown land. When it was determined that coffee, a profitable export crop, could be grown there, the Kandyan lands were sold off to British investors and planters at a mere five shillings per acre, the government even defraying the cost of surveying and road building.[13]

Java is also a prime example of a colonial government seizing territory and then putting it into private foreign hands. In 1870, the Dutch declared all uncultivated land—called waste land—property of the state for lease to Dutch plantation enterprises. In addition, the Agrarian Land Law of 1870 authorized foreign companies to lease village-owned land. The peasants, in chronic need of ready cash for taxes and foreign consumer goods, were only too willing to lease their land to the foreign companies for very modest sums and under terms dictated by the firms. Where land was still held communally, the village

headman was tempted by high cash commissions offered by plantation companies. He would lease the village land even more cheaply than would the individual peasant or, as was frequently the case, sell out the entire village to the company.[14]

The introduction of the plantation meant the divorce of agriculture from nourishment, as the notion of food value was lost to the overriding claim of "market value" in international trade. Crops such as sugar, tobacco, and coffee were selected, not on the basis of how well they feed people, but for their high price value relative to their weight and bulk so that profit margins could be maintained even after the costs of shipping to Europe.

Suppressing Peasant Farming

The stagnation and impoverishment of the peasant food-producing sector was not the mere by-product of benign neglect, that is, the unintended consequence of an overemphasis on export production. Plantations—just like modern "agro-industrial complexes"—needed an abundant and readily available supply of low-wage agricultural workers. Colonial administrations thus devised a variety of tactics, all to undercut self-provisioning agriculture and thus make rural populations dependent on plantation wages. Government services and even the most minimal infrastructure (access to water, roads, seeds, credit, pest and disease control information, and so on) were systematically denied. Plantations usurped most of the good land, either making much of the rural population landless or pushing them onto marginal soils. (Yet the plantations have often held much of their land idle simply to prevent the peasants from using it—even to this day. Del Monte owns 57,000 acres of Guatemala but plants only 9000. The rest lies idle except for a few thousand head of grazing cattle.)[15]

In some cases a colonial administration would go even further to guarantee itself a labor supply. In at least twelve countries in the eastern and southern parts of Africa the exploitation of mineral wealth (gold, diamonds, and copper) and the establishment of cash-crop plantations demanded a continuous supply of low-cost labor. To assure this labor supply, colonial administrations simply expropriated the land of the African communities by violence and drove the people into small reserves.[16] With neither adequate land for their traditional slash-and-burn methods nor access to the means—tools, water, and fertilizer—to make continuous farming of such limited areas viable, the indigenous population could scarcely meet subsistence needs, much less produce surplus to sell in order to cover the colonial taxes. Hundreds of thousands of Africans were forced to become the cheap labor source so "needed" by the colonial plantations. Only by laboring on plantations and in the mines could they hope to pay the colonial taxes.

The tax scheme to produce reserves of cheap plantation and mining labor was particularly effective when the Great Depression hit and the bottom dropped out of cash crop economies. In 1929 the cotton market collapsed, leaving peasant cotton producers, such as those in Upper Volta, unable to pay their colonial taxes. More and more young people, in some years as many as 80,000, were thus forced to migrate to the Gold Coast to compete with each other for low-wage jobs on cocoa plantations.[17]

The forced migration of Africa's most able-bodied workers—stripping village food farming of needed hands—was a recurring feature of colonialism. As late as 1973 the Portuguese "exported" 400,000 Mozambican peasants to work in South Africa in exchange for gold deposited in the Lisbon treasury.

The many techniques of colonialism to undercut self-provisioning agriculture in order to ensure a cheap labor supply are no better illustrated than by the story of how, in the mid-nineteenth century, sugar plantation owners in British Guiana coped with the double blow of the emancipation of slaves and the crash in the world sugar market. The story is graphically recounted by Alan Adamson in *Sugar Without Slaves*.[18]

Would the ex-slaves be allowed to take over the plantation land and grow the food they needed? The planters, many ruined by the sugar slump, were determined they would not. The planter-dominated government devised several schemes for thwarting food self-sufficiency. The price of crown land was kept artificially high, and the purchase of land in parcels smaller than 100 acres was outlawed—two measures guaranteeing that newly organized ex-slave cooperatives could not hope to gain access to much land. The government also prohibited cultivation on as much as 400,000 acres—on the grounds of "uncertain property titles." Moreover, although many planters held part of their land out of sugar production due to the depressed world price, they would not allow any alternative production on them. They feared that once the ex-slaves started growing food it would be difficult to return them to sugar production when world market prices began to recover. In addition, the government taxed peasant production, then turned around and used the funds to subsidize the immigration of laborers from India and Malaysia to replace the freed slaves, thereby making sugar production again profitable for the planters. Finally, the government neglected the infrastructure for subsistence agriculture and denied credit for small farmers.

Perhaps the most insidious tactic to "lure" the peasant away from food production—and the one with profound historical consequences—was a policy of keeping the price of imported food low through the removal of tariffs and subsidies. The policy was double-edged: first, peasants were told they need not grow food because they could always buy it cheaply with their plantation wages; second, cheap food imports destroyed the market for domestic food and thereby impoverished local food producers.

Adamson relates how both the Governor of British Guiana and the Secretary for the Colonies Earl Grey favored low duties on imports in order to erode local food production and thereby release labor for the plantations. In 1851 the governor rushed through a reduction of the duty on cereals in order to "divert" labor to the sugar estates. As Adamson comments, "Without realizing it, he [the governor] had put his finger on the most mordant feature of monoculture: . . . its convulsive need to destroy any other sector of the economy which might compete for 'its' labor."[19]

Many colonial governments succeeded in establishing dependence on imported foodstuffs. In 1647 an observer in the West Indies wrote to Governor Winthrop of Massachusetts: "Men are so intent upon planting sugar that they had rather buy food at very dear rates than produce it by labour, so infinite is the profitt of sugar workes. . . ."[20] By 1770, the West Indies were importing most of the continental colonies' exports of dried fish, grain, beans, and vegetables. A dependence on imported food made the West Indian colonies vulnerable to any disruption in supply. This dependence on imported food stuffs spelled disaster when the thirteen continental colonies gained independence and food exports from the continent to the West Indies were interrupted. With no diversified food system to fall back on, 15,000 plantation workers died of famine between 1780 and 1787 in Jamaica alone.[21] The dependence of the West Indies on imported food persists to this day.

Suppressing Peasant Competition

We have talked about the techniques by which indigenous populations were forced to cultivate cash crops. In some countries with large plantations, however, colonial governments found it necessary to *prevent* peasants from independently growing cash crops not out of concern for their welfare, but so that they would not compete with colonial interests growing the same crop. For peasant farmers, given a modicum of opportunity, proved themselves capable of outproducing the large plantations not only in terms of output per unit of land but, more important, in terms of capital cost per unit produced.

In the Dutch East Indies (Indonesia and Dutch New Guinea) colonial policy in the middle of the nineteenth century forbade the sugar refineries to buy sugar cane from indigenous growers and imposed a discriminatory tax on rubber produced by native smallholders.[22] A recent unpublished United Nations study of agricultural development in Africa concluded that large-scale agricultural operations owned and controlled by foreign commercial interests (such as the rubber plantations of Liberia, the sisal estates of Tanganyika [Tanzania], and the coffee estates of Angola) only survived the competition of peasant producers because "the authorities actively supported them by suppressing indigenous rural development."[23]

The suppression of indigenous agricultural development served the interests of the colonizing powers in two ways. Not only did it prevent direct competition from more efficient native producers of the same crops, but it also guaranteed a labor force to work on the foreign-owned estates. Planters and foreign investors were not unaware that peasants who could survive economically by their own production would be under less pressure to sell their labor cheaply to the large estates.

The answer to the question, then, "Why can't people feed themselves?" must begin with an understanding of how colonialism actively prevented people from doing just that.

Colonialism

- forced peasants to replace food crops with cash crops that were then expropriated at very low rates;
- took over the best agricultural land for export crop plantations and then forced the most able-bodied workers to leave the village fields to work as slaves or for very low wages on plantations;

- encouraged a dependence on imported food;
- blocked native peasant cash crop production from competing with cash crops produced by settlers or foreign firms.

These are concrete examples of the development of underdevelopment that we should have perceived as such even as we read our history schoolbooks. Why didn't we? Somehow our schoolbooks always seemed to make the flow of history appear to have its own logic—as if it could not have been any other way. I, Frances, recall, in particular, a grade-school, social studies pamphlet on the idyllic life of Pedro, a nine-year-old boy on a coffee plantation in South America. The drawings of lush vegetation and "exotic" huts made his life seem romantic indeed. Wasn't it natural and proper that South America should have plantations to supply my mother and father with coffee? Isn't that the way it was *meant* to be?

Author's Note
Why can't people feed themselves— still?

Why hunger in a world of food abundance? This question remains one of the most pressing of the 21st century. On one level, the answer continues to be that extreme power imbalances deny people access to food. What's changing, however, is that on a global level food and farming are now moving rapidly in two directions: Forces creating hunger are intensifying; yet, at the very same time, breakthroughs in human understanding and courage on every continent are attacking hunger at its very roots.

First, the downward spiral: Today roughly a billion of us go hungry—more than ever in history—even though the UN's agricultural arm reports that, compared to four decades ago, the world produces over 30 percent more food for each of us: now almost 3,000 calories per day.[24] That's enough to make us all chubby— and it's only the leftovers, what's left over after we feed more than a third of the world's grain and most of our soy to livestock.[25]

Thus, the recent massive upsurge in hunger does not reflect a supply crisis but a price crisis: In 2008 food commodity prices shot up, and are surging again in 2011. In large measure, prices are reacting to dramatic events far from the fields—some slow developing and some seeming to emerge almost overnight.

Developing countries now spend five to six times more on food imports than they did in the early 1990s, notes Olivier De Schutter, the UN Special Rapporteur on the Right to Food. This deepening dependency reflects powerful human-made forces, including local government defunding of agricultural development—from roads to government agricultural agents educating farmers to subsidized farm inputs—during the 1980s and 1990s. One reason is that foreign aid to poor countries was often tied to their governments' opening doors to imported food while cutting such public supports. At the same time, many farmers in poor countries were encouraged to adopt corporate-controlled seeds and pesticides, often trapping them in debt to moneylenders.

As agriculture in many poor countries faltered, millions of farmers abandoned the land for urban centers. Cities grew, and

poor city folk couldn't find decent work, so their lives depended on cheap food. Feeling that pressure, governments have tried to keep food in cities cheap, which depends on further undercutting profits farmers need to invest in producing more. Voilà, a vicious cycle: Desperate governments opening their doors to cheap food imports only made it harder for their own farming communities to flourish. Speeding the cycle, governments in the Global North—contradicting their own advice—have continued to spend hundreds of billions of dollars annually to subsidize their farmers; making their exports artificially cheap for poor countries to import.[26]

Add to these extreme power imbalances—Wall Street's entry. Over just three years, from 2005 to 2008, the price of hard red wheat, for example, jumped fourfold—even though wheat was plentiful. What was going on? In 1991, Goldman Sachs, followed by other banks, started putting investor dollars into their new commodity indexes—which ballooned from $13 billion in 2003 to $317 billion in 2008. So, "dollars … overwhelmed the actual supply and actual demand for wheat, and rumors began to emerge that someone, somewhere, had cornered the market," explained economics analyst Frederick Kaufman in 2010.[27]

Other factors are also contributing to food-price escalation and price swings: the rising price of oil, climate-change-related flood and drought, as well as world food reserves often kept so low they can't provide a price buffer. Add also the recent government-mandated diversion of grain into making fuel: It amounts to enough sheer calories to meet the needs of a population greater than that of the U.S.

Food-price inflation has also unleashed a long-term hunger-making force, what's now dubbed "land grabs." The World Bank reports that since 2008, speculators and foreign governments have increased by tenfold their purchases of agricultural land in the Global South, especially in Africa.[28] Governments of countries such as Saudi Arabia and South Korea are motivated by fear that their own farming resources will not long support their people; speculators hope to benefit from a rising cost of land as food prices rise.

With all these forces at work, it's clear that the continuing tragedy of hunger, during an extended period of largely excellent world harvests, stems overwhelmingly from concentrated, unaccountable economic power, not from the earth's limits, or, in a significant way, from climate change.[29] As patterns set in place by colonialism continue, the useful questions about food and hunger do not narrowly focus on quantities of food. They are instead:

Do our methods of production enhance ecological relationships that restore—if necessary—and maintain food-producing capacity?

And, do our human relationships enable all people to gain access to what is produced?

These questions take us to the second, profoundly hopeful, food-and-farming path humanity is now charting. Over the last 20 years, scientists, farmers, and social movements worldwide have been proving that ecologically attuned farming can not only achieve desired yields but also support democratic development, enabling people to access what is grown.

Instead of "dependency agriculture"—that is, farming dependent on purchased chemical inputs and commercial seeds—more and more farming communities are embracing agro-ecological approaches in which yields increase dramatically using not purchases but new farming *practices*—such as composting, intercropping, and natural pest control.[30]

In 2011 the UK Office for Science released a study of African farms, covering 10 million acres, demonstrating that on average farmers doubled their yields using largely non-chemical, ecological approaches.[31] A related 2008 UN study showed that such changes in farming practices increase family incomes, improve diets, enhance soil fertility, and empower women. Farmers, freed from dependency on corporate-controlled inputs, are gaining knowledge that makes them more resilient.[32] Also in Africa, farmers in the extremely poor West African nation of Niger have "regreened" 12.5 million acres by re-establishing the ancient practice of keeping trees in fields to restore the soil and provide additional food and fodder.[33] Such breakthroughs are emerging, not in just a few villages, but on millions of acres from Africa to Asia to Latin America.

In parallel, a few societies are coming to see food as a right of citizenship, now enshrined in over twenty constitutions. From this premise, Brazil, for example, cut infant death, an excellent measure of hunger, by 63 percent between 1990 and 2006.[34]

These breakthroughs reflect a revolution in understanding. More and more people throughout the world are realizing that the dominant economic mode—including the economics of food and farming—is not working. Concentrating power, it denies the human need for agency and self-determination—ultimately denying adequate food to a billion of us. In its place, people are creating more ecological and democratic economies. In such "living economies," power is held accountable and continually dispersed so more and more people not only eat, but thrive.

Notes

1. Radha Sinha, *Food and Poverty* (New York: Holmes and Meier, 1976), p. 26.
2. John Stuart Mill, *Political Economy,* Book 3, Chapter 25 (emphasis added).
3. Peter Feldman and David Lawrence, "Social and Economic Implications of the Large-Scale Introduction of New Varieties of Foodgrains," Africa Report, preliminary draft (Geneva: UNRISD, 1975), pp. 107–108.
4. Edgar Owens, *The Right Side of History,* unpublished manuscript, 1976.
5. Walter Rodney, *How Europe Underdeveloped Africa* (London: Bogle-L'Ouverture Publications, 1972), pp. 171–172.
6. Ferdinand Ossendowski, *Slaves of the Sun* (New York: Dutton, 1928), p. 276.
7. Rodney, *How Europe Underdeveloped Africa,* pp. 171–172.
8. Ibid., p. 181.
9. Clifford Geertz, *Agricultural Involution* (Berkeley and Los Angeles: University of California Press, 1963), pp. 52–53.
10. Rodney, *How Europe Underdeveloped Africa,* p. 185.
11. Ibid., p. 184.
12. Ibid., p. 186.
13. George L. Beckford, *Persistent Poverty: Underdevelopment in Plantation Economies of the Third World* (New York: Oxford University Press, 1972), p. 99.
14. Ibid., p. 99, quoting from Erich Jacoby, *Agrarian Unrest in Southeast Asia* (New York: Asia Publishing House, 1961), p. 66.
15. Pat Flynn and Roger Burbach, North American Congress on Latin America, Berkely, California, recent investigation.
16. Feldman and Lawrence, "Social and Economic Implications," p. 103.
17. Special Sahelian Office Report, Food and Agriculture Organization, March 28, 1974, pp. 88–89.
18. Alan Adamson, *Sugar Without Slaves: The Political Economy of British Guiana, 1838–1904* (New Haven and London: Yale University Press, 1972).
19. Ibid., p. 41.
20. Eric Williams, *Capitalism and Slavery* (New York: Putnam, 1966), p. 110.
21. Ibid., p. 121.
22. Gunnar Myrdal, *Asian Drama,* vol. 1 (New York: Pantheon, 1966), pp. 448–449.
23. Feldman and Lawrence, "Social and Economic Implications," p. 189.
24. "Production Indices," FAOSTAT, http://faostat.fao.org/site/612/DesktopDefault.aspx?PageID=612#ancor. This estimate is based on food available after deducting feed and seed. For calories, see Bruno Dorin, Patrick Caron, and Bernard Hubert, "Agrimonde" (PowerPoint presentation at UN Food and Agriculture Organization Expert Meeting on How to Feed the World in 2050, Rome, Italy, June 24–26, 2009), www.fao.org/fileadmin/templates/esa/Global_persepctives/Presentations/Dorin_pres.pdf.
25. *Livestock's Long Shadow: Environmental Issues and Options* (Rome: FAO, 2006), 12, 43, ftp://ftp.fao.org/docrep/fao/010/a0701e/a0701e.pdf.
26. Madeleine Bunting, "How Can We Feed the World and Still Save the Planet?" *Guardian*, January 21, 2011, www.guardian.co.uk/global-development/poverty-matters/2011/jan/21/olivier-de-schutter-food-farming.
27. Fred Kaufman, "The Food Bubble," Harper's, June 2010, 27–28, 32. See also *Commodity Markets Speculation: The Risk to Food Security and Agriculture* (Minneapolis, MN: Institute for Agriculture and Trade Policy, 2008), www.iatp.org/iatp/publication.cfnhefid=104414.
28. Klaus Deininger and Derek Byerlee, *Rising Global Interest in Farmland* (Washington, DC: International Bank for Reconstruction and Development/World Bank, 2011), http://siteresources.worldbank.org/INTARD/Resources/ESW_Sept7_final_final.pdf.
29. "Production Indices," FAOSTAT, http://faostat.fao.org/site/612/DesktopDefault.aspx?PageID=612#ancor.
30. United Nations Environment Program–United Nations Conference on Trade and Development Capacity-Building Task Force on Trade, Environment, and Development, *Organic Agriculture and*

Food Security in Africa (New York: United Nations, 2008), 11–16. www.unctad.org/en/docs/ditcted200715_en.pdf.

31. *Foresight Project on Global Food and Farming Futures: Synthesis Report C9: Sustainable Intensification in African Agriculture—Analysis of Cases and Common Lessons,* The U.K. Government Office for Science, January 2011, 8. http://www .bis.gov.uk/assets/bispartners/foresight/docs/food-and-farming/ synthesis/11-629-c9-sustainable-intensification-in-african- agriculture.pdf.

32. United Nations Environment Program–United Nations Conference on Trade and Development Capacity-Building Task Force on Trade, Environment, and Development, *Organic Agriculture and Food Security in Africa* (New York: United Nations, 2008), 11–16. www.unctad.org/en/docs/ditcted200715_en.pdf.

33. Chris Reij, "Investing in Trees to Mitigate Climate Change," in *State of the World* 2011, ed. Worldwatch Institute (New York: W. W. Norton, 2011), 88.

34. United Nations Children Fund, *The State of the World's Children* 2008: Child Survival (New York: UNICEF, 2007), 114, http://www.unicef.org/publications/files/The_State_of_ the_Worlds_Children_2008.pdf; Marcia C. Castro and Celso C. S. Simões, "Spatio-Temporal Trends of Infant Mortality in Brazil," Paper Presented at the XXVI IUSSP International Population Conference, Marrakech, Morocco, September 2009.

Critical Thinking

1. In relation to hunger, what do the authors mean when they say that "it is the force creating the condition, not the condition itself that must be the target of change"?

2. How did colonizers view agriculture in the subjugated lands? How did they view their own agriculture?

3. What kind of agriculture was practiced prior to colonization? after colonization?

4. What were the two basic strategies to force cash crop production?

5. What were the functions of taxes? Marketing boards?

6. How does Java represent a prime example of how a colonial government seizes land and then puts it into foreign hands? What did the introduction of the plantation mean regarding nourishment?

7. What techniques have been used to actively force peasants off their land?

8. How did British Guiana cope with the "double blow of the emancipation of slaves and the crash in the world sugar market"?

9. Why do some countries prevent peasants from independently growing cash crops?

10. How does the author characterize the level of hunger in the world? the level of food production? What conclusion can we draw from this?

11. What factors have contributed to the inability of developing countries to produce their own food cheaply?

    1. What factors have contributed to food-price escalations and price swings?

    2. What has been a long-term hunger-making force?

    3. How does the author explain the "continuing tragedy of hunger"?

    4. What "useful" questions should we be asking?

    5. What is "dependency agriculture" and what does the author suggest as as an alternative? What evidence does the author cite in favor of such an alternative?

FRANCES MOORE LAPPÉ and **DR. JOSEPH COLLINS** are founders and directors of the Institute for Food and Development Policy, located in San Francisco and New York.

The Arrow of Disease

When Columbus and his successors invaded the Americas, the most potent weapon they carried was their germs. But why didn't deadly disease flow in the other direction, from the New World to the Old?

JARED DIAMOND

The three people talking in the hospital room were already stressed out from having to cope with a mysterious illness, and it didn't help at all that they were having trouble communicating. One of them was the patient, a small, timid man, sick with pneumonia caused by an unidentified microbe and with only a limited command of the English language. The second, acting as translator, was his wife, worried about her husband's condition and frightened by the hospital environment. The third person in the trio was an inexperienced young doctor, trying to figure out what might have brought on the strange illness. Under the stress, the doctor was forgetting everything he had been taught about patient confidentiality. He committed the awful blunder of requesting the woman to ask her husband whether he'd had any sexual experiences that might have caused the infection.

As the young doctor watched, the husband turned red, pulled himself together so that he seemed even smaller, tried to disappear under his bed sheets, and stammered in a barely audible voice. His wife suddenly screamed in rage and drew herself up to tower over him. Before the doctor could stop her, she grabbed a heavy metal bottle, slammed it onto her husband's head, and stormed out of the room. It took a while for the doctor to elicit, through the man's broken English, what he had said to so enrage his wife. The answer slowly emerged: he had admitted to repeated intercourse with sheep on a recent visit to the family farm; perhaps that was how he had contracted the mysterious microbe.

This episode, related to me by a physician friend involved in the case, sounds so bizarrely one of a kind as to be of no possible broader significance. But in fact it illustrates a subject of great importance: human diseases of animal origins. Very few of us may love sheep in the carnal sense. But most of us platonically love our pet animals, like our dogs and cats; and as a society, we certainly appear to have an inordinate fondness for sheep and other livestock, to judge from the vast numbers of them that we keep.

Some of us—most often our children—pick up infectious diseases from our pets. Usually these illnesses remain no more than a nuisance, but a few have evolved into far more. The major killers of humanity throughout our recent history—smallpox, flu, tuberculosis, malaria, plague, measles, and cholera—are all infectious diseases that arose from diseases of animals. Until World War II more victims of war died of microbes than of gunshot or

sword wounds. All those military histories glorifying Alexander the Great and Napoleon ignore the ego-deflating truth: the winners of past wars were not necessarily those armies with the best generals and weapons, but those bearing the worst germs with which to smite their enemies.

The grimmest example of the role of germs in history is much on our minds this month, as we recall the European conquest of the Americas that began with Columbus's voyage of 1492. Numerous as the Indian victims of the murderous Spanish conquistadores were, they were dwarfed in number by the victims of murderous Spanish microbes. These formidable conquerors killed an estimated 95 percent of the New World's pre-Columbian Indian population.

Why was the exchange of nasty germs between the Americas and Europe so unequal? Why didn't the reverse happen instead, with Indian diseases decimating the Spanish invaders, spreading back across the Atlantic, and causing a 95 percent decline in *Europe's* human population?

Similar questions arise regarding the decimation of many other native peoples by European germs, and regarding the decimation of would-be European conquistadores in the tropics of Africa and Asia.

Naturally, we're disposed to think about diseases from our own point of view: What can we do to save ourselves and to kill the microbes? Let's stamp out the scoundrels, and never mind what *their* motives are!

In life, though, one has to understand the enemy to beat him. So for a moment, let's consider disease from the microbes' point of view. Let's look beyond our anger at their making us sick in bizarre ways, like giving us genital sores or diarrhea, and ask why it is that they do such things. After all, microbes are as much a product of natural selection as we are, and so their actions must have come about because they confer some evolutionary benefit.

Basically, of course, evolution selects those individuals that are most effective at producing babies and at helping those babies find suitable places to live. Microbes are marvels at this latter requirement. They have evolved diverse ways of spreading from one person to another, and from animals to people. Many of our symptoms of disease actually represent ways in which some clever bug modifies our bodies or our behavior such that we become enlisted to spread bugs.

The most effortless way a bug can spread is by just waiting to be transmitted passively to the next victim. That's the strategy practiced by microbes that wait for one host to be eaten by the next—salmonella bacteria, for example, which we contract by eating already-infected eggs or meat; or the worm responsible for trichinosis, which waits for us to kill a pig and eat it without properly cooking it.

As a slight modification of this strategy, some microbes don't wait for the old host to die but instead hitchhike in the saliva of an insect that bites the old host and then flies to a new one. The free ride may be provided by mosquitoes, fleas, lice, or tsetse flies, which spread malaria, plague, typhus, and sleeping sickness, respectively. The dirtiest of all passive-carriage tricks is perpetrated by microbes that pass from a woman to her fetus—microbes such as the ones responsible for syphilis, rubella (German measles), and AIDS. By their cunning these microbes can already be infecting an infant before the moment of its birth.

Other bugs take matters into their own hands, figuratively speaking. They actively modify the anatomy or habits of their host to accelerate their transmission. From our perspective, the open genital sores caused by venereal diseases such as syphilis are a vile indignity. From the microbes' point of view, however, they're just a useful device to enlist a host's help in inoculating the body cavity of another host with microbes. The skin lesions caused by smallpox similarly spread microbes by direct or indirect body contact (occasionally very indirect, as when U.S. and Australian whites bent on wiping out "belligerent" native peoples sent them gifts of blankets previously used by smallpox patients).

More vigorous yet is the strategy practiced by the influenza, common cold, and pertussis (whooping cough) microbes, which induce the victim to cough or sneeze, thereby broadcasting the bugs toward prospective new hosts. Similarly the cholera bacterium induces a massive diarrhea that spreads bacteria into the water supplies of potential new victims. For modification of a host's behavior, though, nothing matches the rabies virus, which not only gets into the saliva of an infected dog but drives the dog into a frenzy of biting and thereby infects many new victims.

Thus, from our viewpoint, genital sores, diarrhea, and coughing are "symptoms" of disease. From a bug's viewpoint, they're clever evolutionary strategies to broadcast the bug. That's why it's in the bug's interests to make us "sick." But what does it gain by killing us? That seems self-defeating, since a microbe that kills its host kills itself.

Though you may well think it's of little consolation, our death is really just an unintended by-product of host symptoms that promote the efficient transmission of microbes. Yes, an untreated cholera patient may eventually die from producing diarrheal fluid at a rate of several gallons a day. While the patient lasts, though, the cholera bacterium profits from being massively disseminated into the water supplies of its next victims. As long as each victim thereby infects, on average, more than one new victim, the bacteria will spread, even though the first host happens to die.

So much for the dispassionate examination of the bug's interests. Now let's get back to considering our own selfish interests: to stay alive and healthy, best done by killing the damned bugs. One common response to infection is to develop a fever. Again, we consider fever a "symptom" of disease, as if it developed inevitably without serving any function. But regulation of body temperature is under our genetic control, and a fever doesn't just happen by accident. Because some microbes are more sensitive to heat than our own bodies are, by raising our body temperature we in effect try to bake the bugs to death before we get baked ourselves.

> **We and our pathogens are now locked in an escalating evolutionary contest, with the death of one contestant the price of defeat, and with natural selection playing the role of umpire.**

Another common response is to mobilize our immune system. White blood cells and other cells actively seek out and kill foreign microbes. The specific antibodies we gradually build up against a particular microbe make us less likely to get reinfected once we are cured. As we all know there are some illnesses, such as flu and the common cold, to which our resistance is only temporary; we can eventually contract the illness again. Against other illnesses, though—including measles, mumps, rubella, pertussis, and the now-defeated menace of smallpox—antibodies stimulated by one infection confer lifelong immunity. That's the principle behind vaccination—to stimulate our antibody production without our having to go through the actual experience of the disease.

Alas, some clever bugs don't just cave in to our immune defenses. Some have learned to trick us by changing their antigens, those molecular pieces of the microbe that our antibodies recognize. The constant evolution or recycling of new strains of flu, with differing antigens, explains why the flu you got two years ago didn't protect you against the different strain that arrived this year. Sleeping sickness is an even more slippery customer in its ability to change its antigens rapidly.

Among the slipperiest of all is the virus that causes AIDS, which evolves new antigens even as it sits within an individual patient, until it eventually overwhelms the immune system.

Our slowest defensive response is through natural selection, which changes the relative frequency with which a gene appears from generation to generation. For almost any disease some people prove to be genetically more resistant than others. In an epidemic, those people with genes for resistance to that particular microbe are more likely to survive than are people lacking such genes. As a result, over the course of history human populations repeatedly exposed to a particular pathogen tend to be made up of individuals with genes that resist the appropriate microbe just because unfortunate individuals without those genes were less likely to survive to pass their genes on to their children.

Fat consolation, you may be thinking. This evolutionary response is not one that does the genetically susceptible dying individual any good. It does mean, though, that a human population as a whole becomes better protected.

In short, many bugs have had to evolve tricks to let them spread among potential victims. We've evolved counter-tricks, to which the bugs have responded by evolving counter-counter-tricks. We and our pathogens are now locked in an escalating evolutionary contest, with the death of one contestant the price of defeat, and with natural selection playing the role of umpire.

The form that this deadly contest takes varies with the pathogens: for some it is like a guerrilla war, while for others it is a blitzkrieg. With certain diseases, like malaria or hookworm, there's a more or less steady trickle of new cases in an affected area, and they will appear in any month of any year. Epidemic diseases, though, are different: they produce no cases for a long time, then a whole wave of cases, then no more cases again for a while.

Among such epidemic diseases, influenza is the most familiar to Americans, this year having been a particularly bad one for us (but a great year for the influenza virus). Cholera epidemics come at longer intervals, the 1991 Peruvian epidemic being the first one to reach the New World during the twentieth century. Frightening as today's influenza and cholera epidemics are, though, they pale beside the far more terrifying epidemics of the past, before the rise of modern medicine. The greatest single epidemic in human history was the influenza wave that killed 21 million people at the end of the First World War. The black death, or bubonic plague, killed one-quarter of Europe's population between 1346 and 1352, with death tolls up to 70 percent in some cities.

The infectious diseases that visit us as epidemics share several characteristics. First, they spread quickly and efficiently from an infected person to nearby healthy people, with the result that the whole population gets exposed within a short time. Second, they're "acute" illnesses: within a short time, you either die or recover completely. Third, the fortunate ones of us who do recover develop antibodies that leave us immune against a recurrence of the disease for a long time, possibly our entire lives. Finally, these diseases tend to be restricted to humans; the bugs causing them tend not to live in the soil or in other animals. All four of these characteristics apply to what Americans think of as the once more-familiar acute epidemic diseases of childhood, including measles, rubella, mumps, pertussis, and smallpox.

It is easy to understand why the combination of those four characteristics tends to make a disease run in epidemics. The rapid spread of microbes and the rapid course of symptoms mean that everybody in a local human population is soon infected, and thereafter either dead or else recovered and immune. No one is left alive who could still be infected. But since the microbe can't survive except in the bodies of living people, the disease dies out until a new crop of babies reaches the susceptible age—and until an infectious person arrives from the outside to start a new epidemic.

A classic illustration of the process is given by the history of measles on the isolated Faeroe Islands in the North Atlantic. A severe epidemic of the disease reached the Faeroes in 1781, then died out, leaving the islands measles-free until an infected carpenter arrived on a ship from Denmark in 1846. Within three months almost the whole Faeroes population—7,782 people—had gotten measles and then either died or recovered, leaving the measles virus to disappear once again until the next epidemic. Studies show that measles is likely to die out in any human population numbering less than half a million people. Only in larger populations can measles shift from one local area to another, thereby persisting until enough babies have been born in the originally infected area to permit the disease's return.

Rubella in Australia provides a similar example, on a much larger scale. As of 1917 Australia's population was still only 5 million, with most people living in scattered rural areas. The sea voyage to Britain took two months, and land transport within Australia itself was slow. In effect, Australia didn't even consist of a population of 5 million, but of hundreds of much smaller populations. As a result, rubella hit Australia only as occasional epidemics, when an infected person happened to arrive from overseas and stayed in a densely populated area. By 1938, though, the city of Sydney alone had a population of over one million, and people moved frequently and quickly by air between London, Sydney, and other Australian cities. Around then, rubella for the first time was able to establish itself permanently in Australia.

What's true for rubella in Australia is true for most familiar acute infectious diseases throughout the world. To sustain themselves, they need a human population that is sufficiently numerous and densely packed that a new crop of susceptible children is available for infection by the time the disease would otherwise be waning. Hence the measles and other such diseases are also known as "crowd diseases."

Crowd diseases could not sustain themselves in small bands of hunter-gatherers and slash-and-burn farmers. As tragic recent experience with Amazonian Indians and Pacific Islanders confirms, almost an entire tribelet may be wiped out by an epidemic brought by an outside visitor, because no one in the tribelet has any antibodies against the microbe. In addition, measles and some other "childhood" diseases are more likely to kill infected adults than children, and all adults in the tribelet are susceptible. Having killed most of the tribelet, the epidemic then disappears. The small population size explains why tribelets can't sustain epidemics introduced from the outside; at the same time it explains why they could never evolve epidemic diseases of their own to give back to the visitors.

That's not to say that small human populations are free from all infectious diseases. Some of their infections are caused by microbes capable of maintaining themselves in animals or in soil, so the disease remains constantly available to infect people. For example, the yellow fever virus is carried by African wild monkeys and is constantly available to infect rural human populations of Africa. It was also available to be carried to New World monkeys and people by the transAtlantic slave trade.

Other infections of small human populations are chronic diseases, such as leprosy and yaws, that may take a very long time to kill a victim. The victim thus remains alive as a reservoir of microbes to infect other members of the tribelet. Finally, small human populations are susceptible to nonfatal infections against which we don't develop immunity, with the result that the same person can become reinfected after recovering. That's the case with hookworm and many other parasites.

All these types of diseases, characteristic of small, isolated populations, must be the oldest diseases of humanity. They were the ones that we could evolve and sustain through the early millions of years of our evolutionary history, when the total human population was tiny and fragmented. They are also shared with, or are similar to the diseases of, our closest wild relatives, the African great apes. In contrast, the evolution of our crowd diseases could only have occurred with the buildup of large, dense human populations, first made possible by the rise of agriculture about 10,000 years ago, then by the rise of cities several thousand years ago. Indeed, the first attested dates for many familiar infectious diseases are surprisingly recent: around 1600 B.C. for smallpox (as deduced from pockmarks on an Egyptian mummy), 400 B.C. for mumps, 1840 for polio, and 1959 for AIDS.

Agriculture sustains much higher human population densities than do hunting and gathering—on average, 10 to 100 times higher. In addition, hunter-gatherers frequently shift camp, leaving behind their piles of feces with their accumulated microbes and worm larvae. But farmers are sedentary and live amid their own sewage, providing microbes with a quick path from one person's body into another person's drinking water. Farmers also become surrounded by disease-transmitting rodents attracted by stored food.

> **The explosive increase in world travel by Americans, and in immigration to the United States, is turning us into another melting pot— this time of microbes that we'd dismissed as causing disease in far-off countries.**

Some human populations make it even easier for their own bacteria and worms to infect new victims, by intentionally gathering their feces and urine and spreading it as fertilizer on the fields where people work. Irrigation agriculture and fish farming provide ideal living conditions for the snails carrying schistosomes, and for other flukes that burrow through our skin as we wade through the feces-laden water.

If the rise of farming was a boon for our microbes, the rise of cities was a veritable bonanza, as still more densely packed human populations festered under even worse sanitation conditions. (Not until the beginning of the twentieth century did urban populations finally become self-sustaining; until then, constant immigration of healthy peasants from the countryside was necessary to make good the constant deaths of city dwellers from crowd diseases.) Another bonanza was the development of world trade routes, which by late Roman times effectively joined the populations of Europe, Asia, and North Africa into one giant breeding ground for microbes. That's when smallpox finally reached Rome as the "plague of Antonius," which killed millions of Roman citizens between A.D. 165 and 180.

Similarly, bubonic plague first appeared in Europe as the plague of Justinian (A.D. 542–543). But plague didn't begin to hit Europe with full force, as the black death epidemics, until 1346, when new overland trading with China provided rapid transit for flea-infested furs from plague-ridden areas of Central Asia. Today our jet planes have made even the longest intercontinental flights briefer than the duration of any human infectious disease. That's how an Aerolíneas Argentinas airplane, stopping in Lima, Peru, earlier this year, managed to deliver dozens of cholera-infected people the same day to my city of Los Angeles, over 3,000 miles away. The explosive increase in world travel by Americans, and in immigration to the United States, is turning us into another melting pot—this time of microbes that we previously dismissed as just causing exotic diseases in far-off countries.

When the human population became sufficiently large and concentrated, we reached the stage in our history when we could at last sustain crowd diseases confined to our species. But that presents a paradox: such diseases could never have existed before. Instead they had to evolve as new diseases. Where did those new diseases come from?

Evidence emerges from studies of the disease-causing microbes themselves. In many cases molecular biologists have identified the microbe's closest relative. Those relatives also prove to be agents of infectious crowd diseases—but ones confined to various species of domestic animals and pets! Among animals too, epidemic diseases require dense populations, and they're mainly confined to social animals that provide the necessary large populations. Hence when we domesticated social animals such as cows and pigs, they were already afflicted by epidemic diseases just waiting to be transferred to us.

For example, the measles virus is most closely related to the virus causing rinderpest, a nasty epidemic disease of cattle and many wild cud-chewing mammals. Rinderpest doesn't affect humans. Measles, in turn, doesn't affect cattle. The close similarity of the measles and rinderpest viruses suggests that the rinderpest virus transferred from cattle to humans, then became the measles virus by changing its properties to adapt to us. That transfer isn't surprising, considering how closely many peasant farmers live and sleep next to cows and their accompanying feces, urine, breath, sores, and blood. Our intimacy with cattle has been going on for 8,000 years since we domesticated them—ample time for the rinderpest virus to discover us nearby. Other familiar infectious diseases can similarly be traced back to diseases of our animal friends.

Given our proximity to the animals we love, we must constantly be getting bombarded by animal microbes. Those invaders get winnowed by natural selection, and only a few succeed in establishing themselves as human diseases. A quick survey of current diseases lets us trace four stages in the evolution of a specialized human disease from an animal precursor.

In the first stage, we pick up animal-borne microbes that are still at an early stage in their evolution into specialized human pathogens. They don't get transmitted directly from one person to another, and even their transfer from animals to us remains uncommon. There are dozens of diseases like this that we get directly from pets and domestic animals. They include cat scratch fever from cats, leptospirosis from dogs, psittacosis from chickens and parrots, and brucellosis from cattle. We're similarly susceptible to picking up diseases from wild animals, such as the tularemia that hunters occasionally get from skinning wild rabbits.

In the second stage, a former animal pathogen evolves to the point where it does get transmitted directly between people and causes epidemics. However, the epidemic dies out for several reasons—being cured by modern medicine, stopping when everybody has been infected and died, or stopping when everybody has been infected and become immune. For example, a previously unknown disease termed *o'nyong-nyong* fever appeared in East Africa in 1959 and infected several million Africans. It probably arose from a virus of monkeys and was transmitted to humans by mosquitoes. The fact that patients recovered quickly and became immune to further attack helped cause the new disease to die out quickly.

The annals of medicine are full of diseases that sound like no known disease today but that once caused terrifying epidemics before disappearing as mysteriously as they had come. Who alive today remembers the "English sweating sickness" that swept and terrified Europe between 1485 and 1578, or the "Picardy sweats" of eighteenth- and nineteenth-century France?

A third stage in the evolution of our major diseases is represented by former animal pathogens that establish themselves in humans and that do not die out; until they do, the question of whether they will become major killers of humanity remains up for grabs. The future is still very uncertain for Lassa fever, first observed in 1969 in Nigeria and caused by a virus probably derived from rodents. Better established is Lyme disease, caused by a spirochete that we get from the bite of a tick. Although the first known human cases in the United States appeared only as recently as 1962, Lyme disease is already reaching epidemic proportions in the Northeast, on the West Coast, and in the upper Midwest. The future of AIDS, derived from monkey viruses, is even more secure, from the virus's perspective.

The final stage of this evolution is represented by the major, long-established epidemic diseases confined to humans. These diseases must have been the evolutionary survivors of far more pathogens that tried to make the jump to us from animals—and mostly failed.

Diseases represent evolution in progress, as microbes adapt by natural selection to new hosts. Compared with cows' bodies, though, our bodies offer different immune defenses and different chemistry. In that new environment, a microbe must evolve new ways to live and propagate itself.

The best-studied example of microbes evolving these new ways involves myxomatosis, which hit Australian rabbits in 1950. The myxoma virus, native to a wild species of Brazilian rabbit, was known to cause a lethal epidemic in European domestic rabbits, which are a different species. The virus was intentionally introduced to Australia in the hopes of ridding the continent of its plague of European rabbits, foolishly introduced in the nineteenth century. In the first year, myxoma produced a gratifying (to Australian farmers) 99.8 percent mortality in infected rabbits. Fortunately for the rabbits and unfortunately for the farmers, the death rate then dropped in the second year to 90 percent and eventually to 25 percent, frustrating hopes of eradicating rabbits completely from Australia. The problem was that the myxoma virus evolved to serve its own interest, which differed from the farmers' interests and those of the rabbits. The virus changed to kill fewer rabbits and to permit lethally infected ones to live longer before dying. The result was bad for Australian farmers but good for the virus: a less lethal myxoma virus spreads baby viruses to more rabbits than did the original, highly virulent myxoma.

For a similar example in humans, consider the surprising evolution of syphilis. Today we associate syphilis with genital sores and a very slowly developing disease, leading to the death of untreated victims only after many years. However, when syphilis was first definitely recorded in Europe in 1495, its pustules often covered the body from the head to the knees, caused flesh to fall off people's faces, and led to death within a few months. By 1546 syphilis had evolved into the disease with the symptoms known to us today. Apparently, just as with myxomatosis, those syphilis spirochetes evolved to keep their victims alive longer in order to transmit their spirochete offspring into more victims.

How, then, does all this explain the outcome of 1492—that Europeans conquered and depopulated the New World, instead of Native Americans conquering and depopulating Europe?

In the century or two following Columbus's arrival in the New World, the Indian population declined by about 95 percent. The main killers were European germs, to which the Indians had never been exposed.

Part of the answer, of course, goes back to the invaders' technological advantages. European guns and steel swords were more effective weapons than Native American stone axes and wooden clubs. Only Europeans had ships capable of crossing the ocean and horses that could provide a decisive advantage in battle. But that's not the whole answer. Far more Native Americans died in bed than on the battlefield—the victims of germs, not of guns and swords. Those germs undermined Indian resistance by killing most Indians and their leaders and by demoralizing the survivors.

The role of disease in the Spanish conquests of the Aztec and Inca empires is especially well documented. In 1519 Cortés landed on the coast of Mexico with 600 Spaniards to conquer the fiercely militaristic Aztec Empire, which at the time had a population of many millions. That Cortés reached the Aztec capital of Tenochtitlán, escaped with the loss of "only" two-thirds of his force, and managed to fight his way back to the coast demonstrates both Spanish military advantages and the initial naïveté of the Aztecs. But when Cortés's next onslaught came, in 1521, the Aztecs were no longer naïve; they fought street by street with the utmost tenacity.

What gave the Spaniards a decisive advantage this time was smallpox, which reached Mexico in 1520 with the arrival of one infected slave from Spanish Cuba. The resulting epidemic proceeded to kill nearly half the Aztecs. The survivors were demoralized by the mysterious illness that killed Indians and spared Spaniards, as if advertising the Spaniards' invincibility. By 1618 Mexico's initial population of 20 million had plummeted to about 1.6 million.

Pizarro had similarly grim luck when he landed on the coast of Peru in 1531 with about 200 men to conquer the Inca Empire. Fortunately for Pizarro, and unfortunately for the Incas, smallpox had arrived overland around 1524, killing much of the Inca population, including both Emperor Huayna Capac and his son and designated successor, Ninan Cuyoche. Because of the vacant throne, two other sons of Huayna Capac, Atahuallpa and Huáscar, became embroiled in a civil war that Pizarro exploited to conquer the divided Incas.

When we in the United States think of the most populous New World societies existing in 1492, only the Aztecs and Incas come to mind. We forget that North America also supported populous Indian societies in the Mississippi Valley. Sadly, these societies too would disappear. But in this case conquistadores contributed nothing directly to the societies' destruction; the conquistadores' germs, spreading in advance, did everything. When De Soto marched through the Southeast in 1540, he came across Indian towns abandoned two years previously because nearly all the inhabitants had died in epidemics. However, he was still able to see some of the densely populated towns lining the lower Mississippi. By a century and a half later, though, when French settlers returned to the lower Mississippi, almost all those towns had vanished. Their relics are the great mound sites of the Mississippi Valley. Only recently have we come to realize that the mound-building societies were still largely intact when Columbus arrived, and that they collapsed between 1492 and the systematic European exploration of the Mississippi.

When I was a child in school, we were taught that North America had originally been occupied by about one million Indians. That low number helped justify the white conquest of what could then be viewed as an almost empty continent. However, archeological excavations and descriptions left by the first European explorers on our coasts now suggest an initial number of around 20 million. In the century or two following Columbus's arrival in the New World, the Indian population is estimated to have declined by about 95 percent.

The main killers were European germs, to which the Indians had never been exposed and against which they therefore had neither immunologic nor genetic resistance. Smallpox, measles, influenza, and typhus competed for top rank among the killers. As if those were not enough, pertussis, plague, tuberculosis, diphtheria, mumps, malaria, and yellow fever came close behind. In countless cases Europeans were actually there to witness the decimation that occurred when the germs arrived. For example, in 1837 the Mandan Indian tribe, with one of the most elaborate cultures in the Great Plains, contracted smallpox thanks to a steamboat traveling up the Missouri River from St. Louis. The population of one Mandan village crashed from 2,000 to less than 40 within a few weeks.

The one-sided exchange of lethal germs between the Old and New Worlds is among the most striking and consequence-laden facts of recent history. Whereas over a dozen major infectious diseases of Old World origins became established in the New World, not a single major killer reached Europe from the Americas. The sole possible exception is syphilis, whose area of origin still remains controversial.

That one-sidedness is more striking with the knowledge that large, dense human populations are a prerequisite for the evolution of crowd diseases. If recent reappraisals of the pre-Columbian New World population are correct, that population was not far below the contemporaneous population of Eurasia. Some New World cities, like Tenochtitlán, were among the world's most populous cities at the time. Yet Tenochtitlán didn't have awful germs waiting in store for the Spaniards. Why not?

One possible factor is the rise of dense human populations began somewhat later in the New World than in the Old. Another is that the three most populous American centers—the Andes, Mexico, and the Mississippi Valley—were never connected by regular fast trade into one gigantic breeding ground for microbes, in the way that Europe, North Africa, India, and China became connected in late Roman times.

The main reason becomes clear, however, if we ask a simple question: From what microbes could any crowd diseases of the Americas have evolved? We've seen that Eurasian crowd diseases evolved from diseases of domesticated herd animals. Significantly, there were many such animals in Eurasia. But there were only five animals that became domesticated in the Americas: the turkey in Mexico and parts of North America, the guinea pig and llama/alpaca (probably derived from the same original wild species) in the Andes, and Muscovy duck in tropical South America, and the dog throughout the Americas.

That extreme paucity of New World domestic animals reflects the paucity of wild starting material. About 80 percent of the big wild mammals of the Americas became extinct at the end of the last ice age, around 11,000 years ago, at approximately the same time that the first well-attested wave of Indian hunters spread over the Americas. Among the species that disappeared were ones that would have yielded useful domesticates, such as American horses and camels. Debate still rages as to whether those extinctions were due to climate changes or to the impact of Indian hunters on prey that had never seen humans. Whatever the reason, the extinctions removed most of the basis for Native American animal domestication—and for crowd diseases.

The few domesticates that remained were not likely sources of such diseases. Muscovy ducks and turkeys don't live in enormous flocks, and they're not naturally endearing species (like young lambs) with which we have much physical contact. Guinea pigs may have contributed a trypanosome infection like Chagas' disease or leishmaniasis to our catalog of woes, but that's uncertain.

Initially the most surprising absence is of any human disease derived from llamas (or alpacas), which are tempting to consider as the Andean equivalent of Eurasian livestock. However, llamas had three strikes against them as a source of human pathogens: their wild relatives don't occur in big herds as do wild sheep, goats, and pigs; their total numbers were never remotely as large as the Eurasian populations of domestic livestock, since llamas never spread beyond the Andes; and llamas aren't as cuddly as piglets and lambs and aren't kept in such close association with people. (You may not think of piglets as cuddly, but human mothers in the New Guinea highlands often nurse them, and they frequently live right in the huts of peasant farmers.)

The importance of animal-derived diseases for human history extends far beyond the Americas. Eurasian germs played a key role in decimating native peoples in many other parts of the world as well, including the Pacific islands, Australia, and southern Africa. Racist Europeans used to attribute those conquests to their supposedly better brains. But no evidence for such better brains has been forthcoming. Instead, the conquests were made possible by Europeans' nastier germs, and by the technological advances and denser populations that Europeans ultimately acquired by means of their domesticated plants and animals.

So on this 500th anniversary of Columbus's discovery, let's try to regain our sense of perspective about his hotly debated achievements. There's no doubt that Columbus was a great visionary, seaman, and leader. There's also no doubt that he and his successors often behaved as bestial murderers. But those facts alone don't fully explain why it took so few European immigrants to initially conquer and ultimately supplant so much of the native population of the Americas. Without the germs Europeans brought with them—germs that were derived from their animals—such conquests might have been impossible.

Critical Thinking

1. What are the major killers of humanity and where do they come from? How did most victims of war die before World War II? What determined the winners of past wars? What percentage of the pre-Columbian Indian population was killed by Spanish microbes?

2. How might a bug such as salmonella be passively transmitted to its next victim? What examples does the author provide of microbes getting a "free ride" to its next victim? How might they modify the anatomy or habits of their host in order to accelerate their transmission?

3. How does the author, therefore, describe such "symptoms" of disease? Why is it in the bug's interest to make us "sick?"

Is it in the bug's interest to kill us? How does the author explain death? How do bacteria survive even though the hosts die?

4. What "common responses" do we use to stay alive?

5. Explain the principle of vaccination. How do the bugs "trick us?" Why is the AIDS virus one of the "slipperiest of all?"

6. What is our slowest defense mechanism? How does the author describe the "escalating evolutionary context?"

7. Explain the difference between pathogens that fight a "guerrilla war," creating a steady trickle of new cases, versus those that conduct a "blitzkrieg" and cause epidemics.

8. What characteristics are shared by infectious diseases that visit us as epidemics?

9. Why does measles die out in populations of less than half a million people but persists in larger population?

10. Why can't such "crowd diseases" sustain themselves in small bands of hunter-gatherers and slash-and burn farmers?

11. Does this mean that small human populations are free from all infectious diseases? Explain. Why does the author believe these to be the oldest diseases of humanity?

12. When did crowd diseases first develop and what are the various reasons for their increased frequency?

13. What is the paradox regarding these diseases? Where did they come from? Why does the author say we must be constantly bombarded by them?

14. Describe the four stages in the evolution of a specialized human disease from an animal precursor.

15. In what sense do diseases represent evolution in progress? How do the mixoma virus and the Australian rabbits provide an example?

16. How were Europeans technologically superior to Native Americans? What gave Cortez the decisive advantage over the Aztecs? Why were the surviving Aztecs demoralized? What was Pizarro's similar "grim luck?" What happened to the Mound Builders of the Mississippi Valley?

17. What was the author taught in school that originally justified conquest? What do we know now?

18. Why was there "one-sidedness" to the disease transmission in spite of the large Native American populations? Explain the author's reasoning.

JARED DIAMOND is a contributing editor of *Discover*, a professor of physiology at the UCLA School of Medicine, a recipient of a MacArthur genius award, and a research associate in ornithology at the American Museum of Natural History. Expanded versions of many of his *Discover* articles appear in his book *The Third Chimpanzee: The Evolution and Future of the Human Animal*, which won Britain's 1992 COPUS prize for best science book. Not least among his many accomplishments was his rediscovery in 1981 of the long-lost bowerbird of New Guinea. Diamond wrote about pseudo-hermaphrodites for *Discover's* special June issue on the science of sex.

From *Discover*, October 1992, pp. 64, 66–68, 70–73. Copyright © 1992 by Jared Diamond. Reprinted by permission of the author.

The Americanization of Mental Illness

ETHAN WATTERS

Americans, particularly if they are of a certain leftward-leaning, college-educated type, worry about our country's blunders into other cultures. In some circles, it is easy to make friends with a rousing rant about the McDonald's near Tiananmen Square, the Nike factory in Malaysia or the latest blowback from our political or military interventions abroad. For all our self-recrimination, however, we may have yet to face one of the most remarkable effects of American-led globalization. We have for many years been busily engaged in a grand project of Americanizing the world's understanding of mental health and illness. We may indeed be far along in homogenizing the way the world goes mad.

This unnerving possibility springs from recent research by a loose group of anthropologists and cross-cultural psychiatrists. Swimming against the biomedical currents of the time, they have argued that mental illnesses are not discrete entities like the polio virus with their own natural histories. These researchers have amassed an impressive body of evidence suggesting that mental illnesses have never been the same the world over (either in prevalence or in form) but are inevitably sparked and shaped by the ethos of particular times and places. In some Southeast Asian cultures, men have been known to experience what is called amok, an episode of murderous rage followed by amnesia; men in the region also suffer from koro, which is characterized by the debilitating certainty that their genitals are retracting into their bodies. Across the fertile crescent of the Middle East there is zar, a condition related to spirit-possession beliefs that brings forth dissociative episodes of laughing, shouting and singing.

The diversity that can be found across cultures can be seen across time as well. In his book "Mad Travelers," the philosopher Ian Hacking documents the fleeting appearance in the 1890s of a fugue state in which European men would walk in a trance for hundreds of miles with no knowledge of their identities. The hysterical-leg paralysis that afflicted thousands of middle-class women in the late 19th century not only gives us a visceral understanding of the restrictions set on women's social roles at the time but can also be seen from this distance as a social role itself—the troubled unconscious minds of a certain class of women speaking the idiom of distress of their time.

"We might think of the culture as possessing a 'symptom repertoire'—a range of physical symptoms available to the unconscious mind for the physical expression of psychological conflict," Edward Shorter, a medical historian at the University of Toronto, wrote in his book "Paralysis: The Rise and Fall of a 'Hysterical' Symptom." "In some epochs, convulsions, the sudden inability to speak or terrible leg pain may loom prominently in the repertoire. In other epochs patients may draw chiefly upon such symptoms as abdominal pain, false estimates of body weight and enervating weakness as metaphors for conveying psychic stress."

In any given era, those who minister to the mentally ill—doctors or shamans or priests—inadvertently help to select which symptoms will be recognized as legitimate. Because the troubled mind has been influenced by healers of diverse religious and scientific persuasions, the forms of madness from one place and time often look remarkably different from the forms of madness in another.

That is until recently.

For more than a generation now, we in the West have aggressively spread our modern knowledge of mental illness around the world. We have done this in the name of science, believing that our approaches reveal the biological basis of psychic suffering and dispel prescientific myths and harmful stigma. There is now good evidence to suggest that in the process of teaching the rest of the world to think like us, we've been exporting our Western "symptom repertoire" as well. That is, we've been changing not only the treatments but also the expression of mental illness in other cultures. Indeed, a handful of mental-health disorders—depression, post-traumatic stress disorder and anorexia among them—now appear to be spreading across cultures with the speed of contagious diseases. These symptom clusters are becoming the lingua franca of human suffering, replacing indigenous forms of mental illness.

Dr. Sing Lee, a psychiatrist and researcher at the Chinese University of Hong Kong, watched the Westernization of a mental illness firsthand. In the late 1980s and early 1990s, he was busy documenting a rare and culturally specific form of anorexia nervosa in Hong Kong.

Unlike American anorexics, most of his patients did not intentionally diet nor did they express a fear of becoming fat. The complaints of Lee's patients were typically somatic— they complained most frequently of having bloated stomachs. Lee was trying to understand this indigenous form of anorexia and, at the same time, figure out why the disease remained so rare.

As he was in the midst of publishing his finding that food refusal had a particular expression and meaning in Hong Kong, the public's understanding of anorexia suddenly shifted. On Nov. 24, 1994, a teenage anorexic girl named Charlene Hsu Chi-Ying collapsed and died on a busy downtown street in Hong Kong. The death caught the attention of the media and was featured prominently in local papers. "Anorexia Made Her All Skin and Bones: Schoolgirl Falls on Ground Dead," read one headline in a Chinese-language newspaper. "Thinner Than a Yellow Flower, Weight-Loss Book Found in School Bag, Schoolgirl Falls Dead on Street," reported another Chinese-language paper.

In trying to explain what happened to Charlene, local reporters often simply copied out of American diagnostic manuals. The mental-health experts quoted in the Hong Kong papers and magazines confidently reported that anorexia in Hong Kong was the same disorder that appeared in the United States and Europe. In the wake of Charlene's death, the transfer of knowledge about the nature of anorexia (including how and why it was manifested and who was at risk) went only one way: from West to East.

Western ideas did not simply obscure the understanding of anorexia in Hong Kong; they also may have changed the expression of the illness itself. As the general public and the region's mental-health professionals came to understand the American diagnosis of anorexia, the presentation of the illness in Lee's patient population appeared to transform into the more virulent American standard. Lee once saw two or three anorexic patients a year; by the end of the 1990s he was seeing that many new cases each month. That increase sparked another series of media reports. "Children as Young as 10 Starving Themselves as Eating Ailments Rise," announced a headline in one daily newspaper. By the late 1990s, Lee's studies reported that between 3 and 10 percent of young women in Hong Kong showed disordered eating behavior. In contrast to Lee's earlier patients, these women most often cited fat phobia as the single most important reason for their self-starvation. By 2007 about 90 percent of the anorexics Lee treated reported fat phobia. New patients appeared to be increasingly conforming their experience of anorexia to the Western version of the disease.

What is being missed, Lee and others have suggested, is a deep understanding of how the expectations and beliefs of the sufferer shape their suffering. "Culture shapes the way general psychopathology is going to be translated partially or completely into specific psychopathology," Lee says. "When there is a cultural atmosphere in which professionals, the media, schools, doctors, psychologists all recognize and endorse and talk about and publicize eating disorders, then people can be triggered to consciously or unconsciously pick eating-disorder pathology as a way to express that conflict."

The problem becomes especially worrisome in a time of globalization, when symptom repertoires can cross borders with ease. Having been trained in England and the United States, Lee knows better than most the locomotive force behind Western ideas about mental health and illness. Mental-health professionals in the West, and in the United States in particular, create official categories of mental diseases and promote them in a diagnostic manual that has become the worldwide standard. American researchers and institutions run most of the premier scholarly journals and host top conferences in the fields of psychology and psychiatry. Western drug companies dole out large sums for research and spend billions marketing medications for mental illnesses. In addition, Western-trained traumatologists often rush in where war or natural disasters strike to deliver "psychological first aid," bringing with them their assumptions about how the mind becomes broken by horrible events and how it is best healed. Taken together this is a juggernaut that Lee sees little chance of stopping. "As Western categories for diseases have gained dominance, microcultures that shape the illness experiences of individual patients are being discarded," Lee says. "The current has become too strong."

Would anorexia have so quickly become part of Hong Kong's symptom repertoire without the importation of the Western template for the disease? It seems unlikely. Beginning with scattered European cases in the early 19th century, it took more than 50 years for Western mental-health professionals to name, codify and popularize anorexia as a manifestation of hysteria. By contrast, after Charlene fell onto the sidewalk on Wan Chai Road on that late November day in 1994, it was just a matter of hours before the Hong Kong population learned the name of the disease, who was at risk and what it meant.

The idea that our Western conception of mental health and illness might be shaping the expression of illnesses in other cultures is rarely discussed in the professional literature. Many modern mental-health practitioners and researchers believe that the scientific standing of our drugs, our illness categories and our theories of the mind have put the field beyond the influence of endlessly shifting cultural trends and beliefs. After all, we now have machines that can literally watch the mind at work. We can change the chemistry of the brain in a variety of interesting ways and we can examine DNA sequences for abnormalities. The assumption is that these remarkable scientific advances have allowed modern-day practitioners to avoid the blind spots and cultural biases of their predecessors.

Modern-day mental-health practitioners often look back at previous generations of psychiatrists and psychologists with a thinly veiled pity, wondering how they could have been so swept away by the cultural currents of their time. The confident pronouncements of Victorian-era doctors regarding the epidemic of hysterical women are now dismissed as cultural artifacts. Similarly, illnesses found only in other cultures are often treated like carnival sideshows. Koro, amok and the like can be found far back in the American diagnostic manual (DSM-IV, Pages 845–849) under the heading "culture-bound syndromes." Given the attention they get, they might as well be labeled "Psychiatric Exotica: Two Bits a Gander."

Western mental-health practitioners often prefer to believe that the 844 pages of the DSM-IV prior to the inclusion of culture-bound syndromes describe real disorders of the mind, illnesses with symptomatology and outcomes relatively unaffected by shifting cultural beliefs. And, it logically follows, if these disorders are unaffected by culture, then they are surely universal to humans everywhere. In this view, the DSM is a field guide to the world's psyche, and applying it around the world represents simply the brave march of scientific knowledge.

Of course, we can become psychologically unhinged for many reasons that are common to all, like personal traumas, social upheavals or biochemical imbalances in our brains. Modern science has begun to reveal these causes. Whatever the trigger, however, the ill individual and those around him invariably rely on cultural beliefs and stories to understand what is happening. Those stories, whether they tell of spirit possession, semen loss or serotonin depletion, predict and shape the course of the illness in dramatic and often counterintuitive ways. In the end, what cross-cultural psychiatrists and anthropologists have to tell us is that all mental illnesses, including depression, P.T.S.D. and even schizophrenia, can be every bit as influenced by cultural beliefs and expectations today as hysterical-leg paralysis or the vapors or zar or any other mental illness ever experienced in the history of human madness. This does not mean that these illnesses and the pain associated with them are not real, or that sufferers deliberately shape their symptoms to fit a certain cultural niche. It means that a mental illness is an illness of the mind and cannot be understood without understanding the ideas, habits and predispositions—the idiosyncratic cultural trappings—of the mind that is its host.

Even when the underlying science is sound and the intentions altruistic, the export of Western biomedical ideas can have frustrating and unexpected consequences. For the last 50-odd years, Western mental-health professionals have been pushing what they call "mental-health literacy" on the rest of the world. Cultures became more "literate" as they adopted Western biomedical conceptions of diseases like depression and schizophrenia. One study published in The International Journal of Mental Health, for instance, portrayed those who endorsed the statement that "mental illness is an illness like any other" as having a "knowledgeable, benevolent, supportive orientation toward the mentally ill."

Mental illnesses, it was suggested, should be treated like "brain diseases" over which the patient has little choice or responsibility. This was promoted both as a scientific fact and as a social narrative that would reap great benefits. The logic seemed unassailable: Once people believed that the onset of mental illnesses did not spring from supernatural forces, character flaws, semen loss or some other prescientific notion, the sufferer would be protected from blame and stigma. This idea has been promoted by mental-health providers, drug companies and patient-advocacy groups like the National Alliance on Mental Illness in the United States and SANE in Britain. In a sometimes fractious field, everyone seemed to agree that this modern way of thinking about mental illness would reduce the social isolation and stigma often experienced by those with mental illness. Trampling on indigenous prescientific superstitions about the cause of mental illness seemed a small price to pay to relieve some of the social suffering of the mentally ill.

But does the "brain disease" belief actually reduce stigma?

In 1997, Prof. Sheila Mehta from Auburn University Montgomery in Alabama decided to find out if the "brain disease" narrative had the intended effect. She suspected that the biomedical explanation for mental illness might be influencing our attitudes toward the mentally ill in ways we weren't conscious of, so she thought up a clever experiment.

In her study, test subjects were led to believe that they were participating in a simple learning task with a partner who was, unbeknownst to them, a confederate in the study. Before the experiment started, the partners exchanged some biographical data, and the confederate informed the test subject that he suffered from a mental illness.

The confederate then stated either that the illness occurred because of "the kind of things that happened to me when I was a kid" or that he had "a disease just like any other, which affected my biochemistry." (These were termed the "psychosocial" explanation and the "disease" explanation respectively.) The experiment then called for the test subject to teach the confederate a pattern of button presses. When the confederate pushed the wrong button, the only feedback the test subject could give was a "barely discernible" to "somewhat painful" electrical shock.

Analyzing the data, Mehta found a difference between the group of subjects given the psychosocial explanation for their partner's mental-illness history and those given the brain-disease explanation. Those who believed that their partner suffered a biochemical "disease like any other" increased the severity of the shocks at a faster rate than those who believed they were paired with someone who had a mental disorder caused by an event in the past.

"The results of the current study suggest that we may actually treat people more harshly when their problem is described in disease terms," Mehta wrote. "We say we are being kind, but our actions suggest otherwise." The problem, it appears, is that the biomedical narrative about an illness like schizophrenia carries with it the subtle assumption that a brain made ill through biomedical or genetic abnormalities is more thoroughly broken and permanently abnormal than one made ill though life events. "Viewing those with mental disorders as diseased sets them apart and may lead to our perceiving them as physically distinct. Biochemical aberrations make them almost a different species."

In other words, the belief that was assumed to decrease stigma actually increased it. Was the same true outside the lab in the real world?

The question is important because the Western push for "mental-health literacy" has gained ground. Studies show that much of the world has steadily adopted this medical model of mental illness. Although these changes are most extensive in the United States and Europe, similar shifts have been documented elsewhere. When asked to name the sources of mental illness, people from a variety of cultures are increasingly likely to mention "chemical imbalance" or "brain disease" or "genetic/inherited" factors.

Unfortunately, at the same time that Western mental-health professionals have been convincing the world to think and talk about mental illnesses in biomedical terms, we have been simultaneously losing the war against stigma at home and abroad. Studies of attitudes in the United States from 1950 to 1996 have shown that the perception of dangerousness surrounding people with schizophrenia has steadily increased over this time. Similarly, a study in Germany found that the public's desire to maintain distance from those with a diagnosis of schizophrenia increased from 1990 to 2001.

Researchers hoping to learn what was causing this rise in stigma found the same surprising connection that Mehta discovered in her lab. It turns out that those who adopted biomedical/genetic beliefs about mental disorders were the same people who wanted less contact with the mentally ill and thought of them as more dangerous and unpredictable. This unfortunate relationship has popped up in numerous studies around the world. In a study conducted in Turkey, for example, those who labeled schizophrenic behavior as akil hastaligi (illness of the brain or reasoning abilities) were more inclined to assert that schizophrenics were aggressive and should not live freely in the community than those who saw the disorder as ruhsal hastagi (a disorder of the spiritual or inner self). Another study, which looked at populations in Germany, Russia and Mongolia, found that "irrespective of place . . . endorsing biological factors as the cause of schizophrenia was associated with a greater desire for social distance."

Even as we have congratulated ourselves for becoming more "benevolent and supportive" of the mentally ill, we have steadily backed away from the sufferers themselves. It appears, in short, that the impact of our worldwide anti-stigma campaign may have been the exact opposite of what we intended.

Nowhere are the limitations of Western ideas and treatments more evident than in the case of schizophrenia. Researchers have long sought to understand what may be the most perplexing finding in the cross-cultural study of mental illness: people with schizophrenia in developing countries appear to fare better over time than those living in industrialized nations.

This was the startling result of three large international studies carried out by the World Health Organization over the course of 30 years, starting in the early 1970s. The research showed that patients outside the United States and Europe had significantly lower relapse rates—as much as two-thirds lower in one follow-up study. These findings have been widely discussed and debated in part because of their obvious incongruity: the regions of the world with the most resources to devote to the illness—the best technology, the cutting-edge medicines and the best-financed academic and private-research institutions—had the most troubled and socially marginalized patients.

Trying to unravel this mystery, the anthropologist Juli McGruder from the University of Puget Sound spent years in Zanzibar studying families of schizophrenics. Though the population is predominantly Muslim, Swahili spirit-possession beliefs are still prevalent in the archipelago and commonly evoked to explain the actions of anyone violating social norms—from a sister lashing out at her brother to someone beset by psychotic delusions.

McGruder found that far from being stigmatizing, these beliefs served certain useful functions. The beliefs prescribed a variety of socially accepted interventions and ministrations that kept the ill person bound to the family and kinship group. "Muslim and Swahili spirits are not exorcised in the Christian sense of casting out demons," McGruder determined. "Rather they are coaxed with food and goods, feted with song and dance. They are placated, settled, reduced in malfeasance." McGruder saw this approach in many small acts of kindness. She watched family members use saffron paste to write phrases from the Koran on the rims of drinking bowls so the ill person could literally imbibe the holy words. The spirit-possession beliefs had other unexpected benefits. Critically, the story allowed the person with schizophrenia a cleaner bill of health when the illness went into remission. An ill individual enjoying a time of relative mental health could, at least temporarily, retake his or her responsibilities in the kinship group. Since the illness was seen as the work of outside forces, it was understood as an affliction for the sufferer but not as an identity.

For McGruder, the point was not that these practices or beliefs were effective in curing schizophrenia. Rather, she said she believed that they indirectly helped control the course of the illness. Besides keeping the sick individual in the social group, the religious beliefs in Zanzibar also allowed for a type of calmness and acquiescence in the face of the illness that she had rarely witnessed in the West.

The course of a metastasizing cancer is unlikely to be changed by how we talk about it. With schizophrenia, however, symptoms are inevitably entangled in a person's complex interactions with those around him or her. In fact, researchers have long documented how certain emotional reactions from family members correlate with higher relapse rates for people who have a diagnosis of schizophrenia. Collectively referred to as "high expressed emotion," these reactions include criticism, hostility and emotional overinvolvement (like overprotectiveness or constant intrusiveness in the patient's life). In one study, 67 percent of white American families with a schizophrenic family member were rated as "high EE." (Among British families, 48 percent were high EE; among Mexican families the figure was 41 percent and for Indian families 23 percent.)

Does this high level of "expressed emotion" in the United States mean that we lack sympathy or the desire to care for our mentally ill? Quite the opposite. Relatives who were "high EE" were simply expressing a particularly American view of the self. They tended to believe that individuals are the captains of their own destiny and should be able to overcome their problems by force of personal will. Their critical comments to the mentally ill person didn't mean that these family members were cruel or uncaring; they were simply applying the same assumptions about human nature that they applied to themselves. They were reflecting an "approach to the world that is active, resourceful and that emphasizes personal accountability," Prof. Jill M. Hooley of Harvard University concluded. "Far from high criticism reflecting something negative about the family members of patients with schizophrenia, high criticism (and hence high EE) was associated with a characteristic that is widely regarded as positive."

Widely regarded as positive, that is, in the United States. Many traditional cultures regard the self in different terms—as inseparable from your role in your kinship group, intertwined with the story of your ancestry and permeable to the spirit world. What McGruder found in Zanzibar was that families often drew strength from this more connected and less isolating idea of human nature. Their ability to maintain a low level of expressed emotion relied on these beliefs. And that level of expressed emotion in turn may be key to improving the fortunes of the schizophrenia sufferer.

Of course, to the extent that our modern psychopharmacological drugs can relieve suffering, they should not be denied to the rest of the world. The problem is that our biomedical advances are hard to separate from our particular cultural beliefs. It is difficult to distinguish, for example, the biomedical conception of schizophrenia—the idea that the disease exists within the biochemistry of the brain—from the more inchoate Western assumption that the self resides there as well. "Mental illness is feared and has such a stigma because it represents a reversal of what Western humans . . . have come to value as the essence of human nature," McGruder concludes. "Because our culture so highly values . . . an illusion of self-control and control of circumstance, we become abject when contemplating mentation that seems more changeable, less restrained and less controllable, more open to outside influence, than we imagine our own to be."

Cross-cultural psychiatrists have pointed out that the mental-health ideas we export to the world are rarely unadulterated scientific facts and never culturally neutral. "Western mental-health discourse introduces core components of Western culture, including a theory of human nature, a definition of personhood, a sense of time and memory and a source of moral authority. None of this is universal," Derek Summerfield of the Institute of Psychiatry in London observes. He has also written: "The problem is the overall thrust that comes from being at the heart of the one globalizing culture. It is as if one version of human nature is being presented as definitive, and one set of ideas about pain and suffering. . . . There is no one definitive psychology."

Behind the promotion of Western ideas of mental health and healing lie a variety of cultural assumptions about human nature. Westerners share, for instance, evolving beliefs about what type of life event is likely to make one psychologically traumatized, and we agree that venting emotions by talking is more healthy than stoic silence. We've come to agree that the human mind is rather fragile and that it is best to consider many emotional experiences and mental states as illnesses that require professional intervention. (The National Institute of Mental Health reports that a quarter of Americans have diagnosable mental illnesses each year.) The ideas we export often have at their heart a particularly American brand of hyperintrospection—a penchant for "psychologizing" daily existence. These ideas remain deeply influenced by the Cartesian split between the mind and the body, the Freudian duality between the conscious and unconscious, as well as the many self-help philosophies and schools of therapy that have encouraged Americans to separate the health of the individual from the health of the group. These Western ideas of the mind are proving as seductive to the rest of the world as fast food and rap music, and we are spreading them with speed and vigor.

No one would suggest that we withhold our medical advances from other countries, but it's perhaps past time to admit that even our most remarkable scientific leaps in understanding the brain haven't yet created the sorts of cultural stories from which humans take comfort and meaning. When these scientific advances are translated into popular belief and cultural stories, they are often stripped of the complexity of the science and become comically insubstantial narratives. Take for instance this website text advertising the antidepressant Paxil: "Just as a cake recipe requires you to use flour, sugar and baking powder in the right amounts, your brain needs a fine chemical balance in order to perform at its best." The Western mind, endlessly analyzed by generations of theorists and researchers, has now been reduced to a batter of chemicals we carry around in the mixing bowl of our skulls.

All cultures struggle with intractable mental illnesses with varying degrees of compassion and cruelty, equanimity and fear. Looking at ourselves through the eyes of those living in places where madness and psychological trauma are still embedded in complex religious and cultural narratives, however, we get a glimpse of ourselves as an increasingly insecure and fearful people. Some philosophers and psychiatrists have suggested that we are investing our great wealth in researching and treating mental illness—medicalizing ever larger swaths of human experience—because we have rather suddenly lost older belief systems that once gave meaning and context to mental suffering.

If our rising need for mental-health services does indeed spring from a breakdown of meaning, our insistence that the rest of the world think like us may be all the more problematic. Offering the latest Western mental-health theories, treatments and categories in an attempt to ameliorate the psychological stress sparked by modernization and globalization is not a solution; it may be part of the problem. When we undermine local conceptions of the self and modes of healing, we may be speeding along the disorienting changes that are at the very heart of much of the world's mental distress.

Critical Thinking

1. What evidence is there that mental illness has never been the same the world over?

2. What is meant by the "symptom repertoire" of a culture? How has this been aided by those who minister to the mentally ill?

3. Describe the process by which we in the West have spread our modern knowledge of mental illness along with our "symptom repertoire."

4. How was Dr. Sing Lee able to observe a unique form of anorexia in Hong Kong evolve into a Westernized version of the disease?

5. How has globalization enabled Western symptom repertoires to spread across borders with ease?

6. Why do Western health professionals believe their concepts of mental illness are free of cultural bias? How does the author respond?

7. What is the logic behind seeing mental illness as a "brain disease?" Why does it increase the stigma rather than decrease it?

8. How does the belief that spiritual possession causes schizophrenia illustrate the limitations of Western ideas regarding treatment of the disease? How does this relate to differing concepts of self?

9. How is that "offering the latest Western mental-health theories, treatments and categories in an attempt to ameliorate the psychological stress sparked by modernization and globalization is not a solution; it may be part of the problem?"

ETHAN WATTERS lives in San Francisco. This essay is adapted from his book *Crazy Like Us: The Globalization of the American Psyche.*

The Price of Progress

JOHN BODLEY

*In aiming at progress . . . you must let no one suffer by too
drastic a measure, nor pay too high a price in upheaval
and devastation, for your innovation.*

Maunier, 1949: 725

Until recently, government planners have always considered economic development and progress beneficial goals that all societies should want to strive toward. The social advantage of progress—as defined in terms of increased incomes, higher standards of living, greater security, and better health—are thought to be positive, *universal* goods, to be obtained at any price. Although one may argue that tribal peoples must sacrifice their traditional cultures to obtain these benefits, government planners generally feel that this is a small price to pay for such obvious advantages.

In earlier chapters [in *Victims of Progress,* 3rd ed.], evidence was presented to demonstrate that autonomous tribal peoples have not *chosen* progress to enjoy its advantages, but that governments have *pushed* progress upon them to obtain tribal resources, not primarily to share with the tribal peoples the benefits of progress. It has also been shown that the price of forcing progress on unwilling recipients has involved the deaths of millions of tribal people, as well as their loss of land, political sovereignty, and the right to follow their own life style. This chapter does not attempt to further summarize that aspect of the cost of progress, but instead analyzes the specific effects of the participation of tribal peoples in the world-market economy. In direct opposition to the usual interpretation, it is argued here that the benefits of progress are often both illusory and detrimental to tribal peoples when they have not been allowed to control their own resources and define their relationship to the market economy.

Progress and the Quality of Life

One of the primary difficulties in assessing the benefits of progress and economic development for any culture is that of establishing a meaningful measure of both benefit and detriment. It is widely recognized that *standard of living,* which is the most frequently used measure of progress, is an intrinsically ethnocentric concept relying heavily upon indicators that lack universal cultural relevance. Such factors as GNP, per capita income, capital formation, employment rates, literacy, formal education, consumption of manufactured goods, number of doctors and hospital beds per thousand persons, and the amount of money spent on government welfare and health programs may be irrelevant measures of actual *quality* of life for autonomous or even semiautonomous tribal cultures. In its 1954 report, the Trust Territory government indicated that since the Micronesian population was still largely satisfying its own needs within a cashless subsistence economy, "Money income is not a significant measure of living standards, production, or well-being in this area" (TTR, 1953: 44). Unfortunately, within a short time the government began to rely on an enumeration of certain imported consumer goods as indicators of a higher standard of living in the islands, even though many tradition-oriented islanders felt that these new goods symbolized a lowering of the quality of life.

A more useful measure of the benefits of progress might be based on a formula for evaluating cultures devised by Goldschmidt (1952: 135). According to these less ethnocentric criteria, the important question to ask is: Does progress or economic development increase or decrease a given culture's ability to satisfy the physical and psychological needs of its population, or its stability? This question is a far more direct measure of quality of life than are the standard economic correlates of development, and it is universally relevant. Specific indication of this *standard* of living could be found for any society in the nutritional status and general physical and mental health of its population, the incidence of crime and delinquency, the demographic structure, family stability, and the society's relationship to its natural resource base. A society with high rates of malnutrition and crime, and one degrading its natural environment to the extent of threatening its continued existence, might be described as at a lower standard of living than is another society where these problems did not exist.

Careful examination of the data, which compare, on these specific points, the former condition of self-sufficient tribal peoples with their condition following their incorporation into the world-market economy, leads to the conclusion that their standard of living is *lowered,* not raised, by economic progress—and often to a dramatic degree. This is perhaps the most outstanding and inescapable fact to emerge from the years of research that anthropologists have devoted to the study of culture change and modernization. Despite the best intentions of those who have promoted change and improvement, all too often the results have been poverty, longer working hours, and much greater physical exertion, poor health, social disorder, discontent, discrimination, overpopulation, and environmental deterioration—combined with the destruction of the traditional culture.

Diseases of Development

Perhaps it would be useful for public health specialists to start talking about a new category of diseases. . . . Such diseases could be called the "diseases of development" and would consist of those pathological conditions which are based on the usually unanticipated consequences of the implementation of developmental schemes.

Hughes & Hunter, 1972: 93

Economic development increases the disease rate of affected peoples in at least three ways. First, to the extent that development is successful, it makes developed populations suddenly become vulnerable to all of the diseases suffered almost exclusively by "advanced" peoples. Among these are diabetes, obesity, hypertension, and a variety of circulatory problems. Second, development disturbs traditional environmental balances and may dramatically increase certain bacterial and parasite diseases. Finally, when development goals prove unattainable, an assortment of poverty diseases may appear in association with the crowded conditions of urban slums and the general breakdown in traditional socioeconomic systems.

Outstanding examples of the first situation can be seen in the Pacific, where some of the most successfully developed native peoples are found. In Micronesia, where development has progressed more rapidly than perhaps anywhere else, between 1958 and 1972 the population doubled, but the number of patients treated for heart disease in the local hospitals nearly tripled, mental disorder increased eightfold, and by 1972 hypertension and nutritional deficiencies began to make significant appearances for the first time (TTR, 1959, 1973, statistical tables).

Although some critics argue that the Micronesian figures simply represent better health monitoring due to economic progress, rigorously controlled data from Polynesia show a similar trend. The progressive acquisition of modern degenerative diseases was documented by an eight-member team of New Zealand medical specialists, anthropologists, and nutritionists, whose research was funded by the Medical Research Council of New Zealand and the World Health Organization. These researchers investigated the health status of a genetically related population at various points along a continuum of increasing cash income, modernizing diet, and urbanization. The extremes on this acculturation continuum were represented by the relatively traditional Pukapukans of the Cook Islands and the essentially Europeanized New Zealand Maori, while the busily developing Rarotongans, also of the Cook Islands, occupied the intermediate position. In 1971, after eight years of work, the

team's preliminary findings were summarized by Dr. Ian Prior, cardiologist and leader of the research, as follows:

We are beginning to observe that the more an islander takes on the ways of the West, the more prone he is to succumb to our degenerative diseases. In fact, it does not seem too much to say our evidence now shows that the farther the Pacific natives move from the quiet, carefree life of their ancestors, the closer they come to gout, diabetes, atherosclerosis, obesity, and hypertension.

Prior, 1971: 2

In Pukapuka, where progress was limited by the island's small size and its isolated location some 480 kilometers from the nearest port, the annual per capita income was only about thirty-six dollars and the economy remained essentially at a subsistence level. Resources were limited and the area was visited by trading ships only three or four times a year; thus, there was little opportunity for intensive economic development. Predictably, the population of Pukapuka was characterized by relatively low levels of imported sugar and salt intake, and a presumably related low level of heart disease, high blood pressure, and diabetes. In Rarotonga, where economic success was introducing town life, imported food, and motorcycles, sugar and salt intakes nearly tripled, high blood pressure increased approximately ninefold, diabetes two- to threefold, and heart disease doubled for men and more than quadrupled for women, while the number of grossly obese women increased more than tenfold. Among the New Zealand Maori, sugar intake was nearly eight times that of the Pukapukans, gout in men was nearly double its rate on Pukapuka, and diabetes in men was more than fivefold higher, while heart disease in women had increased more than sixfold. The Maori were, in fact, dying of "European" diseases at a greater rate than was the average New Zealand European.

Government development policies designed to bring about changes in local hydrology, vegetation, and settlement patterns and to increase population mobility, and even programs aimed at reducing certain diseases, have frequently led to dramatic increases in disease rates because of the unforeseen effects of disturbing the preexisting order. Hughes and Hunter (1972) published an excellent survey of cases in which development led directly to increased disease rates in Africa. They concluded that hasty development intervention in relatively balanced local cultures and environments resulted in "a drastic deterioration in the social and economic conditions of life."

Traditional populations in general have presumably learned to live with the endemic pathogens of their environments, and in some cases they have evolved genetic adaptations to specific diseases, such as the sickle-cell trait, which provided an immunity to malaria. Unfortunately, however, outside intervention has entirely changed this picture. In the late 1960s, sleeping sickness suddenly increased in many areas of Africa and even spread to areas where it did not formerly occur, due to the building of new roads and migratory labor, both of which caused increased population movement. Large-scale relocation schemes, such as the Zande Scheme, had disastrous results when natives were moved from their traditional disease-free refuges into infected areas. Dams and irrigation developments inadvertently created ideal conditions for the rapid proliferation of snails carrying schistosomiasis (a liver fluke disease), and major epidemics suddenly occurred in areas where this disease had never before been a problem. DDT spraying programs have been temporarily successful in controlling malaria, but there is often a rebound effect that increases the problem when spraying is discontinued, and the malarial mosquitoes are continually evolving resistant strains.

Urbanization is one of the prime measures of development, but it is a mixed blessing for most former tribal peoples. Urban health standards are abysmally poor and generally worse than in rural areas for the detribalized individuals who have crowded into the towns and cities throughout Africa, Asia, and Latin America seeking wage employment out of new economic necessity. Infectious diseases related to crowding and poor sanitation are rampant in urban centers, while greatly increased stress and poor nutrition aggravate a variety of other health problems. Malnutrition and other diet-related conditions are, in fact, one of the characteristic hazards of progress faced by tribal peoples and are discussed in the following sections.

The Hazards of Dietary Change

The traditional diets of tribal peoples are admirably adapted to their nutritional needs and available food resources. Even though these diets may seem bizarre, absurd, and unpalatable to outsiders, they are unlikely to be improved by drastic modifications. Given the delicate balances and complexities involved in any subsistence system, change always involves risks, but for tribal people the effects of dietary change have been catastrophic.

Under normal conditions, food habits are remarkably resistant to change, and indeed people are unlikely to abandon their traditional diets voluntarily in favor of dependence on difficult-to-obtain exotic imports. In some cases it is true that imported foods may be identified with powerful outsiders and are therefore sought as symbols of greater prestige. This may lead to such absurdities as Amazonian Indians choosing to consume imported canned tunafish when abundant high-quality fish is available in their own rivers. Another example of this situation occurs in tribes where mothers prefer to feed their infants expensive nutritionally inadequate canned milk from unsanitary, but *high status,* baby bottles. The high status of these items is often promoted by clever traders and clever advertising campaigns.

Aside from these apparently voluntary changes, it appears that more often dietary changes are forced upon unwilling tribal peoples by circumstances beyond their control. In some areas, new food crops have been introduced by government decree, or as a consequence of forced relocation or other policies designed to end hunting, pastoralism, or shifting cultivation. Food habits have also been modified by massive disruption of the natural environment by outsiders—as when sheepherders transformed the Australian Aborigines' foraging territory or when European invaders destroyed the bison herds that were the primary element in the Plains Indians' subsistence patterns. Perhaps the most frequent cause of diet change occurs when formerly self-sufficient peoples find that wage labor, cash cropping, and other economic development activities that feed tribal resources into the world-market economy must inevitably divert time and energy away from the production of subsistence foods. Many developing peoples suddenly discover that, like it or not, they are unable to secure traditional foods and must spend their newly acquired cash on costly, and often nutritionally inferior, manufactured foods.

Overall, the available data seem to indicate that the dietary changes that are linked to involvement in the world-market economy have tended to *lower* rather than raise the nutritional levels of the affected tribal peoples. Specifically, the vitamin, mineral, and protein components of their diets are often drastically reduced and replaced by enormous increases in starch and carbohydrates, often in the form of white flour and refined sugar.

Any deterioration in the quality of a given population's diet is almost certain to be reflected in an increase in deficiency diseases and a general decline in health status. Indeed, as tribal peoples have shifted to a diet based on imported manufactured or processed foods, there has been a dramatic rise in malnutrition, a massive increase in dental problems, and a variety of other nutritional-related disorders. Nutritional physiology is so complex that even well-meaning dietary changes have had tragic consequences. In many areas of Southeast Asia, government-sponsored protein supplementation programs supplying milk to protein-deficient populations caused unexpected health problems and increased mortality. Officials failed to anticipate that in cultures where adults do not normally drink milk, the enzymes needed to digest it are no longer produced and milk *intolerance* results (Davis & Bolin, 1972). In Brazil, a similar milk distribution program caused an epidemic of permanent blindness by aggravating a preexisting vitamin A deficiency (Bunce, 1972).

Teeth and Progress

There is nothing new in the observation that savages, or peoples living under primitive conditions, have, in general, excellent teeth. . . . Nor is it news that most civilized populations possess wretched teeth which begin to decay almost before they have erupted completely, and that dental caries is likely to be accompanied by periodontal disease with further reaching complications.

Hooton, 1945: xviii

Anthropologists have long recognized that undisturbed tribal peoples are often in excellent physical condition. And it has often been noted specifically that dental caries and the other dental abnormalities that plague industrialized societies are absent or rare among tribal peoples who have retained their traditional diets. The fact that tribal food habits may contribute to the development of sound teeth, whereas modernized diets may do just the opposite, was illustrated as long ago as 1894 in an article in the *Journal of the Royal Anthropological Institute* that described the results of a comparison between the teeth of ten Sioux Indians who were examined when they came to London as members of Buffalo Bill's Wild West Show and were found to be completely free of caries and in possession of all their teeth, even though half of the group were over thirty-nine years of age. Londoners' teeth were conspicuous for both their caries and their steady reduction in number with advancing age. The difference was attributed primarily to the wear and polishing caused by the traditional Indian diet of coarse food and the fact that they chewed their food longer, encouraged by the absence of tableware.

One of the most remarkable studies of the dental conditions of tribal peoples and the impact of dietary change was conducted in the 1930s by Weston Price (1945), an American dentist who was interested in determining what caused normal, healthy teeth. Between 1931 and 1936, Price systematically explored tribal areas throughout the world to locate and examine the most isolated peoples who were still living on traditional foods. His fieldwork covered Alaska, the Canadian Yukon, Hudson Bay, Vancouver Island, Florida, the Andes, the Amazon, Samoa, Tahiti, New Zealand, Australia, New Caledonia, Fiji, the Torres Strait, East Africa, and the Nile. The study demonstrated both the superior quality of aboriginal dentition and the devastation that occurs as modern diets are adopted. In nearly every area where traditional foods were still being eaten, Price found perfect teeth with normal dental arches and virtually no decay, whereas caries and abnormalities increased steadily as new diets were adopted. In many cases the change was sudden and striking. Among Eskimo groups subsisting entirely on traditional food he found caries totally absent, whereas in groups eating a considerable quantity of store-bought food approximately 20 percent of their teeth were decayed. This figure rose to more than 30 percent with Eskimo groups subsisting almost exclusively on purchased or government-supplied food, and reached an incredible 48 percent among the Vancouver Island Indians. Unfortunately for many of these people, modern dental treatment did not accompany the new food, and their suffering was appalling. The loss of teeth was, of course, bad enough in itself, and it certainly undermined the population's resistance to many new diseases, including tuberculosis. But new foods were also accompanied by crowded, misplaced teeth, gum diseases, distortion of the face, and pinching of the nasal cavity. Abnormalities in the dental arch appeared in the new generation following the change in diet, while caries appeared almost immediately even in adults.

Price reported that in many areas the affected peoples were conscious of their own physical deterioration. At a mission school in Africa, the principal asked him to explain to the native schoolchildren why they were not physically as strong as children who had had no contact with schools. On an island in the Torres Strait the natives knew exactly what was causing their problems and resisted—almost to the point of bloodshed— government efforts to establish a store that would make imported food available. The government prevailed, however, and Price was able to establish a relationship between the length of time the government store had been established and the increasing incidence of caries among a population that showed an almost 100 percent immunity to them before the store had been opened.

In New Zealand, the Maori, who in their aboriginal state are often considered to have been among the healthiest, most perfectly developed of people, were found to have "advanced" the furthest. According to Price:

Their modernization was demonstrated not only by the high incidence of dental caries but also by the fact that 90 percent of the adults and 100 percent of the children had abnormalities of the dental arches.

Price, 1945: 206

Malnutrition

Malnutrition, particularly in the form of protein deficiency, has become a critical problem for tribal peoples who must adopt new economic patterns. Population pressures, cash cropping, and government programs all have tended to encourage the replacement of traditional crops and other food sources that were rich in protein with substitutes, high in calories but low in protein. In Africa, for example, protein-rich staples such as millet and sorghum are being replaced systematically by high-yielding manioc and plantains, which have insignificant amounts of protein. The problem is increased for cash croppers and wage laborers whose earnings are too low and unpredictable to allow purchase of adequate amounts of protein. In some rural areas, agricultural laborers have been forced systematically to deprive nonproductive members (principally children) of their households of their minimal nutritional requirements to satisfy the need of the productive members. This process has been documented in northeastern Brazil following the introduction of large-scale sisal plantations (Gross & Underwood, 1971). In urban centers the difficulties of obtaining nutritionally adequate diets are even more serious for tribal immigrants, because costs are higher and poor quality foods are more tempting.

One of the most tragic, and largely overlooked, aspects of chronic malnutrition is that it can lead to abnormally undersized brain development and apparently irreversible brain damage; it has been associated with various forms of mental impairment or retardation. Malnutrition has been linked clinically with mental retardation in both Africa and Latin America (see, for example, Mönckeberg, 1968), and this appears to be a worldwide phenomenon with serious implications (Montagu, 1972).

Optimistic supporters of progress will surely say that all of these new health problems are being overstressed and that the introduction of hospitals, clinics, and the other modern health institutions will overcome or at least compensate for all of these difficulties. However, it appears that uncontrolled population growth and economic impoverishment probably will keep most of these benefits out of reach for many tribal peoples, and the intervention of modern medicine has at least partly contributed to the problem in the first place.

The generalization that civilization frequently has a broad negative impact on tribal health has found broad empirical support (see especially Kroeger & Barbira-Freedman [1982] on Amazonia; Reinhard [1976] on the Arctic; and Wirsing

[1985] globally), but these conclusions have not gone unchallenged. Some critics argue that tribal health was often poor before modernization, and they point specifically to tribals' low life expectancy and high infant mortality rates. Demographic statistics on tribal populations are often problematic because precise data are scarce, but they do show a less favorable profile than that enjoyed by many industrial societies. However, it should be remembered that our present life expectancy is a recent phenomenon that has been very costly in terms of medical research and technological advances. Furthermore, the benefits of our health system are not enjoyed equally by all members of our society. High infant mortality could be viewed as a relatively inexpensive and egalitarian tribal public health program that offered the reasonable expectation of a healthy and productive life for those surviving to age fifteen.

Some critics also suggest that certain tribal populations, such as the New Guinea highlanders, were "stunted" by nutritional deficiencies created by tribal culture and are "improved" by "acculturation" and cash cropping (Dennett & Connell, 1988). Although this argument does suggest that the health question requires careful evaluation, it does not invalidate the empirical generalizations already established. Nutritional deficiencies undoubtedly occurred in densely populated zones in the central New Guinea highlands. However, the specific case cited above may not be widely representative of other tribal groups even in New Guinea, and it does not address the facts of outside intrusion or the inequities inherent in the contemporary development process.

Ecocide

"How is it," asked a herdsman . . . "how is it that these hills can no longer give pasture to my cattle? In my father's day they were green and cattle thrived there; today there is no grass and my cattle starve." As one looked one saw that what had once been a green hill had become a raw red rock.

Jones, 1934

Progress not only brings new threats to the health of tribal peoples, but it also imposes new strains on the ecosystems upon which they must depend for their ultimate survival. The introduction of new technology, increased consumption, lowered mortality, and the eradication of all traditional controls have combined to replace what for most tribal peoples was a relatively stable balance between population and natural resources, with a new system that is imbalanced. Economic development is forcing *ecocide* on peoples who were once careful stewards of their resources. There is already a trend toward widespread environmental deterioration in tribal areas, involving resource depletion, erosion, plant and animal extinction, and a disturbing series of other previously unforeseen changes.

After the initial depopulation suffered by most tribal peoples during their engulfment by frontiers of national expansion, most tribal populations began to experience rapid growth. Authorities generally attribute this growth to the introduction of modern medicine and new health measures and the termination of intertribal warfare, which lowered morality rates, as well as to new technology, which increased food production. Certainly all of these factors played a part, but merely lowering mortality rates would not have produced the rapid population growth that most tribal areas have experienced if traditional birth-spacing mechanisms had not been eliminated at the same time. Regardless of which factors were most important, it is clear that all of the natural and cultural checks on population growth have suddenly been pushed aside by culture change, while tribal lands have been steadily reduced and consumption levels have risen. In many tribal areas, environmental deterioration due to overuse of resources has set in, and in other areas such deterioration is imminent as resources continue to dwindle relative to the expanding population and increased use. Of course, population expansion by tribal peoples may have positive political consequences, because where tribals can retain or regain their status as local majorities they may be in a more favorable position to defend their resources against intruders.

Swidden systems and pastoralism, both highly successful economic systems under traditional conditions, have proved particularly vulnerable to increased population pressures and outside efforts to raise productivity beyond its natural limits. Research in Amazonia demonstrates that population pressures and related resource depletion can be created indirectly by official policies that restrict swidden peoples to smaller territories. Resource depletion itself can then become a powerful means of forcing tribal people into participating in the world-market economy—thus leading to further resource depletion. For example, Bodley and Benson (1979) showed how the Shipibo Indians in Peru were forced to further deplete their forest resources by cash cropping in the forest area to replace the resources that had been destroyed earlier by the intensive cash cropping necessitated by the narrow confines of their reserve. In this case, certain species of palm trees that had provided critical housing materials were destroyed by forest clearing and had to be replaced by costly purchased materials. Research by Gross (1979) and others showed similar processes at work among four tribal groups in central Brazil and demonstrated that the degree of market involvement increases directly with increases in resource depletion.

The settling of nomadic herders and the removal of prior controls on herd size have often led to serious overgrazing and erosion problems where these had not previously occurred. There are indications that the desertification problem in the Sahel region of Africa was aggravated by programs designed to settle nomads. The first sign of imbalance in a swidden system appears when the planting cycles are shortened to the point that garden plots are reused before sufficient forest regrowth can occur. If reclearing and planting continue in the same area, the natural patterns of forest succession may be disturbed irreversibly and the soil can be impaired permanently. An extensive tract of tropical rainforest in the lower Amazon of Brazil was reduced to a semiarid desert in just fifty years through such a process (Ackermann, 1964). The soils in the Azande area are also now seriously threatened with laterization and other problems as a result of the government-promoted cotton development scheme (McNeil, 1972).

The dangers of overdevelopment and the vulnerability of local resource systems have long been recognized by both anthropologists and tribal peoples themselves. But the pressures for change have been overwhelming. In 1948 the Maya villagers of Chan Kom complained to Redfield (1962) about the shortening of their swidden cycles, which they correctly attributed to increasing population pressures. Redfield told them, however, that they had no choice but to go "forward with technology" (Redfield, 1962: 178). In Assam, swidden cycles were shortened from an average of twelve years to only two or three within just twenty years, and anthropologists warned that the limits of swiddening would soon be reached (Burling, 1963: 311–312). In the Pacific, anthropologists warned of population pressures on limited resources as early as the 1930s (Keesing, 1941: 64–65). These warnings seemed fully justified, considering the fact that the crowded Tikopians were prompted by population pressures on their tiny island to suggest that infanticide be legalized. The warnings have been dramatically reinforced since then by the doubling of Micronesia's population in just the fourteen years between 1958 and 1972, from 70,600 to 114,645, while consumption levels have soared. By 1985 Micronesia's population had reached 162,321.

The environmental hazards of economic development and rapid population growth have become generally recognized only since worldwide concerns over environmental issues began in the early 1970s. Unfortunately, there is as yet little indication that the leaders of the new developing nations are sufficiently concerned with environmental limitations. On the contrary, governments are forcing tribal peoples into a self-reinforcing spiral of population growth and intensified resource exploitation, which may be stopped only by environmental disaster or the total impoverishment of the tribals.

The reality of ecocide certainly focuses attention on the fundamental contrasts between tribal and industrial systems in their use of natural resources, who controls them, and how they are managed. Tribal peoples are victimized because they control resources that outsiders demand. The resources exist because tribals managed them conservatively. However, as with the issue of the health consequences of detribalization, some anthropologists minimize the adaptive achievements of tribal groups and seem unwilling to concede that ecocide might be a consequence of cultural change. Critics attack an exaggerated "noble savage" image of tribals living in perfect harmony with nature and having no visible impact on their surroundings. They then show that tribals do in fact modify the environment, and they conclude that there is no significant difference between how tribals and industrial societies treat their environments. For example, Charles Wagley declared that Brazilian Indians such as the Tapirape

are not "natural men." They have human vices just as we do. . . . They do not live "in tune" with nature any more than I do; in fact, they can often be as destructive of their environment, within their limitations, as some civilized men. The Tapirape are not innocent or childlike in any way.

Wagley, 1977: 302

Anthropologist Terry Rambo demonstrated that the Semang of the Malaysian rain forests have a measurable impact on their environment. In his monograph *Primitive Polluters,* Rambo (1985) reported that the Semang live in smoke-filled houses. They sneeze and spread germs, breathe, and thus emit carbon dioxide. They clear small gardens, contributing "particulate matter" to the air and disturbing the local climate because cleared areas proved measurably warmer and drier than the shady forest. Rambo concluded that his research "demonstrates the essential functional similarity of the environmental interactions of primitive and civilized societies" (1985: 78) in contrast to a "noble savage" view (Bodley, 1983) which, according to Rambo (1985: 2), mistakenly "claims that traditional peoples almost always live in essential harmony with their environment."

This is surely a false issue. To stress, as I do, that tribals tend to manage their resources for sustained yield within relatively self-sufficient subsistence economies is not to make them either innocent children or natural men. Nor is it to deny that tribals "disrupt" their environment and may never be in absolute "balance" with nature.

The ecocide issue is perhaps most dramatically illustrated by two sets of satellite photos taken over the Brazilian rain forests of Rôndonia (Allard & McIntyre, 1988: 780–781). Photos taken in 1973, when Rôndonia was still a tribal domain, show virtually unbroken rain forest. The 1987 satellite photos, taken after just fifteen years of highway construction and "development" by outsiders, show more than 20 percent of the forest destroyed. The surviving Indians were being concentrated by FUNAI (Brazil's national Indian foundation) into what would soon become mere islands of forest in a ravaged landscape. It is irrelevant to quibble about whether tribals are noble, childlike, or innocent, or about the precise meaning of balance with nature, carrying capacity, or adaptation, to recognize that for the past 200 years rapid environmental deterioration on an unprecedented global scale has followed the wresting of control of vast areas of the world from tribal groups by resource-hungry industrial societies.

Deprivation and Discrimination

Contact with European culture has given them a knowledge of great wealth, opportunity and privilege, but only very limited avenues by which to acquire these things.

Crocombe, 1968

Unwittingly, tribal peoples have had the burden of perpetual relative deprivation thrust upon them by acceptance—either by themselves or by the governments administering them—of the standards of socioeconomic progress set for them by industrial civilizations. By comparison with the material wealth of industrial societies, tribal societies become, by definition, impoverished. They are then forced to transform their cultures and work to achieve what many economists now acknowledge to be unattainable goals. Even though in many cases the modest GNP goals set by development planners for the developing nations during the "development decade" of the 1960s were often met, the results were hardly noticeable for most of the tribal people involved. Population growth, environmental limitations, inequitable distribution of wealth, and the continued rapid growth of the industrialized nations have all meant that both the absolute and the relative gap between the rich and poor in the world is steadily widening. The prospect that tribal peoples will actually be able to attain the levels of resource consumption to which they are being encouraged to aspire is remote indeed except for those few groups who have retained effective control over strategic mineral resources.

Tribal peoples feel deprivation not only when the economic goals they have been encouraged to seek fail to materialize, but also when they discover that they are powerless, second-class citizens who are discriminated against and exploited by the dominant society. At the same time, they are denied the satisfactions of their traditional cultures, because these have been sacrificed in the process of modernization. Under the impact of major economic change family life is disrupted, traditional social controls are often lost, and many indicators of social anomie such as alcoholism, crime, delinquency, suicide, emotional disorders, and despair may increase. The inevitable frustration resulting from this continual deprivation finds expression in the cargo cults, revitalization movements, and a variety of other political and religious movements that have been widespread among tribal peoples following their disruption by industrial civilization.

References

Ackermann, F. L. 1964. *Geologia e Fisiografia da Região Bragantina, Estado do Pará.* Manaus, Brazil: Conselho Nacional de Pesquisas, Instituto Nacional de Pesquisas da Amazonia.

Allard, William Albert, and Loren McIntyre. 1988. Rondônia's settlers invade Brazil's imperiled rain forest. *National Geographic* 174(6):772–799.

Bodley, John H. 1970. *Campa Socio-Economic Adaptation.* Ann Arbor: University Microfilms.

———. 1983. *Der Weg der Zerstörung: Stammesvölker und die industrielle Zivilization.* Munich: Trickster-Verlag. (Translation of *Victims of Progress.*)

Bodley, John H., and Foley C. Benson. 1979. Cultural ecology of Amazonian palms. *Reports of Investigations,* no. 56. Pullman: Laboratory of Anthropology, Washington State University.

Bunce, George E. 1972. Aggravation of vitamin A deficiency following distribution of non-fortified skim milk: An example of nutrient interaction. In *The Careless Technology: Ecology and International Development,* ed. M. T. Farvar and John P. Milton, pp. 53–60. Garden City, N.Y.: Natural History Press.

Burling, Robbins. 1963. *Rengsanggri: Family and Kinship in a Garo Village.* Philadelphia: University of Pennsylvania Press.

Davis, A. E., and T. D. Bolin. 1972. Lactose intolerance in Southeast Asia. In *The Careless Technology: Ecology and International Development,* ed. M. T. Farvar and John P. Milton, pp. 61–68. Garden City, N.Y.: Natural History Press.

Dennett, Glenn, and John Connell. 1988. Acculturation and health in the highlands of Papua New Guinea. *Current Anthropology* 29(2):273–299.

Goldschmidt, Walter R. 1972. The interrelations between cultural factors and the acquisition of new technical skills. In *The Progress of Underdeveloped Areas,* ed. Bert F. Hoselitz, pp. 135–151. Chicago: University of Chicago Press.

Gross, Daniel R., et al. 1979. Ecology and acculturation among native peoples of Central Brazil. *Science* 206(4422):1043–1050.

Hughes, Charles C., and John M. Hunter. 1972. The role of technological development in promoting disease in Africa. In *The Careless Technology: Ecology and International Development,* ed. M. T. Farvar and John P. Milton, pp. 69–101. Garden City, N.Y.: Natural History Press.

Keesing, Felix M. 1941. *The South Seas in the Modern World.* Institute of Pacific Relations International Research Series. New York: John Day.

Kroeger, Axel, and François Barbira-Freedman. 1982. *Culture Change and Health: The Case of South American Rainforest Indians.* Frankfurt am Main: Verlag Peter Lang. (Reprinted in Bodley, 1988a:221–236.)

McNeil, Mary. 1972. Lateritic soils in distinct tropical environments: Southern Sudan and Brazil. In *The Careless Technology: Ecology and International Development,* ed. M. T. Farvar and John P. Milton, pp. 591–608. Garden City, N.Y.: Natural History Press.

Mönckeberg, F. 1968. Mental retardation from malnutrition. *Journal of the American Medical Association* 206:30–31.

Montagu, Ashley. 1972. Sociogenic brain damage. *American Anthropologist* 74(5):1045–1061.

Rambo, A. Terry. 1985. *Primitive Polluters: Semang Impact on the Malaysian Tropical Rain Forest Ecosystem.* Anthropological Papers no. 76, Museum of Anthropology, University of Michigan.

Redfield, Robert. 1953. *The Primitive World and Its Transformations.* Ithaca, N.Y.: Cornell University Press.

———. 1962. *A Village That Chose Progress: Chan Kom Revisited.* Chicago: University of Chicago Press, Phoenix Books.

Smith, Wilberforce. 1894. The teeth of ten Sioux Indians. *Journal of the Royal Anthropological Institute* 24:109–116.

TTR: *See under* United States.

United States, Department of the Interior, Office of Territories. 1953. *Report on the Administration of the Trust Territory of the Pacific Islands* (by the United States to the United Nations) for the Period July 1, 1951, to June 30, 1952.

———. 1954. *Annual Report, High Commissioner of the Trust Territory of the Pacific Islands to the Secretary of the Interior* (for 1953).

United States, Department of State. 1955. *Seventh Annual Report to the United Nations on the Administration of the Trust Territory of the Pacific Islands* (July 1, 1953, to June 30, 1954).

———. 1959. *Eleventh Annual Report to the United Nations on the Administration of the Trust Territory of the Pacific Islands* (July 1, 1957, to June 30, 1958).

———. 1964. *Sixteenth Annual Report to the United Nations on the Administration of the Trust Territory of the Pacific Islands* (July 1, 1962 to June 30, 1963).

———. 1973. *Twenty-Fifth Annual Report to the United Nations on the Administration of the Trust Territory of the Pacific Islands* (July 1, 1971, to June 30, 1972).

Critical Thinking

1. Why is "standard of living" an intrinsically ethnocentric concept as a measure of progress? What is a more useful measure and why? What does a careful examination based upon the specific points show?

2. In what ways does economic development increase the disease rate of affected peoples?

3. How does the author answer critics who argue that such figures simply represent better health monitoring? List the examples cited.

4. Explain the effects of government policy on peoples' adaptations to local environmental conditions.

5. Describe the circumstances under which peoples' dietary habits have been changed as a result of outside influences. What has happened to nutritional levels and why?

6. To what was attributed the differences in dental health between the Sioux Indians of Buffalo Bill's Wild West Show and Londoners?

7. What did Weston Price find in his studies?

8. Describe the chain of events that goes from the adoption of new economic patterns to changes in the kinds of crops grown to low wages to nutritional deprivation (principally of children).

9. What is one of the most tragic, and largely overlooked, aspects of chronic malnutrition?

10. What are the prospects that modern health institutions will overcome these problems?

11. How does the author respond to critics who charge that tribal peoples have always had low life expectancies, high infant mortality rates and nutritional deficiencies?

12. What factors have contributed to population growth?

13. What are the consequences for each of the following:
    - Official policy restricting swidden people to smaller territories?
    - Resource depletion forcing people to participate in the world-market economy?
    - The settling of nomadic herders and the removal of prior controls on herd size?
    - Shortening the planting cycles?

14. How does the reality of ecocide focus attention on the fundamental contrasts between tribal and industrial systems in their use of natural resources? Who controls such resources and how they are managed?

15. What do the critics of the "noble savage" image claim? How does the author respond?

16. In what respects do tribal peoples feel deprivation as a result of "modernization"?

Last of Their Kind

The world's cultures have been disappearing, taking valuable knowledge with them, but there is reason to hope.

Wade Davis

Over the past decade geneticists have proved that all people alive today are descendants of a relatively small number of individuals who walked out of Africa some 60,000 years ago and carried the human spirit and imagination to every corner of the habitable world. Our shared heritage implies that all cultures share essentially the same potential, drawing on similar reserves of raw genius. Whether they exercise this intellectual capacity to produce stunning works of technological innovation (as has been the great achievement of the West) or to maintain an incredibly elaborate network of kin relationships (a primary concern, for example, of the Aborigines of Australia) is simply a matter of choice and orientation, adaptive benefits and cultural priorities. Each of the planet's cultures is a unique answer to the question of what it means to be human. And together they make up our repertoire for dealing with the challenges that will confront us as a species in the millennia to come.

But these global voices are being silenced at a frightening rate. The key indicator of this decline in cultural diversity is language loss. A language, of course, is not merely a set of grammatical rules or a vocabulary. It is the vehicle by which the soul of each particular culture comes into the material world. Each one is an old-growth forest of the mind. Linguists agree, however, that 50 percent of the world's 7,000 languages are endangered. Every fortnight an elder dies and carries with him or her into the grave the last syllables of an ancient tongue. Within a generation or two, then, we may be witnessing the loss of fully half of humanity's social, cultural and intellectual legacy. This is the hidden backdrop of our age.

People often ask why it matters if these exotic cultures and their belief systems and rituals disappear. What does a family in New York care if some distant tribe in Africa is extinguished? In truth it probably matters little, no more than the loss of New York would directly affect a tribe in Africa. I would argue that the loss of either way of life does matter to humanity as a whole.

Consider the achievements of the Polynesians. Ten centuries before Christ—at a time when European sailors, incapable of measuring longitude and fearful of the open ocean, hugged the shores of continents—the Polynesians set sail across the Pacific, a diaspora that would eventually bring them to every island from Hawaii to Rapa Nui, the Marquesas to New Zealand. They had no written word. They only knew where they were by remembering how they had got there. Over the length of a long voyage the navigator had to remember every shift of wind, every change of current and speed, every impression from sea, sky and cloud. Even today Polynesian sailors, with whom I have voyaged, readily name 250 stars in the night sky. Their navigators can sense the presence of distant atolls of islands beyond the visible horizon by watching the reverberation of waves across the hull of their vessels, knowing that every island group had its own reflective pattern that can be read with the ease with which a forensic scientist reads a fingerprint. In the darkness they can discern five distinct ocean swells, distinguishing those caused by local weather disturbances from the deep currents that pulsate across the Pacific and can be followed as readily as a terrestrial explorer would follow a river to the sea.

There are many such examples of ancient wisdom. Among the Barasana people of the northwest Amazon in Colombia, for whom all the elements of the natural world are inextricably linked, complex mythologies about the land and its plants and animals have given rise to highly effective land-management practices that serve as a model for how humans can live in the Amazon basin without destroying its forests. The Buddhists of Tibet spend their lives preparing for a moment that we spend most of our lives pretending does not exist: death. Surely their science of the mind—informed by 2,500 years of empirical observation—has something meaningful to contribute to the human patrimony.

This is not to say that cultures should be forced to remain static, that they cannot maintain their identity while changing some of their ways. The Haida did not stop being Native American when they gave up the dugout canoe for the motorboat any more than ranchers in Montana ceased being Americans when they put aside the horse and buggy in favor of the automobile. It is not change or technology that threatens culture; it is domination.

The ultimate tragedy is not that archaic societies are disappearing but rather that avertible forces are driving vibrant peoples and languages out of existence. These external threats take many forms. They may be industrial, as in the case of the egregious forestry practices that have destroyed the subsistence base of the nomadic Penan in the rain forests of Borneo, or the toxic effluents of the petrochemical industry that have compromised the once fertile soils that the Ogoni people of the Niger Delta farmed. Epidemic disease is another menace to culture—to wit, the Yanomamï of the Amazon have suffered dreadful mortality as a result of exotic pathogens brought into their lives by the gold miners who have invaded their lands. Or the threat may be ideology, as in the domination of Tibetan Buddhists by the Communist Chinese.

That cultures do not always fade away but rather may be casualties of other societies' priorities is actually an optimistic observation, because it suggests that if humans are the agents of cultural decline, we can foster cultural survival. Following the Colombian government's 1991 decision to grant land rights to the Indians of the northwest Amazon, for example, the Barasana are now flourishing. Our goal should not be to freeze people in time. Instead we must find ways to ensure that in a pluralistic, interconnected world all peoples may benefit from modernity without that engagement demanding the sacrifice of their ethnicity.

More To Explore

Nomads of the Dawn: The Penan of the Borneo Rain Forest. Wade Davis, Ian MacKenzie and Shane Kennedy. Pomegranate Press, 1995.

Seafaring in the Contemporary Pacific Islands: Studies in Continuity and Change. Edited by Richard Feinberg. Northern Illinois University Press, 1995.

The Search for Shangri-La: A Journey into Tibetan History. Charles Allen. Abacus, 2000.

As Pastoralists Settle: Social, Health, and Economic Consequences of the Pastoral Sedentarization in Marsabit District, Kenya. Edited by Elliot Fratkin and Eric Abella Roth. Springer, 2005.

When Languages Die: The Extinction of the World's Languages and the Erosion of Human Knowledge. K. David Harrison, Oxford University Press, 2007.

Shadows in the Sun: Travels to Landscapes of Spirit and Desire. Wade Davis. Island Press, 2010.

Critical Thinking

1. How many languages and cultures does the world stand to lose within the next generation or two? Why should this matter to us?

2. How were the Polynesians able to settle islands throughout the Pacific?

3. Must cultures remain static in order to maintain ethnic identity? Explain.

4. According to the author, what is the "ultimate tragedy" with regard to the fact that archaic societies are disappearing? Why is this also an "optimistic" observation?

5. Must people reject modernity in order to maintain their ethnicity? Explain.

WADE DAVIS is an anthropologist, ethnobotanist, filmmaker and photographer. His most recent book, *The Wayfinders: Why Ancient Wisdom Matters in the Modern World,* was published in 2009 by Anansi and provided the inspiration for this essay.

Article 39

The Tractor Invasion

For the Indigenous Peoples of the Cerrado, plowshares might as well be swords, as agribusiness increasingly turns their homelands into farmlands.

LAURA GRAHAM

It was evening in the Xavante community of Etéñhiritipa in central Brazil as the moon rose over the Serra do Roncador. We had just finished a refreshing bath in the river and were seated against the wall of a house facing the cleared red-earth plaza in the community's center (clearing the swath of vegetation around the houses and in the central plaza means there are no snakes to deal with near people's homes). Twilight settled over the thatched houses as the adolescent novitiates sang and danced a dreamed song around the semicircular ring of houses and the adult men gathered in the central plaza for their nightly men's council.

The rhythm of daily life felt almost the same as it did more than 25 years ago when, as a graduate student, I began my ethnographic studies of Xavante peoples among this group. The dramatic changes that are taking place in the central Brazilian plateau seemed far away, almost undetectable at a first glance inside the community. But changes there are, and they especially threaten the land rights of the Xavante people. I was in Etéñhiritipa with Cultural Survival Executive Director Ellen Lutz, who came to learn the challenges Xavante now face and to explore ways that Cultural Survival could support their efforts.

The Xavante live in the vast Brazilian savanna called the Cerrado, an area the size of the American Great Plains. A Ge-speaking people, they retreated from contact with national society in the mid-1800s and earned a reputation for fierceness and determined isolationism. Xavante groups did not begin to establish peaceful relationships with representatives of national society until 1946. Even then, some groups refused contact until the mid-1960s.

Fifty years after colonization, the Xavante continue many of their traditional cultural practices, and their spiritual and ceremonial lives are rich. They also face tremendous challenges. Their homeland is now just a 12-hour drive from Brasilia and lies in the heart of Brazil's new agricultural and economic engine. The nine small reserves that the government began carving out for the Xavante in the late 1970s today seem like islands in a sea of soy. And agribusiness has its sights set on even these small reserves where, in indigenous areas such as these, the rich and unique Cerrado ecosystem is still intact.

While large-scale agriculturalists and related corporations are reaping enormous profits from Mato Grosso's burgeoning soy industry and making plans for multimillion-dollar development projects, many Xavante don't have enough to eat, and those who live in the smallest of the Xavante areas can't find sufficient game or even palm fronds to construct their thatched homes. The health situation in Xavante areas is abysmal: infant mortality is high, well above the regional and national averages and close to that of Northeastern Brazil, the nation's poorest region. Xavante mortality rates are high because they are exposed to many infectious diseases and have poor health care; an epidemic of hypertension and diabetes is imminent.

The Xavante are one of many central Brazilian groups whose homelands and livelihoods have been severely affected over the last two decades by the proliferation of colossal agroindustry. In some areas it is soy; in others, sugarcane for biofuels; and in still others, fast-growing eucalyptus for firewood to process soy oil in factories.

"The Cerrado is a source of life to the Indigenous community," says Elcio, from the Terena village of Cachoeirinha. "It is very important to us, and we worry about the devastation of the Cerrado, especially in our region, where the farmers are cutting the forests down. The Cerrado has enormous biodiversity, and it sustains our lives, because our foods come from the Cerrado: it is where we hunt and fish, collect fruits and honey. Burning down the forests is also threatening the biodiversity of the Cerrado. The burnings are destroying the guavira, a delicious fruit that we eat and can also sell."

The Xavante are more fortunate than some because they live in legally protected reserves—even if those protections are frequently disregarded and the areas are small. Many other groups live on lands that have yet not been legally demarcated. For many, their claims have been languishing for decades in the drawers and filing cabinets of the government agency responsible for granting Indigenous Peoples legal title to their lands.

Ellen and I, along with our companions, Hiparidi Top'tiro, a Xavante leader from the Sangradouro Reserve, and activist Daniela Lima, made the trip from Brasilia to the Xavante areas in less than a day. Paved roads carried us to within about

40 miles of the Pimentel Barbosa reserve. This was a journey that in 1982 had taken me a minimum of three days (usually more), traveling in a sturdy four-wheel-drive truck over rough dirt roads and unstable bridges, often no more than two planks precariously set over logs. In the rainy season, when torrential downpours hammer the Cerrado, the road was frequently impassable, and washed-out bridges were common. On this trip, we made rapid time. Our small sedan wove in and out between heavily laden trucks that were barreling down the highway at speeds that made me nervous. These immense truck caravans were transporting agricultural produce, particularly soybeans, out of Mato Grosso, Brazil's largest soy-producing state, to ports and commercial centers where most of these crops would be exported, mainly to markets in Europe, China, and Japan.

Our journey took us past miles and miles of deforested Cerrado fields, much of it owned by large and powerful farming and ranching corporations. We passed huge grain elevators, silos, and storage facilities and billboards with transnational names: Cargill, Bunge, ADM, Maggi, Monsanto. Towns that I previously knew as small hamlets had mushroomed into sizeable cities; municipalities in this region are some of the fastest-growing cities in the nation.

The galloping, massive growth in the agroindustry is putting enormous pressure on the Xavante and other Indigenous groups. The prevailing attitude in the region is pro-development, pro-agribusiness. Anyone who takes an alternative position meets strong resentment and antagonism. This is especially true for Indigenous Peoples who, in defending their constitutionally granted rights to territory, clean environment, and the ability to live according to their traditional ways, are perceived as presenting obstacles to progress.

The Brazilian Cerrado extends across the vast central Brazilian Plateau, stretching over approximately 800,000 square miles, almost one third of the nation's land mass and spanning 12 states. Its total area is equivalent to the combined area of Spain, France, Germany, Italy, and England (or, if you prefer, three times the size of Texas). It is one of the world's most biologically diverse tropical savanna regions and the nation's second major biome, after the Amazon rainforest. Conservation International identifies it as a "Conservation Hotspot," one of "the richest and most threatened reservoirs of plant and animal life on Earth." The Cerrado houses the watersheds for three of South America's major river basins: the Amazon, Sao Francisco, and Paraná/Paraguai. As Xavante leader Cipassé Xavante says, "The fight to save the Cerrado isn't just for us, it is for all humanity." What happens in the Cerrado has broad human and planetary effects.

Soy agribusiness began to aggressively expand into Brazil's central western Cerrado in the late 1980s, when soy varieties that could tolerate the tropical climate became commercially available. This accelerating agricultural boom, together with huge related infrastructure development projects (road construction, hydroelectric dams, colossal hydroengineering projects to transform rivers into water highways), as well as illegal mining and timber extraction in Indigenous areas, is destroying the fragile Cerrado environment and having devastating effects on the region's Indigenous inhabitants.

Socially and culturally diverse Indigenous Peoples have lived in the Cerrado for centuries, but reliable demographic information on the current Indigenous populations does not exist. Brazil's central-west region alone (the states of Mato Grosso, Mato Grosso do Sul, Goiais, Tocantins) is home to some 53,000 Indigenous people who belong to 42 distinct ethnic groups. All of these groups are confronting serious challenges, and some are responding by building alliances with members of other Indigenous groups and other traditional peoples, and also with national and international organizations like Cultural Survival. In the face of formidable foes and challenges, they are asserting themselves to take control over processes that are influencing their lives.

The Rise of Colonization

During the 1960s and into the 1980s, the Brazilian government used large-scale colonization schemes and generous fiscal incentives to attract settlers and commercial cattle ranching from the south into remote Cerrado regions. As the frontier moved westward, there were increasing conflicts between settlers and Indigenous Peoples, and communities were devastated by new diseases, like measles, against which they had no immunity. In a pattern repeated over and over, government agents or missionaries used those problems to attract distressed Indigenous groups to specific locales—government posts or missions—where they received sanctuary and medical treatment. With a region's original inhabitants corralled into defined areas, the state then sold their lands, with titles certifying the land as "free of Indians."

One of the most egregious examples of purging Indigenous Peoples from their lands occurred in the Xavante area known as Maräwaitsede, located in the region of the Suya-Missú River near what is now the Xingu National Park. (The park is Brazil's "postcard" Indigenous Territory, an area of 108,000 square miles that is home to approximately 4,700 people Indigenous Peoples belonging to 14 distinct groups.) After a São Paulo-based rancher fraudulently purchased lands inhabited by Xavante, he flew an airplane over the area everyday and dropped food in a specific location. Eventually the Xavante relocated to the site to receive rations. The rancher then moved the group multiple times and finally settled it close to ranch headquarters, where he forced the Xavante to work for food, and subjected them to continuous harassment by the ranch's non-Indigenous employees. Conditions for Xavante deteriorated so severely that, in 1966, the owners—at that point the powerful Italian-based Olmetto group, whose corporate land holdings reached 6,000 square miles—in collaboration with Salesian missionaries, the government Indian agency, and the Brazilian Air Force, solved their "Indian problem" by airlifting the remaining Xavante some 250 miles away to the Salesian mission at São Marcos. Within two weeks after their arrival, more than 100 Xavante died of a measles epidemic.

In 1994, Xavante from this area finally won a long battle to recoup some of this land when the state demarcated the Maräwäitsede Indigenous Territory. But despite the ruling, ranchers who had moved onto the land refused to leave or allow the Xavante to move back to their territory. They even encouraged settlers to take their place and deforest large tracts. When, in 2004, a determined Xavante group attempted to enter their lands, they were prevented by armed gunmen. The refugees set up camp on the opposite side of the dirt highway (BR-158) and lived for 11 months in improvised shelters. Three babies died of pneumonia exacerbated by the incessant dust from camping alongside the road. When a team carrying out a study for the UN High Commissioner for Human Rights attempted to reach the area by road, ranchers burned bridges in an attempt to stop them. The team hired planes and reached the area by air. This area is still plagued by conflict, and powerful ranchers continue to challenge the Xavante's rights to this land in the courts.

Cattle ranchers continue to deforest huge areas of Cerrado lands for pasture around Indigenous areas as well as within them. Deforestation and the aggressive, intrusive grasses that ranchers plant for cattle severely disrupt the Cerrado flora and fauna, reducing game populations that are important sources of protein in Native peoples' diets. And because hunting is central to many important ceremonials, lack of game has forced many groups, such as the Parecí of western Mato Grosso, to abandon traditional activities that are fundamental to their social organization and culture.

Prior to Brazil's new constitution of 1988, state policy was directed toward assimilating Indigenous Peoples into the nation's social fabric and economy. In the Cerrado area, the government attempted to transform Indigenous Peoples into capitalist ranchers and commercial agriculturalists. For example, in the 1970s, when many Cerrado ranchers were turning to commercial rice cultivation for domestic markets, the National Indian Foundation (FUNAI) implemented colossal mechanized rice cultivation projects in Xavante areas. The state used these projects to justify the creation of their reserves. Instead of "wasting" this land on Indigenous Peoples, these areas (along with Indigenous labor) would contribute to the region's GNP just like other commercial ranches in the region. Many large-scale ranchers and agriculturalists oppose the creation or amplification of Indigenous reserves because, they argue, it removes potentially productive lands from development.

For Xavante, the rice projects were immensely destructive: they created massive technological dependency, exacerbated tensions within and across communities, and, since Xavante substituted rice for nutritious traditional foods, dramatically altered their diet. Malnutrition is now a serious problem, and new diseases are endemic, especially hypertension and diabetes, which are associated with excessive reliance on refined foods and the new sedentary lifestyle. The projects also provided opportunities for corrupt Indian agents to siphon monies in every type of financial transaction, from equipment repair to the sale of crops harvested from Xavante lands. Although these projects were eventually abandoned in the late 1980s, many of the problems they created persist.

1990s—The Soy Boom

Commercial agriculture in the central Brazilian Cerrado began with rice and some soy in the 1970s and exploded into a massive export-oriented agroindustry during the late 1980s and 1990s. Soybean cultivation is highly mechanized, capital intensive, and uses large amounts of chemical fertilizers, herbicides, and pesticides. Its explosion in the Cerrado coincided with increased global demand in the wake of the mad-cow scare, when Europeans turned to soy for high protein animal feed, and with the expansion of world markets for soy oil, especially in China and Japan. In 2000, Mato Grosso became the country's leading soy-producing state, and in 2004, Brazil displaced the United States as the world's leading soy-exporting nation. In Mato Grosso, the area dedicated to soy cultivation increased 81 percent in just three years, between 1991–1994. This area nearly doubled again by 2003, and estimates indicate that the state has the potential to plant 10 times that amount—an area almost the size of California.

The environmental and social consequences of this immense and rapid agricultural explosion are staggering, especially for the region's vulnerable Indigenous inhabitants, particularly those who do not have legal title to their land. Although Brazil's constitution guarantees Indigenous Peoples the right to permanently occupy lands they traditionally inhabited, the government has been lamentably slack in carrying out its obligation to identify and legally demarcate those lands. In many cases, large landholders and corporations tie up the land claims in lawsuits that can drag on for years and, in some cases, such as Serra Raposa do Sol in Roraima, for decades.

And, of course, while the cases are being decided (or not decided), the landholders and corporations can continue developing and profiting from Indigenous land. They build roads, fences, silos, warehouses, buildings, and sometimes even cities in areas that Indigenous Peoples claim. These "improvements" reduce the likelihood that the government will have sufficient political will or the ability to compensate developers for the cost of their investments, and this increases the likelihood that the state will concede to the more powerful party.

There are many cases, like the Xavante in Maräwaitsede who ended up camped on the roadside, in which farmers and ranchers refuse to leave Indigenous lands, even after they have received compensation. One notable case happened on the Ilha do Bananal, an island the size of New Jersey in the middle of the Araguaia River that is home to Karajá, Javaé, and Ava Canoeiro. Despite the ranchers being compensated for having to move, their cattle remain on the island degrading the environment and polluting the waters.

Indigenous groups that challenge powerful landholders are subjected to tremendous pressure. Sometimes they even become martyrs to their cause. In 2007 and 2008, three Xacriabá leaders were assassinated over land disputes. In Mato Grosso do Sul, where Guarani Kaiowa, Nândeva, and other Native communities are squeezed into tiny areas, 80 Indigenous people are imprisoned. Indigenous Peoples in this region suffer extreme social disorganization, and the incidence of suicide is disturbingly high. Eliso da Lopes is one such leader who, because of persecution from ranchers, has not seen his family in over a year. "We want our land returned so that we can plant and produce," he says. "Even though this is our land we are living on the edge of an interstate highway. This is a sad situation, but we are not going to pull back. If the ranchers kill one Indigenous leader, 1,000 leaders will arise."

Some ranchers have taken a more insidious approach to the issue. Among the Parecí of Mato Grosso, for example, neighboring farmers convinced some leaders to become "agricultural partners," even though commercial agriculture within Indigenous areas is illegal. Instead of standing up for Indigenous rights, the state governor, Blairo Maggi, a millionaire farmer whose Maggi Group is the world's largest soy producer, condoned and officially recognized these arrangements. In 1995 the Parecí agreed to allow 130 acres to be planted, an area that has expanded each year. Despite using the term "partners" to describe the Parecí, the farmers take 98 percent of the profits, leaving only 2 percent for the Parecí from the soy grown on their lands with their labor.

Governor Maggi is known in Brazil as O Rei da Soja, "the King of Soy," but environmentalists call him "the King of Deforestation." Mato Grosso leads Brazilian states in the number of agricultural burnings and the rate of deforestation. One hundred and fifteen thousand square miles of forest and savanna (an area the size of Arizona) have been replaced with plantations in the last twenty years, according to the World Wildlife Fund.

Deforestation, especially around the headwaters of rivers and streams, causes severe erosion and increases pollution. During the rainy season heavy rains wash toxic chemicals used in soy agriculture—like the Monsanto herbicide Roundup—directly into rivers where Indigenous Peoples drink, bathe, and catch fish. Because Cerrado soils are acidic and nutrient poor, they demand large amounts of lime and chemical fertilizers to be productive. These, as well as pesticides used in intensive monocropping, seep into water supplies and contaminate groundwater, making even well water dangerous. In the Guarani Aquifer, the world's largest, contaminants have reached 80 percent of the level acceptable for human consumption.

Chemicals are also dropped or carried by wind onto Indigenous lands. This happened during the last planting season in the Xavante territory of Sangradouro, and Paulo Supretaprâ, leader of Etéñhiritipa, reports that this also happens in the Pimentel Barbosa Indigenous Territory. Also, since Brazil's president, Luiz Inácio da Silva, lifted the ban on genetically modified organisms in August 2003, soy farmers plant modified varieties immediately next to, and sometimes inside Indigenous areas, even though their environmental and human impacts are unknown. As Paulo Cipassé says, Xavante are concerned that game animals they hunt and eat may be ingesting toxic substances outside of Indigenous areas. With plans to expand sugarcane planting and installation of factories for converting this crop into biofuels, pressure on Indigenous territories is likely to increase in the future.

Reshaping the Cerrado

With soybean production booming, at more than 4.5 million tons per year in Mato Grosso alone and predictions that production will continue to rise, Brazil has plans for huge infrastructural projects—part of a state plan known as Avança Brasil ("Forward Brazil")—to make the region more accessible and transport the huge harvests to ports and commercial centers. The Tocantins-Araguaia Hidrovia, also known as the Central-Northern Multimodal Transport Corridor, is a multi-million dollar project that would transform the most extensive river basin of central Brazil and the eastern Amazon into a commercial waterway to support barge convoys mostly for transporting soy, but also carrying agricultural toxins, which makes Indigenous Peoples very nervous. In total, the project would alter 1,700 miles of the Tocantins-Araguaia-Rio das Mortes river system. It includes large-scale engineering works including hydroelectric facilities, locks, and dams and the construction of new ports. Two of the planned "small" hydroelectric projects will be constructed in or next to the Xavante areas of São Marcos and Sangradouro, and the project will directly affect the Xavante territories of Areões and Pimentel Barbosa, where Ellen Lutz and I spent the last night of our Xavante trip. A recently constructed dam next to the Parabubure reserve, one of many planned on headwaters to the Xingu River, is already operating.

In addition, the project will affect at least six other Indigenous groups: the Apinajé, Javaé, Karajá, Krahó, Krikati and Tapirapé. In all, the Hidrovia would directly affect the lives of more than 10,000 Indigenous people who depend on the river's flora and fauna for their livelihoods. But the Indigenous Peoples are fighting the project, and a lawsuit filed by the Xavante of Pimentel Barbosa in collaboration with the Brazilian organization, Instituto Socioambiental, has delayed the work. It is not clear, though, whether they will be able to stop it.

Although Ellen and I only visited a few of the 200 Xavante communities that exist today, we were heartened to learn about many positive projects that Xavante are undertaking to improve conditions in their reserves. Cipassé, the leader of the Wederä community in Pimentel Barbosa, gave us a tour of a recently inaugurated school in his community that had been built with government funds, with state-of-the-art kitchen equipment and a room ready for computers. He also told us of the community's project to manage, and hopefully increase, the population of white-lipped peccary in the reserve. Wederä and many other Xavante communities are also undertaking projects, often in collaboration with NGOs, that validate traditional knowledge of Cerrado plants, many of which have medicinal properties. They want to revitalize collecting and processing practices that have been abandoned and encourage the eating of nutritious Cerrado foods. Small projects like these, which can make a tremendous difference in Indigenous Peoples' lives, are underway in many Indigenous communities throughout the Cerrado. The Krahó, for example, are helping to enrich the environment by participating in a Cerrado fruit project and earning some income at the same time.

We were glad that our trip provided opportunities for our companions, Hiparidi Top'tiro and Daniela Lima, to spend time with Xavante leaders and community members. Among other things, they discussed a project known as Marãna Bödödi, or Forest Path, which would unite the disparate Xavante and Bororo Indigenous territories that lie along the Rio das Mortes into a single contiguous protected area.

As part of our effort to understand ways that Cultural Survival may best support Xavante, we met with staff from the National Indian Foundation's department of territorial affairs and the office of the Attorney General that deals with Indigenous affairs. It was very encouraging to find that the officials we met were very supportive of this and other Indigenous efforts to protect their lands.

Brazil's constitution is a strong weapon for Indigenous Peoples, but putting their rights into practice takes dedication and very long, hard work. The Xavante Warä Association and an expanding network called the Mobilization of Indigenous Peoples of the Cerrado are taking action to advance the struggle of Indigenous Peoples of the Cerrado. Kuiusi Kisêdjê, leader of the Ngojwere community in the Xingu, spoke for many when he said, "We fight to recoup this land because it is sacred to us; our ancestors are buried here. A lot of people think that we only care about money, but what we want is our land."

Critical Thinking

1. What is the contrast between the expansion and prosperity of the large-scale agriculturalists and the conditions of the Xavante? How are the Xavante "more fortunate than some?"

2. What evidence is there of massive growth in the agroindustry? What is the prevailing attitude in the region regarding this?

3. What are the other developments destroying the fragile Cerrado?

4. How has the government's policy of colonization affected the indigenous people?

5. How have cattle ranchers changed the land and the ability of the Xavante to hunt?

6. Prior to 1988, what was state policy regarding assimilation and land use?

7. How were the rice projects destructive? What have been the health consequences?

8. How has the legal process failed the Indigenous Peoples?

9. What happens to those who challenge the powerful landholders?

10. What have been the consequences of deforestation and the use of chemicals?

11. How will the water projects affect the people of the area?

12. What are some positive projects being undertaken by the Xavante?

We Are Going Underwater

Susan A. Crate

Siberian Villagers Show the World What Global Climate Change Means

There are no longer any skylarks. They are gone, and we don't hear them. And now we also don't hear the shaman's drum. Before we had shamans, and the woods rang. . . . Humans are not meant to dig down in the earth, but they started to do mining here in the Soviet time, and now with all the water they want to dig down again, this time to make canals. There is too much water. For example, at Chegde there used to be many families working and haying and keeping animals, and now only one family can get enough hay there, because the rest is flooded. But I think all the canals and all the digging will make matters worse. They dug a canal at Tüölbe—a six-meter-deep canal. That is bad; we are not to dig like that. This is a sacred land, and we are not to bother the land so much. - Bahylai (Vasilii) Nikolaev, Khoro, Suntar District, Republic of Sakha (Yakutia), Russian Federation, July 10, 2010.

For me, testimony like this from Viliui Sakha, a horse- and cattle-breeding people of northeastern Siberia, is food for thought. I have lived, worked, and conducted ethnographic research in their communities since 1991 and have witnessed many transformations over the years. But Nikolaev, born in 1926, can look back over a long lifetime of drastic changes. Even though the 1917 October Revolution had already occurred, Nikolaev was born early enough to learn and live his people's preSoviet adaptations—both physical and spiritual—to the extreme Siberian climate. He also witnessed the Soviet transformation of his people's lifeways and culture through the gradual collectivization and further rapid consolidation of Sakha subsistence practices into sovkhozi (agro-industrial state farm operations). Nikolaev was one of several native Sakha hired as local guides for Soviet geological teams exploring the diamond-rich region during the push for industrialization in the late 1950s. His diverse life experience is richly summarized in his view that Sakha laws of nature have been repeatedly and increasingly broken—to the point where the fundamental sounds, the song of the skylark and the echo of the shaman's drum, are now absent from his homeland.

Nikolaev's homeland is the Republic of Sakha (Yakutia), which takes up one-fifth of the Russian Federation's territory. Ethnically, about 45 percent of the republic's 1 million inhabitants are Sakha, formerly called Yakuts, their Russian designation. Most still speak their native Sakha, a Turkic language (readers accustomed to the transliteration of Russian names and words will notice some nonstandard adaptations). Nikolaev is Viliui Sakha, because he lives in one of the districts that lies in the watershed of the Viliui River, a western tributary of the great Lena River, which flows northward through the center of the republic. Viliui Sakha are distinctive from Sakha inhabiting the republic's central regions, mostly on account of their acclaimed music and dance traditions, personified by the late improvisatory singer Sergei Afanas'evich Zverov.

For more than half a millennium Sakha have raised their cattle and horses in an extreme continental climate. Like all place-based peoples (a term used in anthropology circles to refer to groups who depend directly upon their immediate environment for both their physical and spiritual sustenance), their pioneering ancestors developed adaptations to live and flourish within a specific ecosystem. In their case, they faced a subarctic environment with continuous permafrost and annual temperature swings of 180 Fahrenheit degrees, from–75 in the winter to 105 in summer. Also like most place-based peoples, Sakha refined an ancestral belief system that mediates their interactions with their environment. Theirs is an animistic world view, one that recognizes the sentient quality of all of creation and that requires people to perform specific acts and rituals in order to thrive. Shamans, individuals either born or apprenticed into their calling, are the intermediaries for humans with the spirit worlds. "Black" shamans travel from the middle world, the world of human habitation, to the lower world to fight and negotiate with abaalii (evil spirits) in times of crisis. In contrast, "white" shamans interact with sky spirits, most importantly during the Sakha summer festival, to ensure a plentiful harvest.

Not only have Sakha adapted to an extreme climate and subarctic ecosystem, they have also accommodated outside social pressures. In the mid-1600s, during Russian imperial expansion eastward, colonizers forced them to pay iasak (fur tribute) and annexed some of their lands. Their holdings were further taken during the Soviet collectivization process, their environment was despoiled by Soviet-era industrialization—in their case, diamond mining—and since the early 1990s they continue to deal with changes following the fall of the Soviet Union. For most Viliui Sakha, daily life continues to be a full-time job of addressing the immediate needs of family, household, income, and food production.

With the turn of the twenty-first century, however, Sakha face a new challenge, one much less announced or recognized: a subtle and gradually increasing change in cycles and patterns of weather and climate.

I began hearing testimonies about this new change in the summer of 2005, the last field research season of a project focused on local definitions of future sustainability. While analyzing surveys, the project research team, made up of my village research assistants and me, found that in answers to the final, open-ended question, 90 percent of the eighty-five participants had expressed concern about changes in weather patterns, temperature, landscape, and the like. In response, we decided to spend part of the final weeks interviewing elders, since they had the longest continuous period of observation of local weather and climate.

Among the thirty-three elders interviewed, ten mentioned that one of the differences between now and before was that now the Bull of Winter was no longer arriving. I knew they were referring to the mythological beast who, according to the Sakha story, comes bringing with him the cold three-month period when it is too dry to snow and all is held in a frozen silence. Such testimony clarified for me how global climate change was affecting not only the villagers' physical environment, but also their mythological or cosmological adaptation to that environment—a ripe subject for further investigation. Before leaving the field that summer, I asked if the communities wanted to participate in a three-year project focused on understanding these changes of concern. With their approval (and a bit of proposal writing), I returned in 2008 to begin documenting their local experiences and adaptive responses.

During our first summer of research, we focused on gathering local people's observations and perceptions of change, their explanations of the causes of those changes, and their opinions about how the near future would unfold if those changes were to continue. We met with Sakha in the four villages where I had been concentrating my field research since 1991, all located in the Suntar district. In each village, we conducted two six-person focus groups and interviewed fifteen people. Our results showed overall consensus on the following nine changes.

Winters are warm. Most agreed that warmer winters are welcome, since people need less wood to heat their homes, and cows can be outside more and can walk to the water hole instead of people having to haul water to the barns for them. "It is good not to be cold," one young man remarked, "and we youth already expect the winter to be warm!" But with further probing, many also commented that warmer winters mean more sickness, especially for elders and children. The same probing also revealed many favorable views of a cold winter. One elder remarked: "In winter the cold makes your body feel lighter, and you work and move better and go about with enthusiasm. In the warmth, it is

like your bones have melted, and you can't work and move well." This acceptance of cold is even expressed in time-tested proverbs still in use today. For example:

There is increasing water on the land. Standing water and flooding interfere with the villagers' main rural resource: graze for horses and hay as fodder for cows. "I don't recall anything like the water we have had in the past ten years," said one villager. "Before, we hayed all the fields—now we have to go here and there to hay, because all our haylands are underwater." The increased water also ruins roads needed to access resources, and has even begun inundating foundations of low-lying houses. Householders have also been accustomed to creating a bahuts, or underground freezer, by digging a hole down to the permafrost. In it they store meat, milk products, and even ice for summer drinking water. That natural convenience is increasingly flooded, and more and more households have to do without a buluus or use an electric freezer.

There is too much rain, and it falls at the wrong times. Precipitation patterns have changed so that it not only rains more, but rainfall tends to come not in spring but instead during July and August, interfering with the villagers' haying activities. "When it rains, it rains for very long times and at the wrong times of year," said one villager. "When I was ten and went haying, we would wait for rain—it never rained. Back then it only rained for two or three days during the entire haying season—and when it did rain, we would go berrying. But in the last ten years we have not able to finish the hay work because of rain."

Summers are cold. Cold summers prevent the full maturing of many staple garden and forage plants, not to mention hay. Cold summer weather also makes it less inviting to get all the work done to prepare for the long winter. Sakha have a saying: "One day of summer is worth a week of winter." They also feel robbed of a much-deserved recharge of warmth from the hot, dry summers formerly characteristic of their area. "If it is warm," said one elder, "we feel good and wear light clothes and can work hard—and soak up all the Sun's warm rays." Notably, Sakha say both kinds of unseasonable weather—mildness in the cold time and wet chill in the hot time—sap their energy for work.

Seasons come late. The most problematic lagging season is an extended fall, which is interfering with the regular timing of events. For example, the extended periods of freeze and thaw affect the annual cycle of slaughter. Typically, Sakha wait until temperatures are below freezing twenty-four hours a day so that they can store the meat in unheated sheds, utilizing the environment as a natural freezer. That would normally be in the middle of November. With the extended fall, however, they are now having to wait an extra two to four weeks—which means feeding the animals intended for slaughter another two to four weeks' worth of hay, and putting off replenishing household meat stores.

The extended fall also interferes with the gathering of oton (cowberry or lingonberry), the last berry of the season and the one most highly prized by households for its vitamins. Typically those berries are harvested in large quantities, which are poured into cardboard boxes and stored in unheated sheds to gradually freeze for fresh eating during the winter. With the repeated freezing and thawing that now occurs, the skin of the berries is broken, and entire boxes of them turn into unusable mush.

In addition, many natural signs that tell Sakha spring is on its way increasingly appear during the extended fall period. One is n'urguhunnar, or snowdrops, the first spring flower that pushes up through the snow, much as crocuses do in temperate zones of the United States. The formation of icicles and of new needles on larch trees are other "heralds of spring" that, jarringly, are seen in the newly extended fall.

Even as winter finally settles in, problems arise. The extended fall, characterized by cycles of freezing and thawing, often causes formation of a layer of ice beneath the snow that makes it impossible for horses, which forage outside year-round, to continue feeding. Between that and the increase in snowfall, many horse breeders now complain that their herds are suffering. "Horses can't reach their food, so they starve, and many die—and many of the babies inside them die," one villager reported. "Also, this winter some fell through the thin ice."

There is too much snow. Villagers also report that instead of the usual three-month break in snowfall when the Bull of Winter arrived, it now snows all winter, owing to warming. Because of this, they constantly have to clear snow, especially to move it away from their homes before the spring thaw to avoid inundation. As one put it, "With so much snow, falling all winter long, and the winds—we now have to shovel all winter, and sometimes a few times a day."

There are more floods. Inhabitants also talked about how the annual spring flood cycle, characteristic of their ecosystem and resulting from the spring thaw of ice and snow, has increased in volume and duration. This results in broken transportation infrastructure (roads and bridges), sudden inundation of homes and public buildings, and the intensification of the existing problem of increasing water on the land.

Temperatures change suddenly. Many people mentioned this new phenomenon. One elder remarked, "In June it is hot, then very cold and windy. In the fall season it will suddenly snow and then there will be very warm days. In winter it was minus 40 [Celsius], and the next day, very suddenly, it was 3 or 4 degrees [above zero]."

There are fewer birds and animals. The decline was "widely noted." "I hunt, and I can tell you that the wild animals are very few—you can count them on your fingers," said one villager. An elder lamented:

It used to be that you got up in the morning, and your ears were filled with the sounds of birds and animals. In the summer we waited to hear the skylark's song in the hay fields, and in the spring we waited for the cuckoo's talking. We lived on the edge of Kuukei Lake, and the ducks and geese also made a lot of sounds. Now it is totally quiet. I miss the birds' singing—they have been my friends ever since I was a child, we grew up together.

Hares, an important game species for Sakha, will not nest in wet land, and so, to the extent that water is increasing across the land, they have more than likely changed their range. But a decline in the population of hares, or of other wild animals, should not be attributed solely to global climate change.

For example, over the last decade more people have had the time and resources to hunt than in the Soviet period. Not only that, most contemporary youth no longer observe Sakha hunting ethics (as one elder put it, "Young people nowadays kill everything they see"). Such factors play a role in consort with climate-change effects. This dynamic of "multiple stressors" plays a similar role in the other eight changes inhabitants observe.

In discussions of their various observations in the focus groups and in interviews, the increasing water on the land emerged as the inhabitants' greatest concern. But beyond the practical concerns of not enough hay, hampered transportation, and household inundation, Sakha also find the increasing water psychologically unsettling. "I am very scared that we are going underwater," said one villager. "Looking down from a plane you can see that the land has patches of water across it—water is coming up from below. It looks like the land is sinking down." I was reminded how the phrase uuga barabyt ("We are going underwater") had already come up in focus-group and interview discussions. Even I had noticed the increasing water on the land after an absence of three years, and had documented it by taking some snapshots during our 2008 airplane ride to the villages.

As mentioned above, climate change is not the only contributing factor to contemporary local change, and also it is not the first issue Sakha have coped or are coping with. They could be thought of as experts in adapting—to an extreme subarctic climate, to Russian colonization, to sovietization, to post-Soviet times. But how they will adapt to the new changes—particularly the flooding of land and the difficulty of laying up sufficient hay for their herds—remains to be seen. Our 2009 survey revealed that the vast majority do not want to move away, even if it means not keeping cows. Like most place-based peoples, they are tied to their ancestral homelands.

We also know from our investigation that most Sakha do not make the connection between the changes they are seeing locally and global climate change. Their explanations were based on the evidence available to them, which points to contributing factors in the changes they observe, but does not tell the full story. When asked what was the cause, most blamed the Viliui hydroelectric reservoir. Others identified the source as the natural wet and dry cycles of their ecosystem. The third most popular explanation was the recent overabundance of technology and mechanization. The few who mentioned global climate change were either teachers, university students home from the city for the summer, or elders who read every newspaper they could subscribe to.

The unprecedented effects of global climate change—at work to a greater or lesser extent in each of the nine changes—make adaptation a novel challenge for Viliui Sakha, and for all the world's inhabitants. Therefore, finding ways to bring an understanding of that phenomenon into local awareness makes sense as a way to encourage new adaptive strategies, bolster survival, and allay some of the psychological distress. Conversely, the detailed and highly specific observations of place-based peoples such as the Viliui Sakha contribute important information, clarifying the diverse physical and cultural ways that this global phenomenon is having its effect. This kind of local knowledge needs to be brought to the attention of the global community and into the formulation of policy initiatives.

This revelation prompted our team to explore the ways we could both increase local awareness of the role played by climate change and also bring local observations and understanding to the regional science community. Our culminating event for the three-year project was what we called "knowledge exchanges."

One of our regional scientific consultants since the project's outset, Alexander Fedorov, a specialist from the MeInikov Permafrost Institute, quickly agreed to participate in the knowledge exchanges. He himself is Viliui Sakha, from the Nyurba district, which neighbors the Suntar district where our research is based. He told us he was keenly aware of the need to bring scientific information to the affected communities. It was poignant to me that halfway through the knowledge exchange trip, Fedorov shared with me how satisfying the experience was for him—adding that not only was it the first time he had presented his research to a public audience, but also the first time he had done so in his native Sakha language.

In the summer of 2010 we traveled by van from the capital city, Yakutsk, to our four research villages, stopping to hold knowledge exchanges in the four district centers along the way. We began the exchanges by inviting audience participants to talk about changes they had been observing. Here is just one example, from a man who traveled six miles on horseback to attend our event:

> I am a cowboy and hunter—and I see that the land has changed. Where there was never a ravine there now is a ravine, all has caved in. Around the streams, where the flat haylands are located, the same thing is happening—ravines have now formed and all the water goes away very quickly down those ravines, and the lands that never were dry before are now dry. The ducks come very late. Mostly I am speaking about changes in the land's surface: where there never was a hill, there now is a hill; where there never was a hole, there now is. The wet lands are now dry, and there are more and more ravines. Land that never had water now does, and the erosion of our lands is happening very quickly—in just the last few years. And horses have a very hard time in the warm winter. We thought that warm would be good for the horses, but now we understand it is bad for them. Overall, we have come to a time when we cannot predict the weather. Before, things came in the right times, and now they do not.

Alexander Fedorov's Sharing of his research was similarly far-reaching. After providing a concise overview of global climate change and its amplified effect in the polar regions, including the Republic of Sakha (Yakutia), he brought his presentation home by focusing on permafrost. He explained that across the world, global climate change is affecting ecosystems in specific ways, and in the Sakha ecosystem the main indicator of it is the degradation of permafrost. He went on to explain that among the many kinds of permafrost, that which made up most of the Viliui regions was the kind with large ice wedges and, consequently, the most susceptible to temperature change and degradation. His comments were illustrated with photographs of familiar village scenes combined with graphed data.

Fedorov also shared newly developed technologies to help preserve permafrost—methods of building new houses and of retrofitting old ones. For new construction, large pipes are laid under the site where the house will be built and are covered with several feet of soil; then the house is built on top. The pipe ends are left open in winter to allow freezing air to maintain the permafrost, and are closed in summer to prevent warm air from thawing it. For an existing home, an auger is used to dig a hole several yards deep alongside the foundation, down to the permafrost. A pipe is then inserted and filled with diesel fuel or kerosene, which keep the soil cold because of their low freezing points.

Overall, the knowledge exchanges were a success: residents participated actively, adding their local knowledge to the scientific understanding of how the global phenomenon is affecting their locales; reciprocally, specific scientific knowledge helped to fill out local perceptions of contemporary change. Our task now is to integrate local and regional knowledge and to share it more broadly among the region's inhabitants and beyond. Our primary goals in this integration are both to bolster Sakha understandings and adaptations and to inform the science and policy communities about how climate change is affecting local environments and cultures.

Some scientists are developing ways to "scale down" global climate models to make them relevant to local communities. In my work on global climate change and place-based peoples, I am repeatedly asked if we plan to "scale up" our findings to have global significance. Although I do believe the knowledge we have gained can have a wider application, it will not be by scaling it up, but rather by giving the world community a local window into the diverse ways global climate change is unsettling and challenging such time-refined adaptations as those of the Viliui Sakha. Those of us who live within consumer societies may believe that the centralized energy, food, and water systems on which we so depend are on much safer ground than Sakha hayfields, but if our location and technology can delay the full impact of change, they can also make us less adaptable when the floodwaters (figurative or literal) finally reach us. We must recognize our infrastructures'—and our own—ultimate vulnerability to climate impacts, and act in time.

Place-based peoples in climate-sensitive regions, such as the far north, are now feeling the first and most detectable effects of global climate change. We must ask ourselves how we will fare as climate change proceeds to affect the world's temperate zones. We should realize that we are all losing our places. If we can learn to identify, admire, and share the unique adaptive capacities of one another's cultures, we will all have a better chance to weather the storm.

Critical Thinking

1. How do the Viliui Sakha describe the environmental changes taking place in their area and their effects upon their ability to subsist?

2. What nine changes did the author's research show?

3. How have these changes specifically affected the Viliui Sakha and the plants and animals they depend upon?

4. What have been the Sakhu explanations for these changes?

5. Why is it important to increase local awareness of the role played by climate change as well as to bring local observations and understanding to the regional community?

6. How might new technologies help the Viliui Sakhai?

7. Why does the author think that those of us within the consumer society should recognize our own vulnerability to climate change?

SUSAN A. CRATE has worked with indigenous communities in Siberia since 1988, and specifically with Viliui Sakha since 1991. An interdisciplinary scholar specializing in environmental and cognitive anthropology and human ecology, she is an associate professor of anthropology in the Department of Environmental Science and Policy at George Mason University in Fairfax, Virginia. She has published numerous peer-reviewed articles and books, including the monograph *Cows, Kin and Globalization: An Ethnography of Sustainability* (Alta Mira Press, 2006). She is also senior editor of *Anthropology and Climate Change: From Encounters to Actions* (Left Coast Press, 2009). This article is mainly based on research funded by National Science Foundation, Office of Polar Programs, Arctic Social Science Program grant 0710935.

Being Indigenous in the 21st Century

With a shared sense of history and a growing set of tools, the world's Indigenous Peoples are moving into a future of their own making without losing sight of who they are and where they come from.

WILMA MANKILLER

There are more than 300 million indigenous people, in virtually every region of the world, including the Sámi peoples of Scandinavia, the Maya of Guatemala, numerous tribal groups in the Amazonian rainforest, the Dalits in the mountains of Southern India, the San and Kwei of Southern Africa, Aboriginal people in Australia, and, of course the hundreds of Indigenous Peoples in Mexico, Central and South America, as well as here in what is now known as North America.

There is enormous diversity among communities of Indigenous Peoples, each of which has its own distinct culture, language, history, and unique way of life. Despite these differences, Indigenous Peoples across the globe share some common values derived in part from an understanding that their lives are part of and inseparable from the natural world.

Onondaga Faith Keeper Oren Lyons once said, "Our knowledge is profound and comes from living in one place for untold generations. It comes from watching the sun rise in the east and set in the west from the same place over great sections of time. We are as familiar with the lands, rivers, and great seas that surround us as we are with the faces of our mothers. Indeed, we call the earth Etenoha, our mother from whence all life springs."

Indigenous people are not the only people who understand the interconnectedness of all living things. There are many thousands of people from different ethnic groups who care deeply about the environment and fight every day to protect the earth. The difference is that indigenous people have the benefit of being regularly reminded of their responsibilities to the land by stories and ceremonies. They remain close to the land, not only in the way they live, but in their hearts and in the way they view the world. Protecting the environment is not an intellectual exercise; it is a sacred duty. When women like Pauline Whitesinger, an elder at Big Mountain, and Carrie Dann, a Western Shoshone land rights activist, speak of preserving the land for future generations, they are not just talking about future generations of humans. They are talking about future generations of plants, animals, water, and all living things. Pauline and Carrie understand the relative insignificance of human beings in the totality of the planet.

Aside from a different view of their relationship to the natural world, many of the world's Indigenous Peoples also share a fragmented but still-present sense of responsibility for one another. Cooperation always has been necessary for the survival of tribal people, and even today cooperation takes precedence over competition in more traditional communities. It is really quite miraculous that a sense of sharing and reciprocity continues into the 21st century given the staggering amount of adversity Indigenous Peoples have faced. In many communities, the most respected people are not those who have amassed great material wealth or achieved great personal success. The greatest respect is reserved for those who help other people, those who understand that their lives play themselves out within a set of reciprocal relationships.

There is evidence of this sense of reciprocity in Cherokee communities. My husband, Charlie Soap, leads a widespread self-help movement among the Cherokee in which low-income volunteers work together to build walking trails, community centers, sports complexes, water lines, and houses. The self-help movement taps into the traditional Cherokee value of cooperation for the sake of the common good. The projects also build a sense of self-efficacy among the people.

Besides values, the world's Indigenous Peoples are also bound by the common experience of being "discovered" and subjected to colonial expansion into their territories that has led to the loss of an incalculable number of lives and millions and millions of acres of land and resources. The most basic rights of Indigenous Peoples were disregarded, and they were subjected to a series of policies that were designed to dispossess them of their land and resources and assimilate them into colonial society and culture. Too often the policies resulted in poverty, high infant mortality, rampant unemployment, and substance abuse, with all its attendant problems.

The stories are shockingly similar all over the world. When I read Chinua Achebe's *Things Fall Apart,* which chronicled the systematic destruction of an African tribe's social, cultural, and economic structure, it sounded all too familiar: take the land, discredit the leaders, ridicule the traditional healers, and send the children off to distant boarding schools.

And I was sickened by the Stolen Generation report about Aboriginal children in Australia who were forcibly removed from their families and placed in boarding schools far away from their families and communities. My own father and my Aunt Sally were taken from my grandfather by the U.S. government and placed in a government boarding school when they were very young. There is a connection between us. Indigenous Peoples everywhere are connected both by our values and by our oppression.

When contemplating the contemporary challenges and problems faced by Indigenous Peoples worldwide, it is important to remember that the roots of many social, economic, and political problems can be found in colonial policies. And these policies continue today across the globe.

Several years ago Charlie and I visited an indigenous community along the Rio Negro in the Brazilian rainforest. Some of the leaders expressed concern that some environmentalists, who should be natural allies, focus almost exclusively on the land and appear not to see or hear the people at all. One leader pointed out that a few years ago it was popular for famous musicians to wear T-shirts emblazoned with the slogan "Save the Rainforests," but no one ever wore a T-shirt with the slogan "Save the People of the Rainforest," though the people of the forest possess the best knowledge about how to live with and sustain the forests.

With so little accurate information about Indigenous Peoples available in educational institutions, in literature, films, or popular culture, it is not surprising that many people are not even conscious of Indigenous Peoples.

The battle to protect the human and land rights of Indigenous Peoples is made immeasurably more difficult by the fact that so few people know much about either the history or contemporary lives of our people. And without any kind of history or cultural context, it is almost impossible for outsiders to understand the issues and challenges faced by Indigenous Peoples.

This lack of accurate information leaves a void that is often filled with nonsensical stereotypes, which either vilify Indigenous Peoples as troubled descendants of savage peoples, or romanticize them as innocent children of nature, spiritual but incapable of higher thought.

Public perceptions will change in the future as indigenous leaders more fully understand that there is a direct link between public perception and public policies. Indigenous Peoples must frame their own issues, because if they don't frame the issues for themselves, their opponents most certainly will. In the future, as more indigenous people become filmmakers, writers, historians, museum curators, and journalists, they will be able to use a dazzling array of technological tools to tell their own stories, in their own voice, in their own way.

Once, a journalist asked me whether people in the United States had trouble accepting the government of the Cherokee Nation during my tenure as principal chief. I was a little surprised by the question. The government of the Cherokee Nation predated the government of the United States and had treaties with other countries before it executed a treaty with one of the first U.S. colonies.

Cherokee and other tribal leaders sent delegations to meet with the English, Spanish, and French in an effort to protect their lands and people. Traveling to foreign lands with a trusted interpreter, tribal ambassadors took maps that had been painstakingly drawn by hand to show their lands to heads of other governments. They also took along gifts, letters, and proclamations. Though tribal leaders thought they were being dealt with as heads of state and as equals, historical records indicate they were often objects of curiosity, and that there was a great deal of disdain and ridicule of these earnest delegates.

Tribal governments in the United States today exercise a range of sovereign rights. Many tribal governments have their own judicial systems, operate their own police force, run their own schools, administer their own clinics and hospitals, and operate a wide range of business enterprises. There are now more than two dozen tribally controlled community colleges. All these advancements benefit everyone in the community, not just tribal people. The history, contemporary lives, and future of tribal governments is intertwined with that of their neighbors.

One of the most common misperceptions about Indigenous Peoples is that they are all the same. There is not only great diversity among Indigenous Peoples, there is great diversity within each tribal community, just as there is in the larger society. Members of the Cherokee Nation are socially, economically, and culturally stratified. Several thousand Cherokee continue to speak the Cherokee language and live in Cherokee communities in rural northeastern Oklahoma. At the other end of the spectrum, there are enrolled tribal members who have never been to even visit the Cherokee Nation. Intermarriage has created an enrolled Cherokee membership that includes people with Hispanic, Asian, Caucasian, and African American heritage.

So what does the future hold for Indigenous Peoples across the globe? What challenges will they face moving further into the 21st century?

To see the future, one needs only to look at the past. If, as peoples, we have been able to survive a staggering loss of land, of rights, of resources, of lives, and we are still standing in the early 21st century, how can I not be optimistic that we will survive whatever challenges lie ahead, that 100 or 500 years from now we will still have viable indigenous communities? Without question, the combined efforts of government and various religious groups to eradicate traditional knowledge systems has had a profoundly negative impact on the culture as well as the social and economic systems of Indigenous Peoples. But if we have been able to hold onto our sense of community, our languages, culture, and ceremonies, despite everything, how can I not be optimistic about the future?

And though some of our original languages, medicines, and ceremonies have been irretrievably lost, the ceremonial fires of many Indigenous Peoples across the globe have survived all the upheaval. Sometimes indigenous communities have almost had to reinvent themselves as a people but they have never given up their sense of responsibility to one another and to the land. It is this sense of interdependence that has sustained tribal people thus far and I believe it will help sustain them well into the future.

Indigenous Peoples know about change and have proven time and time again they can adapt to change. No matter where they go in the world, they hold onto a strong sense of tribal identity while fully interacting with and participating in the larger society around them. In my state of Oklahoma alone, we have produced an indigenous astronaut, two United States congressmen, a Pulitzer Prize-winning novelist, and countless others who have made great contributions to their people, the state, and the world.

One of the great challenges for Indigenous Peoples in the 21st century will be to develop practical models to capture, maintain, and pass on traditional knowledge systems and values to future generations. Nothing can replace the sense of continuity that a genuine understanding of traditional tribal knowledge brings. Many communities are working on discrete aspects of culture, such as language or medicine, but it is the entire system of knowledge that needs to be maintained, not just for Indigenous Peoples but for the world at large.

Regrettably, in the future the battle for human and land rights will continue. But the future does look somewhat better for tribal people. Last year, after 30 years of advocacy by Indigenous Peoples, the United Nations finally passed a declaration supporting their distinct human rights. The challenge will be to make sure the provisions of the declaration are honored and that the rights of Indigenous Peoples all over the world are protected.

Indigenous Peoples simply do better when they have control of their own lives. In the case of my own people, after we were forcibly removed by the United States military from the southeastern part of the United States to Indian Territory, now Oklahoma, we picked ourselves up and rebuilt our nation, despite the fact that approximately 4,000 Cherokee lives were lost during the forced removal. We started some of the first schools west of the Mississippi, Indian or non-Indian, and built schools for the higher education of women. We printed our own newspapers in Cherokee and English and were more literate than our neighbors in adjoining states. Then, in the early 20th century, the federal government almost abolished the Cherokee Nation, and within two decades, our educational attainment levels dropped dramatically and many of our people were living without the most basic amenities. But our people never gave up the dream of rebuilding

the Cherokee Nation. In my grandfather's time, Cherokee men rode horses from house to house to collect dimes in a mason jar so they could send representatives to Washington to remind the government to honor its treaties with the Cherokee people.

Over the past 35 years, we have revitalized the Cherokee Nation and once again run our own school, and we have an extensive array of successful education programs. The youth at our Sequoyah High School recently won the state trigonometry contest, and several are Gates Millennium Scholars. We simply do better when we have control over our own destiny.

Critical Thinking

1. What do the 300 million indigenous people of the world have in common? Where does such knowledge come from?

2. In what ways do indigenous people differ from others who care about the environment?

3. In what respects is there a "shared sense of responsibility for one another" among indigenous people?

4. Describe the Indigenous People's common experience of "being discovered" and "being subjected to colonial expansion."

5. Why is it important to not just "save the rainforests," but also to "save the people?"

6. How is the battle to protect the human and land rights of Indigenous Peoples made immeasurably more difficult? How does the author suggest that such public perceptions be changed?

7. In what respects were tribal groups, such as the Cherokee, independent entities at one time?

8. In what respects do tribal governments in the United States still exercise a range of sovereign rights?

9. Why is the author optimistic about the future survival of indigenous communities?

10. What challenges lie ahead for Indigenous Peoples and how does the author suggest that they are meeting these challenges?

11. How have the Cherokee shown that "Indigenous Peoples simply do better when they have control over their own lives?"

Population Seven Billion

By 2045 global population is projected to reach nine billion. Can the planet take the strain? As we reach the milestone of seven billion people this year, it's time to take stock. In the coming decades, despite falling birthrates, the population will continue to grow—mostly in poor countries. If the billions of people who want to boost themselves out of poverty follow the path blazed by those in wealthy countries, they too will step hard on the planet's resources. How big will the population actually grow? What will the planet look like in 2045? Throughout the year we'll offer an in-depth series exploring those questions. The answers will depend on the decisions each of us makes.

ROBERT KUNZIG

One day in Delft in the fall of 1677, Antoni van Leeuwenhoek, a cloth merchant who is said to have been the long-haired model for two paintings by Johannes Vermeer—"The Astronomer" and "The Geographer"—abruptly stopped what he was doing with his wife and rushed to his worktable. Cloth was Leeuwenhoek's business but microscopy his passion. He'd had five children already by his first wife (though four had died in infancy), and fatherhood was not on his mind. "Before six beats of the pulse had intervened," as he later wrote to the Royal Society of London, Leeuwenhoek was examining his perishable sample through a tiny magnifying glass. Its lens, no bigger than a small raindrop, magnified objects hundreds of times. Leeuwenhoek had made it himself; nobody else had one so powerful. The learned men in London were still trying to verify Leeuwenhoek's earlier claims that unseen "animalcules" lived by the millions in a single drop of lake water and even in French wine. Now he had something more delicate to report: Human semen contained animalcules too. "Sometimes more than a thousand," he wrote, "in an amount of material the size of a grain of sand." Pressing the glass to his eye like a jeweler, Leeuwenhoek watched his own animalcules swim about, lashing their long tails. One imagines sunlight falling through leaded windows on a face lost in contemplation, as in the Vermeers. One feels for his wife.

Leeuwenhoek became a bit obsessed after that. Though his tiny peephole gave him privileged access to a never-before-seen microscopic universe, he spent an enormous amount of time looking at spermatozoa, as they're now called. Oddly enough, it was the milt he squeezed from a cod one day that inspired him to estimate, almost casually, just how many people might live on Earth.

Nobody then really had any idea; there were few censuses. Leeuwenhoek started with an estimate that around a million people lived in Holland. Using maps and a little spherical geometry, he calculated that the inhabited land area of the planet was 13,385 times as large as Holland. It was hard to imagine the whole planet being as densely peopled as Holland, which seemed crowded even then. Thus, Leeuwenhoek concluded triumphantly, there couldn't be more than 13.385 billion people on Earth—a small number indeed compared with the 150 billion sperm cells of a single codfish! This cheerful little calculation, writes population biologist Joel Cohen in his book *How Many People Can the Earth Support?*, may have been the first attempt to give a quantitative answer to a question that has become far more pressing now than it was in the 17th century. Most answers these days are far from cheerful.

Historians now estimate that in Leeuwenhoek's day there were only half a billion or so humans on Earth. After rising very slowly for millennia, the number was just starting to take off. A century and a half later, when another scientist reported the discovery of human egg cells, the world's population had doubled to more than a billion. A century after that, around 1930, it had doubled again to two billion. The acceleration since then has been astounding. Before the 20th century, no human had lived through a doubling of the human population, but there are people alive today who have seen it triple. Sometime in late 2011, according to the UN Population Division, there will be seven billion of us.

And the explosion, though it is slowing, is far from over. Not only are people living longer, but so many women across the world are now in their childbearing years—1.8 billion—that the global population will keep growing for another few decades at least, even though each woman is having fewer children than she would have had a generation ago. By 2050 the total number could reach 10.5 billion, or it could stop at eight billion—the difference is about one child per woman. UN demographers consider the middle road their best estimate: They now project that the population may reach nine billion before 2050—in 2045. The eventual tally will depend on the choices individual couples make when they engage in that most intimate of human acts, the one Leeuwenhoek interrupted so carelessly for the sake of science.

With the population still growing by about 80 million each year, it's hard not to be alarmed. Right now on Earth, water tables are falling, soil is eroding, glaciers are melting, and fish stocks are vanishing. Close to a billion people go hungry each day. Decades from now, there will likely be two billion more mouths to feed, mostly in poor countries. There will be billions more people wanting and deserving to boost themselves out of poverty. If they follow the path blazed by wealthy countries—clearing forests, burning coal and oil, freely scattering fertilizers and pesticides—they too will be stepping hard on the planet's natural resources. How exactly is this going to work?

There may be some comfort in knowing that people have long been alarmed about population. From the beginning, says French demographer Hervé Le Bras, demography has been steeped in talk of the apocalypse. Some of the field's founding papers

229

were written just a few years after Leeuwenhoek's discovery by Sir William Petty, a founder of the Royal Society. He estimated that world population would double six times by the Last Judgment, which was expected in about 2,000 years. At that point it would exceed 20 billion people—more, Petty thought, than the planet could feed. "And then, according to the prediction of the Scriptures, there must be wars, and great slaughter, &c.," he wrote.

As religious forecasts of the world's end receded, Le Bras argues, population growth itself provided an ersatz mechanism of apocalypse. "It crystallized the ancient fear, and perhaps the ancient hope, of the end of days," he writes. In 1798 Thomas Malthus, an English priest and economist, enunciated his general law of population: that it necessarily grows faster than the food supply, until war, disease, and famine arrive to reduce the number of people. As it turned out, the last plagues great enough to put a dent in global population had already happened when Malthus wrote. World population hasn't fallen, historians think, since the Black Death of the 14th century.

In the two centuries after Malthus declared that population couldn't continue to soar, that's exactly what it did. The process started in what we now call the developed countries, which were then still developing. The spread of New World crops like corn and the potato, along with the discovery of chemical fertilizers, helped banish starvation in Europe. Growing cities remained cesspools of disease at first, but from the mid-19th century on, sewers began to channel human waste away from drinking water, which was then filtered and chlorinated; that dramatically reduced the spread of cholera and typhus.

Moreover in 1798, the same year that Malthus published his dyspeptic tract, his compatriot Edward Jenner described a vaccine for smallpox—the first and most important in a series of vaccines and antibiotics that, along with better nutrition and sanitation, would double life expectancy in the industrializing countries, from 35 years to 77 today. It would take a cranky person to see that trend as gloomy: "The development of medical science was the straw that broke the camel's back," wrote Stanford population biologist Paul Ehrlich in 1968.

Ehrlich's book, *The Population Bomb,* made him the most famous of modern Malthusians. In the 1970s, Ehrlich predicted, "hundreds of millions of people are going to starve to death," and it was too late to do anything about it. "The cancer of population growth . . . must be cut out," Ehrlich wrote, "by compulsion if voluntary methods fail." The very future of the United States was at risk. In spite or perhaps because of such language, the book was a best seller, as Malthus's had been. And this time too the bomb proved a dud. The green revolution—a combination of high-yield seeds, irrigation, pesticides, and fertilizers that enabled grain production to double—was already under way. Today many people are undernourished, but mass starvation is rare.

Ehrlich was right, though, that population would surge as medical science spared many lives. After World War II the developing countries got a sudden transfusion of preventive care, with the help of institutions like the World Health Organization and UNICEF. Penicillin, the smallpox vaccine, DDT (which, though later controversial, saved millions from dying of malaria)—all arrived at once. In India life expectancy went from 38 years in 1952 to 64 today; in China, from 41 to 73. Millions of people in developing countries who would have died in childhood survived to have children themselves. That's why the population explosion spread around the planet: because a great many people were saved from dying.

And because, for a time, women kept giving birth at a high rate. In 18th-century Europe or early 20th-century Asia, when the average woman had six children, she was doing what it took to replace herself and her mate, because most of those children never reached adulthood. When child mortality declines, couples eventually have

fewer children—but that transition usually takes a generation at the very least. Today in developed countries, an average of 2.1 births per woman would maintain a steady population; in the developing world, "replacement fertility" is somewhat higher. In the time it takes for the birthrate to settle into that new balance with the death rate, population explodes.

When child mortality declines, couples eventually have fewer children—but that transition takes a generation.

Demographers call this evolution the demographic transition. All countries go through it in their own time. It's a hallmark of human progress: In a country that has completed the transition, people have wrested from nature at least some control over death and birth. The global population explosion is an inevitable side effect, a huge one that some people are not sure our civilization can survive. But the growth rate was actually at its peak just as Ehrlich was sounding his alarm. By the early 1970s, fertility rates around the world had begun dropping faster than anyone had anticipated. Since then, the population growth rate has fallen by more than 40 percent.

The fertility decline that is now sweeping the planet started at different times in different countries. France was one of the first. By the early 18th century, noblewomen at the French court were knowing carnal pleasures without bearing more than two children. They often relied on the same method Leeuwenhoek used for his studies: withdrawal, or coitus interruptus. Village parish records show the trend had spread to the peasantry by the late 18th century; by the end of the 19th, fertility in France had fallen to three children per woman—without the help of modern contraceptives. The key innovation was conceptual, not contraceptive, says Gilles Pison of the National Institute for Demographic Studies in Paris. Until the Enlightenment, "the number of children you had, it was God who decided. People couldn't fathom that it might be up to them."

Other countries in the West eventually followed France's lead. By the onset of World War II, fertility had fallen close to the replacement level in parts of Europe and the U.S. Then, after the surprising blip known as the baby boom, came the bust, again catching demographers off guard. They assumed some instinct would lead women to keep having enough children to ensure the survival of the species. Instead, in country after developed country, the fertility rate fell below replacement level. In the late 1990s in Europe it fell to 1.4. "The evidence I'm familiar with, which is anecdotal, is that women couldn't care less about replacing the species," Joel Cohen says.

The end of a baby boom can have two big economic effects on a country. The first is the "demographic dividend"—a blissful few decades when the boomers swell the labor force and the number of young and old dependents is relatively small, and there is thus a lot of money for other things. Then the second effect kicks in: The boomers start to retire. What had been considered the enduring demographic order is revealed to be a party that has to end. The sharpening American debate over Social Security and last year's strikes in France over increasing the retirement age are responses to a problem that exists throughout the developed world: how to support an aging population. "In 2050 will there be enough people working to pay for pensions?" asks Frans Willekens, director of the Netherlands Interdisciplinary Demographic Institute in The Hague. "The answer is no."

In industrialized countries it took generations for fertility to fall to the replacement level or below. As that same transition takes place in the rest of the world, what has astonished demographers is how much faster it is happening there. Though its population continues to grow, China, home to a fifth of the world's people, is already below replacement fertility and has been for nearly 20 years, thanks in part to the coercive one-child policy implemented in 1979; Chinese women, who were bearing an average of six children each as recently as 1965, are now having around 1.5. In Iran, with the support of the Islamic regime, fertility has fallen more than 70 percent since the early '80s. In Catholic and democratic Brazil, women have reduced their fertility rate by half over the same quarter century. "We still don't understand why fertility has gone down so fast in so many societies, so many cultures and religions. It's just mind-boggling," says Hania Zlotnik, director of the UN Population Division.

"At this moment, much as I want to say there's still a problem of high fertility rates, it's only about 16 percent of the world population, mostly in Africa," says Zlotnik. South of the Sahara, fertility is still five children per woman; in Niger it is seven. But then, 17 of the countries in the region still have life expectancies of 50 or less; they have just begun the demographic transition. In most of the world, however, family size has shrunk dramatically. The UN projects that the world will reach replacement fertility by 2030. "The population as a whole is on a path toward nonexplosion—which is good news," Zlotnik says.

The bad news is that 2030 is two decades away and that the largest generation of adolescents in history will then be entering their childbearing years. Even if each of those women has only two children, population will coast upward under its own momentum for another quarter century. Is a train wreck in the offing, or will people then be able to live humanely and in a way that doesn't destroy their environment? One thing is certain: Close to one in six of them will live in India.

I have understood the population explosion intellectually for a long time. I came to understand it emotionally one stinking hot night in Delhi a couple of years ago . . . The temperature was well over 100, and the air was a haze of dust and smoke. The streets seemed alive with people. People eating, people washing, people sleeping. People visiting, arguing, and screaming. People thrusting their hands through the taxi window, begging. People defecating and urinating. People clinging to buses. People herding animals. People, people, people, people.

—Paul Ehrlich

In 1966, when Ehrlich took that taxi ride, there were around half a billion Indians. There are 1.2 billion now. Delhi's population has increased even faster, to around 22 million, as people have flooded in from small towns and villages and crowded into sprawling shantytowns. Early last June in the stinking hot city, the summer monsoon had not yet arrived to wash the dust from the innumerable construction sites, which only added to the dust that blows in from the deserts of Rajasthan. On the new divided highways that funnel people into the unplanned city, oxcarts were heading the wrong way in the fast lane. Families of four cruised on motorbikes, the women's scarves flapping like vivid pennants, toddlers dangling from their arms. Families of a dozen or more sardined themselves into buzzing, bumblebee-colored auto rickshaws designed for two passengers. In the stalled traffic, amputees and wasted little children cried for alms. Delhi today is boomingly different from the city Ehrlich visited, and it is also very much the same.

At Lok Nayak Hospital, on the edge of the chaotic and densely peopled nest of lanes that is Old Delhi, a human tide flows through the entrance gate every morning and crowds inside on the lobby floor. "Who could see this and not be worried about the population

of India?" a surgeon named Chandan Bortamuly asked one afternoon as he made his way toward his vasectomy clinic. "Population is our biggest problem." Removing the padlock from the clinic door, Bortamuly stepped into a small operating room. Inside, two men lay stretched out on examination tables, their testicles poking up through holes in the green sheets. A ceiling fan pushed cool air from two window units around the room.

Bortamuly is on the front lines of a battle that has been going on in India for nearly 60 years. In 1952, just five years after it gained independence from Britain, India became the first country to establish a policy for population control. Since then the government has repeatedly set ambitious goals—and repeatedly missed them by a mile. A national policy adopted in 2000 called for the country to reach the replacement fertility of 2.1 by 2010. That won't happen for at least another decade. In the UN's medium projection, India's population will rise to just over 1.6 billion people by 2050. "What's inevitable is that India is going to exceed the population of China by 2030," says A. R. Nanda, former head of the Population Foundation of India, an advocacy group. "Nothing less than a huge catastrophe, nuclear or otherwise, can change that."

China is already below replacement fertility, thanks in part to its coercive one-child policy.

Sterilization is the dominant form of birth control in India today, and the vast majority of the procedures are performed on women. The government is trying to change that; a no-scalpel vasectomy costs far less and is easier on a man than a tubal ligation is on a woman. In the operating theater Bortamuly worked quickly. "They say the needle pricks like an ant bite," he explained, when the first patient flinched at the local anesthetic. "After that it's basically painless, bloodless surgery." Using the pointed tip of a forceps, Bortamuly made a tiny hole in the skin of the scrotum and pulled out an oxbow of white, stringy vas deferens—the sperm conduit from the patient's right testicle. He tied off both ends of the oxbow with fine black thread, snipped them, and pushed them back under the skin. In less than seven minutes—a nurse timed him—the patient was walking out without so much as a Band-Aid. The government will pay him an incentive fee of 1,100 rupees (around $25), a week's wages for a laborer.

The Indian government tried once before to push vasectomies, in the 1970s, when anxiety about the population bomb was at its height. Prime Minister Indira Gandhi and her son Sanjay used state-of-emergency powers to force a dramatic increase in sterilizations. From 1976 to 1977 the number of operations tripled, to more than eight million. Over six million of those were vasectomies. Family planning workers were pressured to meet quotas; in a few states, sterilization became a condition for receiving new housing or other government benefits. In some cases the police simply rounded up poor people and hauled them to sterilization camps.

The excesses gave the whole concept of family planning a bad name. "Successive governments refused to touch the subject," says Shailaja Chandra, former head of the National Population Stabilisation Fund (NPSF). Yet fertility in India has dropped anyway, though not as fast as in China, where it was nose-diving even before the draconian one-child policy took effect. The national average in India is now 2.6 children per woman, less than half what it was when Ehrlich visited. The southern half of the country and a few states in the northern half are already at replacement fertility or below.

In Kerala, on the southwest coast, investments in health and education helped fertility fall to 1.7. The key, demographers there say, is the female literacy rate: At around 90 percent, it's easily the highest in India. Girls who go to school start having children later than ones who don't. They are more open to contraception and more likely to understand their options.

So far this approach, held up as a model internationally, has not caught on in the poor states of northern India—in the "Hindi belt" that stretches across the country just south of Delhi. Nearly half of India's population growth is occurring in Rajasthan, Madhya Pradesh, Bihar, and Uttar Pradesh, where fertility rates still hover between three and four children per woman. More than half the women in the Hindi belt are illiterate, and many marry well before reaching the legal age of 18. They gain social status by bearing children—and usually don't stop until they have at least one son.

As an alternative to the Kerala model, some point to the southern state of Andhra Pradesh, where sterilization "camps"—temporary operating rooms often set up in schools—were introduced during the '70s and where sterilization rates have remained high as improved hospitals have replaced the camps. In a single decade beginning in the early 1990s, the fertility rate fell from around three to less than two. Unlike in Kerala, half of all women in Andhra Pradesh remain illiterate.

Amarjit Singh, the current executive director of the NPSF, calculates that if the four biggest states of the Hindi belt had followed the Andhra Pradesh model, they would have avoided 40 million births—and considerable suffering. "Because 40 million were born, 2.5 million children died," Singh says. He thinks if all India were to adopt high-quality programs to encourage sterilizations, in hospitals rather than camps, it could have 1.4 billion people in 2050 instead of 1.6 billion.

Critics of the Andhra Pradesh model, such as the Population Foundation's Nanda, say Indians need better health care, particularly in rural areas. They are against numerical targets that pressure government workers to sterilize people or cash incentives that distort a couple's choice of family size. "It's a private decision," Nanda says.

In Indian cities today, many couples are making the same choice as their counterparts in Europe or America. Sonalde Desai, a senior fellow at New Delhi's National Council of Applied Economic Research, introduced me to five working women in Delhi who were spending most of their salaries on private-school fees and after-school tutors; each had one or two children and was not planning to have more. In a nationwide survey of 41,554 households, Desai's team identified a small but growing vanguard of urban one-child families. "We were totally blown away at the emphasis parents were placing on their children," she says. "It suddenly makes you understand—that is why fertility is going down." Indian children on average are much better educated than their parents.

That's less true in the countryside. With Desai's team I went to Palanpur, a village in Uttar Pradesh—a Hindi-belt state with as many people as Brazil. Walking into the village we passed a cell phone tower but also rivulets of raw sewage running along the lanes of small brick houses. Under a mango tree, the keeper of the grove said he saw no reason to educate his three daughters. Under a neem tree in the center of the village, I asked a dozen farmers what would improve their lives most. "If we could get a little money, that would be wonderful," one joked.

The goal in India should not be reducing fertility or population, Almas Ali of the Population Foundation told me when I spoke to him a few days later. "The goal should be to make the villages livable," he said. "Whenever we talk of population in India, even today, what comes to our mind is the increasing numbers. And the numbers are looked at with fright. This phobia has penetrated the mind-set so much that all the focus is on reducing the number. The focus on people has been pushed to the background."

It was a four-hour drive back to Delhi from Palanpur, through the gathering night of a Sunday. We sat in traffic in one market town after another, each one hopping with activity that sometimes engulfed the car. As we came down a viaduct into Moradabad, I saw a man pushing a cart up the steep hill, piled with a load so large it blocked his view. I thought of Ehrlich's epiphany on his cab ride all those decades ago. People, people, people, people—yes. But also an overwhelming sense of energy, of striving, of aspiration.

The annual meeting of the Population Association of America (PAA) is one of the premier gatherings of the world's demographers. Last April the global population explosion was not on the agenda. "The problem has become a bit passé," Hervé Le Bras says. Demographers are generally confident that by the second half of this century we will be ending one unique era in history—the population explosion—and entering another, in which population will level out or even fall.

But will there be too many of us? At the PAA meeting, in the Dallas Hyatt Regency, I learned that the current population of the planet could fit into the state of Texas, if Texas were settled as densely as New York City. The comparison made me start thinking like Leeuwenhoek. If in 2045 there are nine billion people living on the six habitable continents, the world population density will be a little more than half that of France today. France is not usually considered a hellish place. Will the world be hellish then?

Some parts of it may well be; some parts of it are hellish today. There are now 21 cities with populations larger than ten million, and by 2050 there will be many more. Delhi adds hundreds of thousands of migrants each year, and those people arrive to find that "no plans have been made for water, sewage, or habitation," says Shailaja Chandra. Dhaka in Bangladesh and Kinshasa in the Democratic Republic of the Congo are 40 times larger today than they were in 1950. Their slums are filled with desperately poor people who have fled worse poverty in the countryside.

Whole countries today face population pressures that seem as insurmountable to us as India's did to Ehrlich in 1966. Bangladesh is among the most densely populated countries in the world and one of the most immediately threatened by climate change; rising seas could displace tens of millions of Bangladeshis. Rwanda is an equally alarming case. In his book *Collapse,* Jared Diamond argued that the genocidal massacre of some 800,000 Rwandans in 1994 was the result of several factors, not only ethnic hatred but also overpopulation—too many farmers dividing the same amount of land into increasingly small pieces that became inadequate to support a farmer's family. "Malthus's worst-case scenario may sometimes be realized," Diamond concluded.

Many people are justifiably worried that Malthus will finally be proved right on a global scale—that the planet won't be able to feed nine billion people. Lester Brown, founder of Worldwatch Institute and now head of the Earth Policy Institute in Washington, believes food shortages could cause a collapse of global civilization. Human beings are living off natural capital, Brown argues, eroding soil and depleting groundwater faster than they can be replenished. All of that will soon be cramping food production. Brown's Plan B to save civilization would put the whole world on a wartime footing, like the U.S. after Pearl Harbor, to stabilize climate and repair the ecological damage. "Filling the family planning gap may be the most urgent item on the global agenda," he writes, so if we don't hold the world's population to eight billion by reducing fertility, the death rate may increase instead.

Eight billion corresponds to the UN's lowest projection for 2050. In that optimistic scenario, Bangladesh has a fertility rate of 1.35 in 2050, but it still has 25 million more people than it does today. Rwanda's fertility rate also falls below the replacement level, but its population still rises to well over twice what it was before the genocide. If that's the optimistic scenario, one might argue, the future is indeed bleak.

But one can also draw a different conclusion—that fixating on population numbers is not the best way to confront the future. People packed into slums need help, but the problem that needs solving is poverty and lack of infrastructure, not overpopulation. Giving every woman access to family planning services is a good idea—"the one strategy that can make the biggest difference to women's lives," Chandra calls it. But the most aggressive population control program imaginable will not save Bangladesh from sea level rise, Rwanda from another genocide, or all of us from our enormous environmental problems.

People packed into slums need help, but the problem that needs solving is poverty, not overpopulation.

Global warming is a good example. Carbon emissions from fossil fuels are growing fastest in China, thanks to its prolonged economic boom, but fertility there is already below replacement; not much more can be done to control population. Where population is growing fastest, in sub-Saharan Africa, emissions per person are only a few percent of what they are in the U.S.—so population control would have little effect on climate. Brian O'Neill of the National Center for Atmospheric Research has calculated that if the population were to reach 7.4 billion in 2050 instead of 8.9 billion, it would reduce emissions by 15 percent. "Those who say the whole problem is population are wrong," Joel Cohen says. "It's not even the dominant factor." To stop global warming we'll have to switch from fossil fuels to alternative energy—regardless of how big the population gets.

The number of people does matter, of course. But how people consume resources matters a lot more. Some of us leave much bigger footprints than others. The central challenge for the future of people and the planet is how to raise more of us out of poverty—the slum dwellers in Delhi, the subsistence farmers in Rwanda—while reducing the impact each of us has on the planet.

The World Bank has predicted that by 2030 more than a billion people in the developing world will belong to the "global middle class," up from just 400 million in 2005. That's a good thing. But it will be a hard thing for the planet if those people are eating meat and driving gasoline-powered cars at the same rate as Americans now do. It's too late to keep the new middle class of 2030 from being born; it's not too late to change how they and the rest of us will produce and consume food and energy. "Eating less meat seems more reasonable to me than saying, 'Have fewer children!'" Le Bras says.

It's too late to keep the new middle class of 2030 from being born. But it's not too late to change the ways we all consume.

How many people can the Earth support? Cohen spent years reviewing all the research, from Leeuwenhoek on. "I wrote the book thinking I would answer the question," he says. "I found out it's unanswerable

in the present state of knowledge." What he found instead was an enormous range of "political numbers, intended to persuade people" one way or the other.

For centuries population pessimists have hurled apocalyptic warnings at the congenital optimists, who believe in their bones that humanity will find ways to cope and even improve its lot. History, on the whole, has so far favored the optimists, but history is no certain guide to the future. Neither is science. It cannot predict the outcome of *People* v. *Planet,* because all the facts of the case—how many of us there will be and how we will live—depend on choices we have yet to make and ideas we have yet to have. We may, for example, says Cohen, "see to it that all children are nourished well enough to learn in school and are educated well enough to solve the problems they will face as adults." That would change the future significantly.

The debate was present at the creation of population alarmism, in the person of Rev. Thomas Malthus himself. Toward the end of the book in which he formulated the iron law by which unchecked population growth leads to famine, he declared that law a good thing: It gets us off our duffs. It leads us to conquer the world. Man, Malthus wrote, and he must have meant woman too, is "inert, sluggish, and averse from labour, unless compelled by necessity." But necessity, he added, gives hope:

"The exertions that men find it necessary to make, in order to support themselves or families, frequently awaken faculties that might otherwise have lain for ever dormant, and it has been commonly remarked that new and extraordinary situations generally create minds adequate to grapple with the difficulties in which they are involved."

Seven billion of us soon, nine billion in 2045. Let's hope that Malthus was right about our ingenuity.

Critical Thinking

1. Why should we be alarmed about continued world population growth?

2. How did Thomas Malthus explain world growth?

3. Discuss the "demographic transition" as an explanation for population growth.

4. How has medical science aided population growth?

5. What is meant by "replacement fertility"? Why do populations continue to expand for a period after reaching replacement fertility?

6. In what parts of the world has fertility fallen significantly? What was the "demographic dividend" and what did it mean for the United States? Where do we still find high fertility rates?

7. What have been some of the key factors in reducing fertility in such places as China and India?

8. Why do critics say is it more important to focus on health, education, and the personal decisions people make regarding fertility rather than on "numerical targets"?

9. Why are many people justifiably worried that Malthus will finally be proved right on a global scale?

10. In what respects do some say the focus on population rather than the environment is wrong? What matters more than simply the number of people, according to the author?

11. In what sense did Malthus express hope?

ROBERT KUNZIG is *National Geographic's* senior editor for the environment.

From *National Geographic*, January 2011, pp. 40, 42–43, 45, 48–49, 60–63. Copyright © 2011 by National Geographic Society. Reprinted by permission.

Test-Your-Knowledge Form

We encourage you to photocopy and use this page as a tool to assess how the articles in *Annual Editions* expand on the information in your textbook. By reflecting on the articles you will gain enhanced text information. You can also access this useful form on a product's book support website at www.mhhe.com/cls

NAME: _____ DATE: _____

_____

TITLE AND NUMBER OF ARTICLE:

_____

BRIEFLY STATE THE MAIN IDEA OF THIS ARTICLE:

_____

LIST THREE IMPORTANT FACTS THAT THE AUTHOR USES TO SUPPORT THE MAIN IDEA:

_____

WHAT INFORMATION OR IDEAS DISCUSSED IN THIS ARTICLE ARE ALSO DISCUSSED IN YOUR TEXTBOOK OR OTHER READINGS THAT YOU HAVE DONE? LIST THE TEXTBOOK CHAPTERS AND PAGE NUMBERS:

_____

LIST ANY EXAMPLES OF BIAS OR FAULTY REASONING THAT YOU FOUND IN THE ARTICLE:

_____

LIST ANY NEW TERMS/CONCEPTS THAT WERE DISCUSSED IN THE ARTICLE, AND WRITE A SHORT DEFINITION: